CONTENTS

S0-AXV-860

SOCIETY IN QUESTION
SOCIOLOGICAL READINGS FOR THE 21ST CENTURY

ROBERT J. BRYM
UNIVERSITY OF TORONTO

SOCIETY IN QUESTION
SOCIOLOGICAL READINGS FOR THE 21ST CENTURY
THIRD EDITION

NELSON

THOMSON LEARNING

Australia • Canada • Mexico • Singapore • Spain • United Kingdom • United States

For more information contact
Nelson Thomson Learning,
1120 Birchmount Road,
Scarborough, Ontario,
M1K 5G4.
Or you can visit our Internet site at
http://www.nelson.com

Canadian Cataloguing in Publication Data

Main entry under title:

Society in question : sociological readings for the 21st century

3rd ed.
Includes bibliographical references and index.
ISBN 0-7747-3437-X

1. Sociology.   2. Canada — Social conditions.   I. Brym, Robert J., 1951–   .

HM51.S6427 2000   301   C00-931104-1

Acquisitions Editor: Brad Lambertus
Developmental Editor: Camille Isaacs
Production Editor: Liz Radojkovic
Production Coordinator: Cheryl Tiongson

Copy Editor: Barbara Tessman
Cover Design: Mighty Design Inc.
Interior Design: Mighty Design Inc./Opus House Inc.
Typesetting and Assembly: Carolyn Sebestyen/Christine Gambin
Printing and Binding: Webcom Printing Ltd.

Cover art: *Market II* by David Armstrong, 22" × 30". Copyright © 1997 David Armstrong. All rights reserved.

This book was printed in Canada.
3 4 5   04 03 02

For my students, who keep inspiring me and challenging me to do better.

— RJB

PREFACE

Society in Question is designed to supplement the main textbook in an introductory sociology course. I have therefore aimed for balanced coverage of major topics, approaches, and methods in current sociology. However, as the title and subtitle suggest, this book also tries to convey more than just a sense of what sociologists do for a living. The readings, and my introductions to them, are intended to speak plainly and vividly to contemporary Canadians about how sociology can help them make sense of their lives in a rapidly changing and often confusing world. The book's title is thus an intentional pun: as the nature of social life is called into question by vast and sometimes frightening forces over which we appear to have little control, sociological questioning offers the prospect of helping us understand those forces and make informed choices about how we can best deal with them.

This is a non-parochial collection of articles. I have not felt obliged to select only the works of authors who are Canadian citizens and hold PhDs in sociology (although the large majority are and do). The sociological imagination has influenced anthropology, political science, history, and law, among other disciplines. I have chosen some works by scholars in these fields because they are particularly striking examples of how cognate disciplines have repaid the favour by enriching sociological thought. Moreover, I strongly believe that, especially in this era of globalization, Canadian sociologists have as much to learn from non-Canadians as from non-sociologists. That is why several non-Canadians are among the authors represented here.

I consider some of the pieces reprinted here to be modern classics, but I have tried wherever possible to select items that speak to key issues of social life today. Specifically, three-quarters of the articles in this book were written between 1990 and 2000 and all but three of the remainder in the 1980s.

Finally, although I selected a few articles just because they cover important topics concisely and clearly, more rigorous criteria guided most of my choices. As I reviewed material for this collection, I tried to place myself in the shoes of a contemporary Canadian undergraduate who, entirely sensibly, takes the time to read only material that says something significant and unobvious. Many of the articles in this book surprised me when I first read them, and they continue to affect the way I see the world. Accordingly, the best indicator of the usefulness of this book will be the number of students who complete it and say that it helped ensure that they can no longer pick up a newspaper without thinking about the broader sociological significance of what they've read. That is just about the highest praise an introductory sociology instructor can receive.

ACKNOWLEDGEMENTS

I am indebted to the Harcourt Canada team of Camille Isaacs and Brad Lambertus for their assistance in shaping this collection. They are an author's dream come true.

ROBERT J. BRYM
University of Toronto

A NOTE FROM THE PUBLISHER

Thank you for selecting *Society in Question: Sociological Readings for the 21st Century*, Third Edition, by Robert J. Brym. The author and publisher have devoted considerable time to the careful development of this book. We appreciate your recognition of this effort and accomplishment.

We want to hear what you think about *Society in Question*. Please take a few minutes to fill in the stamped reader reply card at the back of the book. Your comments and suggestions will be valuable to us as we prepare new editions and other books.

PART 1 | THE FIELD OF SOCIOLOGY

I have been writing my autobiography for over twenty years. As autobiographies go, it is pretty unconventional. It records no personal events or dates, nor does it sketch interesting characters. My friends, enemies, colleagues, parents, wife, and children are not mentioned in it. It is not written as a personal narrative. Yet, indirectly, it is the story of my life.

My life story is embedded in my sociological writings. The pressing issues that trouble me have somehow been transformed into a research agenda. But I alone can plainly see the connection between my life and my writings. To the degree that my writings have any value to others, it lies in their contribution, however slight, to conversations and debates that people who call themselves sociologists have engaged in for more than a century. Those sociologists couldn't care less about whether I have found my research and writing useful in addressing the political, ethnic, and economic issues that have weighed on me over the years.

Nor should they. Sociology is a science — a science that is not as precise as physics, which doesn't have to contend with human caprice, but a science nonetheless. Sociologists try to observe their chosen corner of reality in a systematic and controlled manner and to evaluate the validity of their ideas on the basis of whether their observations confirm or refute them. The origins of those ideas are irrelevant, scientifically speaking. That is, I think, what the American writer Kurt Vonnegut meant when he wrote that the most beautiful marigold he ever saw was growing in a bucket of cat manure.

Here we have the great irony of much scholarship, sociology included. Scholars try to be dispassionate and objective, yet a great deal of scholarly activity is animated by real-life experiences and individual passions. For example, Albert Einstein believed on philosophical grounds that the universe is a deterministic system operating according to iron laws and that it is the physicist's job to discover those laws. When he was confronted by evidence that certain subatomic processes can be described only in terms of probable rather than certain outcomes, he objected: "God does not play dice with the universe." In this case, Einstein was not swayed by the evidence; his personal bent of mind, even his religious outlook, affected his evaluation of the evidence.

In their laudable efforts to be objective, some scholars lose sight of the fact that personal experiences and individual passions help them define certain problems as urgent and certain solutions to those problems as preferable. But few thoughtful and honest scholars can fool themselves for long with pious statements about being purely objective in their research. The plain fact is that objectivity and subjectivity each have an important role to play in science, including sociology. Objectivity is a "reality check"; subjectivity leads us to define which aspect of reality is worth checking on in the first place.

In contrast to those who believe that objectivity is everything, many people are under the equally misguided impression that subjectivity tells all, that their own experience is the sole reliable guide to action, that their personal troubles are theirs and theirs alone. In his 1959 classic work *The Sociological Imagination*, a portion of which is reprinted here as Chapter 1, the late C. Wright Mills shows how wrong this commonsense view is.

When one person in a community is unemployed, says Mills, that is a personal trouble and perhaps a personal failing. When 30 percent of a country's work force is unemployed, as was the case in North America during the Great Depression of 1929–39, that is a massive social issue. The best sociologists try to show how personal troubles are tied to social issues and how social issues, in turn, have developed historically. From Mills's point of view, good sociology is liberating. It promises to broaden your sense of what you can do with your life by showing how your subjective feelings and actions are a product of broad social and historical forces, and how you can act to alter those social and historical forces and thus improve the quality of your life. Although in some respects dated — Mills's tone was influenced by the fact that he wrote at the height of the Cold War; his language is sexist — his main argument is as true and as inspiring today as it was over 40 years ago.

Some students may consider sociology's promise too abstract, theoretical, or impractical. They may immediately see how the health professions, teaching, or engineering can help improve the world, yet sociology's contribution may remain murky. Chapter 2, by Joel Charon, is good medicine for skeptics. Charon says sociology's main practical contribution is that it can improve the workings of democracy. By his definition, a **democracy** is a society in which people (1) think and act as they wish, (2) limit the power of government, (3) respect and protect minority rights, and (4) enjoy equal opportunity for a decent life. Sociology lays bare the social conditions that promote freedom, limit state power, encourage respect for diversity, and undermine privilege. Can there be any more practical tasks for humanity than achieving these goals?

GLOSSARY

A **democracy** is a society in which people think and act as they wish, limit the power of government, respect and protect minority rights, and enjoy equal opportunity for a decent life.

CRITICAL THINKING QUESTIONS

1. What are the key aspects of the sociological perspective? What are the benefits of using this perspective?
2. In what ways can sociology show us how to make society more democratic?
3. What are the roles of objectivity and subjectivity in social scientific research?
4. How is sociology distinct from other disciplines?

ANNOTATED BIBLIOGRAPHY

Robert J. Brym with Bonnie J. Fox, *From Culture to Power: The Sociology of English Canada* (Toronto: Oxford University Press, 1989). An overview of theoretical controversies and empirical findings in several of the main fields of sociological research in Canada outside Quebec.

Robert J. Brym and Céline Saint-Pierre, "Canadian Sociology," *Contemporary Sociology* 26, 4 (1997): 543–6. An update of the preceding item.

Immanuel Wallerstein, ed., *Current Sociology* 46, 2 (1998), The Heritage of Sociology and the Future of the Social Sciences in the 21st Century. This special issue of the journal of the International Sociological Association contains programmatic statements about the future of the discipline by leading scholars, including Canada's Margrit Eichler.

Irving Zeitlin, *Ideology and the Development of Sociological Theory*, 6th ed. (Upper Saddle River, NJ: Prentice-Hall, 1997). A thorough introduction to sociology's classical tradition.

Chapter 1

The Sociological Imagination

C. WRIGHT MILLS

Nowadays men often feel that their private lives are a series of traps. They sense that within their everyday worlds, they cannot overcome their troubles, and in this feeling, they are often quite correct: What ordinary men are directly aware of and what they try to do are bounded by the private orbits in which they live; their visions and their powers are limited to the close-up scenes of job, family, neighbourhood; in other milieux, they move vicariously and remain spectators. And the more aware they become, however vaguely, of ambitions and of threats which transcend their immediate locales, the more trapped they seem to feel.

Underlying this sense of being trapped are seemingly impersonal changes in the very structure of continent-wide societies. The facts of contemporary history are also facts about the success and the failure of individual men and women. When a society is industrialized, a peasant becomes a worker; a feudal lord is liquidated or becomes a businessman. When classes rise or fall, a man is employed or unemployed; when the rate of investment goes up or down, a man takes new heart or goes broke. When wars happen, an insurance salesman becomes a rocket launcher; a store clerk, a radar man; a wife lives alone; a child grows up without a father. Neither the life of an individual nor the history of a society can be understood without understanding both.

Yet men do not usually define the troubles they endure in terms of historical change and institutional contradiction. The well-being they enjoy, they do not usually impute to the big ups and downs of the societies in which they live. Seldom aware of the intricate connection between the patterns of their own lives and the course of world history, ordinary men do not usually know what this connection means for the kinds of men they are becoming and for the kinds of history-making in which they might take part. They do not possess the quality of mind essential to grasp the interplay of man and society, of biography and history, of self and world. They cannot cope with their personal troubles in such ways as to control the structural transformations that usually lie behind them.

Surely it is no wonder. In what period have so many men been so totally exposed at so fast a pace to such earthquakes of change? That Americans have not known such catastrophic changes as have the men and women of other societies is due to historical facts that are now quickly becoming "merely history." The history that now affects every man is world history. Within this scene and this period, in the course of a single generation, one-sixth of mankind is transformed from all that is feudal and backward into all that is modern, advanced, and fearful. Political colonies are freed; new and less visible forms of imperialism installed. Revolutions occur; men feel the intimate grip of new kinds of authority. Totalitarian societies rise, and are smashed to bits—or succeed fabulously. After two centuries of ascendancy, capitalism is shown up as only one way to make society into an industrial apparatus. After two centuries of hope, even formal democracy is restricted to a quite small portion of mankind. Everywhere in the underdeveloped world, ancient ways of life are broken up and vague expectations become urgent demands. Everywhere in the overdeveloped world, the means of authority and of violence become total in scope and bureaucratic in form. Humanity itself now lies before us, the super-nation at either pole concentrating its most coordinated and massive efforts upon the preparation of World War Three.

The very shaping of history now outpaces the ability of men to orient themselves in accordance with cherished values. And which values? Even when they do not panic, men often sense that older ways of feeling and thinking have collapsed and that newer beginnings are ambiguous to the point of moral stasis. Is it any wonder that ordinary men feel they cannot cope with the larger worlds with which they are so suddenly confronted? That they cannot understand the meaning of their epoch for their own lives? That — in defence of selfhood — they become morally insensible, trying to remain altogether private men? Is it any wonder that they come to be possessed by a sense of the trap?

It is not only information that they need — in this Age of Fact, information often dominates their attention and overwhelms their capacities to assimilate it. It is not only the skills of reason that they need — although their struggles to acquire these often exhaust their limited moral energy.

What they need, and what they feel they need, is a quality of mind that will help them to use information and to develop reason in order to achieve lucid summations of what is going on in the world and of what may be happening within themselves. It is this quality, I am going to contend, that journalists and scholars, artists and publics, scientists and editors are coming to expect of what may be called the sociological imagination.

1

The sociological imagination enables its possessor to understand the larger historical scene in terms of its meaning for the inner life and the external career of a variety of individuals. It enables him to take into account how individuals, in the welter of their daily experience, often become falsely conscious of their social positions. Within that welter, the framework of modern society is sought, and within that framework the psychologies of a variety of men and women are formulated. By such means the personal uneasiness of individuals is focused upon explicit troubles, and the indifference of publics is transformed into involvement with public issues.

The first fruit of this imagination — and the first lesson of the social science that embodies it — is the idea that the individual can understand his own experience and gauge his own fate only by locating himself within his period, that he can know his own chances in life only by becoming aware of those of all individuals in his circumstances. In many ways it is a tenable lesson; in many ways a magnificent one. We do not know the limits of man's capacities for supreme effort or willing degradation, for agony or glee, for pleasurable brutality or the sweetness of reason. But in our time we have come to know that the limits of "human nature" are frighteningly broad. We have come to know that every individual lives, from one generation to the next, in some society; that he lives out a biography, and that he lives it out within some historical sequence. By the fact of his living he contributes, however minutely, to the shaping of this society and to the course of its history, even as he is made by society and by its historical push and shove.

The sociological imagination enables us to grasp history and biography and the relations between the two within society. That is its task and its promise. To recognize this task and this promise is the mark of the classic social analyst. It is characteristic of Herbert Spencer — turgid, polysyllabic, comprehensive; of E.A. Ross — graceful, muckraking, upright; of Auguste Comte and Émile Durkheim; of the intricate and subtle Karl Mannheim. It is the quality of all that is intellectually excellent in Karl Marx; it is the clue to Thorstein Veblen's brilliant and ironic insight, to Joseph Schumpeter's many-sided constructions of reality; it is the basis of the psychological sweep of W.E.H. Lecky no less than of the profundity and clarity of Max Weber. And it is the signal of what is best in contemporary studies of man and society.

No social study that does not come back to the problems of biography, of history, and of their intersections within a society has completed its intellectual journey. Whatever the specific problems of the classic social analysts, however limited or however broad the features of social reality they have examined, those who have been imaginatively aware of the promise of their work have consistently asked three sorts of questions:

1. What is the structure of this particular society as a whole? What are its essential components, and how are they related to one another? How does it differ from other varieties of social order? Within it, what is the meaning of any particular feature for its continuance and for its change?

2. Where does this society stand in human history? What are the mechanics by which it is changing? What is its place within and its meaning for the development of humanity as a whole? How does any particular feature we are examining affect, and how is it affected by, the historical period in which it moves? And this period—what are its essential features? How does it differ from other periods? What are its characteristic ways of history-making?

3. What varieties of men and women now prevail in this society and in this period? And what varieties are coming to prevail? In what ways are they selected and formed, liberated and repressed, made sensitive and blunted? What kinds of "human nature" are revealed in the conduct and character we observe in this society in this period? And what is the meaning for "human nature" of each and every feature of the society we are examining?

Whether the point of interest is a great power state or a minor literary mood, a family,

a prison, a creed—these are the kinds of questions the best social analysts have asked. They are the intellectual pivots of classic studies of man in society—and they are the questions inevitably raised by any mind possessing the sociological imagination. For that imagination is the capacity to shift from one perspective to another—from the political to the psychological; from examination of a single family to comparative assessment of the national budgets of the world; from the theological school to the military establishment; from considerations of an oil industry to studies of contemporary poetry. It is the capacity to range from the most impersonal and remote transformations to the most intimate features of the human self—and to see the relations between the two. Back of its use there is always the urge to know the social and historical meaning of the individual in the society and in the period in which he has his quality and his being.

That, in brief, is why it is by means of the sociological imagination that men now hope to grasp what is going on in the world, and to understand what is happening in themselves as minute points of the intersections of biography and history within society. In large part, contemporary man's self-conscious view of himself as at least an outsider, if not a permanent stranger, rests upon an absorbed realization of social relativity and of the transformative power of history. The sociological imagination is the most fruitful form of this self-consciousness. By its use men whose mentalities have swept only a series of limited orbits often come to feel as if suddenly awakened in a house with which they had only supposed themselves to be familiar. Correctly or incorrectly, they often come to feel that they can now provide themselves with adequate summations, cohesive assessments, comprehensive orientations. Older decisions that once appeared sound now seem to them products of a mind unaccountably dense. Their capacity for astonishment is made lively again. They acquire a new way of thinking, they experience a transvaluation of values: in a word, by their reflection and by their sensibility, they realize the cultural meaning of the social sciences.

2

Perhaps the most fruitful distinction with which the sociological imagination works is between "the personal troubles of milieu" and "the public issues of social structure." This distinction is an essential tool of the sociological imagination and a feature of all classic work in social science.

Troubles occur within the character of the individual and within the range of his immediate relations with others; they have to do with his self and with those limited areas of social life of which he is directly and personally aware. Accordingly, the statement and the resolution of troubles properly lie within the individual as a biographical entity and within the scope of his immediate milieu—the social setting that is directly open to his personal experience and to some extent his willful activity. A trouble is a private matter: values cherished by an individual are felt by him to be threatened.

Issues have to do with matters that transcend these local environments of the individual and the range of his inner life. They have to do with the organization of many such milieux into the institutions of an historical society as a whole, with the ways in which various milieux overlap and interpenetrate to form the larger structure of social and historical life. An issue is a public matter: some value cherished by publics is felt to be threatened. Often there is a debate about what that value really is and about what it is that really threatens it. This debate is often without focus if only because it is the very nature of an issue, unlike even widespread trouble, that it cannot very well be defined in terms of the immediate and everyday environments of ordinary men. An issue, in fact, often involves a crisis in institutional arrangements, and often too it involves what Marxists call "contradictions" or "antagonisms."

In these terms, consider unemployment. When, in a city of 100 000, only one man is unemployed, that is his personal trouble, and for its relief we properly look to the character of the man, his skills, and his immediate opportunities. But when in a nation of 50 million employees, 15 million men are unemployed, that is an issue, and we may not hope to find its solution within the range of opportunities open to any one individual. The very structure of opportunities has collapsed. Both the correct statement of the problem and the range of possible solutions require us to consider the economic and political institutions of the society, and not merely the personal situation and character of a scatter of individuals.

Consider war. The personal problem of war, when it occurs, may be how to survive it or how to die in it with honour; how to make money out of it; how to climb into the higher safety of the military apparatus; or how to contribute to the war's termination. In short, according to one's values, to find a set of milieux and within it to survive the war or make one's death in it meaningful. But the structural issues of war have to do with its causes; with what types of men it throws up into command; with its effects upon economic and political, family and religious institutions; with the unorganized irresponsibility of a world of nation-states.

Consider marriage. Inside a marriage a man and a woman may experience personal troubles, but when the divorce rate during the first four years of marriage is 250 out of every 1000 attempts, this is an indication of a structural issue having to do with the institutions of marriage and the family and other institutions that bear upon them.

Or consider the metropolis—the horrible, beautiful, ugly, magnificent sprawl of the great city. For many upper-class people, the personal solution to "the problem of the city" is to have an apartment with private garage under it in the heart of the city, and forty miles out, a house by Henry Hill, garden by Garrett Eckbo, on a hundred acres of private land. In these two controlled environments—with a small staff at each end and a private helicopter connection—most people could solve many of the problems of personal milieux caused by the facts of the city. But all this, however splendid, does not solve the public issues that the structural fact of the city poses. What should be done with this wonderful monstrosity? Break it all up into scattered units, combining residence and work? Refurbish it as it stands? Or, after evacuation, dynamite it and build new cities according to new plans in new places? What should those plans be? And who is to decide and to accomplish whatever choice is made? These are structural issues; to confront them and to solve them requires us to consider political and economic issues that affect innumerable milieux.

In so far as an economy is so arranged that slumps occur, the problem of unemployment becomes incapable of personal solution. In so far as war is inherent in the nation-state system and in the uneven industrialization of the world, the ordinary individual in his restricted milieu will be powerless—with or without psychiatric aid—to solve the troubles this system or lack of system imposes upon him. In so far as the family as an institution turns women into darling little slaves and men into their chief providers and unweaned dependants, the problem of a satisfactory marriage remains incapable of purely private solution. In so far as the overdeveloped megalopolis and the overdeveloped automobile are built-in features of the overdeveloped society, the issues of urban living will not be solved by personal ingenuity and private wealth.

What we experience in various and specific milieux, I have noted, is often caused by structural changes. Accordingly, to understand the changes of many personal milieux we are required to look beyond them. And the number and variety of such structural changes increase as the institutions within which we live become more embracing and more intricately connected with one another. To be aware of the idea of social structure and to use it with sensibility is to be capable of tracing such linkages among a great variety of milieux. To be able to do that is to possess the sociological imagination.

3

What are the major issues for publics and the key troubles of private individuals in our time? To formulate issues and troubles, we must ask what values are cherished yet threatened, and what values are cherished and supported, by the characterizing trends of our period. In the case both of threat and of support we must ask what salient contradictions of structure may be involved.

When people cherish some set of values and do not feel any threat to them, they experience well-being. When they cherish values but do feel them to be threatened, they experience a crisis—either as a personal trouble or as a public issue. And if all their values seem involved, they feel the total threat of panic.

But suppose people are neither aware of any cherished values nor experience any threat. That is the experience of indifference, which, if it seems to involve all their values, becomes apathy. Suppose, finally, they are unaware of any cherished values, but still are very much aware of a threat? That is the experience of uneasiness, of anxiety, which, if it is total enough, becomes a deadly unspecified malaise.

Ours is a time of uneasiness and indifference—not yet formulated in such ways as to permit the work of reason and the play of sensibility. Instead of troubles—defined in terms of values and threats—there is often the misery of vague uneasiness; instead of explicit issues there is often merely the weak feeling that all is somehow not right. Neither the values threatened nor whatever threatens them has been stated; in short, they have not been carved to the point of decision. Much less have they been formulated as problems of social science.

In the thirties there was little doubt—except among certain deluded business circles—that there was an economic issue which was also a pack of personal troubles. In these arguments about "the crisis of capitalism," the formulations of Marx and the many unacknowledged reformulations of his work probably set the leading terms of the issue, and some men came to understand their personal troubles in these terms. The values threatened were plain to see and cherished by all; the structural contradictions that threatened them also seemed plain. Both were widely and deeply experienced. It was a political age.

But the values threatened in the era after World War Two are often neither widely acknowledged as values nor widely felt to be threatened. Much private uneasiness goes unformulated; much public malaise and many decisions of enormous structural relevance never become public issues. For those who accept such inherited values as reason and freedom, it is the uneasiness itself that is the trouble; it is the indifference itself that is the issue. And it is this condition, of uneasiness and indifference, that is the signal feature of our period.

All this is so striking that it is often interpreted by observers as a shift in the very kinds of problems that need now to be formulated. We are frequently told that the problems of our decade, or even the crises of our period, have shifted from the external realm of economics and now have to do with the quality of individual life — in fact with the question of whether there is soon going to be anything that can properly be called individual life. Not child labour but comic books, not poverty but mass leisure, are at the centre of concern. Many great public issues as well as many private troubles are described in terms of "the psychiatric" — often, it seems, in a pathetic attempt to avoid the large issues and problems of modern society. Often this statement seems to rest upon a provincial narrowing of interest to the Western societies, or even to the United States — thus ignoring two-thirds of mankind; often, too, it arbitrarily divorces the individual life from the larger institutions within which that life is enacted, and which on occasion bear upon it

more grievously than do the intimate environments of childhood.

Problems of leisure, for example, cannot even be stated without considering problems of work. Family troubles over comic books cannot be formulated as problems without considering the plight of the contemporary family in its new relations with the newer institutions of the social structure. Neither leisure nor its debilitating uses can be understood as problems without recognition of the extent to which malaise and indifference now form the social and personal climate of contemporary American society. In this climate, no problems of "the private life" can be stated and solved without recognition of the crisis of ambition that is part of the very career of men at work in the incorporated economy.

It is true, as psychoanalysts continually point out, that people do often have "the increasing sense of being moved by obscure forces within themselves which they are unable to define." But it is *not* true, as Ernest Jones asserted, that "man's chief enemy and danger is his own unruly nature and the dark forces pent up within him." On the contrary: "Man's chief danger" today lies in the unruly forces of contemporary society itself, with its alienating methods of production, its enveloping techniques of political domination, its international anarchy — in a word, its pervasive transformations of the very "nature" of man and the conditions and aims of his life.

It is now the social scientist's foremost political and intellectual task — for here the two coincide — to make clear the elements of contemporary uneasiness and indifference. It is the central demand made upon him by other cultural workmen — by physical scientists and artists, by the intellectual community in general. It is because of this task and these demands, I believe, that the social sciences are becoming the common denominator of our cultural period, and the sociological imagination our most needed quality of mind.

Chapter 2

Is Sociology Important? The Need for a Critical Understanding of Society

JOEL CHARON

In the final analysis, it may be true that ignorance is bliss. It may be true that people should be left alone with the myths they happen to pick up in interaction with one another. It may be true that a liberal arts education that does not have immediate practical value is worthless.

SOCIOLOGY AND A LIBERAL ARTS EDUCATION

I do not believe any of the ideas above, but I wonder about them a lot. One can more easily make a case for mathematics, foreign languages, writing, speech, psychology, and economics on the level of practical use. "The student needs to know these if he or she is to get along in life," the argument goes. It is far more difficult to make a case for sociology on the basis of practical use—unless, of course, by practical use one means *thinking about and understanding the world*. If a college education is ultimately an attempt to encourage people to wonder, investigate, and carefully examine their lives, then sociology is one of the most important disciplines.

Note its purpose: to get students to examine an aspect of life carefully and systematically that most people only casually and occasionally think about. It is to get people to understand what culture is and to recognize that what they believe is largely a result of their culture. It is to get them to see that they are born into a society that has a long history, that they are ranked and given roles in that society, and that ultimately they are told who they are, what to think, and how to act. It is to get them to see that the institutions they follow and normally accept are not the only ways in which society can function—that there are always alternatives. It is to get them to realize that those whom they regard a sick, evil, or criminal are often simply different. It is to get them to see that those they hate are often a product of social circumstances that should be understood more carefully and objectively.

In short, the purpose of sociology is to get people to examine objectively their lives and their society. This process is uncomfortable and sometimes unpleasant. I keep asking myself, as I teach the insights of sociology, "Why not just leave those students alone?" And, quite frankly, I do not usually know how to answer this question. We are socialized into society. Shouldn't we simply accept that which we are socialized to

Source: Excerpted from "Is Sociology Important? The Necessity for a Critical Understanding of Society," in Joel M. Charon, *Ten Questions: A Sociological Perspective*, 3rd ed. (Belmont, CA: Wadsworth Publishing, 1998), pp. 227–37. Reprinted with permission.

believe? Isn't it better for society if people believe myth? Isn't it better for people's happiness to let them be?

I usually come back to what many people profess to be one primary purpose of a university education: "liberal arts." To me, the liberal arts should be "liberating." A university education should be liberating; it should help the individual escape the bonds of his or her imprisonment through bringing an understanding of that prison. We should read literature, understand art, and study biology and sociology in order to break through what those who defend society want us to know to reach a plane where we are able to see reality in a more careful and unbiased way. In the end, sociology probably has the greatest potential for liberation in the academic world: At its best, it causes individuals to confront their ideas, actions, and being. We are never the same once we bring sociology into our lives. Life is scrutinized. Truth becomes far more tentative.

SOCIOLOGY AND DEMOCRACY
THE MEANING OF DEMOCRACY

Liberation, as you probably realize, has something to do with democracy. Although democracy is clearly an ideal that North Americans claim for themselves, it is not usually clearly defined or deeply explored.

Sociology, however, explores democracy, and it asks rarely examined questions about the possibility for democracy in this—or any—society. To many people democracy simply means "majority rule," and we too often superficially claim that if people go to a voting booth, then democracy has been established and the majority does, in fact, rule. Democracy, however, is far more than majority rule, and majority rule is far more than the existence of voting booths.

Democracy is very difficult to achieve. No society can become perfectly democratic; few societies really make much progress in that direction. Democracy is also difficult to define. When I try, I usually end up listing four quali-

ties. These describe a whole society, not just the government in that society. Although everyone will not agree that these are the basic qualities of a democracy, I think they offer a good place to begin.

1. *A democratic society is one in which the individual is free in both thinking and action.* People are in control of their own lives. To the extent that a society encourages freedom, we can call it a democratic society.

2. *A democratic society is one where the government is effectively limited.* Those who control government do not do what they choose to do. Voting, law, organization of people, and constitutions effectively limit their power. To the extent that government is effectively limited, we call it a democratic society.

3. *A democratic society is one where human differences are respected and protected.* There is a general agreement that no matter what the majority favours, certain rights are reserved for the individual and for minorities who are different from the majority. Diversity is respected and even encouraged. To the extent that diversity and individuality are respected and protected, we call it a democratic society.

4. *A democratic society is one in which all people have an equal opportunity to live a decent life.* That is, privilege is not inherited, people have equality before the law, in educational opportunity, in opportunity for material success, and in whatever is deemed to be important in society. To the extent that real equality of opportunity exists, we call it a democratic society.

These four qualities that make up the definition of democracy described here must be tentative descriptions, and people should debate their relative significance. Some will regard others to be more important, and some will regard only one or two of these qualities as necessary. I am only trying here to list four qualities that make sense to me and that guide my own estimate of whether societies are democratic.

If these qualities do capture what democracy means, however, it should be obvious that the questions and thinking that are basic to the sociological perspective are relevant to both the understanding of and working toward a democratic society. Because sociology focuses on social organization, structure, culture, institutions, social order, social class, social power, social conflict, socialization, and social change, *sociology must continually examine issues that are relevant to understanding a democratic society.* And, on top of this, because *sociology critically examines people and their society, it encourages the kind of thinking that is necessary for people living in and working for a democratic society.* One might, in truth, argue that *the study of sociology is the study of issues relevant to understanding democratic society.*

SOCIOLOGY: AN APPROACH TO UNDERSTANDING DEMOCRATIC SOCIETY

One of sociology's main concerns is the nature of the human being and the role of socialization and culture in what we all become. To ask questions about human nature is to ask simultaneous questions about the possibility for democratic society, a society built on qualities that are not often widespread in society: respect for individual differences, compromise, and concern over inequality and lack of freedom. The sociological approach to the human being makes no assumption of fixed qualities, but it has a strong tendency to see human beings as living within social conditions that are responsible for forming many of their most important qualities. A society tends to produce certain types of people and certain social conditions, encouraging one value or another, one set of morals or another, one way of doing things or another. Conformity, control of the human being, tyranny, and pursuit of purely selfish interests can be encouraged; but so, too, can freedom, respect for people's rights, limited government, and equality. *The possibilities for and the limits to a human being who can live democratically are part of what sociology investigates through its questions concerning culture, socialization, and human nature.*

Those who think about society must inevitably consider the central problem of social order: How much freedom and how much individuality can we allow and still maintain society? Those who favour greater freedom will occasionally wonder: How can there really be meaningful freedom in any society? As long as society exists, how much freedom can we encourage without destroying the underlying order? Are there limits? If so, how can we discover them? What are the costs, if any, of having a democratic society? Those who fear disorder and the collapse of society might ask: How much does the individual owe to society? Such questions are extremely difficult to answer, but they are investigated throughout the discipline of sociology, and they push the serious student to search for a delicate balance between order and freedom. Too often people are willing to sell out freedom in the name of order; too often people claim so much freedom that they do not seem to care about the continuation of society. The sociologist studies these problems and causes the student to reflect again and again on this dilemma inherent in all societies, especially those that claim to be part of the democratic tradition. There can be no freedom without society, Émile Durkheim reminds us, for a basic agreement over rules must precede the exercise of freedom. *But the problem is: How many rules? How much freedom? There is no more basic question for those who favour democracy, and there is no question more central to the discipline of sociology.*

The question of social order also leads us to the questions of what constitutes a nation and what constitutes a society. These issues may not seem at first to have much relevance to democracy, but they surely do. It is easy for those who profess democracy to favour majority rule. It is much more difficult for any nation to develop institutions that respect the rights of all societies within its borders. A nation is a political state that rules over one or more societies. If it is democratic, then the nation does not simply rule these societies but responds to their needs and rights, from true political representation to a decent standard of living. If it is democratic, the question the nation faces is *not* "How can we mould that society to be like the dominant society?" but "How can we create an order in which many societies can exist?" If it is democratic, then the nation must balance the needs of each society's push for independence with the need for maintaining social order. *The whole meaning of what it is to be a society, as well as the associated problems of order and independence, are central sociological — and democratic — concerns.*

It is the question of control by social forces over the human being that places sociology squarely within the concerns of democracy. Much of sociology questions the possibility for substantial freedom. Democracy teaches that human beings should and can think for themselves. Much of the purpose of sociology, however, is to show us that our thinking is created by our social life, that, although we may claim that our ideas are our own, they really result from our cultures, from our positions in social structure, and from powerful and wealthy people. Even to claim that "we are a democracy!" can simply be part of an ideology, an exaggeration we accept because we are victims of various social forces. Our actions, too, result from a host of social forces that few of us understand or appreciate: institutions, opportunities, class, roles, social controls — to name only some — that quietly work on the individual, pushing him or her in directions not freely chosen. Sociology seems to make democracy an almost impossible dream, and to some extent the more sociology one knows, the more difficult democracy seems. *Indeed, sociology tends to simply uncover more and more ways in which human beings are shaped and controlled. This, in itself, makes sociology very relevant for understanding the limits of democracy. It causes one to seriously wonder if human beings can be free in any sense.*

As I said earlier in this chapter, however, *sociology as a part of a liberal education is an attempt to liberate the individual from many of these controls.*

The first step in liberation is understanding: It is really impossible to think for oneself or to act according to free choice unless one understands the various ways in which we are controlled. For example, it is only when I begin to see that my ideas of what it means to be a "man" have been formed through a careful and calculated process throughout society that I can begin to act in the way I choose. Only when I being to understand how powerful advertising has become in developing my personal tastes as well as my personal values can I begin to step back and direct my own life. And even then, an important sociological question continuously teases the thoughtful person: Can society exist if people are truly liberated? If people question everything, can there still be the unity necessary for order?

The study of social inequality — probably the central concern within all sociology — is, of course, an issue of primary importance to understanding the possibility for a democratic society. It seems that it is the nature of society to be unequal. Many forces create and perpetuate inequality. Indeed, even in our groups and our formal organizations great inequalities are the rule. Why? Why does it happen? And what are its implications for democracy? If society is characterized by great inequalities of wealth and power, then how can free thought and free action prevail among the population? If a society — in name, a democracy — has a small elite that dominates the decision making, then what difference does going to the polls make? If large numbers of people must expend all of their energy to barely survive because of their poverty, where is their freedom, their opportunity to influence the direction of society, their right to improve their lives? If society is characterized by racist and sexist institutions, then how is democracy possible for those who are victims? *More than any other perspective, sociology makes us aware of many problems standing in the way of a democratic society, not the least of which are social, economic, and political inequality.*

This focus on social inequality will cause many individuals to look beyond the political arena to understand democracy. A democratic society requires not only limited government but also a limited military, a limited upper class, limited corporations, and limited interest groups. Limited government may bring freedom to the individual, but it also may simply create more unlimited power for economic elites in society, which is often an even more ruthless tyranny over individual freedom. *Sociology, because its subject is society, broadens our concerns, investigates the individual not only in relation to political institutions but also in relation to many other sources of power that can and do limit real democracy and control much of what we think and do.*

The democratic spirit cares about the welfare of all people. It respects life, values individual rights, encourages quality of life, and seeks justice for all. Sociology studies social problems. It tackles many problems, including those associated with human misery. Many people live lives of misery, characterized by poverty, crime, bad jobs, exploitation, lack of self-worth, stress, repressive institutions, violent conflict, inadequate socialization, and alienation of various kinds. These are more than problems caused by human biology or human genes; these are more than problems caused by the free choices of individual actors. Something social has generally caused misery to occur. *Although it is impossible for sociology — or a democratic society — to rid the world of such problems, it is part of the spirit of both to understand them, to suggest and to carry out ways to deal with them.* Democracy is shallow and cold if large numbers of people continue to live lives of misery.

What does ethnocentrism have to do with democracy? Is this central concern in sociology relevant to understanding and living in a democratic society? We return to the issue of respect for minorities mentioned earlier. Ethnocentrism, although perhaps inevitable and even necessary to some extent, is a way of looking at one's own culture and others in a manner antagonistic to a basic principle of democracy: respect for human diversity and individuality. To claim that our culture is superior to others is to treat other cultures without respect, to reject them for what they are, to believe that everyone must be like us. Such ideas encourage violent conflict and war and justify discrimination, segregation, and exploitation. Sociology challenges us to be careful with ethnocentrism. We must understand what it is, what its causes are, and how it functions. An understanding of ethnocentrism will challenge us to ask: "When are my judgements of others simply cultural and when are they based on some more defensible standards (such as democratic standards)?" "When are my judgements narrow and intolerant; when are they more careful and thought out?" Even then, an understanding of ethnocentrism will not allow us to judge people who are different without seriously questioning our judgements. *Sociology and democracy are perspectives that push us to understand human differences and to be careful in condemning those differences.*

The sociologist's faith in the individual as an agent of social change is not great. Democracy is truly an illusion if it means that the individual has an important say in the direction of society. But if sociology teaches us anything about change that has relevance for democracy, it is that intentionally created change is possible only through a power base. If a democracy is going to be more than a description in a book, people who desire change in society — ideally, toward more freedom, limited government, equality of opportunity, and respect for individual rights — must work together and act from a power base, recognizing that the existing political institutions are usually fixed against them. And before we go off armed with certainty, we should remember that our certainty was probably also socially produced and that through our efforts we may bring change we never intended and may even lose whatever democracy we now have. Social change is complex, depends on social power, and is difficult to bring about in a way we would like. *The sociologist will examine the possibility for intentional social change in a democratic society and will be motivated to isolate the many barriers each society establishes to real social change.*

SUMMARY AND CONCLUSION

Democracy exists at different levels. For some, it is a simplistic, shallow idea. For others, however, it is a complex and challenging idea to investigate and a reality worthwhile to create. If it is going to be more than a shallow idea, however, then people should understand the nature of all society, the nature of power, ethnocentrism, inequality, change, and all the other concepts discussed and investigated in sociology. Whereas other disciplines may study issues relevant to understanding democracy and encourage people to think democratically, in a very basic sense this study is the heart of sociology.

It is important to understand society without bias—that is, even about something so personal as society, human beings should try to be objective, to set aside the cultural reality they have learned, and to understand the world as it actually is. This critical evaluation of what we believe has a lot to do with freedom, because without it we are left with a cultural bias we are barely aware of and one that will influence all that we think. Democracy means that one must understand reality not through accepting authority but through careful, thoughtful investigation. It is through evidence, not bias, that one should understand. It is through open debate, not a closed belief system, that one should try to understand. *The principles of science and democracy are similar. There is no greater test of those principles than the discipline of sociology: an attempt to apply scientific principles to that for which we are all taught to feel a special reverence.*

Because it is a critical perspective that attempts to question what people have internalized from their cultures, sociology is a threat to those people who claim to know the truth. It punctures myth and asks questions that many of use would rather not hear. To see the world sociologically is to wonder about all things human. To see the world sociologically is to see events in a much larger context than the immediate situation, to think of individual events in relation to the larger present, to the past, and to the future. To see the world sociologically is to be suspicious of what those in power do (in our society and in our groups), and it is constantly to ask questions about what is and what can be.

The sociologist wonders about society and asks questions that get at the heart of many of our most sacred ideas. Perhaps this is why it seems so threatening to "those who know"; and perhaps this is why it is so exciting to those who take it seriously.

PART 2 | FOUNDATIONS OF SOCIETY

Imagine standing at the end of a road 30 km long. Allow each metre of the road to represent 100 000 years. The entire road will then signify the amount of time that has passed since life first appeared on the planet: about 3 billion years. From this long view, human beings are very recent arrivals, first assuming their present form only about 100 000 years ago, or just a metre down the road.

Recorded human history spans a much shorter distance. The development of agriculture, undoubtedly the single most important event in human history, took place about 10 000 years ago (only 10 cm down the road). The beginning of modern industry, arguably the second most important event in human history, dates from just over 200 years ago (a mere 2 mm down the road).

The evolution of agriculture and modern industry hint at what makes humans different from other animals: our ability to create symbols (**abstraction**), to make and use tools that improve our ability to take what we want from nature (**production**), and to develop a complex social life (**cooperation**). These are the characteristics that enabled humans to survive and multiply despite a harsh natural environment and poor physical endowments.

The chapters in this part of the book focus on the building blocks of social life, the basic social mechanisms and processes involved in human abstraction, production, and cooperation. You will explore how face-to-face symbolic communication, or **social interaction**, enables people to engage in social learning, or socialization. By means of **socialization** people acquire the languages, laws, science, values, customs, and beliefs—in short, the **culture**—of the groups to which they belong. When social interaction assumes a regular or patterned form, the *relations* among people form a **social structure**. Social structures may be, for example, hierarchical or egalitarian, tightly integrated or loosely organized; and different social-structural forms influence human thoughts and actions in different ways. The patterned behaviour of people embedded in a social structure is called a **role**. For instance, in some types of hierarchy, some people perform the role of slave, others the role of master. You will see that social structures and cultures are paradoxical features of social life. On the one hand, they are constructed anew, and often modified, at least a little, by each person in society. On the other hand, because social structures and cultures exist before any particular individual does, they help define and limit what the individual can think and what he or she can do. Hence the sociologist's answer to the philosopher's debate about whether people are free or determined: They are both.

GLOSSARY

Abstraction is the human ability to create symbols in order to classify experience and generalize from it.

Cooperation is the human ability to give and receive aid from other humans; social structures are typically created in order to facilitate cooperation.

Culture is the stock of human learning, the sum of human creations, as expressed symbolically in custom, language, art, law, science, and so on.

Production is a distinctively human mode of interacting with nature; it involves inventing tools and using them to make and improve the means of survival.

Roles are the behaviour patterns of people embedded in a social structure.

Social interaction is meaningful communication between people.

Socialization is the social process by which culture is learned.

Social structures are the patterns of social relations in which people are embedded and that provide opportunities for, and constrain, action.

PART 2A | INTERACTION AND SOCIALIZATION

In 1995, women working full-time in Canada's paid labour force earned 73 cents for every dollar earned by men. Although that was up from 64 cents a decade earlier, there were still nearly five times more men than women in high-paying jobs (those in which people earned $51 000 or more per year). Meet the **glass ceiling**, a sociological barrier that makes it difficult for most women to rise to the top rungs of the job ladder.

What is the glass ceiling made of? Over 100 male chief executives and 400 female senior managers were asked in a 1998 survey sponsored by the Conference Board of Canada to indicate the top three barriers to women's advancement to senior levels. The barrier most frequently mentioned by the women: male stereotyping and preconceptions of women's roles and abilities. The barrier most frequently mentioned by the men: lack of job experience. These responses are not necessarily contradictory. In corporations and the public bureaucracy, male managers may slot talented women into communications and human resource jobs because of their preconceptions of what women are good at; and because of this bias, women may fail to get the kind of operational experience in the field or on the production line that could lead them to top managerial positions. In any case, the men and women who participated in the survey certainly agreed on one thing. The second most frequently chosen response by both groups was "commitment to family responsibilities." Married women still do most of the housework and child care, while governments and corporations provide little in the way of parental support. The resulting career disruption, absenteeism, use of the part-time job option, and sheer physical and emotional exhaustion are major impediments to the advancement of women in the job hierarchy (see Chapter 18). Not surprisingly, therefore, among full-time workers in the paid labour force in 1991, *never-married* women earned 91 percent as much as never-married men, but *married* women earned only 65 percent as much as married men. Clearly, given current domestic, state, and corporate arrangements, married women, especially those with children, are penalized economically.

In Chapter 3, Deborah Tannen explores another fascinating aspect of the glass ceiling: gender-specific conversational styles. Because the **primary socialization** (or early childhood upbringing) of women usually differs from that of men, they typically communicate in different ways at work. These differences matter in terms of career advancement. According to Tannen, "women's and men's conversational styles affect who gets heard, who gets credit, and what gets done at work." In other words, a great deal of miscommunication between men and women takes place on the job. Due to the distribution of power in the workplace and the nature of this miscommunication, male managers may not notice the important contributions made by women or may even mistake them for incompetence. Tannen's revealing case studies drive home the point that women's careers will benefit if women become more assertive at work and if male managers improve their ability to understand everyday, gendered, face-to-face interaction. Indeed, by assessing the impact of typical male and female conversational styles, Tannen's research contributes to this role change.

Socialization does not, of course, end in early childhood. It is a lifelong process. In Chapter 4, Jack Haas and William Shaffir of McMaster University provide an extended example of **secondary socialization** in their analysis of how medical students learn to perform the role of doctor. They demonstrate that medical students become adept at **impression management** in order not to be judged incompetent by their teachers and patients. That is, they learn to consciously and often cynically manipulate the way they present themselves to others in order to be seen in the best possible light. They adopt a new vocabulary and way of dress to set themselves off from patients. They try to model their behaviour after that of doctors who have authority over them. By engaging in these symbolic interaction practices, they reduce the distance between their selves and the role of doctor. They eventually learn the role so well that, by the time they complete medical school, they fail to see any difference between their selves and their role. They come to take for granted a fact they once had to socially construct, painstakingly and imaginatively: the fact that they are doctors.

In the 1980s and early 1990s, most social scientists believed that social interaction by means of computers would involve only the exchange of information, not the formation of communities. Some science fiction writers saw things differently. In his 1984 novel, *Neuromancer*, Vancouver-based author William Gibson coined the term "cyberspace." He envisioned a set of virtual communities where interaction takes place through computers, "a consensual hallucination experienced daily by billions of legitimate operators, in every nation.... A graphic representation of data abstracted from the banks of every computer in the human system." In his 1992 novel, *Snow Crash*, American science fiction writer Neal Stephenson popularized the idea of "avatars," or fictional representations of individuals in cyberspace. Stephenson believed that individuals in virtual communities could not only engage in a wide range of social interactions, but could also present themselves differently from their real selves. In Stephenson's vision of cyberspace, people assume any persona they like through their avatars.

As MIT sociologist Sherry Turkle argues in Chapter 5, the future envisaged by Gibson and Stephenson is here. The Internet, she writes, has changed fundamentally the way the self is formed during social interaction. This is not just because the Internet creates many new opportunities to interact with people in distant locations. In addition, the Internet has spawned many on-line role-playing games and "chat rooms," where users interact anonymously. Anonymity encourages people to adopt new identities and explore parts of their selves they may have formerly concealed or suppressed. Moreover, the Internet allows people to play many roles simultaneously rather than sequentially. In real life, you might play the role of son in the morning, student in the afternoon, and boyfriend in the evening. But on the Internet you can play different roles in different windows at the same time. Thus, according to Turkle, the Internet not only renders the self more plastic, it also divides it and distributes it over new psychic territory.

The readings in this part show that roles are not handed to people like so many ready-to-wear suits of clothing. Individuals assist in tailoring roles to match their individual needs and capabilities. Learning a role is a creative endeavour, often requiring keen interpersonal skills. Roles are not passively learned but actively negotiated.

GLOSSARY

The **glass ceiling** is a sociological barrier that makes it difficult for most women to rise to the top rungs of the job ladder.

Impression management is the conscious manipulation of how one presents one's self to others for the purpose of achieving a desired result.

Primary socialization is social learning that takes place during early childhood, usually in the family.

Secondary socialization is social learning that takes place after early childhood in public school, during professional training, and so on.

CRITICAL THINKING QUESTIONS

1. According to Deborah Tannen, what factors prevent women from advancing in the work force? Why do men get more recognition and rewards for the work they perform?

2. What is meant by the term "the glass ceiling"? Do you agree with Deborah Tannen that conversational style differences between men and women play a significant role in establishing the glass ceiling? What are some conversational rituals common among women? What are some other examples of language differences in the workplace that make women's experience different from men's experience?

3. How would you change gender socialization to reduce gender inequality in the workplace?

4. To what degree do Deborah Tannen's findings reflect gender inequality and socialization in the workplace? What are some other explanations for gender inequality in the workplace? How could Tannen make her argument more convincing and generalizable?

5. Explain how medical students from McMaster University adopt a professional image as they progress through the secondary socialization process. What are other examples of secondary socialization?

6. According to Jack Haas and William Shaffir, how do medical students demonstrate trustworthiness?

7. What are some professions other than physician that use costumes, props, and linguistic symbols to create a professional image?

8. Do you think Turkle's argument applies to only a small number of people? Do you think her argument is likely to become more relevant over time? Why or why not?

9. On the Web, go to "The Mud Connector" at http://www.mudconnect.com. Visit a MUD. Evaluate Turkle's argument on the basis of your experience.

10. Does social interaction in Web-based virtual communities pose any dangers to the development of the self? Does it, for example, discourage face-to-face interaction and encourage social isolation? If so, what consequences might that have?

ANNOTATED BIBLIOGRAPHY

Robert H. Frank, *Passions within Reason: The Strategic Role of the Emotions* (New York: Norton, 1988). Brilliantly argues that the conscious pursuit of self-interest is incompatible with its attainment. Instead, self-interest is maximized in human interaction by the development of trust, a sense of justice, and other emotions.

Erving Goffman, *The Presentation of Self in Everyday Life* (New York: Anchor Doubleday, 1959). The definitive account of impression management in everyday interaction.

Julia Wood, Ron Sept, and Jane Duncan, *Everyday Encounters: An Introduction to Interpersonal Communication* (Scarborough, ON: ITP Nelson, 1998). An elegantly presented introduction to interpersonal communication, full of Canadian examples.

Chapter 3

The Glass Ceiling

DEBORAH TANNEN

A man who heads up a large division of a multinational corporation was presiding at a meeting devoted to assessing performance and deciding who would be promoted into the ranks of management. One after another, each senior manager got up, went down the list of individuals in his group and evaluated them, explaining whether or not they were promotable, and why. Though there were significant numbers of women in every group, not a single person singled out for advancement was female. One after another, every senior manager pronounced every woman in his group not ready for promotion because she lacked the necessary confidence. The division head began to doubt his ears. How could it be that *all* the talented women in the division suffered from a lack of confidence?

The situation described by this manager seemed to me to hold a clue to one described by a top executive at another multinational corporation who contacted me for help: "We started full of hope but we've reached an impasse. We are very successful at recruiting top women—they're creative, motivated, with fabulous credentials. They look just as good as the men when we hire them, if not better. But they don't get promoted. Years into our affirmative-action program, we still don't have any women in top management." The women who had been hired either were stuck at the level of middle management or had left the company or the field. He was describing what is sometimes referred to as the glass ceiling: an invisible barrier that seems to keep women from rising to the top. The

problem is considered so widespread and serious that a Glass Ceiling Commission was created as part of the U.S. Civil Rights Act of 1991, chaired by the secretary of labor.

Many earnest executives sincerely believe that there is no glass ceiling but only a pipeline problem: When women have been in the pipeline long enough to work their way up, some will reach positions at the top. But the longer this situation prevails, the less tenable the pipeline theory becomes. According to a 1991 report by the United States Department of Labor, progress has been extremely slow. During the ten-year period from 1979 to 1989, the representation of women and minorities in the top executive positions of the one thousand largest American corporations rose from 3 percent to 5 percent. Another 1991 survey based on 94 randomly selected Fortune 1000–sized companies found women comprised 37 percent of employees, 17 percent of managers, but only 6½ percent of executive-level managers.

The temptation is to see the cause of the glass ceiling as "sexism," and surely there is truth in this characterization. But "sexism" tells us where we are without telling us how we got there, and without providing help in getting out. I do not doubt there are men (as well as women) who do not wish to see women advance. It may be that the presence of women in their work lives is a complication that they did not bargain for when they chose their life's work. They may see every woman who fills a job in their field as taking that job from a man (rather than seeing half the men

Source: Excerpted from Deborah Tannen, *You Just Don't Understand* (New York: William Morrow and Company, 1994), pp. 132–59. Copyright © 1990 by Deborah Tannen. Reprinted by permission of HarperCollins Publishers, Inc.

in their field as taking jobs that should have gone to qualified women). They may even feel that women do not belong in positions of authority, certainly not in authority over them. But not all men fit this description. There are many men who sincerely want to see women advance and are trying to do something about it.

In all the companies I visited, I observed what happened at lunchtime. I saw women who ate lunch in their offices and women who skipped lunch to run or exercise in the gym and women who ate in groups with other women or with men. I observed men who ate alone or with colleagues and a few who went home to have lunch with their wives. I observed young men who made a point of having lunch with their bosses, and men at high levels of management who ate lunch with the big boss. I rarely noticed women who sought out the highest-level person they could eat lunch with.

Early on, I became aware of an irony. On one hand, it was from men that I heard that if women weren't promoted, they simply weren't up to snuff, whereas women everywhere agreed that something outside themselves prevents women from advancing. But on the other hand, it was women, more often than men, who seemed to feel that all that was necessary for success was to do a great job, that superior performance would be recognized and rewarded. Yet looking around, I could see that much more seemed to go into getting recognized and rewarded, and I saw men more often than women behaving in these ways.

In addition to doing excellent work, you must make sure that your work is recognized. This may consist of making a point to tell your boss, or your boss's boss, what you have done — either orally, or by sending reports or copies of pertinent correspondence. If a group meets, the person who is the first to report the group's results may get the most credit for them, whether or not that person was the source of the ideas in the first place. When lunchtime comes, the one who eats lunch with the boss may be doing more to get ahead than the one who stays in the office,

eating a sandwich and working. Doing brilliantly at a project that no one knows about will do little good in terms of personal advancement; doing well in a high-profile project, or one that puts you into contact with someone in power who will thereby gain firsthand knowledge of your skill, may make the big difference when that person speaks up in a meeting at which promotions are decided. All of these dynamics could be derisively dismissed as "office politics," but they are simply a matter of human nature. How *are* the bosses to know who's done what? It is understandable (though not necessarily admirable) if they notice what happens before them and fail to notice what they would have to rout around to see. Put another way, influence flows along lines of affiliation and contact.

Here is a brief explanation of how conversational-style differences play a role in installing a glass ceiling. When decisions are made about promotion to management positions, the qualities sought are a high level of competence, decisiveness, and ability to lead. If it is men, or mostly men, who are making the decisions about promotions — as it usually is — they are likely to misinterpret women's ways of talking as showing indecisiveness, inability to assume authority, and even incompetence. A woman who feels it is crucial to preserve the appearance of consensus when making decisions because she feels anything else would appear bossy and arrogant begins by asking those around her for their opinions. This can be interpreted by her bosses as evidence that she doesn't know what she thinks should be done, that she is trying to get others to make decisions for her.

Again and again, I heard from women who knew they were doing a superior job and knew that their immediate co-workers knew it but the higher-ups did not. Either these women did not seem to be doing what was necessary to get recognition outside their immediate circle, or their superiors were not doing what was necessary to discern their achievements and communicate these upward. The kinds of things they were doing, like quietly coming up with the ideas that influence their groups and helping those around them to do their best, were not easily observed in the way that giving an impressive presentation is evident to all.

Even so small a linguistic strategy as the choice of pronouns can have the effect of making one's contributions more or less salient. It is not uncommon for many men to say "I" in situations where many women would say "we." One man told me, "I'm hiring a new manager; I'm going to put him in charge of my marketing division," as if he owned the corporation he worked for and was going to pay the manager's salary himself. Another talked about the work produced by all the members of his group in the same way: "This is what I've come up with on the Lakehill deal." In stark contrast, I heard a woman talking about what "we" had done, but on questioning discovered that it was really she alone who had done the work. By talking in ways that seemed to her appropriate to avoid sounding arrogant, she was inadvertently camouflaging her achievements and lessening the chances they would be recognized.

Sociolinguist Shari Kendall spent two days shadowing the technical director for a news/talk show at a local radio station. The woman, Carol, was responsible for making sure all the technical aspects of the show went smoothly, and she did her job very well. The following incident, presented and analyzed by Kendall, reveals both why Carol was so good at her job and why her excellence was likely to go unrecognized.

Carol knew she had a challenge on her hands: the "board op," the technician who sits at the soundboard (the radio show's control tower), was out sick, and Harold, the man filling in, was very, very nervous. He had to get all the right prerecorded bits of music and talk onto the air at the right time, make sure that callers got on just when the host wanted to talk to them, and generally throw switches in the right direction at the right moment—switches chosen from a dizzying array that made up the soundboard. Though Harold had a thorough technical knowledge of the equipment, he was

unfamiliar with the routines of the show and inexperienced in this role. He was so nervous, he was shaking. For her part, Carol knew that if Harold fouled up, she would be blamed. She also knew that it is hard to throw a switch in the right direction with split-second timing when your hands are shaking. So, in addition to making sure he knew all the routines, she had to help Harold relax, which meant she had to make him feel competent and up to the job.

First Carol made sure that she gave Harold the information he needed to run the show and cautioned him about potential errors, all in a way that did not make him feel incompetent. Kendall points out that Carol gave Harold information phrased so as to imply it was not general technical knowledge (which he should have) but information particular to this show (which he could not be expected to have). For example, instead of saying, "Don't forget that tapes have a one-second lead-in," she said, "On this show everything has that one-second dead roll." Rather than saying, "Don't mix up the tapes; make sure you get them on in the right order," she said, "The only thing that people usually have trouble with is that they end up playing the promos and cassette tags and stuff in the wrong order." She avoided giving direct orders by saying, for example, "Probably we will want to re-cue the switch" when obviously it was he who had to re-cue the switch. In other words, Carol managed to apprise Harold of what he had to do without giving the impression she thought he was in danger of getting it wrong, and without framing him as potentially incompetent.

When she had done all she could to ensure that Harold knew what he had to do, Carol did not consider her job finished. She still wanted to make sure he felt calm and in control. She could have done this directly, by assuring him: "Now, look, you're a techie—you know a lot about this equipment; you'll do just fine," but when you think about it, that sounds condescending. Reassuring him would position her as superior and him as a novice needing reassurance. So she built up his confidence indirectly by framing him as an expert in an area in which he knew he was competent.] She picked up his copy of *Mac Weekly* and engaged him in conversation about computers. He took this opportunity to give her information about purchasing used Macs. Kendall, who was in the room observing, noticed that Harold sat back, put his feet up, and visibly relaxed during this conversation. Right before her eyes, he was transformed from the nervous novice to the self-assured teacher. As I pictured this scene in my mind, it was as if someone had inserted a tube in his foot and blown him back up. Carol remained with Harold throughout the show, and when it proceeded without requiring anything of him, she again asked him questions about computers. She later told Kendall that she sometimes keeps technicians talking during periods when they're not working the soundboard to reduce tension and prevent errors.

[Carol's efforts paid off. The self-confidence she inspired in Harold carried him through the show, which went without a hitch — a success that no one would know was due in part to Carol.] Quite the contrary, imagine the impression their supervisor might have gotten had he come into the studio shortly before airtime and found Harold with his feet up, answering Carol's questions about computers. It is likely he would have thought, even if he didn't think it through, that Harold was very much in command of the situation, and Carol was a rather underqualified technical supervisor who needs technical advice from her pinch-hitting board op. How different this impression would have been had she been less competent — say, if she had rushed into the studio at the last moment, rather than early, and had been busily giving direct orders to the board op right up to airtime. Now that would have created an image of firm control, even as it would have rattled Harold and caused him to make errors.

In two other conversations Kendall analyzed, Carol was working with a colleague named Ron, the manager of another control room. It was Carol's job to see that all went smoothly with the technical aspects of her show; it was Ron's to see that everything went well with all shows. In this instance, Carol foresaw a potential problem with the telephone hookup to be used when her show went on the road the following week. Ron, however, had not foreseen any problem. Carol managed to call the potential problem to Ron's attention and to enlist his aid in heading it off. This show too went off without a hitch.

The proof of the pudding is in the eating. [Carol had a low rate of technical errors on her watch. But the proof of her competence was invisible: the *absence* of errors.] How do you get your bosses to see something that did not happen? Carol herself expressed concern that her excellent work and job skills might not be recognized when new appointments were made.

This example is hauntingly similar to one described by journalist Sharon Barnes, who tells of an office that had to switch from manual to computer operations. Barnes contrasts the way two managers, a man and a woman, handled the switch. [The woman foresaw the need for computerization and gradually hired secretaries with computer experience, so the transfer to computerization took place without a ripple. The man did not prepare, so when the time came to switch to computers, his staff was in revolt. He mollified them by catering a lunch at which a consultant taught them what they needed to know. His troubleshooting was rewarded with a letter of commendation and a bonus. Barnes calls this "the white knight method" — letting problems happen and then ostentatiously solving them. This attracts attention, whereas making sure the problems don't arise in the first place is likely to go unnoticed — and unrewarded. According to Barnes, the white knight method is more common among men, the problem-preventing method more common among women.]

Here is another example of a woman getting others to do their best at the risk of her own credibility. It comes from the curator of a private art collection. The young men who were responsible for constructing the art installations were generally competent with tools, but they were artists, not construction workers, so they did not always know how to execute what she wanted. Her job was complicated by the fact that they would not tell her when they didn't know how to do something. She noticed that one of the three had more knowledge and skill than the other two. He often set about doing a job while the others stood by — not asking, but not working either. She figured out that if *she* asked for an explanation, the other two, hearing the explanation they needed, would start working. In her own words, she got the information out by taking the stance "I'm just a girl who doesn't understand." Like Carol, she framed herself as ignorant in order to get the job done. In this situation, the curator was the boss. There was no one over her to observe the interaction, miss her intent, and conclude that she was underqualified. The knowledgeable man *did* once explode, "Every time we do something, you ask the same stupid questions!" She simply walked away and explained later — in private — what she was doing and why; he immediately understood and apologized.

This corrective was simple enough, but not likely to happen with a boss who might well say nothing but form his opinion and keep his counsel. Once again, there is no harm in assuming the ritual appearance of incompetence so long as everyone knows that it is ritual. When it is taken literally, and when only one person in an interaction is using that style, the strategic use of an appearance of incompetence can be mistaken for the real thing.

In these examples, women adjusted their ways of speaking to make sure the job got done. In a study I conducted, together with a colleague, of doctor–patient communication, I observed a pediatrician who spoke in a seemingly unsure way in order to buffer the emotional impact of what she was saying. Because her work involved not only examining her young patients and consulting with their parents but also reporting to other clinical staff, we had an unusual opportunity to hear her talking about the same information under different circumstances, where she made a very different impression.

My colleague Cynthia Wallat and I analyzed the videotapes of the pediatrician talking in several different contexts about a child with cerebral palsy who had recently been diagnosed as having an arteriovenous malformation in her brain. In one of the videotapes, the doctor was examining the child in the presence of the mother. She pointed out that hemangiomas, visible as red marks on the child's face, were basically the same type of malady as the arteriovenous malformation in the brain. This gave the mother an opportunity to express a concern, and the doctor responded to the indirect question by providing an explanation:

Mother: I've often wondered about how dangerous they — they are to her right now.

Doctor: Well, um, the only danger would be from bleeding. *From* them. If there was any rupture, or anything like that. Which *can* happen. ... um, That would be the danger. *For* that. But they're ... mm ... *not* going to be something that will get worse as time goes on.

Mother: Oh, I see.

Doctor: But they're just *there*. Okay?

The doctor seemed rather insecure in this excerpt. Her talk was full of hesitations ("Well," "um," pauses). She uttered extra verbiage that didn't add meaning ("or anything like that," "which *can* happen"). She added phrases after her sentences were done ("the only danger would be from bleeding. *From* them." "That would be the danger. *For* that.") Emphasis seemed to fall in odd places.

But the doctor's hesitance and circumlocution in this setting contrasts sharply with her fluency and assurance when she talked about the same condition in a meeting with her peers. There she articulated part of the reason for her lack of fluency in speaking to the mother: She did not know how much information the parents already possessed about the danger of the child's condition, and she was not hesitant about the information she was imparting but about the effect it might have on the mother:

> uh, I'm not sure how much counselling has been *done, with* these parents, around the issue ... of the a-v malformation. Mother asked me questions, about the operability, inoperability of it, um, which I was not able to answer. She was told it was inoperable, and I had to say, "Well, yes, some of them are and some of them aren't." And I think that this is a—a—an important point. Because I don't know whether the possibility of sudden death, intracranial hemorrhage, if any of this has ever been dis*cuss*ed with these parents.

The physician, who showed so much hesitation and repetition in explaining the danger of the a-v malformation in the child's brain to the mother, expressed the same information in the staff meeting strongly and directly: There is a possibility of "sudden death, intracranial hemorrhage." When my colleague and I talked to the doctor, we were not surprised to learn that in speaking to the mother, she had been considering the emotional impact of telling a mother that her child might die suddenly because the a-v malformations could cause a hemorrhage in the brain at any time. When the mother asked this question, the doctor was in the midst of examining the child, so she could not take a half hour to discuss the danger and deal with the mother's reaction. Furthermore, the child was not her regular patient; she was examining her in connection with an educational placement. So she wanted to make sure that anything she said was coordinated with what the parents had been told by their own doctors.

The doctor's seeming lack of articulateness stemmed from her sensitivity to the potential impact of her diagnosis on the mother. And the mother appreciated this. She told us that of all the doctors she had taken her daughter to (and there had been many), she found this one to be the most considerate. In contrast, she said, she had been given devastating diagnoses and prognoses by doctors with no regard to how the information might make her feel. For example, early in the child's life one doctor had told her in a matter-of-fact way, "Your child will be a vegetable," and then moved on to other topics.

Considering how the doctor spoke to the mother in comparison with how she spoke in a meeting with other medical staff makes it clear that her hesitance and other disfluencies did not reflect her level of competence but her awareness of the impact of what she was saying on the person she was talking to. But how often do we have a tape recording of the same person talking about the same topic in another setting? And how often, when women talk in tentative, even seemingly confused, ways in order to soften the impact of what they are saying, are they seen as lacking in competence or confidence?

We judge others not only by how they speak, but also by how they are spoken to. If we hear people asking lots of questions and being lectured to, an impression takes root that they don't know much and that those lecturing to them know a lot. This is why girls used to be told to make boys feel good on dates by asking them about subjects they're expert on and listening attentively to their answers. It is also what Japanese subordinates are supposed to do to make the boss feel important when they spend an evening with him, according to Japanese anthropologist Harumi Befu. Ellen Ryan and her colleagues have found that when a health care provider behaves in a patronizing way toward elderly patients, observers evaluate the patient as less competent.

If people are being spoken to as if they know nothing, we assume they know nothing. If people are addressed as if they are pretty smart, we assume they're pretty smart. This probably has some basis in most of the conversations we hear around us; it is a reasonable way to approach the world, trusting it to give us clues. But if women routinely take the position of novice or listener to make others feel smart, it is highly likely that those others, as well as observers, will underestimate their abilities.]

Even worse, how a woman is addressed by others may have little to do with how she spoke in the first place. A consultant who worked fairly regularly with a small company commented to me that the new manager, a woman, was challenged and questioned by her subordinates more than her predecessor had been. He hadn't noticed any direct evidence that would lead him to question her competence, but he didn't really know the area they were working in. He added, "Maybe they know something about her abilities that I don't know." This seemed to me a double whammy. [A woman who assumes a role that has previously been held by men will likely begin work with an aura of suspicion about whether she is up to the job, and this may well lead at least some of her co-workers to press her to justify her decisions. This very questioning then becomes evidence that she lacks competence — regardless of her real abilities.]

Women may get more flak not only because their competence is in question but also because they are perceived as more vulnerable. A man who sails competitively commented that in a race, if he's looking for a hole, he picks a boat skippered by a woman or an older man; if you yell at them, he said, they are more likely to get out of the way. In the same spirit, Nancy Woodhull, a media and workplace consultant, points out that when corporate leadership changes and people jockey for position, they are especially likely to try to move in on turf held by women.

This insight helped me understand an experience that had puzzled and troubled me. I took part in a joint presentation together with a man whose style was different from mine. When I speak alone, as I generally do, I rarely get hostile comments from audience members because I always make sure to show the positive side of every style I mention and show the logic of *both* speakers when I give an example of a misunderstanding. I'm always careful not to make anyone

look bad. My co-speaker, however, was more provocative. Many of his anecdotes made either women or men look foolish.

When the question period came, this different tone had sparked a different response from the audience: some of the questions were hostile — especially from women. But most of the hostile questions were directed at me — including those that took issue with statements he alone had made. At the time, I was hurt and baffled, but in retrospect I could see what probably had happened. These women, riled by his tone and possibly put off by how he talked about women in some of his examples, looked at the stage and saw a large, gray-haired man with a caustic tone who did not hesitate to ruffle feathers, and a younger woman who was always conciliatory and eager not to offend. I was an easier target. My "open" manner left me open to attack.

Conversational rituals common among women involve each saving face for the other. One speaker is freed to take the one-down position (ritually, of course) because she can trust the other to, ritually again, bring her back up. Neither has to worry too much about casting herself in the best possible light because everyone is working together to save face for everyone else. I save your face, and you save mine.

[Put another way, many of the conversational rituals common among women are designed to make others feel comfortable, and this often involves the speaker taking a one-down role herself, though as we have seen, this is usually a ritual the other person is expected to match. At the same time women who observe these rituals are not investing a lot of energy in making sure they themselves do not appear one-down, which means that's just where they may end up.]

A couple of years ago, I arrived at a class I was teaching and found a newspaper journalist waiting outside the door. She told me she had been trying to get me on the phone, but because she had not succeeded in reaching me at my office, she had come ahead to the class because she wanted to sit in and write a short piece about me. Now the number of people who want to sit in on my classes, for various reasons, is considerable, so I have long had a firm policy that I do not permit auditors or visitors for any reason. Since I always conduct classes not as lectures but as discussions among students sitting in a circle, a stranger in our midst is a significant intrusion. There was no question in my mind that had the journalist gotten me on the phone beforehand, I would have told her this. But here I was faced with a poor woman who had made the trek all the way to my class, had waited for a long time, and was now looking at me directly and plaintively. I felt culpable for not having been in my office when she was trying to reach me, and I have a strong impulse to help everyone and inconvenience no one. I had to make a snap decision; I let her in.

At the end of the class, I collected assignments, and a few students had not followed my instructions. To save face for them, I said something like, "I'm sorry if my instructions weren't clear." I suspect some readers will be able to foresee what happened: Lo and behold, in the article she wrote, the journalist took this ritual apology as a literal admission of fault and used it to make me look bad: Imagine, she wrote, here's this expert on communication, and she can't even give comprehensible assignment instructions to her students.

I am sure that some people will think, "It serves her right. She opened herself up to this." And they are correct. The impulses that drove me to make others feel comfortable were driving me in a direction opposite from self-protection, which would have led me to deny the journalist entrance to my class (it was her problem, not mine, if she made the trip without getting permission to sit in), or, once she was there, would have led me to monitor my behaviour so as not to say anything that might appear as weakness — the kind of self-monitoring that leads others (including many men) not to apologize, take blame, admit ignorance, and so on.

It is interesting to consider, however, how well my impulse to accommodate the journalist worked for her. She risked rejection by showing up at the door of my class unannounced. In a way, she was counting on me to observe interactional rituals common among women, and in this case her hunch paid off.

All these examples dramatize how ways in which women are likely to talk may mask their true competence in the view of those who are required to judge their performance. When forced to evaluate people they do not work with day-to-day, executive and high-level managers will necessarily be influenced by what little exposure they have had to the people they are judging. In addition to the fleeting impressions of chance encounters, for many top executives this may mean the few times they have observed lower managers directly — when they are making presentations. And this is yet another situation in which knowing a lot doesn't automatically transfer into showing what you know. If most women's conversational rituals have prepared them for private speaking, the importance of formal presentations is yet another aspect of moving through "the pipeline" that puts many women at a disadvantage.

Public speaking is frightening for almost everyone. But standing up in front of a large group of people, commanding attention, and talking authoritatively are extensions of the socialization most boys have been forced to endure, as boys in groups tend to vie for centre stage, challenge the boys who get it, and deflect the challenges of others. Many of the ways women have learned to be likable and feminine are liabilities when it comes to public presentations. Most girls' groups penalize a girl who stands out or calls attention to herself in an obvious way.

A woman who works as a trainer for business people coming to the United States realized that a disproportionate amount of the criticism she and her colleagues delivered to the trainees was directed at women, especially in the nebulous category of "professional presence." They found themselves telling women, more often than men, that they did not speak loudly enough, did not project their voices, should stop cocking their heads to one side, should try to lower the pitch of their voices. A few women were told that their way of dressing was too sexy, their manner too flirtatious, if they wanted to be taken seriously in the American business environment. In a sense, they were appearing too "feminine." But there were also women who were told that they were too challenging and abrasive. They launched into questions without a lead-in or hedges; they asked too many insistent questions; they did not tilt their heads at all or seemed to be tilting them in challenging ways. Although the trainers did not think of it in these terms, you could say that these women were not "feminine" enough.

In at least one case, a particular trainee had to be told that she was coming across as both too flirtatious and too confrontational. In wondering why such a large percentage of women in her program (a small one to start with) had the basic skills down cold, yet seemed to be undermining their own effectiveness by their nonverbal behaviour, the trainer concluded that they had a very fine line to walk: The range of behaviours considered acceptable for them was extremely narrow. And, perhaps most important, the American professional business culture in which they were learning to fit was not only American but also American male.

All of the factors mentioned by the trainer indicate that making presentations is a prime example of an activity in which behaviour expected of women is at odds with what is expected of an effective professional. In fact, the very act of standing up in front of a group talking about ideas is something that was unthinkable for women not so long ago. The nineteenth-century abolitionist Abby Kelley was reviled as a "Jezebel" and "fornicator" because of her public speaking. Because she was physically attractive, men saw her as a dangerous seductress.

Once a woman (or man) does make public presentations, she (or he) is open to challenge or even attack. Many women have been told they cave in too quickly rather than stand their ground. Being able to deal effectively with pub-

lic challenges is not something that comes easily to many women (or men). And there are regional and cultural differences in styles as well. One man, a sociologist from a small town, was invited to give a lecture at a major East Coast university where he was being considered for a faculty position. The questions from the floor were so authoritative that he became convinced he was talking to people who had obviously done research in his area, research that he had somehow missed in his review of the literature. After the talk, which he was sure he had bombed, he went to the library and scoured the sources for references to these men's work—references that did not exist. To his amazement (he had taken literally the tone of contempt in their questioning), he got the job. So he had occasion to discover that they had done no work in the field at all; they were simply challenging him to see how well he could defend his claims—and were satisfied and pleased with his rebuttals. Although he had successfully defended himself against this ritual assault, he had gotten the impression that they had more basis for their challenges than they actually had.

There are many women who are very successful public speakers. I once noted the different public-speaking styles of two presenters at a meeting—a man and a woman. Both were excellent speakers, but he filled the room with his expansive presence, whereas she brought the room in close. He told stories as if he were in church preaching to a crowd; she told them as if she were sitting in her living room with friends. (An audience member commented on how "natural" she sounded.) She did not tell jokes, as he did, but she was humourous. Whereas he remained straight-faced after saying something funny, she laughed along with her audience. The woman's public speaking was successful in a private-speaking sort of way, whereas his was successful in a more public-speaking, oratorical way.

This is not to say that there is only one way for a woman or a man to give successful presentations. Both women and men must learn to handle this special situation well in order to get recognition for the work they do, but women's socialization is usually more at odds with the requirements of presenting to a group.

If one of the reasons women are not promoted is that they are spending more time doing their jobs and less time promoting themselves, can the solution be for women to begin promoting themselves more? Veronica had an observant boss who noticed that many of the ideas coming out of the group were hers, but it was often someone else in the group who trumpeted the ideas around the office and got credit for them. The boss told Veronica she should take more credit for her ideas. But Veronica wasn't comfortable doing that. She tried and found she simply didn't enjoy work if she had to approach it as a grabbing game. She liked the atmosphere of shared goals and was comfortable in the knowledge that she was part of a group effort. Striving to get credit for herself felt like a lonely and not very admirable endeavour. Trying to follow her boss's advice made coming to work a lot less fun.

In a related pattern, I spoke to many women who claimed they simply were not comfortable standing out. And I spoke to men who had noticed women who seemed to feel that way. For example, a man who headed an educational film company called a woman into his office and told her the good news that one of the clients with whom she had dealt in the past had decided to make a large purchase for a new film library. Rather than saying, "Great! I'll give them a call right away," the woman said, "Maybe someone else should follow up this time, since I've already got the highest sales in the group for the month." Even though the sales staff did not work on commission, the manager was incredulous. "They *asked* for you," he said. "They liked working with you before, and you're the one they want. What kind of a company would I be running if I didn't give my clients the person they ask for?" This convinced her, and she accepted the assignment. But she had to think of it in terms of what was good for the company rather than what was good for her—or at least be *assigned* the job rather than appear to be *taking* it.

I saw this same force at work in a talented graduate student who had been working for me as a research assistant in addition to participating in a seminar I taught. One day I told her, in private, that I owed her two apologies. The first was because she had handed me a bill for her services as research assistant as we were leaving class, and I had misplaced it. The second was that I feared I had embarrassed her in class when I unthinkingly corrected a minor grammatical error she had made while speaking. She told me that, since I was bringing it up, there was something that had bothered her, but it wasn't either of the two things I mentioned. It was something else entirely. The students had gathered around me after the last class meeting of the term, discussing who would take the next course. She had expressed frustration that she could not afford to take the course, and everyone knew my policy against allowing auditors. But I had said, "Maybe I can make an exception for you." She had not been bothered by my publicly correcting her grammar or by my neglecting to pay her on time. What bothered her was my singling her out for special treatment.

Favouritism can wreak havoc in any group. But whereas anyone can see that those not in favour would resent those who are, it seems that many women are uncomfortable not only being out, but also being too obviously in. This has resounding implications for promotability. Unobtrusively doing excellent work does not threaten group belonging. But getting special recognition does. It may well spark resentment from co-workers. Resentment, in fact, can result from almost any action that ensures getting credit, especially from those above. In a large organization, everyone is really the servant of many masters. Whereas you are taking direction, or even orders, from an immediate supervisor, that supervisor is answerable to someone above, who is answerable to someone above that. And somewhere in the upper layers are those who determine your fate when it comes to ranking and promotion. Much depends, therefore, on your ability to make contact with the people above your boss. But if you do, you may well incur the rancour of your immediate boss and your peers. And this may be a burden that more women than men are hesitant to risk.

Besides the danger of provoking peer resentment (or related to it) is the different ways women and man are inclined to view self-aggrandizing talk. Letting others know about what you have done is almost always labelled boasting by women, and boasting is something most women have learned early on to avoid. In contrast, many men assume they have to let others know what they've done in order to get the recognition they deserve. Bragging about his exploits got Othello the hand of Desdemona; Kate had to learn to keep her mouth shut to marry Petruchio—the "shrew" who spoke up had to be "tamed."

The example of a professional couple illustrates the attitudes many women and men have toward displaying or downplaying their own accomplishments. Bridget and Sean were both successful real estate agents, but they had different habits of self-presentation. Sean made sure to let new acquaintances know what he had done; Bridget played down what she had done and assumed people would eventually learn of it from others and like her all the more for her modesty when they did. Bridget thought Sean was boastful; he thought she was foolishly and inappropriately self-deprecating. Neither thought of the other's way of talking as related to gender; they thought they were dealing with issues of personal character.

A widely publicized incident involving political consultant Ed Rollins is evidence that talking about one's accomplishments is a ritual common among men. Rollins managed the campaign of Republican candidate Christine Todd Whitman in her 1993 bid for the governorship of New Jersey. At a breakfast for journalists shortly after Whitman's victory, Rollins boasted that he had won the election for his candidate by his successful efforts to keep blacks from voting—for example, by making donations to African American churches in exchange for the minis-

ters' agreement not to preach get-out-the-vote sermons. When this boast hit the headlines, there was talk of knocking the candidate out of office and sending Rollins to jail. So he quickly explained that his boasts had been groundless, designed to embarrass his opponent James Carville, who was campaign manager for the Democratic candidate Jim Florio.

It is not clear whether Rollins was telling the truth when he first made the boast or when he later claimed it had been baseless. Whichever it was—and this may never be known—the case is a revealing example of the ritualized role of boasting. Rollins saw his role of campaign manager as a head-to-head fight with another man, Carville, and wanted to take ostentatious credit for his victory, so he boasted in a group about what he had done—or felt he could get away with claiming to have done. Another famous (or infamous) instance of boasting occurred when police located one of the men who allegedly had arranged an attack on figure-skater Nancy Kerrigan in part because he—rival skater Tonya Harding's "bodyguard"—had boasted openly to fellow students about what he had accomplished.

This incident, and the story of Ed Rollins's boasting, brought to mind an intriguing statement by Rupert Allason, a British member of Parliament who is an authority on the British intelligence services. He was explaining why he thinks women make better spies than men. On the occasion of the appointment of Stella Rimington as the first female director-general of the British Internal Security Service, Allason commented, "Women have always been good security operatives. While men tend to gossip about their job to impress friends, women gossip about trivia and keep their real secrets."

Linguist Penelope Eckert made similar observations of high school girls' and boys' secret-keeping habits. The high school girls Eckert studied told her that boys were better at keeping secrets than girls. Eckert hypothesized that this is not because boys are morally superior to girls but because, given the sex-separate social structure of the high schools, girls have something to gain by revealing other girls' secrets, whereas boys do not. (Girls gain status by their social network—whom they are friends with. So showing that you know a girl's secrets is a good way to prove to others that you are friends with her. Boys, on the other hand, gain status by their own accomplishments. They gain nothing by demonstrating that they are close friends with girls, so they have no incentive to repeat their secrets. Instead, the boys are tempted to talk about what they've done or can claim to have done.) This explains why, in the situation of a spy or a campaign manager, males' and females' abilities to hold their tongues are not-so-mysteriously reversed.

Whatever the motivation, women are less likely than men to have learned to blow their own horns—which means they may well not get credit for the work they have done, or, as Ed Rollins at least claimed, try to get credit for what they have not done. More women than men seem to have a sense that if they do this, they will not be liked. And the spectre of working in an environment where they are not liked may be more than they are willing to risk. The congeniality of the work environment is important to everyone, but the requirement that everyone like each other may be more central to women's notion of congeniality, whereas men may value other types of congeniality, such as easy banter. One man who heads a large division of a corporation commented that in recruiting for diversity, they usually get the minority men they want by offering them the most generous package of remuneration. In recruiting women, however, they are most successful by sending women to recruit other women. If the recruiter can convince a prospective woman that the company provides a positive work environment, it is successful in recruiting her even if she has competing offers that are more lucrative. In addition to providing evidence that a congenial work environment is very important to many women, this may also say something about why women are chronically paid less than men in comparable positions.

The most eloquent and amusing description I know of why someone fails to get credit for her work and how she changes her behaviour to rectify the situation is in a short story by the Irish writer Maeve Binchy entitled "King's Cross." As the story opens, Sara Gray, an overworked and underappreciated assistant manager in a travel office, is interviewing a prospective secretary named Eve, who turns out to be a mixture of the Lone Ranger and Mary Poppins. Eve swoops into Sara Gray's life and transforms it by showing her how to get recognition—and promotion.

The first thing Eve does is insist on addressing her boss as "Miss Gray," even though Sara protests that it sounds "snooty." Eve points out that the male managers and assistant managers all call Sara by her first name, though she addresses many of them as "Mr." When speaking of Miss Gray to others, she adopts a tone of respect bordering on awe that gradually creeps into the attitudes of others in the office. Eve tells Sara that "it is absolutely intolerable the way that people think they can come barging in here, taking advantage of your good nature and picking your brains, interrupting us and disturbing you from whatever you are doing." To put a stop to this, Eve sets herself up at the door to Sara's office and insists that anyone who wants to see Miss Gray must make an appointment.

Eve discovers that Sara has not been taking advantage of available perks such as an account at a taxi firm, a clothing allowance, and a small fund for redecorating her office. With the latter, Eve acquires a conference table and suggests how Sara might use it. She points out that when Sara last developed a wildly successful marketing idea, no one but her boss, Garry Edwards, knew that it had been hers, so he got the credit and the reward, since it came out of his division. Eve counsels:

> Next time, I suggest you invite Mr. Edwards and his boss and the marketing director and one or two others to drop in quite casually—don't dream of saying you are calling a meet-

ing, just suggest that they might all like to come to your office one afternoon. And then, at a nice table where there is plenty of room and plenty of style, put forward your plans. That way they'll remember you.

When Sara prepares work for Garry Edwards, Eve sends copies to others, so everyone knows it's her work. She encourages Sara to get an assistant who can cover her desk, so indispensability will not be an excuse for failing to send her to conferences or, eventually, promote her. She makes sure that Sara's name is on the list of guests to social events attended by executives. When Garry Edwards tries to undo Sara by blaming her for his own mistake, Eve's filing system yields a document proving that Sara had recommended the correct course of action. Garry Edwards is out, and Sara Gray gets his job, which she had, after all, been doing, without remuneration, all along.

This is, sadly for us all, just a fantasy, a work of fiction, though a delightful one to read. How nice it would be if Eve swept into each of our lives and ensured we got the credit we deserve. But the story, oversimplified (and entertaining) as it is, captures some of what individuals can do (and often fail to do) to achieve that felicitous result on their own.

I do not wish to imply that all inequities in recognition and promotion result from the behaviour—linguistic or otherwise—of individuals. Some forces are out of our hands, or at least extremely difficult to influence. A phenomenon having little to do with conversational style that may handicap women is mentoring.

An academic position was advertised at a major university. Everyone was welcome to apply. But one candidate was a favourite of someone on the faculty. The faculty member saw to it that his candidate was the last one scheduled for a presentation, and he let him know when the other candidates were giving their presentations. This enabled his candidate to attend the others' presentations and gauge the reaction of the audience—what went over well, what fell flat, what concerns were reflected in the questions asked. He took this information into account in planning his own talk, and he wowed the department enough to get the job. At least one woman who had applied for the job felt that she had been locked out by an "old-boy network."

Similar patterns can obtain in promotion, where one candidate has established a relationship with someone involved in the search. He may be informed of the opening earlier, told what is best to emphasize in his application or interview, and given an advantageous position in the queue. Is this illegal preferential treatment or just "mentoring," a system by which a younger person has a supporter and ally higher up who "brings him along"? If such supporter relationships are likely to spring up between someone established in the organization and someone new to it, it is likely that the older person will be male (since he probably entered the organization when there were few or no women in it) and also likely that the established person will be drawn to someone who reminds him of himself at that stage—who is therefore probably male too. It is not intentional "sexism," yet it is a pattern that favours men over women—not all men, of course, but it is a structure women are less likely to fit into.

At the same time that we seek to understand how ways of talking can work against women, we also must bear in mind that it may be harder for women to get promoted regardless of how they speak. Marjorie and Lawrence Nadler list a number of studies that show that stereotypes work against women. They cite, for example, Lea Stewart, who found that women are often given different task assignments than men with similar positions and qualifications, and the ones they are given are not those that lead to advancement. They also cite Cynthia Fink, who shows that there is a widespread belief that men are simply more suited to management. Finally, Garda Bowman, Beatrice Worthy, and Stephen Grayser show that managers believe women just don't have the decision-making skills or aggressiveness needed to succeed in managerial positions.]

Not every woman, or every man, wants to be promoted, though the argument that women don't really want high-pressure jobs has been used to avoid giving them the chance. There are women and men who choose downward mobility, but I do not think there are many people who would choose not to have their work recognized. People whose contributions are appreciated become motivated to continue and increase their efforts, whereas those whose contributions are overlooked are more likely to leave, perhaps citing other reasons for their decision. So failing to recognize the achievements of those with styles that do not call attention to themselves is a loss not only to the individuals but also to the companies.

Talking, like walking, is something we do without stopping to question how we are doing it. Just as we cheerfully take a walk without thinking about which foot to move forward (unless a puddle blocks our path), we simply open our mouths and say what seems self-evidently appropriate, given the situation and person we are talking to. In other words, ordinary conversation has a ritual character, and the conversational rituals typical of women and men, though they obviously have a lot in common—otherwise we couldn't talk to each other—can also be different. And even subtle differences can lead to gross misinterpretation. In a situation in which one person is judging another and holds the key to a gate the other wants to pass through, the consequences of style differences can be dire indeed.

If more and more people understand the workings of conversational style, they will be able to adjust their own ways of talking and stand a better chance of understanding how others mean what they say. But at the same time, the more people gain an understanding of conversational style, the less necessary it will be for others to adjust their style. If supervisors learn to perceive outstanding performance regardless of the performer's style, it will be less necessary for individuals to learn to display their talents. On that happy day, the glass ceiling will become a looking glass through which a fair percentage of Alices will be able to step.

Chapter 4

Impression Management: Becoming a Doctor at McMaster University

JACK HAAS

WILLIAM SHAFFIR

In his seminal work on social interaction, Goffman (1959) draws attention to the significance of impression management in everyday life. In order to explore this dimension of social life, sociologists have focused mainly on people involved in deviant and low status occupations (Ball, 1967; Edgerton, 1967; Goffman, 1961; Henslin, 1968; Maurer, 1962; Prus and Sharper, 1979; Scott, 1968). Yet as Hughes (1951) suggests, a comparative study of occupations often reveals similar adaptive mechanisms. In occupations that demand a measure of trust from clients, participants must convince legitimating audiences of their credibility. The importance of playing an adequate role in order to exact the right kind of response from clients is true of both shady and respectable occupations.

Although impression management and role playing are essential parts of this kind of sociological interaction, effective performance becomes even more crucial when participants perceive an audience that is potentially critical and condemning. This is especially true when an audience has high expectations of competence in others. If those in whom competence is expected also have a concomitant responsibility of making decisions that affect the well-being of others, the situation is even more crucial. Audiences then look for cues and indications of personal and/or collective (institutional) competence, and in response practitioners organize a carefully managed presentation of self intended to create an aura of competence.

Concern about the competence of those granted rights and responsibilities affecting others is very much a part of the relationship existing between patients and medical professionals. Patients look for competent advice and assistance, and medical professionals, particularly doctors, want to convince those they treat that they are indeed competent and trustworthy. It is only when a patient believes a doctor possesses these attributes that diagnostic intervention and prescribed treatment can affect the course of the illness in any positive way.

Studies of professional socialization (Becker et al., 1961; Bloom, 1973; Broadhead, 1983; Light, 1980; Merton et al., 1957; Olesen and Whittaker, 1968; Ross, 1961) show how trainees adopt a professional image as they proceed through the socialization process. Sociological studies of noncollege, school, and other training

Source: *Becoming Doctors: The Adoption of a Cloak of Competence* (Greenwich, CT: JAI Press, 1987), pp. 53–83. Reprinted by permission of the publisher.

situations (Geer, 1972) indicate that the socialization experience involves learning specific skills and techniques as well as taking on an occupational culture that includes a new or altered identity. Such studies describe a process whereby students or trainees adapt in order to develop a new view of the self.

As students are professionalized, they are initiated into a new culture wherein they gradually adopt those symbols that represent the profession and its generally accepted authority. These symbols (language, tools, clothing, and demeanour) establish, identify, and separate the bearer from the outsider, particularly from the client and the paraprofessional audience. Professionalization, as we observed it, involves the adoption and manipulation of symbols and symbolic behaviour that create an imagery of competence. The net result of this process separates the profession from those they are intended to serve.

Faced with inordinately high audience expectations, medical students begin the process of professionalization by distancing themselves from those they interact with. They manipulate the symbols of their new status in order to distinguish their activity as one grounded in mystery and sciences unfathomable to others. Their performance is intended to convince both themselves and others that they are competent and confident to face the immense responsibilities imposed by their privileged role.

This chapter will demonstrate the ways in which the medical students we studied attempted to communicate trustworthiness by impression management. The focus is mainly on the clinical or clerkship experience, this being the critical phase of the ritual ordeal where the professionalization process is most intense. We begin by outlining the general expectations that delineate the physician's role and the perceived expectations of the student in clinical training. Then we describe the importance of the manipulation and control of people, symbols, and ideas that is necessary for meeting both generalized and situational expectations.

As students become successful at controlling and manipulating others' impressions in order to be perceived as competent and trustworthy, they increasingly identify with the role and with the ways that qualified practitioners handle their problems. Successful control of professionalizing situations, it would seem, has a self-fulfilling quality that allows authoritative performances to contribute to the neophytes' changing perceptions of the self. If initiation is rigorous, students learn to adopt a symbolic-ideological cloak of competence that they perceive initiated members of the medical fraternity to wear. It is thus that the image of authority and trustworthiness is created. By way of a conclusion we will point out that the nature of legitimating audience expectations is perceived by newcomers as requiring conformity to a role that is exaggerated and thus demands an exaggerated performance.

GENERALIZED EXPECTATIONS OF COMPETENCE

The medical profession is a unique one in that so much of its authority depends on the effective communication of trust. Freidson (1970: 10–11) outlines the characteristics of this occupation that serve to set it apart from others. These are:

- A general public belief in the consulting occupation's competence, in the value of its professed knowledge and skill.
- The occupational group ... must be the prime source of the criteria that qualify a person to work in an acceptable fashion.
- The occupation has gained command of the exclusive competence to determine the proper content and effective method of performing some tasks.

Medicine's position, Freidson (1970: 5) notes, is equivalent to that of a state religion: "it has an officially approved monopoly of the right to define health and illness and to treat illness."

Doctors possess a special authority because of their accepted expertise about human health. Their work is believed to constitute a social and individual good. Their authority is further enhanced by the historical linking of medicine and religion: the physician mediates the mysteries of scientific research through a ritual system where the doctor assumes a priest-like role (Siegler and Osmond, 1973: 42).[1]

To create a physician's authority requires the manipulation of an effective symbol system that is accepted and shared by participants. The moral authority of the physician is most apparent as being complete and unassailable when the doctor is involved with decisions affecting life and death. The fact that death strikes fear in human beings gives impressive, Aesculapian authority to those who are believed able to ward it off or postpone it (Siegler and Osmond, 1973).[2]

Because of the authority invested in them, medical practitioners, students and physicians alike, must deal with the inordinate and exaggerated demands of those they treat. The problem is somewhat less in magnitude for the medical student, who is generally protected from situations that would prematurely or inappropriately demand his exercise of responsibility. Students, however, realize that the outcome of their socialization will, in the future, require them to deal with life and death situations. It is thus their hope that the socialization process will prepare them to meet the responsibilities imposed by their profession with both confidence and competence. According to one student:

> I think you're faced with a problem, that in a large way the public has unrealistic expectations about the medical profession. It puts the doctor in a very difficult position because you know yourself you don't know it all, but the public thinks you know it all and puts you in a position where you have to be a good actor. (Interview: Winter, second year)

THE PROBLEMS OF PERCEIVED EXPECTATIONS IN CLERKSHIP

During the rotating clerkship assignments, the students are exposed to many different audiences, which all have different expectations about the proper performance of the role. In fact, in the hospital setting, the role itself is ambiguous and raises the question, is the individual primarily student, clerk, or physician? As a result, the "clinical jerk" is constantly faced with new situations that do not relate in a clear way to his or her new status. In consequence he or she finds it difficult to assume an appropriate role and to project a "correct" identity.

Another confusing aspect of the clinical clerk's situation concerns the responsibility he or she is expected to assume. In earlier phases of the program the student examined patients as part of a learning experience; clerkship demands that the students do more than learn. They must assume a degree of responsibility for patient well-being. A student summarizes this difference when he says

> Well, from my perception, even in Phase II and Phase III, we played around with real patients in a Phase I sort of thing. ... It was sort of a game. You were trying to find out what was the interesting clinical sign. Whereas now (clerkship) when you see a patient you are doing a history and physical on a patient and it sort of focuses on you. ... The intern may or may not go over the bloody patient because he's really trusting you to pick up what you should pick up ... so you're always trying to think, "Well, if I don't pick these up, and the resident doesn't get them, I'm the one who has done the history and physical. If I miss something then somebody is going to be after my ass for it." (Interview: Winter, third year)

As students in clerkship become more integral members of a health care team, they are delegated some tasks that require the exercise of personal responsibility, and thus they become accountable in ways almost always new to them. The taking on of increased responsibility and the concomitant exercise of medical judgement makes them accountable to a variety of professionals. The prevalent response of the clinical clerk is to develop an increasingly sympathetic attitude toward his or her future profession. The following examples gleaned from clinical clerks illustrate this point:

> [The conversation centres around clerkship and whether this phase of the program alters one's view of the medical profession.] I think it does from the point of view that you can more or less see other people's situations much more because you're in their boat. ... Having been in it [medicine], I can see why some patients are dealt with quickly perhaps. (Interview: Spring, second year)

> I remember when we were way back in Phase II and Phase I, we would go see a patient with a clinical skills preceptor, and he might have said something to the patient that seemed rude, and I'd get all very indignant about it and say: "My God, you're not being sensitive." While that may have been justified, now that I'm on the ward I can see that in a way it's a bit silly to take that one episode, because what you are seeing is one episode in a long history of the relationship between that patient and his doctor. You're taking this totally out of context and it's really not relevant to criticize unless you really know the relationship. Now I'm much less free with those sorts of criticisms. (Interview: Spring, second year)

Students are confronted with a dilemma. On the one hand they try to prove themselves as competent to others while, on the other, they remain concerned about the limits of their competence, which might cause them to act inappropriately, perhaps with dire consequences. Two students summarize this ambiguous response to the taking on of responsibility this way:

> Jim complains to Claudette that on one of his rotations he was given too much responsibility. He says, "I don't mind it if I'm ready for it, but I just didn't feel I was ready for it. The resident thought I was ready for it. He thought I knew more than I did. Maybe I did, maybe I didn't. If I did, I suppose I was ready for it, but I didn't feel I was ready for it. I didn't feel I knew enough but he tells me I knew enough. I felt

uncomfortable and asked that I not be given the responsibility." (Field notes: Spring, third year)

While students are generally protected from meeting all the expectations of patients, they do face the unpredictable nature of faculty expectations; in fact, faculty become the major reference group or audience that students feel most demand and evaluate competence. The teaching staff is responsible for evaluating and determining the progress of the students. The students, in turn, attempt to estimate teachers' demands, although at times they are ill-defined and sometimes contradictory. Defining and attempting to meet faculty expectations is often difficult. The students' problem is dealing with staff who have widely divergent approaches to the practice of medicine. Faced with a threatening ambiguity, students try to find out the particular biases and special areas of interest of those with whom they must interact (Becker et al., 1961). This is because they soon realize that their teachers are convinced of the correctness and validity of their expertise and approach. In this sort of situation the students find their competence and learning assessed in situations in which they are vulnerable and therefore easily reminded of their incompetence.

For professional students the short-term goal of a "good" evaluation is vital because this kind of assessment demonstrates their developing competence to those who control their careers. To a lesser extent this is also true of students in traditional medical school settings. Although these students initially impress the faculty by their skill at passing examinations, they must eventually demonstrate competence. This is similar to students in the innovative program, through the exercise of selective interactional skills. Both types of students, those in traditional and innovative learning environments, then exhibit a common reaction to evaluation in the face of uncertain expectations. When individuals are uncertain about what they should know or how they should apply it, they "cover" themselves by deflecting others from probing their ignorance

(Edgerton, 1967; Goffman, 1963; Haas, 1972, 1977; Haas and Shaffir, 1977; Olesen and Whittaker, 1968). This "cloaking" behaviour is often accompanied by initiative-taking behaviour intended to impress others with their competence. This phenomenon is well documented. For example, Becker et al. state:

> Perhaps the most noticeable form of attempting to make a good impression is the use of trickery of various kinds to give the appearance of knowing what one thinks the faculty wants one to know or having done what the faculty wants done, even though these appearances are false. (1961: 284)

Bucher and Stelling also report that students, themselves, are aware that impression management is crucial to their progress.

> The residents have learned that they could contribute considerably to the nature and outcome of the supervisory process. ... The most common tactic was that the resident psyched out what the superior wanted to hear and presented his material accordingly. (1977: 107, 109)

THE SYMBOLS OF PROFESSIONALISM

The professionalization of medical students is facilitated and intensified by symbols the neophytes manipulate. The manipulation serves to announce to insiders and outsiders alike how they are to be identified. During the first weeks of their studies students begin wearing white lab jackets with plastic name tags that identify them as medical students. In addition, since from the beginning clinical skills sessions are included in the curriculum, students participate in a variety of settings with the tools of the doctor's trade carried on their person. This attire clearly identifies students to participants and visitors of the hospital/school setting. Then, equipped with their identity kit, students begin to learn and express themselves in the medical vernacular, often referred to as "McBabble" or "medspeak." Distinctive dress, badges, tools, and language provide the students with symbols that announce their role and activity.

The significance of these symbols to the professionalization process is critical. The symbols serve, on the one hand, to identify and unite the bearers as members of a community of shared interests, purpose, and identification (Roth, 1957), and, on the other, these symbols distinguish and separate their possessors from lay people, making their role seem more mysterious, shrouded, and priest-like (Bramson, 1973). The early manipulation of these symbols serves to heighten identification and commitment to the profession, while at the same time facilitates students' separation from the lay world. As one student candidly remarks:

> Wearing the jacket seems to give you carte blanche to just about go anywhere you want in the hospital. People assume that you belong and that you know what you're doing. (Field notes: Spring, second year)

The importance of the white coat as a symbol is reinforced by the faculty and staff who, with the exception of the psychiatry department, mandate that it be worn. As the following incident illustrates, this expectation is rigorously adhered to, and is justified in terms of patients' expectations:

> The rheumatology session tutorial group assembled and walked to the room where Dr. Gordon would be met. Dr. Gordon said, "Well you know in order to see any of the patients you have to wear a white jacket and a tie." The group was very surprised by his remark and, in fact, John and Ken looked at each other in disbelief. John said, "No, I didn't know that."
>
> Dr. Gordon says, "Well you do know that in order to see any of the patients you have to wear a white coat. They expect that. You will agree that they expect that. Wouldn't you agree with that?"
>
> John says, "No, I wouldn't. I mean that hasn't been my experience."
>
> Dr. Gordon says, "Well, have you ever visited any of the patients in the hospital?"

John says, "Yes, for about a year and a half now."

Dr. Gordon says, "Those people who have the white jackets on will be able to visit the patients. Those who don't, won't be able to." (Field notes: Winter, second year)

One of the first difficult tasks that faces students is to begin to learn and communicate within the symbolic system that serves to define medical work and workers. Learning to use the "correct" language is part of this. From the beginning, in tutorials, readings, demonstrations, and rounds, students are exposed to a language in which they are expected to become facile. A student explains the importance of replacing his lay vocabulary:

> When I was just beginning, I would use my own words to describe how a lesion looked or how a patient felt ... because they were more immediate to me and more accessible to me. And on many occasions I was corrected. The way you describe that is such and such because that is the vocabulary of the profession and that is the only way you can be understood. (Interview: Winter, third year)

Another incident that took place in a tutorial captures the students' difficulties in knowing when use of the symbol system may be inappropriate:

> At one point Dr. Smith asked, "What is it, what is the name for this kind of phenomenon that gives this kind of pain?" E.C. volunteered a term and she ended it with a question mark. She was tentatively offering a term. Dr. Smith said, "Just use the plain language. What is the plain everyday word for that?" There was a pause and he said, "Heartburn, that's what everybody calls it and that's good enough." (Field notes: Spring, first year)

The separation between "we" and "they" becomes clearer to the students as they learn the professional symbol system and are absorbed into the medical culture. As they move through the culture, they learn how symbols are used to communicate and enforce certain definitions of the situations they are exposed to. Students must learn how practising physicians manipulate these symbols to this end.

The ability to use the linguistic symbols of medicine defines members of the profession and creates a boundary that is not often crossed. Two students reflect on the significance of technical terminology:

> So you could talk about things in front of a patient that would totally baffle the patient and keep him unaware of issues that you were discussing. I don't think this is unique to medicine. I think this is a general phenomenon of professionalization. [Learning the language] was a matter of establishing some common ground with people you were going to be relating to on a professional basis for the rest of your life. (Interview: Spring, third year)

> You just can't survive if you don't learn the jargon. It's not so much an effort to identify as it is an effort to survive. People in medicine have a world unto themselves and a language unto themselves. It's a world with a vocabulary ... and a vocabulary that, no question about it, creates a fraternity that excludes the rest of the world and it's a real tyranny to lay persons who don't understand it. (Interview: Spring, third year)

In sum, the adoption of special props, costume, and language reinforces the students' identification with and commitment to medicine while it enables them to project an image of having adopted a new and special role. Having learned how to manipulate the symbols to reflect audiences' expectations, they begin to shape and control their professional relationships.

The manipulation of symbolic language and props does more than shape and control professional relationships, it actually changes the neophyte's own perception of himself or herself. Because students wear and manipulate the symbols of their trade, they are presumed by others to possess special knowledge. Not only this, but students, because of a developing facility to manipulate symbols, eventually convince themselves that indeed they are special. One student thoughtfully comments on the dynamic nature of the relationship existing between the symbol system and his own self-image:

> When you wore the jacket, especially in the beginning, people were impressed. After all, it told everyone, including yourself, that you were studying to be a doctor. ... The other thing about wearing the white jacket is that it does make things more obvious. You know what you are, what you are doing sort of thing. You know, it is sort of another way of identifying. There were very few ways that people had to identify with the medical profession and one of the ways was to begin to look like some of the doctors. (Interview: Spring, second year)

MANAGING THE SITUATION

It must be noted, however, that while appropriate medical accoutrements help new clerks manage their new roles, they remain acutely aware of their limitations, and are highly sensitive to a perceived need that they must meet a variety of role expectations. Their short-term goal is to convince their audience of their competence without inviting criticism: they must gain the confidence of those who can affect their reputation. One student discussed the importance of impression management in relation to varying audience expectations in these terms:

> The first day you've got to make a good impression. If you make a bad impression the first day, then that's it. You've got to spend the whole rest of the rotation redeeming yourself for making a boo-boo. Maybe it's just an insignificant thing, but if you do that the first day, then you've had it. (Field notes: Fall, second year)

In their attempt to control their audiences' impressions of them, students usually use two broadly based but intricately related strategies: the first is covering up, a strategy intended to provide protection from charges of incompe-

tence; the second is the necessity of taking initiative. Both strategies are designed to convince others that they are developing the necessary attribute of trustworthy competence. Both strategies require considerable skills in self-presentation. A student describes one of these strategies as a form of initiative taking that provides protection from divergent medical approaches taken by senior personnel:

> Like Dr. Jones who was my advisor or boss for medicine, he always came and did rounds on Tuesday mornings. ... His interest was in endocrinology and ... he was going to pick up that endocrine patient to talk about, and so of course any dummy can read up Monday night like hell on the new American Diabetic Association standards for diabetes or hyperglycemia. ... So the next day you seem fairly knowledgeable. ... But I just wonder how much you remember when you try to read over in a hurry and you try to be keen just for the next day. Because that afternoon you forget about it because you figure Wednesday morning hematology people make their rounds and, of course, you have to read hematology Tuesday night. (Interview: Winter, second year)

The constant need to create and manage the image of a competent self through the process of impression management is sometimes at odds with a basic tenet of the school's philosophy, which encourages learning through problem solving, and the complementary development of a questioning attitude. In order to deal with this contradiction students attempt to manage an appearance of competence while at the same time they control others' impressions of it. This student expresses his handling of the problem this way:

> The best way of impressing others with your competence is asking questions you know the answers to. Because if they ever put it back on you, "Well what do you think?" then you tell them what you think and you'd give a very intelligent answer because you knew it. You

didn't ask to find out information. You ask it to impress people. (Interview: Winter, third year)

The same contradiction gives rise to another strategy that students employ designed to mask uncertainty and anxiety with an image of self-confidence. Projection of the right image is recognized by students as being as important as technical competence. As one student remarks: "We have to be good actors, put across the image of self-confidence, that you know it all." Another student, referring to the importance of creating the right impression, claims:

It's like any fraternity. You've got to know. You've got to have a certain amount of basic knowledge before they think it's worth talking to you. If you display less than that basic knowledge their reflexes come into play and they think this person is an idiot. Let's find out exactly how much they don't know, rather than building on what you do know. That's a different manoeuvre. Being out in the pale, not worth talking to, or within the pale and well-worth talking to. There is image management in every profession. It's very unfortunate because the people who precisely need the help are those who are willing to admit their ignorance, and I've been in tutorials where people who are really willing to admit their ignorance tend to get put down for it. After a while they stop asking questions. That's very unfortunate. (Interview: Spring, third year)

Clinical clerks believe that they must always be aware of the expectations of their audience before they carefully balance a self-confident demeanour with an attitude and gestures of proper deference in the face of those who control their career:

Student A: Sometimes there is a lot of politics involved ... in speaking up because you are aware of your position. ... You don't want to seem too smart. You don't want to show up people. If you happen to know something, you know, that say the resident doesn't know, you

have to be very diplomatic about it because some of these guys are very touchy.

Student B: And you don't want to play the game either of just "I'll be student and you be teacher."

Student A: Yeah, and at the same time you don't want to come off as appearing stupid. If you happen to believe something ... you try to defend yourself but in a very diplomatic manner, all the time being careful not to step on anybody's toes. (Interview: Spring, third year)

The use of presentational skills can be understood only in terms of students' perceptions that impression management offers the most appropriate tactics for successfully negotiating the evaluation system they face (Becker et al., 1961; 1968). Most are quite frank about the importance of consciously impressing others. Two students comment:

In that context [with the clinical skills preceptor] I try to shine. I try to outdo others. It's also good if you raise your hand and give a side-point. ... You guess with confidence. If you don't know, no matter what, you say it with confidence. You'll be much better on rounds if you do that. (Interview: Spring, second year)

If you want to establish a reputation as a great staff man or whatever one of the things is that you know a lot and this is one of the ways you establish your reputation. ... Some people will cover up by bull-shitting very skillfully. People usually don't make the effort to prove them wrong. And it always helps to be ready with a quick snappy answer which is right. ... And what I usually do is I say I don't know, but I usually say it with a very aggressive air, you know, but not in a put-down way. (Interview: Fall, third year)

The relationship between verbal or interactional skills and reputation making is highlighted during these student interviews:

Well, I know people who came across as knowing a lot and they don't do it purposely or they don't do it arrogantly or anything, they just talk a lot. And usually most of these people do know a lot and they talk a lot. But a fair amount of it is also they are just good talkers. They are good with words and if you were to sort of compare them with someone who is less flashier in a different setting, in other words, ask them to do a write-up or ask them to do a written assessment of the patient, the quieter one would probably do just as well. These people are better on their feet so they come across all right. There is definitely that aspect and you see that even more when you get into clinical medicine and really much of what gives a person a reputation is not really how much he knows, although he's got to know a fair amount, he's got to know certainly above average, but really how much of a performer he is. (Interview: Spring, third year)

The way reputations are established on a ward, be it for clinical clerks, interns, residents, or staff is largely on the basis of verbal discussions that occur all over the place. They occur at rounds ... they occur at seminars and so on. And these are all verbal, that's the big thing about them. At these sorts of goings on, it's people who were quick, who jumped in with a diagnosis when only two symptoms were known and were right, who are good with words and that sort of thing—these sorts of people are the ones who tend to establish reputations. Rarely are reputations made on the basis of reading written products of their work. Residents, they do write things. You know, they write discharge summaries, they write admitting histories and physicals. And often times, especially if the patient comes back, these things will be read by another person. In that sense you may get an idea of what the person has done at a quieter time when he hasn't had to perform verbally. By and large, that's a lesser aspect of it than what happens at these sessions. It's really the people who are verbal and sort of aggressive in that way who are known as being good. (Interview: Spring, third year)

Even as they pursue good evaluations through good interactional performances, the students do not ignore their long-term goal of achieving competence. One aptly sums up the relationship of meeting the expectations of frequently changing audiences, and the necessity of impression management, with a lesser but, nonetheless, important concern about his future role as a decision maker:

This week I was at all different places, some of which I had never been to. You're having a constant turnover of patients and a constant turnover of staff people that you run into. Each of them has different expectations towards you, and you're always on guard. You're never exactly sure how each of them wants you to act, so it puts you in a kind of tension situation. I know when I leave work I really feel a big relief that I can finally let my hair down. Most of us present this image that we are comfortable and confident. That's the image you have to present. ... I figure to myself as a doctor you shouldn't have to feel this way, but I think one thing medical school does to you is by the time you graduate you realize how little you do know and how much there is to know. And it's so overwhelming to see your finiteness and limitations, and to recognize when you get the degree, all of a sudden you're going to be expected to know. You're going to be expected to make decisions. (Interview: Winter, third year)

PERFORMANCE SUCCESS AND PROFESSIONALIZING CONFIDENCE AND IDENTIFICATION

As they advance through the program, students continually observe doctors' working habits, listen to their philosophies of medical practice, take note of their competencies and incompetencies, and reflect upon the nature of their own present and future relationships with patients. The physicians with whom they practise their clinical skills become models after which students pattern their own beliefs and behaviour:

Certainly there are people who impress me ... certain aspects of their personality that I would want to incorporate in some way in my practice. It is easy to model yourself after people you see on the wards. ... You don't know anything and you start watching them and before too long you find yourself in a position where you tend to model yourself after these people.

Through observation, role playing, and practice, students begin to identify with the organization and practice of the medical profession.

As students observe and experience the problems of medical care and practice, they develop an understanding of, and learn to identify with, the profession and the means by which its members confront their problems. Consequently, students become less able to voice criticisms of what they see as they adopt the role of those they will emulate in the future. As they assume increased responsibilities and make medical judgements for which they must account to a variety of professionals, they develop an increasingly sympathetic outlook toward their future profession.

Students gain clinical and interactional experience in ward settings that allows them to increase their repertoire of roles played for various audiences and in different situations. A student describes her experiments with various scripts when she says:

Every patient I see gives me more experience. I'll see as many patients as I can because I can learn from seeing them. Like I can try out a different approach and see the reaction that I get. I found that every time I see a patient, I try to ask questions in a different way and test out different approaches. It's like going to see a play that you've already seen many times, but every time you see it you notice something different. In a sense it's the same with the patients. You gain a little more experience every time, and that is really important. (Interview: Spring, second year)

It would appear that nothing succeeds like success; and as the students gain confidence they learn that the projection of a successful image is an effective way of controlling others' impressions of their developing professionalism. A student describes the importance of impression-management skills in easing the relationships with patients, particularly in dealing with the sensitive areas of the physical examination:

I think it's largely a matter of how you present yourself. Now if I go in all shaky and flushed and nervous about it, the patient is going to pick up on this and is going to respond. So I think you have to go in with a confident manner and know your business and go about it in a very clear-cut way, so the patient does not know you have any fears of the situation and therefore you don't transfer those fears to the patient. (Interview: Winter, third year)

Another student graphically describes the ambiguous nature of interactional evaluation and the skills required to handle the ambiguity. Students believe they can deflect others from evaluating cognitive or performance competence negatively:

You see the kind of student that they [faculty] want to see is the strong and the assertive-type person. Medical people like to see people who state their position and take a stand ... a go-getter, an individual who can relate, an individual who on their own can lead a tutorial group, who can take patients and follow them through, who can take initiatives. ... If they see you being decisive and confident and they see you can do something, then they think you're good. I think it's very easy for you to slide by on personality. Sometimes I think I'm at fault ... because I think I have the personality that I can put others in the situation where they won't go and find out if I'm weak in some areas. That's the problem with this place: that they never really separate personality from academics. (Interview: Winter, second year)

As students gain confidence they learn that skillful methods of communication provide an effective way of controlling others' impressions of their professionalism. The intimate relationship between developing confidence and professional success through the projection of confident performances that convey success is indicated in the following student's comments:

> If you act like you know, they treat you like you know. If you act like you don't know what is happening, then that's the way they treat you. It might sound really strange, but that is the way it is. You've got to let them know that you know what you are doing. (Field notes: Fall, third year)

Confidence is often bolstered by the comparisons that students inevitably make with their peers and practising professionals; the clerks realize that other players, too, are involved in the game of impression management. Lack of knowledge and even incompetence are easy to hide in a milieu that emphasizes appearance.[3] A student makes this point:

> The comforting thing about clerkship is that you see that specialists and interns and residents don't know everything. That's kind of reassuring to know that first of all you don't have to know everything and secondly that a lot of people who are beyond you in their training don't know everything. (Field notes: Spring, third year)

Clerks are in continuous contact with other members of the medical hierarchy and thus have ample opportunity to imitate them. Conforming to the model of their evaluators makes them aware that professional practice is a mixture of both science and art. The art of impression management, when mastered, allows the clerks to increase their identification with the practice, and allows them to gain confidence about their ability to demonstrate professional competence. Eventually, successful completion of the clerkship provides a social badge of legitimation, which affirms they have taken another step in the transition from student to professional.

In summary, the students come to realize that, as practising professionals, they will continue to place emphasis on the symbolic communication of competence. Effective reputation-making, for practitioners as well as for students, depends on the successful control and manipulation of symbols, ideas, and legitimators in professional rituals and situations. Donald Light astutely points out the outcome of what amounts to a ritual ordeal in the study of psychiatric residents when he notes:

> By structuring them [training programs] so that the trainees experience feelings of intense anxiety, ignorance, and dependence, such programs may be teaching professionals to treat clients as they have been treated. And by exaggerating their power and expertise, mentors establish a model of omnipotence that their students are fated to repeat. To the extent that laymen accept this mythology, omnipotent tendencies become reinforced in daily life. To the extent they challenge it, professionals like physicians or psychiatrists become embattled and defensive. (1980: 307)

A key factor in the professionalization process is that students learn authoritativeness. It is communicated by means of body language, demeanour, and carefully managed projections of the self-image. They believe that to be a good student-physician is either to be or appear to be competent. They observe that others react to their role playing. A student describes this process when he says:

> To be a good GP, you've got to be a good actor, you've got to respond to a situation. You have to be quick, pick up the dynamics of what is going on at the time and try to make the person leave the office thinking that you know something. And a lot of people, the way they handle that is by letting the patient know that they know it all and only letting out a little bit at a time, and as little as possible. I think that they eventually reach a plateau where they start thinking to themselves they are really great and they know it all, because they have these people who are worshipping at their feet. (Interview: Spring, third year)

The self-fulfilling nature of the conversion process, whereby newcomers attain the higher moral status of a professional, is captured in two separate interview comments:

> People expect you to be the healer and so you have to act like the healer. (Field notes: Spring, third year)

> You know a large part of our role is a God role. You have to act like God. You're supposed to be like God. If you don't inspire confidence in your patients, they are not going to get better even if you know the correct diagnosis and have the correct treatment. If they don't have faith in you, they are not going to get better. (Interview: Winter, second year)

The perception of exaggerated expectations from their audience and the ritual ordeal nature of the professionalization process contribute to the model of omnipotence that students believe is helpful for performance success. There is, however, a fine line and tension between confident acting and audience perceptions of arrogance and abuse of authority. The root of this dilemma is reflected in Lord Acton's famous dictum, "Power tends to corrupt and absolute power tends to corrupt absolutely." A clinical clerk describes the corruptive tendency of the professionalizing process when he says:

> They [the nurses] expect you to act that way [abusively]. If you don't, they won't respect you. They need to know you're the boss or they won't respect you. (Field notes: Spring, third year)

The process of adopting the cloak of competence is ultimately justified by students as being helpful to the patient. A student summarizes the relationship between acting competently and patients responding to such a performance by getting well when he says:

> You know the patients put pressure on you to act as if you are in the know. If you know anything about the placebo effect, you know that a lot of the healing and curing of patients does not involve doing anything that will really help them, but rather creating confidence in the patient that things are being done and will be done. We know that the placebo effect for example has even cured cancer patients. If they have the confidence in the doctor and what doctor and what treatment they are undergoing, they are much more likely to get well, irrespective of the objective effects of the treatment. (Interview: Spring, second year)

CONCLUSION

Students learn the practical importance of assuming the cloak of competence.[4] The cloak allows patients to trust, without question, both the health professional and the prescribed treatment. Successful negotiations of the trial by ordeal through proper performances help newcomers gain control or dominance (Freidson, 1970), which is basic to professionalism. The process has a self-fulfilling quality as neophyte professionals move up the professional ladder. Students recognize the importance of appearing authoritative in professional situations. In turn, as they perceive themselves to be successful, they come to believe in their competence in professional matters. The changing nature of the definition of self and the fragility of control over others' perceptions and reactions lead students to develop and maintain a protective shield.

The posture of authoritativeness in professional matters is an expected outcome of the trial by ordeal. The special status and role of professional is enveloped in a set of expectations that require special demonstrations of "possessed" competence. Practising at playing the role eventually results in its adoption and identification. Newcomers model and imitate their mentors (who are also responsible for evaluating them) and the self-perpetuation of the notion of their having a special authoritativeness proceeds.

Neophytes and professionals are similarly involved in careers based on reputational control. Indeed, many laypeople are not only aware that the professionals they deal with are almost constantly engaged in playing a part, in projecting the "proper" image, they also demand it. The interactional basis for this adaptation to a lifetime role is summarized by Halmos when he says:

> We must conclude that the role-playing of being a professional is a hard social fact, and a potent behavioural model for the nonprofessionals, and thus for society at large. ... The strange thing is that the world cannot afford to dispense with being systematically conned! Of course, the truth is that the world is not being deceived: it demands the professing of values and their embodiment in a culturally defined style and ritual. (1970: 180–81)

In his study of the mentally retarded, Edgerton (1967) maintains that the central and shared commonality of the mentally retarded released from institutions was for them to envelop themselves in a cloak of competence to deny the discomforting reality of their stigma. The development of a cloak of competence is, perhaps, most apparent for those who must meet exaggerated expectations. The problem of meeting others' enlarged expectations is magnified for those uncertain about their ability to manage a convincing performance. Moreover, the performer faces the personal problem of reconciling his or her private self-awareness and uncertainty with his or her publicly displayed image. For those required to perform beyond their capacities, in order to be successful, there is the constant threat of breakdown or exposure. For both retardates and professionals the problem and, ironically, the solution are similar. Expectations of competence are dealt with by strategies of impression management, specifically manipulation and concealment. Interactional competencies depend on convincing presentations, and much of professionalism requires the masking of insecurity and incompetence with the symbolic-interactional cloak of competence.

As Hughes has observed, "a feature of work behavior found in one occupation, even a minor or odd one, will be found in others" (1952: 425). In fact, the basic processes of social life operate throughout the social structure. All social groups create boundaries and differences, view themselves in the most favourable ways.[5] All individuals and groups strive to protect themselves from ridicule and charges of incompetence. Our analysis has captured what is and has been a "taken-for-granted" understanding of social life: much behaviour is performance designed to elicit certain reactions. In fact, as we maintain, professional behaviour is, or can be, understood as performance.[6]

NOTES

1. Ernest Becker (1975) argues that man's innate and all-encompassing fear of death drives him to attempt to transcend death through culturally standardized hero systems and symbols.

2. The complaint that physicians avoid patient death and dying is partly explained in the basic human fear of death (Becker, 1975). Although they may grow more desensitized to others' death and dying, they are, at the same time, more often reminded of their own mortality. Moreover, the doctor facing such a situation of telling patient and/or family of impending death is vulnerable to charges of incompetence or failure, and it is competence or its appearance that defines the doctor's role.

3. One merely has to note the numerous and apparently increasing number of imposters who have been discovered in medical practice. See, for example, *New York Times*, February 20, 1983, p. 24. See also Frank Abnagale, Jr. (1982) for a discussion of how the author posed successfully as a member of various professions.

4. The genre of this script is certainly not unique to the professionalization of medical practitioners. For an analogous example of an occupational group that uses collective adoption of a cloak of competence to deal with anxiety about fateful matters, see Haas, 1977. See also Edgerton's analysis of men-

tal retardates' attempts to pass in conventional society by adoption of such a cloak of competence (1967). These examples suggest that the demand for credible performance is accented in those social roles that are perceived as bearing exaggerated expectations about competence.

5. For an example of an occupation where members shroud themselves in a cloak of competence, see Haas (1972, 1974, 1977). High-steel ironworkers, like physicians, must act competently and confidently in fateful matters. Ironworker apprentices, like student-physicians, were observed attempting to control others' definitions of them by acting competently and not revealing their fear or ignorance. In both situations we find neophytes reluctant to reveal their incompetence.

6. Ernest Becker reminds social scientists about their most important question and responsibility when he says: "how do we get rid of the power to mystify? The talent and processes of mesmerization and mystification have to be exposed. Which is another way of saying that we have to work against both structural and psychological unfreedom in society. The task of science would be to explore both of these dimensions" (1975: 165). Our analysis suggests that demystification requires an appreciation of the interactive, collaborative, and symbolic nature of professional–client relations and definitions of the situation.

REFERENCES

Abnagale, F., Jr. 1982. *Catch Me If You Can*. New York: Pocket Books.

Ball, D. 1967. "The ethnography of an abortion clinic." *Social Problems* 14: 293–301.

Becker, Ernest. 1975. *Escape from Evil*. New York: Free Press.

Becker, H.S., B. Geer, and E.C. Hughes. 1968. *Making the Grade: The Academic Side of College Life*. New York: John Wiley and Sons.

Becker, H.S., B. Geer, E.C. Hughes, and A.L. Strauss. 1961. *Boys in White: Student Culture in Medical School*. Chicago: University of Chicago Press.

Bloom, S. 1973. *Power and Dissent in the Medical School*. New York: Macmillan.

Bramson, R. 1973. "The secularization of American medicine." *Hastings Center Studies* 1: 17–28.

Broadhead, R. 1983. *The Private Lives and Professional Identity of Medical Students*. New Brunswick, NJ: Transaction.

Bucher, R. and J. Stelling. 1977. *Becoming Professional*. Beverly Hills, CA: Sage.

Edgerton, R.B. 1967. *The Cloak of Competence: Stigma in the Lives of the Mentally Retarded*. Berkeley: University of California Press.

Freidson, C. 1970. *Profession of Medicine*. New York: Dodds Mead.

Geer, B. 1972. *Learning to Work*. Beverly Hills, CA: Sage.

Goffman, L. 1959. *The Presentation of Self in Everyday Life*. Garden City, NY: Doubleday-Anchor.

———. 1961. *Asylums*. New York: Doubleday.

———. 1963. *Stigma: Notes on the Management of Spoiled Identity*. Baltimore: Penguin.

Haas, J. 1972. "Binging: Educational control among high-steel ironworkers." *American Behavioral Scientist* 16: 27–34.

———. 1974. "The stages of the high-steel ironworkers apprentice career." *Sociological Quarterly* 15: 93–108.

———. 1977. "Learning real feelings: A study of high-steel ironworkers' reactions to fear and danger." *Sociology of Work and Occupations* 4: 147–70.

Haas, J. and W. Shaffir. 1977. "The professionalization of medical students: Developing competence and a cloak of competence." *Symbolic Interaction* 1: 71–88.

Halmos, P. 1970. *The Personal Service Society*. New York: Schocken.

Henslin, J. 1968. "Trust and the cab driver." Pp. 138–58 in M. Truzzi, ed., *Sociology and Everyday Life*. Englewood Cliffs, NJ: Prentice-Hall.

Hughes, E.C. 1951. "Work and self." In J.H. Rohrer and M. Sherif, eds. *Social Psychology at the Crossroads*. New York: Harper and Row.

———. 1952. "The sociological study of work: an editorial foreword." *American Journal of Sociology* 62.

Light, D.W., Jr. 1980. *Becoming Psychiatrists: The Professional Transformation of Self*. New York: W.W. Norton.

Maurer, D. 1962. *The Big Con*. New York: New American Library.

Merton, R.K., G.C. Reader, and P.L. Kendall, eds. 1957. *The Student Physician*. Cambridge: Harvard University Press.

Olesen, V.L. and E.W. Whittaker. 1968. *The Silent Dialogue: A Study in the Social Psychology of Professional Socialization*. San Francisco: Jossey-Bass.

Prus, R. and C.D. Sharper. 1979. *Road Hustler*. Toronto: Gage.

Ross, A.D. 1961. *Becoming a Nurse*. Toronto: Macmillan.

Roth, J. 1957. "Ritual and magic in the control of contagion." *American Sociological Review* 22: 310–14.

Scott, M.B. 1968. *The Racing Game*. Chicago: Aldine.

Siegler, M. and H. Osmond. 1973. "Aesculapian authority." *Hastings Center Studies* 1: 41–52.

Chapter 5

There was a child went forth every day,
And the first object he look'd upon, that object
he became.

— Walt Whitman

Identity in the Age of the Internet

SHERRY TURKLE

We come to see ourselves differently as we catch sight of our images in the mirror of the machine. A decade ago, when I first called the computer a second self, these identity-transforming relationships were almost always one-on-one, a person alone with a machine. This is no longer the case. A rapidly expanding system of networks, collectively known as the Internet, links millions of people in new spaces that are changing the way we think, the nature of our sexuality, the form of our communities, our very identities.

At one level, the computer is a tool. It helps us write, keep track of our accounts, and communicate with others. Beyond this, the computer offers us both new models of mind and a new medium on which to project our ideas and fantasies. Most recently, the computer has become even more than tool and mirror: We are able to step through the looking glass. We are learning to live in virtual worlds. We may find ourselves alone as we navigate virtual oceans, unravel virtual mysteries, and engineer virtual skyscrapers. But increasingly, when we step through the looking glass, other people are there as well.

The use of the term "cyberspace" to describe virtual worlds grew out of science fiction,[1] but for many of us, cyberspace is now part of the routines of everyday life. When we read our electronic mail or send postings to an electronic bulletin board or make an airline reservation over a computer network, we are in cyberspace. In cyberspace, we can talk, exchange ideas, and assume personae of our own creation. We have the opportunity to build new kinds of communities, virtual communities, in which we participate with people from all over the world, people with whom we converse daily, people with whom we may have fairly intimate relationships but whom we may never physically meet.

A nascent culture of simulation is affecting our ideas about mind, body, self, and machine. In the story of constructing identity in the culture of simulation, experiences on the Internet figure prominently, but these experiences can be understood only as part of a larger cultural context. That context is the story of the eroding boundaries between the real and the virtual, the animate and the inanimate, the unitary and the multiple self, which is occurring both in advanced scientific fields of research and in the patterns of everyday life. From scientists trying to create artificial life to children "morphing" through a series of virtual personae, we see evidence of fundamental shifts in the way we create and experience human identity. But it is on the Internet that our confrontations with technology as it collides with our sense of human identity are fresh, even raw. In the real-time communities of cyberspace, we are dwellers on the threshold between the real and virtual, unsure of our footing, inventing ourselves as we go along.

In an interactive, text-based computer game designed to represent a world inspired by the television series *Star Trek: The Next Generation*, thousands of players spend up to eighty hours a

---

Source: Excerpted from "Introduction: Identity in the Age of the Internet," in Sherry Turkle, *Life on the Screen: Identity in the Age of the Internet* (New York: Touchstone, 1997), pp. 9–21. Reprinted with permission of Simon & Schuster. Copyright © 1995 by Sherry Turkle.

week participating in intergalactic exploration and wars. Through typed descriptions and typed commands, they create characters who have casual and romantic sexual encounters, hold jobs and collect paycheques, attend rituals and celebrations, fall in love and get married. To the participants, such goings-on can be gripping: "This is more real than my real life," says a character who turns out to be a man playing a woman who is pretending to be a man. In this game the self is constructed and the rules of social interaction are built, not received.[2]

In another text-based game, each of nearly ten thousand players creates a character or several characters, specifying their genders and other physical and psychological attributers. The characters need not be human and there are more than two genders. Players are invited to help build the computer world itself. Using a relatively simple programming language, they can create a room in the game space where they are able to set the stage and define the rules. They can fill the room with objects and specify how they work; they can, for instance, create a virtual dog that barks if one types the command "bark Rover." An 11-year-old player built a room she calls the condo. It is beautifully furnished. She has created magical jewellery and makeup for her dressing table. When she visits the condo, she invites her cyberfriends to join her there, she chats, orders a virtual pizza, and flirts.

LIVING IN THE MUD

The *Star Trek* game, TrekMUSE, and the other, LambdaMOO, are both computer programs that can be accessed through the Internet. The Internet was once available only to military personnel and technical researchers. It is now available to anyone who can buy or borrow an account on a commercial on-line service. TrekMUSE and LambdaMOO are known as MUDs, Multi-User Domains or, with greater historical accuracy, Multi-User Dungeons, because of their genealogy from Dungeons and Dragons, the fantasy role-playing game that

swept high schools and colleges in the late 1970s and early 1980s.

The multiuser computer games are based on different kinds of software (this is what the MUSE or MOO or MUSH part of their names stands for). For simplicity, here I use the term MUD to refer to all of them.

MUDs put you in virtual spaces in which you are able to navigate, converse, and build. You join a MUD through a command that links your computer to the computer on which the MUD program resides. Making the connection is not difficult; it requires no particular technical sophistication. The basic commands may seem awkward at first but soon become familiar. For example, if I am playing a character named ST on LambdaMOO, any words I type after the command "say" will appear on all players' screens as "ST says." Any actions I type after the command "emote" will appear after my name just as I type them, as in "ST waves hi" or "ST laughs uncontrollably." I can "whisper" to a designated character and only that character will be able to see my words. [In 2000] there are over 1500 MUDs in which over a million people participate.[3] In some MUDs, players are represented by graphical icons; most MUDs are purely text-based. Most players are middle class. A large majority are male. Some players are over 30, but most are in their early twenties and late teens. However, it is no longer unusual to find MUDs where 8- and 9-year-olds "play" such grade-school icons as Barbie or the Mighty Morphin Power Rangers.

MUDs are a new kind of virtual parlour game and a new form of community. In addition, text-based MUDs are a new form of collaboratively written literature. MUD players are MUD authors, the creators as well as consumers of media content. In this, participating in a MUD has much in common with script writing, performance art, street theatre, improvisational theatre — or even commedia dell'arte. But MUDs are something else as well.

As players participate, they become authors not only of text but of themselves, constructing new selves through social interaction. One player says, "You are the character and you are not the character, both at the same time." Another says, "You are who you pretend to be." MUDs provide worlds for anonymous social interaction in which one can play a role as close to or as far away from one's "real self" as one chooses. Since one participates in MUDs by sending text to a computer that houses the MUD's program and database, MUD selves are constituted in interaction with the machine. Take it away and the MUD selves cease to exist: "Part of me, a very important part of me, only exists inside PernMUD," says one player. Several players joke that they are like "the electrodes in the computer," trying to express the degree to which they feel part of its space.

On MUDs, one's body is represented by one's own textual description, so the obese can be slender, the beautiful plain, the "nerdy" sophisticated. A *New Yorker* cartoon captures the potential for MUDs as laboratories for experimenting with one's identity. In it, one dog, paw on a computer keyboard, explains to another, "On the Internet, nobody knows you're a dog." The anonymity of MUDs—one is known on the MUD only by the name of one's character or characters—gives people the chance to express multiple and often unexplored aspects of the self, to play with their identity and to try out new ones. MUDs make possible the creation of an identity so fluid and multiple that it strains the limits of the notion. Identity, after all, refers to the sameness between two qualities, in this case between a person and his or her persona. But in MUDs, one can be many.

Dedicated MUD players are often people who work all day with computers at their regular jobs—as architects, programmers, secretaries, students, and stockbrokers. From time to time when playing on MUDs, they can put their characters "to sleep" and pursue "real life" (MUD players call this RL) activities on the computer—all the while remaining connected, logged on to the game's virtual world. Some leave special programs running that send them

signals when a particular character logs on or when they are "paged" by a MUD acquaintance. Some leave behind small artificial intelligence programs called bots (derived from the word "robot") running in the MUD that may serve as their alter egos, able to make small talk or answer simple questions. In the course of a day, players move in and out of the active game space. As they do so, some experience their lives as "cycling through" between the real world, RL, and a series of virtual worlds. I say a series because people are frequently connected to several MUDs at a time. In an MIT computer cluster at 2 A.M., an eighteen-year-old freshman sits at a networked machine and points to the four boxed-off areas on his vibrantly coloured computer screen. "On this MUD I'm relaxing, shooting the breeze. On this other MUD I'm in a flame war.[4] On this last one I'm into heavy sexual things. I'm travelling between the MUDs and a physics homework assignment due at 10 tomorrow morning."

This kind of cycling through MUDs and RL is made possible by the existence of those boxed-off areas on the screen, commonly called windows. Windows provide a way for a computer to place you in several contexts at the same time. As a user, you are attentive to only one of the windows on your screen at any given moment, but in a sense you are a presence in all of them at all times. For example, you might be using your computer to help you write a paper about bacteriology. In that case, you would be present to a word-processing program you are using to take notes, to communications software with which you are collecting reference materials from a distant computer, and to a simulation program, which is charting the growth of virtual bacterial colonies. Each of these activities takes place in a window; your identity on the computer is the sum of your distributed presence.

Doug is a midwestern college junior. He plays four characters distributed across three different MUDs. One is a seductive woman. One is a macho, cowboy type whose self-description stresses that he is a "Marlboros rolled in the

T-shirt sleeve kind of guy." The third is a rabbit of unspecified gender who wanders its MUD introducing people to each other, a character he calls Carrot. Doug says, "Carrot is so low key that people let it be around while they are having private conversations. So I think of Carrot as my passive, voyeuristic character." Doug's fourth character is one that he plays only on a MUD in which all the characters are furry animals. "I'd rather not even talk about the character because my anonymity there is very important to me," Doug says. "Let's just say that on FurryMUDs I feel like a sexual tourist."[5] Doug talks about playing his characters in windows and says that using windows has made it possible for him to "turn pieces of my mind on and off."

> I split my mind. I'm getting better at it. I can see myself as being two or three or more. And I just turn on one part of my mind and then another when I go from window to window. I'm in some kind of argument in one window and trying to come on to a girl in a MUD in another, and another window might be running a spreadsheet program or some other technical thing for school. ... And then I'll get a real-time message [that flashes on the screen as soon as it is sent from another system user], and I guess that's RL. It's just one more window.

"RL is just one more window," he repeats, "and it's not usually my best one."

The development of windows for computer interfaces was a technical innovation motivated by the desire to get people working more efficiently by cycling through different applications. But in the daily practice of many computer users, windows have become a powerful metaphor for thinking about the self as a multiple, distributed system. The self is no longer simply playing different roles in different settings at different times, something that a person experiences when, for example, she wakes up as a lover, makes breakfast as a mother, and drives to work as a lawyer. The life practice of windows is that of a decentred self that exists in many worlds and plays many roles at the same time. In traditional theatre and in role-playing games that take place in physical space, one steps in and out of character; MUDs, in contrast, offer parallel identities, parallel lives. The experience of this parallelism encourages treating on-screen and off-screen lives with a surprising degree of equality. Experiences on the Internet extend the metaphor of windows — now RL itself, as Doug said, can be "just one more window."

MUDs are dramatic examples of how computer-mediated communication can serve as a place for the construction and reconstruction of identity. There are many others. On the Internet, Internet Relay Chat (commonly known as IRC) is another widely used conversational forum in which any user can open a channel and attract guests to it, all of whom speak to each other as if in the same room. Commercial services such as America Online and CompuServe provide on-line chat rooms that have much of the appeal of MUDs — a combination of real time interaction with other people, anonymity (or, in some cases, the illusion of anonymity), and the ability to assume a role as close to or as far from one's "real self" as one chooses.

As more people spend more time in these virtual spaces, some go so far as to challenge the idea of giving any priority to RL at all. "After all," says one dedicated MUD player and IRC user, "why grant such superior status to the self that has the body when the selves that don't have bodies are able to have different kinds of experiences?" When people can play at having different genders and different lives, it isn't surprising that for some this play has become as real as what we conventionally think of as their lives, although for them this is no longer a valid distinction.

FROM A CULTURE OF CALCULATION TOWARD A CULTURE OF SIMULATION

Most people over 30 years old (and even many younger ones) have had an introduction to computers similar to the one I received in a programming course. But from today's perspective, the fundamental lessons of computing that I was taught are wrong. First of all, programming is no longer cut and dried. Indeed, even its dimensions have become elusive. Are you programming when you customize your word-processing software? When you design "organisms" to populate a simulation of Darwinian evolution in a computer game called SimLife? Or when you build a room in a MUD so that opening a door to it will cause "Happy UnBirthday" to ring out on all but one day of the year? In a sense, these activities are forms of programming, but that sense is radically different from the one presented in my 1978 computer course.

The lessons of computing today have little to do with calculation and rules; instead they concern simulation, navigation, and interaction. The very image of the computer as a giant calculator has become quaint and dated. Of course, there is still "calculation" going on within the computer, but it is no longer the important or interesting level to think about or interact with. Fifteen years ago, most computer users were limited to typing commands. Today they use off-the-shelf products to manipulate simulated desktops, draw with simulated paints and brushes, and fly in simulated airplane cockpits. The computer culture's centre of gravity has shifted decisively to people who do not think of themselves as programmers. The computer science research community as well as industry pundits maintain that in the near future we can expect to interact with computers by communicating with simulated people on our screens, agents who will help organize our personal and professional lives.

The meaning of the computer presence in people's lives is very different from what most expected in the late 1970s. One way to describe what has happened is to say that we are moving from a modernist culture of calculation toward a postmodernist culture of simulation.

Fifteen years ago in popular culture, people were just getting used to the idea that computers could project and extend a person's intellect. Today people are embracing the notion that computers may extend an individual's physical presence. Some people use computers to extend their physical presence via real-time video links and shared virtual conference rooms. Some use computer-mediated screen communication for sexual encounters. An Internet list of "Frequently Asked Questions" describes the latter activity—known as netsex, cybersex, and (in MUDs) TinySex—as people typing messages with erotic content to each other, "sometimes with one hand on the keyset, sometimes with two."

Many people who engage in netsex say that they are constantly surprised by how emotionally and physically powerful it can be. They insist that it demonstrates the truth of the adage that 90 percent of sex takes place in the mind. This is certainly not a new idea, but netsex has made it commonplace among teenage boys, a social group not usually known for its sophistication about such matters. A 17-year-old high school student tells me that he tries to make his erotic communications on the net "exciting and thrilling and sort of imaginative." In contrast, he admits that before he used computer communication for erotic purposes he thought about his sexual life in terms of "trying [almost always unsuccessfully] to get laid." A 16-year-old has a similar report on his cyberpassage to greater sensitivity: "Before I was on the net, I used to masturbate with *Playboy*; now I do netsex on DinoMUD[6] with a woman in another state." When I ask how the two experiences differ, he replies:

> With netsex, it is fantasies. My MUD lover doesn't want to meet me in RL. With *Playboy*, it was fantasies too, but in the MUD there is also the other person. So I don't think of what I do on the MUD as masturbation. Although, you might say that I'm the only one who's touching me. But in netsex, I have to think of fantasies she will like too. So now, I see fantasies as something that's part of sex with two people, not just me in my room.

Sexual encounters in cyberspace are only one (albeit well-publicized) element of our new lives on the screen. Virtual communities ranging from MUDs to computer bulletin boards allow people to generate experiences, relationships, identities, and living spaces that arise only through interaction with technology. In the many thousands of hours that Mike, a college freshman in Kansas, has been logged on to his favourite MUD, he has created an apartment with rooms, furniture, books, desk, and even a small computer. Its interior is exquisitely detailed, even though it exists only in textual description. A hearth, an easy chair, and a mahogany desk warm his cyberspace. "It's where I live," Mike says. "More than I do in my dingy dorm room. There's no place like home."

As human beings become increasingly intertwined with the technology and with each other via the technology, old distinctions between what is specifically human and specifically technological become more complex. Are we living life *on* the screen or life *in* the screen? Our new technologically enmeshed relationships oblige us to ask to what extent we ourselves have become cyborgs, transgressive mixtures of biology, technology, and code.[7] The traditional distance between people and machines has become harder to maintain.

NOTES

1. William Gibson, *Neuromancer* (New York: Ace, 1984).

2. For a general introduction to LambdaMOO and MUDding, see Pavel Curtis, "Mudding: Social Phenomena in Text-Based Virtual Realities," available via anonymous ftp:// parcftp.xerox.com/pub/MOO/papers/DIAC 92.*; Amy Bruckman, "Identity Workshop: Emergent Social and Psychological Phenomena in Text-Based Virtual Reality," unpub. ms., March 1992, available via anonymous ftp://media.mit.edu/pub/asb/ papers/identity-workshop.*; and the chapter on MUDs in Howard Rheingold's *Virtual Community: Homesteading on the Electronic Frontier* (New York: Addison-Wesley, 1993). On virtual community in general, see Allucquere Rosanne Stone, "Will the Real Body Please Stand Up? Boundary Stories about Virtual Cultures," in *Cyberspace: First Steps*, ed. Michael Benedikt (Cambridge: MIT Press, 1992), 81–118. The asterisk in a net address indicates that the document is available in several forms.

3. The number of MUDs is changing rapidly. Most estimates place it at over 1500 but an increasing number are private and so without any official "listing." The software on which they are based (and which gives them their names as MOOs, MUSHes, MUSEs, etc.) determines several things about the game; among these is the general layout of the game space. For example, in the class of MUDs known as AberMUDs, the centre of town is similar from one game to another, but the mountains, castles, and forests that surround the town are different in different games, because these have been built specifically for that game by its resident "wizards." MUDs also differ in their governance. In MUD parlance, wizards are administrators; they usually achieve this status through virtuosity in the game. In AberMUDs only wizards have the right to build onto the game. In other kinds of MUDs, all players are invited to build. Who has the right to build and how building is monitored (for example, whether the MUD government should allow a player to build a machine that would destroy other players' property or characters) is an important feature that distinguishes types of MUDs. Although it may be technically correct to refer to being in a MUD (as in a dungeon), it is also common to speak of being on a MUD (as in logging on to a program). To me, the dual usage reflects the ambiguity of cyberspace as both space and program. I (and my informants) use both in this chapter.

4. A flame war is computer culture jargon for an incendiary expression of differences of opinion. In flame wars, participants give themselves permission to state their positions in strong, even outrageous terms with little room for compromise.

5. I promised Doug anonymity, a promise I made to all the people I interviewed in researching this book. Doug has been told that his name will be changed, his identity disguised, and the names and distinguishing features of his MUD characters altered. It is striking that even given these reassurances, which enable him to have an open conversation with me about his social and sexual activities on MUDs, he wants to protect his FurryMUD character.

6. Here I have changed the name of the MUD (there is to my knowledge no DinoMUD) to protect the confidentiality I promise all informants. I use the real name of a MUD when it is important to my account and will not compromise confidentiality.

7. See, for example, Donna Haraway, "A Manifesto for Cyborgs: Science, Technology, and Socialist Feminism in the 1980s," *Socialist Review* 80 (March–April 1985): 65–107.

PART 2B | CULTURE

In Chapter 6, Daniel Albas and Cheryl Albas of the University of Manitoba demonstrate that culture is a human invention that is created to fulfill human needs. They make their case by analyzing a situation that generates high anxiety — writing exams in university — and showing that many students invent magical practices in order to cope with the stress. One student they interviewed, for example, felt that she would do well only if she ate a sausage and two eggs sunny-side up on the morning of each exam, and only if the sausage were arranged vertically on the left side of her plate and the eggs placed beside the sausage to form the "100" percent grade for which she was striving. Naturally, the ritual had more direct influence on her cholesterol level than on her grade. But indirectly it may have had something of the desired effect: to the degree that it helped relieve her anxiety and relax her, she may have performed better in exams.

Rites such as those described by Albas and Albas are invented by individuals without the benefit of a pre-existing cultural "script." Therefore, there are nearly as many different magical practices surrounding the writing of exams as there are individuals; and what is good luck for one person (e.g., wearing a pink sweatshirt) may be bad luck for another.

Shared cultures eliminate some of this variety and ambiguity, to some degree establishing standardized practices for groups of individuals. In fact, Albas and Albas note the existence of a continuum ranging from high cultural uniformity to high cultural diversity. At one end of the continuum, cultural beliefs and practices are virtually homogeneous for all members of a group. For example, in preliterate societies, most religious rituals are practised communally by all tribal members and no variation from prescribed practice is allowed. At the other extreme are the highly individualized and unscripted magical rites of students writing exams, soldiers going off to war, and athletes preparing to compete. Between the extremes of standardized culture and individualized magic lie contemporary religions, ethnic customs, political ideologies, professional beliefs, and so forth.

Historically, culture has tended to become more diverse as the variety of occupational roles (or the **division of labour**) has increased, as members of different ethnic groups migrate and come into contact with each other, as inexpensive global communications and accessible mass media make contact between diverse cultures easier, and as new political and intellectual movements crystallize. In general, people are now less obliged to accept the culture into which they are born and freer to choose and combine elements of culture from a wide variety of historical periods and geographical settings.

These developments should not, however, blind us to the fact that **ideologies** — systems of ideas that justify the existing social order — are still pervasive, even if they are not shared by everyone. Until the eighteenth century, *religious* ideas legitimized the social order. In the nineteenth and early twentieth centuries, *liberal* ideas largely took their place. In the second half of the twentieth century, *biological* arguments supplemented the liberal world view.

Until the seventeenth- and eighteenth-century democratic revolutions in England, France, and the United States, it was widely believed that kings and queens ruled by "divine right"; royal authority was justified with reference to God's apparent will. By 1800, however, the foundation of

this ideology had been undermined by the revolutionary notion that all men are created equal.*
A big problem remained nonetheless. Although political and legal equality were beginning to
spread, anyone could plainly see that enormous inequalities of wealth persisted. A new ideology
justifying the social order was needed.

That new ideology was *liberalism*, which became entrenched in the nineteenth century. According to
liberalism, the modern social order is unique in that it creates equality of opportunity. That is, in liberal social systems, everyone supposedly enjoys the same chance of achieving material success. To be
sure, some people wind up more successful than others. Social inequality persists. From the liberal
point of view, however, the only reason for continuing social stratification is that "natural" talents are
not evenly distributed. Some people are simply smarter and more energetic than others, and they
therefore benefit more from equality of opportunity.

From liberalism it was only a short step to **biological determinism**, an ideology that became popular in the twentieth century. Biological determinism holds that our innate biological characteristics
determine, among other things, how intelligent and industrious we are. Since, in turn, our intelligence
and industry supposedly determine our success in life, it follows that the system of social inequality
is ultimately a product of nature, not of human design.

In Chapter 7, R.C. Lewontin, a leading geneticist who holds the Alexander Agassiz chair in zoology
at Harvard University, takes issue with biological determinism. After arguing that biological determinism is an important part of our culture and, indeed, one of the dominant ideologies of our era, Lewontin
brilliantly dissects its logical and empirical fallacies. He shows that variations in intelligence are only
partly genetically determined. Equally important in determining intelligence are the developmental environment (family, school, etc.), which constantly interacts with our genes, and purely chance factors. If
intelligence is not a product just of nature, it follows that neither is social inequality. Thus, without in
any way diminishing the importance of biology in helping to make us who we are, Lewontin returns the
analysis of social inequality to its rightful owners: the members of the sociological community.

Chapter 8 examines another aspect of contemporary culture: consumerism. **Consumerism** is the
practice of defining oneself in terms of the commodities one buys. It is not exactly news that most people buy particular styles of clothes, cars, and other commodities partly to project an image of themselves as powerful, sexy, cool, athletic, learned, or sophisticated. The use of jewellery and clothing to
establish rank is as old as human society (see Chapter 13). Nor will it shock anyone to learn that advertising seeks to sell image more than substance. In the immortal words of one advertising executive in
the 1940s, "It's not the steak we sell. It's the sizzle." Less obvious is the way consumer culture turns
dissent into a commodity, markets it to mass audiences, and thereby tames it. That is, consumer culture often turns expressions of radical protest into harmless commodities. I illustrate this process in
Chapter 8 by examining the evolution of hip-hop music.

---

* "White men" would be more accurate. Blacks were defined by the U.S. Constitution as only 60 percent human, and it was not until 18
October 1929 that the Judicial Committee of the Privy Council in London overruled the Supreme Court of Canada and declared that women
are indeed "qualified persons" for purposes of appointment to the Canadian Senate.

GLOSSARY

Biological determinism holds that innate physiological characteristics (genetic makeup, for example) determine intelligence, industry, and therefore the allocation of people to different positions in the social hierarchy.

Consumerism is the practice of defining oneself in terms of the commodities one buys.

The **division of labour** is the variety of occupational roles in a society; the greater the division of labour, the greater the variety of occupational roles.

An **ideology** is a system of ideas that justifies the existing social order.

CRITICAL THINKING QUESTIONS

1. "Culture is a human invention that is created to fulfill human needs." Do you agree or disagree? Give examples to support your position.
2. What does Daniel and Cheryl Albas's study of the practice of "modern day" magic demonstrate about culture?
3. What are the general characteristics of student magic?
4. "Culture is crucial for human survival." Do you agree or disagree? Explain your position.
5. Is it possible to separate nature from nurture, biology from culture? Explain your argument.
6. According to R.C. Lewontin, what is the ideology of biological determinism?
7. How do you explain the existence of inequality in society? Why do we not give the same rewards to farmers and physicians?
8. On the Web, read the Angus Reid Group's "Why Is It Important to Track Pop Culture?" at http://www.angusreid.com/pdf/publicat/pop.pdf. As a consumer, do you think the kind of research described in this article is valuable? Why or why not?
9. Can you think of elements of consumer culture other than hip-hop that began as forms of radical protest and then developed mass appeal? Was the main force underlying this transformation commercial, or did other forces come into play as well?

ANNOTATED BIBLIOGRAPHY

Martin Albrow, *The Global Age: State and Society Beyond Modernity* (Stanford, CA: Stanford University Press, 1997). A lucid and up-to-date synthesis and critique of theories of globalization, including implications for global culture.

Richard Gruneau and David Whitson, *Hockey Night in Canada: Sport, Identities and Cultural Politics* (Toronto: Garamond, 1993). Canada's national sport is placed under the sociological microscope in this lucid and engaging account, which shows how the global marketplace for commercial spectacle has altered the game and Canadians' sense of themselves.

Mark Anthony Neal, *What the Music Said: Black Popular Music and Black Public Culture* (New York: Routledge, 1999). An intelligent and comprehensive analysis of the social forces that have shaped black popular music for the past 50 years.

Chapter 6	Students' Use of Magic during Examinations
	DANIEL ALBAS
	CHERYL ALBAS

MAGIC AND SUCCESS: THE CASE OF EXAMINATIONS

In a comprehensive study of university student life (Albas and Albas, 1984), still ongoing, we identify a number of practices designed to allay anxiety and so increase chances for success in examinations. We set out to analyze these common but yet to be systematically studied unusual practices as a kind of "modern day" magic.

Magic seems inevitably to be associated with anxiety-causing events, whether its function is to allay the anxiety, as Malinowski suggests, or to generate anxiety where it does not exist and for societal reasons should, as Radcliffe-Brown suggests (Homans, 1941). Examinations are highly tense and anxiety-causing events, and the practices described in this chapter as magic are essentially anxiety-coping mechanisms.

The examination arena is one in which students, no matter how well prepared, encounter a number of uncertainties. These include, for example, whether they have interpreted the questions correctly; whether the professors will interpret their answers as they intend them; and not least, whether they themselves are "up" for the contest in terms of the sharpness of their memories, organizational abilities, and ability to complete the task on time. Accordingly, it is not surprising to find surrounding the examina-tion a number of practices by students that are clearly intended as uncertainty-coping mechanisms and that could be called magic, if magic is defined as an *action directed toward the achievement of a particular outcome with no logical relationships between the action and the outcome or, indeed, any empirical evidence that the one produces the other*. In effect, this is nonrational behaviour in a setting where one might expect maximum rationality. Clearly we are not dealing with the magic of the sleight-of-hand professional magicians intend for entertainment, nor with that of preliterate shamans or urban gypsies (i.e., cultic magic). Such behaviour is directed toward achieving an outcome, involves many everyday and commonplace acts, yet does seem to rely for the achievement of the outcome on some mystical element.

In this chapter we attempt to depict and analyze magical practices students use to allay anxiety and so increase their chances for success. It must be clearly understood that what we are describing as "magic" is behaviour that falls on a continuum between the "heavy magic" of prelit-erate peoples and superstition (Jahoda, 1969). Student magic is more like the kind of supersti-tion practised by athletes (Gmelch, 1971), sol-diers under battle conditions (Stouffer et al.,

1949), miners (Wilson, 1942), and gamblers (Henslin, 1967). It is being described here for its ethnographic interest. We realize that magic among students has been observed in the past, but we are not aware of any previous effort to examine it systematically.

A description of how the study was carried out is followed by a discussion of general and specific characteristics of student magic. In the final section we suggest implications of this modern adaptation of an ancient technique for the wider societal context.

METHOD

We gathered the data over the last thirteen years from over 300 students in our own and others' classes in Manitoba's largest university (now enrolling 24 000 students). The sample represents a complete spectrum of student background as to age, sex, marital status, and social class. We observed and interacted with students as they studied in libraries, took study breaks, and made last-minute preparations before making their way to their respective exam sites. We continued our tracking as students gathered outside the exam centres, entered, chose their seats, and wrote their exams. Finally, we monitored students as they again congregated outside the exam sites and even as they gathered in pubs and local restaurants for the traditional "post-mortems." As a result we were able to record the increased frequency of magical practices culminating on the day of the exam and the dramatical drop (though not entire disappearance) immediately upon completion of the exam.

The methodological process involved triangulation: data of different kinds were collected from a variety of sources in such a way that the weaknesses of one data-collecting technique were compensated for by the strengths of another, thus better ensuring reliability and validity. The four sources employed were: (1) exam logs, (2) surveys, (3) observation and probing for meaning, and (4) student accounts to explain failures.

THE LOGS

The exam logs, which students were asked to keep over the thirteen-year period, were a source of data that proved rich in subjective detail. These logs included descriptions of thoughts, sentiments, and behaviour that they considered significant, from the first day of classes up to and including the return of their examination grades. Over time, such logs were collected from approximately 300 students of all ages, grade levels, achievement levels, and marital statuses. These records served as a valuable source of information about the inner-life of students and other aspects that we were in no position to observe. Although the word magic was never mentioned, approximately one-fifth of the students mentioned practices that could be classified as magical.

THE SURVEY (INTERVIEWS)

In checking these accounts, we asked different students who had never submitted logs whether they had employed any of the forms of magic that were listed in the logs provided by other students. The general form of the question was, "Do you engage in any practices designed to enhance 'good luck' or to ward off 'bad luck'?" About one-third of the approximately 65 students interviewed indicated that they had done so at one time or another.

OBSERVATIONS AND PROBES

Sensitized to the variety and prevalence of magic, we "probed" by asking for explanations whenever we observed some unusual behaviour. A student suddenly breaking the rhythm and length of his stride as he walked into the exam room was avoiding walking on a line of the basketball court in the gym. Another, rolling his study notes into a cylinder and squeezing them, sought to wring knowledge from his notes. We did not code all explanations given for unusual behaviours as descriptions of magic in our sense. Where explanations showed any sort of plausible empirical connection between the practice and the result sought, the practice was not coded as magical.

ADDITIONAL STUDENT ACCOUNTS (WRITTEN AND VERBAL)

Another data source was the accounts given by students in about a dozen counselling sessions subsequent to the exams to explain their failures on examinations. On such occasions some students would sheepishly admit to having neglected some important practice that they had come to regard as necessary for success.

GENERAL CHARACTERISTICS OF STUDENT MAGIC

We found that from one-fifth to one-third of our students used magic, predominantly of the kind intended to bring good luck rather than to ward off bad luck. In Frazer's (1958) terms, it was largely "contagious" magic rather than "imitative" (no more than half a dozen cases of the latter), and there was only a handful of cases in which "omens" were given credence. The descriptions of magic employed by students fall

into the two major categories of Material Items (Figure 6.1) and Behaviours (Figure 6.2). In turn, these categories are further divided into Prescribed for Luck, on the one hand, and Unlucky or Tabooed, on the other. Focusing first on Material Items Prescribed for Luck, these can be sub-classified as Favourite Oldies and Oddities, Lucky Locations, and Miscellaneous. Favourite Oldies and Oddities are represented by Items of Appearance, Books and Pens, and Food. Items of Appearance include not only Clothing but also Jewellery, Perfume, and Modes of Wearing the Hair. Thus, Items Prescribed for Luck exhibit a variety of at least seven different classes of items. If one distinguishes between Dressing Up and Dressing Down, the number of different classes of Items Prescribed for Luck increases to eight. It did not seem feasible to classify Unlucky Items. Accordingly, the total variety of classes into which magical Material Items fall is nine — eight Prescribed for Luck and an unclassified miscellany of Unlucky Items.

Within the other major category, Behaviour, there are five distinct classes prescribed for Luck: Secular Rituals, Religious Rituals, Grooming, Special Music, and a Miscellany of

---

FIGURE 6.1   AREAS OF MAGIC: MATERIAL ITEMS

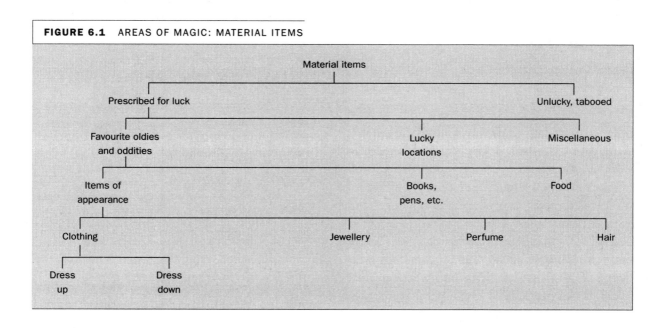

FIGURE 6.2 AREAS OF MAGIC: BEHAVIOURS

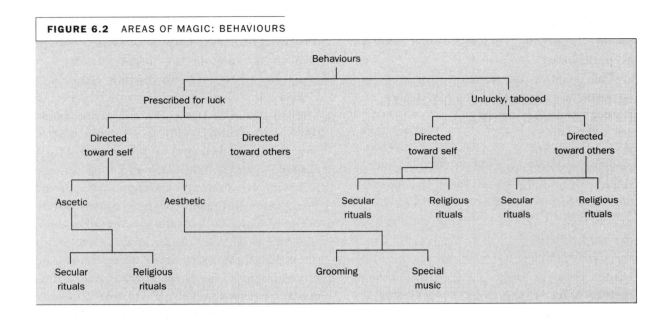

Behaviour Directed toward Others. Under Tabooed Behaviour, in regard to both Behaviour Directed toward Self and Behaviour Directed toward Others, is the twofold classification of Secular Rituals and Religious Rituals. This brings the total number of distinct classes of magical Behaviour to nine. We now turn to specific descriptions of bottom-line Items and Behaviour (those that appear on the bottom line of each of the two figures are not further subclassified).

MAGICAL ITEMS

Items Prescribed for Luck

In regard to Clothing, most students at exam time dress down (i.e., untidily, sloppily), though there are a few who dress up. Among the notable down dressers were: a young woman who always wore to exams her boyfriend's sweatshirt "which was in a deplorable condition with holes everywhere, stretched out of shape and much too big for me"; a science student who always wore an ancient scarf that he insisted "carries parts of my brain in it"; and an engineering student who wore a pink sweatshirt with purported magical qualities. An example of dressing up is the case of a student who always wore a three-piece suit that he had found particularly efficacious when he wore it on one occasion to a job interview. As he indicates, "It's not a very logical thing to wear to an exam because it's hot and restricting." Nevertheless he persists because of his belief in the continuing efficacy of his suit.

Notable items of Jewellery listed by students as bringing them luck were a mother's wedding ring, a mother's RN pin, and a father's class ring. In all of these cases, the students mentioned that the parent was particularly bright and successful, thus implying a faith in magic by contagion.

Under the heading of Perfume, which includes one case of burning incense, all of the accounts suggest a conviction on the part of the students that association with success has the magical power to produce success. One woman wears the perfume that she wore when she met her boyfriend (a lucky event) — "I feel it brings me good luck, as it was luck that brought us together."

Hair is felt by our sample population to possess magical qualities both by its presence and by its absence. One student always has his hair cut short before an exam to permit, as he says, "knowledge to flow freely around my head."

Another student, like Sampson, always allows his hair to grow long before exams "in order to keep the knowledge in."

The general impression is that certain favourite items provide a "security blanket" even if students can only see them (e.g., at the front of the room on the floor) and not actually handle them during the examination. Some "special pens" have written previous successful examinations, and without them students would have less confidence in their ability to do well. For example, an advertisement in a student newspaper read, "Help! I've lost my silver Cross pen. Deep psychological and sentimental value; never written an exam without it. Lost last Friday. If found contact Anna (phone number)." In another instance, the pen had been used to write all of the notes for the course and the student believed that it "knew" the material. Books and notes, although strictly prohibited from use during the exam, are often placed in heaps at the front and along the walls of the room, where students can see them. Many students claim that, in merely looking at the books, "summaries come up through the covers" to them. One student said that on the infrequent occasions she is allowed to take her books with her to her seat, she puts them on the floor and then puts her feet on them. She swears that the knowledge comes up to her through her legs. She adds the disclaimer that she is not crazy and that "it is true."

The magical properties of certain foods or food eaten in a special way at a special time or bought from some particular vendor all have been claimed to bring good luck. One student insists that the purchase of a *carrot muffin* (no other kind) at the "*patty wagon*" (no other vendor) on the way to the examination room is most potent. Failure to secure the right muffin at the right place is an ill omen for her. Another student insists that on examination days she has to have the following breakfast in the following manner: one sausage placed vertically on the left of the plate and beside it two eggs sunny-side up to make the configuration "100" (percent). Still another student stirs his coffee exactly 20 times on examination days. His rationale was that he was taking 5 courses and aspired to an A in each (which is the equivalent of 4 grade points), and 5 times 4 equals 20. This student attained a straight A average over his university career. These student practices resemble what Frazer (1958) refers to in *The Golden Bough* as imitative magic, where the magical method imitates the desired effect.

Examples of Lucky Locations are specific zones of the examination room and may include the back, sides, front, or middle. Students arrive early to secure these Lucky Locations because to sit anywhere else is to court confusion and disaster. Some students insist on a specific seat number that has proved lucky in the past. Some are not particular about the region of the room or a specific seat but they feel they must be in the same cluster with, and close to, those with whom they studied during the term.

Miscellaneous Items include the usual rabbit's feet, dice, coins, as well as tiny teddy bears, kangaroos, and other cuddly toys. One young medical student, very much a positivist in other areas of her life, must, like Christopher Robin, have "Roo" along when she writes her examinations. A young male student is reluctant to write an exam unless he has "found" a coin, which he takes as a sign of "luck." He searches for a coin on the day of the exam, often using up precious study time by "scrounging around bus stops" until he is successful, even at the risk of being late. Another student carries around a lock of his ex-girlfriend's hair in the hope that her extraordinary brightness will illuminate his own efforts.

Unlucky, Tabooed Items

Unlucky Items, interestingly enough, often turn out to be Oldies and Oddities once thought to be lucky but that have failed the owner and so become Tabooed Items. For example, a pink shirt (not the same one mentioned earlier) that had been a lucky talisman was found to be unlucky and thus shunned ever after. What is more, any other student at the same exam who wore a pink shirt was also to be shunned. Another example is the student who reported that in high school he once "crammed" for an exam at home the same day he was to write it and, when he was hungry, heated up a frozen TV dinner. He did unusually well on that exam, so he repeated the pattern of "cramming" at home the day of the exam and eating frozen waffles for breakfast and a TV dinner for lunch. However, when this student arrived at the university he found that studying only on the day of the exam was woefully inadequate and his performance was dreadful. Instead of changing his study habits he changed his "faith" in his lucky food: "It was to the point that even if I ate a whole freezer full of frozen food I would still do poorly on the exam.... I not only stopped eating frozen TV dinners before exams, I now make a point of always avoiding them." Other items, such as a bra (which the student believed to be repressive) and anything new or borrowed, are avoided. (Note the inconsistencies across the sample: one student always borrows her boyfriend's sweatshirt while another will not borrow even a pen.)

Magical Behaviours

Turning now to Magical Behaviours, by far the most prevalent practices—whether directed toward self or others, whether lucky or unlucky —are those that could be termed *rituals*. In turn, these rituals can be subclassified as secular or religious.

Behaviours Directed toward Self Prescribed for Luck

Examples of Secular Rituals Directed toward Self include: knocking on the exam room door three times before entering the room (cf. knocking on wood); stepping over the threshold of the exam room with the right foot first (right in both senses); and making a circuit of the exam building, whatever the weather. However, Behaviours Directed toward Self Prescribed for Luck consist almost entirely of prayer, even in cases where students by their own admission are not particularly religious. Such students nevertheless express a dread of offending God, particularly around examination time, and become compulsively scrupulous in their prayer life and penitent if they forget this duty. There is also, at exam time, an emphasis on virtuous behaviour, particularly toward members of the immediate family, but often also even toward people met on the street. There is a distinct "minding of p's and q's" in the fear that any deviation from the path of righteousness (no matter how occasionally trodden) will be punished. Accordingly, whatever the strength of one's belief, it is not worth taking chances with inexorable fate.

Both the Secular and Religious Rituals Directed toward Self described above could be classified together as being Ascetic in that they involve an element of sacrifice and self-discipline, however unusual. The two other behaviour practices directed toward self, namely Grooming and Special Music, may be classified as Aesthetic in that they have to do with effects that are pleasing to the senses.

Another example of Behaviour Directed toward Self Prescribed for Luck involves students who report that being well groomed contributes to good performance. This in itself may not be magical even by our broad definition. However, when one student states that she puts special care into the manicuring of the three fingers that hold her pen, this begins to seem like magic, certainly the *imitative magic* described by Frazer (i.e., polished fingernails produce polished answers).

A number of students report a Behaviour Directed toward Self Prescribed for Luck that involves "lucky tunes" to which they always listen prior to writing examinations: "then twenty minutes before the exam I drive to school listening to 'Money Changes Everything.' I consistently follow this strategy before I write any exam." The following account is worthy of mention, though not technically a tune or even magic according to our definition (in that there is clearly a thread of empirical connectedness between the act and expected result). One student states that before every exam he listens to a tape by Martin Luther King in which the Reverend King speaks about "his dream" and reiterates the refrain "We shall overcome." Clearly the dream for the student is life success and overcoming this particular exam.

Behaviours Directed toward Others Prescribed for Luck

The category, Behaviours Prescribed for Luck Directed toward Others, might better be described as behaviour required of others by the student. However, since in most cases students go to great ends to elicit such behaviour from family and friends, they may be said indeed to engineer specific forms of behaviour in others. Examples of this are students who insist that before leaving for an examination they be wished good luck by various members of their families according to a formula of specific wording and at a high volume. Quite often it is not sufficient for the formula of the wishes to be secular, they must be invoked by prayer. "At the moment before I walk out of the door I make sure that my parents wish me good luck and especially add 'God Bless You.' The good luck part I could probably do without, but not hearing 'God Bless You' leaves me feeling I'm not getting all the help I could for an exam." In some cases the others who are expected to tender good luck wishes are non-human others. For one student, it was essential for her dog to sit upon his haunches, offer a paw, and "woof" her good luck.

Much as in the case of Lucky Locations, some students seek out lucky people to sit near during the examination (i.e., people whom they think are likely to be star performers). One interesting case of this is a student who stated that he always sought out the ugliest girl to sit next to. By his reasoning, she would not have a boyfriend and would devote all her time to study and be thoroughly well prepared which, in turn, would rub off on him. The magic, of course, is implied in the term "rubbing off" and could best be classified as magic by contagion.

Tabooed Behaviours Directed toward Others

Secular examples of this include refraining from sexual intercourse even, in some cases, by married partners; refraining from discussing the exam, particularly joking about it; and, above all, in this context, avoiding well-wishing. Some students avoid others, even lovers and spouses, who are liable to wish them luck. One student who followed this taboo emphatically avowed that he did not believe in luck. He was nevertheless very upset if someone wished him good luck, and he therefore went out of his way to avoid being so wished.

A few activities were classified as rituals tabooed for religious reasons; for example, refraining from gossip about other people because it is offensive to God, and staying away from entertainment and other secular pursuits because by so doing one acquires virtue, which will be rewarded. These practices, in regard to both items and behaviour, would seem to be most intense when anxiety for the student is at its highest. Similarly, the magic wanes and disappears as the cause for anxiety passes.

DISCUSSION

Examining Figures 6.1 and 6.2 suggests that, among our college students, luck-bringing magic is more prevalent than magic to ward off bad luck. This is particularly the case in Figure 6.1. It is not as immediately apparent in Figure 6.2, but does emerge when one notes that most of the tabooed behaviour described is really directed toward bringing luck rather than warding off misfortune. The point becomes especially clear when we note the prevalence of active manipulative behaviour over passive behaviour, implying the existence of a feeling among the students of being in command of their destinies rather than succumbing to the fate of omens. Of all the accounts of Magical Items and Behaviours, only about ten mentioned the significance of omens. This aspect of student magic is in strong contrast to preliterate magic, where so much credence is placed in omens. Another contrast is that whereas Frazer found imitative magic to be the more prevalent form among preliterates, we found that among students contagious magic is more prevalent.

Another pattern that emerges from these accounts is that items employed and behaviours exhibited are highly private and idiosyncratic. That is, what may be used and considered efficacious by one student may be tabooed by another (e.g., the pink shirts mentioned earlier and careful grooming versus the dishevelled look). This in turn would seem to be related to the fact that student magic is largely invented by the practitioners themselves. It is not traditional or socially shared as is preliterate magic. Student magic is, above all, entirely directed toward self-enhancement, and there is not a single case of magic directed toward the detriment of another, quite unlike the cultic magic of preliterates. Finally, student magic, quite unlike that of preliterate groups, is pragmatic, in that students are willing to abandon any item or behaviour that does not work.

TOWARD A THEORY

On the basis of our information, it appears that student magic can be thought of as being at one end of a continuum that began with preliterate magic and emerged through other forms such as those practised by soldiers in warfare, miners, and sports competitors. At the preliterate-magic end of the continuum, magic is a communal, cooperative enterprise in which the participants have shared meanings in regard to the practices and are motivated by a strong collectivity orientation. Among the soldiers, miners, and athletes, magic is still practised in a community in which there are, to some extent, shared meanings and also, to some extent, but considerably less than among preliterate peoples, a collectivity orienta-

tion. When we come to students writing exams, we have reached the near end of the continuum of magical practices. Here we find magic practised individually and in isolation, without shared meaning (even, to some extent, with contradictory meanings), and completely self-oriented in its motivation. In an attempt to understand these differences along the continuum, it might be suggested that for preliterate peoples living in a less complex and completely homogeneous society, one would expect shared meanings in a way that is not to be expected among heterogeneous, largely anonymous groups of students in contemporary urban society. However, even in contemporary society it is reasonable to expect that, within a group of soldiers who have been trained together to act in unison and whose very lives depend upon the actions of everyone in the group, there would tend to be more of a collectivity orientation than among university students writing exams (although perhaps not as much as within more homogeneous, preliterate groupings). The phenomenon of shared meanings would also be expected to be in an intermediate position, since even though soldiers, miners, and athletes are the products of a heterogeneous socialization compared to preliterate peoples, they nevertheless work together and constitute communities to a greater degree than do exam-writing students. As such, this "middle category" has developed many well-known agreed-upon magical rituals such as "break a leg," "three on a match," not referring to a "winning streak," and "the fatal last shift." In effect then, the particular aspects of student magic that we described earlier, which may seem atypical of magic in the past and in some ways inexplicable, may be partially explained in terms of increasing societal complexity and heterogeneity as well as shifts in cultural values.

In sum, as society moves from preliterate to contemporary, increasing in complexity as well as scientific sophistication, we might expect magic to be transformed from: (1) being publicly performed to being privately and individually performed; (2) being culturally transmitted to being spontaneously generated; (3) being completely shared by the whole community to being utilized privately by individuals; and (4) being unvaryingly uniform and consistent in its rituals to being highly variable and even contradictory. Clearly, with an ideal-type polar construct of this kind, no actual case of magic (including student magic) will in all respects conform to the characteristics of either pole. The burden of this article, however, is that students' magic falls rather toward the latter end of each of these four continua.

REFERENCES

Albas, D., and C. Albas. 1984. *Student Life and Exams: Stresses and Coping Strategies.* Dubuque, IA: Kendall/Hunt.

Frazer, J. 1958. *The Golden Bough: A Study in Magic and Religion.* New York: Macmillan.

Gmelch, G. 1971. "Baseball Magic." *Society* 8(8): 39–41.

Henslin, J. 1967. "Craps and Magic." *American Journal of Sociology* 73: 316–30.

Homans, G. 1941. "Anxiety and Magic." *American Anthropologist* 43: 164–72.

Jahoda, G. 1969. *The Psychology of Superstition.* London: Penguin.

Stouffer, S., A. Lumsdaine, M. Lumsdaine, R. Williams, Jr., M. Smith, I. Janis, and L. Cottrell, Jr. 1949. *Studies in Social Psychology in World War II: The American Soldier, Combat and Its Aftermath.* Princeton, NJ: Princeton University Press.

Wilson, W. 1942. "Miners' Superstitions." *Life and Letters Today* 32: 86–93.

Chapter 7

Biology as Ideology

R.C. LEWONTIN

Our society was born, at least politically, in revolutions of the seventeenth century in Britain and the eighteenth century in France and America. Those revolutions swept out an old order characterized by aristocratic privilege and a relative fixity of persons in the society. The bourgeois revolutions in England, France, and America claimed that this old society and its ideology were illegitimate, and the ideologues of those revolutions produced and legitimized an ideology of liberty and equality. Diderot and the Encylopedists and Tom Paine were the theorists of a society of "liberté, égalité, fraternité," of all men created equal. The writers of the Declaration of Independence asserted that political truths were "self-evident; that all men are created equal; that they are endowed by their creator with certain unalienable rights; that among these are life, liberty, and the pursuit of happiness" (by which, of course, they meant the pursuit of money). They meant literally all *men*, because women were not given the right to vote in the United States until 1920; Canada enfranchised women a little sooner, in 1918—but not in provincial elections in Quebec until 1940. And of course they didn't mean *all* men, because slavery continued in the French dominions and in the Caribbean until the middle of the nineteenth century. Blacks were defined by the United States Constitution as only three-fifths of a person, and for most of the history of English parliamentary democracy, a man had to have money to vote.

To make a revolution, you need slogans that appeal to the great mass of people, and you can hardly get people to shed blood under a banner that reads "Equality for some." So the ideology and the slogans outstrip the reality. For if we look at the society that has been created by those revolutions, we see a great deal of inequality of wealth and power among individuals, between sexes, between races, between nations. Yet we have heard over and over again in school and had it drummed into us by every organ of communication that we live in a society of free equals. The contradiction between the claimed equality of our society and the observation that great inequalities exist has been, for North Americans at least, the major social agony of the last 200 years. It has motivated an extraordinary amount of our political history. How are we to resolve the contradiction of immense inequalities in a society that claims to be founded on equality?

There are two possibilities. We might say that it was all a fake, a set of slogans meant to replace a regime of aristocrats with a regime of wealth and privilege of a different sort, that inequality in our society is structural and an integral aspect of the whole of our political and social life. To say that, however, would be deeply subversive, because it would call for yet another revolution if we wanted to make good on our hopes for liberty and equality for all. It is not a popular idea among teachers, newspaper editors, college professors, successful politicians, indeed anyone who has the power to help form public consciousness.

The alternative, which has been the one taken since the beginning of the nineteenth century, has been to put a new gloss on the notion of equality.

Source: *Biology as Ideology: The Doctrine of DNA* (Toronto: Anansi, 1991), pp. 19–37. Copyright © 1991 by R.C. Lewontin. Reprinted by permission of the House of Anansi Press.

Rather than equality of *result*, what has been meant is equality of *opportunity*. In this view of equality, life is a foot race. In the bad old days of the *ancien régime*, the aristocrats got to start at the finish line whereas all the rest of us had to start at the beginning, so the aristocrats won. In the new society, the race is fair: everyone is to begin at the starting line and everyone has an equal opportunity to finish first. Of course, some people are faster runners than others, and so some get the rewards and others don't. This is the view that the old society was characterized by *artificial* barriers to equality, whereas the new society allows a natural sorting process to decide who is to get the status, wealth, and power and who is not.

Such a view does not threaten the status quo, but on the contrary supports it by telling those who are without power that their position is the inevitable outcome of their own innate deficiencies and that, therefore, nothing can be done about it. A remarkably explicit recent statement of this assertion is the one by Richard Herrnstein, a psychologist from Harvard, who is one of the most outspoken modern ideologues of natural inequality. He wrote,

> the privileged classes of the past were probably not much superior biologically to the downtrodden which is why revolution had a fair chance of success. By removing artificial barriers between classes society has encouraged the creation of biological barriers. When people can take their natural level in society, the upper classes will, by definition, have greater capacity than the lower.[1]

We are not told precisely what principle of biology guarantees that biologically inferior persons cannot seize power from biologically superior ones, but it is not logic that is at issue here. Such statements as Herrnstein's are meant to convince us that although we may not live in the best of all *conceivable* worlds, we live in the best of all *possible* worlds. The social entropy has been maximized so that we have as much equality as possible because the structure is essentially one of equality, and whatever inequalities are left over

are not structural but based on innate differences between individuals. In the nineteenth century this was also the view, and education was seen as the lubricant that would guarantee that the race of life was run smoothly. Lester Frank Ward, a giant of nineteenth-century sociology, wrote, "Universal education is the power which is destined to overthrow every species of hierarchy. It is destined to remove all artificial inequality and leave the natural inequalities to find their true level. The true value of a newborn infant lies in its naked capacity for acquiring the ability to do."[2]

This was echoed 60 years later by Arthur Jensen at the University of California, who wrote about the inequality of intelligence of Blacks and whites: "We have to face it, the assortment of persons into occupational roles simply is not fair in any absolute sense. The best we can hope for is that true merit given equality of opportunity acts as a basis for the natural assorting process."[3]

Simply to assert that the race of life is fair and that different people have different intrinsic abilities to run it is not enough to explain the observations of inequality. Children seem, by and large, to acquire the social status of their parents. About 60 percent of the children of "blue collar" workers remain "blue collar," while about 70 percent of "white collar" workers' children are "white collar." But these figures vastly overestimate the amount of social mobility. Most people who have passed from "blue collar" to "white collar" jobs have passed from factory production-line jobs to office production-line jobs or have become sales clerks, less well paid, less secure, doing work just as numbing of the soul and body as the factory work done by their parents. The children of gas station attendants usually borrow money, and the children of oil magnates usually lend it. The chance that Nelson Rockefeller would have wound up pumping gas was pretty close to zero.

If we live in a meritocracy, in which each person can rise to the status allowed by his or her innate capacities, how do we explain this passage of social power from parent to offspring? Are we really just back in an old aristocratic situation? The naturalistic explanation is to say that not only do we differ in our innate capacities but that these innate capacities are themselves transmitted from generation to generation biologically. That is to say, they are in our genes. The original social and economic notion of inheritance has been turned into biological inheritance.

But even the claim that the intrinsic ability to win success is inherited in the genes is not sufficient to justify an unequal society. After all, we might assert that there ought not to be any particular relationship between what one can accomplish and what social and psychic rewards are given. We might give the same material and psychic rewards to house painters and picture painters, to surgeons and to barbers, to professors who give lectures, and to the janitors who come in and clean up the classroom afterward. We might create a society on whose banners are inscribed, "From each according to his ability, to each according to his need."

To meet this objection to an unequal society there has been developed a biological theory of human nature that says that while the differences between us are in our genes, there are certain inborn similarities among us all. These similarities of human nature guarantee that differences in ability will be converted into differences in status, that society is naturally hierarchical, and that a society of equal reward and status is biologically impossible. We might pass laws requiring such equality, but the moment the vigilance of the state was relaxed we would return to "doing what comes naturally."

These three ideas—that we differ in fundamental abilities because of innate differences, that those innate differences are biologically inherited, and that human nature guarantees the formation of a hierarchical society—when taken together, form what we can call the *ideology of biological determinism.*

The idea that blood will tell was not invented by biologists. It is a dominant theme of nineteenth-century literature, and one can hardly appreciate the most praised and popular writers

of the last century without seeing how a theory of innate difference informed their work. Think of Dickens's *Oliver Twist.* When Oliver first meets young Jack Dawkins, the Artful Dodger, on the road to London, a remarkable contrast in body and spirit is established. The Dodger is described as "a snub-nosed, flat-browed, common-faced boy ... with rather bow-legs, and little, sharp, ugly eyes," and his English was not the best. What can we expect from a 10-year-old street urchin with no family, no education, and only the lowest criminals of London for companions? Oliver's speech, however, is perfect (he knows when to use the subjunctive) and his manner is genteel. He is described as a pale, thin child, but with a good sturdy spirit in his breast. Yet Oliver was raised from birth in the most degrading of nineteenth-century British institutions, the parish workhouse, an orphan with no education and little to eat. He is described as having spent the first nine years of his life rolling about on the floor all day "without the inconvenience of too much food or too much clothing." Where amid the oakumpickings did Oliver garner that sensitivity of soul and perfection of English grammer? *Oliver Twist* is a mystery novel, and that is its mystery. The answer is that although his food was gruel, his blood was upper-middle-class. His mother was the daughter of a naval officer. His father's family was well off and socially ambitious.

A similar theme is central to George Eliot's *Daniel Deronda.* We first meet Daniel, the young stepson of an English baronet, wasting his time in a fashionable gambling spa. When he becomes a bit older, he suddenly has mysterious longings for things Hebrew. He falls in love with a Jewish woman, studies the Talmud, and converts. The reader will not be surprised to learn that he is the son of a Jewish actress whom he has never seen but whose blood tells. Nor is this a madness only of the Anglo-Saxons. The Rougon-Macquart novels of Émile Zola were deliberately written as a kind of experimental literature to illustrate the discoveries of nineteenth-century anthropology. In the preface, Zola tells us that "heredity has its laws just like gravitation." The Rougon-Macquarts are a family descended from the two lovers of one woman, one of whom was a solid, industrious peasant, while the other was a wastrel and degenerate. From the dependable peasant descend solid, honest stock, while from the degenerate ancestor descend a long line of social misfits and criminals including the famous Nana, who was a nymphomaniac from early childhood, and her mother, Gervaise, the laundress, who despite beginning a solid entrepreneurial life, lapses into her natural indolence. When Gervaise's husband, Copeau, the father of Nana, was admitted to hospital with the DTs, the first question the physician asked him was, "Did your father drink?" The public consciousness of the period both in Europe and North America was permeated with the notion that intrinsic differences in temperament and merit will finally dominate any mere effect of education and environment.

The fictional Rougon-Macquarts are seen again in the equally fictional but supposedly real family of Kallikaks, who graced virtually every textbook of American psychology until the Second World War. The Kallikaks were supposed to be two halves of a family descended from two women of contrasting nature and a common father. This piece of academic fiction was meant to convince malleable young minds that criminality, laziness, alcoholism, and incest were inborn and inherited.

Nor were supposedly innate differences restricted to individual variation. Nations and races were said to be characterized by innate temperamental and intellectual differences. These claims were made not by racists, demagogues, and fascist know-nothings but by the leaders of the American academic, psychological, and sociological establishments. In 1923, Carl Brigham, who was later secretary of the College Entrance Examination Board, produced a study of intelligence under the direction of R.M. Yerkes, professor of psychology at Harvard and the president of the American Psychological Association. The study asserted: "We must assume that we are measuring inborn intelligence. We must face the possibility of racial admixture here in America that is infinitely worse than that faced by any European country for we are incorporating the Negro into our racial stock. The decline of the American intelligence will be more rapid ... owing to the presence here of the Negro."[4]

Yet another president of the American Psychological Association said that whenever there has been mixed breeding with the Negro, there has been deterioration of civilizations.[5] Louis Agassiz, one of the most famous zoologists of the nineteenth century, reported that the skull sutures of Negro babies closed earlier than the sutures of white babies, so their brains were entrapped, and it would be dangerous to teach them too much. Perhaps the most extraordinary of claims was that of Henry Fairfield Osborne, president of the American Museum of Natural History and one of America's most eminent and prestigious paleontologists, who worked out the sequence of evolution of the horse. He wrote,

> The northern races invaded the countries to the south, not only as conquerors but as contributors of strong moral and intellectual elements to a more or less decadent civilization. Through the Nordic tide which flowed into Italy came the ancestors of Raphael, Leonardo, Galileo, Titiano; also, according to Günther, of Giotto, Botticelli, Petrarca, and Tasso. Columbus, from his portraits and from busts, *whether authentic or not*, was clearly of Nordic ancestry.[6] [emphasis added]

Whether authentic or not, indeed! Over and over again, leading intellectuals have assured their audiences that modern science shows that there are inborn racial and individual differences in ability. Nor have modern biologists taken a different view. Except for a brief interruption around the time of the Second World War, when the crimes of Nazism made claims of innate inferiority extremely unpopular, biological determinism has been the mainstream commitment of biologists. Yet these claims are made without a shred of evidence and in contradiction to every principle of biology and genetics.

To realize the error of these claims, we need to understand what is involved in the development of an organism. First, we are not determined by our genes, although surely we are influenced by them. Development depends not only on the materials that have been inherited from parents—that is, the genes and other materials in the sperm and egg—but also on the particular temperature, humidity, nutrition, smells, sights, and sounds (including what we call education) that impinge on the developing organism. Even if I knew the complete molecular specification of every gene in an organism, I could not predict what that organism would be. Of course, the difference between lions and lambs is almost entirely a consequence of the differences in genes between them. But variations among individuals within species are a unique consequence of both genes and the developmental environment in a constant interaction. Moreover, curiously enough, even if I knew the genes of a developing organism and the complete sequence of its environments, I could not specify the organism.

There is yet another factor at work. If we count the number of bristles under the wing of a fruitfly, for example, we find that there is a different number on the left side than on the right. Some have more bristles on the left, some more on the right; there is no average difference. So, there is a kind of fluctuating asymmetry. An individual fruitfly, however, has the same genes on its left side as on its right. Moreover, the tiny size of a developing fruitfly and the place it develops guarantee that both left and right sides have had the same humidity, the same oxygen, the same temperature. The differences between left and right side are caused neither by genetic nor by environmental differences but by random variation in growth and division of cells during development: *developmental noise.*

This chance element in development is an important source of variation. Indeed, in the case of the fruitfly bristles, there is as much vari-

ation consequent on developmental noise as there is from genetic and environmental variation. We do not know in human beings, for example, how much of the difference between us is a consequence of the random differences in the growth of neurons during our embryonic life and early childhood. It is our common prejudice that even if one had practised the violin from a very early age, one would not be able to play as well as Menuhin, and we think of him as having special neuronal connections. But that is not the same as saying that those neuronal connections are coded in his genes. There may be large random differences in the growth of our central nervous systems. It is a fundamental principle of developmental genetics that every organism is the outcome of a unique interaction between genes and environmental sequences modulated by the random chances of cell growth and division, and that all these together finally produce an organism. Moreover, an organism changes throughout its entire life. Human beings change their size, not only growing larger as children, but as they grow old, growing smaller as their joints and bones shrink.

A more sophisticated version of genetic determinism agrees that organisms are a consequence of both environmental and genetic influences but describes differences between individuals as differences in *capacity*. This is the empty bucket metaphor. We each begin life as an empty bucket of a different size. If the environment provides only a little water, then all these buckets will have the same amount in them. But if an abundance is provided from the environment, then the small buckets will overflow and the large ones will hold more. In this view, if every person were allowed to develop to his or her genetic capacity, there would indeed be major differences in ability and performance, and these would be fair and natural.

But there is no more biology in the metaphor of innate capacity than there is in the notion of fixed genetic effects. The unique interaction between organism and environment cannot be described by differences in capacity. It is true that if two genetically different organisms developed in exactly the same environment, they would be different, but that difference cannot be described as different capacities because the genetical type that was superior in one environment may be inferior in a second developmental environment. For example, strains of rats can be selected for better or poorer ability to find their way through a maze, and these strains of rats pass on their differential ability to run the maze to their offspring, so they are certainly genetically different in this respect. But if exactly the same strains of rats are given a different task, or if the conditions of learning are changed, the bright rats turn out to be dull and the dull rats turn out to be bright. There is no general genetic superiority of one rat strain over another in finding its way through a problem.

A more subtle and mystifying approach to biological determinism rejects both the genetic fixity of the first view and the capacity metaphor of the second and is, instead, statistical. Essentially, it states the problem as one of partitioning the effects of environment and genes so that we can say that, perhaps, 80 percent of the difference among individuals is caused by their genes and 20 percent by their environment. Of course, these differences must be on a population level rather than an individual level. It would make no sense at all to say that of someone's height of five feet eleven and a half inches, five feet two were a result of her genes and the other nine and a half inches were put there by the food she ate. The statistical view considers the proportion of *variation* among individuals rather than partitioning a particular individual measurement. The statistical approach tries to assign some proportion of all the variation among individuals or groups to variation among their genes, and a second proportion that results from variation among their environments.

The implication is that if most of the variation in, say, intelligence among individuals is a consequence of variation among their genes, then manipulating the environment will not make much difference. If is often said, for example, that 80 percent of the variation among individual children in their IQ performance is caused by variation in their genes and only 20 percent by variation in their environment. The result is that the greatest possible amelioration of environment could not eliminate more than 20 percent of differences among individuals, and the 80 percent would still be there because it is a consequence of genetic variation. This is a completely fallacious although plausible-sounding argument. There is no connection whatsoever between the variation that can be ascribed to genetic differences as opposed to environmental differences and whether a change in environment will affect performance and by how much. We should remember that any very ordinary arithmetic student in primary school in Canada can correctly add a column of figures vastly more quickly than the most intelligent Ancient Roman mathematician, who had to struggle with cumbersome X's, V's, and I's. That same ordinary student can multiply two five-digit numbers with a $10 hand-held calculator more quickly and accurately than a professor of mathematics could have a century ago.

A change in environment, in this case of cultural environment, can change abilities by many orders of magnitude. Moreover, the differences between individuals are abolished by cultural and mechanical inventions. Differences that can be ascribed to genetic differences and that appear in one environment may disappear completely in another. Although there may be biologically based average differences in physique and strength between a random group of men and random group of women (and these are less than usually supposed), these differences rapidly become irrelevant and disappear from practical view in a world of electrically driven hoists, power steering, and electronic controls. So the proportion of variation in a population as a consequence of variation in genes is not a fixed property but one that varies from environment to environment. That is, how much difference among us is a consequence of genetic differences between us depends, curiously enough, on environment.

Conversely, how much difference there is between us that is a consequence of environmental variation in our life histories depends on our genes. We know from experiments that organisms that have some particular genes are very sensitive to environmental variation while other individuals with different genes are insensitive to environmental variation. Environmental variation and genetic variation are not independent causal pathways. Genes affect how sensitive one is to environment, and environment affects how relevant one's genetic differences may be. The interaction between them is indissoluble, and we can separate genetic and environmental effects statistically only in a particular population of organisms at a particular moment with a particular set of specified environments. When an environment changes, all bets are off.

The contrast between genetic and environmental, between nature and nurture, is not a contrast between fixed and changeable. It is a fallacy of biological determinism to say that if differences are in the genes, no change can occur. We know this to be true from medical evidence alone. There are many so-called inborn errors of metabolism in which a defective gene results, in normal circumstances, in a defective physiology. An example is Wilson's disease, a genetic defect that prevents its sufferers from detoxifying the copper that we all consume in minute quantities in our ordinary food. The copper builds up in the body and eventually causes nervous degeneration and finally death, some time in adolescence or early adulthood. Nothing could be more perfectly described as a genetic disorder. Yet people with this defective gene can lead a perfectly normal life and have a normal development by taking a pill that helps them get rid of the copper, and they are then indistinguishable from anyone else.

It is sometimes said that examples of changing the conditions of performance, such as the invention of Arabic numerals, or the calculator, or providing a pill, are beside the point because we are interested in some sort of basic unaided, naked ability. But there are no measures of "unaided" ability, nor are we really interested in them. There are some people who can remember long columns of figures and others who are good at adding and multiplying large numbers in their heads. So why do we give written IQ tests, which, after all, are simply giving the crutch of paper and pencil to people who do not have the "unaided" ability to do mental arithmetic? Indeed, why do we allow people taking mental tests to wear eyeglasses, if we are interested in culturally unmodified "naked" abilities? The answer is that we have no interest in arbitrarily defined abilities, but are concerned with differences in the ability to carry out *socially constructed* tasks that are relevant to the structure of our actual social lives.

Aside from the conceptual difficulties of trying to ascribe separate effects to genes and environment, there are severe experimental difficulties in detecting the influence of genes, especially when we deal with human beings. How do we decide whether genes influence differences in some trait? In all organisms the process is the same. We compare individuals who are differently related to one another, and if more closely related individuals are more similar than are more distantly related ones, we ascribe some power to the genes. But herein lies the deep difficulty of human genetics. Unlike experimental animals, people who are more closely related to each other not only share more genes in common but they also share environment in common because of the family and class structure of human societies. The observation that children resemble their parents in some trait does not distinguish between similarity that comes from genetic similarity and similarity that arises from environmental resemblance. The resemblance of parents and children is the observation to be explained. It is not evidence for genes. For example, the two social traits that have the highest resemblance between parents and children in North America are religious sect and political party. Yet even the most ardent biological determinist would not seriously argue that there is a gene for Episcopalianism or voting Social Credit.

The problem is to distinguish genetic similarity from environmental similarity. It is for this reason that so much emphasis has been put on twin studies in human genetics. The idea is that if twins are more similar than ordinary sibs or if twins raised in completely isolated families are still similar, then this surely must be evidence for genes. In particular, there has been a fascination with a study of identical twins raised apart. If identical twins—that is, twins sharing all the same genes—are similar even though raised apart, then their trait must be strongly genetically influenced. Much of the claim for the high heritability of IQ, for example, comes from studies of identical twins raised apart.

Only three such studies have been published. The first and largest set of studies was reported by Sir Cyril Burt. This was the only study that claimed no similarity between the family circumstances of the families that raised separated twins. It also claimed a heritability of 80 percent for IQ performance. However, careful investigation by Oliver Gillie of the *Times* of London and Professor Leon Kamin at Princeton revealed that Burt had simply made up the numbers and made up the twins.[7] He even made up the collaborators whose names appeared with his in the publications. We need consider these claims no further. They represent one of the great scandals of modern psychology and biology.

When we look at the other studies, which actually give family details of the separated twins, we realize that we live in a real world and not in a Gilbert and Sullivan operetta. The reason that twins are separated at birth may be that their mother has died in childbirth, so that one twin is raised by an aunt and another by a best friend or grandmother. Sometimes the parents cannot afford to keep both children so they give one to a relative. In fact, the studied twins were not raised apart at all. They were raised by members of the same extended family, in the same small village. They went to school together. They played together. Other adoption studies of

human IQ that are said to demonstrate the effect of genes have their own experimental difficulties, including the failure to match children by age, extremely small samples, and biased selection of cases for study.[8] There is a strong effort on the part of parents of many twins to make them as similar as possible. They are given names beginning with the same letter and are dressed alike. International twin conventions give prizes for the most similar twins. One twin study advertised in the newspapers and offered a trip to Chicago for identical twins, thus attracting those who were the most similar.[9] As a consequence of such biases, there is at present simply no convincing measure of the role of genes in influencing human behavioural variation.

One of the major biological ideological weapons used to convince people that their position in society is fixed and unchangeable and, indeed, fair is the constant confusion between inherited and unchangeable. This confusion is nowhere more manifest than in the very studies of adoptions that are meant to measure biological similarities. In human populations, one carries out an adoption study like that of separation of identical twins to try to break the connection between resemblance that comes from genetic sources and resemblance that comes from the sources of family similarity. If adopted children resemble their biological parents more closely than they resemble their adopting parents, then the geneticists quite correctly regard this as evidence for the influence of genes. When one looks at all the studies of adoption in order to study the genetic influence on intelligence, there are two constant results.

First, adopted children do resemble their biological parents in the sense that the higher the IQ score of the biological parent, the higher the IQ score of the child who was adopted. So, biological parents are having some influence on the IQ of their children even though those children are adopted early, and putting aside the possibility of prenatal nutritional differences or extremely early stimulation, it would be reasonable to say that genes have some influence on IQ scores. We can only speculate about the source of genetic influence. There is a premium on speed in IQ testing, and genes might have some influence on reaction times or general speed of central nervous processes.

The second feature of adoption studies is that the IQ test scores of the children are about 20 points higher than those of their biological parents. It is still the case that the biological parents with the higher IQ scores have children with higher scores, but the children as a group have moved well ahead of their biological parents. In fact, the average IQ scores of these adopted children are about equal to the average IQ of the adopting parents, who always do much better on IQ tests than the biological parents. What is at stake here is the difference between *correlation* and *identity*. Two variables are positively correlated if higher values of one are matched with higher values of the other. The ordered set of numbers 100, 101, 102, and 103 is perfectly correlated with the set of 120, 121, 122, and 123 because each increase in one set is perfectly matched by an increase in the other. Yet the two sets of numbers are clearly not identical, differing as they do by 20 units on the average. So the IQ of parents may be excellent predictors of the IQs of their children in the sense that higher values for parents are matched with higher values for offspring, but the *average* IQ value of their children may be much greater. For the geneticist, it is the *correlation* that indicates the role of genes; the heritability predicts nothing about changes in the group average from generation to generation. The adoption studies are a revelation of the meaning of IQ tests and of the social reality of adoption.

First, what do IQ tests actually measure? They are a combination of numerical, vocabulary, education, and attitudinal questions. They ask such things as "Who was Wilkins McCawber?" "What is the meaning of 'sudiferous'?" "What should a girl do if a boy hits her?" (Hitting him back is *not* the right answer!) And how do we know that someone who does well on such a test is *intelligent*? Because, in fact, the tests were originally standardized to pick out precise-

ly those children in a class whom the teacher had already labelled intelligent. That is, IQ tests are instruments for giving an apparently objective and "scientific" gloss to the social prejudices of educational institutions.

Second, people who decide on an early adoption for their children are usually working-class or unemployed people who do not share in the education and culture of the middle class. People who adopt children, on the other hand, are usually middle-class and have an appropriate education and cultural experience for the content and intent of IQ tests. So adopting parents have, as a group, much higher IQ performances than the parents who have chosen adoption for their children. The educational and family environment in which these children are then raised has the expected result of raising all their IQs even though there is evidence for some genetic influence from their biological parents.

These results of adoption studies illustrate perfectly why we cannot answer a question about how much something can be changed by answering a different question, namely, are there genes influencing the trait? If we wanted seriously to ask the question posed by Arthur Jensen in his famous article "How much can we boost IQ and scholastic achievement?"[10] the only way we could answer would be to try to boost IQ and scholastic achievement. We do not answer it by asking, as Jensen did, whether there is a genetic influence on IQ, because to be genetic is not to be unchangeable.

Biological determinists claim that there are not only differences in ability among individuals but that these individual differences explain racial differences in social power and success. It is hard to know how one would get evidence about Black–white differences that did not totally confound genetic and environmental variation. Interracial adoptions, for example, are uncommon, especially of white children adopted by Black foster parents. Occasional evidence does appear, however.

In Dr Barnardo's homes in Britain, where children are taken as orphans soon after birth, a study was done of intelligence testing of children of

Black and white ancestry.[11] Several tests were given at various ages, and small differences were found in the IQ performance between these groups, but these were not statistically significant. If nothing more was said about it, most of the readers would assume that the small differences showed whites were better than Blacks. But in fact the reverse was true. The differences were not statistically significant, but where there were any differences, they were in favour of Blacks. There is not an iota of evidence of any kind that the differences in status, wealth, and power between races in North America have anything to do with the genes, except, of course, for the socially mediated effects of the genes for skin colour. Indeed, there is in general a great deal less difference genetically between races than one might suppose from the superficial cues we all use in distinguishing races. Skin colour, hair form, and nose shape are certainly influenced by genes, but we do not know how many such genes there are, or how they work. On the other hand, when we look at genes we do know something about, genes that influence our blood type, for example, or genes for the various enzyme molecules essential to our physiology, we find that although there is a tremendous amount of variation from individual to individual, there is remarkably little variation on the average between major human groups. In fact, about 85 percent of all identified human genetic variation is between any two individuals from the same ethnic group. Another 8 percent of all the variation is between ethnic groups within a race—say, between Spaniards, Irish, Italians, and Britons—and only 7 percent of all human genetic variation lies on the average between major human races like those of Africa, Asia, Europe, and Oceania.[12]

So we have no reason *a priori* to think that there would be any genetic differentiation between racial groups in characteristics such as behaviour, temperament, and intelligence. Nor is there an iota of evidence that social classes differ in any way in their genes except insofar as ethnic origin or race may be used as a form of economic discrimination. The nonsense propagated by ideologues of biological determinism that the lower classes are biologically inferior to the upper classes, that all the good things in European culture come from the Nordic groups, is precisely nonsense. It is meant to legitimate the structures of inequality in our society by putting a biological gloss on them and by propagating the continual confusion between what may be influenced by genes and what may be changed by social and environmental alternations.

The vulgar error that confuses heritability and fixity has been, over the years, the most powerful single weapon that biological ideologues have had in legitimating a society of inequality. Since as biologists they must know better, one is entitled to at least a suspicion that the beneficiaries of a system of inequality are not to be regarded as objective experts.

NOTES

1. R.J. Herrnstein, *IQ in the Meritocracy* (Boston: Atlantic–Little, Brown, 1973), 221.
2. L.F. Ward, "Education" (manuscript, Special Collection Division, Brown University, Providence, RI, 1873).
3. A.R. Jensen, "How Much Can We Boost IQ and Scholastic Achievement?" *Harvard Educational Review* 39 (1969): 15.
4. C.C. Brigham, *A Study of American Intelligence* (Princeton, NJ: Princeton University Press, 1923), 209–10.
5. H.L. Garrett, *Breeding Down* (Richmond, VA: Patrick Henry Press, n.d.).
6. H.F. Osborne, letter, *New York Times*, 8 April 1924, 18.
7. R.C. Lewontin, S. Rose, and L.J. Kamin, *Not in Our Genes* (New York: Pantheon, 1984), 101–6.
8. L.J. Kamin, *The Science and Politics of IQ* (Potomac, MD: Erlbaum, 1974).
9. Ibid.
10. Jensen, "How Much Can We Boost IQ."
11. B. Tizard. "IQ and Race," *Nature* 247 (1974): 316.
12. R.C. Lewontin, *Human Diversity* (San Francisco: Scientific American Books, 1982).

Chapter 8

Hip-Hop from Dissent to Commodity: A Note on Consumer Culture

ROBERT J. BRYM

MUSIC AS DISSENT AND CONSENT

Music can sometimes act as a kind of social cement. Reflecting the traditions, frustrations, and ambitions of the communities that create it, music can help otherwise isolated voices sing in unison. It can help individuals shape a collective identity. Sometimes, music can even inspire people to engage in concerted political action (Mattern, 1998).

Under some circumstances, however, music can have the opposite effect. It can individualize feelings of collective unrest and thereby moderate dissent. This occurs, for example, when music that originates as an act of rebellion is turned into a mass-marketed commodity. Music that develops in opposition to the mainstream typically gets tamed and declawed when it is transformed into something that can be bought and sold on a wide scale. By commodifying dissent and broadening its appeal to a large and socially heterogeneous audience, consumer culture renders it mainstream. The way it accomplishes this remarkable feat is well illustrated by the musical genre called hip-hop.[1]

THE SOCIAL ORIGINS OF HIP-HOP

Hip-hop originated in the appalling social conditions facing African American inner-city youth in the 1970s and 1980s. During those decades, manufacturing industries left the cities for suburban or foreign locales, where land values were lower and labour was less expensive. Unemployment among African American youth rose to more than 40 percent. Middle-class Blacks left the inner city for the suburbs. This robbed the remaining young people of successful role models they could emulate. The out-migration also eroded the taxing capacity of municipal governments, leading to a decline in public services. Meanwhile, the American public elected conservative governments at the state and federal levels. They slashed school and welfare budgets, thus deepening the destitution of ghetto life (Wilson, 1987).

Understandably, young African Americans grew angrier as the conditions of their existence worsened. With few legitimate prospects for advancement, they turned increasingly to crime and, in particular, to the drug trade.

In the late 1970s, cocaine was expensive and demand for the drug was flat. So, in the early 1980s, Colombia's Medellin drug cartel introduced a less expensive form of cocaine called rock or crack. Crack was not only inexpensive: It offered a quick and intense high, and it was highly addictive. Crack cocaine offered many people a temporary escape from hopelessness and soon became wildly popular in the inner city. Turf wars spread as gangs tried to outgun each other for control of the local traffic. The sale and use of crack became so widespread it corroded much of what was left of the inner-city African American community (Davis, 1990).

The shocking conditions described above gave rise to a shocking musical form: hip-hop. Stridently at odds with the values and tastes of both whites and middle-class African Americans, hip-hop described and glorified the mean streets of the inner city while holding the police, the mass media, and other pillars of society in utter contempt. Furthermore, hip-hop tried to offend middle-class sensibilities, Black and white, by using highly offensive language. In 1988, more than a decade after its first stirrings, hip-hop reached its political high point with the release of the CD *It Takes a Nation to Hold Us Back* by Chuck D and Public Enemy. In "Don't Believe the Hype," Chuck D accused the mass media of maliciously distributing lies. In "Black Steel in the Hour of Chaos," he charged the FBI and the CIA with assassinating the two great leaders of the African American community in the 1960s, Martin Luther King and Malcolm X. In "Party for Your Right to Fight" he blamed the federal government for organizing the fall of the Black Panthers, the radical black nationalist party of the 1960s. Here, it seemed, was an angry expression of subcultural revolt that could not be mollified.

HIP-HOP TRANSFORMED

However, there were elements in hip-hop that soon transformed it (Bayles, 1994: 341–62; Neal, 1999: 144–8). In the first place, early, radical hip-hop was not written as dance music. It therefore cut itself off from a large audience. Moreover, hip-hop entered a self-destructive phase with the emergence of Gangsta rap, which extolled criminal lifestyles, denigrated women, and replaced politics with drugs, guns, and machismo. The release of Ice T's "Cop Killer" in 1992 provoked strong political opposition from Republicans and Democrats, white church groups, and Black middle-class associations. Time/Warner was forced to withdraw the song from circulation. The sense that hip-hop had reached a dead end, or at least a turning point, grew in 1996, when rapper Tupac Shakur was murdered in the culmination of a feud between two hip-hop record labels, Death Row in Los Angeles and Bad Boy in New York (Springhall, 1998: 149–51).

If these events made it seem that hip-hop was self-destructing, the police and insurance industries helped to speed up its demise. In 1988, a group called Niggas with Attitude released "Fuck the Police," a critique of police violence against Black youth. Law enforcement officials in several cities dared the group to perform the song in public, threatening to detain the performers or shut down their shows. Increasingly thereafter, ticket holders at rap concerts were searched for drugs and weapons, and security was tightened. Insurance companies, afraid of violence, substantially raised insurance rates for hip-hop concerts, making them a financial risk. Soon, the number of venues willing to sponsor hip-hop concerts dwindled.

While the developments noted above did much to mute the political force of hip-hop, the seduction of big money did more. As early as 1982, with the release of Grandmaster Flash and the Furious Five's "The Message," hip-hop began to win acclaim from mainstream rock music critics. With the success of Public Enemy in the late 1980s, it became clear there was a big audience for hip-hop. Significantly, much of that audience was composed of white youths. They "relished ... the subversive 'otherness' that the music and its purveyors represented" (Neal, 1999: 144). Sensing the opportunity for profit, major media corporations, such as Time/Warner, Sony, CBS/Columbia, and BMG Entertainment, signed distribution deals with the small independent recording labels that had formerly been the exclusive distributors of hip-hop CDs. In 1988, *Yo! MTV Raps* debuted. The program brought hip-hop to middle America.

Most hip-hop recording artists proved they were more than eager to forego politics for commerce. For instance, the rap group WU-Tang Clan started a line of clothing called WU Wear, and, with the help of major hip-hop recording artists, companies as diverse as Tommy Hilfiger, Timberland, Starter, and Versace began to market clothing influenced by ghetto styles. By the early 1990s, hip-hop was no longer just a musical form but a commodity with spinoffs. Rebellion had been turned into mass consumption.

PUFF DADDY

No rapper has done a better job of turning rebellion into a commodity than Sean Combs, better known as Puff Daddy. Puff Daddy seems to promote rebellion. For example, the liner notes for his 1999 hit CD, *Forever*, advertise his magazine, *Notorious*, as follows:

> There is a revolution out there. Anyone can do anything. There are no rules. There are no restrictions. *Notorious* magazine presents provocative profiles of rebels, rulebreakers and mavericks—*Notorious* people who are changing the world with their unique brand of individuality.
>
> Our goal is to inform and inspire, to educate and elevate the infinite range of individual possibility. ... In essence, *Notorious* is for everyone who wants to live a sexy, daring life—a life that makes a difference. After all, you can't change the world without being a little ... *Notorious* (Combs, 1999).

Although he says he's committed to changing the world, Puff Daddy encourages only individual acts of rebellion, not collective, political solutions. Puff Daddy's brand of dissent thus

appeals to a broad audience, much of it white and middle class. As his video director, Martin Weitz, accurately observed in an interview for *Elle* magazine, Puff Daddy's market is not the ghetto: "No ghetto kid from Harlem is going to buy Puffy. They think he sold out. It's more like the 16-year-old white girls in the Hamptons, baby!" (quoted in Everett-Green, 1999).

It is also important to note that Puff Daddy encourages individual acts of rebellion only to the degree they enrich him and the media conglomerate he works with.[2] And rich he has become. Puff Daddy lives in a US$10 million mansion on Park Avenue in Manhattan and a US$3 million dollar house in the Hamptons. In 1998, *Forbes* magazine ranked him fifteenth among top-earning entertainment figures, with an annual income of US$53.5 million ("Forbes Top...," 1998). Puff Daddy is entirely forthright about his apolitical, self-enriching aims. In his 1997 song "I Got the Power," Puff Daddy referred to himself as "that nigga with the gettin money game plan" (Combs and the Lox, 1997). And on *Forever*, he reminds us: "Nigga get money, that's simply the plan." From this point of view, Puff Daddy has more in common with Martha Stewart than with Chuck D and Public Enemy (Everett-Green, 1999).

POP CULTURE AND THE COMMODIFICATION OF DISSENT

Hip-hop emerged among poor African American inner-city youth as a counsel of despair with strong political overtones. It has become an apolitical commodity that increasingly appeals to a white, middle-class audience. The story of hip-hop is thus testimony to the capacity of consumer culture to constrain expressions of freedom and dissent (Frank and Weiland, 1997).

Interestingly, some sociologists play a big role in this process. In Canada, for example, most of the big public opinion firms (Angus Reid, Goldfarb, and Environics) are owned and run by sociologists. One of the tasks they have set themselves is to better understand the popular culture of North American youth. By conducting surveys and regularly organizing focus groups with young consumers in major North American cities, they identify new tastes and trends that marketers can then use to sell product. The most recent report on pop culture produced by Angus Reid is available for $20 000 a copy (Angus Reid Group, 1999). By producing such reports, public opinion firms help to routinize the commodification of dissent.

Vladimir Lenin, leader of the Russian Revolution of 1917, once said that capitalists are so eager to earn profits they will sell the rope from which they themselves will hang. However, Lenin underestimated his opponents. Savvy entrepreneurs today employ sociologists and other social scientists to help them discover emerging forms of cultural rebellion. They take the edge off these dissenting cultural forms, thereby making them more appealing to a mass market. They then sell them on a wide scale, earning big profits. Young consumers are fooled into thinking they are buying rope to hang owners of big business, political authorities, and cultural conservatives. Really, they're just buying rope to constrain themselves.

NOTES

1. Scholars and music buffs disagree about the exact difference and degree of overlap between hip-hop and rap. They seem to agree, however, that rap refers to a particular tradition of Black rhythmic *lyrics* while hip-hop refers to a particular Black *beat* (often jerky and offbeat) mixed with samples of earlier recordings and LP scratches (now largely *passé*). See Mink-Cee (2000). In this essay, I use the terms interchangeably.

2. *Forever* is marketed, manufactured, and distributed by a unit of BMG Entertainment, the US$6.3 billion entertainment division of Germany's Bertelsmann AG, the third largest media company in the world.

REFERENCES

Angus Reid Group. 1999. "Why Is It Important to Track Pop Culture?" On the World Wide Web at http://www.angusreid.com/pdf/publicat/pop.pdf (March 22, 2000).

Bayles, Martha. 1994. *Hole in Our Soul: The Loss of Beauty and Meaning in American Popular Music*. Chicago: University of Chicago Press.

Combs, Sean "Puffy." 1999. *Forever*. New York: Bad Boy Entertainment (CD).

Combs, Sean "Puffy," and the Lox. 1997. "I Got the Power." On the World Wide Web at http://www.ewsonline.com/badboy/lyrpow.html (March 22, 2000).

Davis, Mike. 1990. *City of Quartz: Excavating the Future in Los Angeles*. New York: Verso.

Everett-Green, Robert. 1999. "Puff Daddy: The Martha Stewart of Hip-Hop." *The Globe and Mail*, 4 September, C7.

"Forbes Top 40 Entertainers." 1998. On the World Wide Web at http://www.forbes.com/tool/toolbox/entertain/ (March 22, 2000).

Frank, Thomas, and Matt Weiland, eds. 1997. *Commodify Your Dissent: Salvos from the Baffler*. New York: W.W. Norton.

Mattern, Mark. 1998. *Acting in Concert: Music, Community, and Political Action*. New Brunswick, NJ: Rutgers University Press.

Mink-Cee. 2000. "Rap vs. Hip-Hop." On the World Wide Web at http://www.geocities.com/BourbonStreet/9459/rapvshiphop.htm (March 23).

Neal, Mark Anthony. 1999. *What the Music Said: Black Popular Music and Black Public Culture*. New York: Routledge.

Springhall, John. 1998. *Youth, Popular Culture and Moral Panics: Penny Gaffs to Gangsta-Rap, 1830–1996*. New York: Routledge.

Wilson, William Julius. 1987. *The Truly Disadvantaged: The Inner City, the Underclass, and Public Policy*. Chicago: University of Chicago Press.

Social structures are the patterns of social relations that bind people together and help to shape their lives. Consider hierarchy, one feature of social structure. Hierarchy refers to the degree to which power is unequally distributed in a social group. The more unequal the distribution of power, the greater the degree of hierarchy. In a family, for instance, the degree of hierarchy and the position of a child in the hierarchy profoundly influence the quality of his or her life. In a very hierarchical family, the child may grow up to resent authority or cringe before it — or both. In a family without hierarchy, the child may be spoiled and remain selfish. As these examples illustrate, who you are is partly the result of the social structures through which you pass.

Despite its importance in shaping who we are, we seldom notice social structure in our everyday lives. In fact, we often deny its significance. That is because our culture places such strong emphasis on individual freedom and responsibility. Accordingly, from an early age, we learn three rules about human behaviour:

1. People are free to act as they wish.
2. People can therefore choose right over wrong.
3. If people choose wrong, we should judge them as moral inferiors.

Such thinking may be good for our egos, but it has little in common with sociology and is one of prejudice's most stubborn roots.

A striking illustration of the fallacy of these commonsense rules of human behaviour is an experiment on obedience to authority conducted by social psychologist Stanley Milgram in the early 1970s. Milgram informed his experimental subjects they were taking part in a study on punishment and learning. He brought each subject to a room where a man was strapped to a chair. An electrode was attached to the man's wrist. The experimental subject sat in front of a console. It contained 30 switches with labels ranging from "15 volts" to "450 volts" in 15-volt increments. Labels ranging from "SLIGHT SHOCK" to "DANGER: SEVERE SHOCK" were pasted below the switches. The experimental subjects were told to administer a 15-volt shock for the man's first wrong answer and then increase the voltage each time he made an error. The man strapped in the chair was in fact an actor who received no actual shock. But as the experimental subject increased the current, the actor began to writhe in pain, shouting for mercy and begging to be released. If the experimental subjects grew reluctant to administer more current, Milgram assured them that the man strapped in the chair would be just fine and insisted that the success of the experiment depended on the subject's obedience. The subjects were, however, free to abort the experiment at any time.

Remarkably, 71 percent of experimental subjects were prepared to administer shocks of 285 volts or more even though the switches at that level were labelled "INTENSE SHOCK," "EXTREME INTENSITY SHOCK," and "DANGER: SEVERE SHOCK" and despite the actor's apparently great distress at these shock levels. When subject and actor were in the same room and the subject was told to force the actor's hand onto the electrode, 30 percent of subjects administered the maximum 450-volt shock. When subject and actor were merely in the same room, 40 percent of subjects administered the maximum shock. When subject and actor were in different rooms but the subject could still see and hear the actor, 62.5 percent of subjects administered the maximum shock. When subject and actor were in different rooms and the actor could be seen but not heard, 65 percent of subjects administered the maximum shock.

Milgram's experiment teaches us that as soon as we are introduced to a structure of authority, we are inclined to obey those in power. This is the case even if the authority structure is brand new and highly artificial, even if we are free to walk away from it without penalty, even if we think that by remaining in its grip we are inflicting terrible pain on another human being. Clearly, social structures are powerful, and we are only deluding ourselves if we continue to insist that everyone is perfectly free to do what he or she wants.

Chapter 9 offers another chilling illustration of the power of social structures. It reports an experiment in which middle-class American and Canadian university students were assigned the role of prisoner or guard in an artificial jail constructed by the experimenter. Almost immediately, the subjects were unable to distinguish between their roles and their real selves. Even though none of the subjects was instructed how to behave, the "guards" quickly learned to take pleasure in causing pain while the "prisoners" were wracked with hatred as they planned their escape. A lifetime of learning was suspended. The experiment had to be abandoned within a few days. Social structure again revealed its influence.

Émile Durkheim's *Suicide* is a forceful, classical exposition of how one aspect of social structure — **social solidarity** — helps to shape us. A group's level of social solidarity is higher to the degree that its members share the same values and interact frequently and intimately. In the section reprinted here as Chapter 10, Durkheim argues that social solidarity anchors people to the social world. It follows that the lower the level of social solidarity in a group, the more a group member will be inclined to take his or her own life if he or she is in deep distress. Durkheim tests this argument by examining the level of social solidarity that characterizes the major religious groups in Europe. He demonstrates that the propensity of group members to take their own lives does indeed vary inversely with social solidarity. On the strength of Durkheim's argument, one is obliged to conclude that social structure powerfully affects even an uncommon, antisocial action that is committed in private.

GLOSSARY

Social solidarity is higher in a group to the degree that its members share the same values and interact frequently and intimately.

Social structures are the patterns of social relations that bind people together and help to shape their lives.

CRITICAL THINKING QUESTIONS

1. *Hitler's Willing Executioners* (New York: Alfred A. Knopf, 1996) is a controversial book by American historian Daniel Goldhagen. He argues that Germans during the Second World War for the most

part participated enthusiastically in the systematic destruction of European Jewry. Read the book and decide whether Goldhagen's argument needs to be qualified in light of the research by Zimbardo and Milgram.

2. Have you ever felt compelled to act against your will? What elements of social structure caused you to do so?

3. "The superiority of Protestantism with respect to suicide results from its being a less strongly integrated church than the Catholic Church." What does Émile Durkheim mean by this statement?

4. "Suicide varies inversely with the degree of integration of the social groups of which the individual forms a part." Explain this statement and give examples to support your answer.

ANNOTATED BIBLIOGRAPHY

Mark Granovetter, "The Strength of Weak Ties," *American Journal of Sociology* 76 (1973): 1360–80. An often-cited article that shows, counterintuitively, how an abundance of weak rather than strong social ties maximizes the probability of finding a job.

Barry Wellman and Stephen Berkowitz, eds., *Social Structures: A Network Approach*, 2nd ed. (Greenwich, CT: JAI Press, 1997). A useful collection that highlights network analysis, a recent and influential approach to the analysis of social structures.

William Foote Whyte, *Street Corner Society: The Social Structure of an Italian Slum*, 3rd ed. (Chicago: University of Chicago Press, 1981). In one of the most highly regarded studies of its type, Whyte elicits the shape of social structure from his keen participant-observations.

Chapter 9

Pathology of Imprisonment

PHILIP E. ZIMBARDO

In an attempt to understand just what it means psychologically to be a prisoner or prison guard, Craig Haney, Curt Banks, Dave Jaffe, and I created our own prison. We carefully screened over 70 volunteers who answered an ad in a Palo Alto city newspaper and ended up with about two dozen young men who were selected to be part of this study. They were mature, emotionally stable, normal, intelligent college students from middle-class homes throughout the United States and Canada. They appeared to represent the cream of the crop of this generation. None had any criminal record, and initially all were relatively homogeneous on many dimensions.

Half were arbitrarily designated as prisoners by a flip of a coin, the others as guards. These were the roles they were to play in our simulated prison. The guards were made aware of the potential seriousness and danger of the situation and their own vulnerability. They made up their own formal rules for maintaining law, order, and respect, and were generally free to improvise new ones during their eight-hour, three-man shifts. The prisoners were unexpectedly picked up at their homes by a city policeman in a squad car, searched, handcuffed, fingerprinted, booked at the Palo Alto station house, and taken blindfolded to our jail. There they were stripped, deloused, put into a uniform, given a number, and put into a cell with two other prisoners, where they expected to live for the next two weeks. The pay was good ($15 a day) and their motivation was to make money.

We observed and recorded on videotape the events that occurred in the prison, and we interviewed and tested the prisoners and guards at various points throughout the study. Some of the videotapes of the actual encounters between the prisoners and guards were seen on the NBC News feature "Chronolog" on November 26, 1971.

At the end of only six days, we had to close down our mock prison because what we saw was frightening. It was no longer apparent to most of the subjects (or to us) where reality ended and their roles began. The majority had indeed become prisoners or guards, no longer able to clearly differentiate between role playing and self. There were dramatic changes in virtually every aspect of their behaviour, thinking, and feeling. In less than a week, the experience of imprisonment undid (temporarily) a lifetime of learning; human values were suspended, self-concepts were challenged, and the ugliest, most base, pathological side of human nature surfaced. We were horrified because we saw some boys (guards) treat others as if they were despicable animals, taking pleasure in cruelty, while other boys (prisoners) became servile, dehumanized robots who thought only of escape, of their own individual survival, and of their mounting hatred for the guards.

We had to release three prisoners in the first four days because they had such acute situational traumatic reactions as hysterical crying, confusion in thinking, and severe depression. Others begged to be paroled, and all but three were willing to forfeit all the money they had earned if they could be paroled. By then (the fifth day), they had been so programmed to

---

Source: Excerpted from "Pathology of Imprisonment," *Society* 9, 6 (1972): 4–8. Reprinted with permission.

think of themselves as prisoners that when their request for parole was denied, they returned docilely to their cells. Now, had they been thinking as college students acting in an oppressive experiment, they would have quit once they no longer wanted the $15 a day we used as our only incentive. However, the reality was not quitting an experiment but "being paroled by the parole board from the Stanford County Jail." By the last days, the earlier solidarity among the prisoners (systematically broken by the guards) dissolved into "each man for himself." Finally, when one of their fellows was put in solitary confinement (a small closet) for refusing to eat, the prisoners were given a choice by one of the guards: give up their blankets and the incorrigible prisoner would be let out, or keep their blankets and he would be kept in all night. They voted to keep their blankets and to abandon their brother.

About a third of the guards became tyrannical in their arbitrary use of power, in enjoying their control over other people. They were corrupted by the power of their roles and became quite inventive in their techniques of breaking the spirit of the prisoners and making them feel they were worthless. Some of the guards merely did their jobs as tough but fair correctional officers, and several were good guards from the prisoners' point of view because they did them small favours and were friendly. However, no good guard ever interfered with a command by any of the bad guards; they never intervened on the side of the prisoners, they never told the others to ease off because it was only an experiment, and they never even came to me as prison superintendent or experimenter in charge to complain. In part, they were good because the others were bad; they needed the others to help establish their own egos in a positive light. In a sense, the good guards perpetuated the prison more than the other guards because their own needs to be liked prevented them from disobeying or violating the implicit guards' code. At the same time, the act of befriending the prisoners created a social reality that made the prisoners less likely to rebel.

By the end of the week, the experiment had become a reality, as if it were a Pirandello play directed by Kafka that just keeps going after the audience has left. The consultant for our prison, Carlo Prescot, an ex-convict with sixteen years of imprisonment in California's jails, would get so depressed and furious each time he visited our prison, because of its psychological similarity to his experiences, that he would have to leave. A Catholic priest, who was a former prison chaplain in Washington, DC, talked to our prisoners after four days and said they were just like the other first-timers he had seen.

But in the end, I called off the experiment, not because of the horror I saw out there in the prison yard, but because of the horror of realizing that *I* could have easily traded places with the most brutal guard or become the weakest prisoner full of hatred at being so powerless that I could not eat, sleep, or go to the toilet without permission of the authorities. *I* could have become Calley at My Lai, George Jackson at San Quentin, one of the men at Attica.

Individual behaviour is largely under the control of social forces and environmental contingencies rather than personality traits, character, will power, or other empirically unvalidated constructs. Thus we create an illusion of freedom by attributing more internal control to ourselves, to the individual, than actually exists. We thus underestimate the power and pervasiveness of situational controls over behaviour because (a) they are often non-obvious and subtle, (b) we can often avoid entering situations in which we might be so controlled, and (c) we label as "weak" or "deviant" people in those situations who do behave differently from how we believe we would.

Each of us carries around in our heads a favourable self-image in which we are essentially just, fair, humane, and understanding. For example, we could not imagine inflicting pain on others without much provocation or hurting people who had done nothing to us, who in fact were even liked by us. However, there is a growing body of social psychological research that underscores the conclusion derived from this prison study. Many people, perhaps the majority, can be made to do almost anything when put into psychologically compelling situations—regardless of their morals, ethics, values, attitudes, beliefs, or personal convictions. My colleague, Stanley Milgram, has shown that more than 60 percent of the population will deliver what they think is a series of painful electric shocks to another person even after the victim cries for mercy, begs them to stop, and then apparently passes out. The subjects complained that they did not want to inflict more pain but blindly obeyed the command of the authority figure (the experimenter) who said that they must go on. In my own research on violence, I have seen mild-mannered coeds repeatedly give shocks (which they thought were causing pain) to another girl, a stranger whom they had rated very favourably, simply by being made to feel anonymous and put in a situation in which they were expected to engage in this activity.

Observers of these and similar experimental situations never predict their outcomes and esti-mate that it is unlikely that they themselves would behave similarly. They can be so confident only when they are outside the situation. However, because the majority of people in these studies do act in non-rational, non-obvious ways, it follows that the majority of observers would also succumb to the social psychological forces in the situation.

With regard to prisons, we can state that the mere act of assigning labels to people and putting them into a situation in which those labels acquire validity and meaning is sufficient to elicit pathological behaviour. This pathology is not predictable from any available diagnostic indicators we have in the social sciences, and it is extreme enough to modify in very significant ways fundamental attitudes and behaviour. The prison situation, as presently arranged, is guaranteed to generate severe enough pathological reactions in both guards and prisoners as to debase their humanity, lower their feelings of self-worth, and make it difficult for them to be part of a society outside their prison.

Chapter 10

Egoistic Suicide

ÉMILE DURKHEIM

If one casts a glance at the map of European suicide, it is at once clear that in purely Catholic countries like Spain, Portugal, Italy, suicide is very little developed, while it is at its maximum in Protestant countries, in Prussia, Saxony, Denmark. The averages in Table 10.1 compiled by Morselli confirm this first conclusion.

The only essential difference between Catholicism and Protestantism is that the second permits free inquiry to a far greater degree than the first. The Catholic accepts his faith ready made, without scrutiny. He may not even submit it to historical examination since the original texts that serve as its basis are proscribed. A whole hierarchical system of authority is devised, with marvelous ingenuity, to render tradition invariable. All *variation* is abhorrent to Catholic thought. The Protestant is far more the author of his faith. The Bible is put in his hands and no interpretation is imposed upon him. The very structure of the reformed cult stresses this state of religious individualism. Nowhere but in England is the Protestant clergy a hierarchy; like the worshippers, the priest has no other source but himself and his conscience. He is a more instructed guide than the run of worshippers but with no special authority for fixing dogma. But what best proves that this freedom of inquiry proclaimed by the founders of the Reformation has not remained a Platonic affirmation is the increased multiplicity of all sorts of sects so strikingly in contrast with the indivisible unity of the Catholic Church.

We thus reach our first conclusion, that the proclivity of Protestantism for suicide must relate to the spirit of free inquiry that animates this religion. Let us understand this relationship correctly. Free inquiry itself is only the effect of another cause. When it appears, when men, after having long received their ready-made faith from tradition, claim the right to shape it for themselves, this is not because of the intrinsic desirability of free inquiry, for the latter involves as much sorrow as happiness. But it is because men henceforth need this liberty. This very need can have only one cause: the overthrow of traditional beliefs. If they still asserted themselves with equal energy, it would never occur to men to criticize them. If they still had the same authority, men would not demand the right to verify the source of this authority. Reflection develops only if its development becomes imperative, that is, if certain ideas and instinctive sentiments that have hitherto adequately guided conduct are found to have lost their efficacy. Then reflection intervenes to fill the gap that has appeared, but which it has not created. Just as reflection disappears to the extent that thought and action take the form of automatic

TABLE 10.1 SUICIDE RATE BY RELIGIOUS COMPOSITION OF COUNTRY

RELIGIOUS COMPOSITION OF COUNTRY	SUICIDES PER MILLION INHABITANTS
Protestant	190
Mixed (Protestant and Catholic)	96
Catholic	58
Greek Catholic	40

Source: Excerpted from *Suicide: A Study in Sociology*, George Simpson, ed., John A. Spaulding and George Simpson, trans. (New York: Free Press, 1951 [1897]), pp. 152, 157–60, 170, and 209–15. Copyright © 1951, copyright renewed 1979 by The Free Press. Reprinted by permission of The Free Press, a division of Simon & Schuster, Inc.

habits, it awakes only when accepted habits become disorganized. It asserts its rights against public opinion only when the latter loses strength, that is, when it is no longer prevalent to the same extent. If these assertions occur not merely occasionally and as passing crises, but become chronic; if individual consciences keep reaffirming their autonomy, it is because they are constantly subject to conflicting impulses, because a new opinion has not been formed to replace the one no longer existing. If a new system of beliefs were constituted that seemed as indisputable to everyone as the old, no one would think of discussing it any longer. Its discussion would no longer even be permitted; for ideas shared by an entire society draw from this consensus an authority that makes them sacrosanct and raises them above dispute. For them to have become more tolerant, they must first already have become the object of less general and complete assent and been weakened by preliminary controversy.

Thus, if it is correct to say that free inquiry, once proclaimed, multiplies schisms, it must be added that it presupposes them and derives from them, for it is claimed and instituted as a principle only in order to permit latent or half-declared schisms to develop more freely. So if Protestantism concedes a greater freedom to individual thought than does Catholicism, it is because it has fewer common beliefs and practices. Now, a religious society cannot exist without a collective *credo*, and the more extensive the *credo* the more unified and strong is the society. For it does not unite men by an exchange and reciprocity of services, a temporal bond of union that permits and even presupposes differences, but that a religious society cannot form. It socializes men only by attaching them completely to an identical body of doctrine and socializes them in proportion as this body of doctrine is extensive and firm. The more numerous the manners of action and thought of a religious character are, which are accordingly removed from free inquiry, the more the idea of God presents itself in all details of existence, and makes individual wills converge to one identical

goal. Inversely, the greater concessions a confessional group makes to individual judgement, the less it dominates lives, the less its cohesion and vitality. We thus reach the conclusion that the superiority of Protestantism with respect to suicide results from its being a less strongly integrated church than the Catholic Church.

This also explains the situation of Judaism. Indeed, the reproach to which the Jews have for so long been exposed by Christianity has created feelings of unusual solidarity among them. Their need of resisting a general hostility, the very impossibility of free communication with the rest of the population, has forced them to strict union among themselves. Consequently, each community became a small, compact and coherent society with a strong feeling of self-consciousness and unity. Everyone thought and lived alike; individual divergences were made almost impossible by the community of existence and the close and constant surveillance of all over each. The Jewish church has thus been more strongly united than any other, from its dependence on itself because of being the object of intolerance. By analogy with what has just been observed apropos of Protestantism, the same cause must therefore be assumed for the slight tendency of the Jews to suicide in spite of all sorts of circumstances that might on the contrary incline them to it. Doubtless they owe this immunity in a sense to the hostility surrounding them. But if this is its influence, it is not because it imposes a higher morality but because it obliges them to live in greater union. They are immune to this degree because their religious society is of such solidarity. Besides, the ostracism to which they are subject is only one of the causes producing this result; the very nature of Jewish beliefs must contribute largely to it. Judaism, in fact, like all early religions, consists basically of a body of practices minutely governing all the details of life and leaving little free room to individual judgement.

The beneficent influence of religion is therefore not due to the special nature of religious conceptions. If religion protects man against the desire for self-destruction, it is not that it preaches the respect for his own person to him with arguments *sui generis;* but because it is a society. What constitutes this society is the existence of a certain number of beliefs and practices common to all the faithful, traditional and thus obligatory. The more numerous and strong these collective states of mind are, the stronger the integration of the religious community, and also the greater its preservative value. The details of dogmas and rites are secondary. The essential thing is that they be capable of supporting a sufficiently intense collective life.

So we reach the general conclusion: suicide varies inversely with the degree of integration of the social groups of which the individual forms a part.

But society cannot disintegrate without the individual simultaneously detaching himself from social life, without his own goals becoming preponderant over those of the community, in a word without his personality tending to surmount the collective personality. The more weakened the groups to which he belongs, the less he depends on them, the more he consequently depends only on himself and recognizes no other rules of conduct than what are founded on his private interests. If we agree to call this state egoism, in which the individual ego asserts itself to excess in the face of the social ego and at its expense, we may call egoistic the special type of suicide springing from excessive individualism.

But how can suicide have such an origin?

First of all, it can be said that, as collective force is one of the obstacles best calculated to restrain suicide, its weakening involves a development of suicide. When society is strongly integrated, it holds individuals under its control, considers them at its service, and thus forbids them to dispose willfully of themselves. Accordingly it opposes their evading their duties to it through death. But how could society impose its supremacy upon them when they refuse to accept this subordination as legitimate? It no longer then possesses the requisite authori-

ty to retain them in their duty if they wish to desert; and conscious of its own weakness, it even recognizes their right to do freely what it can no longer prevent. So far as they are the admitted masters of their destinies, it is their privilege to end their lives. They, on their part, have no reason to endure life's sufferings patiently. For they cling to life more resolutely when belonging to a group they love, so as not to betray interests they put before their own. The bond that unites them with the common cause attaches them to life, and the lofty goal they envisage prevents their feeling personal troubles so deeply. There is, in short, in a cohesive and animated society a constant interchange of ideas and feelings from all to each and each to all, something like a mutual moral support, which instead of throwing the individual on his own resources, leads him to share in the collective energy and supports his own when exhausted.

But these reasons are purely secondary. Excessive individualism not only results in favouring the action of suicidogenic causes, but it is itself such a cause. It not only frees man's inclination to do away with himself from a protective obstacle, but creates this inclination out of whole cloth and thus gives birth to a special suicide that bears its mark. This must be clearly understood for this is what constitutes the special character of the type of suicide just distinguished and justifies the name we have given it. What is there then in individualism that explains this result?

A whole range of functions concerns only the individual; these are the ones indispensable for physical life. Since they are made for this purpose only, they are perfected by its attainment. In everything concerning them, therefore, man can act reasonably without thought of transcendental purposes. These functions serve by merely serving him. In so far as he has no other needs, he is therefore self-sufficient and can live happily with no other objective than living. This is not the case, however, with the civilized adult. He has many ideas, feelings, and practices unrelated to organic needs. The roles of art, morality, religion, political faith, science itself are not to repair organic exhaustion nor to provide sound functioning of the organs. All this supra-physical life is built and expanded not because of the demands of the cosmic environment but because of the demands of the social environment. The influence of society is what has aroused in us the sentiments of sympathy and solidarity drawing us toward others; it is society that, fashioning us in its image, fills us with religious, political, and moral beliefs that control our actions. To play our social role, we have striven to extend our intelligence, and it is still society that has supplied us with tools for this development by transmitting to us its trust fund of knowledge.

Through the very fact that these superior forms of human activity have a collective origin, they have a collective purpose. As they derive from society they have reference to it; rather they are society itself incarnated and individualized in each one of us. But for them to have a raison d'être in our eyes, the purpose they envisage must be one not indifferent to us. We can cling to these forms of human activity only to the degree that we cling to society itself. Contrariwise, in the same measure as we feel detached from society we become detached from that life whose source and aim is society. For what purpose do these rules of morality, these precepts of law binding us to all sorts of sacrifices, these restrictive dogmas exist, if there is no being outside us whom they serve and in whom we participate? What is the purpose of science itself? If its only use is to increase our chances for survival, it does not deserve the trouble it entails. Instinct acquits itself better of this role; animals prove this. Why substitute for it a more hesitant and uncertain reflection? What is the end of suffering, above all? If the value of things can be estimated only by their relation to this positive evil for the individual, it is without reward and incomprehensible. This problem does not exist for the believer firm in his faith or the man strongly bound by ties of domestic or political society. Instinctively and unreflectively they ascribe all that they are and do, the one to his Church or his God, the living symbol of the Church, the other to his family, the third to his country or party. Even in their sufferings they see only a means of glorifying the group to which they belong and thus do homage to it. So, the Christian ultimately desires and seeks suffering to testify more fully to his contempt for the flesh and more fully resemble his divine model. But the more the believer doubts, that is, the less he feels himself a real participant in the religious faith to which he belongs, and from which he is freeing himself; the more the family and community become foreign to the individual, so much the more does he become a mystery to himself, unable to escape the exasperating and agonizing question: to what purpose?

If, in other words, as has often been said, man is double, it is because social man superimposes himself upon physical man. Social man necessarily presupposes a society that he expresses and serves. If this dissolves, if we no longer feel it in existence and action about and above us, whatever is social in us is deprived of all objective foundation. All that remains is an artificial combination of illusory images, a phantasmagoria vanishing at the least reflection; that is, nothing that can be a goal for our action. Yet this social man is the essence of civilized man; he is the masterpiece of existence. Thus we are bereft of reasons for existence; for the only life to which we could cling no longer corresponds to anything actual; the only existence still based upon reality no longer meets our needs. Because we have been initiated into a higher existence, the one that satisfies an animal or a child can satisfy us no more and the other itself fades and leaves us helpless. So there is nothing more for our efforts to lay hold of, and we feel them lose themselves in emptiness. In this sense it is true to say that our activity needs an object transcending it. We do not need it to maintain ourselves in the illusion of an impossible immortality; it is implicit in our moral constitution and cannot be even partially lost without this losing its raison d'être in the same degree. No proof is needed that in such a state of confusion the least cause of discouragement may easily give birth to desperate resolutions. If life is not worth the trouble of being lived, everything becomes a pretext to rid ourselves of it.

But this is not all. This detachment occurs not only in single individuals. One of the constitutive elements of every national temperament consists of a certain way of estimating the value of existence. There is a collective as well as an individual humour inclining peoples to sadness or cheerfulness, making them see things in bright or sombre lights. In fact, only society can pass a collective opinion on the value of human life; for this the individual is incompetent. The latter knows nothing but himself and his own little horizon; thus his experience is too limited to serve as a basis for a general appraisal. He may indeed consider his own life to be aimless; he can say nothing applicable to others. On the contrary, without sophistry, society may generalize its own feeling as to itself, its state of health, or lack of health. For individuals share too deeply in the life of society for it to be diseased without their suffering infection. What it suffers they necessarily suffer. Because it is the whole, its ills are communicated to its parts. Hence it cannot disintegrate without awareness that the regular conditions of general existence are equally disturbed. Because society is the end on which our better selves depend, it cannot feel us escaping it without a simultaneous realization that our activity is purposeless. Since we are its handiwork, society cannot be conscious of its own decadence without the feeling that henceforth this work is of no value. Thence are formed currents of depression and disillusionment emanating from no particular individual but expressing society's state of disintegration. They reflect the relaxation of social bonds, a sort of collective asthenia, or social malaise, just as individual sadness, when chronic, in its way reflects the poor organic state of the individual.

Then metaphysical and religious systems spring up that, by reducing these obscure sentiments to formulae, attempt to prove to men the senselessness of life and that it is self-deception to believe that it has purpose. Then new moralities originate that, by elevating facts to ethics, commend suicide or at least tend in that direction by suggesting a minimal existence. On their appearance they seem to have been created out of whole cloth by their makers, who are sometimes blamed for the pessimism of their doctrines. In reality they are an effect rather than a cause; they merely symbolize in abstract language and systematic form the physiological distress of the body social. As these currents are collective, they have, by virtue of their origin, an authority that they impose upon the individual and they drive him more vigorously on the way to which he is already inclined by the state of moral distress directly aroused in him by the disintegration of society. Thus, at the very moment that, with excessive zeal, he frees himself from the social environment, he still submits to its influence. However individualized a man may be, there is always something collective remaining — the very depression and melancholy resulting from this same exaggerated individualism. He effects communion through sadness when he no longer has anything else with which to achieve it.

Hence this type of suicide well deserves the name we have given it. Egoism is not merely a contributing factor in it; it is its generating cause. In this case the bond attaching man to life relaxes because that attaching him to society is itself slack. The incidents of private life that seem the direct inspiration of suicide and are considered its determining causes are in reality only incidental causes. The individual yields to the slightest shock of circumstance because the state of society has made him a ready prey to suicide.

PART 3 | SOCIAL INEQUALITY

Social inequality is a core — some would say the central — sociological problem. It has provoked and confounded analysts since the founding of the discipline.

For example, the simplification of the capitalist class system forecast by Marx never took place. Instead of polarizing around a large class of impoverished workers and a tiny class of wealthy capitalists, the stratification system became more complex. Small business owners did not disappear. In recent years they have actually become more numerous as a proportion of the economically active population. What C. Wright Mills called an "occupational salad" of "white-collar" personnel — professionals, educated office-holders, clerks, and so forth — became the largest component of the stratification system. Manual or "blue-collar" workers experienced a rising standard of living (at least until the early 1970s) while their numbers as a proportion of the total labour force shrunk. The revolution that Marx expected never happened.

Poverty nonetheless persists. According to the government-funded National Council of Welfare, about one out of six Canadians is poor. Moreover, poverty has been feminized: the substantial majority of poor adults are women. True, most adult women now work for a wage in the paid labour force, a development totally unforeseen by Marx (and, for that matter, Weber and others). On the other hand, women tend to be segregated in "pink-collar" jobs — occupations that pay relatively low wages and are analogous to women's traditional family roles as servers, teachers, and nurturers. Even today, it is uncommon for women to have authority over men in the workplace, and even intimate relations between women and men are strongly influenced by the distribution of authority between the sexes.

Another unanticipated development in the realm of social stratification concerns the tenacity of ethnic and racial inequality, which the founders of sociology expected to disappear under capitalism. They believed that large factories and bureaucracies would, in effect, homogenize people, forcing them to work together, treating them all the same, and making cultural differences between them less pronounced. Actually, although ethnic and racial stratification have declined in Canada and elsewhere, different ethnic and racial groups still tend to occupy definite niches in the social hierarchy.

These are some of the key problems in stratification research and some of the chief issues examined in the chapters that follow.

PART 3A

CLASS AND GENDER INEQUALITY

Since the early 1970s, the average real income (or "purchasing power") of Canadians has fallen, reversing the trend to higher real incomes following the Second World War. Also since the early 1970s, income inequality has increased: the richest 20 percent of Canadians earn a larger share of total national income than they did 25 years ago, the middle 60 percent earn less, and the poorest 20 percent earn about the same. The share of total after-tax national income earned by the richest 20 percent of Canadians is now about 42 percent. The middle 60 percent of Canadians earn about 50 percent of total after-tax national income. The share of total after-tax national income earned by the bottom 20 percent of Canadians is about 8 percent.

Little wonder, then, that poverty remains a serious and persistent problem, as Ann Duffy of Brock University and Nancy Mandell of York University show in Chapter 11. The **poverty rate** is usually defined as the proportion of Canadian families whose members spend more than 58.5 percent of their gross income on the necessities of food, clothing, and shelter. Using that standard, the poverty rate fell between the end of the Second World War and the early 1970s, remained fairly steady at about one-eighth of the population until 1992, and then rose again to over one-sixth of the population. Most poor people work for a living, but more of the poor are lone women and their small children than used to be the case. As Duffy and Mandell document, the social and personal costs of poverty remain staggering.

In Chapter 12, Wallace Clement of Carleton University and John Myles of Florida State University analyze the gendered nature of the working and professional/managerial classes in postindustrial societies. They derive their data from a large sociological survey conducted in Canada, the United States, Sweden, Norway, and Finland. Postindustrial society is characterized by a small and shrinking blue-collar or manual working class and a large and expanding service sector that employs white-collar workers. Clement and Myles argue that the decline of the manual working class is attributable to both an increasingly efficient manufacturing sector (which requires less manual labour) and the entry of most adult women into the paid labour force (especially the service sector). This pattern of recruitment of women into the paid work force suggests that the capitalist labour market is not gender-blind. One reaches the same conclusion if one considers the consequence of women's labour force recruitment: once in the paid work force, women start to make gender-specific demands for labour market reform, such as expanded daycare facilities and pay equity with men.

It is in the category of clerical and related occupations that one finds the biggest gender discrepancy in employment patterns. In 1991, 31.6 percent of women in Canada's paid labour force worked in clerical and related occupations, compared with just 7.0 percent of men. This pattern repeats itself, although to a lesser degree, in all occupational categories. A gendered division of labour is pervasive, and in general women get jobs with less income, less status, and less authority than men.

In all of the countries analyzed by Clement and Myles, women are much more likely to hold authority and decision making positions in the service sector than in the manufacturing sector. However, even in the service sector, the proportion of women in authority and decision making positions is less than the overall proportion of women in that sector. In fact, for most industries, the gender gap between men in authority and women in subordinate roles is bigger in services than in manufacturing. Thus, postindustrialism has so far consolidated, not eroded, the traditional sexual division of labour. True, women have been gaining ground in middle-management positions, where they have authority mainly over other women. But they have been losing ground in upper-management positions, where male authority is even more entrenched than it was a couple of decades ago.

Women's progress in the labour market is hampered by their disproportionately large share of domestic responsibilities. Without an affordable and accessible daycare system, for example, women continue to shoulder most of the responsibility for raising children. They therefore tend to have less energy, time, and emotion to invest in paid work than do men. Yet Clement and Myles demonstrate that the greater the share of women's contribution to family income, the more decision making power women have at home. In addition, they discuss national and class differences in the level of household equality.

Social inequality is not just about money and power. It is also about status. Twenty years ago, American writer Alison Lurie wrote a fascinating social history of clothing, a chapter of which is reprinted here as Chapter 13. With Lurie we move from the economic side of social inequality to its culture and symbols — in Weber's terms, Lurie focusses on how people use clothing to demonstrate their social status and thereby evoke esteem and gain prestige. By wearing clothes made of expensive materials, sporting many different outfits, keeping up with style changes dictated by expensive fashion houses, and conspicuously displaying labels, the better-off are able to demonstrate their perceived superiority (and the less well-to-do are sometimes able to pass for something they are not). Lurie argues that many of the clothes we wear are uncomfortable, poorly designed for the activities that occupy us, wasteful of materials, and priced far above reasonable profit margins. But if they convey high status we put them on, put up with them, and even come to regard them as beautiful. That is because clothes are an important vehicle for the presentation of self in everyday social interaction, the conscious manipulation of how others see us and how we see ourselves. Because clothing performs this function, personality shifts often accompany a change in costume; people dress to look and feel sexy, athletic, casual, formal, rich, and so forth.

GLOSSARY

The **poverty rate** is the proportion of Canadian families whose members spend more than 58.5 percent of their gross income on the necessities of food, clothing, and shelter.

CRITICAL THINKING QUESTIONS

1. What is meant by the feminization of poverty? Is the feminization of poverty an issue in Canadian society? Give examples from your reading to support your answer.
2. "Poverty is most often experienced by women and children." What social factors account for this finding?

3. What are the main crossnational differences in stratification discussed by Clement and Myles? What accounts for these differences?
4. How has the working class changed in postindustrial society according to Clement and Myles?
5. Outline the different ways clothing shows the social position of the wearer.
6. According to Alison Lurie, people use clothing to demonstrate social status and prestige. What are some other symbols of social status that people commonly use?

ANNOTATED BIBLIOGRAPHY

Pat Armstrong and Hugh Armstrong, *The Double Ghetto: Canadian Women and Their Segregated Work*, 3rd ed. (Toronto: McClelland and Stewart, 1994 [1978]). A classic account of gender inequality in Canada.

Richard Breen and David B. Rottman, *Class Stratification: A Comparative Perspective* (New York: Harvester Wheatsheaf, 1995). A concise and incisive overview of theories.

Gøsta Esping-Andersen, *Changing Classes: Stratification and Mobility in Post-Industrial Societies* (London: Sage, 1993). Cutting-edge comparative research on how postindustrialism affects class structures and mobility patterns.

Alan Frizell and Jon H. Pammett, eds., *Social Inequality in Canada* (Ottawa: Carleton University Press, 1996). This book is actually about Canadians' *perceptions* of inequality as compared to the perceptions of people in eighteen other countries. A unique crossnational perspective.

Chapter 11 | Poverty in Canada

ANN DUFFY

NANCY MANDELL

THE POOR IN CANADA TODAY

Any discussion of poverty inevitably must confront the contentious issues of definition and measurement. It is easy to see that homeless, starving children in nineteenth-century Montreal were poor; it is more difficult to identify those contemporary Canadians who have too little to get by and who are unable to participate in any meaningful fashion in the social, political, educational, or spiritual life of the nation. While these individuals are not (necessarily) starving or homeless, they are "relatively deprived" in the nation and community in which they live.

For years, government agencies, social researchers, and advocacy groups have struggled to arrive at objective standards of impoverishment—level of family income, costs of housing, food, clothing, fuel, etc.—that distinguish the poor. To date Canada has not arrived at an "official" definition of poverty. Statistics Canada, the Canadian Council on Social Development, the Senate's Special Committee on Poverty, various metropolitan centres, and other groups and organizations have all devised independent measures.

The best-known measure is the Statistics Canada definition (adopted in 1973) that establishes income cut-offs below which people are considered to live in "straitened circumstances." The cut-offs are based on the notion that poor families are those who spend more than 58.5 percent of their gross income on food, clothing, and shelter, leaving few or no funds for transportation, health, personal care, education, household operation, recreation, or insurance. These income cut-offs vary in terms of the size of the household and the size of the area of residence (more than 500 000, 100 000–499 999, and so on). For example, a single person living in Toronto on less than $13 414 in 1989, by StatsCan's definition, was considered poor, while a single person living on less than $9135 in a rural area was poor (Ross and Shillington, 1989: 5–7; see also National Council of Welfare, 1989).

It is important to keep in mind that the sources of income for the poor are varied. Many are poor because the social assistance they receive is below the low-income cut-offs. An Ontario couple with two children in 1989 would have received $16 478 in total welfare income (including basic social assistance, additional benefits, family allowances, child tax credit, child-related benefits, federal sales tax credit, and provincial tax credits). This income placed them $10 323 *below* Statistics Canada's low-income cut-off. In general, incomes from welfare payments for two-parent families with two children ranged between 44 percent and 78 percent of the poverty line; for single-parent families they constituted 50 to 75 percent of the poverty line (National Council of Welfare, 1990b: 29, 31).

Many other Canadians are poor because their earnings from employment are below the low-income cut-offs. The overwhelming majority (98 percent) of poor families have members who are in the labour force for some period during the year (Economic Council of Canada, 1992: 14; see also National Council of Welfare, 1988: 78).[1] When the worker lives alone or is a single parent, when only the husband in the family is employed, when the work is part-time, contract, short-term, irregular, low-wage, unskilled (young, immigrant, and/or poorly educated workers), and when there are dependent children in the home, employment frequently fails to provide an escape from poverty (Ross and Shillington, 1989: 57–64; Gunderson, Muszynski, and Keck, 1990: 68–71).

There are serious shortcomings with the Statistics Canada measure of Canadian poverty. It leaves out all Natives living on reserves, institutional inmates, residents of the Yukon and Northwest Territories, and the homeless. It tells us nothing about the duration or depth of poverty; that is, how long any one individual is poor and how poor he/she is. There is considerable debate about the locational adjustments, which assume it costs less (as much as 32 percent less) to live in rural areas than in a large metropolitan area. Others argue that with the increasing tax bite, income cut-offs should be based on after-tax income. Finally, the measure ignores differences in the actual level of need in the household. For example, severe disability and lack of access to subsidized services may significantly increase household needs (Ross and Shillington, 1989).

Despite these flaws, the low-income cut-offs provide a sobering portrait of poverty in Canada today. In all, 13.1 percent of Canadian families in 1991 (949 000 families) were poor.[2] Among unattached individuals, 36.5 percent (1.26 million individuals) lived below the low-income cut-offs. Predictably, there is a distinct regional dimension to Canadian poverty. In 1991, only 13.5 percent of Ontario families were poor, while poverty was a fact of life for 21.1 percent of Manitoba families. Almost 40 percent (1990) of families headed by young people (under 25 years of age) and more than 50 percent of unattached young people are poor. Families and

individuals with low levels of education are more likely to be poor, as are families with only one wage-earner (National Council of Welfare, 1992, 1993; Ross and Shillington, 1989: 21–29).

THE FEMINIZATION OF POVERTY

Canadian women are particularly at risk of being poor. The term "feminization of poverty" refers to the fact that women in many of the industrialized Western nations are more likely to be poor than men (Pearce, 1978; Goldberg, 1990). Though Canadian women are better off than their American counterparts (as a result of lower rates of single parenthood and more expansive social policies), over 15 percent of Canadian women compared to 11 percent of Canadian men lived in poverty in 1987. Women constitute 59 percent of the Canadian adults who are poor (National Council of Welfare, 1990a). Nor is this a new problem; the ranks of the poor have long been populated by women who were deserted, widowed, or orphaned (Katz, 1975: 60; Simmons, 1986).[3] Evidence suggests, too, that women figure among the poorest of the poor. For example, the largest poverty gap for poor families (how far below the poverty line an individual or family lives) is found among female-headed single-parent families (National Council of Welfare, 1993: 14; 1990a: 9–14; Ross and Shillington, 1989: 54).

While the reasons behind women's impoverishment are complex, they have much to do with traditional gender ideologies, inequities in the labour force, and flaws in our family law and responses to marriage breakdown. For generations, women have been expected to devote their lives to their unpaid duties in marriage and motherhood. Although many wives and mothers also worked for pay, this was generally seen as undesirable. Lower pay rates for women, rules against the employment of married women, and the peripheralization and stigmatization of "women's work" all reinforced the notion that women's place was in the home (Duffy and Pupo, 1992: 13–40).

Throughout the twentieth century, however, these notions have come under increasing attack. The first and second waves of the women's movement, advanced education for women, and the reduction in family size, among other factors, have undermined the traditional sexual division of labour. In particular, increasing numbers of Canadians have found that they simply cannot survive on the uncertain income of a single male (or female) breadwinner. The failure of wages to keep pace with inflation, increases in taxation, high rates of unemployment, and the loss of high-paying industrial and resource extraction jobs have made the male-breadwinner family increasingly anachronistic.[4] Today, 59 percent (1988) of married women and 62 percent of wives with preschool children are in the paid work force (Statistics Canada, 1990: 74, 80). Indeed, the poverty rate among two-parent families would double (to 16 percent of Canadian families) if these wives and mothers were not in the paid labour force (National Council of Welfare, 1990a: 40).[5]

While much has changed, much remains the same. Women are still encouraged to focus their energies on marriage and motherhood; women's employment is still less well paid than men's, with full-time women workers earning about 65 percent of male wages; patterns of sexual and gender harassment continue to maintain female job ghettos. Women are still occupationally segregated into work with lower wages, less prestige, and less opportunity for advancement. Women workers are less likely to be protected by union organizations in their places of employment. Finally, and most importantly, women are still considered responsible for most child care and housework. In the absence of adequate child-care and parental leave policies, juggling the conflicting demands of child care, housework, and paid work often means costly interruptions[6] in labour force participation and/or peripheral employment as a part-time, casual, or contract employee (Gunderson, Muszynski, and Keck, 1990). Being employed in "women's work" or taking several years off to

care for young children can translate into disaster when marriages end in divorce, when women face long years of widowhood, or when never-married women opt for single parenthood.

An astounding 75 percent of never-married single-parent mothers and 52 percent of women who head single-parent families because of divorce, death, or desertion are poor (National Council of Welfare, 1990a: 9).[7] Without a male breadwinner in the family and with inadequate or non-existent support payments, many women cannot provide sufficient income for their families. The Economic Council of Canada's five-year survey of Canadian incomes found women's incomes (adjusted for family size) dropped by about 39 percent when they separated or divorced and thereafter rose only slightly. Three years after the marriage breakup, women's incomes were still 27 percent below their earlier level. Men's income (adjusted for family size), in contrast, increased by an average of 7 percent. Along with the labour force inequalities discussed above, inadequate support payments produce the inequity. In 1989, only 68 percent of divorces involving dependent children resulted in a child-support order, and those orders averaged a scant $250 per child per month (Economic Council of Canada, 1992: 49).[8]

Similarly, elderly women (65 and over) who are widowed, divorced, or never married face high rates of poverty. In 1990, almost half (47.1 percent), compared with 33.6 percent for unattached elderly men, lived below the low-income cut-offs.[9] As these women age, their rate of impoverishment increases; 50 percent of unattached women 75 or over are poor.[10] While being unattached jeopardizes both male and female seniors, women are particularly at risk because they are less likely to receive income from occupational pension plans, the Canada/Quebec Pension Plan, and investments. The traditional patterns of women's work, with its work interruptions to take care of family responsibilities, work in low-paying, poorly benefited jobs, along with high rates of part-time and contractual work, contribute to high rates of female impoverishment whenever women find themselves without a spouse (National Council of Welfare, 1992: 68; 1990a: 98–103).[11]

Based on current trends in marriage, divorce, and life expectancy, an estimated 84 percent of all Canadian women can expect to spend some portion of their adult lives without a male breadwinner in the home[12] – as pregnant teens, single mothers, divorced middle-aged workers, and/or elderly widows (National Council of Welfare, 1990a: 17). In these situations they will have to support themselves and, possibly, their children. Yet, few Canadian women live with these expectations, and fewer still plan their work and marital lives to bring them financial independence and solvency (Duffy, Mandell, and Pupo, 1988). In a society that perpetuates unrealistic notions of romantic love, marital life, and parenting, and in an economy premised on the peripheralized, low-wage, ghettoized work of women, many women continue to be set up for poverty.

Predictably, certain groups of women — immigrant women, disabled women, minority women, and Native Canadians — are at greater risk. Native women, for example, have lower than average labour force participation rates, lower than average earnings, and substantially higher rates of unemployment, partly because of the remote, rural areas in which many live (Abella, 1984). Visible minority and immigrant women frequently find that racial and ethnic discrimination, along with language difficulties and inadequate government policy, translate into long hours of low-wage work (National Council of Welfare, 1990a: 118–27). Foreign-born elderly women (65 and over), in all marital categories, have lower average incomes than their Canadian-born counterparts. Elderly women who are recent immigrants and/or who come from the Third World receive particularly low incomes (Boyd, 1989). Although the majority (57 percent) of disabled people are poor, disabled women are, generally, worse off than their male counterparts (Ross and Shillington, 1989: 28; Barile, 1992).

THE POVERTY OF CHILDREN

Hand in hand with the impoverishment of women and families has gone the poverty of children. More than 1.2 million children[13] are growing up poor (1991), and Canadian children are more likely to be poor than adults aged 16–64 (National Council of Welfare, 1993: 4; Cregheur and Devereaux, 1991: 4). Children constitute more than one-quarter of our poor[14] and the child poverty rate in Canada is the second highest in the industrialized world, topped only by that of the United States (Kitchen et al., 1991: 2, 15).

Although most (56 percent) poor children are growing up in two-parent families, an increasing proportion live in lone-parent (usually mother-led) families (Kitchen et al., 1991: 17). Today (1991), when almost two-thirds (61.9 percent) of female-headed single-parent families (along with one-quarter of the many fewer male-headed single-parent families) are poor, one child in eight is growing up in a lone-parent family (National Council of Welfare, 1993: 8; Economic Council of Canada, 1992: 47).

THE CHANGING FACE OF POVERTY

Poverty patterns are not static. In the last quarter-century there have been significant reductions in the rate and depth of poverty (Economic Council of Canada, 1992: 2). Progress slowed during the 1970s, and since 1973 the poverty rate has tended to fluctuate with the health of the economy[15] (Ross and Shillington, 1989: 21; National Council of Welfare, 1988: 1). Although the rate of family poverty has remained about the same from 1973 to 1986, the rate among unattached individuals "dropped considerably" between 1979 and 1986. The regional distribution of poverty has also shifted, with less poverty in Atlantic Canada, Ontario, and the Prairies and more in Quebec and British Columbia between 1973 and 1986.[16] Also, poverty has increasingly become an urban phenomenon.

Predictably, a weakened economy resulted in higher figures overall in the early 1990s.

An increasing proportion of poor families are headed by young people[17] and more and more poor families are headed by a single parent, most frequently a woman.[18] From 1973 to 1986 there was also an increase in the number of poor families with two or more earners. This reflects, in part, the failure of real family wages to keep pace with rising costs, along with a failed commitment to maintain an adequate minimum wage. In 1973 minimum-wage legislation meant that a worker who worked 40 hours a week over 52 weeks could earn a yearly income 20 percent over the poverty line. By 1991 the same worker would have to work 50 hours a week for 52 weeks simply to reach the poverty line (Kitchen et al., 1991: 36). During this same period, education has become less of a barrier to impoverishment; by 1990, 6 percent of poor families were headed by a person with a university degree (National Council of Welfare, 1992: 37).

The poverty success story has been the marked decrease in poverty among the elderly. Policy changes, including the federal Guaranteed Income Supplement, have meant that instead of 33.6 percent of seniors being poor (1980), only 20.0 percent have low incomes (1991). Similarly, the poverty rate for families headed by individuals 65 or older went from 41.4 percent in 1969 to 9.0 percent in 1991 (National Council of Welfare, 1988: 14; 1993: 6, 8).

Finally, important recent research has given us a better understanding of Canadian poverty and cleared up a variety of misconceptions. Poor families are not necessarily mired in an endless cycle of poverty. By tracking the income of a sample of Canadians for a five-year period (1982–86), the Economic Council of Canada determined that more than 27 percent of Canadians who were poor one year were not poor the next year. However, for every Canadian escaping poverty, another fell into poverty (1992: 22; see also Bouchard, 1988: 9). It appears that poverty is much more volatile than commonly assumed and the line between

"us" and "them" is much murkier. Some families and individuals fall in and out of poverty several times over a five-year span. Indeed, almost one-third of all Canadians will experience at least one episode of poverty during their working lives.

Any number of common events can precipitate poverty for a family or individual: family breakdown, disability, job loss, death of wage-earner. The duration of that impoverishment will depend on a number of individual, societal, and economic factors. Those who are particularly disadvantaged, such as disabled people, lone-parent families, and older single individuals, are more likely to experience longer durations of poverty. For example, it is estimated that lone-parent families average in excess of six years of poverty (Economic Council of Canada, 1992: 19–27, 47).

STRUGGLING WITH POVERTY: THE PERSONAL EXPERIENCE

Being poor has always meant much more than getting by at some arbitrary level of income, and understanding poverty demands more than a statistical overview. Poverty often affects people's lives, their sense of self, and their most important relationships with others. The emotional, physical, and social toll that poverty frequently takes is most apparent among children.

For children and their families, poverty still generally translates into inadequate housing. In Calgary, Edmonton, Vancouver, and Toronto, poor children are likely to live with substandard heating, too little hot water, improper ventilation, generally unsafe conditions (exposed wiring and electrical outlets, and so on), and too little space in which to play or study. Housing problems are frequently compounded by neighbourhoods plagued with high rates of crime and vandalism, inadequate play facilities, and/or hazardous traffic conditions (Marsden, 1991: 8; Kitchen et al., 1991: 6). Echoing nineteenth-century Montreal, recent research indicates that there are New Brunswick children living in

Third World conditions in dwellings with mud floors, leaking roofs, and no running water (Spears, 1991: A21).

Housing problems combine with inadequate nutrition. Poor families often lack the income to maintain a nutritious diet. High housing costs and the spectre of homelessness mean that food budgets are stretched to the limit:

> Juice wars we have at our place. "You can't have that extra glass of juice." They bring somebody in the house and the three of them are having a glass of juice and that's all the juice there is for the rest of the week. And there they are just drinking it down, and you're going, "Oh my God, don't they understand anything?" (Women for Economic Survival, 1984: 13)

While Canada's many food banks[19] and soup kitchens provide a stopgap solution for many families, many poor children clearly get by on too little or low-quality (high fat-sugar content) food (Kitchen et al., 1991: 7).

Predictably, dangerous neighbourhoods, inadequate housing, and insufficient nutrition take a toll on the health of poor children. As in the past, the youngest are the most vulnerable. Infants born into Canada's poorest families are twice as likely to die during the first year of life than infants born into our wealthiest families (Boyle, 1991: 100). Surviving infancy means that poor children will face higher rates of disability and physical and mental health problems than other Canadian children. For example, they are twice as likely to suffer chronic health problems and more than twice as likely to have a psychiatric disorder (Boyle, 1991: 105; Kitchen et al., 1991: 7; Offord, 1991: 10).

Certain groups of economically disadvantaged children are particularly at risk. The infancy death rate among Native Canadians is five times higher than it is for non-Native children. At each age level beyond infancy, Native children are four times more likely to die than other Canadian children. Being forced to live on the economic and social periphery exacts a heavy psychological toll as well as a physical cost. Native children (aged 10–19) are between five and seven times more likely to commit suicide than the total Canadian population (Boyle, 1991: 99–100).

The psychological health of poor children, in turn, reflects the painful social and emotional environment in which many live. The pressure of poverty contributes to family breakdown and dislocation. Some evidence suggests that poorer families are more subject to family violence, including child abuse and neglect (MacLeod, 1987: 20–21; Gelles and Cornell, 1990: 14–15).[20] Growing up poor often means coping with a parent or parents who are themselves struggling with fear, anger, frustration, isolation, and despair.

The emotional and psychological realities of poverty are complex, and reactions to poverty reflect the particular personal circumstances and history of each individual. Many poor adults and children cope with courage, resourcefulness, and a sense of humour, and many poor children grow up with positive adult role models and a strong sense of family loyalty. However, most poor children do not live on Walton Mountain and the adults in their lives are also often deeply troubled by their economic straits.

Poverty typically means more than doing without; it means feeling cut off from the mainstream of our consumer society. With a few exceptions, the lives and experiences of the poor are not reflected on television or in the movies: the advertisements in magazines and on subway trains simply underscore the insufficiencies of their lifestyle. Life becomes an observer sport: watching other people get new jobs, buy new houses, or take their families to Disneyland. A 50-year-old woman, on her own, who had been looking for work for five months, voiced the alienation felt by so many: "I need a job. I want to work. I want to be able to pay my bills. I want to be solvent. I want to live!" (Burman, 1988: 54).

Each day small and large events underscore the poor person's marginalization in society. When the school organizes a bike hike, any children without bikes have to sit in the classroom and do worksheets. Frustrated parents see their children left out and humiliated: "It visually stamps them as poor. You can hide many things, but when visually you're made poor, then something's bloody wrong" (Women for Economic Survival, 1984: 16). A woman buys food with a food voucher at her local grocery store and when change is owed, the cashiers engage in a loud conversation about whether "you're supposed to give them any money." Not surprisingly, the woman ends up feeling "like they were talking about somebody who wasn't a person. I just wanted to tell them to forget about it, keep the damn change" (Carniol, 1987: 90). Day by day and incident by incident, the chasm grows between being poor and "normal life," leaving poor adults and their children feeling more isolated, stereotyped, and rejected:

> I could read their mind, right, so that I know what they're saying, "Well he's unemployed, he's getting nowhere," right? Because that's what I'm doing right now, getting nowhere. (Burman, 1988: 204)

> People never really think of what it's like to be poor until they are poor themselves. It's a sad fact but it's true. ... They have to live it. My husband is not one of those "welfare bums." He tries; he tries really hard. (Baxter, 1988: 41)

When people become poor themselves, it comes as a shock that the negative stereotype now applies to them:

> When I went down there, I felt that I just stuck right out. I thought, "Oh my God, people think I'm on welfare." Typical stereotype I guess you're led to believe. You used to think, "It's those people who are on welfare," and now you discover you're one of those people. (Burman, 1988: 86)

Being one of *those* people often means living with a stigma. Many poor are ashamed of their identity as poor, seek to hide it whenever possible, and feel there is something "wrong" with them:

> At the beginning [of being unemployed] I was feeling so good about myself that that was a lot

easier. ... Towards the end I was feeling like such a loser. ... You portray this, it's written all over your face. (Burman, 1988: 196)

> I need to move to a better place. There are so many losers living around me but being on welfare people think you're a loser anyway. (Baxter, 1988: 165)

Coping with stigmatization may mean being filled with anger at the injustices of a social system that seems to benefit so many other people:

> I walked down the street one day — God, how do people buy their clothes, where are they getting their money, how come they have a job? ... Like, I just thought shit! (Burman, 1988: 203)

For some, when the impoverishment seems to grind on endlessly or when their personal situations deteriorate, anger and frustration give way to despair and depression. Over and over poor people talk of periods of hopelessness and of suicidal depression.

Being poor and being on welfare can be a double whammy. Many of the poor, who must rely on social assistance for all or part of their income, report that dealing with the social work apparatus compounds feelings of stigmatization and vulnerability. Even when individual welfare workers are helpful and supportive, the relationship between worker and client is structured to erode the autonomy, power, and privacy of the poor. The negativity of some welfare workers merely exacerbates a bad situation:

> Social assistance is based on the notion that women need help and can't make decisions. The system makes you feel like you failed at your role in life. (Blouin, 1992)

> My worker is very strict. It's like being with my parents when I was younger ... the worker controls my life. I hate it. (Blouin, 1992)

> They have a real looking-down-on-you attitude, and my back just gets right up. I don't

find them very pleasant people. I keep thinking how people less assertive than me deal with that. I bet there's a lot of people that cry. (Burman, 1988: 85)

Home visits by welfare workers, personal questions from workers, and the constant fear of being "reported to welfare" for having not followed all the rules tend to undermine clients' sense of personal power and self-confidence:

> I never want to go back on welfare. Self-esteem while you are on welfare is really low. You end up being dependent on somebody you don't want to be dependent on. You don't have any say or any control over your own life. When I was a single parent on welfare and my kids were here, welfare was always checking up on me, social workers were pulling these short-notice visits, like five minutes notice, to see who was living at my house. (Baxter, 1988: 31)

Problems with the welfare apparatus are further complicated by the negative reactions of the general public to welfare recipients. Commonly, landlords will not rent to individuals on welfare, and women on welfare may find themselves labelled as desperate and available: "He wants to go to bed with me! I refuse and he says, 'You'll be sorry.' He figures I'm on welfare, I'm a single parent—I'm fair game" (Carniol, 1987: 86–87). Most commonly, the social assistance recipient has to confront the still popular belief, held by much of the general public as well as many social assistance workers, that people on welfare cheat (Blouin, 1992). Informed by the historical notions that many of the poor are not deserving and/or should be punished for their plight, attitudes toward the provision of adequate social assistance remain ambivalent at best.

As welfare cases soar in the recession of the early 1990s, public preoccupation with welfare fraud has intensified. In 1991 *The Toronto Star* ran at least two major stories on welfare cheating, followed in 1992 by a front-page article on welfare abuse. Although a survey of welfare fraud by independent researchers indicated that less than 3 percent of the welfare caseload involved cheating, prominent members of the community continue to protest that the welfare rules on eligibility are too lax and that penalties for welfare abusers are too lenient (Armstrong, 1992: A18; Sweet, 1991: B1). The poor, who after all receive welfare benefits that leave them below the low-income cut-offs, must face the knowledge that numerous Canadians (some 20 percent of whom admit to cheating on their income tax) think of them as cheats.[21] Even when the issue of cheating is left aside, many Canadians continue to evidence a harsh and unsympathetic attitude toward welfare recipients. Despite the proliferation of food banks and homelessness, a full one-third of the Canadian public think the government spends too much money on welfare, and one-quarter feel that most people on welfare could get along without it if they tried (*The Toronto Star*, January 10, 1991: A12).

Being poor means living with the knowledge that in many ways one is despised or pitied by our consumer society, or, at best, considered to be irrelevant. Not surprisingly, this takes a heavy toll on personal and family life:

> There are times when I am so scared that I'm not going to find a job, I think, "What the hell is wrong with me?" ... I can get scared to death. ... I'll have periods of insomnia. I'll get very short-tempered with my husband and with the children. (Burman, 1988: 195)

> My husband and I are very close. In the past year with the pressure of his job when he suddenly turned 55, he's got very sharp with me. He yelled at me twice and he's never yelled at me in his life. We're fighting for our relationship and we're fighting to survive. What's happening financially can destroy couples that are so close. (Women for Economic Survival, 1984: 14)

> If I say "no" to the children, they feel very depressed when they see other children taking things to school. The children feel very disappointed. They kind of lose love for you. They think that you don't love them. (Women for Economic Survival, 1984: 23)

The child, lacking the life experience and acquired coping skills of adults, is often most deeply wounded by poverty and its personal and familial consequences. When the adults in his/her life are filled with confusion, frustration, anger, rage, humiliation, and fear, when their lives seem beyond their control and beyond hope, the child grows up truly impoverished.

The burdens placed on many poor children serve to perpetuate poverty and economic vulnerability. Predictably, poor children tend to do more poorly in school. By age 11, one in three girls from families on social assistance evidences poor school performance (for example, repeating a grade or being placed in a special class). Four of ten children (aged 12–16) living in subsidized housing have poor school performance (Offord, 1991).[22]

Inevitably, children who do not do well in school are more likely to drop out, and dropouts are more likely to come from single-parent, minority group, and/or poorly educated families (Denton and Hunter, 1991: 133). Children from poor families are almost twice as likely to drop out of school as non-poor children. While children of average and low ability from well-to-do families are likely to stay in school, even children of high ability from poor families are likely to succumb to the pressures. Without a private place to study, with parents who are preoccupied with their economic plight, and with the ever-apparent need for more family income, students from poor families often see immediate employment as the best option (Kitchen et al., 1991: 10–11). Unfortunately, in the long run their lack of education and skills may simply perpetuate their own and, later, their children's economic and social marginalization.

NOTES

1. Kitchen et al. report that in 1987, 32 percent of poor families had one or more earners (1991: 20).

2. Research suggests that few of the poor are destitute; that is, with no yearly income at all. Under 5 percent of the poor fall into this category; an additional 6 percent are "marginally employed"; that is, they earn 50 percent or less of the low-income cut-offs (Economic Council of Canada, 1992: 14).

3. It is interesting to note, for example, that the proportion of single-parent families was about the same 50 years ago. In the 1940s most of these families were headed by widows (66 percent); today, most are headed by separated, divorced, or never-married women (Economic Council of Canada, 1992: 16).

4. Despite the mass movement of women into paid employment, real family wages have not increased significantly since the mid-1970s (Kitchen et al., 1991: 19).

5. The dramatic increase in two-earner families has produced only a slight decline in the incidence of poverty in intact families (Economic Council of Canada, 1992: 17). However, if wives had not participated in the paid labour force, the number of poor families would have more than doubled (National Council of Welfare, 1992: 70).

6. While women today are "dropping out" of the labour force less frequently and for shorter periods of time, the majority of women still interrupt their paid labour at least once (Robinson, 1986). A recent federal government study indicates that when women stay home to raise their children, they lose tens of thousands of dollars of earning capacity, resulting in significant and long-term earning losses. In the event of divorce, these losses are rarely compensated (*The Toronto Star*, July 7, 1992: A9).

7. In 1986, 11 percent of Canadian families were lone-parent families. Of this group, 83 percent were led by women (Statistics Canada, 1990: 15). The poverty rate in female-headed lone-parent families is considerably higher than that in other types of families. Only about 10 percent of two-parent families and 23 percent of male-headed, single-parent families are poor (Ross and Shillington, 1989: 44).

8. The problem has often been further compounded by the half to three-quarters of spouses who default on support orders. While enforcement measures have improved, they do not solve the problem of spouses who cannot be found or simply cannot afford to pay (Kitchen et al., 1991: 17).

9. In 1979 two-thirds of elderly widows were living in poverty. Improvements in these rates have been effected by Guaranteed Income Supplements and other measures (National Council of Welfare, 1979: 13).

10. Even middle-aged (55–64) women who find themselves on their own (because of divorce, separation, widowhood, or never marrying) report incomes 24 percent below those of comparable men and 56 percent lower than incomes of all families and unattached individuals (Burke and Spector, 1991: 16).

11. Further, an unfair tax structure functions to reinforce women's economic disadvantages. For example, women earn 32 percent of all pre-tax income and men earn 68 percent. After all taxes are taken into account, women earn only 26.8 percent of post-tax income and men's share increases to 73.2 percent (Lahey, 1992).

12. As the divorce rate increases, the probability of women being without a spouse is also increasing (National Council of Welfare, 1990a: 17).

13. Not included in these figures are the 51 percent of Native children (living on and off reserves) who are poor (Kitchen et al., 1991: 15).

14. This is down from 1971, when children constituted 36 percent of all poor Canadians (National Council of Welfare, 1975).

15. However, since the overall population has grown, the number of poor in Canada increased between 1973 and 1986 to 2.03 million (Ross and Shillington, 1989: 22). An estimated 3.8 million were poor by 1990 (National Council of Welfare, 1992: 71).

16. Currently (1991), poverty rates are highest in the Prairie provinces, Quebec, and Newfoundland, and lowest in Ontario and Prince Edward Island (National Council of Welfare, 1993: 10).

17. Between 1973 and 1986 the poverty rate among families headed by someone 25 or under almost doubled (Ross and Shillington, 1989: 43).

18. Female lone-parents who are poor are typically younger, less educated, and less likely to be employed, have more and younger children, and are more likely to live in cities than non-poor lone-parent mothers (Ross and Shillington, 1989: 45–47).

19. In Metropolitan Toronto, 40 percent of the 124 000 people who rely on food banks each month are children (Reid, 1991: A10).

20. Higher rates of reported violence among poorer families may reflect, at least in part, the greater vulnerability of many poor families to public scrutiny and the stigmatization of the poor.

21. It is estimated that the federal government loses about $90 billion per year as a result of tax evasion and the underground economy (McCarthy, 1992: A1).

22. Research now suggests that poverty, not separation and divorce, is the key factor contributing to children's low self-esteem and behaviour problems, which are then clearly implicated in educational difficulties (Cox, 1991: C1).

REFERENCES

Abella, R.S. (1984). *Equality in Employment: A Royal Commission Report*. Ottawa: Ministry of Supply and Services.

Armstrong, Jane (1992). "Is Our Welfare System Being Abused?" *The Toronto Star*, March 7: A1, A18.

Barile, Maria (1992). "Dis-Abled Women: An Exploited Genderless Underclass." *Canadian Woman Studies* (Summer): 32–33.

Baxter, Sheila (1988). *No Way to Live: Poor Women Speak Out*. Vancouver: New Star Books.

Blouin, Barbara (1992). "Welfare Workers and Clients: Problems of Sexism and Paternalism." *Canadian Woman Studies* (Summer): 64–65.

Bouchard, Camil (1988). "Poverty: A Dangerous Curve." *Transition*, Vanier Institute of the Family (September): 9–12.

Boyd, Monica (1989). "Immigration and Income Security Policies in Canada: Implications for Elderly Immigrant Women." *Population Research and Policy Review* 8: 5–24.

Boyle, Michael (1991). "Child Health in Ontario," in Richard Barnhorst and Laura C. Johnson, eds., *The State of the Child in Ontario*. Toronto: Oxford University Press.

Bradbury, Bettina (1982). "The Fragmented Family: Family Strategies in the Face of Death, Illness, and Poverty, Montreal, 1860–1885," in Joy Parr, ed., *Childhood and Family in Canadian History*. Toronto: McClelland and Stewart.

Braun, Denny (1991). *The Rich Get Richer: The Rise of Income Inequality in the United States and the World*. Chicago: Nelson-Hall.

Burke, Mary Anne, and Aron Spector (1991). "Falling through the Cracks: Women Aged 55–64 Living On Their Own." *Canadian Social Trends* (Winter): 14–17.

Burman, Patrick (1988). *Killing Time, Losing Ground: Experiences of Unemployment*. Toronto: Wall and Thompson.

Carniol, Ben (1987). *Case Critical: The Dilemma of Social Work in Canada*. Toronto: Between the Lines.

Cox, Bob (1991). "Poverty, Not Divorce, Blamed for Youth's Bad Behavior." *The Toronto Star*, August 15: C1.

Cregheur, Alain, and Mary Sue Devereaux (1991). "Canada's Children." *Canadian Social Trends* (Summer): 2–5.

Denton, Margaret, and Alfred Hunter (1991). "Education and the Child," in Richard Barnhorst and Laura C. Johnson, eds., *The State of the Child in Ontario*. Toronto: Oxford University Press.

Duffy, Ann, Nancy Mandell, and Norene Pupo (1988). *Few Choices: Women, Work and Family*. Toronto: Garamond.

Duffy, Ann, and Norene Pupo (1992). *Part-Time Paradox: Connecting Gender, Work, and Family*. Toronto: McClelland and Stewart.

Duncan, Kenneth (1974). "Irish Famine Immigration and the Social Structure of Canada West," in Michiel Horn and Ronald Sabourin, eds., *Studies in Canadian Social History*. Toronto: McClelland and Stewart.

Economic Council of Canada (1992). *The New Face of Poverty: Income Security Needs of Canadian Families*. Ottawa: Ministry of Supply and Services.

Fuchs, Rachel Ginnis (1984). *Abandoned Children: Foundlings and Child Welfare in Nineteenth-Century France*. Albany, NY: State University of New York Press.

Gelles, Richard J., and Claire P. Cornell (1990). *Intimate Violence in Families*, 2nd ed. Newbury Park, CA: Sage Publications.

Goldberg, Gertrude Schaffner (1990). "Canada: Bordering on the Feminization of Poverty," in Gertrude Schaffner Goldberg and Eleanor Kremen, eds., *The Feminization of Poverty: Only in America?* New York: Praeger.

Gunderson, Morley, and Leon Muszynski with Jennifer Keck (1990). *Women and Labour Market Poverty*. Ottawa: Canadian Advisory Council on the Status of Women.

Katz, Michael B. (1975). *The People of Hamilton, Canada West: Family and Class in a Mid-Nineteenth Century City*. Cambridge: Harvard University Press.

Kitchen, Brigitte, Andrew Mitchell, Peter Clutterbuck, and Marvyn Novick (1991). *Unequal Futures: The Legacies of Child Poverty in Canada*. Toronto: Child Poverty Action Group and the Social Planning Council of Metropolitan Toronto.

Lahey, Kathleen A. (1992). "The Impoverishment of Women in Canada: The Role of Taxation." *Canadian Woman Studies*.

MacLeod, Linda (1987). *Battered but Not Beaten: Preventing Wife Battering in Canada*.

Ottawa: Canadian Advisory Council on the Status of Women.

Marsden, Lorna, chair (1991). *Children in Poverty: Toward a Better Future*. Standing Senate Committee on Social Affairs, Science and Technology. Ottawa: Ministry of Supply and Services.

McCarthy, Shawn (1992). "Ottawa Missing $90 Billion a Year as Cheaters Use Cash to Dodge Taxes." *The Toronto Star*, April 30: A1, A32.

National Council of Welfare (1975). *Poor Kids*. Ottawa: Ministry of Supply and Services.

———. (1979). *Women and Poverty*. Ottawa: Ministry of Supply and Services.

———. (1988). *Poverty Profile 1988*. Ottawa: Ministry of Supply and Services.

———. (1989). *1989 Poverty Lines*. Ottawa: Ministry of Supply and Services.

———. (1990a). *Women and Poverty Revisited*. Ottawa: Ministry of Supply and Services.

———. (1990b). *Welfare Incomes 1989*. Ottawa: Ministry of Supply and Services.

———. (1992). *Poverty Profile 1980–1990*. Ottawa: Ministry of Supply and Services.

———. (1993). *Poverty Profile Update for 1991*. Ottawa: Ministry of Supply and Services.

Offord, Dan (1991). "Growing Up Poor in Ontario." *Transition*, Vanier Institute of the Family, June: 10–11.

Pearce, Diana (1978). "The Feminization of Poverty: Women, Work and Welfare." *Urban and Social Change Review* 11 (February): 28–36.

Reid, Susan (1991). "Facing Up to Poverty in Metro." *The Toronto Star*, November 5: A10.

Robinson, Patricia (1986). Ottawa: Ministry of Supply and Services.

Ross, David, and Richard Shillington (1989). *The Canadian Fact Book on Poverty*. Ottawa: Canadian Council on Social Development.

Simmons, Christina (1986). " 'Helping the Poorer Sisters': The Women of the Jost Mission, Halifax, 1905–1945," in Veronica Strong-Boag and Anita Clair Fellman, eds., *Rethinking Canada: The Promise of Women's History*. Toronto: Copp Clark Pitman.

Spears, John (1991). "N.B. Seeks Answer to Childhood Poverty." *The Toronto Star*, May 31: A21.

Special Senate Committee on Poverty (1976). *Poverty in Canada*. Ottawa: Ministry of Supply and Services.

Statistics Canada (1990). *Women in Canada: A Statistical Report*, 2nd ed. Ottawa: Ministry of Supply and Services.

Sweet, Lois (1991). "Is Welfare Cheating Running Wild?" *The Toronto Star*, June 2: B1, B7.

Women for Economic Survival (1984). *Women and Economic Hard Times: A Record*. Victoria: Women for Economic Survival and the University of Victoria.

Chapter 12

Gender, Class, and Postindustrialism in Canada, Scandinavia, and the United States

WALLACE CLEMENT

JOHN MYLES

There are two reasons why the male blue-collar worker is no longer symbolic of the class structure of the advanced capitalist economies. The first is the revolution in the forces of production that makes the direct producer of most goods increasingly redundant. The second, and equally important, reason has been the incorporation of women into the paid labour force. The massive entry of women into paid work in the latter part of the twentieth century has been as dramatic as the changes in industry composition and virtually inseparable from it. As Table 12.1 shows, from about the end of the Second World War until 1982 (about the time of our surveys), women increased their share of employment from approximately one-quarter to over two-fifths of the labour force. Finland is the exception to this pattern. By 1950 women already made up over two-fifths of the Finnish labour force, compared with a quarter or less of the labour force of the other countries.

As Table 12.2 indicates, the labour-force participation of women tends to be rather higher in the Nordic countries than in North America. In the mid-1970s, the Norwegian level was closer to the North American pattern than to that of Sweden or Finland. By the early 1980s, however, Norway had drawn closer to the Swedish-Finnish levels.

Almost all of this growth in female employment occurred in services.[1] Indeed, if unpaid domestic labour were counted as an industry in the usual classifications, we might describe postindustrialism more in terms of the shift from unpaid to paid service work and put less emphasis on the "goods to services" metaphor.

TABLE 12.1 WOMEN'S SHARE OF THE LABOUR FORCE, 1950 AND 1982

	1950	1982
United States	28	42
Canada	21	40
Norway	27	42
Sweden	26	46
Finland	41	47

SOURCE: Compiled from data in Organisation for Economic Co-operation and Development (OECD), *The Integration of Women into the Economy* (Paris: OECD, 1985), p. 14.

Source: *Relations of Ruling: Class and Gender in Postindustrial Societies* (Montreal: McGill–Queen's University Press, 1994), pp. 33–37, 135–40, and 201–10. Reprinted by permission of the publisher.

TABLE 12.2   LABOUR-FORCE PARTICIPATION BY SEX

	WOMEN		MEN	
	1975	1983	1975	1983
United States	53	62	85	85
Canada	50	60	86	85
Norway	53	67	86	86
Sweden	68	77	89	86
Finland	66	74	80	83

SOURCE: Compiled from data in Organisation for Economic Co-operation and Development (OECD), *The Integration of Women into the Economy* (Paris: OECD, 1985), p. 13.

Most men (56 percent or more) continue to be employed in the traditional sectors associated with an "industrial" economy: goods and distribution. Most women—approximately two-thirds—are employed in the growing postindustrial sectors of the labour market, especially personal/retail, business, and social services.

As a result, the "new"—postindustrial—working class is predominantly female labour employed in clerical, sales, and service occupations in the service industries (see Table 12.3). And consequently the working class now has two prototypes rather than one: the traditional blue-collar male and the postindustrial female service worker. Moreover, variations in postindustrial employment patterns are experienced mainly by women. The large welfare states of Sweden and Norway, in particular, result in the fact that most

women workers are employed by the state in those countries. Half of all employed Swedish women are in social services, compared with only a quarter of American women.

The significant fact about the postindustrial division of labour, then, is not so much that the working class of industrial capitalism has come to an end. Rather, a new working class employed in services has grown up alongside it. Superimposed on this material division of labour is a social division based on gender.

As we show in Figure 12.1, the working class in advanced capitalism has two sexes. In all five countries, women are more likely to be working class than men and less likely to be in any of the other three classes that exercise significant powers over production. In all five countries, women make up 50 percent or more of the working class and a minority of all other classes. But just what historical, social, or political significance should we attach to this fact?

Since the 1970s, it has been commonplace for feminist scholars to comment upon the "gender-blind" character of conventional class theory, but such a charge has had two rather different meanings. Sometimes the charge implies that the "male" preoccupation with class relations results in a disciplinary bias leading to the systematic neglect of gender relations—structured relations of domination and inequality between the sexes. To such a charge, class analysts can plead guilty without necessarily conceding that there are serious flaws in their theories or empirical claims *about* classes. There is no inherent reason why theories about classes must

TABLE 12.3   SELECTED CHARACTERISTICS OF WORKING-CLASS WOMEN

PERCENTAGE OF WORKING-CLASS WOMEN WHO ARE IN:	UNITED STATES	CANADA	NORWAY	SWEDEN	FINLAND
Clerical, sales, and service occupations	66	64	60	66	66
Goods and distributive industries	34	24	28	26	40
State employment	31	38	55	63	38
Unskilled jobs	86	79	81	77	83

FIGURE 12.1   CLASS DISTRIBUTIONS BY SEX AND NATION

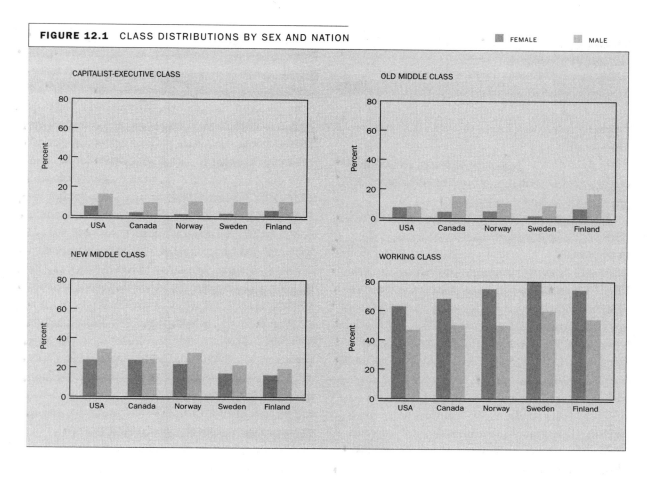

explain all forms of social domination and inequality.

The charge of being gender-blind, on the other hand, can also mean that analyses of classes and processes of class formation that overlook the gendered structure of class relations are both incomplete and incorrect. In short, class analyses that are gender-blind are incomplete on their own terms, not just when measured against the criteria of an alternative problematic. Capitalism and the labour market are not inherently gender-blind, as the conventional wisdom of both neoclassical and Marxian economic theory would have it.

The fact that a "worker" is female rather than male, that she comes to work in a skirt and blouse rather than in overalls, alters the relation between capital and labour in fundamental ways.[2] An example will suffice to illustrate.

The patriarchal organization of households means that most women sell their labour under very different conditions from those of most men. The burden of the "double day" of paid labour and unpaid domestic labour circumscribes both how much labour power women can sell in the market and the timing of its availability. One result is to transform the conditions under which the capital–labour wage relation is negotiated and the agenda of labour when it confronts capital at the bargaining table. The focus of "class struggle" now expands to include new labour-force practices and state policies such as pay equity and daycare. In effect, the struggle over the price of labour and the conditions of its employment is transformed as a result of the conditions and extra-market social relations of the persons (women) who offer their labour for sale in the market. The upshot is irrevocably to alter the trajectory of class formation in *postindustrial* capitalism. Employers are faced with novel demands about the form of the pay packet, work schedules, and the fringe benefits they must negotiate. The state is faced with new demands for legislation and social programs to protect women against the market. As a result, labour unions and labour parties that fail to take up these demands, to incorporate the material interests of a working class that is predominantly female, become doomed to extinction. Likewise, a *class* analysis that does not take account of the changed conditions of the class struggle is doomed to failure.

Numerically, the labour force of traditional industrial labour markets was and is predominantly male (Table 12.4). In contrast, the labour force of the postindustrial sectors is dominated by women. Men are in the majority in both goods production (manufacturing, construction) and distribution (transport, utilities, communication, and wholesale trade), the sectors associated with both the first and the second "industrial revolutions." Here we would expect few women to achieve significant positions within capitalist relations of ruling. In contrast, women dominate in the more "modern" business, consumer, and public services. Female-dominated work sites are more numerous (schools, health care agencies), and there is less likelihood that women in authority will be required to exercise their authority over male subordinates.

There are reasons other than numbers to expect that gender differences in the distribution of positions of power and authority might abate in postindustrial labour markets. The first is the very "modernity" of the service industries. The growth of personal, business, and social services is a contemporary phenomenon, and, as Stinchcombe has shown, the organization of labour within firms, industries, and occupations tends to bear the imprint of the historical period of their foundation and growth.[3] Baron and Newman, for example, show that wage differentials between men and women are greater in "old" than in "new" job categories.[4] Second, state employment is more prevalent in the service sector, and studies of earnings differentials between men and women have shown that the gender gap narrows in the public sector, a result of both public policy and stronger labour unions.[5] Finally, postindustrial labour markets —and especially social and business services— tend to be not only "knowledge-intensive" but also "credential-intensive." Job-relevant skills in services tend to be acquired through the educational system rather than through on-going training and apprenticeship programs. This should benefit women, who are typically excluded from on-the-job training programs but who tend to have high levels of formal education.[6]

There is little question that postindustrialism has brought women into the exercise of economic power to a degree unprecedented in history (Table 12.5). In the United States, for example, women in postindustrial services fill almost half of all positions with power and

TABLE 12.4 PERCENT FEMALE BY INDUSTRY SECTOR, EMPLOYED LABOUR FORCE, FULL-TIME AND PART-TIME EMPLOYEES

SECTORS	UNITED STATES	CANADA	NORWAY	SWEDEN	FINLAND
Goods and Distribution	31	24	24	24	35
Goods	32	21	24	23	36
Distributive services	28	31	23	25	33
Postindustrial Services	61	61	57	67	68
Business, personal, and retail services	60	61	52	60	63
Social services and public administration	62	60	60	70	71

authority, compared with less than 20 percent of such positions in goods and distribution. And as the pattern of consistently positive signs in Table 12.5 indicates, women in all countries have greater access to positions of power and authority in postindustrial services than in the traditional industrial core. But the question remains as to whether postindustrialism also means that the rules of the game have changed. Have postindustrial work sites been "degendered"? Does women's *representation* in positions of power and authority more closely reflect their numbers? Has the law of anti-matriarchy been eroded?

The answer to the first of these questions is a clear no. In general, our results for all five countries do not support our postindustrial expectations. Women have not closed the gender gap in the more "modern" sectors of the economy. Of the twenty possible contrasts in Table 12.6, only

three indicate that women are better represented in postindustrial services, four indicate no difference between sectors, and thirteen indicate that women's underrepresentation is greater in the postindustrial, than in the industrial, sector of the economy. In Sweden and the United States, postindustrial services provide somewhat more scope for women to participate in decision making, but these gains are not reflected in greater access to the formal managerial hierarchy. Rather than eroding the traditional sexual division of power, postindustrial labour markets appear to be the site of its consolidation (in the United States and Finland) and even growth (in Canada, Sweden, and Norway).

Some of the reasons for these results can be interpolated from closer inspection of differences among service industries. In those sectors of the service economy characterized by an unusual number of "good jobs," men have tend-

TABLE 12.5   WOMEN'S SHARE OF DECISION MAKING AND AUTHORITY POSITIONS BY INDUSTRY, FULL-TIME EMPLOYEES ONLY (PERCENTAGES)

POSITIONS AND SECTORS	UNITED STATES	CANADA	NORWAY	SWEDEN	FINLAND
Middle and Upper Management					
Goods and distribution	18	19	5	5	15
Postindustrial services	46	44	20	35	52
Difference	+28	+25	+15	+20	+37
Decision Makers					
Goods and distribution	9	13	7	8	27
Postindustrial services	45	39	22	38	57
Difference	+36	+26	+15	+30	+30
Sanctioning Authority					
Goods and distribution	19	24	5	4	16
Postindustrial services	47	43	19	36	50
Difference	+28	+19	+14	+32	+24
Task Authority					
Goods and distribution	19	15	8	6	16
Postindustrial services	46	47	24	37	53
Difference	+27	+32	+16	+31	+37

TABLE 12.6 WOMEN'S REPRESENTATION IN DECISION MAKING AND AUTHORITY POSITIONS BY INDUSTRY, FULL-TIME EMPLOYEES ONLY*

POSITIONS AND SECTORS	UNITED STATES	CANADA	NORWAY	SWEDEN	FINLAND
Middle and Upper Management					
Goods and distribution	−12	−4	−16	−17	−27
Postindustrial services	−16	−20	−24	−27	−27
Decision Makers					
Goods and distribution	−17	−7	−10	−11	−10
Postindustrial services	−9	−15	−14	−6	−17
Sanctioning Authority					
Goods and distribution	−10	−7	−11	−13	−21
Postindustrial services	−10	−13	−19	−17	−22
Task Authority					
Goods and distribution	−11	−7	−8	−11	−22
Postindustrial services	−11	−9	−14	−16	−19

*Calculation of representation is simply percent female within a class subtracted from the female share of the total labour force. Calculated scores may show slight discrepancies; these are the result of rounding procedures.

ed to appropriate an even larger share of power and authority, so that gender differences are augmented rather than diminished. Women's gains in postindustrial services are largely confined to the low-wage and unskilled sectors of the service economy.

To demonstrate the point, we divide the postindustrial sector into high-end (business and public) services, where wages and job skills are above average, and low-end (personal and retail) services, characterized by low wages and limited job skills. As the results in Table 12.7 show (Finland is excluded because of small sample size), women do comparatively well in the low end of the service economy but very poorly in high-end business and public services.

Here, however, our conclusions run into technical limitations imposed by the relatively small size of our national samples. Although our data *suggest* that gender differences are larger in postindustrial services than in goods and distribution, the number of cases involved is not suf-ficient to provide statistically robust evidence for this conclusion.[7] Quite simply, it may be that our conclusions are a result of sampling error. To test this assumption, Boyd, Mulvihill, and Myles examined Canadian census data to determine if similar results could be reproduced using census occupations.[8] The results were remarkably similar. For example, the "gender gap"—the percentage difference between men and women—in upper-management occupations in 1981 (the time of our survey) was largest in business services (−6.6), followed by social services (−5.0), public services (−3.3), distributive services (−2.9), retail services (−1.8), manufacturing (−1.5), and personal services (−0.6).

None of this implies that women have not been gaining ground in the class hierarchy, but there have been two offsetting trends in the labour market: women have been improving their position relative to men in lower-level management and supervisory jobs but losing ground relative to men in upper-level management. As Boyd, Mulvihill, and Myles

TABLE 12.7 WOMEN'S REPRESENTATION IN DECISION MAKING AND AUTHORITY POSITIONS BY POSTINDUSTRIAL SERVICE SECTOR, FULL-TIME EMPLOYEES ONLY

POSITIONS AND SECTORS	UNITED STATES	CANADA	NORWAY	SWEDEN
Middle and Upper Management				
Personal and retail services	–6	–2	(–7)	(–13)
Business and public services	–11	–16	–22	–20
Decision Makers				
Personal and retail services	–4	–11	(–2)	(+8)
Business and public services	–11	–16	–18	–9
Sanctioning Authority				
Personal and retail services	–6	–7	(–12)	(–5)
Business and public services	–11	–16	–22	(–22)
Task Authority				
Personal and retail services	–5	–5	(–7)	(+1)
Business and public services	–13	–11	–17	–21

( ) indicates estimates based on an underlying industry sample of less than 50. For Sweden, cell counts in personal and retail services are based on less than 20 cases. All other ( ) cells are based on 38 or more cases.

show, the gender gap has fallen among middle managers and supervisors in all industries except retail trade since 1971. In contrast, the gender gap in senior-management occupations has risen in all industries except social services.

Bringing these results together suggests the following. As women have entered the labour force in ever larger numbers, a rising share of supervisory and middle-management positions have also opened to them. Women have acquired real economic powers in the public sphere to a degree unprecedented in Western history. Our Canadian results indicate that women encounter the "glass ceiling" to further advancement near the top of the class pyramid, where they begin to compete for positions that involve the exercise of significant authority over men, particularly over senior men. The result, as Mann suggests, is a form of neo-patriarchy, an economy ruled by senior males in which women may rule women but not men. Postindustrialism matters for women because the concentration of women in postindustrial services provides many more opportunities for the exercise of power over other women but not because the glass ceiling has been broken. Indeed, despite their small numbers in services, men have, if anything, been more effective at appropriating class powers in postindustrial, than in traditional industrial, work sites.

The division of domestic responsibilities is intimately associated with people's relationship to the labour force. For women, this has meant that these responsibilities have inhibited their paid working lives, while men have benefited both within the household by being relieved of an equitable responsibility for domestic work *and* within the paid labour force, where they have been advantaged over women burdened by their household duties. Employers have used women's weaker labour-market positions to keep wages down, thus further weakening women's economic power within the household. This entire system is reinforced by patriarchal ideologies and practices that privilege men over women.

Still, there are important gender differences within this broad pattern based upon nation, class, and status. The more economic clout a woman has within the household, as determined by her relative income contribution, the more say she has in making key financial and budgetary decisions. This economic clout is closely associated with her class position, especially for a few capitalist-executive women but more notably for a substantial number of new-middle-class women. There are some key national differences that transcend class and gender. Overall, the Nordic countries are much more equitable in their household decision making than is the United States, with Canada suspended in the middle. This pattern holds across classes and between sexes, whether in conventional or unconventional households, as indicated by spouse's income contribution.

In terms of actual practices, Swedish men stand out as the least progressive in sharing child-care responsibilities, while U.S. men resemble Canadian men. Norwegian men are the most equitable. For household tasks, however, Swedish men become more involved and U.S. men are the least likely to share responsibilities. Nevertheless, women in all these countries overwhelmingly carry the greatest load of domestic responsibilities.

Men in the propertied classes have made the least contribution to domestic work, while new-middle-class women were able to command greater sharing than those from other classes. Most sharing occurs when both partners are working class or a new-middle-class woman is living with a working-class man. The least occurs when women are housewives. These general patterns were upheld for all four countries, but again the overwhelming share of domestic work falls to women in every case.

Household responsibilities disrupt women's labour-force participation in Canada, especially for those currently other than full-time workers. A majority of women in all age groups had some disruption. Number of children affected the experience of disruptions, but even women without children were much more likely to be disrupted in their careers than all types of men by a margin of 43 percent to 17 percent. These disruptions affected women from all classes, although working-class women were most severely impacted. Progressive households where there is a more equal sharing of household tasks have the twin effects of decreasing women's labour-force disruptions rather substantially (by −13 percentage points) and increasing men's disruptions by a like amount (+11 percentage points).

Canadian men in unconventional households have attitudes toward traditional families very similar to the progressive attitudes of Nordic men and women; indeed, men in these unconventional income positions (where their wives earn as much or more than they do) are more progressive in some ways than Canadian women. Canadian women, while more progressive than U.S. women, are not as progressive as Nordic women on a variety of gender-related issues. Canadian men in unconventional income situations are therefore a key bridgehead for progressive gender issues.

The employment status of men matters little to their gender attitudes, but status matters a great deal for women, especially since many women are housewives (the least progressive women's status), while women employed full-time are the most progressive. Full-time working Canadian women more closely resemble Nordic women working full-time in terms of their gender attitudes than do their U.S. counterparts. The greater a woman's attachment to the labour force, the more her attraction to feminism.

Women are empowered *inside* the home when their class power exceeds men's (as in households with working-class men and new-middle-class women). When partners are of the same class, there are different effects: both working class is more liberating for women than both new middle class. When both have new-middle-class careers, it is the man's that takes priority.

Women with relatively more class power than men have a positive influence on their partner's attitudes toward gender issues, and, inversely, men with relatively more power have a reverse effect on women's attitudes. More powerful men tend to dampen women's feminist expectations.

Household-class combinations strongly influenced the attitudes of men toward traditional families, while men living with women working outside the home are much more progressive than those living with housewives. Housewives everywhere tend to be the least progressive women on gender issues. Again, men are more homogeneous in their views and women more diverse with respect to gender attitudes. The lack of unity on the part of women follows from their much more diverse statuses since some women obviously are housewives and others much more likely to be part-time workers, while men are concentrated in full-time status. At the foundation of the differences between men and women, however, is their radically distinct attachment to household responsibilities both on a day-to-day domestic level and at the broader level of careers. The basic gender difference in the intersection between domestic and paid work is fundamental to an understanding of work performed by both sexes.

So, how are families changing? We summarized the changes in income and domestic labour contributions into household types. For women we were able to examine three types: "traditional," where the woman does most of the domestic work and the man brings in most of the money; "transitional," where the woman contributes equally to the household income but there is no reciprocity in men's contribution to domestic labour; and "modern," where there is basic equality in both income and domestic work. It was more difficult to identify "modern" men because they are more reluctant than women to state that their wives contributed as much financially as they do. Still, it was possible to highlight some directions of change. The most modern relationships occur when a working-class man is with a new-middle-class woman, followed by homogeneous working-class families.

Men's gender attitudes are especially influenced by household types, with a major increase in support for feminist issues in all four countries in transitional situations. Women tend to be more strongly influenced by modern arrangements when they are most feminist.

Households are complex sites, where class and gender relations meet to mediate a variety of demands on an individual's behaviour and attitudes. These demands greatly influence the way Nordic and North American women experience the world since households tend to weaken their powers while enhancing men's. We have shown that the more women are attached to the labour force, the more progressive they are on feminist issues and the more influence they exert on their husbands' ideas and—however gradually—their practices in sharing domestic responsibilities. Age and, to some extent, education appear to work toward a more favourable approach to feminist issues, but the way remains contested by traditional men, who have the most power to lose. Before equality can be achieved in the paid labour force, much more attention to equality in the domestic sphere will be required. The point will be to change not only the attitudes of men but their domestic practices. The ongoing sites of struggle include the workplace and the household. In every case, it is the combination of class and gender factors that mediates the practice of inequality.

NOTES

1. For detailed analysis of the Canadian case see Monica Boyd, Mary Ann Mulvihill, and John Myles, "Gender, Power and Postindustrialism," *Canadian Review of Sociology and Anthropology* 28, 4 (1991): 407–36.

2. See Joan Acker, "Gender, Class and the Relations of Distribution," *Signs* 13, 3 (1988): 473–97.

3. A.L. Stinchcombe, "Social Structure and Organizations," in *Handbook of Organizations*, J.G. March, ed. (Chicago: McNally, 1965).

4. James Baron and Andrew Newman, "For What It's Worth: Organizations, Occupations

and the Value of Work Done by Women and Nonwhites," *American Sociological Review* 55 (1990): 155–75.

5. See Monica Boyd and Elizabeth Humphreys, *Labour Markets and Sex Differences in Canadian Incomes,* Discussion Paper no. 143 (Ottawa: Economic Council of Canada, 1979); Margaret Denton and Alfred A. Hunter, *Equality in the Workplace Economic Sectors and Gender Discrimination in Canada*, Discussion Paper, Ser. A., no. 6 (Ottawa: Labour Canada, Women's Bureau, 1982).

6. See John Myles and Gail Fawcett, *Job Skills and the Service Economy*, Working Paper no. 4 (Ottawa: Economic Council of Canada, 1990).

7. In technical terms, tests for interactions across industrial sectors are not statistically significant.

8. Boyd, Mulvihill, and Myles, "Gender, Power and Postindustrialism."

Chapter 13

The Class Language of Clothes

ALISON LURIE

Clothing designed to show the social position of its wearer has a long history. Just as the oldest languages are full of elaborate titles and forms of address, so for thousands of years certain modes of dress have indicated high or royal rank. Many societies passed decrees known as *sumptuary laws* to prescribe or forbid the wearing of specific styles by specific classes of persons. In ancient Egypt only those in high positions could wear sandals; the Greeks and Romans controlled the type, colour, and number of garments worn and the sorts of embroidery with which they could be trimmed. During the Middle Ages almost every aspect of dress was regulated at some place or time — though not always with much success. The common features of all sumptuary laws — like those of edicts against the use of certain words — seem to be that they are difficult to enforce for very long.

Laws about what could be worn by whom continued to be passed in Europe until about 1700. But as class barriers weakened and wealth could be more easily and rapidly converted into gentility, the system by which colour and shape indicated social status began to break down. What came to designate high rank instead was the evident cost of a costume: rich materials, superfluous trimmings, and difficult-to-care-for styles; or, as Thorstein Veblen later put it, Conspicuous Consumption, Conspicuous Waste, and Conspicuous Leisure. As a result, it was assumed that the people you met would be dressed as lavishly as their income permitted. In

Fielding's *Tom Jones*, for instance, everyone judges strangers by their clothing and treats them accordingly; this is presented as natural. It is a world in which rank is very exactly indicated by costume, from the rags of Molly, the gamekeeper's daughter, to Sophia Western's riding habit, "which was so very richly laced" that "Partridge and the post-boy instantly started from their chairs, and my landlady fell to her curtsies, and her ladyships, with great eagerness." The elaborate wigs characteristic of this period conferred status partly because they were both expensive to buy and expensive to maintain.

By the early eighteenth century the social advantages of conspicuous dress were such that even those who could not afford it often spent their money on finery. This development was naturally deplored by supporters of the status quo. In colonial America the Massachusetts General Court declared its "utter detestation and dislike, that men or women of mean condition, should take upon them the garb of Gentlemen, by wearing Gold or Silver lace, or Buttons, or Points at their knees, or to walk in great Boots; or Women of the same rank to wear Silk or Tiffiny hoods, or Scarfes. ..."[1] What "men or women of mean condition" — farmers or artisans — were supposed to wear were coarse linen or wool, leather aprons, deerskin jackets, flannel petticoats, and the like.

To dress above one's station was considered not only foolishly extravagant, but deliberately

Source: *The Language of Clothes* (New York: Random House, 1981), pp. 115–39. Copyright © 1981 by Alison Lurie. Reprinted by permission of Melanie Jackson Agency, LLC.

deceptive. In 1878 an American etiquette book complained,

> It is ... unfortunately the fact that, in the United States, but too much attention is paid to dress by those who have neither the excuse of ample means nor of social claims. ... We Americans are lavish, generous, and ostentatious. The wives of our wealthy men are glorious in garb as are princesses and queens. They have a right so to be. But when those who can ill afford to wear alpaca persist in arraying themselves in silk ... the matter is a sad one.[2]

CONTEMPORARY STATUS: FINE FEATHERS AND TATTERED SOULS

Today simple ostentation in dress, like gold or silver lace, is less common than it used to be; but clothes are as much a sign of status as ever. The wives of our wealthy men are no longer praised for being glorious in garb; indeed, they constantly declare in interviews that they choose their clothes for ease, comfort, convenience, and practicality. But, as Tom Wolfe has remarked, these comfortable, practical clothes always turn out to have been bought very recently from the most expensive shops; moreover, they always follow the current rules of Conspicuous Consumption, Waste, and Leisure.

At the same time, as high-status clothes have become superficially less gorgeous they have increasingly tended to take on an aura of moral virtue. A 1924 guide to good manners clearly suggests this:

> An honest heart may beat beneath the ragged coat, a brilliant intellect may rise above the bright checked suit and the yellow tie, the man in the shabby suit may be a famous writer, the girl in the untidy blouse may be an artist of great promise, but as a general rule, the chances are against it and such people are dull, flat, stale and unprofitable both to themselves and to other people.[3]

The implication is that an ill-dressed person is also probably dishonest, stupid, and without talent. Today this idea is so well established that one of our foremost historians of costume, Anne Hollander, has refused to admit that true virtue can shine through ugly or ragged clothes, as in the tale of Cinderella:

> In real life ... rags obviously cannot be "seen through" to something lovely underneath because they themselves express and also create a tattered condition of soul. The habit of fine clothes, however, can actually produce a true personal grace.[4]

In a society that believes this, it is no wonder that many of those who can ill afford to wear alpaca — or its modern equivalent, polyester — are doing their best to array themselves in silk. Popular writers no longer complain that those of modest means wear clothes above their rank; instead they explain how best to do so: how to, as the title of one such book puts it, *Dress for Success*. At the moment there are so many such guidebooks it may seem surprising that their advice is not followed by more people. However, as my friend the lady executive remarks, "wardrobe engineering won't do much for you if your work is lousy ... or if you're one of an army of aspirants in impeccable skirted suits all competing for the same spot. As with investment advice, once everyone agrees that it's the thing to do, it's time to look for value somewhere else."

There are other problems with dressing to advance your status professionally. First and most obviously, it is very expensive. The young executive who buys a high-priced suit instead of a stereo system or a week's vacation in Portugal or the Caribbean is giving up certain present pleasure for possible future success in a society that regards hedonistic self-fulfillment as a right. Second, there are one's colleagues to consider. For many people, agreeable working conditions and well-disposed birds are worth more than a possible promotion in the bush. The clerk who dresses like his boss is apt to be regarded by other clerks as a cold fish or an ass-kisser; the secretary in her severe skirted suit is seen as snotty and pretentious: Who does she think she is, in that getup? Moreover, somebody who is distrusted and disliked by his or her equals is very unlikely ever to become their superior. It is also a rare boss who wants to have employees who dress exactly as he or she does—especially since they are usually younger and may already have the edge in appearance. Fortunately for the manufacturers, however, there are more ways than one of advertising high status. Today, "simple," "easy-care," and "active" may be the bywords of fashion copy; but fashionable luxury, waste, and inconvenience continue to flourish in new forms.

CONSPICUOUS ADDITION: EATING AND LAYERING

The most primitive form of Conspicuous Consumption is simply to consume so much food that one becomes conspicuous by one's bulk, a walking proof of having dined often and well. Fatness, frequently a sign of high status in primitive tribes, has also been admired in more civilized societies. In late-nineteenth-century Europe and America it was common among well-to-do men, who often, as Robert Brain has remarked, "were as proud of their girth as a Bangwa chief, the big belly being a sign of imposing male power. It was a culture trait among German men, for whom fatness reflected wealth and status."[5] The late-Victorian woman, too, was often as handsomely solid and well-upholstered as her furniture.

In general, the fashionable size seems to vary according to real or imagined scarcity of food. When a large proportion of the population is known to be actually going hungry, it is chic to be well padded and to dine lavishly. When (as in England and America in the 1960s) there seems to be at least enough starchy food to go around, it becomes chic to be thin, thus demonstrating that one is existing on an expensive protein diet rather than on proletarian bread, potatoes, franks, and beans.

Another simple and time-honoured way of consuming conspicuously is to wear more clothes than other people do. "More" of course is relative: when most people went naked, the mere wearing of garments conferred prestige. In ancient Egypt, for instance, slaves and servants often wore nothing, or at most a brief loincloth; aristocrats put on clothes not out of modesty or for warmth, but to indicate rank. Even in colder climates and more puritanical societies it has generally been true that the more clothes someone has on, the higher his or her status. This principle can be observed in medieval and Renaissance art, where peasants wear relatively few garments, while kings and queens (including the King and Queen of Heaven) are burdened with layers of gowns and robes and mantles, even in indoor scenes. The recent fashion for "layered" clothes may be related, as is sometimes claimed, to the energy shortage; it is also a fine way of displaying a large wardrobe.

In any contemporary gathering, no matter what its occasion, the well-to-do can be observed to have on more clothes. The men are more likely to wear vests; the women are more apt to wear panty hose, superfluous scarves, and useless little wraps. Even in hot weather the difference is plain. At an outdoor restaurant on a summer day the customers who have more money and have had it longer will be the ones in jackets and/or long-sleeved shirts and dresses. If it gets frightfully hot they may roll up their sleeves, but in such a way that there is no doubt about their actual length. On the beach, though the rich may splash into the waves in suits as skimpy as anyone else's, the moment they emerge they will make a dash for the conspicuous raw-silk beach kimono, terry swim dress, or linen shirt that matches their bathing suit and restores the status quo.

CONSPICUOUS DIVISION

It is also possible to advertise one's rank by wearing more clothes consecutively rather than simultaneously. Traditionally, the more different outfits one can display, the higher one's status; high society in the past has made this sort of display possible by the division of daily life into many different types of activity, each of which demands a special costume. As a 1924 book on etiquette puts it:

> In the world of good society, dress plays an important part in the expression of culture. There is proper dress for afternoon wear, and another for evening functions. There are certain costumes for the wedding, and others for the garden fête. The gentleman wears one suit to business, and another to dinner. Where civilization has reached its highest point, there has dress and fashion reached its finest and most exquisite development.[6]

The contemporary man does not need to have a morning coat, a frock coat, a dress coat, and a dinner jacket (and the appropriate trousers, shirts, and shoes) as he did in the early 1900s. Nor must the contemporary woman possess morning costumes, walking costumes, afternoon costumes, tea gowns, motoring outfits, and evening dresses—all of which it would have been considered extremely improper and embarrassing to wear at the wrong time or place. Today, the conspicuous multiplication of clothing continues to thrive, but now the emphasis is on sports rather than on social life. The truly fashionable person will have separate getups for tennis, jogging, hiking (winter and summer), bicycling, swimming, skiing, golf, and that anonymous and disagreeable sport known simply as "exercise." If he or she also goes in for team sports or dancing (ballet, modern, tap, folk, or disco) yet more costumes must be acquired, each one unique. From a utilitarian point of view there is no reason not to play golf in jogging clothes, or ride your bike in a bathing suit on a hot day—except of course that it would cause a drastic loss of prestige.

In order to maintain (or better yet to advance) status, it is not merely necessary to have separate costumes for each sporting activity; one must also have costumes—and where relevant, equipment—of properly high prestige. Just any jogging shoes, tennis racket, or leotards will not do; they must bear the currently correct brand and model names, which tend to change so fast that if I were to list them here they would be out of date by the time this book appears.

CONSPICUOUS MULTIPLICATION

Wearing a great many clothes at once is a burdensome and often unpleasantly hot form of Conspicuous Consumption; changing into different outfits for different activities is a nuisance. An alternative or supplementary way of demonstrating high status is to own many similar garments, so that you almost never wear exactly the same costume. The extreme case of this is the person who—like Marie Antoinette—never wears the same thing twice. Today such extravagance is rare and felt to be excessive, but the possession of a very large wardrobe is still considered charming by those who follow what Veblen called "pecuniary canons of taste."

F. Scott Fitzgerald, in a famous scene, describes the effect of Jay Gatsby's extensive collection of shirts on Daisy Buchanan:

> He took out a pile of shirts and began throwing them, one by one, before us, shirts of sheer linen and thick silk and fine flannel, which lost their folds as they fell and covered the table in many-colored disarray. While we admired, he brought more and the soft rich heap mounted higher—shirts with stripes and scrolls and plaids in coral and apple-green and lavender and faint orange, with monograms of Indian blue. Suddenly, with a strained sound, Daisy bent her head into the shirts and began to cry stormily. "They're such beautiful shirts," she sobbed, her voice muffled in the thick folds. "It makes me sad because I've never seen such—such beautiful shirts before."

The particular type of Conspicuous Consumption that consists in the multiplication of similar garments is most common among women. In men it is more rare, and usually associated either with dandyism or with great and rapidly acquired wealth, as in the case of the bootlegger Gatsby. A man who gets a raise or a windfall usually buys better clothes rather than more of them, and he has no need to wear a different outfit each day. Indeed, if he were seen to vary his costume as often as his female colleagues do he would be thought vain and capricious — perhaps even unstable. Monotony of dress is only a minor fault, though a man who wore the same tie to the office every day for a week would probably be considered a dull fellow.

For a woman, on the other hand, variety in dress is essential, and the demand for it starts very early. In America many girls in secondary school or even younger feel acute embarrassment about wearing the same outfit twice in the same week — let alone on consecutive days. Even if they own relatively few garments they will go to great lengths to combine them differently and to alter the total effect with accessories. So strong is this compulsion that quantity is usually preferred to quality, and shoddy new garments to well-made old ones. In terms of the struggle for status, this may be the right decision: young girls may not be able to recognize good clothes, but they can certainly count.

This female sense of the shamefulness of repetition persists into adult life. One of the most double-edged compliments one woman can give another is "Oh, you're wearing that pretty dress *again!*" (Men, who know no better, are forgiven such remarks.) Often the compulsion continues into old age: my mother, when nearly 90, still liked to appear in a different outfit each day "so as not to be boring." But it seems to be strongest among women in offices, for whom the fact that a colleague arrives at work on Tuesday in the same costume she was wearing on Monday is positive proof that she spent the intervening night unexpectedly at somebody else's apartment.

The constant wearing of new and different garments is most effective when those you wish to impress see you constantly — ideally, every day. It is also more effective if these people are relative strangers. If you live and work in an isolated country village, most of the people you meet will already have a pretty good idea of your rank and income, and they will not be much impressed if you keep changing your clothes. If you live in or near a city and work in a large organization, however, you will be seen often by the same people, but most of them will know little about you. Having a large and up-to-date sartorial vocabulary then becomes a matter of the first importance, especially if you have not yet established yourself socially or professionally. For this reason, it is not surprising that the most active supporters of the fashion industry today are young women in places like London and New York.

What is surprising, though, is the lengths to which this support can go. Many young working women now seem to take it for granted that they will spend most of their income on dress. "It's awfully important to look right," a secretary in a London advertising agency explained to me. "If a girl lives at home it'll be her main expense. If she's living in town, even sharing a flat, it's much harder. I'm always in debt for clothes; when I want something I just put it on my credit card. I know things cost more that way. But, well, take these boots. They were £89, but they were so beautiful, I just had to have them, and they make me feel fantastic, like a deb or a film star. All my friends are the same."

CONSPICUOUS MATERIALS: FUR AND LEATHER

Through the centuries, the most popular form of Conspicuous Consumption has been the use of expensive materials. For a long time this meant heavy damasked satins, patterned brocades, and velvets that were hand-woven at tremendous expense of time and labour. Today, when the machine-weaving of such fabrics is relatively simple, but hand labour and natural resources scarce, the desirable materials are wool, silk, leather, and hand-knits. When "artificial silk" (rayon) and nylon first appeared they were expensive and highly fashionable. But since the prestige of any fabric tends to vary in direct relation to its price per yard, the synthetic materials lost distinction as they became cheaper to produce; today "polyester" is a dirty word in many circles. "Natural" fabrics are chic now not only because of the current prestige of nature, but because they cost more than the synthetic alternatives.

The wearing of the skins and pelts of animals to indicate wealth has a varied history. In the past, when the world population of beasts was larger in proportion to that of people, only the furs of the least common animals conferred prestige. Those who had been enriched by their rapacity in war or trade might cover their floors or their beds with rugs made from the skins of the larger and more rapacious beasts, such as the tiger and the bear; or they might on formal occasions wear garments decorated or lined with the pelts of rare animals. Merchants wore robes trimmed with beaver, noblemen preferred sable, kings and queens (as they still do on ceremonial occasions) decked themselves in ermine. But common hides and furs were the dress of the common people. A leather jerkin meant a peasant, a sheepskin jacket a shepherd; the furs of common wild animals like the fox and the rabbit were associated with hunters and outlaws.

In the nineteenth century, however, as wildlife grew rarer, fur collars and cuffs began to appear on outdoor clothing, and fur muffs and tippets became popular. In the 1880s it suddenly became fashionable to decorate women's costumes and accessories with real or imitation dead animals, birds and even insects, and little capes of opossum, raccoon, and marten fur were worn. By the 1890s an entire coat made of or lined with fur had begun to suggest a large bank account rather than too great a familiarity with life in the backwoods.

The first fur coats were usually worn by men; it was not until the turn of the century that they were generally seen on women. For a while the fashion was unisexual; a stylish couple, for instance, might appear in public in identical raccoon coats. After the Depression, however—in spite of the efforts of manufacturers and fashion columnists—a fur coat on a man was a sign either of personal eccentricity or of sports or entertainment stardom—often of both. On a woman it was a conventional way of displaying wealth, with the rarer and more expensive furs such as mink and sable naturally ranking above the pelts of more common beasts.

Leather, particularly that of domestic animals like the cow and the sheep, took somewhat longer to become fashionable. Even today, garments made of hide have real status only if they come from rare and disagreeable animals like the llama and the alligator, or if they can be seen at a glance to have necessitated much tedious hand labour (dyeing, piecing, tooling, etc.).

In the sixties and seventies, when it became clear that many species of animals were threatened with extinction, fur coats became less popular. Many women refused to buy them, and hid any furs they already owned in the closet. Today, though coats made of the skins of rare wild beasts continue to be sold and worn, they have become associated with disregard for environmental values and a slightly murderous disposition. Wearing the fleece of sheep or the skins of cattle, on the other hand, is thought to be consistent with humanitarian views, and is still acceptable except to vegetarians.

CONSPICUOUS WEALTH: WEARING MONEY

Another primitive and simple way of displaying wealth is the wearing of actual money. In the past sharks' teeth, wampum, and coins, as well as many other forms of legal tender, have been made into jewellery or used to trim garments. Today, even in parts of the world where they cannot be used to buy lunch, such pieces retain some of their original prestige, and are often worn as accessories to high-fashion dress, to which they are believed to lend a bar-

baric glamour. Contemporary currency, which has no intrinsic value, is seldom or never made into jewelry, though the silver dimes and sixpences that have now been replaced by cheaper alloys are occasionally attached to bracelets and necklaces.

More common today, as well as in the past, is the decoration of the person with lumps of high-priced rock and metal. This method of announcing one's wealth also has the advantage of simplicity, since more people are aware of the approximate cost of such substances, especially when the local currency is based on them. The recent rise in the price of gold has made gold jewellery far more chic than it used to be, and diamonds, though their rise has not been so spectacular, retain their appeal. Materials such as rubies and emeralds, whose market price is less well-known, or which can more easily be imitated, are naturally less popular. Instant identification is desirable: platinum, though more costly than gold, never really caught on because most people couldn't tell it from silver or aluminum.

IN-GROUP SIGNALS

Sheer bulk and the wearing of many or obviously expensive garments and decorations are signs of status that can be read by almost anyone. More subtle sorts of Conspicuous Consumption are directed toward one's peers rather than toward the world in general; they are intended not to impress the multitude but to identify one as a member of some "in" group.

The costume of the upper-class British male, for example, is a mass of semiotic indicators. According to my informants,[7] he customarily wears striped shirts, sometimes with white collars, leaving plenty of cuff showing and always fastening at the wrist with cuff links. The shirt collars must be neither too long and pointed nor too round, and never button-down: "In fact, the obsession of the gentleman is to avoid all extremes at all times." His suits, made by a "good"—i.e., superb—Savile Row tailor, are embellished in a number of small ways that will

be noted by observant people: for instance, they may have extra buttons on the jacket cuff that can actually be buttoned, and a ticket pocket. The trousers will be cut fairly high in the waist and usually provided with buttons to which to attach braces or suspenders: "Wearing a belt is not done except with country suits, sometimes in the City called 'Friday suits,' since they are worn preparatory to going out of town. Older public-school men prefer to wear a tie around the waist rather than a belt." Ideally, the suit will be a dark pin stripe with a vest. The latter must never have lapels, which are "flashy" and "suggest the dandy or even the pouf." Recently, when one British politician became involved in a homosexual scandal, my informants remarked to one another that they were not really all that surprised: though his suit, hat, and watch chain were very reputable, "the lapels on his waistcoats were a nasty giveaway."

It is not only the clothes themselves that must be correct, but the haircut and the accessories. "A gentleman practically never wears sideburns or a hairstyle that covers his ears"; if he has a mustache it must be of moderate size. His eyeglasses must be of real tortoise shell or gold-rimmed, and he must carry the right umbrella. "Umbrellas are as talismanically magic as fairies' wands. They must be tightly rolled, and preferably never unrolled even in heavy rain." Old Etonians, however, always carry an unrolled umbrella.

Though the ordinary casual observer might miss or misinterpret these details, those in the know will recognize proper London tailoring—just as they will recognize the accent that means someone has gone to the right (i.e., sufficiently expensive) sort of school. Since they too have shopped abroad, they will also notice expensive foreign-made clothes, just as they would notice foreign words that happened to be dropped in conversation. To be acceptable, these must be the right sort of clothes, and from a currently fashionable country. Ideally, they should not be available at home; foreign fashions, like foreign words, are most prestigious when not too familiar. Once they have become naturalized they are no longer very chic—like the word chic itself. French T-shirts and Italian sandals, once high fashion, now cause no more thrill than the words boutique and espresso.

A similar law of diminishing returns affects foreign *types* of garment. The triangular head scarf tied under the chin, originally featured in *Vogue* as an exotic accessory, was so useful and soon became so familiar that it was a negative status indicator. The Oriental kimono, a glamorous import at the turn of the century, was by the 1930s associated with slatternly females of easy virtue, and today is one standard pattern for terry-cloth bathrobes. If such styles are to retain any of their initial prestige they must be made up in very costly materials: the head scarf must be of hand-woven wool and sprout hand-printed roses; the kimono must be of silk embroidered with golden dragons.

CONSPICUOUS LABELLING

Not long ago, expensive materials could be identified on sight, and fashionable men and women recognized Savile Row tailoring or a Paris designer dress at a glance. In the twentieth century, however, synthetics began to counterfeit wool, silk, linen, leather, fur, gold, and precious stones more and more successfully. At the same time, manufacturing processes became more efficient, so that a new and fashionable style could be copied in a few months and sold at a fraction of its original price. Meanwhile, the economic ability to consume conspicuously had been extended to millions of people who were ignorant of the subtleties of dress, who could not tell wool from Orlon or Schiaparelli from Sears Roebuck. As a result there was a world crisis in Conspicuous Consumption. For a while it seemed as if it might actually become impossible for most of us to distinguish the very rich from the moderately rich or the merely well-off by looking at what they were wearing.

This awful possibility was averted by a bold and ingenious move. It was realized that a high-status garment need not be recognizably of better quality or more difficult to produce than other garments; it need only be recognizably more expensive. What was necessary was somehow to incorporate the price of each garment into the design. This was accomplished very simply: by moving the maker's name from its former modest inward retirement to a place of outward prominence. Ordinary shoes, shirts, dresses, pants, and scarves were clearly and indelibly marked with the names, monograms, or insignia of their manufacturers. The names or trademarks were then exhaustively publicized—a sort of saturation bombing technique was used—so that they might become household words and serve as an instant guide to the price of the clothes they adorned. These prices were very high, not because the clothes were made of superior materials or constructed more carefully, but because advertising budgets were so immense.

When this system was first tried, certain critics scoffed, averring that nobody in their right mind would pay $60 for a pair of jeans labelled Gloria Vanderbilt when a more or less identical pair labelled Montgomery Ward could be purchased for $12. Others claimed that consumers who wanted a monogram on their shirts and bags would want it to be their own monogram and not that of some industrialist they had never met. As everyone now knows, they were wrong. Indeed, it soon became apparent that even obviously inferior merchandise, if clearly labelled and known to be extravagantly priced, would be enthusiastically purchased. There was, for instance, a great boom in the sale of very ugly brown plastic handbags, which, because they were boldly stamped with the letters "LV," were known to cost far more than similar but less ugly brown leather handbags. Cotton T-shirts that faded or shrank out of shape after a few washings but had the word Dior printed on them were preferred to better-behaved but anonymous T-shirts. Those who wore them said (or were claimed in advertisements to say) that they felt "secure." After all, even if the shirt was blotchy and tight, everyone knew it had cost a lot of money, and if it got too bad you could always buy another of the same kind. Thus Conspicuous Consumption, as it so often does, merged into Veblen's second type of sartorial status.

CONSPICUOUS WASTE: SUPERFLUOUS DRAPERY

Historically speaking, Conspicuous Waste has most often involved the use of obviously unnecessary material and trimmings in the construction of clothing. The classical toga portrayed in Greek and Roman sculpture, for instance, used much more fabric than was really needed to cover the body, the excess being artistically if inconveniently draped over one arm.

Anne Hollander has written most perceptively about the use of superfluous draped cloth in medieval, Renaissance, and Baroque art. In preindustrial Europe, as she points out, cloth was the most important manufactured commodity, "the primary worldly good." Beautiful material was as admirable as gold or blown glass, and occupied far more space. The ownership of elaborate and expensive clothing was an important proof of social dominance. A single aristocrat sitting for his portrait, however, could wear only one luxurious outfit at a time. The display of many yards of velvet or satin behind him would suggest that he owned more such stuff and was able, in modern terms, to fling it around. Even after immensely full and trailing garments ceased to be worn, at least by men, excess drapery survived in art: it is notable, for example, in the paintings of Hals and Van Dyck and the sculptures of Bernini. The Frick Collection portrait of the Earl of Derby and his family "shows the family out of doors, standing on bare earth with shrubbery in the foreground and trees behind. But on the right side of the painting, behind the earl, next to a column that might conceivably be part of a house, fifty yards of dark red stuff cascade to the ground from

nowhere. So skillfully does Van Dyck fling down these folds that their ludicrous inconsequence is unnoticeable."[8]

Traditionally, as Ms. Hollander remarks, superfluous drapery has been a sign not only of wealth and high rank but of moral worth: angels, saints, martyrs, and Biblical characters in medieval and Renaissance art often wear yards and yards of extra silk and velvet. Drapery derived additional prestige from its association with classical art, and thus with nobility, dignity, and the ideal. Marble columns and togalike folds (occasionally, actual togas) were felt to transform the political hack into a national statesman and the grabby businessman into a Captain of Industry. As Ms. Hollander notes, Westminster Abbey and the Capitol in Washington, DC, are full of such attempted metamorphoses, frozen into soapy marble.

Excess drapery survives today in middlebrow portrait painting, causing over-the-hill industrialists, mayors, and society women to appear against stage backgrounds of draped velvet or brocade, the moral and economic prestige of which is somehow felt to transfer itself to them. Successful academics, I have noticed, are often painted in this manner: posed before velvet curtains, with their gowns and hoods and mortarboards treated in a way that recalls the idealized drapery and stiffened halos of Renaissance saints. (Appropriately, the halos of professors and college presidents are square rather than round.)

The use of superfluous fabric in costume never died out completely. During most of the period between 1600 and 1900, for instance, respectable middle-class and upper-class women wore a minimum of three petticoats; fewer than this was thought pathetic, and indicated negligence or poverty. Skirts were inflated with hoops or bustles to provide a framework on which to display great quantities of cloth, while overskirts, panniers, flounces, and trains demanded additional superfluous fabric. A fashionable dress might easily require twenty or thirty metres of material. Elaborate trimmings of bows, ribbons, lace, braid, and artificial flowers permitted yet more prestigious waste of goods. Men's clothing during the same period used relatively little excess fabric except in outerwear, where long, full coats and heavy capes employed yards of unnecessary cloth, adding greatly to their cost and to the apparent bulk of their wearers.

A glance through any current fashion magazine will show that the use of superfluous fabric today, though on a much more modest scale, is by no means outmoded. Expensive clothes are often cut more generously, and fashion photography tends to make the most of whatever extra material the designer provides, spreading it over prop sofas or blowing it about in the air. Even the most miserly excess of cloth may now be touted as a sign of prestige: a recent advertisement in *The New York Times* boasts of an extra inch in the back yoke of Hathaway shirts which, the manufacturer sobs, costs them $52 000 a year.

Wastage of material in the form of trimming, though less striking than it was in the past, still persists. Today, however, it is often thinly distinguished as practical. A prestigious shirt, for instance, has a breast pocket into which nothing must ever be put; the habit of filling it with pens and pencils is a lower-middle-class indicator, and also suggests a fussy personality. A related ploy, especially popular between the two World Wars, was the custom of embroidering everything with the owner's initials. This may in some cases have had a practical function, as in the separation of laundry, but—and more importantly—it also added conspicuously to the cost of the garment.

SUPERFLUOUS PERSONALITIES

Changing styles, of course, are another and very effective form of Conspicuous Waste. Although I do not believe that fashions alter at the whim of designers and manufacturers—otherwise they would do so far more often—it is certainly true that, when social and cultural changes prompt a shift in the way we look, the fashion industry is quick to take advantage of it, and to hint in advertising copy that last year's dress will do our reputation no good. When new styles do not catch on, other ploys are tried. A recent one is to announce with disingenuous enthusiasm that fashion is dead; that instead of the tyranny of "this year's look" we now have a range of "individual" looks—which are given such names as Classic, Feminine, Sporty, Sophisticate, and Ingenue. The task of the well-dressed liberated woman, the ads suggest, is to choose the look—or, much better and more liberated, *looks*—that suit her "lifestyle." She is encouraged, for instance, to be sleek and refined on the job, glowingly energetic on holiday, sweetly domestic at home with her children, and irresistibly sexy in the presence of what one department at my university has taken to calling her "spouse-equivalent." Thus, most ingeniously, life itself has been turned into a series of fashionable games, each of which, like jogging or scuba-diving or tennis, demands a different costume—or, in this case, a different set of costumes (winter/summer, day/night, formal/informal). The more different looks a woman can assume, the more fascinating she is supposed to be: personality itself has become an adjunct of Conspicuous Waste.

Men traditionally are not supposed to have more than one personality, one real self. Lately, however, they have been encouraged by self-styled "wardrobe engineers" to diversify their outward appearance for practical reasons. According to these experts, the successful businessman needs different sets of clothes in order to "inspire confidence in" (or deceive) other businessmen who inhabit different regions of the United States. This idea is not new, nor has it been limited to the mercantile professions. A former journalist has reported that as a young man he consciously varied his costume to suit his assignment. When sent to interview rich and powerful Easterners, he wore clothes to suggest that he was one of them: a dark-grey flannel Savile Row suit, a shirt from André Oliver or Turnbull & Asser, a Cartier watch of a sort never available at Bloomingdale's, and John Lobb shoes. "What you have to convey to rich people anywhere," he explained, "is that you don't have to try; so what you're wearing shouldn't ever be brand-new." New clothes, on the other hand, were appropriate when interviewing the *nouveau riche*; and since they might not recognize understated wealth, he (somewhat reluctantly, but a job is a job) would also put on a monogrammed shirt and Italian shoes with tassels.

When assigned to official Washington, this particular journalist took care to be three or four years behind current New York modes. "Washington hates fashion, especially New York fashion. The message should be, I am not attempting style; I am a man of the people, a regular fellow." He would therefore wear a somewhat rumpled pin-striped suit, a white shirt and a nondescript tie. Before leaving Manhattan he would get his hair cut shorter than usual. On the other hand, if he were sent to California, or were interviewing a writer, artist, or musician anywhere in the country, he would try to let his hair grow or rumple it up a bit. He would wear slacks and a good tweed jacket over a turtleneck shirt; if the interviewee were financially successful he would add an expensive watch or pair of shoes to this costume. Still other getups were appropriate and available — for the Midwest, Texas, the South, Continental Europe, and Britain.

When this system works it is no longer Waste; nor, since the clothes are deliberately chosen to blend into their surroundings, can they be called Conspicuous. But as the journalist himself remarked, clothes alone cannot disguise anyone, and the travelling salesman or saleswoman who engineers his or her wardrobe but not his or her voice, vocabulary, or manners may simply be practising Conspicuous Waste without its usual reward of enhanced status — let alone a rise in sales figures.

CONSPICUOUS LEISURE: DISCOMFORT AND HELPLESSNESS

Once upon a time leisure was far more conspicuous than it usually is today. The history of European costume is rich in styles in which it was literally impossible to perform any useful activity: sleeves that trailed on the floor; curled and powdered wigs the size, colour, and texture of a large white poodle; skirts two metres in diameter or with two-metre dragging trains; clanking ceremonial swords; starched wimples and cuffs and cravats that prevented their wearers from turning their heads or looking at anything below waist level; high-heeled pointed shoes that made walking agony; and corsets so tight that it was impossible to bend at the waist or take a normal breath. Such clothes proclaimed, indeed demanded, an unproductive life and the constant assistance of servants.

These conspicuously uncomfortable and leisurely styles reached an extreme in the late eighteenth century at the court of Versailles. The political and sartorial revolution that followed freed both sexes temporarily, and men permanently, from the need to advertise their aristocratic helplessness. Men's clothes became, and have remained ever since, at least moderately comfortable. Women's fashions, on the other hand, after barely ten years of ease and simplicity, rapidly became burdensome again and continued so for the next hundred years.

Urban middle-class clothing today, though it does not usually cause pain, makes anything more than limited activity awkward. It is hard to run or climb in a business suit and slick-soled shoes; and the easily soiled white or pale-coloured shirt that signifies freedom from manual labour is in constant danger of embarrassing its wearer with grimy cuffs or ring-around-the-collar. Urban women's dress is equally inconvenient. It should be pointed out, however, that inconvenience may be an advantage in some situations. A friend who often does historical research in libraries tells me that she always gets dressed up for it. If she is obviously handicapped by high heels, a pale, elegant suit, and a ruffled white blouse, the librarians will search the stacks for the heavy volumes of documents and old newspapers she needs and carry them to her, dusting them on the way. If she wears a sweater, casual slacks, and sensible shoes, they will let her do it herself. The same ploy would probably work for a man if he were middle-aged or older.

NOTES

1. Gerald Carson, *The Polite Americans: A Wide-Angle View of Our More or Less Good Manners over 300 Years* (Westport, CT: Greenwood Press, 1980), pp. 12–13.

2. Henrietta O. Ward, *Sensible Etiquette of the Best Society*, 18th ed. (Philadelphia: n.p., 1878), pp. 251–53.

3. Lillian Eichler, *Book of Etiquette*, vol. ii (Oyster Bay, NY: Nelson Doubleday, 1921), p. 147.

4. Anne Hollander, *Seeing through Clothes* (New York: Viking, 1978), p. 443.

5. Robert Brain, *The Decorated Body* (London: Hutchinson, 1979), p. 99.

6. Eichler, *Book of Etiquette*, p. 154.

7. The costume of the upper-class British male; I am indebted to Roland Gant and Nigel Hollis for this information.

8. Hollander, *Seeing through Clothes*, pp. 38–39.

PART 3B

ETHNIC AND RACIAL INEQUALITY

Ethnic groups are usually defined as social collectivities that are distinguished by ancestry and culture. **Races** have relatively unique ancestries and cultures too. In addition, races differ from ethnic groups and from each other in terms of visible physical characteristics, such as skin colour, that are socially defined as significant and that are significant in their social consequences.

Many people assume that cultural differences explain why some ethnic and racial groups are more economically and politically successful than others. In this view, only some groups are blessed with cultures that generate supportive families, respect for education, and an ethic of diligence and hard work. Other groups, culturally less well endowed, are condemned to broken families, low educational attainment, and limited occupational success. In Chapter 14, Stephen Steinberg of Queen's College in New York questions these easy assumptions about the role of culture in determining ethnic and racial fortunes. He focuses on the successes of Asians and Jews in American society, the presumed successes of West Indian Blacks, and the failure of nearly 30 percent of American-born Blacks to escape poverty. Steinberg shows that, as a result of a selective immigration policy in the United States, the successful groups in American society arrived with a head start compared with relatively unsuccessful groups. These successful groups came with occupational experiences, educational backgrounds, and, in some cases, capital that enabled them to achieve rapid movement up the socioeconomic hierarchy. In sharp contrast, American-born Blacks start their climb up the social hierarchy saddled with heavy historical and current liabilities: 200 years of slavery, 300 years of forced segregation, and continuing discrimination in employment, housing, and everyday life. Of course, there are cultural differences between American-born Blacks and, say, Korean and Japanese Americans. But Steinberg's point is that these cultural differences are rooted in different historical and class experiences. In his judgement, culture is not an important *independent cause* of ethnic and racial success or failure.

In Chapter 15, Frances Henry of York University and her colleagues provide an overview of how discrimination affects members of Canada's racial minorities. (While **prejudice** refers to negative *attitudes* toward members of an ethnic or racial group, **discrimination** refers to *behaviour* that has negative consequences for such groups.) They first sketch the changing racial composition of Canadian society. In the early years of the twenty-first century, nearly 18 percent of Canadians are members of racial minorities. The proportion is much higher in large cities, reaching roughly 25 percent in Montreal, Edmonton, Calgary, and Winnipeg, roughly 40 percent in Vancouver, and nearly 50 percent in Toronto. Chinese, Blacks, and South Asians each account for roughly a fifth of the racial-minority population. Henry and her colleagues summarize government-sponsored studies and public opinion polls that have found evidence of widespread racism in Canada, concluding that somewhere between 30 and 55 percent of Canadians hold racist views. They also describe the several white supremacist hate groups that have sprung up in Canada and they report on field experiments and statistical census studies that demonstrate significant racial discrimination in employment, particularly against Black Canadians.

Canada's Aboriginal peoples have fared worse than any other ethnic or racial group in the country. Their way of life was virtually destroyed by European colonization. They were robbed of land, culture, community, and even children. As a result, they now suffer more unemployment, poverty, alcoholism, infant mortality, and day-to-day violence than any other group in the land. Yet, ironically, some

Canadians fail entirely to recognize the historical and social context in which Aboriginal people became victims, instead blaming *them* for their plight. As J. Rick Ponting and Jerilynn Kiely of the University of Calgary note in Chapter 16, a 1994 survey showed that 31 percent of Canadians believe that "most of the problems of aboriginal peoples are brought on by themselves." Ponting and Kiely go on to review the results of the three main surveys on Aboriginal issues conducted in Canada between 1976 and 1994. They paint a picture full of irony and contradiction. Most Canadians are sympathetic to Aboriginals in the abstract, but they know little about them and give Aboriginal issues a low policy priority. On average, Canadians are opposed to "special status" for Aboriginal peoples yet on the whole they favour Native self-government. Most Canadians want action to solve Native problems — but only in the form of royal commissions to study the issues, not in the form of boycotts, demonstrations, and other assertive actions on the part of Native people themselves. Ponting and Kiely also note substantial regional variation in anti-Aboriginal feeling. Quebec stands out as the province most hostile to Aboriginal Canadians, especially their land claims. Ontario is most sympathetic. The overall pattern seems to be that Aboriginal Canadians are viewed as especially problematic where they conflict with questions of ethno-national territorial control and least problematic in areas where they compose a small proportion of the population and make less threatening claims.

Racial and ethnic prejudice and discrimination are quite widespread in Canada, and are by no means directed only against Native peoples. Yet most of Canada's racial and ethnic minorities have fared surprisingly well economically. This is a tribute to their resourcefulness and industry, and it is largely a consequence of their social background. Thus, according to the 1986 census, the median annual income of Black Canadians was 92.1 percent of the median annual income of Canadians of British origin. In contrast, the median annual income of Black Americans was only 67.3 percent of the median annual income of white Americans in 1990. Of the twelve ethnic and racial groups in Canada with a population over 250 000, East Indians had the third-highest median income in 1986; the British ranked fourth. The economic achievement of most of Canada's racial minorities is due largely to the country's selective immigration policy, which favours immigrants with higher education and money. In brief, credentials and capital help to overcome the worst economic consequences of discrimination.

Nonetheless, there are persistent economic differences among racial and ethnic groups in Canada. These are explored in depth in Chapter 17, by Hugh Lautard of the University of New Brunswick and Neil Guppy of the University of British Columbia. Lautard and Guppy critically review past studies of ethnic and racial stratification in Canada, and they analyze Canadian census data from 1931 to 1991. They conclude that occupational differences between ethnic and racial groups have decreased by 50 percent over the 60-year period they studied but that they still remain substantial. Why? Mainly because some groups continue to be augmented by substantial numbers of immigrants, and immigrants suffer more disadvantages than native-born Canadians. For example, immigrants may lack English and French language skills and contacts in the wider community that could help them find better jobs. The Canadian-born children of immigrants are less disadvantaged in this regard, and their movement up the stratification system is therefore somewhat easier, even though discrimination persists, especially for members of racial minority groups.

The results of a study based on the 1986 Canadian census illustrate the effect of immigration status on income. Samples of immigrant and Canadian-born adults were first matched. That is, the members of both groups who were compared had the same distribution of ages, areas of residence, marital statuses, educational levels, occupations, full-time and part-time work statuses, and number of weeks worked in the preceding year. Next, the annual incomes of Canadian-born and foreign-born men and women, both visible-minority and non-visible-minority, were calculated. Table P3B.1 shows the results, expressed in dollars above or below the national average for men and women. Examine the left-hand column first. Note that all immigrants earned below-average incomes and that visible-minority immi-

TABLE P3B.1 ANNUAL INCOME BY IMMIGRATION STATUS, SEX, AND VISIBLE-MINORITY STATUS FOR CANADIANS AGE 25–64 IN 1986 (DEVIATIONS FROM MALE AND FEMALE AVERAGES IN DOLLARS)

	IMMIGRANT	CANADIAN-BORN	AVERAGE
Men			
Visible minority	–5307	–627	
Non-visible minority	–424	436	27 019
Women			
Visible minority	–1634	474	
Non-visible minority	–198	154	15 080

SOURCE: Adapted from Monica Boyd, "Gender, Visible Minority, and Immigrant Earnings Inequality: Reassessing an Employment Equity Premise," in Vic Satzewich, ed., *Deconstructing a Nation: Immigration, Multiculturalism and Racism in '90s Canada* (Halifax: Fernwood, 1992), p. 298.

grants earned less than non-visible-minority immigrants. Turn now to the right-hand column, which contains data on Canadian-born adults. There we see that the group differences are much smaller than in the left-hand column. Moreover, three of the four Canadian-born groups earned more than the national average. Among Canadian-born adults, visible-minority women actually earned more than non-visible-minority women. Only Canadian-born, visible-minority men earned less than the national average for men. But even for them, substantial improvement is evident; while the immigrant generation of visible-minority men earned 19.6 percent less than the average for men, the Canadian-born generation of visible-minority men earned only 2.3 percent less than the average for men. Clearly, being an immigrant carries with it an economic liability. Just as clearly, the liability diminishes for the first Canadian-born generation.

GLOSSARY

Discrimination refers to behaviour that has negative consequences for members of an ethnic or racial group.
Ethnic groups are social collectivities that are distinguished by relatively unique ancestry and culture.
Prejudice refers to negative attitudes toward members of an ethnic or racial group.
Races have relatively unique ancestries and cultures but they also differ from ethnic groups and from each other in terms of physical characteristics (e.g., skin colour) that are socially defined as important and that are important in their social consequences.

CRITICAL THINKING QUESTIONS

1. Do cultural differences explain why some ethnic and racial groups are more economically and politically successful than others? Give examples from your readings to support your answer.

2. What factors account for economic differences among racial and ethnic groups?

3. Identify the major racial minorities in Canada. How does discrimination affect them? Outline some explanations for racial discrimination in Canada.

4. Is it still accurate to portray Canada as a vertical mosaic? Explain your answer using examples from your readings.

5. From a sociological perspective, how do you explain the problems of high alcohol and drug use and low education among Aboriginal peoples?

6. How do Canadians' attitudes toward Aboriginal people vary on different issues? Why do they vary in this way?

7. How do attitudes toward Aboriginal people vary among different groups of Canadians? Why do they vary in this way?

ANNOTATED BIBLIOGRAPHY

Augie Fleras and Jean Elliott, *Unequal Relations: An Introduction to Race, Ethnic and Aboriginal Dynamics in Canada*, 2nd ed. (Scarborough, ON: Prentice-Hall, 1996). A comprehensive introduction to all aspects of race and ethnicity in Canada.

Stephen Jay Gould, *The Mismeasure of Man* (New York: W.W. Norton, 1981). A brilliant, award-winning study of how the measurement of human intelligence has been intimately connected with racist assumptions about human nature.

Jeffrey Reitz and Raymond Breton, *The Illusion of Difference: Realities of Ethnicity in Canada and the United States* (Toronto: C.D. Howe Institute, 1994). Canadians often think that Canada's "ethnic mosaic" differs from the American "melting pot." This book explodes the myth.

Chapter 14

Ethnic Heroes and Racial Villains

STEPHEN STEINBERG

Myths die hard, as the saying goes. To be sure, myths about race and ethnicity are deep-seated and often appear immune to change, but this is not because of some inherent potency or appeal. Myths are socially constructed. They arise in specific times and places, in response to identifiable circumstances and needs, and they are passed on through processes that can be readily observed. Whether a myth prospers or withers is always problematic; most, in fact, are relinquished or forgotten. To explain why some myths persist, we have to explore the relationship that these myths have to larger social institutions that promote and sustain them, and that in turn are served by them.

This chapter deals with myths that purport to explain why racial and ethnic groups occupy higher or lower places in the class system—why, in the popular idiom, "we have made it and they have not." The popular explanation, translated into respectable academic language by mainstream social scientists, is that "we" had the cultural virtues and moral fibre that "they" are lacking. If this theory were predicated on fact alone, it would be fairly easy to dispense with—for example, by showing that Jews, the archetype of ethnic success, arrived with occupational experiences and skills that gave them a headstart relative to other immigrants from eastern and southern Europe, that these latter groups were favourably positioned relative to Blacks, who were excluded from industrial employment altogether during the critical early phases of industrialization, and that racial minorities—Blacks in particular—have been encumbered across generations by discriminatory barriers that constitute the chief reason for their current economic plight. However compelling these facts might be, even when fully documented and analyzed, they are overpowered by other assumptions and beliefs that are almost universally shared in American society and that pervade American social science as well.

My point is that racial and ethnic myths about "making it" are embedded in a larger "success myth," one that is deeply rooted in American history and culture, and not easily countervailed. As Richard Weiss writes at the outset of his book on *The American Myth of Success*:

> the idea that ours is an open society, where birth, family, and class do not significantly circumscribe individual possibilities, has a strong hold on the popular imagination. The belief that all men, in accordance with certain rules, but exclusively by their own efforts, can make of their lives what they will has been widely popularized for well over a century. The cluster of ideas surrounding this conviction makes up the American myth of success.[1]

As Weiss goes on to say, the word "myth" does not imply something entirely false. The success myth was forged when the United States was a nation of yeomen and artisans, and it was sustained through two centuries of virtually uninterrupted territorial expansion and economic growth. There is much in our national experience to sustain notions of America as an open society where the individual can surmount impediments of "birth, family, and class." The problem arises when this simple schema glosses over major contradictions. To wit, colonial

Source: Excerpted from *The Ethnic Myth: Race, Ethnicity, and Class in America* (New York: Atheneum Press, 1989), pp. 263–80. Copyright © 1981, 1989 by Stephen Steinberg. Reprinted with the permission of Scribner, a division of Simon & Schuster, Inc.

America was not just a nation of yeomen and artisans—one-fifth of its inhabitants were slaves, and the wealth that flowed from slavery had a great deal to do with the expanding opportunities for those early Americans who exemplified Puritan virtues of industry, frugality, and prudence. A problem also arises when success is equated with virtue, and failure with sin and personal inadequacy. Not only does this individualize success or failure, thus obscuring the whole issue of social justice, but it also treats virtue and its opposite as a matter of personal endowment, rather than as traits that need to be explained in terms of their historical and social sources.

It has never been easy to accommodate the success myth to the embarrassing realities of racial inequality. If the United States is an open society where the individual is not irreparably handicapped by "birth, family, and class," then how is racial hierarchy to be explained? When Gunnar Myrdal suggested in the 1950s that racism constituted an unhappy contradiction between American ideals and practices, this was heralded as a major advance. Indeed, the thrust of previous research had been to find in the cephalic index or in intelligence tests clear evidence of a biological inferiority that predestined Blacks to subordinate status. The discrediting of scientific racism is unquestionably one of the great triumphs of liberal social science. However, subsequent theorists developed a social-scientific variant of scientific racism that essentially substituted culture for genes. Now it was held that groups that occupy the lowest strata of society are saddled by cultural systems that prevent them from climbing the social ladder. As before, failure is explained not in terms of societal structures, but in terms of traits endemic to the groups themselves.

For the exponents of social-scientific racism, furthermore, culture is almost as immutable as the genes themselves. Thus, for example, Thomas Sowell writes:

> Specific skills are a prerequisite in many kinds of work. But history shows new skills being rather readily acquired in a few years, as compared to the generations—or centuries—required for attitude changes. Groups today plagued by absenteeism, tardiness, and a need for constant supervision at work or in school are typically descendants of people with the same habits a century or more ago. *The cultural inheritance can be more important than biological inheritance,* although the latter stirs more controversy.[2]

As Sowell contends in this passage and his more extended disquisitions, a defective culture is the chief reason why Blacks have not followed in the footsteps of immigrants in their pursuit of the American Dream. Jews, on the other hand, are the perfect counter example—"the classic American success story—from rags to riches against all opposition."[3] Their formula for success amounts to having a certain cultural magic, called "human capital." To quote Sowell again:

> Whether in an ethnic context or among peoples and nations in general, much depends on the whole constellation of values, attitudes, skills, and contacts that many call a culture and that economists call "human capital." ... The importance of human capital in an ethnic context is shown in many ways. Groups that arrived in America financially destitute have rapidly risen to affluence, when their cultures stressed the values and behavior required in an industrial and commercial economy. Even when color and racial prejudices confronted them—as in the case of the Chinese and Japanese—this proved to be an impediment but was ultimately unable to stop them.[4]

In the hands of Thomas Sowell, "human capital" is little more than an obfuscation for writing a morality tale whereby groups—notably Jews and Asians—who have "the right stuff" overcome every impediment of race and class to reach the economic pinnacle. Other groups—especially Blacks—suffer from historically conditioned cultural defects that condemn them to lag behind in the economic competition. Of course, Sowell's morality tale is not an original creation. His ethnic heroes and racial villains are merely an updated version of traditional folklore that pitted rugged cowboys against treacherous Indians (which also had racist overtones).

Nor is this racist folklore, masked as social science, politically innocent. Its covert ideological function is to legitimize existing racial inequalities. By placing cultural blame on the victims, the nation's vaunted ideals are reconciled with patently undemocratic divisions and inequities. By projecting collective Horatio Algers, in the unlikely forms of Jews and Asians, it is demonstrated that "success" is attainable by everyone, without regard to "birth, family, and class." Like all myths, the ethnic myth has an implicit moral: "we" are not responsible, morally or politically, for "their" misfortune.

NEW HEROES: ASIANS AND WEST INDIANS

Social science's enchantment with the success myth, replete with its cast of heroes and villains, has been renewed in recent years with the arrival of millions of immigrants, the majority of whom are Asians, West Indians, and Hispanics. That these new immigrants have generally settled in cities with large concentrations of poverty-stricken Blacks has only highlighted the contrast between upwardly mobile immigrants and inner-city Blacks. Invidious comparisons have been common in the popular press, and social scientists have churned out more spurious scholarship extolling cultural virtue and reciting the stock tale of triumph over adversity. That these new heroes—Asians and West Indians—belong to racial minorities has thickened the plot, since it demonstrates, according to these scholars, that "race" is not an insurmountable obstacle and cannot explain why so many Blacks are still mired in poverty.

Thomas Sowell is prominent among those who have advanced this point of view. In the passage quoted earlier, Sowell notes that Chinese and Japanese confronted "color and racial prejudices," but asserts that this "was ultimately unable to stop them." It is the West Indians, however, who provide Sowell with the clincher to his argument that it is culture, not race, that explains why Blacks languish in poverty:

> While not racially distinct from American Negroes, West Indians have had a different cultural background. ... These differences provide some clues as to how much of the situation of American Negroes in general can be attributed to color prejudice by whites and how much to cultural patterns among blacks.[5]

Several pages later Sowell is less equivocal:

> The contrast between the West Indians and American Negroes was not so much in their occupational backgrounds as in their behavioral patterns. West Indians were much more frugal, hard-working, and entrepreneurial. Their children worked harder and outperformed native black children in school.[6]

The passages above are examples of a unique logical fallacy, which might be called a "Sowellgism." It goes as follows:

Premise 1: Blacks, Asians, and West Indians are all races.
Premise 2: Asians and West Indians have succeeded.
Conclusion: Race cannot explain why Blacks have not succeeded.

The trouble with this reasoning is that it uses an overgeneralized abstraction, "race," to gloss over crucial differences among the racial groups being compared with one another. Only in the most general sense can it be claimed that Asians, West Indians, and African Americans are all "races" that have been victims of racial stereotyping and discrimination. Although true, this proposition obscures the unique oppression that Blacks have endured throughout American history, beginning with two centuries of slavery and another century of official segregation, reinforced by the lynch mob and systematically unequal treatment in all major institutions. West Indians, of course, were also slaves, but living in island homelands that were predominantly Black, they have been insulated from the legalized and all-encompassing segregation that is unique to the African American experience.

Nor can this be dismissed as "history" that has no bearing on the present generation. If mobility is placed in correct sociological perspective, and regarded not as an individual event but as a process that occurs incrementally across generations, it becomes clear that America's legacy of racism has had a significant impact on the life chances even of today's Black youth. To say this is not to engage in "comparative suffering." It is merely to acknowledge the unique oppression that Blacks have experienced on American soil. Otherwise it is scarcely possible to explain why Blacks have been a perennial underclass in American society, and why they continue to lag behind other "racial" minorities.

THE MYTH OF ASIAN SUCCESS

In 1986 the five top recipients of the prestigious Westinghouse Science Talent Search were of Asian descent. This prompted a spate of articles in magazines and newspapers seeking to explain how a tiny minority, representing less than 2 percent of the national population, could achieve such bewildering success. The question, as framed by Malcolm Browne in an op-ed piece in *The New York Times*, is: "Do Asians have genetic advantages, or does their apparent edge in scientific skills stem from their special cultural tradition?"[7] Thus are we offered a choice between genes and culture as explanations for the academic excellence among Asians. Browne rejects genetic determinism, but has no such qualms with respect to cultural determinism. Paraphrasing an unnamed Westinghouse spokesman, he writes: "Tightly knit families and high respect for all forms of learning are traditional characteristics of Asian societies ... as they are for Jewish societies; in the past a very high proportion of top Westinghouse winners were Jewish." Of course, as Browne himself remarks, "the odd

thing is that until the twentieth century, real science scarcely existed in Asia." Undaunted by this apparent contradiction, he argues that Asian children are endowed with "an underlying devotion to scholarship—the kind of devotion imprinted on Asian children by a pantheon of ancestors"—that has made them receptive to Western scientific thought. Thus is a theory bent to accommodate inconvenient facts.

Two years later *The New York Times* ran another piece under the heading, "Why Do Asian Pupils Win Those Prizes?"[8] The author, Stephen Graubard, a professor of history at Brown University and editor of *Daedalus*, opines that Asians, who were eleven of the fourteen Westinghouse finalists from Cardozo High School in Queens, New York, have the advantage of stable families and Asian mothers who rear their children for success. With an air of resignation, he then turns the question onto Blacks and Puerto Ricans: "What is to be done for those hundreds of thousands of other New York children, many of illegitimate birth, who live with one parent, often in public housing, knowing little outside their dilapidated and decaying neighborhoods?" Since Graubard does not believe that the schools can do much to compensate for the defective culture of children from poverty backgrounds, these children are presumably condemned to languish in the cultural wasteland.

The same single-minded preoccupation with culture is found in yet another article in *The New York Times Magazine* on "Why Asians Succeed Here." The author, Robert Oxnam, president of the prestigious Asia Society, writes as follows:

> The story of these new immigrants goes far beyond the high school valedictorians and Westinghouse Science scholars we read about in our newspapers. It is the story of a broader cultural interaction, a pairing of old Asian values with American individualism, Asian work ethics with American entrepreneurship. And, where those cultural elements have collided, it has also been a story of sharp disappointments and frustration.[9]

Once again, culture is the fulcrum of success. Like the other writers quoted earlier, Oxnam identifies "the strong family ties and powerful work ethics of Asian cultures" as "key factors in Asian-American achievement."

This theory of Asian success is a new spin on earlier theories about Jews, to whom Asians are explicitly compared. As with the theory of Jewish success, there are a number of conceptual and empirical problems that throw the theory into question:

1. The theory of "Asian" success lumps together some twenty-five nationalities that are very disparate in history and culture. It is only in the United States that they are assumed to share a common "Asian" heritage. Little or no evidence is put forward to substantiate claims that they share common values with respect to family and work, that these values are significantly different from those found among non-Asian groups, or that these values are the key factors in explaining which Asians get ahead or why more Asians do so than others. Here is a classic case of circular reasoning. Values are not measured independently, but inferred from success, and then posited as the cause of success.

2. Theories of Asian success gloss over the fact that large segments of the Asian populations in the United States are far from prosperous. Alongside dramatic and visible success, touted in the popular media, are deep pockets of poverty, exploitation, and despair. Moreover, if successful Asians are presumed to owe their success to distinctively Asian values with respect to family and work, then are we to assume that less affluent Asians are deficient in these values? Are they therefore less "Asian"?

3. As in the case of Jewish success, the prevailing theory of Asian success overlooks the operation of premigration class factors that go a long way toward explaining the destinies of these immigrants after their arrival. The issue here has to do with selective

migration—that is, with who decides to emigrate and who is permitted entry. As Ezra Vogel, a scholar of China and Japan, has noted, Asian immigrants "are a very biased sample, the cream of their own societies."[10] They are drawn disproportionately from the intellectual and professional elites that, for one reason or another, have restricted opportunity in their home countries. Many of them have been admitted under the occupational preferences built into the new immigration law. In short, they are "successful" even before their arrival in America.

Data collected by the Immigration and Naturalization Service demonstrate the class character of Asian immigration. Table 14.1 reports the percentage of immigrant workers classified as professionals.[11] In the case of Indians, over three-quarters of immigrants with occupations are professionals; this reached a high point in 1969–71, when nine out of every ten Indians with occupations were professionals. Among Filipinos, Koreans, and Japanese the figures range between half and three-quarters; among Chinese, the figures are somewhat lower, but still much higher than for non-Asians. The influx of professionals of all nationalities reached a peak between 1969 and 1971, and declined thereafter. Nevertheless, the evidence is clear that a major segment of Asian immigration represents an educational and occupational elite.

Other data indicate that between 1965 and 1981 some 70 000 medical professionals— physicians, nurses, and pharmacists—came from the Philippines, South Korea, and India.[12] Another major source of immigrants has been students who enter the United States with student visas and then do not return to their home country. Of the 70 000 Chinese students from Taiwan between 1950 and 1983, it is estimated that 90 percent remained in the United States. The same is true of tens of thousands of students from Hong Kong, Korea, and other Asian countries. What these figures indicate is not a dra-

TABLE 14.1   PERCENTAGE OF PROFESSIONALS AMONG ASIAN IMMIGRANTS WITH OCCUPATIONS

	1961–65	1966–68	1969–71	1972–74	1975–77
China	31	35	47	37	31
India	68	67	89	84	73
Japan	44	50	45	37	28
Korea	71	75	70	51	38
Philippines	48	60	70	63	47
All Asians	40	52	62	54	44
All Immigrants	20	25	29	27	25

SOURCE: Adapted from Morrison G. Wong and Charles Hirschman, "The New Asian Immigrants," in *Culture, Ethnicity, and Identity*, William McCready, ed. (New York: Academic Press, 1983), pp. 395–97.

matic success story, but merely the transfer of intellectual and professional elites from less developed nations.

These immigrants start out with the educational and occupational resources that are generally associated with educational achievement in the next generation. To put the cultural theory to a fair empirical test, one would have to compare the children of Asian professionals with the children of other professionals. Only in this way could we assess the significance of distinctive ethnic factors. It is hardly valid to compare the children of upper-middle-class Asian professionals with the children of unemployed Black workers, as is done when "Asians" are compared with "Blacks."[13]

Not all Asian immigrants, however, come from advantaged backgrounds. Indeed, in recent years the flow of immigrants has included large numbers of uneducated and unskilled workers. These are the "downtown Chinese," as Peter Kwong calls them in his book, *The New Chinatown*.[14] These immigrants have difficulty finding employment in the racially segmented labour market outside of Chinatown, and are forced to accept jobs, commonly in sweatshops and restaurants, that match their nineteenth-century counterparts in their debasing exploitation. It has yet to be demonstrated that the children of these super-exploited workers are part of an Asian success story. Indeed, the outbreak of gang violence among Chinatown youth has exploded another myth that had great currency in the 1950s; namely, that because of their close-knit families, delinquency is virtually non-existent among the Chinese.[15]

In demystifying and explaining Asian success, we come again to a simple truth: that what is inherited is not genes, and not culture, but class advantage and disadvantage. If not for the extraordinary selectivity of the Asian immigrant population, there would be no commentaries in the popular press and the social science literature extolling Confucian values and "the pantheon of ancestors" who supposedly inspire the current generation of Asian youth. After all, no such claims are made about the Asian youth who inhabit the slums of Manila, Hong Kong, and Bombay, or, for that matter, San Francisco and New York.

THE MYTH OF WEST INDIAN SUCCESS

The mythical aspects of West Indian success, and the invidious comparisons between West Indians and Blacks, predate the current wave of immigration. In *Beyond the Melting Pot*, published in 1963, Glazer and Moynihan wrote that "the ethos of the West Indians, in contrast to that of the Southern Negro, emphasized saving, hard work, investment and education."[16] Although Glazer and Moynihan offer no evidence to support their claims, their observations are consistent with those made by other observers over several decades.[17] The key issue, though, is not whether West Indians in New York had the exemplary cultural traits that were ascribed to them. The issue is whether these cultural traits *explain* West Indian success, or whether, on the contrary, West Indians were more middle-class to begin with, and this explains their different attitudes with respect to "saving, hard work, investment and education."

As with Asians, the factor of selective migration must be considered. To begin with, we need to distinguish between two waves of West Indian immigration: the first, during the 1920s; the second, after the 1965 Hart-Celler Act. The first wave of immigrants was a highly selective group. According to immigration records, almost all of the adults — 89 percent — were literate, a figure far higher than that for West Indians who did not emigrate, or for the southern Blacks to whom they are compared.[18] Over 40 percent of the West Indian immigrants were classified as skilled, and some of these were highly educated professionals. Thus, once again, in drawing overall comparisons between West Indians and African Americans, we are comparing groups that differ in their social class as well as their ethnicity. It has never been shown that West Indians are different in terms of "saving, hard work, investment and education" when compared with their social class equals who are not West Indian.[19]

In other words, before generalizing about "West Indian cultural values," we need to be clear about which West Indians we have in mind. This is sharply illustrated by Nancy Foner's study of West Indians in New York City and London.[20] Since both groups have the same cultural heritage, this factor cannot explain why West Indians in New York have been more successful than those in Britain. Foner shows that the two immigrant pools are different in occupational background. Those who flocked to Britain during the 1950s were responding to labour shortages and an open-door immigration policy for Commonwealth nations. Although many were skilled workers, only about 10 percent were classified as white-collar. In contrast, among West Indian legal emigrants to the United States between 1962 and 1971, 15 percent were professional workers and another 12 percent worked in other white-collar occupations. For this reason alone, it is not surprising that West Indians in New York have been conspicuously more successful than those in London.[21]

The selective character of West Indian immigration to the United States, as already suggested, "stacks the deck" in terms of any comparisons to African Americans. Especially at a time when there was virtually no indigenous Black middle class, the influx of a small West Indian elite of professionals, businessmen, and prominent individuals did in fact stand out, and seemed to support notions of West Indian cultural superiority. Two things have changed since the migration of the 1920s, however. In the first place, there is a sizable African American middle class. Second, West Indian migration has become more occupationally diverse than was previously the case. Therefore, we have to reconsider our assumptions regarding the social status of West Indians in relation to African Americans.

In a paper entitled "West Indian Success: Myth or Fact?" Reynolds Farley undertakes an extensive analysis of 1980 census data.[22] He concludes that there is more myth than fact in suppositions about West Indian success.

Farley divided his sample into five groups: native whites, native Blacks, Black immigrants pre-1970, Black immigrants post-1970, and Blacks of West Indian ancestry (born in the United States but of West Indian parents or grandparents). On all relevant social and economic indicators, the four Black cohorts differ little among themselves, and where differences exist, they are small in comparison to the differences between Blacks and whites. For example, the figures below indicate the percentages of families that are female-headed:

Whites	11%
Native Blacks	37%
Black immigrants pre-1970	33%
Black immigrants post-1970	25%
West Indian ancestry	38%

Except for recent immigrants, female-headed households are as prevalent among West Indians as among native Blacks. Thus, the data do not support the widespread notion that West Indians have "strong families" in comparison to African Americans.

Nor do the data support the notion that West Indians are endowed with an entrepreneurial spirit that leads to business success. The following figures, adjusted for age, report the rate (per thousand) of self-employment among men:

Whites	87
Native Blacks	30
Black immigrants pre-1970	41
Black immigrants post-1970	22
West Indian ancestry	35

The rate of self-employment among recent West Indian immigrants is strikingly low (in contrast to what is found among recent Korean immigrants, for example). It is true that earlier West Indian immigrants and their descendants have a higher rate of self-employment than do native Blacks, but the levels are still much lower than that for whites. In short, self-employment is not so pronounced among West Indians as to support crude popular notions concerning "Jewmaicans," or, for that matter, more refined claims of "ethnic enterprise" and "entrepreneurial spirit" supposedly endemic to West Indian culture.

Similar patterns are found with respect to education, occupation, and income. West Indians are generally higher on these measures of social class than native Blacks, but the differences are not great and there is always the suspicion that they are an artifact of selective migration. For example, the figures below report the average earnings in 1979 of employed males between the ages of 25 and 64:

Whites	15 170
Native Blacks	9 380
Black immigrants pre-1970	7 460
Black immigrants post-1970	11 170
West Indian ancestry	10 720

Again, West Indians are much closer to native Blacks in their earnings than they are to whites, and recent West Indian immigrants have the lowest incomes of all five groups. On the basis of his analysis of these 1980 census data, Farley reached the following conclusion:

> We have shown that black immigrants and West Indians in 1980 were quite similar to native blacks on the most important indicators of social and economic status. There is no basis now—and apparently there was none in the past—for arguing that the success of West Indians in the United States "proves" that culture, rather than racial discrimination, determines the current status of blacks.[23]

The critical role that premigration factors play in a group's "adjustment" is even more vividly illustrated by the two waves of Cuban immigration. The first wave, occurring in the aftermath of the Cuban Revolution, consisted largely of Cuba's economic elites—professionals, businessmen, shopkeepers, and others disenchanted with Cuban socialism. The second wave, "the Mariel invasion," consisted of ordinary Cubans, including a small number of criminals and mental patients whom the Cuban government cynically placed aboard the boats. The first wave was welcomed, especially in southern Florida's depressed economy, and inspired exuberant articles, like the one in *Fortune* magazine on "Those Amazing Cuban Emigres."[24] The second wave received a far less hospitable reception, and were besmirched by sensational press reports suggesting that the

Mariel Cubans were mostly criminals, lunatics, and degenerates.[25] The Cuban cultural magic seemed to have vanished.

In the final analysis, the attempt to use Asians and West Indians to prove that "race" cannot explain the plight of Black America is fallacious at best, and sinister at worst. It is based on an untenable juxtaposition of groups that look alike in terms of a simplistic racial classification (they are all "racial" minorities), but who are very different in terms of their social class origins, in terms of the structures of opportunity they encounter after their arrival, and even in terms of the depth of racism that limits access to these opportunities. This is not to deny that Asians and West Indian immigrants confront a difficult situation, one that calls forth all their cultural and personal resources. Nor is it to deny that both groups encounter racist barriers in their quest for a better life. It does not do them or ourselves any good, however, to use these struggling minorities to make specious comparisons to African Americans, and to minimize the significance of racism.

NOTES

1. Richard Weiss, *The American Myth of Success* (New York: Basic Books, 1969).

2. Thomas Sowell, *Ethnic America* (New York: Basic Books, 1981), p. 284. Emphasis added.

3. Ibid., p. 98.

4. Ibid., p. 282. For another view, see Stephen Steinberg, "Human Capital: A Critique," *Review of Black Political Economy* 14, 1 (Summer 1985), pp. 67–74.

5. Sowell, *Ethnic America,* p. 216.

6. Ibid., p. 219. For a similar popular account, see "America's Super Minority," *Fortune* 114 (November 24, 1986), p. 148.

7. Malcolm W. Browne, "A Look at Success of Young Asians," *The New York Times* (March 25, 1986), p. A31.

8. Stephen G. Graubard, "Why Do Asian Pupils Win Those Prizes?" *The New York Times* (January 29, 1988), p. A35.

9. Robert B. Oxnam, "Why Asians Succeed Here," *The New York Times Magazine* (November 30, 1986), p. 70.

10. Quoted in Fox Butterfield, "Why Asians Are Going to the Head of the Class," Education Supplement, *The New York Times* (August 3, 1986), section 12, p. 20.

11. These percentages are based on the number of immigrants who report having a job, thereby excluding nonworking women, as well as the old and young.

12. Illsoo Kim, "Ethnic Class Division among Asian Immigrants: Its Implications for Social Welfare Policies," unpublished paper presented at the Conference on Asian American Studies, Cornell University, October 24, 1986, p. 3.

13. If there is a distinctively ethnic factor in patterns of Asian mobility, it is that, like Jews of earlier generations, Asians realize that their channels of opportunity are restricted by prejudice. Closed off from the corporate fast lane, they are drawn to the professions. The sciences are particularly attractive to individuals who lack fluency in English. Data reporting SAT scores indicate that Asian American students score far above average on the math test, but far below average on the verbal test. *The New York Times*, section 12: "Education Life" (August 3, 1986), p. 3.

14. Peter Kwong, *The New Chinatown* (New York: Hill and Wang, 1987), pp. 5–6.

15. For example, see Henry Beckett, "How Parents Help Chinese Kids Stay Out of Trouble," series in the *New York Post* (July 11–13, 1955), and Betty Lee Sung, *The Story of the Chinese in America* (New York: Collier, 1971), p. 156.

16. Nathan Glazer and Daniel Patrick Moynihan, *Beyond the Melting Pot* (Cambridge: MIT Press, 1963), p. 35.

17. For example, Ira Reid, *The Negro Immigrant* (New York: Arno Press, 1969), originally pub-

lished in 1939; James Weldon Johnson, *Black Manhattan* (New York: Knopf, 1930).

18. Nancy Foner, "West Indians in New York City and London: A Comparative Analysis," in Constance R. Sutton and Elsa M. Chaney, eds., *Caribbean Life in New York City* (New York: Center for Migration Studies, 1987), p. 123.

19. In their study of Jamaican and Black American migrant farm workers, Nancy Foner and Richard Napoli observed differences between the two groups that, at first glance, appear to support the cultural thesis. The Black American farm workers were frequently apathetic on the job, and squandered part of their wages on liquor and gambling. In contrast, the Jamaican workers "worked very hard, were extremely productive, and saved most of their earnings" (p. 492).

    To their credit, Foner and Napoli probe beneath surface behaviour, and show that the two groups have different origins and are recruited through different procedures. For Black Americans, migrant labour was a last resort and a dead end, whereas for Jamaicans the wages meant a higher living standard when they returned home, and the possibility of purchasing land or establishing a small business. Thus, the same work attracted a different calibre of worker, and the same pay provided different incentives.

    Second, as offshore workers, Jamaicans were recruited under a program that not only included a physical exam, but also considered their previous work record. They also had to meet a work quota to remain in the camp and to ensure that they would be hired again. In these ways the Jamaican recruiting system "seemed to weed out the kinds of workers who frequently travelled North in the Black American migrant stream" (p. 501). Nancy Foner and Richard Napoli, "Jamaican and Black-American Migrant Farm Workers: A Comparative Analysis," *Social Problems* 25 (June 1978), pp. 491–503.

20. Foner, "West Indians." Also, see Roy Simon Bryce-Laporte, "New York City and the New Caribbean Immigration: A Contextual Statement," *International Migration Review* 13, 2 (1979), pp. 214–34.

21. Foner, "West Indians," 123. In addition to differences in the occupational background of the two West Indian cohorts, Foner cites two other factors that help to explain why West Indians have fared better in the United States: (1) the migration spans a much longer period, and is already into the second generation, and (2) they benefited from having a pre-existing Black community that provided patronage for West Indian professionals and entrepreneurs, and that allowed West Indians to be cast into a privileged intermediary position between Black and white America (comparable in some ways to the position of the coloureds in South Africa).

22. Reynolds Farley, "West Indian Success: Myth or Fact?" unpublished manuscript (Ann Arbor: Population Studies Center, University of Michigan, 1987). Statistical data are taken from pp. 8, 11, and 13. Also see Reynolds Farley and Walter R. Allen, *The Color Line and the Quality of Life in America* (New York: Russel Sage, 1987), chapter 12.

23. Reynolds Farley, "West Indian Success: Myth or Fact?" p. 15.

24. Tom Alexander, "Those Amazing Cuban Emigres," *Fortune* 74 (October 1966), pp. 144–49.

25. Actually, less than 5 percent of the Mariel migrants were hardened criminals, mental patients, or other undesirables. See Robert L. Bach, Jennifer B. Bach, and Timothy Triplett, "The Flotilla 'Entrants': Latest and Most Controversial," *Cuban Studies* 11 (1981), pp. 29–48.

Chapter 15

The Victimization of Racial Minorities in Canada

FRANCES HENRY

CAROL TATOR

WINSTON MATTIS

TIM REES

Canada's population has become increasingly racially diverse. From what was a country inhabited largely by whites and Aboriginal peoples, the population has changed to include people from more than 70 countries. In addition, the source countries from which immigrants come have dramatically altered. In 1961, 90 percent of Canada's immigrants came from European countries; between 1981 and 1991, this figure declined to 25 percent. Almost half of all immigrants who came to Canada between 1981 and 1991 were Asian-born.

By 1986, 38 percent of Canadians had at least one ancestor who was neither French nor English. In the same year, racial minorities accounted for 6.3 percent, or 1.6 million, of Canada's population. Most members of racial-minority groups lived in Ontario (see Figure 15.1). In 1991, the figure had increased to 9.6 percent, or 2.6 million. Recent projections indicate that the racial minority population will rise to 17.7 percent—5.7 million people—in the year 2001.

More than two-thirds of racial-minority immigrants to Canada come from Asia (see Figures 15.2, 15.3, and 15.4). Chinese constitute the most numerous group, with 1.3 million people, followed by South Asians (East Indians, Pakistanis, Sri Lankans, and Bangladeshis) and Blacks, with 1.1 million each. The next most numerous groups are West Asians and Arabs, Filipinos, Southeast Asians (Indochinese), and Latin Americans. The number of Latin American immigrants was expected to expand dramatically by the turn of the century.

By 2001, about half of the population of Toronto and two-fifths of the population of Vancouver are expected to be racial minorities. About one-quarter of the populations of Montreal, Edmonton, Calgary, and Winnipeg are expected to be racial minorities. In Ottawa–Hull and Windsor, one-sixth of the populations will consist of racial minorities. Halifax, Kitchener, Hamilton, Victoria, and Regina will have 10–14 percent (see Figure 15.5).

These figures are taken from the Samuel projection of the numbers of racial minorities expected to live in Canada by the year 2001. Actual figures according to the most recent cen-

Source: Excerpted from Frances Henry, Carol Tator, Winston Mattis, and Tim Rees, *The Colour of Democracy: Racism in Canadian Society*, 2nd ed. (Toronto: Harcourt Canada, 2000), pp. 86–91, 96–117. Reprinted by permission of the publisher.

FIGURE 15.1   RACIAL MINORITIES BY PROVINCE, 1986–2001 (PROJECTED)

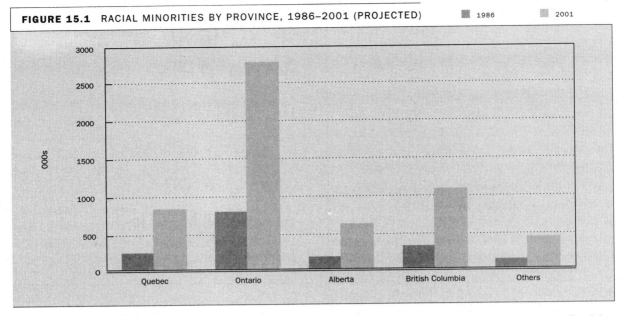

1986   2001

SOURCE: T.J. Samuel, *Visible Minorities in Canada: A Projection* (Toronto: Race Relations Advisory Council on Advertising, Canadian Advertising Foundation, 1992).

sus (1996) show that about 10.7 percent of Canada's total population in 1996 was classified as "visible minority" by the census.[1] As in the earlier figures, Asians, including those from Southeast Asia and South Asia, predominate (see Table 15.1). The provinces of Ontario, British Columbia, and Quebec have the most racial-minority inhabitants (see Table 15.2). There are

FIGURE 15.2   ETHNICITY OF RACIAL MINORITIES, 1986

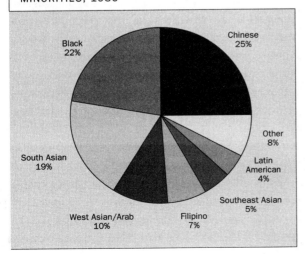

SOURCE: T.J. Samuel, *Visible Minorities in Canada: A Projection* (Toronto: Race Relations Advisory Council on Advertising, Canadian Advertising Foundation, 1992).

FIGURE 15.3   ETHNICITY OF RACIAL MINORITIES, 1991

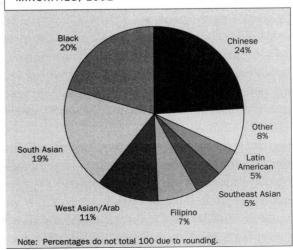

Note: Percentages do not total 100 due to rounding.

SOURCE: T.J. Samuel, *Visible Minorities in Canada: A Projection* (Toronto: Race Relations Advisory Council on Advertising, Canadian Advertising Foundation, 1992).

FIGURE 15.4 ETHNICITY OF RACIAL MINORITIES, 2001 (PROJECTED)

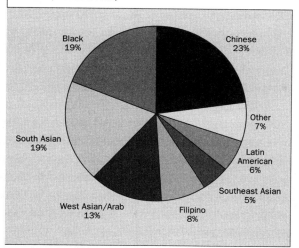

SOURCE: T.J. Samuel, *Visible Minorities in Canada: A Projection* (Toronto: Race Relations Advisory Council on Advertising, Canadian Advertising Foundation, 1992).

also nearly 800 000 Aboriginal people in Canada. The largest cities in Canada also contain the most racial-minority people. In 1996, Toronto led the list with 1 338 095, followed by Vancouver with 564 600 and Montreal with 401 425 (see Table 15.3).

There are many kinds of data one can turn to in assessing the impact of these changes on the composition and complexion of immigrants to Canada. One source of data is the polls and surveys that seek to measure racist attitudes among individuals or groups. In the past two decades, many such surveys have been initiated by government agencies, politicians, the media, and academics.

A second source is the research findings of government commissions, academics, and commissioned studies by universities and other public-sector agencies.

POLLS AND SURVEYS

One of the first surveys of racist attitudes in Canada contained 57 attitudinal items pertaining to racial prejudice (Henry, 1978). The findings revealed that 16 percent of the white mainstream population was extremely intolerant

FIGURE 15.5 RACIAL MINORITIES IN SELECTED CENSUS METROPOLITAN AREAS, 1991 AND 2001 (PROJECTED)

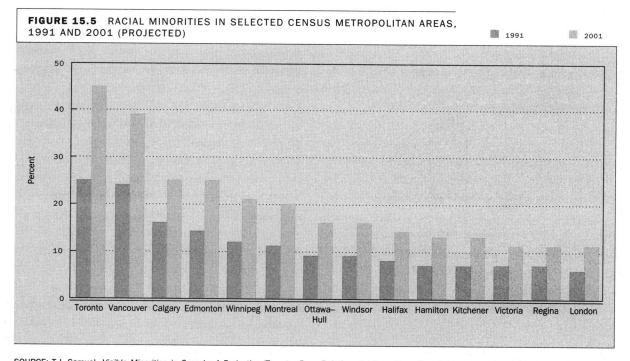

SOURCE: T.J. Samuel, *Visible Minorities in Canada: A Projection* (Toronto: Race Relations Advisory Council on Advertising, Canadian Advertising Foundation, 1992).

TABLE 15.1   VISIBLE MINORITIES IN CANADA BY ETHNIC GROUP, 1996

	NUMBER	PERCENTAGE
Total visible-minority population	3 197 480	99.9
Chinese	860 150	26.9
South Asian	670 585	21.0
Black	573 860	17.9
Arab/West Asian	244 665	7.7
Filipino	234 200	7.3
Latin American	176 975	5.5
Southeast Asian	172 765	5.4
Japanese	68 135	2.1
Korean	64 835	2.0
Visible minority, n.i.e.*	69 745	2.2
Multiple visible minority**	61 570	1.9

*Includes Pacific Islanders and other visible-minority groups; n.i.e. = not included elsewhere.
**Includes respondents who reported more than one visible-minority group.
Note: Percentages do not total 100 due to rounding.

SOURCE: Data from Statistics Canada, *The Daily*, Catalogue no. 11-001, February 17, 1998. Downloaded June 4, 1998, from http://www.statcan.ca/Daily/English/980217/d980217.htm.

and 35 percent somewhat racist. At least 18 percent had very liberal views about race, and a further 30 percent were somewhat liberal.[2]

The attitudinal survey literature has been remarkably consistent over the more than 20 years since that first survey was done. Most of the surveys show that between 10 and 20 percent of Canadians are extremely intolerant of racial minorities. Another 20–35 percent are somewhat racist. Combining these two findings suggests that a large segment of the population could be characterized as racist.

A decade after the Henry study, another survey found that between 7 and 20 percent of Canadians could be described as strongly racist in their views (Environics, 1988). Evidence of "hard core" racism included the following findings: 19 percent of Canadians agreed with

"research findings" that Orientals were superior to whites, who were, in turn, superior to Blacks. Moreover, 13 percent of Canadians would exclude non-white groups from immigrating to Canada, 7 percent would not vote for a Black political candidate, and 9 percent would not vote for a Chinese candidate.

A 1989 survey conducted by researchers at the University of Toronto and York University was designed to determine whether there was a significant difference between the racial attitudes of decision makers—legislators, lawyers, administrators, and police officers—and those of the general population. The survey found that 23 percent of the "elite" Canadians thought minority groups needed to get rid of "harmful and irritating faults," compared with 39 percent of the general population who held the same view. Half of the decision makers and 70 percent of the general population felt that immigrants often bring discrimination upon themselves; 16 percent of the "elites" and almost one-third of the general citizenry believed that "races are naturally unequal" (Gould, 1990).

A 1989 poll in British Columbia, which receives most racial-minority immigrants settling in the West, indicated that many residents believed that immigration does not bring economic advantages to the province. These perceptions were held despite the fact that, shortly before, a highly publicized report by Employment and Immigration Canada found exactly the opposite to be the case. The report demonstrated that after ten years in Canada, Third World immigrants paid more taxes per capita than did western European immigrants. These perceptions were also not shaken by the well-reported findings of the province's central statistics bureau, which showed that Asian entrepreneurial immigrants contributed $122.9 million to the BC economy and $5.4 million to the Alberta economy in 1988. Although entrepreneurial immigrants from Asia created 15 000 jobs in Canada in 1988, nearly half of British Columbia's population thought there were too many immigrants of colour moving into the province.

TABLE 15.2   VISIBLE-MINORITY POPULATION OF CANADA BY PROVINCE, 1996

	TOTAL POPULATION	TOTAL VISIBLE-MINORITY POPULATION	VISIBLE MINORITIES AS % OF TOTAL POPULATION	GEOGRAPHIC DISTRIBUTION OF VISIBLE MINORITIES
Canada	28 528 125	3 197 480	11.2	100.0
Newfoundland	547 155	3 815	0.7	0.1
Prince Edward Island	132 855	1 520	1.1	0.0
Nova Scotia	899 970	31 320	3.5	1.0
New Brunswick	729 625	7 995	1.1	0.3
Quebec	7 045 085	433 985	6.2	13.6
Ontario	10 542 790	1 682 045	15.8	52.6
Manitoba	1 100 295	77 355	7.0	2.4
Saskatchewan	976 615	26 945	2.8	0.8
Alberta	2 669 195	269 280	10.1	8.4
British Columbia	3 589 760	660 545	17.9	20.7
Yukon Territory	30 650	1 000	3.3	0.0
Northwest Territories	64 125	1 670	2.6	0.1

SOURCE: Data from Statistics Canada, *The Daily*, Catalogue no. 11-001, February 17, 1998. Downloaded June 4, 1998, from http://www.statcan.ca/Daily/English/980217/d980217.htm.

In a Toronto survey in 1992, when asked how well their racial or cultural group was accepted, 80 percent of those surveyed in the Black Canadian community, 63 percent in the Chinese Canadian community, and 62 percent of the East Indian–Pakistani Canadian community felt there was some prejudice toward them in Toronto. Also, 73 percent of Blacks, 48 percent of Chinese, and 47 percent of East Indians–Pakistanis felt discriminated against in obtaining work, compared with 31 percent of Jews, 16 percent of Portuguese, and 15 percent of Italians. In terms of discrimination in the legal or court system, the survey found that 49 percent of Blacks felt they were discriminated against. Twenty-one percent of East Indians–Pakistanis felt this way, as did 9 percent of Chinese (*Toronto Star*, 1992).

A report by the Economic Council of Canada (1991) attempted to measure the changing attitudes toward prejudice over time by analyzing the results of 62 surveys taken from 1975 to 1990 by Gallup, Decima, Environics, and other polling organizations. The report found that respondents from communities with greater proportions of visible-minority immigrants were "likely to be more tolerant of racial and ethnic differences." The report also concluded that over time there were "diminishing levels of prejudice." However, the results should be approached with some caution, considering the unreliability and validity of the many data sources as well as the kind of statistical analysis performed, which tends to obscure important variables, such as the unit of analysis, the nature of the questions, the age distribution of the sample, and the socioeconomic status, educational background, and gender of the respondents.

A survey by the federal immigration department of 1800 adults and fourteen focus groups showed a "growing acceptance" of attitudes and practices that show a dislike for "foreign-

TABLE 15.3   VISIBLE-MINORITY POPULATION* OF CANADA, BY CENSUS METROPOLITAN AREAS, 1996

	TORONTO	VANCOUVER	MONTREAL
Total population	4 232 905	1 813 935	3 287 645
Total visible-minority population**	1 338 095	564 600	401 425
Black	274 935	16 400	122 320
South Asian	329 840	120 140	46 165
Chinese	335 185	279 040	46 115
Korean	28 555	17 085	3 505
Japanese	17 055	21 880	2 310
Southeast Asian	46 510	20 370	37 600
Filipino	99 115	40 715	14 385
Arab/West Asian	72 160	18 155	73 950
Latin American	61 655	13 830	46 705
Visible minority, n.i.e.†	45 655	6 775	3 485
Multiple visible minority†	27 435	10 215	1 885

*The Employment Equity Act defines the visible-minority population as persons, other than Aboriginal peoples, who are non-Caucasian in race or non-white in colour.
**The visible-minority groups are based on categories used to define the visible-minority population under the Regulations to the Employment Equity Act.
†Not included elsewhere. Includes Pacific Islander groups or another write-in response likely to be a visible minority (e.g., West Indian, South American).
‡Includes respondents who reported more than one visible-minority group.

SOURCE: Data from Statistics Canada, *1996 Census of Canada*. Downloaded June 4, 1998, from http://www.statcan.ca:80/english/Pgdb/People/Population/demo40e.htm.

ers." One-third of the respondents agreed it was important to "keep out people who are different from most Canadians," while more than half were "really worried that they may become a minority if immigration is unchecked." Almost half admitted there were too many immigrants, even though most underestimated how many people were admitted (*Globe and Mail*, 1992).

Given the extent of ethnocentrism in Canadian society, it is not surprising that these concerns are expressed. However, the number of people who hold these negative attitudes but are not expressing them far exceed those who do, for "fear of being stamped racists" (Samuel, 1988; Wellman, 1978).

In a national survey undertaken by Decima Research in October 1993 for the Canadian Council of Christian and Jews, many myths were reflected in the responses of 1200 respon-

dents. Nearly three-quarters of respondents rejected the concept of Canada as a multicultural mosaic, and 72 percent believed that different racial and ethnic groups should try to adapt to Canadian society rather than preserve their original cultures. The survey found that 41 percent of respondents thought that Canada's immigration policy "allows too many people of different cultures and races to come to Canada," and 53 percent agreed with the statement that "some racial and ethnic groups don't make enough of an effort to fit into Canada." Half agreed with the statement: "I am sick and tired of some groups complaining about racism being directed at them," and 41 percent agreed they are "tired of ethnic minorities being given special treatment."

Ekos Research Associates conducted a number of surveys on immigration and used their results to advise the federal government on immigration policy. Their results in 1992 showed that 43 percent of Canadians believed that too many immigrants took advantage of social programs. By 1994, their polls revealed a steady increase (from 30 percent in 1988 to 53 percent in 1994) in Canadians who believed that there were "too many immigrants." More than one-quarter of the sample also thought that too many "visible minorities" were being accepted. A 1996 poll indicated that 44 percent of respondents found immigration levels too high, and the same number said the levels were about right (*Globe and Mail*, 1996). The population appears to be evenly split on this issue, which has resulted in government policy to maintain the status quo.

A more sophisticated series of surveys have been undertaken by Berry and Kalin, who conducted two national surveys on attitudes toward multiculturalism. Although many more respondents were tolerant than intolerant, the latter group gave less positive ratings to visible-minority groups. This provides evidence of "differential evaluations of ethnic groups along racial lines, but predominately among those who are the most generally prejudiced" (Berry and Kalin, 1997: 9). Aboriginal people and those of Chinese origin were rated nearly as positively as those of European origin. Berry and Kalin's explanation is that while racism may be a factor in explaining why European groups are rated more positively than non-European groups, "it is clear that Canadians are not generally racist in the sense that they rate all non-European origin Canadians in the same way" (1997: 10). Their general conclusions are in keeping with the less sophisticated polls reported above: that 5–20 percent of Canadians "respond negatively to attitude statements about inclusion and acceptance of racial others" (Berry and Kalin, 1997: 11).

The findings of many of the polls and surveys undertaken on this subject demonstrate some of the paradoxes of racism in Canadian society.

HATE GROUPS

An ideology of white supremacy has long been considered within the bounds of respectable, defensible opinion in Canada. In the colonial era, Aboriginal peoples were portrayed by church and state as "heathens" and "savages" and somehow less than human. These images provided justification for the extermination, segregation, and subjugation of Aboriginal peoples. The dehumanizing impact of such blatant propaganda is clearly evident today in the conditions of many Aboriginal communities (Frideres, 1983).

The 1920s and the 1930s saw the development of racist organizations such as the Ku Klux Klan (KKK), which openly promoted hatred against Catholics, Jews, Blacks, and other minorities. The original Klan was founded in Tennessee in 1866. It established bases in Alberta, Manitoba, Saskatchewan, British Columbia, and Ontario, feeding on Canadian anti-Semitism and the fear of Blacks and southern Europeans. While the KKK in Canada today appears to have only a handful of members, a network of other groups peddle hate propaganda, including the Heritage Front, the Liberty Lobby, the Church of the Creator, the Church of Jesus Christ–Aryan Nation, the Aryan Resistance Movement, and the Western Guard. All these groups share an ideology that supports the view that the Aryan, or white, race is superior to all others morally, intellectually, and culturally and that it is whites' manifest destiny to dominate society.

Barrett (1987) has made a significant contribution to understanding the recent activities of the extreme right in Canada. He found 130 organizations but under 600 members, many of whom belonged to more than one organization. Hate groups are usually coteries centred on a leader with a mailing list. Aside from holding meetings, they promote their ideology through distributing their literature widely. They hold rallies and parades, distribute buttons, paint slogans, establish dial-a-message telephone lines, demonstrate, and hold counter-demonstrations at the rallies of others. They may engage in paramilitary training, hold church services, or engage in political canvassing.

Another strategy used by these groups is to defend their activities by presenting themselves as defenders of free expression. Since they consider themselves to be promoting the principles of civil libertarianism, any attempts to curb their activities are portrayed as censorship and therefore anti-democratic.

Barrett (1987) suggests that the main elements of white supremacist ideology are anti-communism, anti-liberalism, racism, and anti-Semitism. White supremacists perceive themselves as the "saviours of the white race and Western Christian civilization" (Barrett, 1987: 90). They believe that the survival of white society in Canada is in jeopardy because of the practice of allowing "non-Aryans" into the country. The Ku Klux Klan suggests that one alternative to the problem of too many racial minorities in Canada is for the government to give "$35 000 to each coloured family as inducement to return to Pakistan, Africa, and elsewhere in the Third World" (Barrett, 1987). It suggests that Jews, too, should be included in this form of "ethnic cleansing," and that the expansion of the white race should be encouraged by providing financial incentives for white parents to have more children.

Barrett concludes that the ideology of the radical right does, to some extent, reflect "what the majority of people think and feel privately, albeit often unconsciously." While hate groups and hate propaganda may be regarded as marginal phenomena, the impact of such extremists is, according to Barrett, disproportionate to their numbers. They gain notoriety and apparent influence by combining strong stances on sensitive policies (such as immigration), which are controversial and have a substantial popular base, with continuous racist appeals couched in emotional, inflammatory rhetoric and threats of violence.

Since the publication of Barrett's pioneering work, the numbers of right-wing groups have proliferated in Canada. KKK branches are active in all of Canada's major cities. Offshoot groups such as the Heritage Front, the Church of the Creator, the Knights for White Rights, and the Aryan Nation are flourishing. Their presence is felt in the many telephone "hot lines" established throughout the country that spew forth hate messages, many of which are directed at Aboriginal peoples and racial minorities. Multiculturalism and immigration policies are also frequently criticized. The messages hammer home the theme "Keep Canada White."

In the past decade, the League for Human Rights of B'nai B'rith (1992) has monitored the number and types of anti-Semitic incidents that have occurred in all regions of Canada. The data file includes a large variety of incidents, ranging from non-violent ones such as anti-Semitic graffiti to more violent incidents that involve damage to persons or property and the desecration of synagogues. A recent analysis of this file showed a "significant increase ... in the numbers of incidents of all kinds." The report noted that this may reflect a "growing tendency of intolerance." But, since longitudinal studies of intolerance are non-existent in Canada, it is not possible to determine whether intolerance or racist behaviour has increased (Economic Council of Canada, 1991).

These racist incidents target not only the Jewish community. Hate-group activity and hate propaganda are directed at members of the Black, Chinese, and South Asian communities. Reports from various multicultural and anti-racist organizations and networks, as well as the cases before the human-rights commissions and courts, support the findings of the League for Human Rights of B'nai B'rith (British Columbia Organization to Fight Racism, 1992; Mock, 1992).

In the early 1990s, the Canadian Human Rights Commission began launching actions to prohibit telephone hate lines. In Vancouver, its action resulted in a tribunal ordering a telephone hate line off the air. Similarly, in Toronto, the Heritage Front was issued with an injunction to stop producing hate messages. In Winnipeg, a human-rights tribunal ordered the Manitoba Knights of the KKK to cease airing its messages. The tribunal found "overwhelming uncontradicted evidence that the messages were likely to expose the persons involved to hatred and contempt by reason of their race, religion, national or ethnic origin, colour or sexual orientation." This decision included not only the Manitoba chapter of the KKK, but also "any other individuals who are members of or act in the name of the Knights of the Ku Klux Klan." In recent years, the Internet has been used as a primary vehicle for the dissemination of hate propaganda (Anti-Defamation League, 1997). One prominent Web site was controlled by Canadian Ernst Zundel, using a base in California. The Canadian Human Rights Commission had, at the time of this writing, launched a tribunal hearing challenging the legitimacy of this method of distributing hate materials.

By 1992, racist violence was seen to be increasing in many Canadian urban centres. For example, over a period of a few weeks in 1993, three Tamil refugees were beaten in Toronto. One died as the result of the injuries inflicted by his white assailants, and one was paralyzed. These incidents must be considered in the context of a long history of racist attitudes toward immigrants and refugees (or those perceived to be "foreigners" by virtue of the colour of their skin). In 1987, Canadians reacted vehemently to the arrival of a few boatloads of Tamil and Sikh refugees who entered Canada without following the normal procedures, while at the same time expressing little concern about the equally unorthodox arrival of significant numbers of Polish refugees.

RECENT RESEARCH

The research on hate crimes and hate or bias incidents has increased in the last few years. Data from the United States, as well as the more limited data available in Canada, indicate that the majority of perpetrators of hate crimes or hate or bias incidents constitute a relatively homogeneous group. They are young, male, and tend to be involved in gangs (Gilmour, 1994).

There is also some evidence that skinheads have been involved in anti-Semitic hate crimes. Further evidence was found in a study that documented that most right-wing violence was committed by skinheads, "and members of other neo-fascist groups such as the Western Guard and anti-communist nationalists." The majority of attacks were motivated by racism, anti-communism, and anti-Semitism (Ross, 1992).

Research also indicates that actual acts of violence or hate crimes committed against racial and other minorities have increased. A study commissioned to determine the nature and extent of hate activity in Metro Toronto (Mock, 1996) offered the following definitions of hate activity:

- hate/bias crime: "criminal offense against a person or property that is based solely on the victim's race, religion, nationality, ethnic origin or sexual orientation"; and
- hate/bias incidents: "incidents of harassment and other biased activity that is not criminal, including name calling, taunting, slurs, graffiti, derogatory or offensive material, vandalism, and threatening or offensive behaviour based on the victim's race, creed, ethnicity or sexual orientation." (Mock, 1996: 14)

The study examined a wide variety of statistical indicators. These included the data from the only three agencies that keep such records, including the Metro Toronto Police Hate Crimes Unit. Qualitative measures such as interviews, focus-group discussions, and reviews of other available literature were also used. The findings reveal that

as the population of Metropolitan Toronto continues to become more diverse, and as difficult economic times continue to fuel the backlash against immigrants and minority groups, the reported incidents of hate motivated activity have steadily increased. While these findings could be the result of increased awareness of reporting mechanisms ... it is unlikely, since the anecdotal evidence of the perceptions of community workers and caseworkers corroborates the statistical findings. (Mock, 1996: 57)

Moreover, the groups most singled out were Jews, Blacks, and homosexuals.

> Reported anti-Semitic incidents are at an all time high, in 14 years of documentation by the League for Human Rights of B'nai B'rith Canada; and according to statistics gathered by the Metro Police, racially motivated incidents against Blacks and other people of colour, and hate motivated attacks on Gays and Lesbians have increased steadily over the last few years. (Mock, 1996: 49)

In a comprehensive statistical analysis of hate crimes in Canada, Roberts (1995) estimated that the total number of hate crimes committed in 1994 in nine major urban centres in Canada was approximately 60 000, including crimes motivated by race hatred as well as ethnicity and religion.

In sum, although the research evidence does not generally support an increase in negative attitudes, there has apparently been an increase in actual behaviour as measured by the escalation of hate-related criminal activity.

It also appears that media reports may generate more hate crimes and incidents. This is known as "the copy-cat effect." For example, an increase in anti-Semitic vandalism was reported after the airing of a program on racism, *Hearts of Hate*, on CTV. Members of the Jewish community and Jewish organizations also report an increase in hate activity whenever a "hate monger such as Zundel, Droege, or Burdi was featured prominently in the media without any counterbalance." Other minority groups report similar events (Mock, 1996).

Thus, racist behaviour stretches along a wide continuum. At one end are the overt and covert daily acts of discrimination involving a significant proportion of the mainstream community. At the other end of the continuum, one finds far more explicit and extreme racist activity in the form of hate propaganda and racial violence perpetrated by a small minority of the population.

DISCRIMINATION IN THE WORKPLACE

Concern over employment discrimination against people of colour, women, persons with disabilities, and Aboriginal peoples led the federal government to establish a royal commission on equality in employment (Abella, 1984). Its task was to inquire into the employment practices of eleven designated Crown and government-owned corporations and to explore the most effective means of promoting equality in employment for four groups: women, Native peoples, disabled persons, and racial minorities. Its findings echoed the conclusions of the report of the Task Force on the Participation of Visible Minorities in Canada (*Equality Now*, 1984) that racial bias and discrimination were a pervasive reality in the employment system. The commissioner, Judge Rosalie Abella, observed that "strong measures were needed to remedy the impact of discriminatory attitudes and behaviour." The remedy she recommended was employment equity legislation (Abella, 1984).

Federal employment equity legislation for the four target groups identified by the Abella Commission was first introduced in 1986 and strengthened in 1995. In that year, the annual report of the president of the Treasury Board revealed that small progress had been made with respect to the hiring of members of employment equity targeted groups. For example, the percentage of women in the public service increased from 42.9 percent in 1988 to 47.4 percent in 1995. The percentage of Aboriginal representation increased from 1.7 to 2.2 percent, while visible-minority representation increased from 2.9 to 4.1 percent. In all of these categories, the available labour pool is much higher.

Although the federal government has attempted to increase the representation of minorities in the public service, downsizing as well as residual racist attitudes have not led to significant gains. In addition, minority-group employees complained in a survey that employment practices were unfair and racially biased. A number of complaints to the Canadian Human Rights Commission, including a class action representing more than 100 employees of Health Canada, were made in the 1990s. Most involved professional employees who believed that they had not had equal access to promotional opportunities in the public service, particularly with respect to managerial positions. A tribunal of the commission found in favour of the complainants in the class action against Health Canada. In sum, there has been little real progress for minorities in the federal public service, largely due to the inability and unwillingness of this institution to respond to social and demographic imperatives.

At the level of the federally regulated private sector, more hiring has taken place. For example, in the banking sector, which has the best record of minority hiring, visible-minority representation has increased from 12.1 percent in 1989 to 13.7 percent in 1994. Communications rose from 5.3 to 7.2 percent, transportation from 3.8 to 4.3 percent, and all other areas from 3.7 to 6.2 percent (Samuel and Karam, 1996). Despite improvements in the overall position of racial minorities in employment regulated by the federal legislation, these groups are still concentrated in the lower sectors of the industries. For example, in banking, visible minorities are overrepresented in lower-level positions, such as tellers, and underrepresented in the managerial ranks.

In the late 1990s, responding to an aging and short-staffed bureaucracy, the Public Service Commission announced that it was hiring more than 2000 new employees. Since a report showed that the availability rate of visible minorities in the labour force was 12 percent but only 4.1 percent were represented in the public service, it might be thought that such minorities were likely to be especially recruited (Samuel, 1998).

Members of racial-minority groups have higher levels of education than do other Canadians. For example, in the late 1990s, 23 percent had university degrees, compared with 14 percent of other Canadians. Moreover, racial minorities had consistently higher levels of education than did other workers in the lower-paying occupations. In the category of "semi-professionals and technicians," for instance, 32.3 percent of racial-minority employees had university degrees, compared with 18.3 percent of others.

Despite higher levels of education, members of racial-minority groups were paid lower salaries than were other Canadians. Reitz, Calzavara, and Dasko (1981) demonstrated that considerable income disparities existed among various ethno-racial groups. People of colour, such as West Indians, and more recently arrived groups such as Portuguese, ranked lowest in incomes.

A decade later, the average salary for all levels of education for a member of a racial minority in both the upper and middle levels and other management occupations was approximately 18 percent lower than that of the total population (Employment and Immigration Canada, 1992: 57). Even in the "other manual workers" category, including all levels of education, members of racial minorities earned nearly 10 percent less than all other manual workers. Another study, issued in 1995 and provocatively entitled *The Colour of Money*, found that Aboriginal and visible-minority men earned significantly less income than did native-born and immigrant white men in Canada. The earnings differentials were not explained by socioeconomic variables such as education, place of schooling, occupation, and others, which were controlled for in this study. Even visible-minority men born in Canada suffered about a 10 percent earnings penalty. These differences were, however, not found among visible-minority women as compared with Canadian-born or immigrant white women. The researchers also noted that while there were clear-cut earning differentials between whites and visible minorities, there was also a considerable degree of heterogeneity within each of these categories (Pendakur and Pendakur, 1995).

One of the key barriers preventing immigrants of colour from access and equity in the labour market is credentialism. Studies in Ontario (Ontario Ministry of Citizenship, 1989) and British Columbia (Fernando and Prasad, 1986) showed that there is little recognition in Canada of the professional qualifications, credentials, and experience of immigrants. Thousands of immigrants find their university degrees and trade diplomas of little value in Canada. These barriers affect doctors, teachers, social workers, nurses, engineers, and others.

Public-sector agencies also show a lack of representation of racial minorities. An audit done for the Ontario public service in 1986 showed that 77 percent of civil servants were white and only 11.9 percent were racial minorities, most of whom were clustered in lower-level positions. In 1989, racial minorities formed only 4 percent of the Metropolitan Toronto Police Force. Almost all of them were cadets, constables, or in training; only three had the rank of inspector (Small, 1992). In 1998, the representation of racial minorities had shown insignificant gains: three staff inspectors, three senior police officers, and only 7.4 percent of the total uniformed employees were racial minorities (Metro Toronto Police Services, 1998). In the late 1980s at the Toronto Board of Education, only 5 percent of the teaching staff were from racial minorities, but this figure increased to 8.5 percent with the inclusion of non-teaching staff. Only 6 percent were classified as managers. The Ontario Human Rights Commission has only one racial-minority director. The Metropolitan Toronto Housing Authority, which deals with large numbers of minority clients, has a minority contingent of only 16.7 percent, of whom 11 percent are at a middle- or senior-management level.

A survey of 672 corporate recruiters ("Canada's Employment Discriminators," 1989), hiring managers, and agency recruiters across Canada conducted by the Canadian Recruiters Guild concluded that there were gross deficiencies in Canada's recruitment and selection practices. It revealed that the moral, legal, and economic impact of recruitment was either not understood or simply ignored by recruiters.

A study undertaken by the Maritime School of Social Work at Dalhousie University in Halifax (Bambrough, Bowden, and Wien, 1992) tracked its racial-minority and Aboriginal graduates and found that minorities experienced considerable difficulty in obtaining employment after graduation. Acadian and Black graduates took several more weeks than non-minority students to find their first job, and Blacks had to apply to many more employers and undertake many more interviews to get a job offer.

The study also found that upon graduation, Blacks found less desirable jobs than others, including limited or term positions and more part-time jobs. Of particular interest was the fact that Blacks were more often in jobs in which the chances for advancement were relatively low, as were salaries. The report concluded that "Black graduates have been less successful than the majority group in accessing the more prestigious social work jobs, such as those to be found in family counselling, hospital social work and in administrative/supervisory positions" (Bambrough et al., 1992).

Harish Jain, who has done extensive research (Jain, 1988; Jain and Hackett, 1989) on employment discrimination in Canada, suggested that racial minorities, as well as women, Aboriginal peoples, and people with disabilities, encounter both entry-level and postemployment discrimination in the workplace. Jain (1985) argued that human-rights statutes across Canada were ineffective in ensuring equality of opportunity in the workplace. Jain identified numerous job barriers in the employment system, including narrow recruitment channels and procedures (such as word-of-mouth recruitment, inflated educational qualifications, biased testing, prejudice and stereotyping in the job interview process, poor performance evaluation, lack of promotions, transfers, and/or salary increases). Unions are another potential source of both racism and sexism (Leah, 1989).

Non-English speaking and racial-minority immigrant women are part of a segregated and marginalized work force and are employed mainly in three areas: private domestic service, service industries, and light manufacturing. Many immigrant racial-minority women working in the public sector are employed as cleaners, cafeteria workers, nurses' aides, and lower-level clerical workers (Vorst et al., 1989). Brand (1987) observed that most Black women work at low-status jobs in homes and institutions and do "Black women's work."

Research on the Caribbean communities in Toronto (Henry, 1994) has yielded some interesting information on the continuing impact of racial discrimination on employment. More than 100 in-depth interviews and many hundreds of hours of participant observation among persons of Caribbean origin in Toronto indicated that the community shows a fairly high level of institutional completeness, considering the recentness of Caribbean migration to Canada. Although there are no Caribbean-owned financial institutions within the community, most service and retail sectors have developed to the extent that goods and services of many kinds can be obtained from Caribbean-owned and -managed businesses.

One of the main reasons for private entrepreneurship among the community was the racial discrimination experienced by job seekers and workers employed in mainstream-owned and -managed firms. Difficulty in obtaining employment was often cited as a major reason for dissatisfaction with living in Canada. In addition, racial harassment on the job and the inability to advance in the company were cited as contributory factors in private entrepreneurship. Restaurateurs, clothiers, and variety-shop owners said they were "fed up" with racial harassment.

A research project focusing on diversity, mobility, and change among Black communities in Canada used primarily census data and made similar findings. It found that although Black people in Canada had levels of education similar to those of the total population, they had substantially lower incomes, were less likely to be self-employed, and were less likely to occupy senior-management positions. Many more Blacks than whites lived in poverty, and Black women had greater poverty rates than men (Torczyner, 1997).

A report on socioeconomic indicators of equality conducted among ethno-racial communities in Toronto in the early 1990s found that while the overall rate of unemployment in Metro Toronto was 9.6 percent, the unemployment rate of non-Europeans far exceeded this (Ornstein, 1997). For example, Africans had a 25.8 percent unemployment rate, followed by Mexicans and Central Americans at 24 percent and Tamils at 23.9 percent. Other groups with a higher than average unemployment rate included Arabs and West Asians, Sri Lankans, Vietnamese, and Aboriginal people. Jamaicans, especially youth between the ages of 15 and 24, had high rates of unemployment as compared with other youth in the same age category. The study also found a weak link between employment and education and concluded that groups with the most unemployment were not those with the least education; many non-European groups found it difficult to convert their educational qualifications into jobs.

Income is closely related to employment, and in the early 1990s Tamils, Sri Lankans, and Africans in Toronto had the lowest earnings (about $19 000), followed closely by East and Southeast Asians, Jamaicans, and South Americans. This figure is in sharp contrast to the average annual employment income of $31 300 and a mean annual income of $50 000. With respect to general indicators of poverty, 19 percent of all families in Toronto were living at or below the poverty line. The highest levels of poverty (33–37 percent) existed among Arabs, West Asians, Latin Americans, Blacks, and Africans. Three in five Toronto children from African nations lived in poverty, as did more than half the children of Jamaican, Iranian, other Arab and West Asian, and Central

American parents. More than two-fifths of Aboriginal children, as well as those of Tamil and Vietnamese origin, lived in poverty.

Ornstein (1997) concluded that many people in Toronto were affected by poverty and inequality. The report acknowledged that the groups most affected were those who found access to employment, housing, education, and other resources constrained due to a variety of economic and social factors.

EMPLOYMENT AGENCIES

Allegations of racial discrimination in the operations of employment agencies in accepting and referring certain clients have been a concern for almost two decades. In 1975, the Canadian Civil Liberties Association (CCLA) conducted a survey of randomly selected employment agencies. The CCLA told agency representatives that it represented an out-of-town firm planning to locate in their community and asked whether, among the services provided, the agencies would agree to refer only white people for the jobs that had to be filled. Of the fifteen employment agencies in Metro Toronto that received this request, eleven said they would screen out persons of colour.

The study was repeated in 1976, surveying employment agencies in Hamilton, Ottawa, and London. Again, eleven of the fifteen agencies indicated their willingness to fulfill discriminatory requests. In 1980, the CCLA surveyed ten agencies in Toronto, seven of whom expressed a willingness to abide by a "whites only" restriction. In 1991, the CCLA repeated the survey for the fourth time, and of the fifteen agencies surveyed in four cities in Ontario, only three declared their unwillingness to accept discriminatory job orders.

Following are some examples of the agencies' responses.

It is discrimination, but it can be done discreetly without anyone knowing. No problem with that.

That's no problem, it's between you and me. I don't tell anyone; you don't tell anyone.

You are paying to see the people you want to see.

Absolutely — definitely ... that request is pretty standard here.

That's not a problem. Appearance means a lot, whether it's colour or overweight people. (Rees, 1991)

Although the role of employment agencies in colluding with discriminatory employers had long been known to those who monitor race relations in Canada, the publicity surrounding a complaint laid with the Ontario Human Rights Commission against two employment agencies in Toronto brought this issue into the public arena. Although the commission found discriminatory information about job applicants in some files, it maintained that the agencies did not have a deliberate policy of discriminating against job applicants. Accordingly, a settlement was reached in which the agencies agreed to develop written policies against accepting discriminatory job requests from employers and to provide training for their employees in race relations and employment equity.

Both agencies also said they would establish three-year employment equity plans, with goals and timetables that provided for the elimination of barriers in recruiting, referral, and placement services. The chief commissioner of the human rights commission was quoted as saying that this settlement "will provide a blueprint for all employment agencies in the province." A number of critics, however, noted that the settlement was fairly limited and did not adequately encompass all the aspects of this complex issue.

NOTES

1. The term "visible minority" is used in the Census of Canada as well as in publications that use census or other government-generated data. It is used in this chapter when discussing such research.

2. Polling and survey data from other countries are similar to those of Canada. For example, a survey conducted in the European Union countries revealed that racism is rampant. The data showed that one-third of respondents are racist; some admitted that they were "very" racist, and others reported being "quite racist" (*North Africa Journal*, 1998). Surveys on racism and attitudes toward immigrants in Australia revealed similar figures to those of Canada (see Adelman et al., 1994).

REFERENCES

Abella, R. (1984). *Report of the Commission on Equality in Employment.* Ottawa: Supply and Services Canada.

Adelman, H., A. Borowski, M. Burnstein, and L. Foster (eds.). (1994). *Immigration and Refugee Policy: Australia and Canada Compared.* Melbourne: Melbourne University Press.

Anti-Defamation League. (1997). *High Tech Hate: Extremist Use of the Internet.* New York: ADL.

Bambrough, J., W. Bowden, and F. Wein. (1992). *Preliminary Results from the Survey of Graduates from the Maritime School of Social Work.* Halifax: Maritime School of Social Work, Dalhousie University.

Barrett, S. (1987). *Is God a Racist? The Right Wing in Canada.* Toronto: University of Toronto Press.

Berry, J.W., and R. Kalin. (1997). "Racism in Canada: Evidence from National Surveys." In L. Driedger and S. Halli (eds.), *Visible Minorities: Race and Racism in Canada.* Ottawa: Carleton University Press.

Brand, D. (1987). "Black Women and Work: The Impact of Racially Constructed Gender Roles on the Sexual Division of Labour." *Fireweed* 25: 35.

British Columbia Organization to Fight Racism. (1992). *Canada 125.* Surrey, BC: BCOFR.

"Canada's Employment Discriminators." (1989). *Currents: Readings in Race Relations* 5(2): 18–21. Toronto: Urban Alliance on Race Relations.

Canadian Civil Liberties Association. (1991). *Survey of Employment Agencies.* Toronto: CCLA.

Canadian Council of Christian and Jews. (1993). *Survey of Canadian Attitudes towards Ethnic and Race Relations in Canada.* Toronto: Decima Research.

Economic Council of Canada. (1991). *Report.* Ottawa.

Employment and Immigration Canada. (1992). *Annual Report, Employment Equity.* Ottawa: Minister of Supply and Services.

Environics. (1988). *Focus Canada Survey.*

Equality Now: Report of the Parliamentary Task Force on the Participation of Visible Minorities in Canada. (1984). Ottawa: Queen's Printer.

Fernando, T., and K. Prasad. (1986). *Multiculturalism and Employment Equity: Problems Facing Foreign-Trained Professionals and Tradespeople in British Columbia.* Vancouver: Affiliation of Multicultural Societies and Service Agencies of British Columbia.

Frideres, J. (1983). *Native Peoples in Conflict.* Scarborough, ON: Prentice-Hall.

Gilmour, G.A. (1994). *Hate-Motivated Violence: A Working Document.* Ottawa: Department of Justice (May).

Globe and Mail. (1992). (October 14).

Globe and Mail. (1996). "Immigrant Levels Reflect Backlash." (October 30): A1.

Gould, T. (1990). "Who Do You Hate?" *Toronto Life* (October).

Henry, F. (1978). *Dynamics of Racism.* Ottawa: Secretary of State.

———. (1994). *The Caribbean Diaspora in Toronto: Learning to Live with Racism.* Toronto: University of Toronto Press.

Jain, H. (1985). *Anti-Discrimination Staffing Policies: Implications of Human Rights Legislation for Employers and Trade Unions.* Ottawa: Secretary of State.

———. (1988). "Affirmative Action/Employment Equity Programmes and Visible Minorities in

Canada." *Currents: Readings in Race Relations* 5(1): 3–7.

Jain, H., and R. Hackett. (1989). "Measuring Effectiveness of Employment Equity Programmes in Canada: Public Policy and a Survey." *Canadian Public Policy* 15(2): 189–204.

League for Human Rights of B'nai B'rith. (1992). *Annual Audit of Anti-Semitic Incidents.* Toronto: B'nai B'rith.

Leah, R. (1989). "Linking the Struggles: Racism, Sexism and the Union Movement." In Vorst et al., (eds.), *Race, Class, Gender: Bonds and Barriers.* Toronto: Between the Lines.

Metro Toronto Police Services. (1998). *Reporting Data.* Toronto.

Mock, K. (1992). *Combatting Hate: Canadian Realities and Remedies.* Toronto: League for Human Rights, B'nai B'rith Canada.

———. (1996). *The Extent of Hate Activity and Racism in Metropolitan Toronto.* Toronto: Access and Equity Centre of the Municipality of Metropolitan Toronto.

North Africa Journal. (1998). 18 (February 21).

Ontario Ministry of Citizenship. (1989). *Access: Task Force on Access to Professions and Trades in Ontario.* Toronto.

Ornstein, M. (1997). *Report on Ethno-Racial Inequality in Metropolitan Toronto: Analysis of the 1991 Census.* Access and Equity Centre of the (former) Municipality of Metropolitan Toronto.

Pendakur, K., and R. Pendakur. (1995). *The Colour of Money: Earnings Differentials among Ethnic Groups in Canada.* Strategic Research and Analysis. Ottawa: Department of Canadian Heritage.

Rees, T. (1991). "Racial Discrimination and Employment Agencies." *Currents: Readings in Race Relations* (Toronto) 7(2): 16–19.

Reitz, J., L. Calzavara, and D. Dasko. (1981). *Ethnic Inequality and Segregation in Jobs.* Toronto: Centre for Urban and Community Studies, University of Toronto.

Roberts, J. (1995). "Disproportionate Harm: Hate Crime in Canada: An Analysis of Recent Statistics." Ottawa: Department of Justice, Research, Statistics and Evaluation Directorate.

Ross, J.L. (1992). "Research Note: Contemporary Radical Right Wing Violence in Canada: A Quantitative Analysis." *Terrorism and Political Violence* 72(3) (Autumn).

Samuel, T.J. (1988). *Immigration and Visible Minorities in the Year 2001: A Projection.* Ottawa: Centre for Immigration and Ethnocultural Studies.

———. (1998). "Debunking Myths of Immigrants." *The Toronto Star*, June 17.

Samuel, T.J., and A. Karam. (1996). "Employment Equity and Visible Minorities in the Federal Workforce." Paper presented to Symposium on Immigration and Integration. Winnipeg (October 25–27).

Small, P. (1992). "Promote Minorities, Report Tells Police." *The Toronto Star* (September 11): A6.

Torczyner, J.L. (1997). *Diversity, Mobility and Change: The Dynamics of Black Communities in Canada.* Montreal: McGill School of Social Work.

Toronto Star. (1992). "Minority Community Survey."

Vorst, J., et al. (eds.). (1989). *Race, Class, Gender: Bonds and Barriers.* Toronto: Between the Lines.

Wellman, D. (1978). *Portraits of White Racism.* Cambridge: Cambridge University Press.

Chapter 16

Public Opinion on Aboriginal Rights

J. RICK PONTING

JERILYNN KIELY

The first national survey on Aboriginal issues was conducted by Ponting and Gibbins in 1976. With few exceptions, such as significant deterioration of support for First Nations in Quebec and British Columbia, the findings from that comprehensive survey still hold true today, as evidenced by the findings from Ponting's detailed, ten-year follow-up national study and an even more detailed 1994 national survey kindly provided to the authors by the Angus Reid Group. We shall discuss the main themes that emerge from those studies. In order to retain focus on the "big picture" and to avoid getting bogged down in detail, we usually report percentages only parenthetically, if at all. Similarly, readers are referred elsewhere (Ponting and Gibbins, 1980: 71–72; Ponting, 1987a: A1–A7) for the methodological details of the surveys. Suffice it to say here that in all three surveys the samples were large (over 1800) and the 1976 and 1986 surveys were conducted using face-to-face interviews in respondents' homes in the official language of the respondent's choice, while the 1994 survey differed by using telephone interviews. All three surveys were conducted by reputable polling firms.[1]

LITTLE KNOWLEDGE, LOW PRIORITY

Canadians know very little about Aboriginal affairs. In part, that is because we tend to pay little attention to most Aboriginal matters in the mass media and attach a low priority to Aboriginal issues, except when they touch close to home by involving personal inconvenience or threat to our livelihood. The evidence of this widespread ignorance is overwhelming, as measured by such indicators as not knowing the meaning of the term "Aboriginal people," not being aware of the existence of the Indian Act, not being aware of the existence of Aboriginal rights in the Constitution, and over-estimating by a factor of at least two the proportion of Native people in the Canadian population. Around 15 percent of Canadians are almost totally oblivious to Aboriginal matters in this country.

OPPOSITION TO SPECIAL STATUS

With the exception of a select few situations, such as First Nations' special relationship with

Source: Excerpted from "Disempowerment: 'Justice,' Racism, and Public Opinion," in *First Nations in Canada: Perspectives on Opportunity, Empowerment, and Self-Determination*, J. Rick Ponting, ed. (Toronto: McGraw-Hill Ryerson, 1997), pp. 174–92. Reprinted by permission of the publisher.

FIGURE 16.1   DISTRIBUTION OF THE SAMPLE ON THE INDEX OF SUPPORT FOR SPECIAL STATUS AND ON THE INDEX OF SUPPORT FOR NATIVE SELF-GOVERNMENT

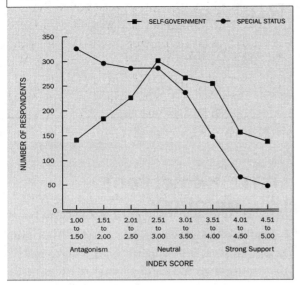

the land, Canadians manifest a pronounced tendency to reject what they view as "special status" for Native people. This is shown in the curve in Figure 16.1, which plots the distribution of the sample on two indexes, one of which is the Index of Support for Special Status for Natives, in the 1986 survey. A respondent's score on this index is his or her average score on four items dealing with special institutional arrangements for Native people. As with most of the indexes reported in this chapter, this one comprises statements with which respondents are asked to indicate their degree of agreement or disagreement, on a scale ranging from "strongly agree" to "strongly disagree."[2]

In Figure 16.1 we shall observe that most respondents fall at the unsupportive end of the scale measuring support for special status for Native people. In 1986 even stronger opposition to special status was found in most questions that explicitly use the word "special." For instance, in 1986, when respondents were given two statements—one of which described special institutional arrangements for Native people and one of which did not—and were asked

to choose the one that came closer to their views, it was repeatedly found that almost two-thirds of respondents opted for the statement that denied special status to Native people. One concrete example of this involved the two statements: "For crimes committed by Indians on Indian reserves, there should be special courts with Indian judges" (only 27 percent chose this); and "Crimes committed by Indians on Indian reserves should be handled in the same way as crimes committed elsewhere" (65 percent chose this). By 1994, there was some softening of this antagonism to special status[3] and the issue had become less clear-cut. Some ambivalence had entered Canadians' minds. On some questions, Canadians were still more antagonistic than supportive.[4] On other questions, though, there was more support than antagonism.[5] Our interpretation of this discrepancy is that it is an indication of Canadians' opinions on Aboriginal issues being rather inchoate. Although opinions on Aboriginal issues are not exactly formless, because Aboriginal issues are so peripheral to most Canadians we should expect a less consistently structured set of opinions on these issues than on some other issues such as the environment or national unity.

Such opposition to "special status" as does exist is probably rooted both in the long-standing opposition of many Canadians outside Quebec to special status in Confederation for Quebec, and in a norm of equality that is widely held among Canadians.

Obviously, Canadians' orientation to "special status" for First Nations could have important implications for the degree of self-determination that is attainable under the federal government's "self-government" legislation. The division of public opinion on this is captured nicely by a 1994 question (L1) pertaining to "self-government for Canada's aboriginal peoples—that is, both status and non-status Indians, the Métis and the Inuit." The remainder of the question, and the equal division of respondents across the three response options, follows:

Which of the following three broad statements best describes how you feel about aboriginal self-government, or the right of aboriginals to govern themselves?

- Aboriginal peoples in Canada have an historic, existing, inherent right to self-government. (29%)
- The federal and provincial governments should allow aboriginal peoples to govern themselves. (27%)
- Aboriginal people have no more right to self-government than other ethnic groups in Canada. (28%)

We pursue these issues of rights and self-government in more detail below.

SUPPORT FOR SELF-GOVERNMENT AND ABORIGINAL RIGHTS

Paradoxically, antagonism toward special status coexists with a support for Native self-government and even for recognition of the inherent right to self-government as an existing Aboriginal or treaty right. For many Canadians, self-government is less a manifestation of special status than a basic democratic right of self-determination. This interpretation is suggested by the fact that in Figure 16.1 the curve representing the distribution of the sample on an Index of Support for Native Self-Government[6] exhibits a markedly different shape than the curve for the Index of Support for Special Status for Natives. The curve depicting support for Native self-government is akin to the famous bell-shaped curve, and the average score is slightly to the supportive side of the mid-point of the scale. The curve for support for special status is highly skewed.

Surprisingly, even when the notion of the inherent right to self-government was linked with the Charlottetown Accord, defeated in the 1992 nationwide referendum, a small majority of the 1994 sample favoured its recognition as an Aboriginal and treaty right.

The degree of autonomy of First Nations governments from provincial governments is of pivotal importance in defining the fundamental character of First Nations governments. Replacing non-Native bureaucrats with brown-faced bureaucrats who administer essentially the same provincial policies is not self-determination. Yet, that is precisely what a substantial majority (akin to the 1986 survey's two-thirds disapproving of special status) of the 1994 respondents preferred when given the option between two statements, as follows:

Aboriginals could develop and run their own programs in [such areas as health, education and child welfare] without the province having any authority. (19%)

versus

Aboriginals could manage the programs in these areas but they would still be subject to provincial laws and standards. (65%)

Canadians' views of the capability of Aboriginal governments are improving.[7] When Canadians were asked in 1994 "how much confidence you have ... in terms of the role they might play in working towards some solutions to aboriginal peoples' concerns," the chiefs of large bands garnered majority support, as did national Aboriginal organizations.[8] Also, there is plurality support for the eventual dismantling of the Department of Indian Affairs and Northern Development (DIAND) and strong majority support for the Manitoba approach of transferring DIAND responsibilities to Aboriginal control as "a model for moving towards aboriginal self-government across the country." However, indications are that on the matter of the representativeness of Aboriginal leaders, by 1994 the skeptics had closed the gap on the believers, such that the population had come to be evenly divided.[9]

GENERAL SYMPATHY

To some extent, support for Native self-government and Native rights is a reflection of a more general positive orientation toward, or attitudinal support for, Natives. This might be called "sympathy," if that word can be stripped of connotations of condescension. Overall, the Canadian population in both 1976 and 1986 tended to be more sympathetic than antagonistic toward Native people. This observation is based on respondents' scores on composite indexes of several questions in each survey.[10] In 1986 two separate indexes were used. Only 10–15 percent of Canadians were *consistently* antagonistic (strongly or mildly) toward Native people across both scales. Twice as many were *consistently* supportive. On both indexes, as on the 1976 index, the average score for the sample was well above the mid-point of the scale. Further evidence of a generalized sympathy comes from other questions not included in any of the indexes. For instance, in 1986 a majority (57 percent) disagreed with the statement "Indians are a bunch of complainers" (only 23 percent agreed), and a large majority (71 percent) disagreed with the statement "The more I hear and see about Indians in the news media, the less respect I have for them" (only 13 percent agreed).

However, there has been a deterioration in support for Native people over the almost two decades covered by the surveys. For instance, in 1976 an overwhelming majority (72 percent) agreed with the statement "Indians deserve to be a lot better off economically than they are now." By 1986, only a plurality agreed (48 percent versus 29 percent disagreeing). The question was not asked on the 1994 survey, but it was a smaller plurality that took the pro-Aboriginal stance in response to the following somewhat similar statement: "Most of the problems of aboriginal people are brought on by themselves" (40 percent disagreed; 31 percent agreed). Yet, on another question that might carry moral overtones to respondents who adhere to the Protestant work ethic, a solid majority of the 1994 sample agreed (57 percent versus 15 percent who disagreed) with the statement "Aboriginal people are hard-working and industrious, and capable of earning their way if given a chance."

The deterioration in support for Native people can be seen in Table 16.1. There we observe that in Canada as a whole, the victimization stereotype of Indians/Aboriginal people lost about half of its adherents (as a percentage of the total population) between 1976 and 1994, while the alcohol and drug-abuse stereotype almost doubled in prevalence during that period, to the point of reaching parity with the victimization view. Note that in 1976, British Columbia was right at the national average level of sympathy for Native people, but a decade later it was well below the national average. Whereas a majority of Quebeckers, perhaps expressing a shared sense of deprivation as an ethnic minority in Canada, viewed Indians as victims of racism or discrimination in 1976, by 1994 only one-fifth did. The view that alcohol or drugs was the main problem facing Indians was scarcely detectable in Quebec in 1976, but eighteen years later it was not only held by a large minority of Quebeckers, but was notably more prevalent in Quebec than the view of Aboriginal people as victims of racism and discrimination.

SENSITIVITY TO NATIVE PEOPLE'S SPECIAL RELATIONSHIP TO THE LAND

Respondents exhibited a generally supportive opinion for Native people on matters related to land and land-use conflict. Two examples, from among several available in the 1986 survey, are:

- a (slight) majority of Canadians agreed (versus one-third who disagreed) with the statement: "Where Natives' use of land conflicts with natural resource development, Native use should be given priority."
- a near majority disagreed (48 percent versus 37 percent agreeing) that giving Native people special hunting rights "just isn't fair."[11]

On a 1994 question a plurality agreed (44 percent versus 29 percent disagreeing) with the

TABLE 16.1   REGIONAL VARIATION IN PUBLIC OPINION ON ABORIGINAL ISSUES

ITEM OR STATEMENT	CANADA	ATL. CAN.	MTL.	REST OF QUE.	TOR.	REST OF ON	MB	SK	AB	VANC.	REST OF BC
Mean Score on Index of:											
Sympathy for Natives, 1976*	3.31	3.10	3.56		3.25		3.15	2.90	3.00	3.30	
Sympathy for Natives, 1986*	3.22	3.12	3.17	3.31	3.47	3.30	3.13	2.96	3.13	3.09	2.97
Sympathy for Indians, 1986*	3.29	3.09	3.42	3.45	3.48	3.38	3.39	2.91	3.08	3.04	3.04
Support for Special Status for Native People, 1986*	2.56	2.38	2.15	2.96	2.34	2.45	2.44	2.14	2.07	2.11	2.07
1994 Statement											
It just isn't right for Natives to have special rights that other Canadians don't have.											
% agreeing	41	47	57		24		53	55	47	41	
% disagreeing	34	36	32		30		37	34	36	46	
1994 Question											
Generally speaking, do you think Canada's aboriginal people are being reasonable or unreasonable in terms of their current land claims?											
Reasonable (%)	38	34	30		32		55	53	50	49	
Unreasonable (%)	41	45	66		21		41	43	38	46	
Main (1976)/Most Serious (1994) Problem Facing Indians (1976)/Canada's Aboriginal People (1994) Today?											
% citing racism or discrimination											
1976	39	27	51		36			31		44	
1994	21	20	20		18		23	28	22	24	
% citing alcohol or drugs											
1976	12	7	1		13			28		12	
1994	23	25	30		17		29	21	29	13	

*Denotes possible range is 1.0 to 5.0, where 5.0 is most sympathetic.

statement: "Aboriginals have a special relationship to the land and can be trusted as better caretakers of the environment."

OPPOSITION TO TACTICAL ASSERTIVENESS

Canadians tend not to be accepting of any escalation of First Nations' protest tactics beyond a rather tame level. Protest was a major focus of the 1976 survey (Ponting and Gibbins, 1981), and the 1994 survey also included several questions on the topic. The results are broadly similar over the two decades. In 1976, the use of the courts and of protest marches received majority approval, as did "requesting that a royal commission be formed to study Indians' problems."

The majority disapproved of the more assertive tactics of barricading roads or railroads crossing Indian reserves, and threatening violence. Even boycotting private businesses elicited strong disapproval ratings.

In 1994, among five tactics listed, the only one for which approvers outnumbered disapprovers was the blockading of natural resource extraction on land claimed by Aboriginal people.[12] A "peaceful blockade of a major highway to press for speedier action on land claims" met with resounding disapproval as did the strategy of unilaterally asserting sovereignty.[13] Even making a formal complaint to the United Nations was approved by only a little more than a third of the sample (37 percent versus 45 percent disapproving). Similarly, only one-third approved of delaying completion of a resource megaproject.

REGIONAL VARIATION

To this point, discussion of public opinion has been couched in terms of Canada as a whole. That, however, obscures important variations from one region of the country to another. Those regional variations take on considerable practical significance when one remembers that many of the reforms sought by First Nations require the approval of provincial governments.

In some provinces, notably Saskatchewan and now Quebec, support for Aboriginal people is clearly rather low, while in Ontario support is comparatively high. Table 16.1 provides examples from the three surveys. Note how Quebeckers stand out as thinking Aboriginal people are being unreasonable in their land claims and how a high proportion of people from that province, along with Manitobans and Albertans, view alcohol or drugs as the most serious problem or issue facing Aboriginal people in Canada. Conversely, alcohol and drugs rank as only the seventh most serious Aboriginal problem in British Columbians' view. All four western provinces also stand apart from the rest of Canada in thinking that Aboriginal people are being reasonable in their land claims.

Table 16.2 depicts regional variation in answers to the open-ended question asking respondents to name the Aboriginal issue or problem that they think is most serious. In numerous ways, this table reveals that Canadians in different regions have a very different picture of Aboriginal matters. For instance, "Integration into society" is most commonly identified by Quebeckers as the most serious Aboriginal issue or problem, whereas, at the other extreme, it ranks ninth in importance in Saskatchewan. Ontarians and British Columbians rank education as the most serious Aboriginal issue or problem, whereas in Quebec it ranks seventh. Prairie residents stand apart as being more likely to see self-government as a more serious issue

than do residents of other provinces. Regional subcultures are reflected in other ways, too. For instance, Alberta, with its frontier ideology's emphasis on self-reliance and "rugged individualism," has a notably higher proportion of respondents citing "lack of initiative or motivation" than do the Atlantic provinces and Quebec, where structural barriers to personal success are more widely recognized and acknowledged.

Regional variation is also pronounced on other measures not shown in Table 16.1 or 16.2. For instance, the proportion of the public that is oblivious to Native issues is much larger in Quebec than in the other provinces. In addition, familiarity with Native matters tends to be regionally specific. To the extent that Canadians are familiar with Native matters at all, that familiarity is usually confined to matters in their own region. The 1986 survey found that even on issues that are clearly of national applicability, such as Aboriginal rights in the Constitution or the 1985 amendments to the Indian Act to remove sex discrimination, regional variation emerges in respondents' degree of familiarity.

CAUSES OF HOSTILITY

The 1986 national survey offers some important insights into the causes of hostility toward government policies designed to help Aboriginal people. Using advanced statistical techniques, Langford and Ponting (1992) determined that ethnocentrism is a minor to negligible determinant of hostility. Instead, economic conservatism (the "free enterprise" belief that government should minimize its role in economic relations), prejudice, and perceptions of conflicting group interests[14] between Aboriginals and themselves are key determinants of respondents' policy preferences. Furthermore, there is an important *interaction effect* between prejudice and perceived group conflict. That is, to take a hypothetical example, if a British Columbia logger has a low level of prejudice toward Natives, her perception that

TABLE 16.2   MOST SERIOUS ABORIGINAL ISSUE OR PROBLEM, BY PROVINCE, 1994

PROBLEM	CANADA Rank	%	ATLANTIC CANADA Rank	%	QUEBEC Rank	%	ONTARIO Rank	%	MANITOBA Rank	%	SASKAT. Rank	%	ALBERTA Rank	%	BC Rank	%
Alcohol/ drugs	1	23.2	2	24.8	2	29.9	5	17.4	2	28.6	5	20.6	1	28.6	7	13.4
Integration in society	2	22.4	6	14.4	1	38.2	6	16.6	6	14.2	9	8.3	5	18.0	6	15.6
Racism/ discrimination	3	20.8	3	20.4	3	19.6	3	18.4	3	23.3	2	27.7	2.5	21.8	1.5	24.0
Unemployment/ jobs	4	20.2	1	31.2	5	13.7	2	20.4	1	29.4	1	30.5	4	21.3	4	19.8
Education	5	18.9	5	15.1	7	12.6	1	24.6	5	16.3	3	24.1	6	17.7	1.5	24.1
Land claims	6	16.3	10	10.0	4	16.9	4	17.6	8	10.5	8	8.8	7	13.4	3	23.1
Self-government	7	14.8	7	14.1	8.3	10.8	7	14.0	4	20.5	4	21.0	2.5	21.7	5	16.3
Culture/ traditions	8	12.7	4	15.3	6	13.2	8	13.8	10.5	9.8	10	8.0	8	10.6	8	12.0
Poverty	9	10.1	8	11.6	8.3	10.8	9	8.4	10.5	9.9	6	12.6	9	9.3	9.5	11.1
Dependency on gov't/want everything for nothing/too much gov't funding/ handouts	10	8.6	9	10.3	8.3	10.8	12	4.7	7	11.4	12	3.7	11	7.8	9.5	11.1
People don't understand them	11	5.5	11	8.9	11	4.9	10	7.5	13	4.2	13	2.8	13	2.6	12	4.3
Lack of initiative or motivation	12.5	4.3	—	0.0	12	2.3	11	5.4	12	7.1	7	11.1	10	8.9	13	2.6
Low self-esteem/ self-worth/ self-respect	12.5	4.3	12	3.7	13	1.2	13	3.3	9	10.2	11	7.2	12	7.4	11	8.2
Valid cases	**1493**		**139**		**451**		**395**		**66**		**66**		**160**		**209**	

SOURCE: Angus Reid Group Ltd.

Native land claims threaten her livelihood from logging would have little impact on her support for Native self-government or on her support for special status for Natives. However, for another logger in whom the level of prejudice against Native people is high, that same perception that his livelihood is threatened by Native land claims will produce a dramatically lower level of support for both Native self-government and special status for Native people.

It is also possible to analyze these relationships from the opposite side. In doing so, we found that prejudice has very little impact on the dependent variables (support for Native self-government; support for special status for Native people) when the level of perceived group conflict is low. However, when perceived group conflict is high, prejudice again becomes an important determinant of Canadians' policy preferences toward Aboriginal people.

Our findings suggest the utility of distinguishing between two types of prejudice: dormant and activated. Prejudice against a group is dormant when it is unattached to any sense of conflict with that outgroup. Dormant prejudice has minimal effects on policy preferences vis-à-vis that outgroup. On the other hand, prejudice against a group is activated when it is linked to a perception of contemporary conflict with the outgroup. Such activated prejudice has important effects on policy preferences.

Regardless of whether prejudice is dormant, activated, or absent, economic conservatism was found statistically to produce antagonism toward Aboriginals and their preferred policies. Aboriginal people and their supporters might despair at that finding, in light of the contemporary influence of economic conservatism and the fact that substantial state financial participation will be necessary to overcome the effects of past and present racism, as the final report of the Royal Commission on Aboriginal Peoples asserted.

CONCLUSION

Although public opinion has softened slightly over the years on the issue of "special status" for First Nations, debilitating stereotypes remain alive in a significant minority of the non-Native population. In its broader contours, public opinion is no longer the ally that it was when social scientists first began monitoring it over two decades ago. Canadians have a low tolerance for precisely the kinds of protest strategies and tactics that create leverage for otherwise disempowered peoples. Aboriginal peoples have had to resort to those strategies and tactics and have paid the price in a deteriorating level of support from non-

Native people. Furthermore, the very assertiveness that Aboriginal peoples are finding necessary to attain concrete results is likely to bring Aboriginal people into competition with private and commercial interests in the larger society. Non-Native people's perception of such competition as a threat is associated with opposition to government policies favoured by Aboriginal leaders.

Non-Native politicians might seek to discount non-Native public opinion on Aboriginal issues as uninformed, uninterested, and inconsistent. It is all three of those things. However, there are limits to how far politicians in office are willing to go when, as was the case in Canada in the mid-1990s, the courts are waivering, political opponents are seeking to reap political gain from government's policies toward Native people, financial costs increase relentlessly, and the recommended reforms veer off at a 180° angle from the increased level of accountability that the public seeks from the state.

Violence-prone right-wing extremist organizations do exist in Canada, but they have little influence and their main focus has not been on Aboriginal people. Of more concern should be the more influential right-wing ideologues. Their ethnocentric, anti-statist, pro–individual rights, radical egalitarian, fiscal retrenchment philosophy is profoundly antithetical to First Nations' needs. The probability is that they will inject partisan politics into Aboriginal issues such that Aboriginal people, lacking electoral clout, will again be buffeted by political forces that are largely beyond their ability to control. A real danger is that the political atmosphere created by right-wing ideologues will lead the state to offer either mere incremental, tokenistic change, which would exacerbate the problems of distrust of government, or conversely, to offer in desperation some drastic "solution" of radical equality. Neither approach offers true justice in the sense of arrangements that permit the survival and well-being of Indians as Indians (Boldt, 1993: 57).

NOTES

1. The 1986 national survey reported here was conducted with the aid of a Sabbatical Leave Fellowship from the Social Sciences and Humanities Research Council of Canada (SSHRCC) and with funding from SSHRCC (Research Grants Division), the Multiculturalism Directorate of the federal Department of the Secretary of State (Canadian Ethnic Studies Research Program), the University of Calgary, and the sale of reports issuing from the study. Data for the 1976 study reported here were collected under a generous grant from the Donner Canadian Foundation. The Angus Reid Group conducted the 1994 study reported here. The authors express their sincere appreciation to these supporters of the projects and to the respondents, research assistants, and other support staff members without whose assistance the projects would not have been possible. Data collection in 1976 and 1986 was done under contract by Complan Research Associates Ltd. and Decima Research Ltd., respectively. Percentages cited in this section do not sum to 100 percent because "Don't Know; No Response" is usually not reported here. In the 1994 survey, the "Don't Know; No Response" category was remarkably constant at about 15 percent of the sample.

2. The statements in the 1986 Index of Support for Special Status for Natives are shown below, and are followed by the percentage of the sample agreeing (strongly or moderately) and then the percentage disagreeing (strongly or moderately) with each one:

"If Parliament and the elected leaders of the Native people agreed that some Canadian laws would not apply in Native communities, it would be all right with me" (38 percent vs 44 percent);

"Native schools should not have to follow provincial guidelines on what is taught" (22 percent vs 67 percent);

"Native governments should have powers equivalent to those of provincial governments" (31 percent vs 51 percent); and

"Native governments should be responsible to elected Native politicians, rather than to Parliament, for the federal government money they receive" (28 percent vs 44 percent).

3. Given a choice of the RCMP having the "responsibility to enforce the law on aboriginal land reserves regardless of what the band leaders might want" and the RCMP "respect[ing] the wishes of the band leaders and leaving law enforcement up to the members of the reserve," a majority (56 percent of the 1994 sample) chose the former and only 25 percent chose the latter option.

4. For instance, given the statement "It just isn't right for natives to have special rights that other Canadians don't have," 41 percent of the 1994 sample agreed and 34 percent disagreed. Similarly, in that same survey 51 percent agreed with the statement "Aboriginal Canadians who eventually have self-government on their own land base should no longer have any special status or rights," while only half as many (26 percent) disagreed.

5. For instance, almost half (46 percent) of the 1994 sample agreed that "Aboriginals should have certain formally recognized rights such as these [exemption from certain taxes, special hunting and fishing rights]," while only 37 percent disagreed.

6. The Index of Support for Native Self-Government is made up of four items. A respondent's index score is his or her average score across the four items. The items are listed below, and are followed by the percentage of the sample agreeing (strongly or moderately) and then the percentage disagreeing (strongly or moderately):

"It is important to the future well-being of Canadian society that the aspirations of Native people for self-government be met" (42 percent vs 33 percent);

"Those provincial premiers who oppose putting the right to Native self-government in the Constitution are harming Native people" (38 percent vs 34 percent);

"Most Native leaders who call for self-government for Native people are more interested in promoting their own personal career than in helping Native people" (30 percent vs 41 percent); and

"The Constitution of Canada should specifically recognize the right of Indians to self-government" (41 percent vs 40 percent).

7. In 1986, 30 percent of respondents thought that, if Native governments were adequately funded, they would be more capable than the federal government of meeting Native people's needs, while 18 percent thought the federal government would be more capable, and 37 percent thought that the two would be equally capable. In 1994, a large plurality (46 percent) was of the opinion that "if aboriginal self-government becomes a reality ... the overall standard of living and living conditions of Canada's aboriginal peoples, let's say 10 years down the road," will improve, whereas 19 percent thought it would stay the same and 18 percent thought it would get worse. Eighteen percent did not express an opinion. The stability of the "anti-Aboriginal" opinion (at 18 percent) over the eight years is noteworthy.

8. The question also asked 1994 respondents how much confidence they have in each of several other players. The full results are as follows, with the numbers in parentheses representing "a lot of confidence," "a fair amount of confidence," "not much confidence," and "no confidence at all," respec-

tively: Chiefs of large Indian bands (9 percent, 45 percent, 19 percent, and 9 percent); your provincial government (6 percent, 43 percent, 24 percent, and 10 percent); the federal government (8 percent, 45 percent, 23 percent, and 8 percent); Canada's justice system (10 percent, 43 percent, 23 percent, and 8 percent); the federal Department of Indian and Northern Affairs (5 percent, 42 percent, 26 percent, and 7 percent); Ovide Mercredi, leader of the Assembly of First Nations (15 percent, 40 percent, 14 percent, and 8 percent); Ron Irwin, the federal Minister of Indian and Northern Affairs (4 percent, 36 percent, 18 percent, and 7 percent); the Royal Commission on Aboriginal Peoples (7 percent, 40 percent, 19 percent, and 7 percent); and national Aboriginal organizations (9 percent, 50 percent, 15 percent, and 5 percent).

9. In 1986, in response to the statement "Most Native leaders who call for self-government for Native people are more interested in promoting their own personal career than in helping Native people," 30 percent agreed (anti-Native) and 41 percent disagreed (pro-Native). The 1994 survey asked: "Now, thinking about Canada's aboriginal leadership as a whole, based on your own impressions, do you think they represent the views and concerns of: all, most, some, or only a few of the aboriginal people in this country?" The responses were: 4 percent for "all"; 38 percent for "most"; 29 percent for "some"; and 13 percent for "only a few."

10. See Ponting and Gibbins (1980: 84–85) and Ponting (1987c: B11–B12) for the items constituting these indexes and for the distribution of the samples on those items.

11. In a 1988 national follow-up study, when the question was reworded to deal with special fishing rights, rather than special hunting rights, the results were virtually identical.

12. The item was phrased as follows: "blocking resource companies from taking natural resources such as timber and minerals from

lands claimed by aboriginals." Approval was given by 41.6 percent of the 1994 respondents, while 41.2 percent disapproved.

13. The item read: "Indian bands establishing gaming houses and other gambling facilities on their reserve lands without the approval of other government"; 70 percent disapproved; 15 percent approved.

14. Perceptions of conflicting group interests were measured in terms of such dimensions as the belief that Native people already receive excessive financial assistance from government, and the belief that Native people already exercise considerable power and influence with the federal or provincial government.

REFERENCES

Boldt, Menno. 1993. *Surviving as Indians. The Challenge of Self-Government.* Toronto: University of Toronto Press.

Decima Research Limited. 1987. *A Study of Canadian Attitudes toward Aboriginal Self-Government.* Toronto: Decima.

Langford, Tom, and J. Rick Ponting. 1992. "Canadians' Responses to Aboriginal Issues: The Role of Prejudice, Perceived Group Conflict, and Economic Conservatism," *Canadian Review of Sociology and Anthropology* 24, 2: 140–66.

Ponting, J. Rick. 1986. *Arduous Journey.* Toronto: McClelland and Stewart.

———. 1987a. *Profiles of Public Opinion on Canadian Natives and Native Issues.* Module 1. *Constitutional Issues.* Calgary: Research Report #87-01, Research Unit for Public Policy Studies, the University of Calgary.

———. 1987b. *Profiles of Public Opinion on Canadian Natives and Native Issues.* Module 2. *Special Status and Self-Government.* Calgary: Research Report #87-02, Research Unit for Public Policy Studies, the University of Calgary.

———. 1987c. *Profiles of Public Opinion on Canadian Natives and Native Issues.* Module 3. *Knowledge, Perceptions, and Sympathy.* Calgary: Research Report #87-03, Research Unit for Public Policy Studies, the University of Calgary.

———. 1988a. *Profiles of Public Opinion on Canadian Natives and Native Issues.* Module 4. *Native People, Finances, and Services.* Calgary: Research Report #88-01, Research Unit for Public Policy Studies, the University of Calgary.

———. 1988b. *Profiles of Public Opinion on Canadian Natives and Native Issues.* Module 5. *Land, Land Claims, and Treaties.* Calgary: Research Report #88-02, Research Unit for Public Policy Studies, the University of Calgary.

Ponting, J. Rick, and Roger Gibbins. 1980. *Out of Irrelevance: A Socio-Political Introduction to Indian Affairs in Canada.* Scarborough, ON: Butterworth.

———. 1981. "The Reactions of English Canadians and French Québécois to Native Indian Protest," *Canadian Review of Sociology and Anthropology* 18, 2: 222–38.

Chapter 17

Revisiting the Vertical Mosaic: Occupational Stratification among Canadian Ethnic Groups

HUGH LAUTARD

NEIL GUPPY

John Porter's idea of a "vertical mosaic" remains a powerful image of Canadian society (Porter, 1965). Porter depicts Canada as a composite of enduring social groups, where membership is defined principally by class and ethnicity, but also by language and religion. Porter also demonstrated the vertical ranking of these groups on a series of inequality dimensions. In the context of ethnicity, the distinctive groups in the mosaic reflect the potent force of ethnic identity, whereas the vertical alignment accentuates the hierarchy of ethnic inequality. It is an argument first of social differentiation, and second of social stratification.

The composition of the Canadian population has changed since Porter wrote, but social cleavages based on ethnicity remain important. In recent decades the vertical mosaic imagery has been reinterpreted in government circles (Abella, 1984; Boyer, 1985), where the subordinate positions of women, disabled people, Aboriginal peoples, and visible minorities have been highlighted. The "politics of difference" focuses less on class and broadly defined ethnic-ity and more on gender, disability, and "race." Responding to a growing human rights movement, new policies (e.g., the Charter of Rights and Freedoms and the 1986 Employment Equity Act) have been enacted to facilitate equality and erode the vertical mosaic.

Ironically, at a time when governments are reacting to appeals concerning human rights, some sociologists have begun questioning the durability of ethnicity as an organizing principle in the vertical mosaic. Indeed, two decades after publishing *The Vertical Mosaic*, Porter himself coauthored a paper proclaiming "the collapse of the vertical mosaic" (Pineo and Porter, 1985: 390; see also Darroch, 1979; Denis, 1986; Pineo, 1976).[1] This view runs counter to new government policies and against the grain of other sociological research demonstrating the continuation of intense ethnic antagonism and discriminatory behaviour (Henry, 1999; Robson and Breems, 1986).

Sorting out the reasons for this divergence of opinion in the current literature is our starting

Source: Excerpted from Hugh Lautard and Neil Guppy, "Revisiting the Vertical Mosaic: Occupational Stratification among Canadian Ethnic Groups," in *Race and Ethnic Relations in Canada*, 2nd ed., Peter S. Li, ed. (Toronto: Oxford University Press, 1999), pp. 219–52. Reprinted by permission of Oxford University Press.

point (see also Reitz, 1988). In reviewing that literature, we pay particular attention to research findings concerned with historical trends in the salience of ethnicity as a central component of the vertical mosaic. Is there a causal link between your ethnicity and your socioeconomic fortunes (or misfortunes)? We present new data, providing the longest historical perspective yet available on the association between ethnicity and occupation, using 60 years of census data, from 1931 to 1991. Like Porter, we stress both social differentiation and social stratification, although clearly the latter is the key to debates about the vertical mosaic.

THE DECLINING SIGNIFICANCE OF ETHNICITY?

In *The Vertical Mosaic* Porter offered three distinct observations about ethnic inequality. First, he argued that "charter status" groups, the French and English, commanded greater power and privilege than did "entrance status" groups (i.e., other immigrants) arriving later. Second, he noted an asymmetry of power favouring the English over the French. Third, he claimed that among non-charter immigrant groups, ethnic inequality persisted. For him, these three aspects of inequality were core features in the distribution of power and privilege in Canada.

Porter's most renowned evidence highlighted the economic elite; he found that "economic power belong[ed] almost exclusively to those of British origin" (Porter, 1965: 286). While the French were significantly underrepresented, members of non-charter minority groups were virtually absent among economic powerbrokers. Clement's more recent (1975) sketch of the economic elite suggested a waning of British dominance, although of 775 elite members, 86.2 percent still were English Canadian, 8.4 percent were French Canadian, and only 5.4 percent were of other ethnic origins. However, more recent data suggest that the exclusivity of the British among various Canadian elites has eroded further in the last

few decades (Ogmundson and McLaughlin, 1992). While anglophone families like the Thomsons, Westons, and Blacks continue as dominant forces in Canada, other powerbrokers from non-Anglo backgrounds, such as Frank Stronach and Li Ka-shing, compete for elite status. Relative to the proportion of people of British origin in the population, elite members of British origin are still overrepresented among the elite (Nakhaie, 1997). However, a Canadian elite that was at one time almost exclusively British now has more representation from other ethnic groups.

Porter (1965) also presented data from the 1931, 1951, and 1961 censuses. Crossclassifying ethnic origin and occupation, he determined the extent to which various groups were over- and underrepresented in different job categories. In the 1931 census he found that British and Jewish groups ranked high (i.e., they were overrepresented in professional and financial occupations, and underrepresented in low-level, unskilled, and primary jobs); and that the "French, German, and Dutch would probably rank next, followed by Scandinavian, Eastern European, Italian, Japanese, 'Other Central European,' Chinese, and Native Indian" (Porter, 1965: 81). He concluded that by 1961 and "except for the French [who had slipped], the rough rank order [had] persisted over time" (Porter, 1965: 90).

Porter offered two complementary, although independent, explanations for the differential representation of ethnic groups by occupation level. First, immigrants constitute a significant portion of the Canadian labour force (more than one in five as late as 1971), and traditionally Canada has attracted a polarized population of both the well educated and the poorly educated, with relatively few people in between.[2] New immigrants in Canada reinforce traditional patterns of occupational inequality since one difference between ethnic groups is the occupation level of their immigrants (Porter, 1965: 86; 1985: 40–51). For instance, new British immigrants acquire professional and financial jobs more often then do recent Eastern European immigrants, who disproportionately take up unskilled, lower-level positions.

Second, Porter also suggested that, once in Canada, ethnic groups differed in the extent to which they aspired to upward occupational mobility. Some ethnic groups valued achievement less than others, either because of cultural differences (e.g., less emphasis on material reward) or because of perceived or experienced discriminatory barriers (for a recent statement, see Pineo and Porter, 1985: 360–1). However, to the extent that ethnic assimilation occurred, Porter reasoned that ethnic origin exerted less impact on individual occupational mobility. Conversely, in the face of continued ethnic affiliations, mobility was limited or blocked.

Darroch (1979) undertook an ambitious revision of Porter's original interpretation. He suggests that Porter paid too much attention to the persistence of a "rough rank order" over the three censuses, and failed to note the diminishing strength of the association between ethnicity and occupation level. Quite simply, Porter was not sensitive enough to the fact that the occupational over- and underrepresentation of ethnic groups was much less in 1961 than had been the case in 1931. Darroch reviewed other evidence, including data from the 1971 census, to show that the salience of ethnicity for occupational allocation had diminished over time. He concluded that the idea of blocked ethnic mobility had no foundation in fact and that we should be "skeptical of the idea that ethnic affiliations are a basic factor in generally limiting mobility opportunities in Canada" (Darroch, 1979: 16).

These sentiments were echoed by Winn (1985) in the context of government policy debates. He was sharply critical of the Abella Commission's call for the introduction of affirmative-action programs to augment mobility prospects for groups whose progress had remained "unjustifiably in perpetual slow motion" (Abella, 1984: 4). Winn reviewed data from the 1971 and 1981 censuses, concluding that his evidence provided "no empirical support for the premise that Canadian society is immobile and that visible or low prestige groups cannot make economic progress" (1985: 689). Affirmative action was unnecessary, he said, because the ethnic inequality implied by the vertical mosaic was exaggerated.

A more pessimistic conclusion concerning the continuing salience of ethnicity as a basis for inequality appears in Lautard and Loree (1984). Using more detailed occupation data, they agreed with Darroch's finding that occupational inequality among ethnic groups had declined over time. But whereas Darroch (1979: 22) was willing to conclude that ethnicity was no longer a fundamental source of inequality, Lautard and Loree (1984: 342) maintained that "occupational inequality is still substantial enough to justify the use of the concept 'vertical mosaic' to characterize this aspect of ethnic relations in Canada."

Porter (1985: 44–51) repeated his earlier analysis with the 1971 census and, agreeing with Lautard and Loree, claimed that "ethnic stratification has persisted through to 1971" (Porter, 1985: 48). Here he offers no hints about a "collapse" of the vertical mosaic. The census, however, contains data for both the foreign-born and the native-born, and so it confounds the two explanations that Porter offered for the association between ethnicity and occupation.

Working with Pineo (Pineo and Porter, 1985), Porter demonstrated that the strength of the association between ethnic origin and occupational status had attenuated in recent decades (up to 1973), at least for males from the major European ethnic groups.[3] They also showed that for native-born Canadian men, ethnic origin had no significant influence on individual occupational mobility. This latter finding suggests that the thesis of blocked ethnic mobility does not persist for second- and third-generation Canadian men from the major European ethnic groups.

If, as these data show, occupational mobility is *not* limited by ethnic origin for many groups, then of Porter's two explanations for the ethnicity-occupation link, immigration would seem now to be the remaining factor. Boyd's (1985) research on the influence of birthplace on occupational attainment supports this interpretation. For foreign-born men and women, she showed that ethnic origin had a definite effect on occupational attainment, even after controlling for differences in the average age, education, social origin, and place of residence of ethnic groups. For women she found evidence of sex and birthplace as factors underlying the Canadian mosaic (Boyd, 1985: 441).

If education attainment is used to measure the ethnic vertical mosaic, clear evidence exists that British dominance has eroded. As Herberg (1990) reports when examining the possession of postsecondary credentials, "of the top one-third of groups, ... five of the six highest are visible minority groups" (with Jews as the sixth group). Similarly, using only people born in Canada, Geschwender and Guppy (1995: 80) conclude that "the vertical mosaic, at least on the dimension of education, has undergone a significant reshuffling in recent times." However, both these studies also report "ethnic penalties" when it comes to translating education into occupational position and income attainment. Herberg (1990: 218) speaks of "brutal income inequality" for visible minorities, while Geschwender and Guppy (1995: 81) point to "financial penalties" for members of specific ethnic groups (e.g., French, First Nations, Italian, Jewish, Chinese), although these penalties are paid more by men than women (see also Agocs and Boyd, 1993).

Part of the dispute over whether an ethnic component to the vertical mosaic has persisted in Canada is reflected in the proverbial "Is the glass half full or half empty?" Exactly how much inequality is enough to attribute it "fundamental" status? However, a far larger part of the dispute turns on matters of both theoretical definition and methodological procedure. For example, both Winn and Porter (in his early work) relied mainly on rank-ordered data, and Darroch was correct in contending that the size

of the gap between ranks is crucial. But further, as Lautard and Loree insisted, the gap's size depends on the number of occupations considered, and so they improved the quality of evidence by looking at a wider range of occupation levels. In addition, the use of differing ethnic categories (especially notable in survey-based as opposed to census data) makes comparison and definitive conclusion precarious.

Key issues of theoretical and methodological dispute revolve around three aspects: the ethnic groups studied, the occupation levels considered, and the purity of historical comparability. These are reviewed in turn.

ETHNIC GROUPS

The definition of ethnicity remains contentious in the social science literature, and this debate touches directly on ethnic inequality and the vertical mosaic. Census data have been among the principal sources of evidence in evaluating the association between ethnic origin and occupation level. However, until 1981 the census definition of ethnicity relied on tracing ancestral male lineage, often a difficult task after several generations, especially given interethnic marriages and historical changes in national boundaries around the world.

In addition, Statistics Canada is reluctant about releasing detailed information for relatively small groups, and so ethnic categories have frequently been combined to form groups of mixed origin (e.g., Asian, Scandinavian). Typically the following ethnic categories have been used in the census: British (English, Irish, Scottish), French, German, Italian, Jewish, Dutch, Scandinavian, Eastern European (Polish, Ukrainian), Other European, Asian, and Native Indian.[4]

OCCUPATIONS

Porter (1965) relied on five broad occupation groups and a residual category for his 1931 to 1961 census analysis: professional and financial, clerical, personal service, primary and unskilled, agriculture, and all others. By 1961 the residual category ("all others") had swollen to 58 percent of the total. For the sake of comparability, Darroch's (1979) reanalysis was forced to employ these crude groupings, but Lautard and Loree (1984) began afresh and used more refined occupation distinctions, amounting to hundreds of separate job categories for each census.

Also at issue is how occupation differences are understood. Attention can centre on whether or not ethnic groups tend to be concentrated in different occupations (a focus on the ethnic division of labour, i.e., social differentiation). Alternatively, if ethnic groups tend to congregate in different occupations, then the relative placement of occupations in the status hierarchy is crucial (a focus on the occupational prestige hierarchy, i.e., social stratification).

HISTORICAL COMPARABILITY

Changes in the occupation structure and in the countries of origin of immigrants have meant that census procedures have had to be revised over the years. For occupation, this has meant both the addition and deletion of job titles (e.g., computer programmer). For ethnicity, one crucial change is in reporting procedures. For instance, in the early years when European groups dominated, little detail was made available for such visible minorities as Blacks or Indo-Pakistanis (even though both groups have a long history in Canada). Also, questions for ethnicity change with almost every recent census (see Kralt, 1980).[5]

Since census definitions of occupations have changed over time there are advantages and disadvantages in the use of both broad and narrow occupational groups. The broad groups maximize comparability over time because most specific jobs are still classified in the same broad categories from one census to the next. However, the broad categories obscure crucial status gradations and are thus more useful in distinguishing social differentiation than social stratification, and the latter is the more important component in the current debate. Using more occupations gives a more refined calibration of inequality at any one point in time, although it does so by sacrificing comparability over time.

MEASURING ETHNIC OCCUPATIONAL STRATIFICATION

We need a method of summarizing the general pattern of occupational stratification to make comparisons among groups, to determine trends across census years, and to compare our results with those of previous studies (e.g., Darroch, 1979). The most widely used summary measure is the index of dissimilarity. This index is calculated by subtracting the percentage of an ethnic group in each occupational category from that of the total labour force. Separate analyses are conducted for men and women. Normally, in a pair of distributions, there will be the same number of positive differences as negative differences, subject to rounding. The total of all positive differences (or all negative differences) is the percentage of ethnic group members who would have to have a different occupation in order for the group's occupational distribution to match that of the total labour force. Thus, the greater the index value, the greater the occupational differentiation.[6]

For example, say the index of dissimilarity for British males is 3. This means that only 3 percent of the British men in the labour force would have to be in a different occupational category for there to be no difference between their occupational distribution and that of the total male labour force. If the index of dissimilarity for Portuguese women is 27 percent, this indicates much greater differentiation. It means that more than one Portuguese woman in four would have to be in a different occupational group in order for them to have the same occupational distribution as the total female labour force.

Finally, measures such as the index of dissimilarity are most appropriately calculated for a group in comparison with the total labour force *minus that group* to correct for the presence of the group itself in the total (Duncan and Duncan, 1955: 494). Accordingly, the results presented in the next section indicate the differentials between each ethnic group and the rest of the labour force rather than between groups and the total labour force (as in the examples given earlier).

Dissimilarity, however, does not necessarily mean disadvantage. As a method of capturing stratification, as opposed to differentiation, another measure is appropriate—the index of net difference. This measure is calculated with occupational data ranked according to socioeconomic scales such as those prepared by Blishen (1958) for 1951; Blishen (1967) for 1961; Blishen and McRoberts (1976) and Blishen and Carroll (1978) for males and females, respectively, for 1971; and Blishen, Carroll, and Moore (1987) for 1981 and 1991.

Related to the index of dissimilarity but more complicated in its calculation, the index of net difference provides a measure of the overall occupational ranking of a group in relation to the rest of the labour force. Indexes of net difference may be negative as well as positive, with a minus sign indicating comparatively lower occupational status and a positive sign comparatively higher status. In either case, the greater the absolute value of the index, the greater the degree of occupational inequality. A net difference of zero would indicate overall equality of occupational status.[7] If we use the image of an occupational "ladder," members of an ethnic group with a positive index of net difference would on average be positioned higher on the ladder than the rest of the labour force. A negative index would indicate that on balance the group is lower on the occupational ladder than the rest of the labour force. Finally, zero net difference would indicate that on average members of the group are neither higher nor lower on the ladder than the rest of the total labour force. We now turn to the results of the analysis of ethnic occupational differentiation and stratification

in Canada, using the indexes of dissimilarity and net difference.[8]

OCCUPATIONAL STRATIFICATION AMONG CANADIAN ETHNIC GROUPS, 1931–1991

Table 17.1 contains Lautard and Loree's (1984) indexes of occupational dissimilarity for the ethnic groups examined by Porter (1965) and Darroch (1979) for the census years 1931 through 1971. The higher the measured occupational dissimilarity, the more unlike are the occupational profiles of different ethnic groups. Our indexes show the decline in occupational differentiation found by Darroch, although we show higher levels of dissimilarity because we include more occupations. The indexes for men in 1961, for example, include no values lower than 15 percent, and the mean (29) is more than double that yielded by Darroch's analysis (14). By 1971 there is one value for men lower than 15 percent, but again the mean (24) is nearly double that calculated by Darroch (14) for both sexes combined.

After 1931, when the average dissimilarity for females is the same as that for males (37 percent), ethnic differentiation among women in the paid labour force is less than that among men, but even by 1971 only four groups (German, Dutch, Scandinavian, and Polish) have indexes of 15 percent or less, and all these are above 10 percent; the mean for women in 1971 is 21 percent. Thus, on average, in 1971 a quarter of the male labour force and a fifth of the female labour force would have to have had different occupations in order for there to have been no occupational dissimilarity among ethnic groups. It is also evident from Table 17.1 that while the standard deviations, like the means, decline between 1931 and 1971, relative variation (V) undergoes a net increase for both sexes. The rankings of ethnic groups by degree of dissimilarity, moreover, remain remarkably stable, with the Italian, Jewish, Asian, and Native

TABLE 17.1   OCCUPATIONAL DISSIMILARITY BETWEEN SELECTED ETHNIC GROUPS AND THE REST OF THE LABOUR FORCE, BY SEX: 1931, 1951, 1961, AND 1971

ETHNIC GROUP	MALE				FEMALE			
	1931	1951	1961	1971	1931	1951	1961	1971
British	22	20	19	15	27	23	22	16
French	15	17	16	14	26	23	17	17
German*	24	23	17	15	20	14	13	11
Italian	48	34	40	35	39	24	45	38
Jewish	65	63	59	51	51	40	34	32
Dutch	21	20	17	17	14	17	15	15
Scandinavian	29	23	18	17	25	13	10	12
Polish	34**	23	18	15	45**	21	17	14
Ukrainian		28	21	15		22	21	16
Other European†	43	21	19	21	49	18	20	23
Asian‡	61	46	45	36	50	25	20	25
Native Indian††	49	57	57	41	59	53	48	31
Mean (x̄)	37	31	29	24	37	24	24	21
Standard deviation(s)	17	16	17	13	15	11	12	9
V (s/x̄)	.46	.52	.59	.54	.41	.46	.50	.43
(Number of occupations)	(388)	(278)	(332)	(496)	(265)	(226)	(277)	(412)

*Includes Austrian in 1931.
**Eastern European (Polish and Ukrainian combined).
†Other Central European in 1931.
‡Weighted average of Chinese and Japanese in 1931.
††Includes Eskimos in 1951.

SOURCES: 1931: Dominion Bureau of Statistics, *Seventh Census of Canada, 1931*, vol. 7, *Occupations and Industries* (Ottawa: King's Printer, 1936), Table 49; 1951: Dominion Bureau of Statistics, *Ninth Census of Canada, 1951*, vol. 4, *Labour Force: Occupations and Industries* (Ottawa: Queen's Printer, 1953), Table 12; 1961: Dominion Bureau of Statistics, *1961 Census of Canada*, vol. 3, Part 1 (Bulletin 3.1-15), *Labour Force: Occupations by Sex, Showing Birthplace, Period of Immigration and Ethnic Group: Canada and Provinces*, Catalogue no. 94-515 (Ottawa: Queen's Printer, 1964), Table 21; 1971: Statistics Canada, *1971 Census of Canada*, vol. 3, Part 3 (Bulletin 3.3-7), *Occupations: Occupations by Sex, Showing Birthplace, Period of Immigration and Ethnic Group, for Canada and Regions*, Catalogue no. 94-734 (Ottawa: Information Canada, 1975), Table 4. This table is reproduced from Lautard and Loree (1984, Table 1).

Indian groups tending to be more dissimilar from the rest.

As noted above, occupational dissimilarity does not necessarily involve inequality of occupational status. Table 17.2 presents Lautard and Loree's (1984) indexes of net difference in occupational status between each ethnic group and the total labour force for 1951 through 1971.[9]

The few positive indexes reflect the relatively high occupational rank of the British, Jewish, and, by 1971, Asian groups, as well as a relative advantage in 1951 and 1961 for Scandinavian females. The negative values indicate the relatively low status of the other groups. With one exception (women of Italian origin in 1971), the largest negative indexes are those for Native

Indians, for whom even the 1971 indexes exceed −.30 for males and −.20 for females. Between 1951 and 1971, mean ethnic inequality declined, as did the standard deviations and the relative variation (V), but the latter remains very high for both sexes. The most pronounced shifts in the rank-order of the ethnic groups by relative occupational status include the Asian and Polish men, rising from a tie at third lowest in 1951 to second- and sixth-highest respectively in 1971; and Italian females dropping from fifth-highest

in 1951 to lowest in 1971. Otherwise, the ranking of ethnic groups by relative occupational status is about as stable as that by occupational dissimilarity.

Table 17.3 contains indexes of dissimilarity for sixteen ethnic groups as of 1971, and seventeen as of 1981 and 1991. The replacement of "Other European" with Hungarian, Portuguese, Greek, and Yugoslav, and "Asian" with Chinese and South Asian, results in higher average dissimilarity for 1971 than in Table 17.1: 30 and 27 per-

TABLE 17.2   NET DIFFERENCE IN OCCUPATIONAL STATUS BETWEEN ETHNIC GROUPS AND THE TOTAL LABOUR FORCE, BY SEX: 1951, 1961, AND 1971

	MALE			FEMALE		
ETHNIC GROUP	1951	1961	1971	1951	1961	1971
British	.09	.11	.07	.11	.12	.07
French	−.11	−.10	−.04	−.11	−.07	−.01
German	−.03	−.06	−.07	−.13	−.11	−.09
Italian	−.15	−.28	−.21	−.08	−.37	−.34
Jewish	.41	.42	.35	.20	.21	.24
Dutch	−.10	−.09	−.09	−.15	−.12	−.10
Scandinavian	−.04	−.05	−.08	−.01	−.03	−.01
Polish	−.14	−.07	−.07	−.20	−.16	−.12
Ukrainian	−.11	−.10	−.09	−.20	−.19	−.12
Other European	−.12	−.11	−.11	−.17	−.19	−.20
Asian	−.14	−.03	−.10	−.06	−.05	−.01
Native Indian*	−.68	−.63	−.34	−.55	−.47	−.23
Mean ($\bar{x}$)	.18	.17	.14	.16	.17	.13
Standard deviation(s)	.19	.18	.11	.14	.13	.10
V ($s/\bar{x}$)	1.06	1.06	.79	.88	.76	.77
(Number of occupational ranks**)	(208)	(298)	(496)	(178)	(252)	(412)

*Includes Eskimo in 1951.
**May not equal the number of occupations in Table 17.1 because of ties.

SOURCES: 1951: Dominion Bureau of Statistics, *Ninth Census of Canada, 1951*, vol. 4, *Labour Force: Occupations and Industries* (Ottawa: Queen's Printer, 1953), Table 12; 1961: Dominion Bureau of Statistics, *1961 Census of Canada*, vol. 3, Part 1 (Bulletin 3.1-15), *Labour Force: Occupations by Sex, Showing Birthplace, Period of Immigration and Ethnic Group: Canada and Provinces*, Catalogue no. 94-515 (Ottawa: Queen's Printer, 1964), Table 21; 1971: Statistics Canada, *1971 Census of Canada*, vol. 3, Part 3 (Bulletin 3.3-7), *Occupations: Occupations by Sex, Showing Birthplace, Period of Immigration and Ethnic Group, for Canada and Regions*, Catalogue no. 94-734 (Ottawa: Information Canada, 1975), Table 4. This table is reproduced from Lautard and Loree (1984, Table 2).

cent, for males and females respectively, compared with 24 and 21 percent. Between 1971 and 1981 ethnic occupational differentiation generally declined. The only exceptions are the indexes for men of Dutch and Scandinavian origin and Jewish women, each of which are one point higher in 1981 than 1971, and the indexes for men of French and German origin and for Scandinavian women, which are the same for both years. Over

the 1970s, average ethnic dissimilarity declined 3 points among men and 4 points among women, to 27 and 23 percent, respectively, as of 1981.

Over the 1980s, occupational dissimilarity declined among both men and women for nine of the seventeen ethnic groups, including the Southern European, Jewish, Chinese, and South Asian groups, as well as for the Native Indians and Métis and for Blacks; women of Hungarian

TABLE 17.3   OCCUPATIONAL DISSIMILARITY* BETWEEN SELECTED ETHNIC GROUPS AND THE REST OF THE LABOUR FORCE, BY SEX: 1971, 1981, AND 1991

ETHNIC GROUP	MALE			FEMALE		
	1971	1981	1991	1971	1981	1991
British	15	10	10	16	9	7
French	14	14	15	18	14	14
German	15	15	16	11	9	11
Dutch	16	17	19	15	13	14
Scandinavian	17	18	19	12	12	14
Ukrainian	15	13	15	16	9	11
Polish	15	14	17	14	10	15
Hungarian	21	19	19	20	15	14
Italian	35	26	21	38	25	18
Portuguese	46	42	36	57	48	33
Greek	48	45	36	51	42	31
Yugoslav	33	31	26	35	29	23
Jewish	51	49	47	32	33	31
Chinese	52	44	38	34	30	27
South Asian	46	34	29	31	27	24
Indian and Métis	41	37	36	32	29	27
Black	NI	32	28	NI	30	27
Mean ($\bar{x}$)	30	27	25	27	23	20
Standard deviation(s)	15	13	10	14	12	8
V ($s/\bar{x}$)	.50	.48	.41	.52	.52	.41
(Number of occupations)	(498)	(496)	(512)	(464)	(495)	(512)

*Each figure in the table indicates the percentage of the ethnic group that would have to have a different occupation in order for there to be no difference between the occupational distribution of that group and the rest of the labour force.
NI: Not included.

SOURCE: Special tabulations of census data.

origin also have a lower index in 1991 than in 1981. The indexes for men of British and Hungarian origin and for women of French origin show no change, while those for men of French origin and for both men and women of German, Dutch, Scandinavian, Ukrainian, and Polish origin are higher in 1991 than 1981. Average ethnic dissimilarity declined by 2 points for men and 3 points for women between 1981 and 1991. As of 1991, on average, one-quarter (25 percent) of the men and one-fifth (20 percent) of the women would have to have a different occupation in order for there to be no occupational differentiation among these ethnic groups.

Thus, with the exception of the indexes for men and women of Scandinavian and Polish origin and for men of French, German, and Dutch origin, which are higher in 1991 than 1971, and those for men of Ukrainian and women of German origin, which are the same in 1991 as in 1971, the figures in Table 17.3 indicate continuing declines in ethnic occupational differentiation. Nevertheless, relative variation in occupational dissimilarity among ethnic groups remained over 40 percent, with the Northern and Eastern European groups generally below the means, while, with a few exceptions, the Southern European, Jewish, and Asian groups, as well as the Blacks and Native Indians and Métis, are above the means for each of the three census years under consideration. In addition, 1991 data for people of Arab, Filipino, and Indo-Chinese origins yield indexes generally in the 40s, which, if included in the analysis, would raise the means for men and women to 27 and 23, respectively.

Table 17.4 presents indexes of net difference in occupational status between each of the ethnic groups and the rest of the labour force as of 1971, 1981, and 1991. The results for 1971 are consistent with those in Table 17.2. With the exception of the indexes for those of British, Jewish, and South Asian origin, all values for 1971 are negative. As well, in 1971 those of Southern European origins, along with Native Indians and Métis, have lower overall occupa-

tional status than the rest of the groups examined. While occupational inequality among ethnic groups continued to decline among both men and women over the 1970s and 1980s, there have been some shifts in the relative rank order of the groups. The indexes for men of British and Jewish origin remain positive, while those for men of Eastern European and Scandinavian origin become positive in 1981. By 1991, men of South Asian origin have lower overall occupational status than the rest of the male labour force, while those of Italian and Yugoslav origin rank with those of German and Dutch origin. Black men have a negative index in 1981 and even lower occupational status in 1991 when, along with men of Portuguese and Greek origin and Native Indian and Métis men, they have lower overall occupational status than men of all other ethnic origins. The relative occupational status of Chinese men drops over the 1970s but rises over the 1980s, with the indexing becoming positive in 1991.

Among women, the indexes for those of British and Jewish origin remain positive over the 1970s and 1980s, while those for women of Scandinavian and Ukrainian origin become positive. No overall difference in occupational status vis-à-vis the rest of the female labour force is indicated for women of French origin in 1981 or 1991, or for women of Hungarian origin in 1991. Not unlike that of men of Italian origin, overall occupational status of Italian women increases to the point that by 1991 they rank with women of German and Dutch origin, while other women of Southern European origin, along with women of South Asian origin and Native Indian and Métis women, have lower overall occupational status than women of all other origins, including Black women. The occupational status of Black women declined much less, while that of South Asian women declined much more, in both absolute and relative terms and with respect to change in rank order. By 1991 there was a clear tendency for non-European and Native Indian and Métis women, along with Southern European (except

TABLE 17.4   NET DIFFERENCE IN OCCUPATIONAL STATUS* BETWEEN SELECTED ETHNIC GROUPS AND THE REST OF THE LABOUR FORCE, BY SEX: 1971, 1981, AND 1991

ETHNIC GROUP	MALE			FEMALE		
	1971	1981	1991	1971	1981	1991
British	.13	.06	.04	.14	.06	.04
French	−.06	−.04	−.01	−.02	.00	.00
German	−.08	−.02	−.04	−.09	−.04	−.06
Dutch	−.09	−.06	−.04	−.10	−.06	−.04
Scandinavian	−.08	.01	−.01	−.01	.03	.01
Ukrainian	−.09	.01	.01	−.13	.00	.02
Polish	−.08	.03	.01	−.12	−.01	−.03
Hungarian	−.06	.03	.03	−.13	−.03	−.00
Italian	−.22	−.12	−.04	−.35	−.19	−.05
Portuguese	−.38	−.33	−.27	−.62	−.40	−.29
Greek	−.27	−.31	−.20	−.48	−.36	−.22
Yugoslav	−.12	−.05	−.04	−.29	−.18	−.10
Jewish	.36	.30	.34	.24	.27	.29
Chinese	−.04	−.08	.02	−.20	−.14	−.07
South Asian	.26	.09	−.03	.19	−.09	−.14
Indian and Métis	−.35	−.25	−.25	−.23	−.18	−.15
Black	NI	−.02	−.12	NI	−.02	−.07
Mean ($\bar{x}$)	.17	.11	.09	.21	.12	.09
Standard deviation(s)	.12	.11	.11	.16	.13	.09
V ($s/\bar{x}$)	.71	1.00	1.21	.76	1.08	1.01
(Number of occupational ranks**)	(498)	(468)	(485)	(464)	(467)	(485)

*A negative figure indicates relatively lower overall occupational status, a positive figure relatively higher status. Zero indicates overall equality of occupational status. The greater the absolute size of the index, the greater the inequality.

**May not equal the number of occupations in Table 17.3 because of tied ranks.

NI: Not included.

SOURCE: Special tabulations of census data.

for Italian) women, to have the lowest overall occupational statuses.

Although for both women and men average occupational inequality among ethnic groups continued to decline, almost all of the decrease occurred over the 1970s, and as of 1981 and 1991 relative variation in ethnic inequality was at or above unity. Moreover, 1991 data for people of Arab, Filipino, and Indo-Chinese origins yielded negative indexes (except for that of Arab men [+.03]), which, if included in the analysis, would raise average occupational inequality for women to .11, while leaving that for men unchanged, and maintain relative variation at the comparatively high levels of unity for both.

THE VERTICAL MOSAIC, 1931–1991

The historical comparison of ethnic inequality, as measured by occupational differences, suggests that between 1931 and 1991 there has been a decline in the significance of ethnicity. The decline has been moderate, however, with ethnic origin continuing to influence occupational destination.

The trend in occupational dissimilarity indicates a reduction in the ethnic division of labour of roughly 30 percent for men and 40 percent for women in 60 years. Social differentiation based on ethnicity is slowly eroding. The comparable results in ethnic occupational stratification reveal a reduction of 50 percent for men and 44 percent for women, although over a shorter time span (from 1951 to 1991). These historical comparisons are admittedly crude, and we caution that precise calculations are impossible.

Do these results imply a "collapse" in the vertical mosaic? Using 1971 census data, Porter himself felt that "ethnic stratification" had persisted. For males, Tables 17.3 and 17.4 both reveal very small declines in differentiation and stratification between 1971 and 1991, affording no firm grounds for repudiating Porter's claim. For females, the 1971 to 1991 changes have been larger, but by 1991 levels of differentiation and stratification among women of various ethnic groups are still similar to those for men.

An alternative method of illustrating how large or how small the reported differences are is to compare the differentiation and stratification among ethnic groups with similar differences between women and men. Our 1991 data set yields an index of dissimilarity between the occupational distributions of men and women of 54 percent. This figure is greater than the 1991 ethnic averages we report (25 percent among men; 20 percent among women) and

indeed is greater than the dissimilarity measured for any single ethnic group. Still, certain groups (Jewish men and women of both Filipino and Indo-Chinese origins) have dissimilarity scores closer to figures for gender than to the respective ethnic mean.

Using socioeconomic status (SES) as the dimension that best illustrates the vertical mosaic, the ethnic distribution can once more be compared with differences between women and men. In this case, ethnic inequality is greater than gender inequality (see, e.g., Darroch, 1979: 13). This comparison obscures much of the known inequality between women and men (SES scores combine education and income, and typically women in the labour force are paid less but have higher levels of schooling than men). Thus, the index of net difference in women's overall occupational status compared with that of men is –.07 in 1991, whereas the average absolute value for ethnicity is .09 among both men and women (.11 for women if people of Arab, Filipino, and Indo-Chinese origins are included).

What these two comparisons of gender differences with ethnic differences suggest is that the gendered division of labour is more marked than is the ethnic division of labour. That is, men and women tend to be clustered in "sex-typed" jobs more often than members of specific ethnic groups are concentrated in "ethnic-linked" jobs. However, when the comparison is made on the dimension of socioeconomic status, inequality is more marked among ethnic groups than it is between the genders (granting, however, the limitations of SES comparisons between women and men).

Porter's "vertical mosaic" interpretation of Canadian society rested upon far more than ethnic occupational differentiation. As we noted earlier, the penetration of ethnic members into elite groups, a key element of the vertical mosaic, has remained limited. Nevertheless, some progress has been made here too, as the new "entrepreneurial" immigration category suggests, and certainly visible minorities have done well in selected occupational niches—among professionals, for example (Lambert, Ledoux, and Pendakur, 1989).

The research design that we have employed prohibits us from investigating which of Porter's two dynamics best explains the continuing level of ethnic inequality: differential immigration or blocked mobility. Our reading of the research literature suggests that immigration continues as the more important factor, especially in terms of visible minorities (McDade, 1988; Sorensen, 1995). But even here, the bimodal character of Canadian immigration, to which Porter initially drew attention, continues. However, immigration patterns cannot be the sole explanation because our results are also consistent with research showing that visible minorities face earning penalties in the labour market, penalties that are consistent with the blocked mobility thesis (see e.g., Geschwender and Guppy, 1995; Li, 1988; Lian and Matthews, 1998).

Finally, whatever the actual extent and sources of the vertical mosaic, it coexists with other aspects of ethnic and racial inequality beyond the scope of our analysis, including prejudice, hate, and violence, as well as systematic and systemic discrimination in recruitment, interviewing, hiring, promotion, training, and termination practices. Similarly, among the "paradoxes of racism in Canadian society" is the "invisibility" of visible minorities, who "are excluded from ... political, social, and economic institutions ... [as well as from] the official history of Canada" (Henry et al., 1995: 85).

NOTES

The authors gratefully acknowledge the assistance of Donnalouise Watts and the contributions of the editor, Peter Li, and an anonymous reviewer to the development of this chapter. The research reported here was supported by an SSHRCC Leave Fellowship and an SSHRCC Research Grant awarded to Hugh Lautard, a Killam Research Fellowship awarded to Neil Guppy, and grants from the University of New Brunswick Research Fund.

1. Porter died before this paper was published, and it is unclear whether he saw the concluding section, from which this quotation is taken, before his death.

2. For much of Canada's history, foreign-born workers have had a higher level of education than have native-born Canadians (see Boyd, 1985; Légacé, 1968). What this average hides, however, is the tendency for immigrants to be either relatively well or relatively poorly educated.

3. In this particular analysis Porter included the following ethnic groups: English, Irish, Scottish, French, German, Dutch, Italian, Jewish, Polish, Ukrainian, Norwegian, Russian, and a residual (other) category.

4. Winn's work is the exception here in that he reports on only "selected" ethnic groups; from the 1981 census, he reports on neither the British nor the Germans, for example.

5. Prior to 1981 the census question to determine ethnic origin was: "To which ethnic or cultural group did you or your ancestor (on the male side) belong on coming to this continent?" In 1981 the question was: "To which ethnic or cultural group did you or your ancestors belong on first coming to this continent?" Notice, especially, how difficult it is for Native Indians to accurately answer this question. Also in 1981, and for the first time, multiple origins were accepted. The 1991 question read "To which ethnic or cultural group(s) did this person's ancestors belong?"

6. The index of dissimilarity may also be obtained by adding all the differences between two percentage distributions, without regard to signs, and dividing the sum by two (Duncan and Duncan, 1955: 494). For the present study, each ethnic group was compared with the rest of the labour force (i.e., the total labour force, less the group in question).

7. Specifically, a negative index of net difference indicates the extent to which the probability of a member of the ethnic group in question will have a lower occupational rank than a member of the rest of the labour force exceeds the opposite probability, assuming random pairing. A positive value indicates the opposite relation, while zero would indicate that the two probabilities are the same (Lieberson, 1975: 279–80).

8. As summary measures, of course, the index of dissimilarity and the index of net difference are not without limitations in their ability to reflect occupational differentiation and inequality, respectively. For example, the index of dissimilarity is insensitive to variation in the pattern of differences between two distributions, while the index of net difference is less than ideal for analyzing inequality among groups polarized with respect to occupational status, as ethnic groups containing substantial numbers of immigrants will be.

9. Because there is no occupational ranking for 1931, there are no indexes of net difference in occupational status for that year.

REFERENCES

Abella, Rosalie. 1984. *Equality in Employment: A Royal Commission Report.* Ottawa: Minister of Supply and Services.

Agocs, Carol, and Monica Boyd. 1993. "The Canadian Ethnic Mosaic Recast: Theory, Research and Policy Frameworks for the 1990s." Pp. 330–52 in James Curtis, Edward Grabb, and Neil Guppy, eds., *Social Inequality in Canada: Patterns, Problems, Policies,* 2nd ed. Toronto: Prentice-Hall.

Blishen, Bernard R. 1958. "The Construction and Use of an Occupational Class Scale." *Canadian Journal of Economics and Political Science* 24, no. 4: 519–31.

———. 1967. "A Socio-economic Index for Occupations in Canada." *Canadian Review of Sociology and Anthropology* 4, no. 1: 41–53.

Blishen, Bernard R., and William K. Carroll. 1978. "Sex Differences in a Socio-economic Index for Occupations in Canada." *Canadian Review of Sociology and Anthropology* 15, no. 3: 352–71.

Blishen, Bernard R., William K. Carroll, and Catherine Moore. 1987. "The 1981 Socio-economic Index for Occupations in Canada." *Canadian Review of Sociology and Anthropology* 24, no. 4: 465–88.

Blishen, Bernard R., and Hugh A. McRoberts. 1976. "A Revised Socio-economic Index for Occupations in Canada." *Canadian Review of Sociology and Anthropology* 13, no. 1: 71–9.

Boyd, Monica. 1985. "Immigration and Occupational Attainment." Pp. 393–446 in M. Boyd, ed., *Ascription and Attainment: Studies in Mobility and Status Attainment in Canada.* Ottawa: Carleton University Press.

Boyer, J. Patrick. 1985. *Equality for All. Report of the Parliamentary Committee on Equal Rights.* Ottawa: Minister of Supply and Services.

Clement, Wallace. 1975. *The Canadian Corporate Elite.* Toronto: McClelland and Stewart.

Darroch, Gordon. 1979. "Another Look at Ethnicity, Stratification and Social Mobility in Canada." *Canadian Journal of Sociology* 4, no. 1: 1–25.

Denis, Ann. 1986. "Adaptation to Multiple Subordination? Women in the Vertical Mosaic." *Canadian Ethnic Studies* 18, no. 3: 61–74.

Dominion Bureau of Statistics. 1936. *Seventh Census of Canada*, 1931. Vol. 7. Ottawa: King's Printer.

———. 1953. *Ninth Census of Canada*, 1951. Vol. 4. *Labour Force: Occupations and Industries.* Ottawa: Queen's Printer.

———. 1964. *1961 Census of Canada.* Vol. 3, Part 1 (Bulletin 3.1-15). *Labour Force: Occupations by Sex, Showing Birthplace, Period of Immigration and Ethnic Group:*

Canada and Provinces. Catalogue no. 94-515. Ottawa: Queen's Printer.

Duncan, Otis Dudley, and Beverly Duncan. 1955. "Residential Distribution and Occupational Stratification." *American Journal of Sociology* 60, no. 5: 493–503.

Geschwender, Jim, and Neil Guppy. 1995. "Ethnicity, Educational Attainment, and Earned Income among Canadian-Born Men and Women." *Canadian Ethnic Studies* 27, no. 1: 67–83.

Henry, Frances. 1999. "Two Studies of Racial Discrimination in Employment." James Curtis, Edward Grabb, and Neil Guppy, eds., in *Social Inequality in Canada: Patterns, Problems, Policies*, 3rd ed. Toronto: Prentice-Hall.

Henry, Frances, Carol Tator, Winston Mattis, and Tim Rees. 1995. *The Colour of Democracy in Canadian Society.* Toronto: Harcourt Brace.

Herberg, Edward N. 1990. "Ethno-Racial Socio-economic Hierarchy in Canada: Theory and Analysis of the New Vertical Mosaic." *International Journal of Comparative Sociology* 31, no. 3–4: 206–21.

Kralt, John. 1980. "Ethnic Origin in the Canadian Census: 1871–1981." Pp. 18–49 in Roman Petryshyn, ed., *Changing Realities: Social Trends among Ukrainian Canadians.* Edmonton: Canadian Institute of Ukrainian Studies.

Lambert, M., M. Ledoux, and R. Pendakur. 1989. "Visible Minorities in Canada 1986: A Graphic Overview." Policy and Research Unit, Multiculturalism and Citizenship.

Lautard, Hugh, and Donald Loree. 1984. "Ethnic Stratification in Canada, 1931–1971." *Canadian Journal of Sociology* 9, no. 3: 333–44.

Légacé, Michael D. 1968. "Educational Attainment in Canada." Dominion Bureau of Statistics, Special Labour Force Survey No. 7. Ottawa: Queen's Printer.

Li, Peter. 1988. *Ethnic Inequality in a Class Society.* Toronto: Thompson.

Lian, Jason, and David Ralph Matthews. 1998. "Does the Vertical Mosaic Still Exist? Ethnicity and Income in Canada, 1991." *Canadian Review of Sociology and Anthropology*, forthcoming.

Lieberson, Stanley. 1975. "Rank-Sum Comparisons between Groups." Pp. 276–91 in David R. Heise, ed., *Sociological Methodology.* San Francisco: Jossey-Bass.

McDade, Kathryn. 1988. "Barriers to Recognition of the Credentials of Immigrants in Canada." Discussion Paper 88.B.1. Ottawa: Institute for Research on Public Policy.

Nakhaie, M. Reza. 1997. "Vertical Mosaic among the Elites: The New Imagery Revisited." *Canadian Review of Sociology and Anthropology* 34, no. 1: 1–24.

Ogmundson, Richard, and J. McLaughlin. 1992. "Trends in the Ethnic Origins of Canadian Elites: The Decline of the BRITS." *Canadian Review of Sociology and Anthropology* 29, no. 2: 227–42.

Pineo, Peter. 1976. "Social Mobility in Canada: The Current Picture." *Sociological Focus* 9, no. 2: 109–23.

Pineo, Peter, and John Porter. 1985. "Ethnic Origin and Occupational Attachment." Pp. 357–92 in M. Boyd, ed., *Ascription and Attainment: Studies in Mobility and Status Attainment in Canada.* Ottawa: Carleton University Press.

Porter, John. 1965. *The Vertical Mosaic: An Analysis of Social Class and Power in Canada.* Toronto: University of Toronto Press.

———. 1985. "Canada: The Social Context of Occupational Allocation." Pp. 29–65 in M. Boyd, ed., *Ascription and Achievement: Studies in Mobility and Status Attainment in Canada.* Ottawa: Carleton University Press.

Reitz, Jeffrey. 1988. "Less Racial Discrimination in Canada, or Simply Less Racial Conflict? Implications of Comparisons with Britain." *Canadian Public Policy* 14, no. 4: 424–41.

Robson, Reginald, and Brad Breems. 1986. *Ethnic Conflict in Vancouver.* Vancouver: British Columbia Civil Liberties Association.

Satzewich, Vic, and Peter S. Li. 1987. "Immigrant Labour in Canada: The Cost and Benefit of

Ethnic Origin in the Job Market." *Canadian Journal of Sociology* 12, no. 3: 229–41.

Sorensen, Marianne. 1995. "The Match between Education and Occupation for Immigrant Women in Canada." *Canadian Ethnic Studies* 27, no. 1: 48–66.

Statistics Canada. 1975. *1971 Census of Canada*. Vol. 3, Part 3 (Bulletin 3.3-7). *Occupations: Occupations by Sex, Showing Birthplace, Period of Immigration and Ethnic Group, for Canada and Regions.* Catalogue no. 94-734. Ottawa: Information Canada.

———. 1993. *1991 Census of Canada, The Nation: Ethnic Origin.* Catalogue no. 93-315. Ottawa: Industry, Science and Technology Canada.

Winn, Conrad. 1985. "Affirmative Action and Visible Minorities: Eight Premises in Quest of Evidence." *Canadian Public Policy* 11, no. 4: 684–700.

PART 4 | SOCIAL INSTITUTIONS

The social structures that constitute human societies are nested like Russian dolls or Chinese boxes (see Figure P4.1). There are structures within structures within structures. The smallest are known as **microstructures**. Microstructures are small, localized sites of face-to-face interaction, such as families. Social relations in microstructures tend to be emotionally deep and enduring, which is why people value them for their own sake. **Macrostructures**, in contrast, are larger, less localized, and more impersonal. People participate in macrostructures for specific, instrumental reasons — to earn money, get an education, and so on. **Global structures** are even larger, more remote, and more impersonal. They involve relations between whole societies and between nations.

As Figure P4.1 shows, **institutions** are found at both the micro- and macrostructural levels of society. Institutions are social structures that, to varying degrees, fulfill basic human needs. These needs include:

- the reproduction of the species and the nurturance and primary socialization of small children, a set of functions that is usually performed by the family (see Part 4A);
- the maintenance and renewal of legitimate authority, a set of functions that is performed by the political system (see Part 4B); and
- the production and distribution of material resources, a set of functions that is performed by the economy (see Part 4C).

FIGURE P4.1   THE NESTED STRUCTURES OF SOCIETY

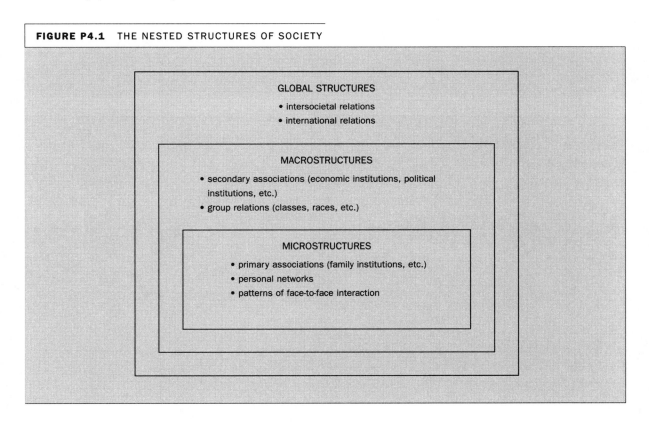

GLOBAL STRUCTURES
- intersocietal relations
- international relations

MACROSTRUCTURES
- secondary associations (economic institutions, political institutions, etc.)
- group relations (classes, races, etc.)

MICROSTRUCTURES
- primary associations (family institutions, etc.)
- personal networks
- patterns of face-to-face interaction

In keeping with the overall theme of this book, the chapters in this part focus on how powerful social forces, such as the entry of most adult women into the paid labour force, the rise of "neo-nationalist" movements, and global economic competition are reshaping major social institutions. The chapters highlight not just the fact that social institutions fulfill basic human needs, but that basic human needs are flexible and may therefore be fulfilled by a wide variety of institutional forms. The chapters also show that the adaptation of families, political systems, and economies to new conditions is often disorienting for the people who live and work in them. Some people react by organizing resistance to change and attempting to return to the old state of affairs. The very term "institution" may suggest a solid and stable establishment, but in reality social conflict is never far below the surface of any modern institution.

GLOSSARY

Global structures are the largest and most impersonal patterns of social relations, including relations between societies and nations.

Institutions are micro- and macro-level social structures that address basic human needs, such as reproduction, nurturance, and primary socialization (the family), the maintenance and renewal of legitimate authority (the political system), and the production and distribution of material resources (the economy).

Macrostructures are large, non-localized, impersonal sets of social relations. People participate in them for specific, instrumental reasons.

Microstructures are small, localized, emotionally intense patterns of social relations. People value such relations for their own sake.

The **nuclear family** consists of a husband and a wife living in the same household with at least one child. In the **traditional nuclear family** (comprising about one out of eight Canadian households), only the husband is employed in the paid work force. In the **non-traditional nuclear family** (comprising about a quarter of Canadian households), both the husband and the wife are employed in the paid work force. In addition, about a third of households are **non-nuclear families**: childless couples, lone parents living with at least one child, and husbands and wives with no children living at home. Finally, about a quarter of Canadian households are not recognized as families by the Canadian census. These **non-family households** include people living alone and people who are living together but who are neither married nor bound by common law (e.g., gay couples).

As one descends this list of household types, one moves from shrinking to expanding categories. The traditional nuclear family is no longer the predominant family form because so many women have entered the paid work force, especially since the 1960s. Non-nuclear families are increasingly common for several reasons. More women are deciding not to have children so that they can pursue higher education and careers. Others cannot have children with their spouses because they or their spouses are infertile. Infertility affects up to 15 percent of couples and is on the rise, largely, some medical scientists suspect, due to worsening environmental conditions. Non-nuclear families are also more common because the proportion of Canadians who marry is down (from over 90 percent in 1971 to under 85 percent today), the divorce rate is up (by over 700 percent since the early 1950s), and the rate of remarriage after divorce is down (from over 80 percent of divorcees in 1971 to under 70 percent today). Finally, non-family households are more common since more single people (including the elderly) can afford to live on their own and since gay lifestyles are more widely accepted than they used to be, at least in large urban areas.

The facts listed above should not lead one to conclude that the family is in a state of collapse. A countrywide poll taken in 1987 found that over three-quarters of Canadians regard the family as the most important thing in their lives, more important than career and religion. Ninety-two percent of respondents with children at home said that the family is becoming more important to them. The overwhelming majority of adults still want to marry and have children. The family is not a crumbling institution. What is happening, however, is that people are freer than they once were to establish the kinds of family arrangements that best suit them. For instance, because most adult women are now employed in the paid work force, and because changes in divorce laws have made the division of property after divorce more equitable, women now have a measure of economic independence, which gives them greater freedom to end unsatisfying marriages and seek more gratifying relationships. This does not spell the end of the family but the possibility that improved family forms can take shape.

Whether one is optimistic or pessimistic about the future of the family, one thing is clear. Women's increasing labour force participation has not resulted in a substantial change in the division of household labour. Today, both husband and wife work in the paid labour force in nearly two-thirds of husband–wife families, yet men's participation in domestic work has increased only slightly since the 1970s and 1980s. Several surveys show that Canadian women continue to be chiefly responsible for meal preparation, meal cleanup, laundry, general household cleaning, and grocery shopping, regardless of whether they are employed in the paid labour force. As a result, Canadian women in dual-earner families now work on average over thirteen hours per day on paid and unpaid labour.

In Chapter 18, Norene Pupo of York University discusses some of the impediments to a more egalitarian division of household labour. Pupo notes how unequal power relations between husbands and wives are embedded in popular conceptions of appropriate role behaviour. She then shows how household work has changed to increase demands on women's time despite the availability of new appliances and other conveniences. Although the government has recently reformed Canadian divorce law (to recognize the importance of women's unpaid work in the home) and some corporations are slowly introducing "family-friendly" workplace policies, Pupo questions the degree to which these changes will result in a substantial shift in the gendered division of domestic labour.

Another more disturbing aspect of unequal power relations between men and women is male violence against women, including wife battering and sexual assault. Although battering is now viewed more as a public issue than a personal problem, much wife beating still goes unreported and many marriages are still the site of abuse. In Chapter 19, Holly Johnson of Statistics Canada analyzes violence against women. Rates of violence against women are shockingly high. Fifty-one percent of the 12 300 women interviewed in the 1993 Statistics Canada survey discussed by Johnson reported they had been physically or sexually assaulted at least once by a man. True, several other surveys have shown that rates of female violence against men are about the same as rates of male violence against women. However, Canadian, American, and Scottish research have shown that when women commit acts of violence against men they tend overwhelmingly to be acting in self-defence. Moreover, women's violent acts are in general far less injurious than men's. These findings evoke the power asymmetry that continues to plague relations between women and men.

Part of Newton's third law of motion states that the exertion of physical force on an object evokes an opposite reaction from that object. Analogously, every social change evokes a reaction on the part of those who are deeply entrenched in the status quo. In Chapter 20, Lorna Erwin of York University discusses one such case. In the early 1980s, the pro-family movement was organized in Canada in defence of the traditional nuclear family and conservative moral values. Its members spoke out passionately in opposition to feminism, gay rights, abortion, and so forth. Erwin conducted a survey in the late 1980s to determine who the supporters of the pro-family movement are and the likelihood of their developing a broader, **neoconservative** agenda, as they have in the United States. (Neoconservatism is a political ideology that attributes most social problems to too much state involvement in the lives of the citizenry.) She shows that the supporters of the pro-family movement tend to be relatively well-educated, middle-class, female homemakers over the age of 45 who were raised in traditional nuclear families in small towns or on farms and who practise Catholicism or fundamentalist Protestantism. Erwin also finds that pro-family movement members are more likely than most Canadians to hold *liberal* views on general political and economic issues. She therefore concludes that Canada is unlikely to follow the American pattern: the chance of a neoconservative movement emerging from the pro-family movement in Canada is small.

GLOSSARY

Neoconservatism is a political ideology that attributes most social problems to too much state involvement in the lives of the citizenry.

Non-family households include people living alone and people who are living together but who are neither married nor bound by a common-law union (e.g., gay couples).

Non-nuclear families include childless couples, lone parents living with at least one child, and husbands and wives with no children living at home.

A **non-traditional nuclear family** is a nuclear family in which both the husband and the wife are employed in the paid work force.

A **nuclear family** consists of a husband and a wife living in the same household with at least one child.

A **traditional nuclear family** is a nuclear family in which only the husband is employed in the paid work force.

CRITICAL THINKING QUESTIONS

1. Why do most women continue to be responsible for most domestic work even after they take on full-time employment?
2. How does women's unpaid work in the home hamper their opportunities in the labour market? Has the division of household labour changed much in the last three decades?
3. How do rates of wife assault and sexual assault vary with the age, marital status, household income, and educational attainment of the victim? How do you explain these variations?
4. What are the chances of a neoconservative movement emerging from the pro-family movement in Canada? Explain your answer.

ANNOTATED BIBLIOGRAPHY

Margrit Eichler, *Families in Canada Today: Recent Changes and Their Policy Consequences*, 2nd ed. (Toronto: Gage, 1988). A penetrating analysis of how Canadian families have changed and how public policies need to be reformed to take account of new realities.

Meg Luxton, *More Than a Labour of Love: Three Generations of Women's Work in the Home* (Toronto: Women's Press, 1980). A Canadian classic. Shows how changes in the capitalist economy affect women's domestic labour and gender relations by focusing on households in Flin Flon, Manitoba.

Carol Stack, *All Our Kin: Strategies for Survival in a Black Community* (New York: Harper and Row, 1974). This highly regarded participant-observation study shows how kinship networks adapt to conditions of extreme poverty. The author convincingly demonstrates that there are functional alternatives to the nuclear family that are required by non-middle-class social settings.

Chapter 18

The Expanding Double Day

NORENE PUPO

WORK–FAMILY INTERFACES

Today most married women with children remain in the paid labour force, returning to their jobs following maternity leaves. In 1991 among women aged 25 to 44, 68 percent with preschool children, 84 percent with older children at home, and 90 percent without children were in the paid labour force (Marshall, 1994, p. 29). Although women with very young children tend to decrease their paid work hours, their total number of work hours does not change given the increased load of unpaid household work. For example, wives in dual-earner families whose youngest child is 0 to 5 years of age on average spend 7.3 hours per day in paid work and 6.9 hours doing domestic work. When the youngest child is 6 to 15, women spend 7.4 hours at paid work and 5.0 hours at unpaid work. Those whose youngest child is between 16 and 24 years of age increase their paid work hours to 8.4, while doing 4.1 hours of unpaid household work daily. Among women with no children under age 25, 8.9 hours are spent in paid work, while unpaid work is reduced on average to 3.3 hours daily (Marshall, p. 29).

These long hours of work may tax family members' physical and mental health. A significant number of Canadians experience time-crunch stress, and women are consistently more time stressed than men (Frederick, 1993, p. 7). Dual-earning couples working full time are the most time-stressed group, 57 percent experience feeling time crunched, while 22 percent describe themselves as severely time crunched. In this situation, there are significant differences between men and women: Over 28 percent of women compared with less than 16 percent of men report being severely time crunched (Frederick, p. 8).

Women's levels of stress are higher than their partners' because they are charged with the primary responsibility for children and housework. A recent study in Quebec of 575 unionized telephone operators and workers in energy and health care sectors found that 56 percent of the women and 42 percent of the men in large companies have difficulty reconciling their childcare responsibilities and their jobs, and as a result they suffer high levels of stress, feel overworked and irritable, and are extremely fatigued ("Workers struggle," 1995).

According to the 1990 General Social Survey, only a small minority of dual-earner couples with both partners working full-time and with children at home had an equal division of housework. In younger families, men tend to be somewhat more involved in household work. Almost half (47 percent) of wives under age 35 in dual-earner families and employed full-time were solely responsible for daily housework, compared with 69 percent of wives aged 45 to 64 (Marshall, 1993, pp. 13–14). The higher rates of participation in household work by men in younger families may relate to the ages of the children, the volume of household work, or more liberal attitudes toward domestic work.

Source: Adapted from "Always Working, Never Done: The Expansion of the Double Day," in *Good Jobs, Bad Jobs, No Jobs: The Transformation of Work in the 21st Century*, Ann Duffy, Daniel Glenday, and Norene Pupo, eds. (Toronto: Harcourt Brace, 1997), pp. 155–65. Reprinted by permission of the publisher.

There is a tendency to separate private and public spheres, which presents an intricate balancing problem to parents, especially women, as they cope with the pushes and pulls of workplace and family simultaneously. On the job, workers are usually not defined as family members and are expected not to pull their private concerns into their (public) work space. In workplaces where personal calls are not permitted, parents are unable to receive messages from their child's daycare in an emergency or from their school-age children, who may wish to "check in" with their mother at work once they get home from school. Messing (1995, p. 258) points out that women in such situations are forced to spend much time and effort devising methods of communication, contingency plans, and fall-back scenarios. She recommends that occupational health programs take into account family obligations when devising workplace standards.

Participation in domestic work is not necessarily contingent on employment. McAllister (1990) found that men adjust their domestic labour to the demands of the outside labour market, while women adjust their domestic work to avoid conflict with their mates and their employment situations. For example, one woman who works part-time as a receptionist and whose husband works shifts explained:

> I do the housework. My husband's hours are long, and he's on shift. He'll babysit and do things when I ask him to, but it's really my job. I get it done as much as I can during the week. On the weekends when he's off, he doesn't like me doing housework.

Unemployed men participate more in household work than employed men. But the relationship between men's employment status and domestic work is not straightforward. Brayfield (1992) found that unemployed men who have employed wives undertake almost 40 percent of the traditionally female housekeeping tasks and that their contribution to household work is therefore substantially greater than other men's. However, unemployed men whose wives are employed should undertake more than half of the domestic work in order to balance the overall division of labour between partners. Regardless of their actual employment status, men are regarded as breadwinners, and because they usually have greater earning potential than women, they are more insulated from the domestic sphere, ready for the labour market (Brayfield, 1992). In this way, families preserve inequality in the division of domestic labour.

POWER, GENDER, AND THE HOUSEHOLD

Popular discourse presents household labour as women's work. Women discuss ways in which their partners "help out," while men often refer to themselves as "pitching in" to "help" their wives by "babysitting" or doing other household chores. A waitress and mother of two girls related her story:

> I used to do everything on my own because I want things done a certain way. ... I'd rather do it myself and do it right. ... But now, when you live in such a busy lifestyle, ... anyone who pitches in and does something, you love it.

That some wives must ask their husbands to help out implies that they are responsible for the work but may require help from their husbands on occasion. Even when men undertake certain household tasks on a regular basis (starting the evening meal, for example), there may be an air of impermanence about the arrangement. In interviews with married women about the ways in which they divide household work with their husbands, many refer to their husbands engaging in housework because of their own absence from the home, not because the couple considered the tasks to be his job.

Remaining outside the labour force in unpaid work sometimes displaces women from the centre of decision making in the family. For example, women who earn some wages, even meagre amounts, report that having their own earnings gives them more say in family matters than when they stay at home full-time. A woman who works in sales and has one child said:

> I think of my income as the family's, but I find when I work if I want to buy something for myself, I do it much more readily because I know we can afford it and I put money in.

In her study of working-class, single-earner families in Flin Flon, Manitoba, Luxton (1980) found that there were heavy personal consequences for women as economic dependants. Meeting their husbands' needs was a household priority, and they had to accommodate these needs at high costs to themselves.

THE CHANGING NATURE OF HOUSEHOLD WORK

While the nature of household work has changed remarkably from earlier times, the volume of work has not diminished, as expectations of frequently washed clothes, multiple-dish meals, freshly vacuumed carpets, and home craftwork and decorating (the Martha Stewart influence) increase. Cowan (1983) argues that women today spend as much time on household work as their predecessors in the nineteenth century despite the availability of household appliances and newer technologies. Modern appliances are not necessarily labour-saving (although they may be advertised as such). Having them does not decrease the hours spent overall on household chores, but they may make certain tasks (chopping vegetables, for example) easier and faster to complete.

Because household work is not defined as an occupation, there is no protection for workers who are injured while performing their domestic duties. If a woman is injured while working the second shift at home and cannot return to the workplace, she will face the loss of her income. In addition, a worker may be denied occupational health benefits or workers' compensation if a health problem or injury is related to domestic work (Messing, 1995, p. 257; Weisberg, 1988). Workers' Compensation Board officers investigate exactly where an injury took place. If they suspect that a woman injured her back at home (e.g., by carrying a hamper of wet clothes while doing laundry), instead of at her workplace, they will rule that she is ineligible for compensation (Weisberg, 1988). Such decisions act as a powerful reminder of social disregard for and trivialization of the value of housework.

When interviewed by Compensation Board adjudicators at their workplaces about a claim, some women report that they have been asked if their injury prevents them from doing their housework. Despite the fact that it was extremely difficult and painful for her to carry out her housework, one woman acknowledged that she did carry out her household chores because there was no one else in the family to do them. Her honesty prompted the adjudicator to note that there was an inconsistency in her claim and to recommend that her benefits be terminated because she was not totally disabled (Weisberg, 1988).

TIME OUT, TIME OFF

The pattern of dividing household work seems to indicate that wives, particularly employed wives, have little time for leisure for themselves and are therefore subject to time stress and burnout. In fact, much of their leisure time is tied to children's activities, and the line between work and leisure is often blurred. Some of this work-leisure involves attending children's hockey practices and baseball games or volunteering in their classrooms. One mother, who is employed full-time and spends at least six hours a week taxiing her children to and from various sporting activities (team practices and games), said:

> The only way I could make time for myself is to combine an hour of exercise for myself with my daughter's swim practices. So instead of joining an aerobics class, I go on an hour's long power walk during the three or four practices a week [my daughter] goes to. One day I'd like to

join aerobics, or volleyball, or something else on my own, not something makeshift during the practices, but I can't fit it all in right now.

Mothers' work is greatly affected by the involvement of their children in community activities and organized sports. Spontaneous games of hockey and baseball have been replaced by associations such as Minor Hockey and Little League, which require players to attend multiple events (games and practices) weekly. This situation taxes parents' time considerably, not only because it requires elaborate schemes of taxiing children to meet their schedules, but also because it affects processes and rituals surrounding the evening meal. With extracurricular and (paid) work schedules to juggle, family members may have to eat at different times, thus affecting both meal preparation and cleanup.

COOKING, CONSUMING, AND CLEANING: THE SUBSTANCE OF DOMESTIC WORK

Devices such as bread-baking machines are making their way into Canadian kitchens, reestablishing a practice long forsaken given the availability of affordable ready-baked goods. While specialized kitchen appliances are expensive and beyond the reach of many Canadians' household budgets, what is significant is the rebirth of lost practices (bread baking, jam making) and the pressure they may put on women who are primarily responsible for meal preparation to adopt these time-consuming chores.

In 1994, 81.5 percent of Canadian households had a microwave oven (Statistics Canada, 1995, p. 48). There is evidence from a study in the United States that microwaves were first adopted by households with employed wives (Oropesa, 1991). Microwave technology has not dramatically altered the burden of meal preparation, which is one of the most time-consuming tasks within the household, nor has it been used to its fullest by household members. However, with the growth in the number of microwave-

able products in grocery stores and the increasing familiarity of all but the youngest members of the household with its use, the microwave has the potential to increase the involvement of husbands and even children in meal preparation (Oropesa, 1991).

The new household technologies have not had a great impact upon the amount of work done because their introduction runs up against other processes directing yet more work to the home. Glazer (1993) refers to a process she calls the "work transfer," whereby tasks previously performed in paid labour have been shifted to the unpaid sphere. The work transfer, she argues, is part of the process undertaken by managements to reduce their labour costs, by shifting the expense of (women's) paid work to unpaid household labour, again to be borne by women. This labour transfer, Glazer suggests, is simply one step in a series of cost-saving measures undertaken by business, measures that include deskilling, speedups, and job consolidation.

In the retail industry, for example, tasks once performed by clerks for pay are now a large part of the routine of unpaid household work, and the task of shopping for food and other household items has been enlarged. In earlier times, middle-class women would order groceries and other household items by phone. Store clerks would then collect the items, which would in turn be delivered by paid employees. This service is no longer available on a broad basis. When it is, there are usually service charges or higher markups on items purchased. To avoid these charges, most people undertake the work themselves.

While daily trips to the market may no longer be necessary, shopping is nevertheless very time-consuming. The trend is toward warehouse-type stores of 90 000 square m or more. While these stores offer consumers thousands of items under one roof, along with a variety of services (restaurants, hair salons, optical outlets, etc.), their size sometimes overwhelms consumers who find it costly in time and energy to walk through them to find the items needed. In these self-serve stores, consumers are enticed to buy in bulk as a way of saving time. But since regular trips to markets are still needed for perishable items, bulk buying may simply prove to be a costly exercise.

Retail outlets usually no longer offer shoppers help in locating and demonstrating items. This cutback in service saves the retail industry labour costs, because employees are increasingly hired simply as clerks and checkers rather than as salespersons who assist customers. In this intensified work situation, retail employees are not trained adequately about the goods sold in the stores, nor are they expected to spend long periods of time waiting on customers; their job is to process orders and move customers in and out of the store as quickly and efficiently as possible.

As a result, the "work" of retailing once performed by store clerks and salespersons is now done by the customers themselves. Clerks are frequently unavailable to answer questions about products, to lift heavy items into shopping carts, to carry orders out to the car, or to assemble goods. Numerous household items—from lawn mowers and barbecues to kitchen appliances and toys and sporting goods—require assembly at home. To some extent, even the assembly of furniture has been passed on to the consumer.

CARING AND CARETAKING

Particularly in periods of economic stagnation and high rates of unemployment, many grown children return to their parents' home. Although a recent study has found that these "boomerang children" are welcomed back by parents, who like to help out in times of need, there are increased domestic pressures on the household, reminiscent of the kinds of pressure, particularly on the mothers, when the children were younger. One woman, whose two grown sons (30 and 32) moved back in following layoffs from their jobs, said:

All of a sudden I had two kids at home. When they returned, we became mommy and daddy

and two kids over again. They wanted chocolate-chip cookies and I wanted to know what time they'd be in for dinner (as cited in Lipovenko, 1995, A14).

The work of caring has grown in recent years due to fiscal crises and retrenchment within health and social services. For example, hospital patients are routinely sent home sooner after surgery or illness. The size of hospitals' short-stay units has increased. While this approach has served to intensify the work of nurses, in that the patients under their care are sicker, it has also shifted a great deal of routine nursing to the unpaid members of the household (Glazer, 1993). Even when the patient is discharged and requires some professional care from community nurses, unpaid family members are instructed in a number of aspects of the patient's care, including sterilizing instruments required for dressing, changing bandages, and bathing.

The same fiscal pressures are serving to prevent families from shifting child care and educational work from the home to the public sector. The state has never seriously taken up the cause of child care, assuming that it is essentially unpaid women's work. With deficit-cutting measures, caring work is thrust back to the family and mainly onto the shoulders of women. And this movement of work into the home is reaching further into the stages of childhood, affecting the number of years women may remain at home full-time or accept only minimal part-time or casual employment. In Ontario, for example, the provincial government's severe deficit-cutting measures have now threatened junior kindergarten programs.

With the absence of teacher's paid helpers and the growing size of classes, in the primary grades there are greater expectations that parents (read mothers) will participate on a voluntary basis in their children's classrooms or as lunchroom monitors or playground supervisors. Cutbacks have forced reductions in the number of lunchtime supervisors in many schools. As a result, children eat their lunch on the gymnasium floor, where there is a 60:1 ratio of children to supervisors, unless parents volunteer to supervise the kids in the more orderly and comfortable classroom environment (McQuaig, 1993).

RECOGNITION UNDER FAMILY LAW AND FAMILY-FRIENDLY POLICIES

There is some recognition of women's work in the home through family law. Whereas women were previously left out of the financial picture in the family, family law now recognizes their contribution to the household through unpaid domestic labour (Pupo, 1988). A number of landmark divorce cases (e.g., *Murdoch vs. Murdoch*) awarded wives who remained non-employed half of the marital property.

A provision in the Ontario Family Law Act allows a judge to use his or her discretion in divisions of marital property and assets. The judge need not equally divide assets "if to do so would be unconscionable" (Haliechuk, 1988, p. A24). Some lawyers representing tycoons and others among the super wealthy feel their clients are paying too high a price for divorce. Following the award of $6 million to Mariellen Black, ex-wife of industrialist Montegu Black, the case lawyer argued that the "standard is an extremely high one to meet" and unnecessarily penalizes "the 'super person,' the business genius, rock star or athlete who accumulates enormous wealth more because of his or her own talent than because of the help of the partner" (as cited in Haliechuk, 1988, p. A24).

In another effort to promote inclusiveness by dissociating gender from family work, there has been some attention paid recently to transforming workplaces into more family-friendly organizations. Family-friendly employers are beginning to develop policies and workplace practices that take into account workers' family responsibilities, ranging from their need for short-term absences to care for their children on school holidays or sick days, to flexible hours to accommodate school schedules, to long-term requirements for on-site child care (Duffy & Pupo, 1996). Again, we might question what impact the family-friendly workplace (or the discourse around gender and inclusion in the workplace) may have in practice on how family members participate in and are affected by household work.

CONCLUSION

Compared with their predecessors, men today may be participating more in household work, but this may largely be a function of their wives' increased workloads. Attitudes toward men engaging in housework and being openly involved in their children's lives have softened, but the level of their participation in domestic work and the types of work around the home they do are largely related to their identity as breadwinners.

While individual couples engage in the ongoing process of establishing as reasonable a division of domestic labour as their circumstances allow, they require the structures and conditions that will support more egalitarian arrangements. Along with resocialization and educational campaigns aimed at shattering gender role stereotyping, households require material and social support from the state and employers. Mending the separation between public and private spheres will require, among other measures, high-quality, accessible child care, revised respite and health care programs, and workplace policies (supported in turn by state legislation such as provisions for extended parental leave) that take into account workers' family commitments. While these measures alone will not guarantee fairer arrangements between partners, they may provide more adequate parameters within which to move toward more equitable divisions.

REFERENCES

Brayfield, A.A. (1992, February). Employment resources and housework in Canada. *Journal of Marriage and the Family*, 54, 19–30.

Cowan, R.S. (1983). *More work for mother: The ironies of household technology from the open hearth to the microwave*. New York: Basic Books.

Duffy, A., & Pupo, N. (1996). Family friendly organizations and beyond: Proposals for policy directions with women in mind. In National Forum on Family Security (Ed.), *Family security in insecure times* (Vol. 2) (pp. 1–24). Ottawa: Canada Council for Social Development.

Frederick, J. (1993, Winter). Are you time crunched? In *Canadian social trends* (pp. 6–9). Statistics Canada Catalogue 11-008E.

Glazer, N.Y. (1993). *Women's paid and unpaid labor: The work transfer in health care and retailing*. Philadelphia: Temple University Press.

Haliechuk, R. (1988, December 23). Tycoon's $6 million divorce a lesson in new law. *The Toronto Star*, p. A24.

Lipovenko, D. (1995, December 7). Grown children flocking home to save money. *The Globe and Mail*, p. A14.

Luxton, M. (1980). *More than a labour of love: Three generations of women's work in the home*. Toronto: Women's Press.

Marshall. (1993, Winter). Dual earners: Who's responsible for house work? In *Canadian social trends* (pp. 11–14). Statistics Canada Catalogue 11-008E.

Marshall. (1994, Spring). Balancing work and family responsibilities. In *Perspectives on labour and income* (pp. 26–30). Statistics Canada Catalogue 75-001E.

McAllister, I. (1990, February). Gender and the household division of labor. *Work and occupations*, 17 (1), 79–99.

McQuaig, L. (1993). *The wealthy banker's wife: The assault on equality in Canada*. Toronto: Penguin Books.

Messing, K. (1995). Don't use a wrench to peel potatoes: Biological science constructed on male model systems is a risk to women workers' health. In S. Burt & L. Code (Eds.), *Changing methods: Feminists transforming practice* (pp. 217–63). Peterborough, ON: Broadview Press.

Oropesa, R.S. (1991, August). Female labour force participation and time-saving household technology: A case study of the microwave from 1978 to 1989. Paper presented at the Annual Meeting of the American Sociological Association, Cincinnati, OH.

Pupo, N. (1988). Preserving patriarchy: Women, the family and the state. In N. Mandell & A. Duffy (Eds.), *Reconstructing the Canadian family: Feminist perspectives* (pp. 207–37). Toronto: Butterworths.

Statistics Canada. (1995, Summer). Key labour and income facts. In *Perspectives on labour and income* (pp. 41–52). Statistics Canada Catalogue 75-001E.

Weisberg, K. (1988). Board games: Sexist bias at the Workers' Compensation Board. *Healthsharing*, 9 (4), 25–28.

Workers struggle for balance in jobs, child care at big firms. (1995, November 30). *The Globe and Mail*, p. A10.

Chapter 19 | Violence against Women

HOLLY JOHNSON

INTRODUCTION

Victimization surveys were designed initially to address the need for information about crimes not reported to the police and to provide a source of crime statistics that complement the long-standing Uniform Crime Reporting survey of police-reported data. Canada has a history of crime victimization surveys dating back to the late 1970s; however, it had become apparent that, while they are proficient at measuring property offences and perceptions of crime, these surveys were not designed to measure the more sensitive kinds of victimizations that primarily affect women, such as wife assault and sexual violence. In attempting to measure a wide variety of crimes, these omnibus surveys did not allow for detailed analysis of all types of violence and threats to women, the emotional and physical consequences, the decisions women make to use support services and their satisfaction with these services, and other detailed information that is necessary for the development of public policy around this issue. Thus, the federal Department of Health commissioned the Violence against Women survey in recognition of the lack of reliable statistical data on which to test theories and develop policies and programs to address violence against women. Canada's first national survey on male violence against women was conducted by Statistics Canada early in 1993.

The design of this survey evolved out of the tradition of victimization surveys, whereby a random sample of the population is interviewed about their perceptions of crime and their experiences of victimization, and their responses are weighted to represent the population at large. A total of 12 300 women 18 years of age and over across the ten provinces were interviewed for this survey. Random selection helps ensure that those who respond are statistically representative of everyone in the population and that the results can be generalized to the population at large. The Violence against Women survey differs, however, from traditional victimization surveys, such as Canada's General Social Survey (GSS), the National Crime Survey in the United States, and the British Crime Survey, in important ways. Drawing on his experience with two telephone surveys of women in Toronto, Smith (1994) articulates a number of strategies designed to improve the accuracy of survey data on sensitive subjects such as wife assault and sexual assault. "Violence" in crime surveys is typically defined in legalistic terms through a single question embedded among a series of other crimes. Non-traditional surveys, on the other hand, tend to use broader definitions that "take women's subjective experiences seriously." Smith advocates, for example, the use of multiple measures at different points in the survey to offer many opportunities for respondents to divulge a previously forgotten incident or one that may be painful to recall. He also recommends giving greater attention to building rapport between respondents and interviewers through open-ended questions that allow respondents to speak in their own words, and through the careful selection of interviewers.

Source: Adapted from "Violence against Women," in *Crime in Canadian Society*, 5th ed., Robert A. Silverman, James J. Teevan, and Vincent F. Sacco, eds. (Toronto: Harcourt Brace, 1996), pp. 210–21. Reprinted by permission of the publisher.

Smith also criticizes traditional crime victimization surveys for a narrow emphasis on annual victimization rates. The GSS asks respondents about incidents that took place during the twelve months preceding the interview. While twelve-month rates avoid problems of memory recall and are useful for tracking trends over time, they can obscure the scope of the problem. Eighty percent of violent incidents reported to the Violence against Women survey occurred *before* the twelve months leading up to the survey. Arbitrarily assigning one year as the cutoff point for victim or non-victim status may skew the analysis of correlations and consequences of victimization. Many women designated non-victims may continue to suffer serious consequences of previous victimization, and the comparison of their responses with those of recent victims may produce misleading results.

Careful testing of survey questions, multiple measures, selection and training of interviewers, and lifetime victimization rates were all incorporated into the design of the survey. In addition, the approach that was developed was particularly sensitive to the constraints that apply to surveying women about their experiences of violence over the telephone in a household setting, including respondent burden, the sensitivity of the information being sought, and the difficulty of responding to questions while the abuser may be present in the home. In discussions with women who had been victims of violence, the survey designers felt strongly that the appropriate approach would take account of the many realities of the women responding, and should be flexible, sensitive, and offer options as to when and where the women would participate.

One unique aspect of the Violence against Women survey was the extensive consultation process undertaken during the design and development phases. Advice and recommendations on the methodology and content of the survey were sought through ongoing discussions with a wide variety of experts, academics, government representatives, the police community, shelter workers, counsellors and advocates for battered women, as well as victims of violence seeking support in shelters and sexual assault counselling groups. These groups were instrumental in helping to design question wording that is sensitive, and that respondents can understand as reflective of their experiences. This was accomplished through lengthy discussions over the content of the questionnaire and issues to be addressed, focus group testing of question wording, one-on-one interviews with drafts of the questionnaire, and two large field tests.

A common concern among survey researchers is one of biased results if a large proportion of respondents refuse to participate in the survey or refuse to answer specific questions. There are a number of reasons why a woman may not wish to reveal her experiences to an interviewer over the telephone: she may feel her experience is too personal or painful to discuss; she may be embarrassed or ashamed about it; she may fear further violence from her abuser should he find out; or, she may have forgotten about it if it was minor or happened a long time ago (Smith, 1994). A survey of this nature asks the women responding to disclose the most intimate and perhaps the most troubling details of their lives to a stranger over the telephone. Even more important, from an ethical point of view, researchers must never lose sight of the possibility that with every telephone call the respondent could be living with an abusive man and that her safety could be jeopardized should he learn of the content of the survey. The selection and training of interviewers are critical factors in enabling a relationship of trust to develop between interviewers and respondents, a climate in which respondents feel safe and comfortable enough to discuss their experiences. Another important aspect of the approach developed for this survey, from the point of view of respondents' safety, was to provide options as to when and where they would participate. At the outset of the interview, every woman was provided with a toll-free telephone number that she could use to call back to resume the interview in the event that she had to hang up suddenly. A great many women took advantage of this option. A total of 1000 calls were received on the toll-free line over the five-month period of interviewing, and 150 were women wanting to continue an uncompleted interview that they had had to interrupt or calling to add additional information to a completed interview. This kind of interest and commitment to the interview process indicates an exceptional level of emotional commitment that this line of questioning can provoke and to which survey researchers must respond. Over one-half of all calls were from women wanting to verify the legitimacy of the survey, many at the point of sensitive questions about violence in their lives. One-quarter wanted more information about the sponsorship of the survey and how they could obtain the results. Many women called to express their appreciation for the opportunity to be involved in the survey and commended the government for taking the issue seriously.

This chapter presents the results of the Violence against Women survey as they relate to the prevalence of violence and emotional abuse by marital partners and sexual violence by men other than spouses. But this survey goes beyond quantifying women's experiences of criminal violence. The importance of this survey lies in its ability to put women's experiences of violence into a context that recognizes the parallels among violence inside and outside the home, threats to women's feelings of security that they experience routinely through sexual harassment, women's fear of victimization, and how women manage threats to their safety in their everyday lives. It allows an elaboration of our understanding of violence against women and the impact it has on their lives. Much recent scholarship recognizes the links between women's experiences of all types of violence and threats to women's personal security in the public and private spheres (Kelly, 1988; Stanko, 1990; Dekeseredy and MacLean, 1990). Criminal violence is only one dimension of a much broader problem manifest in the day-to-day lives of all women. To address only one type of violence, wife assault or

specific forms of sexual assault, for example, is to deny the wider social context in which women routinely feel threatened by male violence. It is to disregard the very real connections between the violence in women's lives by intimates, men they know and trust, perhaps a work colleague, a doctor, or a relative, and men they fear as strangers. Frightening and potentially volatile situations, such as being followed or leered at, with the implied threat of sexual violence, are very threatening experiences that cause women to feel fearful and insecure. These factors play a central role in shaping women's perceptions of their safety, and yet most traditional crime victimization surveys or family violence surveys do not consider them an important component of women's victimization. Some writers have described this range of violent and intimidating behaviours as a "continuum" of violence in women's lives because of the similar effects of these experiences on the female victim (Kelly, 1988; Stanko, 1990). It is this continuum that this survey is attempting to address.

CONSTRUCTING DEFINITIONS OF VIOLENCE

The broad objectives of this survey were to provide reliable statistical information about the extent and the nature of violence against women and women's fear of violence. Definitions of violence against women used in statistical surveys vary widely. They include psychological and emotional abuse, financial abuse, and sexual coercion, as well as physical and sexual assault as legally defined (Dekeseredy and Kelly, 1993; Koss and Gidycz, 1985). The prevalence of "violence" was estimated by this survey using questions based on legal definitions of physical and sexual assault as contained in the Canadian Criminal Code. These strict definitions were necessary in view of the fact that respondents would be asked a series of questions about the actions they took to get help, including reporting to the police, whether the incident resulted in an offender appearing in court, and their satisfaction with the action taken by the police and the courts.

The range of behaviours considered sexual assault under Canadian law include unwanted sexual touching up to violent sexual attacks with severe injury to the victim. Physical assaults range from face-to-face threat of imminent attack up to and including attacks with serious injury. Sexual violence outside marriage was measured through responses to two questions:

Sexual Attack

Has a male stranger (date or boyfriend or other man known to you) ever forced you or attempted to force you into any sexual activity by threatening you, holding you down or hurting you in some way?

Unwanted Sexual Touching

Has a male stranger (other man known to you) ever touched you against your will in any sexual way, such as unwanted touching, grabbing, kissing or fondling?

Physical violence by men other than marital partners was measured through the following two questions:

Physical Attack

Now I'm going to ask you some questions about physical attacks you may have had since the age of 16. By this I mean any use of force such as being hit, slapped, kicked or grabbed to being beaten, knifed or shot. Has a male stranger (date or boyfriend or other man known to you) ever physically attacked you?

Threats of Attack

The next few questions are about face-to-face threats you may have experienced. By threats I mean any time you have been threatened with physical harm since you were 16. Has a male stranger (date or boyfriend or other man known to you) ever threatened to harm you? Did you believe he would do it?

Incidents that involved both sexual and physical attack were counted only once as a sexual assault.

Women were not asked about unwanted sexual touching in dating and marital relationships. While technically these behaviours are legally crime, in the testing of the questionnaire the majority of respondents found this concept to be ambiguous and confusing and there was a concern among the survey designers that the responses to these questions would be of questionable validity. Coercive sexuality is the norm in North American society, where young men are expected to initiate sexual activity and to apply a certain amount of pressure on women, and women are expected to resist and to agree to sex only reluctantly (Clark and Lewis, 1977). The lines around "unwanted sexual touching" in intimate or dating relationships thus become blurred. Still, the data are included below.

Ten questions were used to measure violence by a marital partner (including legally married and common-law partners), taking account of Smith's advice to offer many opportunities for disclosure in order to overcome hesitancy on the part of the woman responding. Development of these items began with the violence items listed in the Conflict Tactics Scale (CTS), which was developed by Murray Straus and his colleagues at the University of New Hampshire (Straus, 1990). These items were then tested in focus groups of abused women, and two pilot tests were undertaken with random samples of women. A number of modifications were made throughout the testing phase in response to ambiguity in the question wording. The original CTS item "threatened to hit or throw something at you" was altered to read "threatened to hit you with his fist or anything else that could hurt you." Similarly, the item "threw something at you" has been clarified to read "thrown anything at you that could hurt you." The item "hit you with something" now reads "hit you with something that could hurt you." These modifications were made following field testing in which some respondents were clearly confused about whether to include incidents in which they were threatened or hit in a playful way with harmless objects that could not possibly hurt them. The addition of an item on forced sexual activity recognizes the reality of sexual violence in marriage.[1] (The complete list of items is contained in Table 19.1.)

THE PREVALENCE OF VIOLENCE AGAINST WOMEN

According to the Violence against Women survey, 51 percent of Canadian women have experienced at least one incident of physical or sexual assault since the age of 18 (Table 19.2). Women are at greater risk of violence by men they know than by strangers. Almost one-half of all women (45 percent) have been victimized by men known to them (spouses, dates, boyfriends, family, acquaintances, etc.) while 23 percent have experienced violence by a stranger. These percentages add to more than 51 percent because of the very high number of women who reported violence by both strangers and known men.

TABLE 19.1 NUMBER AND PERCENTAGE OF EVER-MARRIED WOMEN 18 YEARS AND OVER WHO REPORTED VIOLENCE BY A MARITAL PARTNER,* BY TYPE OF ASSAULT

TYPE OF ASSAULT	NUMBER (000s)**	PERCENT**
Total	2652	29
1. Threatened to hit her with his fist or anything else that could hurt her	1688	19
2. Thrown anything at her that could hurt her	1018	11
3. Pushed, grabbed, or shoved her	2221	25
4. Slapped her	1359	15
5. Kicked, bit, or hit her with his fist	955	11
6. Hit her with something that could hurt her	508	6
7. Beat her up	794	9
8. Choked her	607	7
9. Threatened to use or used a gun or knife on her	417	5
10. Forced her into any sexual activity when she did not want to by threatening her, holding her down, or hurting her in some way	729	8

*Includes common-law partners.
**Figures do not add to totals because of multiple response.

TABLE 19.2 NUMBER AND PERCENTAGE OF WOMEN 18 YEARS OF AGE AND OVER WHO HAVE BEEN PHYSICALLY OR SEXUALLY ASSAULTED, BY RELATIONSHIP OF PERPETRATOR

RELATIONSHIP	NUMBER (000s)**	PERCENT**
Total	5377	51
Spouse or ex-spouse	2652	29*
Date-boyfriend	1724	16
Other known man	2461	23
Stranger	2456	23

*Based on the number of women who have ever been married or lived with a man in a common-law relationship.
**Figures do not add to totals because of multiple response.

Almost four women in ten (39 percent) have been victims of sexual assault. One in four women reported unwanted sexual touching, and the same proportion reported a violent sexual attack. A much smaller proportion, 17 percent, have been physically threatened or assaulted by men other than spouses.

The percentage of women who have been assaulted by a spouse or live-in partner is 29 percent. Overall, rates of violence in previous marriages were estimated to be 48 percent compared with 15 percent in marriages that were current at the time of the interview. There is a continued risk of violence to women from ex-partners despite a divorce or separation. In fact, 19 percent of women assaulted by a previous partner said the man was violent during a period of separation, and in one-third of these cases the violence became more severe during that time.

As Table 19.1 illustrates, the most common forms of violence inflicted on women by marital partners were pushing, grabbing, and shoving followed by threats of hitting, slapping, throwing something at them, kicking, biting, and hit-ting with fists. While the percentage of women who have been beaten up, choked, sexually assaulted, or had a gun or knife used against them are all less than 10 percent, in each of these categories, between 400 000 and 800 000 Canadian women have been affected.

Not only do Canadian women report significant levels of violence, a majority of those who have been physically or sexually assaulted have been victimized more than once. The greatest risk of repeat victimization is in the area of sexual violence. Sixty percent of women who have been sexually assaulted by someone other than a spouse reported more than one such incident, and 26 percent were assaulted *four times or more*. Four in ten women who have been violently sexually attacked, and six in ten who reported unwanted sexual touching, said it happened to them more than once.

Women are at risk of sexual violence in a variety of locations and situations. As Figure 19.1 illustrates, almost one-half of all sexual assaults (46 percent) occurred in a private place such as the woman's home, the man's home, someone else's home, or in a car. For some, sexual assault

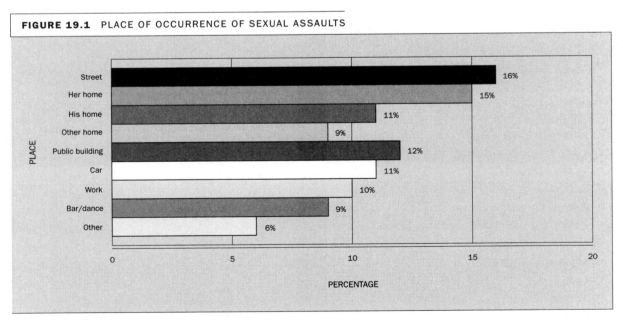

FIGURE 19.1   PLACE OF OCCURRENCE OF SEXUAL ASSAULTS

SOURCE: Based on material from Violence against Women survey, 1993.

is an occupational hazard (10 percent occurred at the woman's place of work) and not an uncommon risk of being on the street, at a bar or dance, and using public buildings.

In the majority of cases, wife assault is characterized by this survey as ongoing or repeated acts of violence, in which incidents recur and increase in severity over time. Although pushing, grabbing, and shoving were the most commonly reported type of violence, only 5 percent of women said this was the only thing that happened to them, and only 4 percent said they were just threatened. As Table 19.3 shows, the majority of abused women said they were assaulted on more than one occasion, and one-third were assaulted more than ten times. This table also shows how much more violent men from previous marital relationships were. Ten percent of women reporting violence by a current partner said it happened more than ten times compared with 41 percent of women who were assaulted by a previous partner.

EMOTIONAL ABUSE BY MARITAL PARTNERS

Research shows that a great deal of violence against wives occurs in the context of the man's possessiveness, jealousy, and demands or criticisms over her domestic performance (Dobash and Dobash, 1984; Hart, 1988; Walker, 1979). The man's obsessiveness about his wife and his

desire to control her have also been cited as precursors to wife killings (Daly and Wilson, 1988; Walker, 1984; Wilson and Daly, 1992, 1994). Emotionally abusive behaviour, therefore, is important contextual information about wife battering. Emotional abuse was measured in this survey through responses to statements about the partner's efforts to jealously guard the woman's contact with other men, to isolate her from outside support, to control her whereabouts, or to degrade her through name-calling and put-downs. As Table 19.4 illustrates, the percentage of ever-married women reporting emotional abuse by a spouse is higher than the percentage reporting violence: 35 percent said their partner has done one or more of these things to them compared with 29 percent who experienced physical or sexual violence. Emotional abuse was used in conjunction with violence by the majority of violent men: three-quarters of women who were assaulted by a spouse were also emotionally abused. A much smaller proportion (18 percent) who reported no physical violence by a marital partner were nonetheless emotionally abused.

Obsessive and controlling behaviour feature prominently in serious battering relationships. Emotional abuse is present in the majority of violent relationships, but the frequency of emotionally abusive and controlling behaviours on the part of violent men increases dramatically as the seriousness of the battering increases (Wilson,

TABLE 19.3   PERCENTAGE OF WOMEN 18 YEARS AND OVER WHO HAVE EXPERIENCED VIOLENCE BY A SPOUSE, BY NUMBER OF OCCURRENCES

NUMBER OF OCCURRENCES	EVER-MARRIED WOMEN	CURRENT PARTNER	PREVIOUS PARTNER
Total	100	100	100
1	35	59	24
2–5	22	22	22
6–10	9	7	11
11 or more	32	10	41
Not stated	2	—*	2

* Not statistically reliable.

TABLE 19.4 PERCENTAGE OF EVER-MARRIED WOMEN REPORTING EMOTIONAL ABUSE, BY TYPE OF PHYSICAL VIOLENCE

TYPE OF EMOTIONAL ABUSE	ALL WOMEN	LESS SEVERE VIOLENCE*	MORE SEVERE VIOLENCE*
Total**	35	79	95
1. He is jealous and doesn't want her to talk to other men	19	48	72
2. He tries to limit her contact with family or friends	16	39	65
3. He insists on knowing who she is with and where she is at all times	22	44	70
4. He calls her names to put her down or make her feel bad	21	49	81
5. He prevents her from knowing about or having access to the family income, even if she asks	10	24	44

*Previous spouses only.
**Figures do not add to totals because of multiple response.

Johnson, and Daly, 1995). In cases of severe violence by an ex-spouse, emotionally abusive and controlling behaviours were used by 95 percent of abusers (Table 19.4). Severe violence was defined as being beaten up or worse or receiving injuries that required medical attention.

For a controlling and abusive man, his partner's pregnancy may represent to him a threat to his exclusive control over her and to her exclusive attention and affection toward him. Overall, 21 percent of women physically or sexually assaulted by a spouse were assaulted during pregnancy. Violence during pregnancy was four times more frequent among women who experienced the most severe forms of violence than among others victimized less severely (33 percent as compared with 8 percent). These findings add important empirical support to theories that explain wife assault as a function of gender relations, male dominance and power, and control in marital relationships.

CORRELATES OF VIOLENT VICTIMIZATION

Sample surveys like the Violence against Women survey lend themselves to an analysis of the distribution of violent victimization within the population. In other words, they allow us to describe who is at greatest risk of being victimized according to certain social characteristics of Canadian women. Table 19.5 outlines the percentage of women who have ever been physically or sexually assaulted by a spouse or sexually assaulted by someone other than a spouse according to their age, marital status, household income, and education. Since these characteristics are subject to change over time and may have changed significantly between the time of the assault and the time of the interview, these calculations are based on a snap-shot of experiences in the twelve months preceding the survey.

Women learn about sexual violence and threats to their safety at a young age. Young women 18 to 24 years of age experienced rates of sexual assault twice that of women in the next age group (25 to 34) and had rates of wife assault that were three times higher. Although characteristics of perpetrators are not shown in this table, the same distinct age effect is evident in men who are violent toward their wives. The rate of wife assault in newer marriages, that is, relationships of two years or less, was almost three times the national average.

TABLE 19.5 TWELVE-MONTH RATES OF WIFE ASSAULT AND SEXUAL ASSAULT, BY SOCIODEMOGRAPHIC
CHARACTERISTICS OF WOMEN

SOCIODEMOGRAPHIC CHARACTERISTICS	WIFE ASSAULT*	SEXUAL ASSAULT
Twelve-month rate	3 *percentage*	5
Age Group		
18–24	12	18
25–34	4	8
35–44	3	5
45 and over	1	1
Marital Status		
Married	2	2
Common-law	9	7
Separated	n/a	10
Divorced	n/a	13
Single	n/a	15
Widowed	—**	—
Household Income		
Less than $15 000	6	7
$15 000–$29 999	3	6
$30 000–$59 999	3	5
$60 000 or more	3	5
Education		
Less than high school	3	4
High school diploma	3	5
Some postsecondary education	3	8
University degree	3	4

*Based on women who were married or living with a man in a common-law relationship in the twelve months preceding the survey.
** Not statistically reliable.

Other personal characteristics that are associated with age also show up as strong predictors of risk of sexual assault. For example, single women and those with some postsecondary education (the largest proportion of whom are in the youngest age group) report the highest rates of sexual assault. In the case of wife assault, a woman's education has no bearing on her risk, although her partner's education does seem to have an effect: men without a high school education assaulted their wives at twice the rate of men with a university degree. Men who were out of work in the year prior to the survey committed assaults against their wives at twice the rate of employed men. Finally, women living in common-law relationships had rates of violence by a spouse that were four times as high as women legally married.

Contrary to common stereotypes of battered women, household income is not as strong a factor in wife assault as some others. Women living in households with incomes under $15 000 have rates of wife assault that are twice the national average; however, rates for women in high-income households ($60 000 and over) are the same as rates for women in the middle-income range. Rates of sexual assault also decline slightly as the woman's household income increases, but not markedly.

Rates of violent victimization vary depending on the geographic area in which a woman lives. Women living in urban areas have somewhat higher rates of wife assault and sexual violence; women living in British Columbia and Alberta report the highest provincial rates and Newfoundland women the lowest (Table 19.6). It is not clear to what extent these provincial differences may be attributed to cultural differences and the willingness or reluctance of the women responding to report their experiences to an

interviewer, or whether these are indicators of real differences in the levels of violence against women. The general east–west pattern with rising rates in the western provinces is consistent with police statistics and theories that the greater migration into British Columbia and Alberta results in fewer social controls in these provinces and subsequent increases in criminal activity. Newfoundland, on the other hand, is a province with much higher out-migration and lower in-migration than others, which may produce greater social cohesion and controls against behaving violently. These provincial patterns, together with the relatively weak relationship between wife assault and household income, must cause us to question certain assumptions about the links between poverty and abuse, since Newfoundland, one of the most economically depressed areas of the country, has the lowest rates of violence against women.

TABLE 19.6   LIFETIME RATES OF WIFE ASSAULT AND SEXUAL ASSAULT, BY PLACE OF RESIDENCE

PLACE OF RESIDENCE	WIFE ASSAULT*	SEXUAL ASSAULT
Total ever assaulted	29	37
Urban/Rural		
Urban	30	38
Rural	26	30
Province		
British Columbia	32	45
Alberta	30	42
Saskatchewan	25	32
Manitoba	26	35
Ontario	25	38
Quebec	22	31
New Brunswick	23	33
Nova Scotia	27	35
Prince Edward Island	22	39
Newfoundland	14	25

(percentage)

*Based on women who have ever been married or lived with a man in a common-law relationship.

CONCLUSIONS

The Violence against Women survey provides empirical evidence of widespread violence against women in Canadian society. Three in ten women who have ever been married or lived with a man in a common-law relationship have experienced violence by a marital partner, and almost four in ten women have been sexually assaulted. A great many women have been victimized more than once.

Violence and the threat of violence are lessons learned early in life. Young women have the highest rates of sexual assault, and young women in new marriages are at greatest risk of violence from their equally young male partners. Common-law marital status elevates the risk of wife assault. The highest rates of wife assault are reported to have occurred in relationships that have ended, quite often from estranged spouses. Emotionally abusive and controlling behaviour is common in men who assault their wives, especially as the severity of the violence escalates.

Some writers would argue that "lifestyle" and "routine activities" are central to developing an explanation of how personal characteristics affect rates of violent victimization. Adherents of this position maintain that victimization rates reflect differences in exposure to risk that result from occupational and leisure activities. To the extent that lifestyle puts people in dangerous places, or out on the street late at night, their risk of victimization will increase. Crime victimization surveys have shown that young people have fewer family responsibilities and a more active lifestyle than older people, which allow them to engage in evening activities outside the home. In the context of the lifestyle/routine activities perspective, the higher victimization rates of young women would be explained by the greater likelihood that these women are unmarried, free from family responsibilities, and active in evening activities that put them in close proximity to offenders.

There are problems in attempting to apply the lifestyle/routine activities approach to violent victimization of women, however. As the Violence against Women survey indicates, women face a greater risk of violence in familiar places by men they know. While lifestyle and routine activities may play a role in stranger attacks, or in understanding sexual assault as an occupational hazard for some women, they cannot account for the very high rate of violence involving intimates. Clearly, a different perspective is necessary to explain the causes of wife assault and dating violence, since the greatest risk factor, according to lifestyle/routine activities, is to be married, dating, or living with a man. This is the "activity" that puts women in close proximity to an offender and at risk of violence. Similarly, in a significant proportion of cases of sexual assault, the risky activity is dating, or having a father, a colleague, or a neighbour. The victim-blaming focus of this perspective, when applied to situations of sexual violence and wife assault, helps perpetuate negative stereotypes about women who "ask for it" by their appearance or style of dress or who stay with a violent man because somehow they enjoy it, relieving men of the responsibility for their violence. What is needed for a clearer understanding of why so many men are violent toward women is a focus on the offender and on societal factors that legitimate male dominance over women in so many aspects of life. For example, what is the role of emotional abuse in battering relationships, and how does it keep women from leaving the men who abuse them? What assumptions do men make about the "availability" of young women in particular as acceptable targets for sexual violence? How have the criminal justice system and other helping systems reinforced cultural messages that violence against women will be tolerated? These are the questions and the orientation necessary to tackle the important research issues and policy decisions ahead in the area of violence against women.

NOTE

The author wishes to thank Karen Rodgers, Canadian Centre for Justice Statistics, and the editors for their comments and suggestions on an earlier draft.

1. The manner in which the Conflict Tactics Scale is typically introduced to respondents, as a list of ways of settling differences, is problematic: it is potentially very confusing to respondents and not appropriate for orienting them toward thinking about violence they have suffered at the hands of their partners. While some respondents may think about experiences of violence as ways of settling differences, a great many may not, which must cause us to question the reliability and validity of a scale to measure violence that was, in fact, designed to address ways of resolving conflict. There is substantial evidence that many acts of aggression by men against their wives are not precipitated by an argument or disagreement between them, and it is questionable whether respondents would think them appropriate to include. The Violence against Women survey represents a significant departure from other surveys employing the CTS in that it has an extensive lead-up to questions about spousal violence through detailed questions about fear of violence in public places, precautionary behaviour, sexual harassment, and sexual and physical violence by strangers, dates and boyfriends, and other known men. This survey is concerned not with ways of settling disagreements but with violence against women, and this context will have been established at this point.

Traditional usage of the CTS asks respondents to quantify each violent act or blow, a seemingly impossible task for victims of repeated or ongoing violence. Emphasis throughout the Violence against Women survey is on the number of different occasions a marital partner has been violent, the types

of violent acts, and the level of injury and emotional upset suffered by the victim, and not on counting each threat or blow.

REFERENCES

Clark, Lorenne, and Debra Lewis. 1977. *Rape: The Price of Coercive Sexuality*. Toronto: The Women's Press.

Daly, M., and M. Wilson. 1988. *Homicide*. New York: Aldine de Gruyter.

Dekeseredy, Walter, and Katharine Kelly. 1993. "The Incidence and Prevalence of Woman Abuse in Canadian University and College Dating Relationships." *Canadian Journal of Sociology* 18(2): 137–59.

Dekeseredy, Walter, and Brian MacLean. 1990. "Research Women Abuse in Canada: A Realist Critique of the Conflict Tactics Scale." *Canadian Review of Social Policy* 25: 19–27.

Dobash, R., and R. Dobash. 1984. "The Nature and Antecedents of Violent Events." *British Journal of Criminology* 24: 269–88.

Hart, B. 1988. "Beyond the 'Duty to Warn': A Therapist's 'Duty to Protect' Battered Women and Children." In K. Yllo and M. Bograd (eds.), *Feminist Perspectives on Wife Abuse*. Beverly Hills: Sage.

Kelly, Liz. 1988. *Surviving Sexual Violence*. Minneapolis: University of Minnesota Press.

Koss, Mary, and C. Gidycz. 1985. "Sexual Experiences Survey: Reliability and Validity." *Journal of Consulting and Clinical Psychology* 53: 422–23.

Smith, Michael. 1994. "Enhancing the Quality of Survey Data on Violence against Women: A Feminist Approach." *Gender and Society* 8(1): 109–27.

Stanko, Elizabeth. 1990. *Everyday Violence: How Men and Women Experience Sexual and Physical Danger*. London: Pandora.

Straus, Murray. 1990. "Measuring Intrafamily Conflict and Violence: The Conflict Tactics (CTS) Scales." In Murray Straus and Richard

Gelles (eds.), *Physical Violence in American Families: Risk Factors and Adaptations to Violence in 8145 Families.* New Brunswick, NJ: Transaction.

Walker, L. 1979. *The Battered Woman.* New York: Harper Perennial.

———. 1984. *Battered Woman Syndrome.* New York: Springer.

Wilson, M., and M. Daly. 1992. "Who Kills Whom in Spouse Killings? On the Exceptional Sex Ratio of Spousal Homicides in the United States." *Criminology* 30(2): 189–215.

———. 1994. "Spousal Homicide." *Juristat* 14: 8.

Wilson, M., H. Johnson, and M. Daly. 1995. "Lethal and Nonlethal Violence against Wives." *Canadian Journal of Criminology* 37: 331–61.

Chapter 20

Neoconservatism and the Canadian Pro-Family Movement

LORNA ERWIN

Unlike their American counterparts, Canada's anti-feminist forces—the pro-family movement—were not initially hostile to the welfare state. In the early and mid-1980s when REAL (an acronym standing for Realistic Equal Active for Life) Women and a handful of kindred organizations[1] arose to denounce feminist influences on the schools, the courts, the media, and even the governments of the day, there was little attempt in the pro-family defence of the traditional housewife to tie feminists to the alleged excesses of "runaway" social spending or "confiscatory" taxation. While in the United States, the very emergence of a "New Right" during the Carter and Reagan presidencies was predicated on the fusion of a cultural politics of family, sexuality, and reproduction with a backlash against welfare and government spending,[2] the leaders and publications of Canadian anti-feminism paid little attention to state programs per se. And even when they opposed new initiatives, as they consistently have in the case of a national daycare program, they eschewed neoconservative rhetoric.

For such leaders, no less than for our former prime minister, social programs remained a "sacred trust." There was no New Right during the 1980s to bolster the neoconservative agenda of the Mulroney government, which meant that what the government managed to achieve in cutting back income-maintenance and social-assistance programs, and in other deregulatory and redistributory measures, had to be achieved mainly by stealth. Nevertheless, since 1987 a notable shift toward neoconservative discourse has occurred in pro-family ideology. Where once it was sexual liberation and women's employment outside the home that were at the centre of movement discourse, now it is the intrusive, feminist-driven state with its confiscatory levels of taxation.

With frequent acknowledgements to the Hoover Institution and the Fraser Institute, pro-family leaders now present the family as a self-sufficient unit needing little help from governments. Social welfare "give-aways" only demoralize the family while fiscally conservative policies strengthen it. That such a shift in rhetoric comes at a time of rapid changes of leadership and a kind of stasis in movement affairs raises inevitable questions about the movement's likely impact on Canada's political life. Are we now, finally, to see a full-blown religious right in English-speaking Canada, just as this phenomenon has suffered a major defeat in the U.S. presidential election? This question is all the more compelling in light of recent reports of the Reform Party's success in appealing to evangelical Protestants (*The Globe and Mail*, December 30, 1992: 1).

Source: "Neoconservatism and the Canadian Pro-Family Movement," *Canadian Review of Sociology and Anthropology* 30, 3 (1993): 401–20. Reprinted by permission of the publisher.

This chapter explores the likelihood of the pro-family leadership succeeding in this endeavour. To this end, the origins and the ideological development of the movement are discussed, and empirical data on the sociodemographic background and the political beliefs of the membership are presented. In light of these data, the movement's potential to generate a consensus among its membership in support of a broad attack on social services and welfare spending is explored.

SOCIAL MOVEMENTS AND CONSENSUS MOBILIZATION

Linked to the question of national impact is a prior question of mobilization. While the literature on social movements is rich in theories concerning how movements get started, there is little to guide explorations of the maintenance and reactivation of membership commitment — especially when leaders of existing movements attempt to redefine the groups and social influences that are to be opposed. Even the more recent theoretical developments in the field, resource mobilization theory and the new social movement approach, shed little light on such matters. While the first concentrates on the mobilization of resources and the costs and benefits of participation, it does not concern itself with the formation of mobilization potentials at all. As for new social movement theory, this paradigm does focus on the mobilization potential of contemporary social movements, but it assumes that mobilization potentials form spontaneously through societal developments. Overlooked is the part that social movements themselves play in defining situations that move individuals to action (Klandermans, 1988). Moreover, both these approaches are chiefly concerned with the emergence of social movements, rather than with how commitment is sustained or redirected.

This lacuna in the literature is curious given that the success of any particular movement campaign is usually dependent upon its staying power — that is, on its ability to affect both consensus and action mobilization (i.e., the activation of commitment by individuals who already belong to the movement). It cannot be taken for granted that rank-and-file members feel that the concrete goals of leaders and movement organizations are related to their dissatisfactions and aspirations; nor can it be assumed that such adherents will consistently believe that participation in the movement's activities is effective (Klandermans, 1988). Even in the case of en bloc engagement, individuals have to decide whether and to what degree they will conform to the collectivity, particularly if the movement is promoting views that differ from those around which it originally mobilized.

In one of the few attempts to illuminate the relationship between ideology and participant mobilization, Snow, Rochford, Worden, and Benford (1986) develop a series of useful concepts in their cross-cultural analysis of the peace movement. The term *framing*, an extension of Goffman's frame analysis (Goffman, 1974), is used to illuminate the signifying work that social movements do. It focuses, in other words, on the process of mobilizing adherents by assigning meaning to relevant events and conditions. In this view, the mobilization or activation of adherents is contingent upon the linkage of individual and movement interpretive orientations, such that "some sets of individual interests, values, and beliefs and social movement activities, goals, and ideology are congruent and complementary" (Snow et al., 1986: 464). While Snow et al. identify various sets of factors that affect the "mobilizing potential" of a movement's framing efforts, only one set — what they refer to as *phenomenological constraints* — will be drawn on here.[3]

Phenomenological constraints involve three interrelated but analytically distinct factors: (1) *empirical credibility*; (2) *experiential commensurability*; and (3) *narrative fidelity*. Empirical credibility refers to the fit between the framing and events in the world. Are there events or occurrences that can be pointed to as legitimating evidence for the claims of the movement to its supporters? Experiential commensurability refers to the interpretive lens through which the "evidence" is filtered, especially in light of the personal experiences of individuals, which usually act as an important screening mechanism. Do the framing efforts interpret threatening events and developments in ways that harmonize with the ways in which these events, etc., are currently being experienced? Or are such framing efforts too abstract, too distant from the everyday existence of participants? To illustrate, Snow et al. (1986: 209) suggest that it was precisely such a lack of experiential commensurability in the peace movement's "doomsday campaign" in the United States that explains the difficulties American peace activists encountered, compared with European and Japanese activists, in concretizing the nuclear threat to their compatriots. Apparently a "doomsday" frame did not resonate among Americans as it did among European and Japanese citizens, and, consequently, was a weak prod to action. As for the third of Snow, Rochford, Worden, and Benford's phenomenological constraints, narrative fidelity, this refers to the degree to which framings strike a responsive chord with the cultural heritage of movement supporters. In sum, the more credible, experientially commensurable, and culturally resonant a leadership's framing efforts are, the more likely action mobilization will occur.

Or as Antonio Gramsci (1971) argues in his discussions of hegemony and revolution, "political education" must begin with and be linked to the nature and structure of the belief system that is the objective of transformation. It follows that when these linkages are effective, new symbols or goals can become the unifying points in the organization of the collective struggle. When they fail, the future of the movement is threatened.

DATA AND METHODS

The primary data for this examination of the pro-family movement were gathered in 1986–87 in a mail-out questionnaire survey of English-speaking supporters from across Canada ($N = 812$). When I undertook this research there was an absence of data on the national membership of the anti-abortion/pro-family forces in both Canada and the United States. Generalizations about movement participants were almost entirely based on small and localized samples of leaders, or "activists" —an unsatisfactory strategy for my purposes, since it was precisely the differences that usually divided leaders and followers, and the tensions that marked their relations, that I found problematic. These differences and tensions would be especially crucial, I felt, in any assessment of the likely impact of the movement on Canadian politics generally. But this entailed the problem of establishing the outer boundary of the movement. I needed some way of distinguishing between individuals who did identify with and contribute to the movement, however minimally, and those who were simply passive well-wishers.

It was, in any case, with these considerations in mind that I sought to make use of the subscription list of *The Interim*. This is a non-sectarian monthly publication, begun in 1983 and edited in Toronto, which bills itself as "Canada's Pro-Life, Pro-Family Newspaper." Without a rival in the field, *The Interim* already had a readership that numbered in the tens of thousands by 1986. It circulated in all parts of English-speaking Canada, and was not tied to any particular organization or subsection of the pro-family universe. Its claim of being the national voice of the movement was thus a reasonable one. Hence my assumption that its subscribers (almost all of whom had paid $9.00 for an annual subscription) were supporters of the cause it served—an expectation that was well borne out by the data that the survey yielded on pro-family activities.

To obtain a random sample of names and addresses from *The Interim*'s computerized list of subscribers ($N = 46\,683$) every thirty-ninth name was selected, producing a total of 1197 names and addresses. Questionnaires were sent to each of these, as were reminder cards. Deaths, vacated dwellings, and inaccurate addresses eliminated 118 of these selections, reducing the base to 1079. From this base, 812 questionnaires were returned, a response rate of 75 percent.

The questionnaire was divided into four sections: (1) participation in the movement; (2) social and moral attitudes; (3) political attitudes and behaviour; and (4) socioeconomic information. Where feasible, the survey included questions that allowed comparisons between pro-family adherents and the Canadian public. These questions were taken from various attitudinal and behavioural studies, such as the National Election Survey (1984), the Quality of Life Survey (1981), the Canadian Census (1985), and various years of the Gallup Poll.[4]

In addition to the survey, the analysis that follows is informed by interviews carried out with 28 movement leaders from across Canada and with 40 ordinary members mostly from Southern Ontario, and by my own observation of pro-family conferences, rallies, and workshops.

ORIGINS AND FRAMING STRATEGY

Although it is often the case that the inconspicuous protests and refusals that characterize the behaviour of future activists make it difficult to determine just when a movement begins (Freeman, 1983: 8–10), this is hardly true of the pro-family movement in Canada. In fact, the movement was organized by a number of key anti-abortion activists, whose initial idea was to broaden the base of their cause, chiefly by targeting feminists and their handmaidens in the schools, the government, and the media. That these activists were drawn from the hardline, no-compromise sector of the anti-abortion movement is significant, especially in light of a conventional association of intransigence on moral issues with religious fundamentalism.

In fact, the hardliners set out to deemphasize the movement's ethical and religious vocabulary,

though not to eliminate it altogether. The point was to frame the issue of abortion as a manifest symptom of social decay and elite irresponsibility. The rising toll of abortions, in this view, was the most visible evidence of a widespread rejection of the values associated with the breadwinner ethic and the traditional family — a rejection that was rooted in the movement of women into paid employment, in the social derogation of housewives, and especially in the increasing legitimacy of feminism and feminists. This latter focus became increasingly salient from the late 1970s on, as the hardliners split from the more moderate anti-abortionists in order to become more actively involved in politics. In Ontario, this was reflected in efforts, undertaken in the early 1980s, to oppose Bill 7, the homosexual rights bill. It was also reflected in attempts throughout the decade to elect anti-abortion and pro-family candidates in provincial and federal elections.

It was in 1983, however, that the dissident anti-abortionists were presented with the opportunity they needed, when a proposal to scrap the tax exemption for dependent spouses was put forward by federal cabinet minister Judy Erola. The upshot was REAL Women. "I felt tremendous indignation," one of REAL Women's founders told me about Erola's proposal.

> What feminists had always implied, that a woman who stays home is a second-class citizen, was now being translated into public policy. I called some of my pro-life friends and got in touch with some of the local groups and they were just fuming too. ... So they called other pro-lifers, and it just kind of snowballed. We decided to form our own group, one that would speak for the silent majority, the real women of Canada.

Equally shocking to REAL Women's founders were the constitutional developments of a year or so earlier, when feminists dramatically succeeded in writing gender-equality provisions into the new Canadian Charter of Rights and Freedoms. Society, it was claimed by the new organization, was now embroiled in an "undeclared civil war," one that pitted an "anti-family," materialistic "vocal minority" against an antimaterialistic "silent majority." Led by elite feminists and gay rights activists, "anti-family" groups had seized control of mainstream institutions and were launching a "wholesale, frontal attack" on traditional values. As for the policy goals of the new movement, these were largely restricted to measures aimed at shoring up the position of full-time homemakers (by improving their tax exemptions and pension benefits, increasing family allowances, and the like — proposals that for the most part were deemphasized after the movement entered its neoconservative phase). But apart from insistent demands that the federal and provincial grants sustaining women's organizations be ended, which was the centrepiece of its campaign to delegitimize feminism, the pro-family founders weren't all that interested in policy. Rather, their analyses of Canada's deteriorating social fabric seemed designed to lend rhetorical encouragement to the idea that sacrifice to family was still a woman's surest path to happiness and fulfillment. Finally, it is important to point out that appeals to potential recruits continued to be framed in religious terms, even if the main emphasis was a kind of secularized patriotism. It was still the Christian duty of those who believed in "the family" to fight for its survival. By the same token, if the "anti-family" forces were not successfully challenged, then both "the nation and the foundation of individual well-being" would be lost.

PROFILE OF THE PRO-FAMILY MEMBERSHIP

So much for the initial framing efforts of the pro-family leadership. Let us now address Snow and Benford's questions about the phenomenological fit between these framing efforts and the interests, experiences, and cultural-political heritage of the movement's early recruits.

Among the most striking findings to emerge from the survey data collected for this study are those that underscore the homogeneity of pro-family supporters, especially in terms of their generational experiences and religious commitments.[5] A solid majority of this predominantly female constituency is middle-aged (58 percent are women, and 62 percent of all respondents, women and men, are 45 years or older). Equally significant, 69 percent of them were raised in small towns or on farms, and 71 percent grew up in families whose mothers did not work outside the home.

And despite these Depression-era, rural, small-town beginnings (or perhaps because of them), they are relatively middle class and well educated. Thus 35 percent of pro-family individuals have a university degree (46 percent of the men and 27 percent of the women), compared with only 10 percent of Canadians generally, according to Quality of Life (QOL) data. (Unless otherwise specified, all comparisons of this kind are based on QOL surveys.) Likewise, 27 percent are professionals or semiprofessionals, compared with only 14 percent of Canadians generally. Indeed, of the 50 percent of pro-family respondents who are employed, some 54 percent are professionals or semiprofessionals, compared with 23 percent of all Canadians.

Regarding both individual and family income, here comparisons are less revealing — chiefly, I would speculate, because so many of this relatively aged group are either retired or full-time homemakers. Thus 41 percent of the male respondents earned at least $40 000 annually (again in 1986–87 dollars), compared with only 8 percent for all Canadian men (Census of Canada, 1986: 93–114). Yet median family income for all pro-family respondents was only $250 higher than the 1986 Canadian average: $35 000 versus $34 750 (Census of Canada, 1986: 93). Such modest family incomes would seem to validate the movement's claim that its members espouse antimaterialist values. They, at any rate, reflect the fact that 51 percent of women respondents are full-time homemakers, with 25 percent indicating they are "satisfied" and 75 percent saying they are "very satisfied" in this role. By the same token, very few indicate a desire for employment on either a full-time or part-time basis (.2 percent want a full-time job versus 8 percent of all Canadian homemakers; and 6 percent a part-time job versus 29 percent of all Canadian homemakers). Not surprisingly, pro-family members have large families and stable marriages: 74 percent are currently married, only 3 percent have ever experienced divorce or separation, and 57 percent have three children or more.[6]

Turning now to religion, the mainstream Protestant denominations (United and Anglican) are very poorly represented among pro-family supporters, with 95 percent being either Catholic or fundamentalist. Ninety-three percent say that their religious beliefs are important to them, while 96 percent report church attendance of at least once a week. Given this exceptional level of commitment, it is hardly surprising that a majority of them (56 percent) got involved in the movement through their church. Significantly enough, 72 percent had never been politically active prior to their involvement in one of the anti-abortion/pro-family organizations.

Indeed, the beliefs and motivations underlying their participation in the movement are remarkably similar — and also highly congruent with the initial framing efforts of the movement (see Table

20.1). Thus a common belief — expressed in both the questionnaires and in the 68 interviews undertaken for this study — is that pro-family supporters are engaged in a righteous crusade against adversaries variously depicted as "wealthy," "well-educated," "anti-family," "materialistic," and "sexually promiscuous." They are likewise described as "atheists," or "secular humanists" and "radical feminists who hate men." Associated with the anti-family forces are a number of prominent organizations: the United Church, the New Democratic Party, the National Action Committee on the Status of Women, and Planned Parenthood, as well as all feminist, pro-choice, and gay rights groups.

As for the extent of this constituency's participation in the movement, here too there is evidence that the framing efforts of the leadership were highly successful. Forty-four percent of the survey respondents report giving their time on a regular basis; 76 percent say they have gone to the trouble of contacting a politician, and 48 percent have protested at a clinic or hospital where abortions are being performed. Ninety percent also report making financial contributions beyond the membership fees charged by REAL Women and most of the other groups. (The average donation was $75, with 31 percent donating $100 or more.) Finally, while 31 percent voiced disapproval of movement actions,

TABLE 20.1 RESPONSES OF PRO-FAMILY RESPONDENTS TO THE QUESTION: "PLEASE INDICATE HOW IMPORTANT THE FOLLOWING CONCERNS WERE TO YOU IN YOUR DECISION TO BECOME INVOLVED IN THE PRO-FAMILY MOVEMENT."

	VERY IMPORTANT	FAIRLY IMPORTANT	NOT IMPORTANT	TOTAL %	NUMBER OF CASES
Opposition to abortion	99	.3	.2	100	810
Support for traditional values	67	22.0	11.0	100	806
Opposition to pornography	62	23.0	15.0	100	802
Opposition to secular humanism	55	28.0	17.0	100	803
Opposition to the gay rights movement	52	26.0	22.0	100	800
Opposition to the feminist movement	48	33.0	19.0	100	802
Opposition to sex education in schools	46	34.0	20.0	100	796

only 8 percent had Canadian activities in mind. The rest exclusively cited tactics used in the United States, particularly the fire-bombing of abortion clinics.

THE TURN TOWARD NEOCONSERVATISM

By 1987, after four years of existence, REAL Women could plausibly claim a groundswell of national support. Affiliates had been established in every province and region of the country, and —to judge by the circulation figures of *The Interim*—a national membership of roughly 100 000 had been recruited to the various pro-family groups. Clearly, the leaders' framing strategy, which had linked a decline of support for the traditional family to an elitist feminist ascendancy, had struck a responsive chord. Indeed, despite a partial downplaying of religion, there is every indication, to judge by the data presented above, that the leadership succeeded very well in evoking and projecting themes that accorded with the marked religiosity and the unusual "life worlds" of the membership. In Snow, Rochford, Worden, and Benford's terms, these ideological frames acted as effective prods to mobilization because of the large extent to which they were commensurate with both the lived realities and "inherent ideology" of a large constituency of Canadians.

In December 1987, however, this framing strategy was altered. A statement entitled "Towards a Pro-Family Economy," appearing in the newsletter of REAL Women, marked the change. In the past, it began,

> the pro-family movement has emerged in Canada to battle the "social issues," i.e., abortion, pornography, ... radical feminism, etc. With but few exceptions, we have given little attention to the monetary issues affecting Canadian families—the government tax and spend machine. Among economists, Canadians are defined as a people whose attitudes display little sympathy towards reducing government

spending programs and reducing individual tax rates. The Department of Finance holds the idea that the "Canadian psyche" is such that we are willing to pay substantially higher rates to maintain the government programs and giveaways we have come to expect. Hasn't the time come to tell the Department of Finance they are reading the Canadian public wrong? (*REALity*, 1987: 1)

This statement went on to comment on a White Paper on tax reform issued by the Conservative government in Ottawa, praising its proposals for lowering corporate taxes, while suggesting that its projected reduction of personal income taxes didn't go far enough.

Then, a few months later, another change was registered, when the organization's newsletter dropped the scriptural passages that framed its masthead. We have gone through "a year of difficulties over changing our original directions," a May 1988 *REALity Update* stated, cryptically, in an announcement that the organization was moving its national office to Ottawa. The difficulties, which had come to a head at a February 1988 conference, involved infighting between old and new board members over the role that "Christian" and "family" values would play in the organization's campaign to become more policy oriented (read neoconservative). After the ousting of REAL Women's president and several board members, *The Interim* published a highly negative account of the recent takeover, and it and other anti-abortion groups began distancing themselves from the Ottawa-based board. This didn't seem to phase the new board members, however, as notes and articles in the newsletter became peppered with references to entrepreneurial freedom, the free market economy, high taxes, and government intrusions. Pay equity and affirmative action, the Spring 1988 issue of *REALity* states,

> are a blueprint for the radical restructuring of our society. ... The philosophy underlying this proposed legislation is just another factor introduced to undermine our free market. ... It

is an attempt at the wholesale redistribution of income implemented and watched over by a vast unprecedented bureaucracy with great power and little accountability. (*REALity*, 1988: 1–2)

Regarding daycare, a similar note was being struck:

> Free universally available daycare ... will direct national finances straight towards a catastrophe of appalling dimensions with unimagined repercussions. National bankruptcy is the hillside to which the aircraft is headed. ... The debt picture of Canada is such that ... the burden of a daycare tax would shock and oppress the nation. (*REALity*, 1988: 8)

Underlying this new emphasis on state intrusiveness and fiscal calamity was the notion that the family worked best as a self-sufficient unit. Social welfare "give-aways" only weakened the family, while fiscally conservative policies tended to strengthen it. Was this new framing venture one that played well with the membership? Did it lend itself to the tasks of building consen-

sus and action mobilization? Unfortunately, there exist no longitudinal survey data that might answer this question definitively. There is, however, considerable evidence from the 1986–87 survey to suggest why the movement has lost its momentum.

POLITICAL ATTITUDES OF THE PRO-FAMILY MEMBERSHIP

While the causal link between feminist influences and the incidence of family pathology and breakdown is widely believed within the pro-family movement, pro-family adherents are much more accepting of what they perceive to be the impact of feminism in the public realm. Thus, as Table 20.2 indicates, over 90 percent of respondents "agree" or "strongly agree" that feminism has "devalued motherhood" and "undermined traditional family values"; some 78 percent agree that "feminists do not understand the needs of homemakers"; and 91 percent either "agree" or "strongly agree" that "most Canadian women do not support feminist goals." Yet

TABLE 20.2   RESPONSES OF PRO-FAMILY RESPONDENTS TO THE QUESTION: "HERE ARE SOME OPINIONS THAT YOU HEAR DIFFERENT PEOPLE GIVING ABOUT THE FEMINIST MOVEMENT. PLEASE INDICATE WHETHER YOU STRONGLY AGREE, AGREE, DISAGREE, OR STRONGLY DISAGREE WITH THE FOLLOWING STATEMENTS."

	STRONGLY AGREE	AGREE	STRONGLY DISAGREE	DISAGREE	TOTAL %	NUMBER OF CASES
			(Percentages)			
Feminism has led to a devaluation of motherhood	61	31	2	6	100	782
Feminism has undermined traditional family values	53	38	2	7	100	762
Feminists don't understand the needs of homemakers	28	50	3	19	100	701
The majority of Canadian women don't support the goals of the feminist movement	41	50	2	7	100	649
Feminism has helped women in the work force	9	65	5	21	100	683
Feminism has contributed to an improvement in the status of women	7	42	16	35	100	709

there is also a perception among 74 percent of pro-family respondents that "feminism has helped women in the work force"; and almost half (49 percent) say that it has "contributed to an improvement in the status of women."

The membership's feelings about government involvement in daycare, a policy the movement is vehemently opposed to, are also mixed. While there is almost no support for the idea of a state-funded national scheme, subsidies for families that require daycare and live below the poverty line are acceptable to 42 percent of the membership—a view that is seemingly at odds with the movement's concern for eliminating all daycare funding. At the very least, such attitudes suggest that the movement's inflexible

views in this area are not widely shared by the membership.

And as with daycare, so too with attitudes toward government generally. Consider the findings of Table 20.3, in which there is little to suggest the complex of pro-business/anti-government attitudes that has been prevalent among the religious right in the United States. Pro-family respondents are somewhat more distrustful of unions than their QOL counterparts (81 percent versus 70 percent); they are more distrustful of big business, too (84 percent versus 74 percent). Both groups are roughly equal in their feelings about the federal government (47 percent versus 50 percent). But this last finding is not a distrust of government per se, to judge

TABLE 20.3 RESPONSES OF PRO-FAMILY AND QUALITY OF LIFE RESPONDENTS TO THE QUESTION: "SOME GROUPS IN CANADA HAVE MORE POWER THAN OTHERS TO GET THE THINGS THEY WANT. PLEASE INDICATE IF YOU THINK EACH OF THE GROUPS LISTED BELOW HAS TOO MUCH POWER FOR THE GOOD OF THE COUNTRY, TOO LITTLE POWER, OR ABOUT THE RIGHT AMOUNT OF POWER."

	TOO MUCH POWER	ABOUT RIGHT AMT. OF POWER	TOO LITTLE POWER	TOTAL %	NUMBER OF CASES
	(Percentages)				
The Media					
Pro-family	85	13	2	100	770
Large Corporations					
Pro-family	84	15	1	100	752
Quality of Life	74	23	3	100	2948
Labour Unions					
Pro-family	81	17	2	100	770
Quality of Life	70	22	8	100	2948
Federal Government					
Pro-family	47	47	6	100	725
Quality of Life	50	39	11	100	2948
Provincial Government					
Pro-family	29	61	10	100	727
Quality of Life	28	52	20	100	2948
Religious Leaders					
Pro-family	.05	36	62	100	721

Note: The "much, too much power" and "too much power" and the "much, much too little" and "much too little" categories are combined.

by the much lower figures for provincial governments (29 percent versus 28 percent for QOL respondents). Significantly enough, only religious leaders are felt—by 62 percent of pro-family respondents—to have "much too little" or "too little" power.

In Table 20.4 there is also little evidence of neoconservative tendencies among the pro-

TABLE 20.4   RESPONSES OF PRO-FAMILY AND QUALITY OF LIFE RESPONDENTS TO THE QUESTION: "HOW MUCH EFFORT DO YOU THINK THE GOVERNMENT SHOULD PUT INTO THE ACTIVITIES LISTED BELOW?"

	MORE EFFORT	SAME AMOUNT OF EFFORT	LESS EFFORT	TOTAL %	NUMBER OF CASES
		(Percentages)			
Fighting Pornography					
Pro-family	89	9	2	100	787
Helping the Poor					
Pro-family	77	21	2	100	781
Quality of Life	64	32	4	100	2840
Crime Prevention					
Pro-family	66	33	1	100	772
Quality of Life	74	24	2	100	2887
Education					
Pro-family	40	33	8	100	765
Quality of Life	55	42	3	100	2880
Assisting the Unemployed					
Pro-family	37	44	18	100	768
Quality of Life	36	40	24	100	2808
Protecting the Rights of the Disabled					
Pro-family	60	39	1	100	753
Protecting the Rights of Native People					
Pro-family	43	42	13	100	742
Quality of Life	48	41	11	100	2791
Establishing Equal Pay for Work of Equal Value Programs					
Pro-family	33	33	32	100	759
Eliminating Discrimination against Women					
Pro-family	19	33	42	100	722
Quality of Life	56	35	9	100	2836
Protecting Homosexuals from Discrimination in Employment					
Pro-family	5	24	63	100	721

Note: The "much more effort" and "more effort" and the "much less effort" and "less effort" categories are combined.

family supporters. Indeed, on some indicators they appear to be as liberal as, or even more liberal than, Canadians generally. Thus pro-family respondents want more government commitment to help the poor (77 percent versus 64 percent for QOL respondents); less to fight crime (66 percent versus 74 percent); and about the same for assisting the unemployed (37 percent versus 36 percent). Only when an issue identified with feminism is raised does the pro-family group digress sharply from the Canadian norm, with only 19 percent (versus 56 percent) wanting more government effort to eliminate discrimination against women.

Finally, consider the responses to the statements featured in Table 20.5. On two out of three questions, the pro-family respondents are stronger on what might be called the egalitarian position; and on the third—concerning the desirability of the gap between the rich and the poor—there is little to choose between them and Canadians generally (63 percent versus 67 percent for QOL respondents).

DISCUSSION

All told, these data on political attitudes suggest that if the pro-family constituency is not all that enthusiastic about extending income supports and social services, neither are they about to be mobilized for a campaign against the "government tax and spend machine." Except where sexual, reproductive, and family issues are concerned, their economic and political attitudes would seem to be somewhat more liberal than those of Canadians generally. "We live in a very prosperous country," I was told by one of the ordinary members I interviewed,

one in which no child should ever go hungry. I'd like to see the government revise the tax system: tax low income families much, much less and increase the taxes on the wealthy, particularly if they're single. And what about charity—people are so materialistic today, they have garage sales instead of giving stuff to the poor. It just makes me sick. We were poor during the Depression. My dad had died, but we

TABLE 20.5 RESPONSES OF PRO-FAMILY AND QUALITY OF LIFE RESPONDENTS TO THE QUESTION: "HERE ARE A SERIES OF STATEMENTS ABOUT SOCIAL ECONOMIC ISSUES. CHOOSE THE ANSWER THAT COMES CLOSEST TO YOUR OWN OPINION."

	AGREE	NEITHER AGREE NOR DISAGREE	DISAGREE	TOTAL %	NUMBER OF CASES
		(Percentages)			
People with High Incomes Should Pay more Taxes					
Pro-family	77	8	14	100	760
Quality of Life	57	13	30	100	2836
Too Much Difference between Rich and Poor					
Pro-family	63	23	13	100	767
Quality of Life	67	15	17	100	2841
Unemployment Is High because Welfare Is Too Easy to Get					
Pro-family	50	16	32	100	772
Quality of Life	67	11	22	100	2860

Note: The "strongly agree" and "agree" and the "strongly disagree" and "disagree" categories are combined.

never went hungry. The church and our neighbours helped us out until we got on our feet again.

Genuine as they are, such sentiments are still likely to be overwhelmed by the exceptional sexual, reproductive, and family concerns mentioned above. We see this especially in the fact that, despite the centrality of so much of their political thinking, pro-family individuals are deeply distrustful of the mainstream parties, including the federal Conservatives, whom they might be expected to support.

Thus, in response to a question on federal voting intentions (as of 1986–87), only 23 percent were prepared to vote for one of the three main parties, with the Conservatives (11 percent) and Liberals (10 percent) roughly splitting this vote equally. This would seem to auger well for the Reform Party (which hadn't been launched at the time the survey was completed). And this indeed is what some of the movement's leaders devoutly wish. "I'm very enthusiastic about the Reform Party," the current president of REAL Women stated in a recent interview.

> We don't tell our members how to vote but ... [w]e're both against equal pay for work of equal value, we're against so much government intervention into family and private life, which is what the radical feminists want. If they got their way, there'd be no private life left. The Reform Party seems to support many of the philosophical ideas that we have. (Sharpe and Braid, 1992: 145–46)

Leaders of the Alberta Federation of Women United for Families have also publicly endorsed Preston Manning, whose fundamentalist background and anti-abortion/pro-family views are well known in Alberta and perhaps elsewhere in the West. So far, however, the Reform Party has accented its neoconservative orthodoxy over its pro-family appeals. And Manning's promise of dealing with "moral" issues (like abortion) by referenda (Manning, 1992: 108) is a compromise that may not win that many votes from the pro-family constituency, especially in light of the recent work done by the federal Conservatives' Family Caucus to shore up the party's appeal to the religious right.

Consisting of some 32 backbench MPs, the Family Caucus, like the Reform Party, was launched since the survey data for this study were collected. (In fact, some 86 percent of pro-family respondents were of the opinion that, since their electoral sweep in 1984, the Tories had done little or nothing about pro-family concerns.) Caucus members meet with pro-family leaders, and some of its members have addressed pro-family functions. (The Caucus quietly bills itself as a "defender of Christian values.") Moreover, it supports various pro-family positions, including the recriminalization of abortion, the elimination of tax breaks for common-law couples, and the development of a child tax benefit program weighted in favour of the working poor rather than welfare recipients. It has also been credited with preventing amendments to the Human Rights Act that would recognize same-sex marriages, and with killing the Tory's national daycare scheme (*The Ottawa Citizen*, March 2, 1993: A3). Given all this, the Family Caucus might well outbid the Reform Party and draw pro-family voters to the Tories—though this isn't likely to happen if "feminist" Kim Campbell becomes the next Conservative leader. (Campbell's two divorces and her resignation from William Vander Zalm's cabinet over the abortion issue are not likely to endear her to pro-family supporters.)

Clearly, it is the Reform Party that has the best chance of corralling the pro-family vote (in the sense that President Reagan was able to corral the religious right in the United States). Nevertheless, if the survey data of this study are any guide, it won't happen. Essentially, we are dealing with a constituency of militant single-issue (or cluster-issue) voters, whose sympathy for the economic program of Manning's neoconservatism is too weak to induce them to abandon their normal practice of voting for pro-family candidates—Tory, Liberal, Reform, or independent—wherever such candidates may present themselves. As a political force, they may help to defeat feminist-backed measures—like the national daycare scheme promised by the Tories in 1988. That in itself is no small achievement, but it is not a sign that an American-style New Right is in the offing.

CONCLUSION

The outlook of pro-family supporters is clearly reflective of their material and social interests; more specifically, both their world view and lifestyles are characterized by a deep-seated traditionalism that rests on the economic privileges of the middle class and strict adherence to a conservative, religiously based moral code. The ideology of familialism (Barrett and McIntosh, 1982) that largely defines their world view is also embedded in their traditional family and gender arrangements. Indeed, it presents these relations as normal and right. In this light, their consciousness of the cultural and moral differences that separate them from mainstream society is not false. Indeed, the issues that concern pro-family adherents most deeply—i.e., women's abandonment of full-time homemaking, easier divorce legislation, the increasing secularization of society, and changing sexual mores and practices—do represent a threat to their way of life. Hence their sense of disquiet and righteous anger as the schools, courts, media, and other institutions that once upheld their values have become more tolerant of unconventional living arrangements and non-conforming groups.

The structural and cultural location of pro-family supporters, their experiences, and their religious and moral outlook therefore predisposed them to the initial framing efforts of the movement. Yet, coexisting with the moral traditionalism and religious populism of movement supporters is a kind of political conservatism that, paradoxically enough, is supportive of Canada's long-standing public-enterprise traditions, especially as these traditions mandate collective provision for basic needs. Hence, for example, their opposition to universal daycare, on the one hand, and their acceptance of some public subsidization in this area, on the other. By the same token, it is not the government or the state per se that is distrusted or reviled, as it is metropolitan elites and institutions: feminists above all, but also media and large corporations.

Given that the majority of the membership were political neophytes, the movement was clearly successful in its initial mobilization efforts. The likelihood, however, of its sustaining that commitment is now less certain. To revisit Snow, Rochford, Worden, and Benford's categories, the data reported here suggest that the movement's turn toward neoconservatism will not have empirical credibility, experiential commensurability, or narrative fidelity with the rank and file. The membership's lack of support for cutbacks in social services coupled with their acknowledgement of the structural factors, particularly economic hardship, that influence contemporary family relations, may lead them to view the leadership's demand for social welfare cutbacks as misplaced and unduly harsh. Again in Snow, Rochford, Worden, and Benford's term, the pro-family movement may well be confronted with the problem of "frame over-extension"; that is, an expansion of the boundaries of their primary framework to incorporate positions that have little resonance with the membership and may indeed run counter to the "inherent ideology" of many of them (1986: 206).

One theoretical implication of this analysis is the support it lends to Snow et al. (1986) and Klandermans (1988) to the effect that the process of sustaining consensus or redirecting a movement's participants may be a more interactive, multi-dimensional, and ultimately hazardous undertaking than is generally appreciated. Finally, apropos of the future of the pro-family movement, the data suggest that its neoconservative prospects are limited. Despite the leadership's current flirtation with the Reform Party, a full-blown New Right on the American model, with its fusion of a cultural and economic offensive, is unlikely. Our neoconservatives will have to continue to use stealth and indirection (as in the free trade agreements) if the dismantling of the Canadian welfare state is to proceed apace.

NOTES

Funding for the research reported herein was provided by the Faculty of Arts Research Grant (York University). I'm also grateful for the comments on earlier versions of this chapter provided by S.A. Longstaff, Michael D. Ornstein, Gordon Darroch, and three anonymous reviewers.

1. REAL Women is the most visible and active pro-family group in Canada. It is a national organization, which began in Toronto and quickly established affiliates in each of the provinces. Later, in 1988, it moved its headquarters to Ottawa. Other pro-family organizations include: the Coalition for Family Values, Renaissance Canada, the Alberta Federation of Women United for Families (AFWUF), Positive Parents, and various anti-abortion and religiously based groups.

2. See Eisenstein, 1989; Whitaker, 1987; Gordon and Hunter, 1977–78; and Petchesky, 1985 for discussions of the New Right's successful fusionist strategy in the United States.

3. The other sets of constraints discussed by Snow and Benford include: (1) the robustness, completeness, and thoroughness of the framing effort; (2) the internal structure of the larger belief system with which the movement seeks to affect some kind of cognitive ideational alignment; and (3) cycles of protest.

4. The 1981 Quality of Life (QOL) study was conducted by the Institute for Social Research at York University. The 1984 National Election Survey was conducted by Canadian Facts, a private survey and marketing firm. The Canadian Gallup Polls are national polls conducted by the Canadian Institute of Public Opinion, and Census of Canada data are published by Statistics Canada. Respondents in each of these surveys are selected randomly, and the target population includes all Canadian residents 18 years or older.

5. For a more detailed discussion of the class backgrounds of the pro-family leadership and rank and file, see Erwin (1988).

6. The respondents in this sample tend to fit the demographic profile and lifestyle pattern characteristic of participants in anti-abortion, anti-ERA, and anti-pornography organizations. Studies of these groups have found that growing up in a smaller-sized community, having a large family, being in stable marriages, and being a Catholic or Protestant fundamentalist with a high level of religiosity correlates with support for moral reform movements (Page and Clelland, 1978; Zurcher and Kirkpatrick, 1976; Wood and Hughes, 1984; Brady and Tedin, 1976; Leahy, Snow, and Worden, 1983; Petersen and Mauss, 1976; Singh and Leahy, 1978; and Luker, 1984).

REFERENCES

Barrett, Michèle, and Mary McIntosh. 1982. *The Anti-Social Family*. London: Verso.

Brady, David W., and Kent L. Tedin. 1976. "Ladies in Pink: Religion and Political Ideology in the Anti-ERA Movement." *Social Science Quarterly* 59 (March): 198–205.

Census of Canada. 1986. *Estimates of Families in Canada*. Catalogue no. 99-526.

Eisenstein, Zillah. 1989. "Liberalism, Feminism and the Reagan State: The Neo-Conservative Assault on (Sexual) Equality." Pp. 236–62 in Ralph Milliband, Leo Panitc, and John Seville, eds., *The Socialist Register*. London: Merlin Press.

Erwin, Lorna. 1988. "The Pro-Family Movement in Canada." Pp. 266–78 in Peta Tancred-

Sheriff, ed., *Feminist Research: Prospect and Retrospect*. Kingston: McGill-Queen's University Press.

Freeman, Jo, ed. 1983. *Social Movements of the Sixties and Seventies*. New York: Longman.

Goffman, Erving. 1974. *Frame Analysis*. New York: Harper Colophon.

Gordon, Linda, and Allen Hunter. 1977–78. "Sex, Family, and the New Right: Anti-feminism as a Political Force." *Socialist Review* 12 (November–February): 9–25.

Gramsci, Antonio. 1971. *Selections from the Prison Notebooks*. Translated by Q. Hoare and G. Nowell-Smith. London: Lawrence and Wishart.

Klandermans, Bert. 1988. "The Formation and Mobilization of Consensus." Pp. 173–96 in Bert Klandermans, Hanspeter Kriesi, and Sidney Tarrow, eds., *International Social Movement Research*. London: JAI Press.

Leahy, Peter J., David A. Snow, and Steven Worden. 1983. "The Anti-abortion Movement and Symbolic Crusades: Reappraisal of a Popular Theory." *Alternative Lifestyles* 6 (Fall): 27–47.

Luker, Kristin. 1984. *Abortion and the Politics of Motherhood*. Berkeley: University of California Press.

Manning, Preston. 1992. *The New Canada*. Toronto: Macmillan.

Page, Ann L., and Donald A. Clelland. 1978. "The Kanawha County Textbook Controversy: A Study of the Politics of Lifestyle Concern." *Social Forces* 57: 265–81.

Petchesky, Rosalind. 1985. *Abortion and Woman's Choice: The State, Sexuality, and Reproductive Freedom*. Boston: Northeastern University Press.

Petersen, Larry R., and Armand L. Mauss. 1976. "Religion and the 'Right to Life': Correlates of Opposition to Abortion." *Sociological Analysis* 37: 243–54.

REALity 1984. 2, No. 2 (Fall).

———. 1985. 3, No. 3.

———. 1986. 4, No. 4 (Summer).

———. 1987. 5, No. 1 (Christmas).

———. 1988. 6, No. 1 (Spring).

REALity Update. 1986. January (no volume indicated).

———. 1988. May (no volume indicated).

Sharpe, Sydney, and Don Braid. 1992. *Storming Babylon: Preston Manning and the Rise of the Reform Party*. Toronto: Key Porter Books.

Singh, Khrisna B., and Peter J. Leahy. 1978. "Contextual and Ideological Dimensions of Attitudes toward Discretionary Abortion." *Demography* 15 (August): 381–88.

Snow, David A., E. Burke Rochford, Jr., Steven K. Worden, and Robert D. Benford. 1986. "Frame Alignment Processes, Micromobilization, and Movement Participation." *American Sociological Review* 51, no. 4: 464–81.

Whitaker, Reg. 1987. "Neo-conservatism and the State." Pp. 1–31 in Ralph Milliband, Leo Panitch, and John Saville, eds., *The Socialist Register*. London: Merlin Press.

Wood, Michael, and Michael Hughes. 1984. "The Moral Basis of Moral Reform: Status Discontent vs. Culture and Socialization as Explanations of Anti-Pornography Social Movement Adherence." *American Sociological Review* 49: 86–99.

Zurcher, Louis A., and George R. Kirkpatrick. 1976. *Citizens for Decency: Antipornography Crusades as Status Defense*. Austin: University of Texas Press.

Voters are unhappy, in Canada no less than in other democratic countries. Surveys repeatedly show that Canadians are growing increasingly cynical about politics and distrustful of politicians. As a result, fewer Canadians are voting; while three-quarters of eligible voters cast ballots in the 1984 federal election, only two-thirds did so in 1997. In addition, political loyalty is becoming antique. That is, voters are more willing than ever to switch their allegiance from one party to the next in succeeding elections. They are swayed less by ideologies, principles, and programs than by personalities and fleeting issues. Consequently, Canada's political landscape gyrates wildly from one election to the next. The fortunes of some parties rise as quickly as the fortunes of other parties decline (see Figure P4B.1).

Despite the widespread discontent that mars Canadian politics, voters are more highly educated than ever and they are just as interested in politics as past generations of voters. However, they are more likely than past generations to express their interest and sophistication by participating in nonconventional forms of politics. Thus, in a 1980 survey, 24 percent of Canadians said they had joined in a boycott, attended an unlawful demonstration, joined an unofficial strike, or occupied a building or a factory at least once. In a 1990 survey, the comparable figure was nearly 33 percent. Participation in nonconventional politics is most common among young, highly educated people. If present trends continue, therefore, one may reasonably expect participation in nonconventional forms of politics to increase in coming years.

In Chapter 21, political scientist Harold Clarke and his associates document the growing cynicism of the Canadian electorate and blame it squarely on the growth of what they call brokerage politics. Brokerage politics involves party leaders organizing focus groups, public opinion polls, and informal canvasses of voters to determine the hot issues of the day. With this information in hand, party leaders delineate the varied

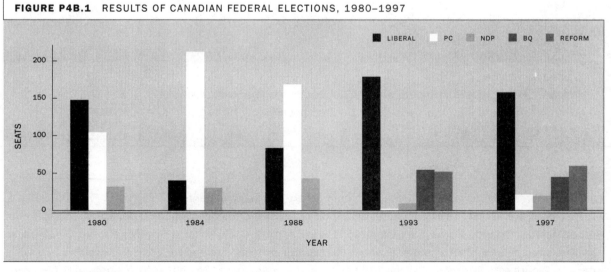

FIGURE P4B.1 RESULTS OF CANADIAN FEDERAL ELECTIONS, 1980–1997

SOURCE: Adapted from Library of Parliament, "Distribution of House of Commons Seats at General Elections," *Canadian Parliamentary Guide, 1997,* downloaded from Statistics Canada at http://www.statcan.ca:80/english/Pgdb/State/Government/govt10.htm, May 2, 2000.

interests of the electorate. They then work out a strategy for organizing a coalition of diverse interests that, they hope, will support their party. They use advertising firms, public relations experts, and "spin doctors" to help them project an image of the party and its leaders that will appeal to the diverse interests in their desired coalition. In this way, party leaders "broker" a coalition of supporters.

The components of the brokered coalition change over time. That is because new political exigencies emerge, and they often require that parties strengthen their ties to some interest groups and weaken their ties to others. As a result, party policies are also in flux. The goal of parties in a system of brokerage politics is not to adhere to relatively fixed sets of principles but to manipulate the electorate in order to gain and maintain power. (That is why, for example, the Liberals did a quick flip-flop on the free trade issue in the early 1990s; they felt they had to switch from an anti–free trade to a pro–free trade position in order to win office.) The system of brokerage politics seems highly democratic because parties listen intently to the opinions of groups of voters. But the system is in fact unresponsive to voters' group interests, which are likely to be watered down or sacrificed entirely as parties seek to broker coalitions between diverse groups. This is the main source of voters' cynicism.

Because brokerage politics fails to bring together stable coalitions of interests, the party system lacks a mechanism that reliably identifies possible solutions for big new political problems. How, then, do Canadian citizens deal with big new political problems? One method was noted above: they engage in nonconventional politics. A second method involves forming new parties. In the 1930s, the Co-operative Commonwealth Federation (CCF) and Social Credit emerged in the West when the Liberal and Conservative parties failed to accommodate Western interests. Similarly, in the 1990s, the Reform Party (now the Canadian Alliance) and the Bloc Québécois emerged to represent distinct regional interests that could not find a voice inside the existing parties.

The Bloc Québécois is not just the voice of Quebec in Ottawa. It is the *sovereignist* voice of Quebec at the federal level. Since the 1970s, a large number of Quebeckers have organized to opt out of Confederation. This is Canada's perennial and biggest political problem. Chapter 22 by Robert Brym briefly recaps the circumstances that led to the emergence of widespread sovereignist sentiment in Quebec.

CRITICAL THINKING QUESTIONS

1. What is more democratic — a system of brokerage politics or a system in which various group interests are firmly aligned with specific parties?
2. Can nonconventional politics and new parties adequately express the interests of dissenting Canadian citizens?
3. What would the costs and benefits of Quebec sovereignty be to Quebec?
4. What would the costs and benefits of Quebec sovereignty be to the rest of Canada?

ANNOTATED BIBLIOGRAPHY

William K. Carroll, ed., *Organizing Dissent: Contemporary Social Movements in Theory and Practice*, 2nd ed. (Toronto: Garamond, 1997). A useful collection of articles on nonconventional politics in Canada.

Baruch Kimmerling, ed., *Current Sociology* 45, 1 (1996), pp. 1–222, Political Sociology at the Crossroads. This special issue contains a critical assessment of political sociology around the world.

Kenneth McRoberts, *Quebec: Social Change and Political Crisis*, 3rd ed. with a postscript (Toronto: Oxford University Press, 1999). The definitive account in English of the political, economic, and social dimensions of the Quebec question.

Chapter 21

Canadian Elections and the Limits of Brokerage Politics

HAROLD D. CLARKE

JANE JENSON

LAWRENCE LEDUC

JON H. PAMMETT

AN ANGRY AND CYNICAL ELECTORATE

For a number of years politicians have been the target of a dissatisfied citizenry, which feels left out of the political process and unhappy about its outcomes. In 1992, an angry electorate rejected the Charlottetown Accord, a proposal to get Quebec to sign the constitution of Canada. Other population consultations, such as those carried out by the Spicer Commission after the defeat of the Meech Lake Accord, turned up high levels of public grumpiness, which fed into the whole subsequent discussion of constitutional politics. In addition, in the 1993 election campaign, much was made by the Reform Party of its promise to make politicians more responsive and more responsible. The populist agenda of the new party resonated for many voters who were dissatisfied with old-style politics.

Canadians do not believe that the problem is of their own making. They place the blame squarely on politicians and the political process. The public remains interested in elections, and most citizens cast a ballot when given the opportunity to do so. Yet voters give the parties exceedingly low marks for their contribution to democratic debate and the presentation of alternative futures. Figure 21.1 shows that, despite the array of new issues and long-running controversies that crowd the agenda, citizens do not exhibit any growing tendency to feel that politics is too complicated for them to understand. Indeed there has been a slight increase in feelings of subjective political competence. If anything, voters feel more rather than less capable of understanding politics, despite the abandonment of the familiar discourse of postwar Keynesianism and the adoption of unfamiliar neoconservative frameworks.

Source: Excerpted from Harold D. Clarke, Jane Jenson, Lawrence LeDuc, and Jon H. Pammett, "The Politics of Discontent," in *Absent Mandate: Canadian Electoral Politics in an Era of Restructuring*, 3rd ed. (Toronto: Gage Educational Publishing, 1996), pp. 176–87. Reprinted with permission.

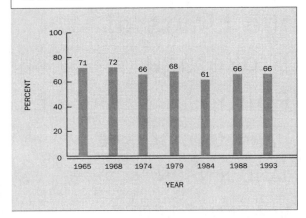

FIGURE 21.1 PERCENTAGE BELIEVING "POLITICS IS TOO COMPLICATED TO UNDERSTAND," 1965–1993

SOURCE: *Canadian National Election Studies* (1965–79), *Political Support in Canada Studies* (1984–93) Inter-University Consortium for Political and Social Research (Ann Arbor, MI).

Nor are Canadians turning away from politics. Many of them take an interest in elections. In 1993 a majority (52 percent) of the voters reported that they were "very interested" in that election, while an additional 32 percent said they were "fairly interested." Levels of interest in elections have remained high over the last decade, therefore providing no evidence that the years of political and economic turbulence have caused the voters to withdraw their attention or concern.

Election interest also translated into rates of participation in campaign-related activities, which were generally as high as in the previous election in 1988, which was itself an election that provoked a great deal of attention. In spite of the slightly lower voting turnout in 1993, Figure 21.2 shows that the various other dimensions of political participation remained at or near the same level. Many people continue to discuss politics with others, and the percentage of the population that reported attempting to influence their friends' vote jumped from 18 percent to 23 percent. Four-fifths of the electorate had watched a television program about the campaign, while similar numbers reported reading about the election in a newspaper or hearing about it on the radio. The portrait of the voters that emerges from these data is one of a reasonably interested, active group, not discouraged by the complexity of the issues or fearful of discussing the new economic schemas.

Yet, voters are not happy, and they place the blame for their distress squarely at the door of politicians, especially those practising *brokerage politics*. In brokerage politics, parties do not have a fixed and predictable position on issues. Instead, before each election, parties canvass the electorate to learn how public opinion is distributed on a range of salient issues. Parties then try to negotiate or "broker" a coalition of supporters that will lead them to electoral victory.

If we examine additional measures of voters' sense of external efficacy as well as of their sense of trust, we see that all these indicators have moved in the direction of greater dissatisfaction. As Figure 21.3 shows, the percentage of people feeling they had no say in government hovered in the range of 49 percent to 57 percent from 1965 to 1988, but in 1993 it shot up to 65 percent. Two-thirds of the electorate, rather than a

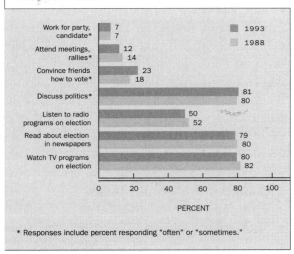

FIGURE 21.2 ELECTORALLY RELATED ACTIVITIES, 1988 AND 1993

* Responses include percent responding "often" or "sometimes."

SOURCE: *Political Support in Canada Studies* (1988, 1993) Inter-University Consortium for Political and Social Research (Ann Arbor, MI).

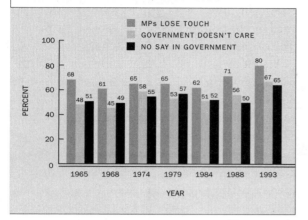

FIGURE 21.3 PERCENTAGES BELIEVING MPs LOSE TOUCH WITH CONSTITUENTS, GOVERNMENT DOESN'T CARE WHAT THEY THINK, AND PEOPLE LIKE THEM HAVE NO SAY, 1965–1993

SOURCE: *Canadian National Election Studies* (1965–79), *Political Support in Canada Studies* (1984–93) Inter-University Consortium for Political and Social Research (Ann Arbor, MI).

In giving such evaluations the Canadian electorate is not expressing a generalized cynicism to all things political, however. Both post-election and inter-electoral public opinion surveys reveal a capacity and a willingness among voters to make choices about *where* to direct their criticisms. Voters do recognize that political parties make a significant contribution to democratic politics. As Table 21.1 shows, parties are most often valued as facilitators of representation and participation.[1] Levels of approval of activities such as representing "everybody," encouraging people to become politically active, and finding consensus are substantially higher than other characteristics of parties, even if they remain distressingly low in absolute terms (only about a third of the population, after all, gives parties high marks on these general democratic activities).

But voters are profoundly and almost universally dissatisfied with brokerage politics. Almost two-thirds of respondents consider that the parties do not offer real choices, while 69 percent think that the parties fail to tell the voters about the really important problems facing the coun-

half, now report strong feelings of being ignored. Over the same period the perception that the system itself was unresponsive showed a steady increase, reaching even greater heights in 1993 than the already elevated levels of 1988. In 1993 four-fifths of the voters said they believed that their elected representatives, the members of Parliament, quickly lose touch with their constituents. Two-thirds felt that the government did not care about people like them. In both cases, the reported levels of external political inefficacy in 1993 were the highest on record.

Many voters also believe that the political authorities are untrustworthy, and survey evidence suggests that these beliefs have become more widespread in recent years. Between 1988 and 1993, the size of the group considering authorities to be "smart" dropped by 9 percent, while that which thought them trustworthy declined by 17 percent (Figure 21.4). When asked about authorities' stewardship of the taxpayers' dollars, fully 93 percent of the voters in 1993 believed that money was being wasted, climbing to that level from an already high 80 percent in 1988.

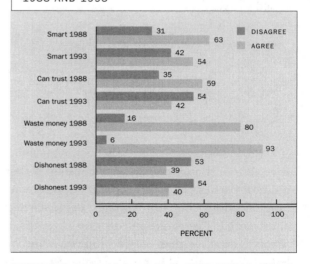

FIGURE 21.4 TRUST IN POLITICAL AUTHORITIES, 1988 AND 1993

SOURCE: *Political Support in Canada Studies* (1988, 1993) Inter-University Consortium for Political and Social Research (Ann Arbor, MI).

TABLE 21.1   EVALUATIONS OF POLITICAL PARTIES, 1991

	AGREE (%)	DISAGREE (%)	DON'T KNOW (%)
Parties spend too much time bickering and quarrelling rather than solving important problems facing the country	**89**	6	5
In elections political parties don't tell people about the really important problems facing the country	**69**	21	11
Political parties and democracy always go together — no parties, no democracy	50	**26**	24
Political parties generally try to look after the best interests of everybody and not just the interests of those who vote for them	33	**57**	10
Parties give people a say in politics that they couldn't have as individuals	44	**41**	15
There is often a big difference between what a party says it will do, and what it actually does if it wins an election	**91**	4	5
Parties usually are more interested in winning elections than in governing afterwards	**81**	12	7
Parties do a good job of encouraging people to become active in politics	31	**51**	18
Political parties do more to divide the country than to unite it	**56**	28	17
Parties don't offer voters real choices in elections because their policies are all pretty much the same	**63**	26	10
Parties generally do a good job in helping groups reach agreement about what government should be doing	29	**50**	21

Note: Boldface percentages indicate negative response.

SOURCE: *Political Support in Canada Studies* (1991) Inter-University Consortium for Political and Social Research (Ann Arbor, MI).

try. Moreover, there is virtual consensus that political parties pay too much attention to winning elections and not enough to governing afterwards (81 percent) and to gaining partisan advantage rather than solving important problems (89 percent). The most dramatic result in Table 21.1, and the one that most clearly indicates that the practices of brokerage politics contribute to the public's cynicism, is the 91 percent of the respondents who report that they anticipate a "big difference" between "what a party says it will do, and what it actually does if it wins an election."

Other surveys confirm this finding. In a 1991 study, André Blais and Elisabeth Gidengil found that the highest level of political cynicism over twelve different measures were recorded in response to a statement that "most candidates in federal elections make campaign promises they have no intention of fulfilling.[2] They also found that the electorate reserved its harshest judgement for the parties' capacity to provoke meaningful consideration of the issues. Fully 87 percent of their respondents agreed with the statement that "the parties confuse the issues rather than provide a clear choice on them" while 81 percent thought the parties "squabbled" too much.[3]

In commenting on such findings, the Royal Commission on Electoral Reform and Party Financing indicted the parties and their behaviour, saying that "feelings about confusing issues and squabbling may ... partly reflect the limited efforts by parties to engage in political education and discussion of policy issues."[4] Indeed, the message is quite clear. Canadian citizens are not "turned off" electoral politics per se. They are interested and they want to be involved. Yet, they feel that they do not have access to the political process and that politicians and governments are neither sufficiently responsive nor reliable. Oftentimes, voters behave as if they feel they have no choice but to "throw the rascals out," even if the replacements are not likely to be very different. Thus, the electorate is not simply cynical. It is angry and exhibits high levels of dissatisfaction with brokerage politics.

THE LEGACY OF BROKERAGE POLITICS: PERMANENT DEALIGNMENT

Crucial to the story of Canadian voters is the longstanding legacy of a party system characterized, from the beginning of the twentieth century, by a style of politics that has minimized real debate about alternatives. It is a system that has frequently focused more on leaders and image politics, and in which parties have taken over each other's policies. Thus, the economic and social positions adopted by the two main parties

have often been indistinguishable from each other. Moreover, when there were policy differences, it was often hard to predict on the basis of its past actions which position any party would adopt. That the Liberals carried on much of the neoconservatism of the Tories after 1993 is only the most recent example of policy flip-flops and convergence over the years.

Accompanying the pliability in programmatic stances and policy positions of parties has been a high level of flexibility in the responses of Canadian voters when elections invite them to make choices. As we might expect in a party system in which much of the public has not developed enduring ties to political parties rooted in ideology or group loyalties, Canadian voters exhibit few qualms about switching from one party to another as the winds of approval change. The electorate has been willing to abandon earlier decisions on short notice and it has become accustomed to shifting easily among alternative parties, candidates, leaders, and party policies once it decides that it is time to try something new. Few voters have been patient enough to wait out an extended stretch of time before abandoning a position, person, or party. This unwillingness to think long-term has been encouraged by parties that have promised quick-fix solutions. As such, it has now become a real constraint on any party's ability to experiment with proposing alternative projects for the future.

Moreover, in part because of the fluidity of issues, leaders and their ability to stitch together policy stances have become an important factor accounting for voting choice, especially among flexible partisans. When parties emphasize leadership and voters focus on the leaders, discussion is deflected toward general considerations of public confidence in these individuals. Popular evaluations of the leaders are, of course, based partly on their stance on issues and partly on their perceived personal characteristics. Nevertheless, the prominent role frequently accorded the leaders during election campaigns ensures that any policy discussion occurs around the public utterances and personal skills of these few persons, and that their character and public confidence in their ability to carry out policy become inextricably intertwined with the consideration of the electoral issues themselves. This emphasis on leaders and leadership may enable parties to avoid discussion of conflict-creating or unpopular policy alternatives that might damage their fortunes during the campaign. Yet, it also ensures that leaders bear the brunt of public displeasure when the quick-fix policies produced in this way do not work. Individual party leaders have become both the anchors of the brokerage system and its major casualties. The fate of former Conservative prime minister Kim Campbell in the 1993 election is only the most recent, and perhaps most dramatic, manifestation of this aspect of brokerage politics.

Whether the behaviour of the parties or the flexibility of partisan ties in the electorate is the ultimate source of brokerage politics is a question that can never be answered satisfactorily. Indeed, any question about ultimate cause is incorrectly posed. The process over time has been one of learning by both voters and politicians. Political parties have learned that their electoral coalitions are fragile creations, requiring constant and careful tending. For their part voters have learned that they will not be offered clear choices about the future in elections and therefore often seek only to bring about a "change."

The impact of this interactive learning process has been clearly visible in elections since the mid-1960s. Canadians have been fickle in their attachments to political parties, changing not only their votes but also their party identification. Such a situation can be characterized as one of *dealignment*. A dealigned party system is one in which volatility is paramount, where there are frequent changes in electoral outcomes as well as lots of individual flexibility. The 1993 election, which decimated the Conservatives' parliamentary delegation at the same time as it fractured the House of Commons into five parts, is an obvious result of such dealignment. It is, however, only the most recent manifestation of

what has been a long-standing characteristic of federal electoral politics, revealed earlier in the big swings of 1958, 1968, and 1984.

An alternative kind of party system is one that is *aligned*. Where alignment exists, large numbers of people believe that their interests and those of others like them are best served, over the long haul, by a particular party that offers something different from its competitors. Voters in an aligned party system consider that a particular party advances the cause of specific social groups and espouse readily identifiable ideological positions. Moreover, parties can be differentiated by their ties to *particular* groups and commitments to *specific* alternatives. One result is that in an aligned party system voters settle into recurrent patterns of political thought and behaviour.

As these patterns begin to break down, a process of dealignment takes hold. A variety of factors may give rise to dealignment, including shifts in the parties' links to social groups, abandonment of ideological commitments, or changes in the composition of the electorate. Thus, the retreat from postwar Keynesian economics in many countries has been associated with a dealignment of party systems, as social classes and other social groups found themselves bereft of allies or abandoned by their previously favoured party. Other analyses have identified a dealignment following the "new politics" preferred by the baby-boom generations first voting in the 1970s and 1980s in Western Europe and North America.[5]

Configurations of support for Canadian parties have not been adequately explained by long-term forces such as social class, religion, or other group characteristics. nor has ideology been a strong correlate of either partisanship or voting, and the party system has long defied a simple left/right depiction.[6] Moreover, if federal politics has always been characterized by strong regional patterns of party and electoral support, these have never been stable over time. For example, the Liberal "stronghold" of Quebec crumbled before the Tories led by their new leader from Quebec, Brian Mulroney, in 1984. Only two elections later, that party virtually disappeared from that province's electoral map following the overwhelming victory of the Bloc Québécois. The map of the West has been similarly reconfigured since the Reform Party came on the scene.

We have seen that parties are not able to call on loyal electorates and instead have attempted to harness a variety of less predictable short-term forces to achieve victory. It is the predominance of short-term forces that has led us to be skeptical about whether 1993 marks any realignment, despite the dramatic changes and the appearance of new parties. For a party system to be realigned, changes would have to be more than temporary and patterns would have to begin to jell into a stable shape. The specific circumstances of the 1993 events as well as the history of earlier elections suggest a cautious assessment.

First, the Bloc Québécois, despite its success in becoming the official opposition, has publicly proclaimed that it has little intention of being a contender in the next election.[7] Thus, federal politics in Quebec is destined to undergo another major shift. History gives us even more reason to expect continued instability. For example, before the Conservatives were returned to power in the turbulent election of 1988, three successive governing parties had gone down to defeat—the Liberals in 1979, the Tories in 1980, and the Liberals in 1984. Indeed, prior to 1988, the only post-1945 federal election to produce consecutive majority governments was that of 1953. Moreover, if the Tories' back-to-back victories in 1984 and 1988 led to speculation about a realignment in which the Conservatives would replace the Liberals as the "government party," their spectacular defeat in 1993 quickly undermined that proposition.

Another possible suggestion is that the Tories' electoral successes in the 1980s simply started a process of dealignment that became evident in 1993. It is difficult to sustain such a hypothesis. Over the last two decades, at least,

there is abundant evidence of widespread flexibility in partisan attachments and volatility in electoral behaviour and results. Thus, unlike other party systems in which a convergence of specific events and changes in the electorate in the 1970s and 1980s triggered a dealignment, it is quite likely that the current dealignment of the Canadian party system is rooted in now distant events and conditions.

Election results over several decades reinforce the story told by the survey evidence; the Canadian situation is one of *permanent dealignment*. Whatever its sources, the consequences of this ongoing phenomenon are very visible in the contemporary volatility of electoral politics. Nonetheless, a situation of permanent dealignment does not imply that nothing has changed. Rather, it means that change itself is a key strand of the fabric of federal politics. In 1993, as in previous years, we have seen that levels of partisan identification remained high, at the same time that large numbers of voters shifted the direction of their allegiance. They moved to the new parties and thereby produced the 1993 successes of the Bloc Québécois and the Reform Party. It is far too early—and on the basis of past experience quite unlikely—that these voters will be any more than the "fair-weather friends" that they have already been for the Liberals, Conservatives, or NDP. Massive shifts from party to party from one election to another are not unusual, nor have they proved to be a reliable indicator that a realignment had occurred or was in the offing.

INTO THE FUTURE

Despite the change in government in 1993, the project for restructuring the Canadian economy and its place in the world continues. Continuity may be observed in both the Liberal government's willingness to pick up the neoconservative torch passed to it by the soundly defeated Tories and its decision to do so in ways that will contribute little if anything to lessening the electorate's dissatisfaction with brokerage politics. A number of policy reversals as well as dramatic initiatives hardly hinted at in the campaign took place. The Liberal government has acted in this way despite the exceedingly high levels of dissatisfaction with such party behaviour already evident in the various public opinion data.

The Liberals of course are not the only party that has been criticized for failing to live up to its campaign promises. In the aftermath of its 1993 success, some observes chastised the Reform Party, which had pledged a new approach to politics, for accepting the perks of office and softening some of its policy positions. Although Reform leaders insist that the essentials of their agenda will remain intact, the forces that encourage parties, new or old, to play the traditional brokerage game did not disappear in 1993. One of the most important of these forces is the flexibility of voters' partisan attachments. This flexibility will continue to generate a strong potential for electoral volatility in the years ahead, and parties ignore it at their peril. If the party system fragmented in 1993, past experience gives us little guide as to whether the patterns yielded by this fragmentation will endure. Rather it encourages a good deal of skepticism about their durability. All parties will continue to face the challenge of building winning coalitions in elections, and dramatic reversals of fortune for *any* party can readily occur.

Despite these continuities there have been changes. The most dramatic and consequential is the consolidation of the restructuring project. The postwar commitment to Keynesian economic policies and constitutional reform has given way to neoconservative economics and constitutional stalemate. These have produced their own responses among the electorate. High levels of dissatisfaction with traditional political forms have not led to alienation or demobilization. Rather, as the events of constitutional debate in the early 1980s first demonstrated and then as the conflicts over free trade and Meech Lake confirmed, Canadians have been seeking new routes to representation. Sometimes this

has led to demands for forms of direct democracy, such as the constitutional referendum in 1992. Sometimes it has been expressed in support for a political party, such as the Reform Party, which promises to change the old ways of doing things. And sometimes it has generated new routes to representation, which by-pass the party system and channel energy in the direction of interest groups and social movements.

All of these are signs that there is a serious public thirst for maintaining and extending the spaces of democratic politics. Whether the party system and electoral politics will quench this thirst remains the great unknown as we face the next century. The challenge put to parties and elections, the traditional institutions of democratic governance, is to rise to the occasion and finally begin to fulfill their assigned task of organizing choice and mobilizing change.

NOTES

1. Harold D. Clarke and Allan Kornberg, "Evaluations and Evolution: Public Attitudes toward Canada's Federal Parties, 1965–1991," *Canadian Journal of Political Science* 26 (1993): 292.
2. André Blais and Elisabeth Gidengil, *Making Representative Democracy Work: The Views of Canadians*, vol. 17 of the Research Studies of the Royal Commission on Electoral Reform and Party Financing (Toronto: Dundurn Press, 1991), Table 3.1, p. 35.
3. Ibid., Table 3.5, p. 42
4. Royal Commission on Electoral Reform and Party Financing (RCERPF), *Reforming Electoral Democracy* (Ottawa: Supply and Services, 1991), vol. 1, p. 226.
5. For a detailed overview of this literature, comparing Western Europe to Canada, see Maureen Covell, "Parties as Institutions of National Governance," in Herman Bakvis, ed., *Representation, Integration and Political Parties in Canada*, vol. 14 of the Research

Studies of the RCERPF (Toronto: Dundurn Press, 1991).

6. See Harold D. Clark and Marianne Stewart, "Canada," in Mark Franklin et al., eds., *Electoral Change: Responses to Evolving Social and Attitudinal Structures in Western Countries* (Cambridge: Cambridge University Press, 1992), and Janine Brodie and Jane Jenson, "Piercing the Smokescreen: Brokerage Parties and Class Politics," in A.-G. Gagnon and A.B. Tanguay, eds., *Canadian Parties in Transition: Discourse, Organization, Representation* (Toronto: Nelson, 1988).

7. The BQ did run in the 1997 election.

Chapter 22

The Quebec Question

ROBERT J. BRYM

ORIGINS OF ETHNIC STRATIFICATION

As part of their centuries-long struggle to control North America, the British conquered New France in 1760. They imposed a policy of strict domination and, eventually, assimilation on the Aboriginal peoples. They could not, however, adopt a similar policy in their dealings with the *Canadiens* in Quebec. The *Canadiens* were greater in number, more densely settled, and more technologically advanced than the Aboriginal population. The British recognized that any attempt to impose the Church of England, the English language, and English civil law in the former French colony could result in unacceptably high levels of resistance and conflict. Therefore, they tried to accommodate two *Canadien* elite groups, the agricultural landowners and the Catholic clergy, by reinforcing their rights and privileges. The British believed this would win the allegiance of the two elites, whose members would in turn help build loyalty to Britain among the population as a whole.

In contrast, the British undermined the rights and privileges of a third elite, the *Canadien* merchants engaged mainly in the fur trade. The British took over virtually all large-scale commerce. As a result, wealthy *Canadien* merchants returned to France. Only their less prosperous colleagues stayed. However, those who remained behind were not allowed to take delivery of goods from France nor to establish ties with British trading firms. As a result, most of the remaining *Canadien* merchants became farmers.

In this manner, business in Quebec became a British domain. Agriculture, religion, and politics remained the province of the French. This pattern of ethnic stratification remained intact for two hundred years. True, by 1950 most farmers had been transformed into urban, industrial workers. A contingent of Québécois had become physicians, lawyers, and members of the "new middle class" of administrators, technicians, scientists, and intellectuals. However, the upper reaches of the stratification system remained overwhelmingly British. Thus, in 1961, men of British origin in Montreal earned 49 percent more on average than men of French origin. In the province of Quebec, people of English origin were 57 percent more likely than those of French origin to be professionals and managers and 45 percent less likely to be blue-collar workers. In Canada as a whole, only a handful of captains of industry were of French origin.[1]

THE QUIET REVOLUTION AND ITS UNRESOLVED PROBLEMS

Apart from its rigid system of ethnic stratification, Quebec in the middle of the twentieth century was remarkable because of its undeveloped government services. Health, education, and welfare were controlled largely by the Catholic Church. Intervention of the government in economic matters was almost unknown.

241

In the late 1940s, members of Quebec's new middle class, together with blue-collar workers, began campaigning to modernize the provincial political system. They pressed for more liberal labour laws that would recognize the right of all workers to form unions and strike. They wanted state control over education and a new curriculum that stressed the natural and social sciences rather than classical languages and catechism. They desired a government that would supply a wide range of social services to the population. They demanded that the state provide better infrastructure for economic development and assist francophone entrepreneurs to expand their businesses. The partial realization of these aims in the course of the 1960s came to be known as the Quiet Revolution. Due to the Quiet Revolution, by the early 1970s, Quebec could boast a political system as advanced as that of any other Canadian province.

Nonetheless, the modernization of the Quebec state failed to resolve four interrelated issues.

1. *The potential demographic decline of the Québécois.* In 1956, women in Quebec gave birth to more children on average than women in any other province. By 1981, however, they gave birth to *fewer* children on average than women in any other province. In fact, they were having fewer than the 2.1 children women must bear on average to ensure that the size of the population does not decline.[2] Noticing this trend in the 1970s, many Québécois felt they were becoming an endangered species.

2. *The assimilation of immigrants into English culture.* Fears of demographic decline were reinforced by the preference of most new immigrants to have their children educated in English-language schools. Together with the falling birth rate, this development threatened to diminish the size—and therefore, potentially, the power—of Quebec's francophone population.

3. *Persistent ethnic stratification.* The Quiet Revolution helped create many thousands of jobs for highly educated francophones

—but only in the government bureaucracy, the educational system, and in new Crown corporations such as Hydro-Québec. It became apparent in the 1970s that management positions in the private sector remained the preserve of Canadians of British origin.

4. *The continued use of English as the language of private industry.* English remained the language of choice in the private sector because the largest and technologically most advanced businesses were controlled by English Canadians and Americans. This situation was felt particularly keenly when the expansion of the state sector, and therefore the upward mobility of the new francophone middle class, slowed in the 1970s. Figures on the ethnic distribution of income illustrate the problem. In 1961, Canadians of English origin earned on average 28 percent more than Canadians of French origin. By 1971, the occupational effects of the Quiet Revolution had reduced the English advantage to 10 percent. Fifteen years later, improvement in the French position had halted and even reversed. Canadians of English origin were earning 11 percent more than Canadians of French origin.[3]

THE RISE OF SEPARATISM

In the 1960s, the Quebec state had intervened energetically in the life of the francophone community to ensure its survival and improve its status. However, because of the unresolved issues just listed, it became clear to many Québécois during the 1970s and 1980s that the survival and prosperity of their community also required active state intervention in non-francophone institutions. For example, many Québécois came to believe that most shares of banks, trust companies, and insurance firms should be held in Quebec and that these financial institutions should be obliged to reinvest their profits in the province. They argued that the state should increase its role as economic planner and initiator of development and should forbid foreign ownership of cultural enterprises. Finally, the Québécois increasingly demanded compulsory French-language education for the children of most immigrants, obligatory use of French among private-sector managers, and French-only signs in public places.

Most Québécois regarded these proposals as the only means by which their community could survive and attain equality with other groups. Because the Quebec state did not have the legal authority to enact some of the proposed changes, most Québécois felt that the province ought to negotiate broader constitutional powers with the federal government. A substantial minority of Québécois went a step further. They became convinced that Quebec ought to become a politically sovereign nation, albeit a nation economically associated with Canada.

In contrast, the great majority of non-francophone Quebeckers viewed separation as a danger to their economic well-being, an infringement on their minority rights, and a dangerous fragmenting principle if applied universally. Their economic fear was that separatism would scare away foreign investment and isolate Quebec from the North American market. Their fear of losing minority rights was well expressed by Aboriginal groups in Quebec. They noted that the idea of Quebec sovereignty "rests on the erasure of the political status of aboriginal peoples and the denial of their most fundamental rights to self-determination."[4] Thus, Aboriginal treaties signed with the federal government would necessarily be nullified if Quebec separated because Ottawa would no longer have authority in Quebec. Such nullification, argued Aboriginal lawyers, is illegal under international law. Certain English-rights advocates emphasized the political dangers of fragmentation. They provocatively asked: If Quebec can separate from Canada, why can't areas of Quebec with a non-francophone majority separate from Quebec?

In the midst of these controversies, the pro-independence Parti Québécois won the provincial election in 1976. In 1980, it held a refer-endum to see whether Quebeckers favoured "sovereignty-association." On the whole, they did not. The vote was nearly 60 percent against the government's proposition. Among francophones, 52 percent voted "no." The francophones most likely to support sovereignty-association were between 21 and 35 years of age. Voting "yes" was also associated with having a higher education, being a union member, working in the public sector, and not practising Catholicism.[5]

THE DEFEAT OF RECONCILIATION

The referendum defeat weakened Quebec nationalism. Partly for that reason, the Parti Québécois lost the 1985 provincial election. Shortly thereafter, the new Liberal government of the province demonstrated it was willing to soften Quebec's constitutional demands. In 1982, all the provinces except Quebec had signed the Canadian Constitution. The Quebec Liberals now agreed to endorse that document, thereby giving up the decades-long struggle to increase Quebec's constitutional powers.

Before signing, Quebec asked only that a few principles be endorsed by the federal government and the other provinces. These principles were set out in the 1987 Meech Lake Accord. Among the most important provisions of the accord was a declaration that Quebec is a "distinct society" that has the right to preserve and promote its identity. The accord recognized minority language rights throughout Canada. It stressed that acknowledgement of Quebec's unique status would in no way diminish either provincial or federal powers. Most of the other provisions merely entrenched established practices. In short, compared with Quebec's demands in the 1960s and 1970s for more constitutional authority, the Meech Lake Accord was weak broth.

Nonetheless, Manitoba and Newfoundland refused to sign the accord. As the June 1990 ratification deadline approached, it became clear that other segments of Canadian society also opposed granting Quebec special status in Confederation. Some women's organizations, Aboriginal associations, members of some minority ethnic groups, and many Canadians in Newfoundland and the Prairies argued that ratifying the Meech Lake Accord would amount to sacrificing their rights and special interests for the sake of Quebec. Consequently, the accord was not ratified.

The Québécois, for their part, felt rejected, insulted, and enraged. In their view, they had asked for little and received nothing. They began to sense there might not be a place for them in Confederation after all. In July 1990, a public opinion poll conducted in Quebec showed that over 62 percent of the province's population favoured sovereignty — far more than at any other time in Quebec history.

In the 1994 Quebec provincial election, the Parti Québécois was reelected. It immediately began planning a second referendum on sovereignty-association. The referendum was held in 1995. The forces opposed to separation won by the narrowest of margins — about 1 percent. Subsequently, the charismatic Lucien Bouchard became head of the Parti Québécois. He promised a third referendum under "winning conditions" — that is, when the chance of victory is good. Thus, as Canada entered the twenty-first century, its future remained uncertain.

THE ROLE OF OUTSIDE FORCES: FEDERALISM AND GLOBALIZATION

Above, we considered the circumstances *in* Quebec that led to the growth of separatism. However, *external* forces have also played an important role in Quebec's political development. In concluding, let us briefly consider two of the most important of these external forces: the decentralized nature of the Canadian federation and the increasing tempo of globalization.

Federalism is a system of government that divides state power between central and provincial governments. Canada was a loosely struc-

tured federation from the start. Power was decentralized because the country was created from diverse elements that lacked a deep and unifying sense of nationhood. It was a creation not of the people of British North America but of its business and political leaders, who conceived the country as a pragmatic means of escape from untenable economic and political circumstances.

In the mid-1860s, British North American business leaders faced the loss of export markets because the British were dismantling the protected market known as the British Empire while the Americans had turned against free trade. The colonies had also accumulated a crippling debt load, due mainly to borrowing money to help finance railroad construction. Meanwhile, certain elements in the United States were threatening to expand the borders of their country northward. In this context, the business and political leaders of British North America regarded Confederation as a means of creating a new market and an expanded tax base by encouraging mass immigration and promoting economic growth. In order to forge a union, the Fathers of Confederation were careful to avoid consulting ordinary citizens for fear of having their plan rejected. In the end, they drafted a founding document, the British North America Act, that played down the deep conflicts of interest and culture that distinguished the British North American colonies. Significantly, they left ambiguous the question of how power would be distributed between federal and provincial governments.

This pragmatic vagueness left the door open to the bickering and bargaining that has characterized federal–provincial relations ever since 1867. Quebec has led the fight to further decentralize federal authority by gaining more control over taxation, resource revenues, immigration policy, language use, and so on, but other provinces have not been far behind. It is thus clear that the growth of separatism has been encouraged by the decentralized nature of Canadian federalism.[6]

A second external factor fuelling the growth of separatism is the increased tempo of globalization.[7] Globalization is a phenomenon of many parts. Among the most important are flourishing worldwide markets for standardized goods; increasing dependence of countries on each others' resources; wave upon wave of international investment; the growth of fast and widely accessible international transportation and communication; increasing recognition that ecological problems are global in character; and the creation of transnational organizations with the authority to make economic and other decisions that are binding on countries. All these forces erode the sovereignty of existing nation-states, breaking down their borders in many parts of the world.

The impact of globalization is certainly evident in the 1989 free trade deal between Canada and the United States. The free trade agreement promotes the untaxed movement of goods, services, capital, and labour between the two countries. As the Canadian and U.S. economies become more highly integrated, Canada is becoming more like the United States. For example, the removal of trade barriers between the two countries means that Canadian workers have to compete with American workers for jobs. If Canadians demand higher wages and superior social services, then jobs will drift southward, where wages and taxes are lower. It is therefore no coincidence that fewer Canadian workers are unionized now than in the mid-1980s, average wage levels relative to those in the United States have dropped, and social services are being cut. All this promotes the decline of Canada as an independent political community. With less money available for national rail services, public broadcasting, and a social safety net, many of the institutions that tie Canada's regions together are getting weaker.

Worldwide, the erosion of existing national borders due to globalization allows old animosities based on nation, ethnicity, race, and religion to intensify. In Russia, the former Yugoslavia, the United Kingdom, France, Spain, and Indonesia, various groups are trying to reestablish ancient borders. Separatism is thus not a phenomenon that is unique to Quebec. It has deep roots inside the province, but it is also part of a worldwide phenomenon.

NOTES

1. Robert J. Brym with Bonnie J. Fox, *From Culture to Power: The Sociology of English Canada* (Toronto: Oxford University Press, 1989), 108.

2. A. Romaniuc, "Fertility in Canada: From Baby-boom to Baby-bust," *Current Demographic Analysis* (Ottawa: Statistics Canada, 1984), 14–18. This figure assumes a stable population in which the number of emigrants equals the number of immigrants.

3. Brym with Fox, *Culture to Power*, 108; *Dimensions: Profile of Ethnic Groups: Census Canada 1986* (Ottawa: Statistics Canada, 1989), 1–7, 1–8; *1971 Census of Canada: Profile Studies: Ethnic Origins of Canadians*, Vol. 5, Part 1 (Ottawa: Statistics Canada, 1977), 68, 76; *Royal Commission on Bilingualism and Biculturalism Report: The Work World*, Book 3A, Parts 1 and 2 (Ottawa: Queen's Printer, 1969), 16. Income data for 1961 are for males only. Canada-wide figures are given because breakdowns for Quebec and Montreal in 1986 have not been published.

4. Mary Ellen Turpel, "Does the Road to Quebec Sovereignty Run through Aboriginal Territory?" in Daniel Drache and Roberto Perin, eds., *Negotiating with a Sovereign Quebec* (Toronto: James Lorimer, 1992), 93.

5. Kenneth McRoberts, *Quebec: Social Change and Political Crisis*, 3rd ed. (Toronto: McClelland and Stewart, 1988), 327–29.

6. Robert J. Brym, "Some Advantages of Canadian Disunity: How Quebec Sovereignty Might Aid Economic Development in English-Speaking Canada," *Canadian Review of Sociology and Anthropology* 29, 2 (1992): 210–26.

7. Benjamin R. Barber, *Jihad vs. McWorld: How Globalism and Tribalism Are Reshaping the World* (New York: Ballantine, 1995).

PART 4C | THE ECONOMY AND WORK

When the twentieth century was still young, the celebrated German sociologist Max Weber wrote admiringly of the "technical superiority" of bureaucracies "over any other form of organization." **Bureaucracies**, wrote Weber, are more precise, faster, less ambiguous, more discrete, and cheaper than all other ways of organizing business, education, law, the military, and so forth. They achieve their efficiency because they embody a specialized division of labour, a strict hierarchy of authority, clear regulations, impersonality, and a staff that is technically qualified to do its job.

Weber also recognized the dark underside of bureaucracy. Bureaucracies, he wrote, create cadres of powerful non-elected officials, thus making the world less democratic. Bureaucracies also lead people to focus on the means of achieving goals that have been specified by their superiors, not on questioning and helping to decide those goals. For these reasons, Weber likened the modern era to an "iron cage." In Chapter 23, George Ritzer of the University of Maryland carries Weber's analysis a step further. He argues that the rationalization of the world is occurring in much the way Weber predicted. However, argues Ritzer, the model for this process is not bureaucracy so much as the fast-food restaurant. "McDonaldization," as Ritzer calls it, combines the principles of bureaucracy with those of the assembly line and "scientific management." Ritzer shows that, since the mid-1950s, McDonaldization has spread to larger and larger areas of life, and is now taking over prebirth and postdeath as well. He discusses several countervailing forces, but concludes that they are not sufficiently powerful to overwhelm the continued McDonaldization of the world.

Bureaucratization is one master trend governing the social organization of work. A second such trend is **job polarization**. Job polarization refers to the rapid growth of "bad jobs," the slower growth of "good jobs," and the still slower growth of medium-quality jobs. Bad jobs don't pay much and require the performance of routine tasks under close supervision. Working conditions are unpleasant and sometimes dangerous. Bad jobs require little formal education. In contrast, good jobs often require higher education. They pay well. They are not closely supervised, are carried out in pleasant surroundings, and encourage the worker to be creative. Good jobs offer secure employment, opportunities for promotion, and fringe benefits. In a bad job, you can easily be fired, receive few if any fringe benefits, and have few prospects for promotion. If, over a decade or more, the number of bad jobs grows quickly, the number of medium-quality jobs grows slowly, and the number of good jobs grows at an intermediate rate, the occupational structure will start to assume the shape of an hourglass. Increasingly, jobs will be polarized, or concentrated at the high and low ends of the occupational structure. This sort of polarization appears to have taken place in Canada in the 1990s.

In Chapter 24, Wallace Clement of Carleton University analyzes one of the main forces that led to the creation of many bad jobs in Canada in the 1990s: the free trade agreements that Canada signed with the United States and Mexico. Before free trade, Canadian workers enjoyed higher wages and more state benefits than workers in the other North American countries. However, by making cross-border trade and investment easier, the free trade agreements put downward pressure on both wages and benefits. If employers in Canada continued paying high wages, and if Canadian governments continued taxing citizens at high rates to pay for generous state benefits, employers under free trade could simply shift their investment to more hospitable regimes. That is just what some employers did in the

1990s. Consequently, unemployment remained high throughout the decade. As Clement shows, to prevent further deterioration of the Canadian job market, wage levels were forced down and governments slashed their budgets. Bad jobs proliferated.

Ritzer and Clement sketch only part of the recent history of jobs. A more complete picture would give more weight to countervailing trends. It would also sketch the range of policy choices available to Canadian governments.

One countervailing trend is "debureaucratization." Many sociologists think Ritzer exaggerates the efficiency of bureaucracy and the scientific management of work, just as Weber did before him. Heavily bureaucratized industrial organizations, assembly-line production, and a highly fragmented division of labour often create alienated workers, high absenteeism and turnover, slow adaptation to changing market conditions, and low productivity. In response to these inefficiencies, Japanese- and Swedish-inspired **quality of working life** (QWL) programs recommend several innovations:

- eliminating various levels of middle management (establishing "flat" organizational structures);
- allowing worker participation in a variety of tasks and jobs related to their main functions;
- creating teams of a dozen or so workers who are delegated authority to make a variety of work-related decisions themselves; and
- forming "quality circles" of workers to monitor and correct defects in products and services.

The implementation of such ideas in Canada has been limited and has met with mixed results. But in the opinion of many sociologists, valuable lessons can be learned from these new forms of work organization that can help to improve the quality of working life and make the Canadian economy more productive.

A second trend that has helped to balance the rapid growth of bad jobs in Canada is the (less rapid) growth of good jobs at the top of the occupational structure. This has been stimulated by the postindustrial revolution. **Postindustrialism** refers to the relative decline of agriculture and manufacturing as sources of employment and the corresponding growth and recent rise to dominance of the economy's service sector. In Chapter 25, Harvey Krahn and Graham Lowe provide a bird's-eye view of postindustrialism and its effects on jobs. They show that the postindustrial revolution is taking place in the context of a global movement to promote free trade and investment. Their sketch is not entirely rosy. They do, however, note that the postindustrial revolution has created many good jobs in education, health, social services, entertainment, government, and business.

Krahn and Lowe also make the important point that the globalizing forces promoting free trade form a *political* movement that seeks to influence government policy. The free trade movement is led by big business. However, big business is not the only influential political actor. Ordinary citizens also influence governments to varying degrees. And in response to political pressures, governments can adopt public policies that modify the free trade movement's impact. For example, government policy can encourage global competitiveness at the low end of the wage scale. That is, governments can use their taxation and other powers to lower the income and benefits of people with bad jobs so they can compete more effectively against low-wage workers in other countries. Alternatively, governments can use their taxation and other powers to encourage a reduction in the number of bad jobs and stimulate the citizenry to compete in international markets at the high end of the wage scale. Starkly stated, the big economic question Canadians face is whether the country should be trying to compete against countries like Mexico or countries like Germany. This is a political choice. To a degree, therefore, Canada's economic future is in the hands of its citizens.

GLOSSARY

Bureaucracies are secondary associations that operate relatively precisely, quickly, unambiguously, discretely, and inexpensively. They achieve their efficiency because they embody a specialized division of labour, a strict hierarchy of authority, clear regulations, impersonality, and a staff that is technically qualified to do its job.

Job polarization refers to the rapid growth of "bad jobs," the slower growth of "good jobs," and the still slower growth of medium-quality jobs.

Postindustrialism refers to the relative decline of agriculture and manufacturing as sources of employment and the corresponding growth and recent rise to dominance of the economy's service sector.

The **quality of working life** movement recommends eliminating various levels of middle management, allowing worker participation in a variety of tasks and jobs related to their main functions, the creation of teams of workers who are delegated authority to make a variety of work-related decisions themselves, and the formation of "quality circles" of workers to monitor and correct defects in products and services.

CRITICAL THINKING QUESTIONS

1. What does George Ritzer mean by the statement, "McDonaldization is expanding both in time and space"? Give examples to support your answer.
2. "McDonaldization is a global phenomenon even though it is at odds with many of the basic tenets of globalization theory." Explain what Ritzer means by this statement.
3. The American unemployment rate fell during the 1990s but the Canadian unemployment rate remained high. Why?
4. In what sense is the free trade movement a political movement subject to political pressures?

ANNOTATED BIBLIOGRAPHY

Ann Duffy, Daniel Glenday, and Norene Pupo, eds., *Good Jobs, Bad Jobs, No Jobs: The Transformation of Work in the 21st Century* (Toronto: Harcourt Brace, 1997). This collection shows how structural changes in the Canadian economy have transformed the traditional workplace, created new types of work, influenced women and families, and altered patterns of unemployment and retraining.

Gordon Laxer, *Open for Business: The Roots of Foreign Ownership in Canada* (Toronto: Oxford University Press, 1989). An award-winning socio-historical explanation of Canada's economic structure.

James Rinehart, *The Tyranny of Work: Alienation and the Labour Process*, 3rd ed. (Toronto: Harcourt Brace, 1996). A highly regarded Marxist account of the sociology of work, containing Canadian data and illustrations.

Chapter 23

The McDonaldization Thesis: Is Expansion Inevitable?

GEORGE RITZER

The "McDonaldization thesis" (Ritzer, 1983; 1993; 1996) is derived, most directly, from Max Weber's (1968 [1921]) theory of the rationalization of the Occident and ultimately the rest of the world (Kalberg, 1980). Weber tended to see this process as inexorable, leading, in the end, to the iron cage of rationalization from which there was less and less possibility of escape. Furthermore, with the corresponding decline in the possibility of individual or revolutionary charisma, Weber believed that there was a decreasing possibility of the emergence of a revolutionary counterforce.

Time has been kind to the Weberian thesis, if not to the social world. Rationalization has progressed dramatically in the century or so since Weber developed his ideas. The social world does seem to be more of an iron cage and, as a result, there does seem to be less possibility of escape. And it does appear less likely that any counterrevolution can upset the march toward increasing rationalization.

It is this theory and empirical reality that forms the background for the development of what has been termed the "McDonaldization thesis." This thesis accepts the basic premises of rationalization as well as Weber's basic theses about the inexorable character of the process. Its major point of departure from the Weberian theory of rationalization is to argue that the paradigm of the process is no longer, as Weber argued, the bureaucracy, but it is rather the fast-food restaurant. The fast-food restaurant has combined the principles of the bureaucracy with those of other rationalized precursors (for example, the assembly line, scientific management) to create a particularly powerful model of the rationalization process. It is a relatively new paradigm, traceable to the opening of the first restaurant in the McDonald's chain in 1955. While there were a number of predecessors to the first McDonald's outlet in the fast-food industry, it is McDonald's that was the truly revolutionary development in not only that industry, but in the history of the rationalization process.

Embodying perfectly the principles of rationalization, McDonald's became the model to be emulated first by other fast-food chains and later by other types of chain stores. It was not long before the success of McDonald's caught the eye of those in other types of businesses, and ultimately in virtually every other sector of society. Today, not only is McDonald's

Source: Adapted from "The McDonaldization Thesis: Is Expansion Inevitable?" *International Sociology* 11, 3 (September 1996): 291–307. Reprinted by permission of the author.

a worldwide success, but it offers an alluring model to those in a wide variety of leadership positions. It is in this role that McDonald's is playing the key role in the still-further expansion of the process of rationalization. Indeed its participation is so central that the contemporary manifestations of this process can be aptly labelled "McDonaldization."

Like Weber I have tended to view this process as inexorable in a variety of senses. First, it is seen as migrating from its roots in the fast-food industry in America to other types of businesses and other social institutions. Second, McDonaldization is spreading from the United States to more and more societies around the world. Third, McDonaldization is viewed as having first concentrated on the rationalization of processes central to life itself, but more recently it has moved to encompass the birth process (and before) as well as the process of death (and beyond).

To put this expansionism in contemporary theoretical terms, McDonaldization is expanding in both space and time (Giddens, 1984; Harvey, 1989). Spatially, McDonaldization is encompassing more and more chains, industries, social institutions and geographic areas of the world. Temporally, McDonaldization has moved from the core of life itself both backward to the birth process as well as the steps leading up to it and forward to the process of dying and its aftermath.

The evidence on the spatial and temporal advance of McDonaldization is overwhelming. However, in this essay I want to do more than review this evidence. I want to reexamine the issue of inexorability. Do its past and present successes mean that McDonaldization is truly inexorable? Is there no hope that the process can be slowed down or even stopped? Is it possible to avoid an iron cage of rationalization that encompasses time (from birth and before to death and beyond) and space (geographic areas within the United States and throughout the world)? Before getting to these issues, I need to review the basic parameters of the McDonaldization thesis.

McDONALDIZATION

I begin with a foundational definition: *McDonaldization is the process by which the principles of the fast-food restaurant are coming to dominate more and more sectors of American society, as well as of the rest of the world.* The nature of the McDonaldization process may be delineated by outlining its five basic dimensions: efficiency, calculability, predictability, control through the substitution of technology for people, and, paradoxically, the irrationality of rationality.

First, a McDonaldizing society emphasizes *efficiency*, or the effort to discover the best possible means to whatever end is desired. Workers in fast-food restaurants clearly must work efficiently; for example, burgers are assembled, and sometimes even cooked, in an assembly-line fashion. Customers want, and are expected, to acquire and consume their meals efficiently. The drive-through window is a highly efficient means for customers to obtain, and employees to dole out, meals. Overall, a variety of norms, rules, regulations, procedures, and structures have been put in place in the fast-food restaurant in order to ensure that *both* employees and customers act in an efficient manner. Furthermore, the efficiency of one party helps to ensure that the other will behave in a similar manner.

Second, there is great importance given to *calculability*, to an emphasis on quantity, often to the detriment of quality. Various aspects of the work of employees at fast-food restaurants are timed, and this emphasis on speed often serves to adversely affect the quality of the work, from the point of view of the employee, resulting in dissatisfaction, alienation, and high turnover rates. Only slightly over half the predominantly part-time, teenage, non-unionized, generally minimum-wage work force remains on the job for one year or more (Van Giezen, 1994). Similarly, customers are expected to spend as little time as possible in the fast-food restauarant. In fact, the drive-through window reduces this time to zero, but if the customers desire to eat in the restaurant, the chairs are designed to impel them to leave after about twenty minutes. All of this emphasis on speed clearly has a negative effect on the quality of the "dining experience" at a fast-food restaurant. Furthermore, the emphasis on how fast the work is to be done means that customers cannot be served high-quality food, which, almost by definition, requires a good deal of time to prepare.

Third, McDonaldization involves an emphasis on *predictability*. Employees are expected to perform their work in a predictable manner, and customers are expected to respond with similarly predictable behaviour. Thus, when customers enter, employees will ask, following scripts (Leidner, 1993), what they wish to order. For their part, customers are expected to know what they want, or where to look to find what they want, and they are expected to order, pay, and leave quickly. Employees (following another script) are expected to thank them when they do leave. A highly predictable ritual is played out in the fast-food restaurant, and it is one that involves highly predictable foods that vary little from one time or place to another.

Fourth, there is great *control* in a McDonaldizing society, and a good deal of that control comes from technologies. While these technologies currently dominate employees, increasingly they will be replacing humans. Employees are clearly controlled by such technologies as French-fry machines that ring when the fries are done and even automatically lift the fries out of the hot oil. For their part, customers are controlled both by the employees, who are constrained by such technologies, as well as more directly by the technologies themselves. Thus, the automatic fry machine makes it impossible for a customer to request well-done, well-browned fries.

Finally, both employees and customers suffer from the various *irrationalities of rationality* that seem inevitably to accompany McDonaldization. Many of these irrationalities involve the oppposite of the basic principles of McDonaldization. For example, the efficiency of the fast-food restaurant is often replaced by the inefficiencies associated with long lines of people at the counters or long lines of cars at the drive-through window. While there are many others, the ultimate irrationality of rationality is dehumanization. Employees are forced to work in dehumanizing jobs and customers are forced to eat in dehumanizing settings and circumstances. In Harry Braverman's terms, the fast-food restaurant is a source of degradation for employees and customers alike (Braverman, 1974).

EXPANSIONISM

McDonald's has continually extended its reach, within American society and beyond. As McDonald's chairman put the company's objective, "Our goal: to totally dominate the quick service restaurant industry worldwide. ... I want McDonald's to be more than a leader. I want McDonald's to dominate" (Papiernik, 1994).

McDonald's began as a suburban and medium-sized-town phenomenon, but in recent years it has moved into big cities and smaller towns (Kleinfeld, 1985; L. Shapiro, 1990) that supposedly could not support such a restaurant, not only in the United States but also in many other parts of the world. A huge growth area is in small satellite, express, or remote outlets opened in areas that are not able to support full-scale fast-food restaurants. These are beginning to appear in small store fronts in large cities, as well as in non-traditional settings like department stores and even schools. These satellites typically offer only limited menus and may rely on larger outlets for food storage and preparation (Rigg, 1994). McDonald's is considering opening express outlets in such locations as museums, office buildings, and corporate cafeterias.

Another significant expansion has occurred as fast-food restaurants have moved onto college campuses (the first such facility opened at the University of Cincinnati in 1973), instead of being content merely to dominate the strips that surround many campuses. In conjunction with a variety of "branded partners" (for example, Pizza Hut and Subway), Marriott now supplies food to almost 500 colleges and universities (Sugarman, 1995).

Another, even more recent, incursion has occurred: we no longer need to leave the highway to dine in our favourite fast-food restaurant. We can obtain fast food quickly and easily at convenient rest stops along the highway and then proceed with our trip. Fast food is also increasingly available *in* service stations (Chan, 1994). Also in the travel realm, fast-food restaurants are more and more apt to be found in hotels (E. McDowell, 1992), railway stations, and airports, and their products are appearing even on the trays of in-flight meals. The following newspaper advertisement appeared a few years ago: "Where else at 35,000 feet can you get a McDonald's meal like this for your kids? Only on United's Orlando flights." Now, McDonald's so-called Friendly Skies Meals are generally available to children on Delta flights. In addition, in December 1994, Delta began offering Blimpie sandwiches on its North American flights (*Phoenix Gazette*, 1994). (Subway sandwiches are also now offered on Continental flights.) How much longer before McDonaldized meals will be available on all flights everywhere by every carrier? In fact, on an increasing number of flights, prepackaged "snacks" have already replaced hot main courses.

In other sectors of society, the influence of fast-food restaurants has been more subtle, but no less profound. While we are now beginning to see the appearance of McDonald's and other fast-food restaurants in high schools and trade schools (Albright, 1995), few lower-grade schools as yet have in-house fast-food restaurants, but many have had to alter school cafeteria menus and procedures so that fast food is readily and continually available to children and teenagers (Berry, 1995). We are even beginning to see efforts by fast-food chains to market their products in these school cafeterias (Farhi, 1990).

The military has been pressed into offering fast-food menus on its bases and ships. Despite the criticisms by physicians and nutritionists, fast-food outlets are increasingly turning up *inside* hospitals. No homes have a McDonald's of their own, but dining within the home has been influenced by the fast-food restaurant. Home-cooked meals often resemble those available in fast-food restaurants. Frozen, microwavable, and pre-prepared foods, also bearing a striking resemblance to McDonald's meals and increasingly modelled after them, often find their way to the dinner table. Then there is the home delivery of fast foods, especially pizza, as revolutionized by Domino's.

As powerful as it is, McDonald's has not been alone in pressing the fast-food model on American society and the rest of the world. Other fast-food giants, such as Burger King, Wendy's, Hardee's, Arby's, Big-Boy, Diary Queen, TCBY, Denny's, Sizzler, Kentucky Fried Chicken, Popeye's, Subway, Taco Bell, Chi Chi's, Pizza Hut, Domino's, Long John Silver, Baskin-Robbins and Dunkin' Donuts, have played a key role, as have the innumerable other businesses built on the principles of the fast-food restaurant.

Even the derivatives of McDonald's and the fast-food industry more generally are, in turn, having their own influence. For example, the success of *USA Today* has led to changes in many newspapers across the nation, with shorter stories and colour weather maps, for example. As one *USA Today* editor put it: "The same newspaper editors who call us McPaper have been stealing our McNuggets" (Prichard, 1987: 232–33).

Sex, like virtually every other sector of society, has undergone a process of McDonaldization. In the movie *Sleeper*, Woody Allen not only created a futuristic world in which McDonald's was an important and highly visible element, but he also envisioned a society in which even sex underwent the process of McDonaldization. The denizens of his future world were able to enter a machine called an "orgasmatron" that allowed them to experience an orgasm without going through the muss and fuss of sexual intercourse. In fact, we already have things like high-ly specialized pornographic movies (heterosexu-al, homosexual, sex with children, sex with animals) that can be seen at urban multiplexes and are available at local video stores for viewing in the comfort of our living rooms. In New York City, an official called a three-story pornograph-ic centre "the McDonald's of sex" because of its "cookie-cutter cleanliness and compliance with the law" (*New York Times*, 1986: 6). The McDon-aldization of sex suggests that no aspect of our lives is immune to its influence.

IS McDONALDIZATION TRULY INEXORABLE?

I want to discuss this issue both spatially and temporally. First, there is the spatial issue of whether McDonaldization is destined to spread from its American roots and become a global phenomenon. Second, there is the temporal issue of whether McDonaldization will inev-itably spread from its control over the core of life to colonize birth and before as well as death and beyond.

GLOBALIZATION

We can discuss the first issue under the heading of globalization, or the spread of McDonald's, and more importantly the principles of McDon-aldization, around the world. However, in using the term globalization here, it should be pointed out that, as we will see below, there are some dif-ferences between its usage here and the way it has been used in the currently voguish global-ization theory.

While there are significant differences among globalization theorists, most if not all would accept Robertson's advocacy of the idea that social scientists adopt "a specifically global point of view," and "treat the global condition as such" (Robertson, 1992: 61, 64). Elsewhere, Robertson (1990: 18) talks of the "study of the world as a whole." More specifically, Robertson argues that we need to concern ourselves with global pro-

cesses that operate in relative independence of societal sociocultural processes. Thus, Robertson (1992: 60) argues, "there is a general autonomy and 'logic' to the globalization process, which operates in *relative* independence of strictly soci-etal and other conventionally studied sociocultu-ral processes." Similarly, Featherstone (1990: 1) discusses the interest in processes that "gain some autonomy on a global level."

While the reach of McDonaldization is glob-al, it does not quite fit the model proposed by globalization theorists. The differences between them are clear when we outline those things rejected by globalization theorists:

1. A focus on any single nation-state.
2. A focus on the West in general, or the United States in particular.
3. A concern with the impact of the West (westernization) or the United States (Amer-icanization) on the rest of the world.
4. A concern with homogenization (rather than heterogenization).
5. A concern with modernity (as contrasted with postmodernity).
6. An interest in what used to be called mod-ernization theory (Tiryakian, 1991).

The fact is that while McDonaldization *is* a global process, it has all of the characteristics *rejected* by globalization theorists: it does have its source in a single nation-state; it does focus on the West in general and the United States in particular; it is concerned with the impact of westernization and Americanization on the rest of the world; it is attentive to the homogeniza-tion of the world's products and services; it is better thought of as a modern than a postmod-ern phenomenon (because of its rationality, which is a central characteristic of modernity); and it does have some affinity with moderniza-tion theory (although it is not presented in the positive light modernization theory tended to cast on all western phenomena). Thus, McDon-aldization is a global phenomenon even though it is at odds with many of the basic tenets of globalization theory.

The global character of this American institution is clear in the fact that it is making increasing inroads around the world (B. McDowell, 1994). For example, in 1991, for the first time, McDonald's opened more restaurants abroad than in the United States (Shapiro, 1992). This trend continues and, as we move toward the next century, McDonald's expects to build twice as many restaurants each year overseas as it does in the United States. Already by the end of 1993 over a third of McDonald's restaurants were overseas. As of the beginning of 1995, about half of McDonald's profits came from its overseas operations. As of this writing, one of McDonald's latest advances was the opening of a restaurant in Mecca, Saudi Arabia (*Tampa Tribune*, 1995).

Other nations have developed their own variants of this American institution, as is best exemplified by the now large number of fast-food croissanteries in Paris, a city whose love of fine cuisine might have led one to think that it would prove immune to the fast-food restaurant. India has a chain of fast-food restaurants, Nirula's, which sells mutton burgers (about 80 percent of Indians are Hindus who eat no beef) as well as local Indian cuisine (Reitman, 1993). Perhaps the most unlikely spot for an indigenous fast-food restaurant was then war-ravaged Beirut, Lebanon; but in 1984 Juicy Burger opened there (with a rainbow instead of golden arches and J.B. the clown replacing Ronald McDonald), with its owners hoping that it would become the "McDonald's of the Arab world" (Cowan, 1984).

Other countries not only now have their own McDonaldized institutions, but they have also begun to export them to the United States. For example, the Body Shop is an ecologically sensitive British cosmetics chain with, as of early 1993, 893 shops in many countries; 120 of those shops were in the United States, with 40 more scheduled to open that year (Elmer-Dewitt, 1993; E. Shapiro, 1991). Furthermore, American firms are now opening copies of this British chain, such as the Limited, Inc.'s, Bath and Body Works.

This kind of obvious spread of McDonaldization is only a small part of that process's broader impact around the world. Far more subtle and important are the ways in which McDonaldization and its various dimensions have affected the way in which many institutions and systems throughout the world operate. That is, they have come to adopt, and adapt to their needs: efficiency, predictability, calculability, and control through the replacement of human by non-human technology (and they have experienced the irrationalities of rationality).

How do we account for the global spread of McDonaldization? The first and most obvious answer is that material interests are impelling the process. That is, there is a great deal of money to be made by McDonaldizing systems, and those who stand to profit are the major motor force behind it.

Culture is a second factor in the spread of McDonaldization. There appears to be a growing passion around the world for things American, and few things reflect American culture better than McDonald's and its various clones. Thus, when Pizza Hut opened in Moscow in 1990, a Russian student said: "It's a piece of America" (*Washington Post*, 1990: B10). Reflecting on the growth of Pizza Hut and other fast-food restaurants in Brazil, the president of Pepsico (of which Pizza Hut is part) said of Brazil that this nation "is experiencing a passion for things American" (Blount, 1994: F1). Many people around the world identify strongly with McDonald's; in fact to some it has become a sacred institution (Kottak, 1983). On the opening of the McDonald's in Moscow, one journalist described it as the "ultimate icon of Americans," while a worker spoke of it "as if it were the Cathedral in Chartres ... a place to experience 'celestial joy'" (Keller, 1990: 12).

A third explanation of the rush toward McDonaldization is that it meshes well with other changes occurring in American society as well as around the world. Among other things, it fits in well with the increase in dual-career families, mobility, and affluence and with a society in which the mass media play an increasingly important role.

A fourth factor in the spread of McDonaldization and other aspects of American culture (the credit card [Ritzer, 1995], for example), is the absence of any viable alternative on the world stage. The path to worldwide McDonaldization has been laid bare, at least in part, because of the death of communism. With the demise of communism the only organized resistance can come from local cultures and communities. While the latter can mobilize significant opposition, it is not likely to be nearly as powerful as one embedded in an alternate worldwide movement.

Given the spread of McDonaldization and the powerful reasons behind it, what can serve to impede this global development? First, there is the fact that many areas of the world offer little in the way of profits to those who push McDonaldization. Many economies are so poor that there is little to be gained by pushing McDonaldized systems on them. Other institutions within such societies may want to McDonaldize their operations, but they are likely to be so overwhelmed by day-to-day concerns that they will have little time and energy to overhaul their systems. Furthermore, they are apt to lack the funds needed for such an overhaul. Thus their very economic weakness serves to protect many areas of the world from McDonaldization.

Second, we cannot overlook the importance and resilience of local culture. Globalization theorists, in particular, have emphasized the strength of such cultures. While it is true that McDonaldization has the power to sweep away much of local culture, it is not omnipotent. For example, while the eating habits of some will change dramatically, many others will continue to eat much as they always have. Then, even if the eating habits of an entire culture change (a highly unlikely occurrence), other aspects of life may be partly or even wholly unaffected by McDonaldization. It is also likely that too high a degree of McDonaldization will lead to a counterreaction and a reassertion of local cul-

ture. Also worth mentioning are the many ways in which local cultures affect McDonaldizing systems, forcing them to adapt in various ways to local demands and customs (for example, as discussed above, the mutton burgers in India).

The combination of a comparative lack of economic incentive to the forces behind McDonaldization and the opposition of local cultures will serve to impede the global spread of McDonaldization. However, when a given local culture advances economically, those who profit from McDonaldization will begin to move into that domain. In such cases, only local resistance will remain as a barrier to McDonaldization. It seems clear that while some local cultures will successfully resist, most will fail. In the end, and in the main, the only areas of the world that will be free of McDonaldization are those that lack the economic base to make it profitable.

The only hope on the horizon might be international groups like those interested in health and environmental issues. McDonaldized systems do tend to pose health risks for people and do tend to threaten the environment in various ways. There has, in fact, been some organized opposition to McDonaldized systems on health and environmental grounds. One could envision more such opposition, organized on a worldwide basis, in the future. However, it is worth noting that McDonaldized systems have proven to be quite adaptable when faced with opposition on these grounds. That is, they have modified their systems to eliminate the greatest threats to their customers' health and the greatest environmental dangers. Such adaptations have thus far served to keep health and environmental groups at bay.

THE COLONIZATION OF LIFE AND DEATH

While spatial expansion is covered in the previous section under the heading of globalization, in this section I deal with temporal expansion. McDonaldization first focused on a variety of things associated with *life*. That is, it is the day-to-day aspects of living — food, drink, clothing, shelter, and so on — that were initially McDonaldized. Firmly ensconced in the centre of the process of living, McDonaldization has pressed outward in both directions until it has come to encompass as many aspects as possible of both the beginning (birth) and the end of life (death). Indeed, as we will see, the process has not stopped there, but has moved beyond what would, at first glance, appear to be its absolute limits to encompass (again, to the degree that such a thing is possible) "prebirth" and "post-death." Thus, this section is devoted to what might be termed the "colonization" (Habermas, 1987) of birth (and its antecedents) and death (and its aftermath) by the forces of McDonaldization.

In recent years a variety of steps have been taken to rationalize the process leading up to birth: burgeoning impotence clinics, including chains (Jackson, 1995), or soon-to-be-chains; artificial or, better, "donor" (Baran and Pannor, 1989) insemination; in vitro fertilization (DeWitt, 1993); surrogate mothers (Pretorius, 1994); "granny pregnancies" (*Daily Mail*, 1994); home pregnancy and ovulation-predictor tests (Cain, 1995); sex-selection clinics (Bennett, 1983); sex-determination tests like amniocentesis (Rapp, 1994); and tests including chorionic villus sampling, maternal serum alpha-fetoprotein, and ultrasound to determine whether the fetus is carrying such genetic defects as Down's syndrome, hemophilia, Tay-Sachs, and sickle-cell disease. All of these techniques are collectively leading to "high-tech baby making" (Baran and Pannor, 1989), which can be used to produce what have been called "designer pregnancies" (Kolker and Burke, 1994) and "designer babies" (Daley, 1994).

The rationalization process is also manifest in the process of giving birth. One measure of this is the decline in the very human and personal practice of midwifery. In 1900 about half of American births were attended by midwives, but by 1986 that had declined to only 4 percent (Mitford, 1993). Then there is the bureaucratization of childbirth. In 1900, less than 5 percent of births in the United States took place in hospitals, by 1940 it was 55 percent, and by 1960 the process was all but complete with nearly 100 percent of births taking place in hospitals (Leavitt, 1986: 190).

Hospitals and the medical profession developed standard, routinized (McDonaldized) procedures for handling childbirth. One of the best-known viewed childbirth as a disease (a "pathologic process") and its procedures were to be followed even in the case of low-risk births (Treichler, 1990). First, the patient was to be placed in the lithotomy position, "lying supine with legs in air, bent and wide apart, supported by stirrups" (Mitford, 1993: 59). Second, the mother-to-be was to be sedated from the first stage of labour on. Third, an episiotomy[1] was to be performed to enlarge the area through which the baby must pass. Finally, forceps were to be used to make the delivery more efficient. Describing this type of procedure, one woman wrote "Women are herded like sheep through an obstetrical assembly line [needless to say, one of the precursors of McDonaldization], are drugged and strapped on tables where their babies are forceps delivered" (Mitford, 1993: 61). This procedure had most of the elements of McDonaldization, but it lacked calculability, but that was added in the form of the "Friedman Curve" created in 1978. This curve envisioned three rigid stages of labour with, for example, the first stage allocated exactly 8.6 hours during which cervical dilation went from 2 to 4 cm (Mitford, 1993: 143).

A variety of non-human technologies (e.g., forceps) have been employed in the delivery of babies. One of the most widespread is the scalpel. Many doctors routinely perform episiotomies during delivery so that the walls of the vagina are not stretched unduly during pregnancy.

The scalpel is also a key tool in caesareans. A perfectly human process has come, in a large number of cases, to be controlled by this technology and those who wield it (Guillemin,

1989). The first modern caesarean took place in 1882, but as late as 1970 only 5 percent of all births involved caesareans. The use skyrocketed in the 1970s and 1980s, reaching 25 percent of all births in 1987 in what has been described as a "national epidemic" (Silver and Wolfe, 1989). (By 1989 there had been a slight decline to just under 24 percent).

Once the baby comes into the world, there is a calculable scoring system, Apgar, used on newborns. The babies are given scores of 1 to 2 on five factors (for example, heart rate, colour), with 10 being the top (healthiest) total score. Most babies have scores between 7 and 9 a minute after birth, and 8 to 10 after five minutes. Babies with scores of 0 to 3 are in distress.

We move now to the other frontier: from the process of being born to that of dying. The McDonaldization of death begins long before a person dies; it commences in the efforts by the medical system to keep the person alive as long as possible: the increasing array of technologies designed to keep people alive; the focus of medicine on maximizing the *quantity* of days, weeks, or years a patient remains alive, and the lack of emphasis on the *quality* of life during that extra time; computer systems that assess a patient's chances of survival; and the *rationing* in the treatment of the dying person.

Turning to death itself, it has followed much the same path as birth. That is, it has been moved out of the home and beyond the control of the dying and their family members and into the hands of medical personnel and hospitals. Physicians have played a key role here by gaining a large measure of control of death just as they won control over birth. And death, like birth, is increasingly likely to take place in the hospital. In 1900, only 20 percent of deaths took place in hospitals, in 1949 it was up to 50 percent, by 1958 it was at 61 percent, and by 1977 it had reached 70 percent. By 1993 the number of hospital deaths was down slightly (65 percent), but to that must be added the increasing number of people who die in nursing homes (11 percent) and residences such as hospices (22 per-

cent) (National Center for Health Statistics, 1995). Thus, death has been bureaucratized, which means it has been rationalized, even McDonaldized. The latter is quite explicit in the growth of hospital chains and even chains of hospices, using principles derived from the fast-food restaurant, which are increasingly controlling death. One result of all of this is the dehumanization of the very human process of death, as we are increasingly likely to die (as we are likely to be born) impersonally, in the presence of total strangers.

However, even the best efforts of modern, rationalized medicine inevitably fail and patients die. But we are not free of McDonaldization even after we die. For example, we are beginning to witness the development of the changeover from largely family-owned to chains of funeral homes (Corcoran, 1992; Finn, 1991). The chains are leaping into this lucrative and growing market often offering not only funeral services, but cemetery property and merchandise such as caskets and markers.

Perhaps the best example of the rationalization of death is the cremation. It is the parallel to caesareans in the realm of birth. Cremations are clearly more efficient than conventional funerals and burials. Ritual is minimized, and cremations have a kind of assembly-line quality; they lead to "conveyor belt funerals." Cremations also lend themselves to greater calculability than traditional funerals and burials. For example, instead of allowing lying in state for a day, or more, the city of London crematorium has the following sign: "Please restrict service to 15 minutes" (Grice, 1992: 10). Then there is the irrationality of the highly rational cremation, which tends to eliminate much of the human ceremony associated with a traditional funeral-burial.

The period after one dies has been rationalized in other ways, at least to some degree. There are, for example, the pre-arranged funerals that allow people to manage their affairs even after they are dead. Another example is the harvesting of the organs of the deceased so that others might live. Then there is cryogenics, where people are having themselves, or perhaps just their heads, frozen so that they might be brought back to life when anticipated advances in the rationalization of life make such a thing possible.

Given the rationalization of birth and before as well as death and beyond, are there any limits to this expansion? Several are worth mentioning:

- The uniqueness of every death (and birth): "Every life is different from any that has gone before it, and so is every death. The uniqueness of each of us extends even to the way we die" (Nuland, 1994: 3).

- The often highly nonrational character of the things that cause death (and cause problems at birth):

  Cancer, far from being a clandestine foe, is in fact berserk with the malicious exuberance of killing. The disease pursues a continuous, uninhibited, circumferential, barn-burning expedition of destructiveness, in which it heeds no rules, follows no commands and explodes all resistance in a homicidal riot of devastation. Its cells behave like members of a barbarian horde run amok—leaderless and undirected, but with a single-minded purpose: to plunder everything within reach. (Nuland, 1994: 207)

  If ever there was a daunting nonrational enemy of rationalization, cancer (and the death it often causes) is it.

- Midwifery has enjoyed a slight renaissance *because* of the dehumanization and rationalization of modern childbirth practices. When asked why they have sought out midwives, women complain about things like the "callous and neglectful treatment by the hospital staff," "labour unnecessarily induced for the convenience of the doctor," and "unnecessary caesareans for the same reason" (Mitford, 1993: 13).

- The slight decline in caesareans is reflective of the growing concern over the epidemic of caesareans as well as the fact that the American College of Obstetricians came out for abandoning the time-honoured idea, "once a caesarean, always a caesarean."

- Advance directives and living wills tell hospitals and medical personnel what they may or may not do during the dying process.

- The growth of suicide societies and books like Derek Humphrey's *Final Exit* give people instructions on how to kill themselves; on how to control their own deaths.

- The growing interest in euthanasia, most notably the work of "Dr. Death," Jack Kevorkian, shows that more people wish to exercise control over their own deaths.

CONCLUSION

I have discussed the spatial and temporal expansion of McDonaldization under the headings of globalization and the colonization of birth and death. It is abundantly clear that McDonaldization is expanding dramatically over time and space. However, there remains the issue of whether or not this growth is inexorable. A number of the barriers to, and limits on, the expansion of McDonaldization have been discussed in this chapter. There clearly are such limits and, perhaps more importantly, McDonaldization seems to lead to various counterreactions that serve to limit this spread. The issue, of course, is whether or not these counterreactions can themselves avoid being McDonaldized.

While there is some hope in all of this, there is not enough to allow us to abandon the Weberian hypothesis about the inexorable march toward the iron cage of, in this case, McDonaldization. In spite of this likely scenario, I think there are several reasons why it is important for people to continue to try to contain this process. First, it will serve to mitigate the worst excesses of McDonaldized systems. Second, it will lead to the discovery, creation, and use of niches where people who are so inclined can escape McDonaldization for at least a part of their day or even a larger portion of their lives.

Finally, and perhaps most important, the struggle itself is ennobling. As a general rule, such struggles are nonrationalized, individual, and collective activities. It is in such struggles that people can express genuinely human reason in a world that in virtually all other ways has set up rationalized systems to deny people the ability to behave in human ways; to paraphrase Dylan Thomas, instead of going gently into that next McDonaldized system, rage, rage against the way it's destroying that which makes life worth living.

NOTE

1. An episiotomy is an incision between the vagina and the anus to enlarge the opening needed for a baby to pass.

REFERENCES

Albright, M. (1995) "Inside Job: Fast-food Chains Serve a Captive Audience," *St Petersburg Times* 15 January: 1H.

Baran, A. and Pannor, R. (1989) *Lethal Secrets: The Shocking Consequences and Unresolved Problems of Artificial Insemination.* New York: Warner Boks.

Bennett, N., ed. (1983) *Sex Selection of Children.* New York: Academic Press.

Berry, M. (1995) "Redoing School Cafeterias to Favor Fast-Food Eateries," *The Orlando Sentinel* 12 January: 11.

Blount, J. (1994) "Frying Down to Rio," *Washington Post-Business* 18 May: F1, F5.

Braverman, H. (1974) *Labor and Monopoly Capital: The Degradation of Work in the Twentieth Century.* New York: Monthly Review Press.

Cain, A. (1995) "Home-Test Kits Fill an Expanding Health Niche," *The Times Union-Life and Leisure* (Albany, NY) 12 February: 11.

Chan, G. (1994) "Fast-Food Chains Pump Profits at Gas Stations," *The Fresno Bee* 10 October: F4.

Corcoran, J. (1992) "Chain Buys Funeral Home in Mt Holly," *Burlington County Times* 26 January.

Cowan, A. (1984) "Unlikely Spot for Fast Food," *The New York Times* 29 April: 3: 5.

Daily Mail (1994) "A New Mama, Aged 62," 19 July: 12.

Daley, J. (1994) "Is Birth Ever Natural?" *The Times* (London) 16 March.

DeWitt, P. (1993) "In Pursuit of Pregnancy," *American Demographics* May: 48ff.

Elmer-Dewitt, P. (1993) "Anita the Agitator," *Time* 25 January: 52ff.

Farhi, P. (1990) "Domino's Is Going to School," *Washington Post* 21 September: F3.

Featherstone, M. (1990) "Global Culture: An Introduction," in M. Featherstone (ed.) *Global Culture: Nationalism, Globalization and Modernity*, pp. 1–14. London: Sage.

Finn, K. (1991) "Funeral Trends Favor Stewart IPO," *New Orleans City Business* 9 September.

Giddens, A. (1984) *The Constitution of Society: Outline of the Theory of Structuration.* Berkeley: University of California Press.

Grice, E. (1992) "The Last Show on Earth," *The Times* (London) 11 January: 10.

Guillemin, J. (1989) "Babies by Caesarean: Who Chooses, Who Controls?" in P. Brown (ed.) *Perspectives in Medical Sociology*, pp. 549–58. Prospect Heights, IL: Waveland Press.

Habermas, J. (1987) *The Theory of Communicative Action. Vol. 2., Lifeworld and System: A Critique of Functionalist Reason.* Boston, MA: Beacon Press.

Harvey, D. (1989) *The Condition of Postmodernity: An Inquiry into the Origins of Cultural Change.* Oxford: Blackwell.

Jackson, C. (1995) "Impotence Clinic Grows into Chain," *The Tampa Tribune–Business and Finance* 18 February: 1.

Kalberg, S. (1980) "Max Weber's Types of Rationality: Cornerstones for the Analysis of Rationalization Processes in History," *American Journal of Sociology* 85: 1145–79.

Keller, B. (1990) "Of Famous Arches, Beeg Meks and Rubles," *The New York Times* 28 January: 1: 1, 12.

Kleinfeld, N. (1985) "Fast Food's Changing Landscape," *The New York Times* 14 April: 3: 1, 6.

Kolker, A. and Burke, B. (1994) *Prenatal Testing: A Sociological Perspective*. Westport, CT: Bergin and Garvey.

Kottak, C. (1983) "Rituals at McDonald's," in M. Fishwick (ed.) *Ronald Revisited: The World of Ronald McDonald*, pp. 52–58. Bowling Green, OH: Bowling Green University Press.

Leavitt, J. (1986) *Brought to Bed: Childbearing in America, 1750–1950*. New York: Oxford University Press.

Leidner, R. (1993) *Fast Food, Fast Talk: Service Work and the Routinization of Everyday Life*. Berkeley: University of California Press.

McDowell, B. (1994) "The Global Market Challenge," *Restaurants & Institutions* 104, 26: 52ff.

McDowell, E. (1992) "Fast Food Fills Menu for Many Hotel Chains," *The New York Times* 9 January: D1, D6.

Mitford, J. (1993) *The American Way of Birth*. New York: Plume.

National Center for Health Statistics (1995) *Vital Statistics of the United States, 1992–1993, Volume II — Mortality, Part A*. Hyattsville, MD: Public Health Service.

The New York Times (1986) 5 October: 3: 6.

Nuland, S. (1994) *How We Die: Reflections on Life's Final Chapter*. New York: Knopf.

Papiernik, R. (1994) "Mac Attack?" *Financial World* 12 April.

Phoenix Gazette (1994) "Fast-Food Flights," 25 November: D1.

Pretorius, D. (1994) *Surrogate Motherhood: A Worldwide View of the Issues*. Springfield, IL: Charles C. Thomas.

Prichard, P. (1987) *The Making of McPaper: The Inside Story of USA Today*. Kansas City, MO: Andrews, McMeel and Parker.

Rapp, R. (1994) "The Power of 'Positive' Diagnosis: Medical and Maternal Discourses on Amniocentesis," in D. Bassin, M. Honey and M. Kaplan (eds.) *Representations of Motherhood*, pp. 204–19. New Haven, CT: Yale University Press.

Reitman, V. (1993) "India Anticipates the Arrival of the Beefless Big Mac," *Wall Street Journal* 20 October: B1, B3.

Rigg, C. (1994) "McDonald's Lean Units Beef Up NY Presence," *Crain's New York Business* 31 October: 1.

Ritzer, G. (1983) "The McDonaldization of Society," *Journal of American Culture* 6: 100–7.

——. (1993) *The McDonaldization of Society*. Thousand Oaks, CA: Pine Forge Press.

——. (1995) *Expressing America: A Critique of the Global Credit Card Society*. Thousand Oaks, CA: Pine Forge Press.

——. (1996) *The McDonaldization of Society*, rev. ed. Thousand Oaks, CA: Pine Forge Press.

Robertson, R. (1990) "Mapping the Global Condition: Globalization as the Central Concept," in M. Featherstone (ed.) *Global Culture: Nationalism, Globalization and Modernity*, pp. 15–30. London: Sage.

——. (1992) *Globalization: Social Theory and Global Culture*. London: Sage.

Shapiro, E. (1991) "The Sincerest Form of Rivalry," *The New York Times* 19 October: 35, 46.

——. (1992) "Overseas Sizzle for McDonald's," *The New York Times* April 17: D1, D4.

Shapiro, L. (1990) "Ready for McCatfish?" *Newsweek* 15 October: 76–7.

Silver, L. and Wolfe, S. (1989) *Unnecessary Cesarian Sections: How to Cure a National Epidemic*. Washington, DC: Public Citizen Health Research Group.

Sugarman, C. (1995) "Dining Out on Campus," *Washington Post/Health* 14 February: 20.

Tampa Tribune (1995) "Investors with Taste for Growth Looking to Golden Arches," *Business and Finance* 11 January: 7.

Thomas, D. (1952) "Do Not Go Gentle into That Good Night," in D. Thomas *The Collected Poems of Dylan Thomas*, p. 128. New York: New Directions.

Tiryakian, E. (1991) "Modernisation: Exhumetur in Pace (Rethinking Macrosociology in the 1990s)," *International Sociology* 6: 165–80.

Treichler, P. (1990) "Feminism, Medicine, and the Meaning of Childbirth," in M. Jacobus, E. Keller and S. Shuttleworth (eds.) *Body Politics: Women and the Discourses of Science*, pp. 113–38. New York: Routledge.

Van Giezen, R. (1994) "Occupational Wages in the Fast-Food Industry," *Monthly Labor Review* August: 24–30.

Washington Post (1990) "Wedge of Americana: In Moscow, Pizza Hut Opens 2 Restaurants," 12 September: B10.

Weber, M. (1968 [1921]) *Economy and Society*. Totowa, NJ: Bedminster Press.

Chapter 24

Work and Society: Canada in Continental Context

WALLACE CLEMENT

THE WORST OF BOTH WORLDS

In the late 1980s and 1990s, Canada became increasingly integrated into the United States economy through several free trade agreements. These agreements facilitated cross-border trade and investment. Closer integration of the two countries had some paradoxical effects. On the one hand, Canadians witnessed an erosion of their hard-won rights to various welfare-state benefits — state-funded medical services, subsidized higher education, and the like. In this sense, Canada became more like the United States, where citizens have historically enjoyed fewer welfare-state entitlements than Canadians. On the other hand, Canada failed to participate fully in the "boom" economy of the United States, at least until 2000. For example, while the proportion of working-age Americans in the labour force remained exceptionally high throughout the 1990s, the corresponding proportion in Canada fell. Similarly, while Canadian Gross Domestic Product per capita (GDPpc) was 82 percent of American GDPpc in 1989, it fell to 76 percent by 1997. Thus, the Canadian labour market failed to emulate the American model, while the system of Canadian citizenship entitlements began to do so. In terms of labour market and state benefits, then, Canada experienced the worst of both worlds.

COMPARING LABOUR MARKETS

Before 1981, Canada and the United States had nearly identical unemployment rates. During the 1980s, however, a 2 percent gap in unemployment rates opened between the two countries. The gap grew to 5 percent in the early 1990s and reached nearly 8 percent in 1999.[1]

The growing gap between Canadian and U.S. unemployment rates was due in part to the extraordinary capacity of the United States to create new jobs and the failure of Canada to follow suit. However, other factors were at work too. For one thing, the United States imprisons more of its citizens per 100 000 population than any other country save Russia. Incarceration became particularly popular in the United States in the 1980s and 1990s. Today, nearly 2 million Americans are behind bars, and the rate of incarceration is about 4.5 times higher than in Canada. The high incarceration rate keeps many hard-to-employ Americans out of the labour force while providing many jobs for police and prison guards.[2] Also helping to keep the United States unemployment rate low is the growing population of "illegal immigrants." There are about 5 million illegal immigrants in the United States, nearly half from Mexico.[3] This is proportionately far more than in Canada. Illegal immigrants are likely to experience higher

Source: Excerpted from Wallace Clement, "Work and Society: Canada in a Continental and Comparative Context," Presentation, Department of Sociology, Bishop's University, Lennoxville, Quebec, November 9, 1999. Reprinted by permission of the author.

unemployment rates than legal immigrants and non-immigrants, yet they are not calculated among the officially unemployed because they are in the country illegally.

Compared to the United States, Canada was more deeply affected by the recession of the early 1990s and its population grew more quickly. These factors also contributed to the growing gap in unemployment rates between the two countries. True, by the middle of 1999, Canada's unemployment rate fell to its lowest level in nine years (7.6 percent) and continued to decline in 2000. But it is important to note that much of this decline was due to the growth of part-time, not full-time, jobs; part-time jobs are less secure, pay less, and offer fewer benefits than full-time jobs. Moreover, some of the decline was due to people dropping out of the labour force. Declining unemployment rates due to people dropping out of the labour force and taking part-time work are less impressive and less beneficial than declining unemployment rates due to the growth of full-time jobs.

One of the strongest patterns of change in Canada's labour force during the free trade era is the rise in self-employment. Self-employment accounted for three-quarters of all new jobs created between 1989 and 1997. The self-employed now constitute 18 percent of Canada's labour force. Ninety percent of these new jobs are in the service sector, led by business services and health and social services. Significantly, earnings of self-employed workers are more polarized than earnings of employees. Thus, 45 percent of self-employed workers, compared to 26 percent of employees, earn less than $20 000 annually. At the other extreme, only 1 percent of employees, compared to 4 percent of self-employed workers, earn more than $100 000 annually.[4]

A major Statistics Canada study contrasting labour market developments in Canada and the United States between 1989 and 1997 found that self-employment grew by 39 percent in Canada while the number of employed people rose by only 1.6 percent. In the United States over the same period, both self-employment and

employment in general grew by about 10 percent (see Table 24.1). The difference in self-employment in the two labour markets is striking when one considers that self-employment accounted for four-fifths of total job growth in Canada and only one-tenth in the United States between 1989 and 1997.[5] Equally stunning is the share of growth coming from part-time employment in Canada contrasted with the United States. Canada's full-time employees took a major hit over the period. Thus, not only was Canada's job growth much slower than in the United States, it was characterized by the more rapid growth of so-called marginal or "contingent" jobs that offer less job security, lower wages, more seasonal work, and fewer benefits.

The growth of contingent jobs affects different segments of the labour force to varying degrees. Compare women and men, for example. A recent Canadian study reports that nearly two-thirds of women who have been employed in the paid labour force have had their work interrupted for six or more months. This compares to just over a quarter of men. Moreover, while 88 percent of women's labour force interruptions were due to family responsibilities in

TABLE 24.1 PERCENTAGE EMPLOYMENT GROWTH, CANADA AND THE UNITED STATES, 1989–1997

	CANADA	UNITED STATES
Total Employment Growth	6.5	10.4
Percent of Total Growth from:		
Self-employment	79.4	9.5
Part-time	47.8	6.2
Full-time	31.8	3.3
Employees	20.6	90.5
Part-time	47.3	20.4
Full-time	−26.7	70.1

SOURCE: Adapted from Statistics Canada, *Labour Force Update* Catalogue no. 71-005-XPB (Autumn 1998), Table 4, p. 17.

the 1950s, this figure fell to 47 percent in the 1990s. Meanwhile, economic reasons such as layoffs accounted for nearly a quarter of female labour force interruptions in the 1990s.[6] Another gender difference is evident in the proportion of women and men who work part-time. In all countries, women are more likely than men to work fewer than 30 hours a week. In the United States, for example, about 8 percent of men and 19 percent of women work less than 30 hours a week. In Canada, the respective figures are about 11 percent and 29 percent.[7]

Finally, it should be noted that part-time work may be voluntary or involuntary. In Canada, an increasingly large share of the part-time labour force is involuntary, which is to say it consists of people who want to work full-time but cannot find full-time jobs. Thus, between 1975 and 1994, part-time employment rose from 11 percent to 17 percent of the labour force, while those seeking full-time employment but having to settle for part-time work rose from 11 percent to 35 percent. In 40 percent of cases, the involuntary part-time worker was the primary earner in the family.[8]

CITIZENSHIP AND THE WELFARE STATE

On the basis of the foregoing discussion, it seems safe to conclude that, since the advent of free trade in the late 1980s, Canada has not participated in many aspects of the boom economy enjoyed by its southern neighbour. Whether we examine labour force participation rates, unemployment rates, change in GDPpc, or growth in full-time non-contingent jobs, Canada has lagged behind the United States. That, however, is only half the story I want to tell. The other half has to do with the decline of welfare-state benefits or entitlements. Here Canada *has* begun to resemble the United States. That is largely because of free trade. If Canada kept welfare-state benefits much higher than U.S. levels, investment capital would tend to flow out of the country because total labour costs would be so

much higher in Canada. Free trade thus puts downward pressure on Canadian welfare-state benefits.

The main differences between Canadian and U.S. entitlements are in the realm of health care and postsecondary education. In the mid-1990s, just under 45 percent of American health care costs were covered by government. In Canada, the comparable figure was just over 70 percent. Similarly, the Canadian government heavily subsidizes postsecondary education, while American postsecondary education is largely private. However, these and other differences between the Canadian and American welfare states are weakening in the free trade era. Canadian government spending on health care and post-secondary education was cut throughout the 1990s. Tuition fees have gone up, and private health care is making inroads, especially in Alberta.

Here I must distinguish entitlements based on employment from those based on citizenship. To the extent that access to health care is based on private insurance plans or plans paid by employers rather than awarded as a right of citizenship, health care insurance is turned into a commodity. In Canada, basic health care, including doctors' fees and hospitalization, is covered by a nationally financed health insurance scheme. Other features of health care —dentistry, drugs, eyewear, types of hospital rooms, and so on—are covered either privately or through employment benefits. In Canada, employers face modest demands for health care coverage in labour negotiations whereas in the United States health care insurance demands are high because state funding covers only the elderly and the poor. The link between work and society is weaker in Canada than in the United States in this respect.

For education, Canada's primary and secondary levels are fully state-funded with near-universal utilization of the system. Preschool child care is a private responsibility, and a once-promised national daycare program remains only a dream. Postsecondary education is fee-based, but tuition has traditionally been modest and all universities are public institutions. In the United States, an increasing share of primary and secondary students are in private schools because of the low quality of state-funded schools. Postsecondary education is sharply divided between state-sponsored institutions with high tuition fees and private colleges with extremely high tuition fees.

In Canada, the contributory "employment insurance" scheme became more restrictive in the 1990s as eligibility criteria were tightened and a shrinking share of the unemployed were deemed entitled to benefits. People excluded from employment insurance are pushed into the means-tested welfare system. Although 83 percent of unemployed Canadians qualified for unemployment insurance benefits in 1989, only 43 percent were eligible in 1997. This declining coverage resulted from 1996 reforms disqualifying "voluntary" job-leavers and seasonal and part-time workers. Benefits were cut from 67 percent of previous salary to 55 percent. The result was a cash cow for the government: $19.5 billion in employment insurance contri-

butions were collected in 1997, but only $12.5 billion were paid in benefits and administration.[9]

In terms of public expenditures on labour markets, Canada and the United States are not in the same league. Active labour market measures facilitate people's ability to find work. Passive measures compensate them for not working. While active labour market support diminished in Germany and Sweden in the 1990s, these countries remained active in their labour market support throughout the decade. Canada and Australia were high on passive support but low on active support and moderate overall. Japan and the United States were inactive and provided little even in the way of passive labour market support (see Table 24.2).

Compared to the United States, Canada spends more on employment services and labour market training. However, Canada follows the meagre United States pattern for youth measures, subsidized employment, and disability measures. During the 1990s, countries like Australia, Germany, and Sweden dedicated more resources to actively combatting unem-

TABLE 24.2   PUBLIC EXPENDITURES ON LABOUR MARKET PROGRAMS, 1997, AS PERCENTAGE OF GDP

	CANADA	USA	AUSTRALIA	JAPAN	GERMANY	SWEDEN
Employment services	0.20	0.06	0.24	0.03	0.21	0.26
Labour market training	0.17	0.04	0.09	0.03	0.36	0.43
Youth measures	0.02	0.03	0.06	0.00	0.07	0.02
Subsidized employment	0.06	0.01	0.21	0.04	0.34	0.70
Disability measures	0.03	0.03	0.06	0.00	0.28	0.67
Total Active	0.48	0.17	0.66	0.10	1.25	2.09
Unemployment compensation	1.17	0.26	1.30	0.40	2.49	2.16
Early retirement	0.01	0.00	0.00	0.00	0.05	0.00
Total Passive	1.18	0.26	1.30	0.40	2.54	2.16
TOTAL	1.65	0.43	1.97	0.50	3.79	4.25
% change in total, 1990–97	–0.78	–0.30	0.59	0.19	1.56	1.68

SOURCE: Adapted from Organisation for Economic Co-operation and Development, *Employment Outlook* (Paris: OECD, July 1994, July 1996, June 1998).

ployment. Canada is in the same league as the United States and Japan in this respect. Still, it is exceptional because, unlike these two low-unemployment countries, Canada suffers from chronically high unemployment.

Canada's dramatic reduction in passive payments was achieved by cutting coverage, not by reducing unemployment, as in the United States. Indeed, Canada's unemployment increased as its expenditures decreased. In terms of its welfare-state expenditures, it is acting like the United States, but it is doing so on a labour market foundation dramatically different from its neighbour's.

CONCLUSION

What, in the final analysis, can be said about the relationship between work and society during the free trade era in Canada? Work in Canada has become more marginal or contingent in many respects. There are more self-employed workers, more part-time workers, and more unemployed workers. Instead of becoming more like the American labour market, where people tend to work longer hours during longer work lives, Canada has become a place where people work less because less work is available, especially good work in the public sector and large corporations. Postindustrialism has not been kind to the Canadian labour force.

In areas like employment insurance, the Canadian government is putting more stress on employment-based benefits that are not typically available for the self-employed and part-time workers. The Canadian state has not yet withered away to American levels, because its citizens continue to insist on a modicum of social support. Canada stands between the American job machine with its abundance of cheap labour and the more supportive labour markets of Sweden and Germany.

Are Canadians, as citizens and workers, better off under free trade? We cannot answer this question fully because we will never know the outcome of alternative policy choices. Nonetheless, it seems clear that many Canadians have paid dearly for the path Canada's political leaders chose and its economic leaders demanded.

NOTES

1. See Statistics Canada, *Labour Force Update*, Autumn 1998, p. 3.
2. Bruce Western and Katherine Beckett, "The Penal System as a Labor-Market Institution: The Dynamics of Jobs and Jails, 1980–1995" paper presented to the American Sociology Association, Toronto 1997; H.L. Ginsburg, J. Zaccone, G.S. Goldberg, S.D. Collins, and S.M. Rosen, *Economic and Industrial Democracy* 18 (1997), Special Issue on the Challenge of Full Employment in the Global Economy, Editorial Introduction, p. 24.
3. See Min Zhou, "Growing Up American: The Challenge Confronting Immigrant Children and the Children of Immigrants," *Annual Review of Sociology* 23 (1997): 63–95; *New York Times,* August 31, 1997.
4. See *Canadian Social Trends* (Ottawa: Statistics Canada, Spring 1998), p. 28.
5. See *Labour Force Update*, Autumn 1998, p. 13.
6. See Janet Fast and Moreno Da Pont, "Changes in Women's Work Continuity," *Canadian Social Trends* (Ottawa: Statistics Canada, Autumn 1997), pp. 3–5.
7. See Rianne Mahon, "Women Wage Earners and the Future of Swedish Union," *Economic and Industrial Democracy* 17 (1996): 555, 574. Also see Jacqueline O'Reilly and Claudia Spree, "The Future Regulation of Work and Welfare: Time for a Revised Social and Gender Contract?" *European Journal of Industrial Relations* 4, 3 (1998): 259–81.
8. Grant Schellenberg, "'Involuntary' Part-Time Workers," *Perception* 18, 3/4 (1996).
9. See *The Globe and Mail* February 13, 1998: A3.

Chapter 25

Postindustrialism and Globalization

HARVEY J. KRAHN

GRAHAM S. LOWE

POSTINDUSTRIALISM

Continuing social and economic change has led some social scientists to argue that we have moved out of the industrial era into a *postindustrial society*. Daniel Bell, writing in the early 1970s, was among the first to note these transformations in the U.S. occupational structure.[1] The Industrial Revolution had seen jobs in the manufacturing and processing sectors replace agricultural jobs. After the Second World War II, jobs in the service sector had become much more prominent. The number of factory workers was decreasing, while employment in the areas of education, health, social welfare, entertainment, government, trade, finance, and a variety of other business sectors was rising. White-collar workers were beginning to outnumber blue-collar workers.

Bell argued that postindustrial societies would engage most workers in the production and dissemination of knowledge, rather than in goods-production as in industrial capitalism. While industrialization had brought increased productivity and living standards, postindustrial society would usher in an era of reduced concentration of power (Bell, 1973: 358–67). Power would no longer reside merely in the ownership of property, but also in access to knowledge and in the ability to think and to solve problems. *Knowledge workers*—technicians, professionals, and scientists—would become a large and important class. Their presence would begin to reduce the polarization of classes that had typi-

fied the arrival of the industrial age. Bell proposed that knowledge workers would become the elite of the postindustrial age.

A decade after Bell published his ideas about postindustrial society, John Naisbitt popularized them in *Megatrends*. By including occupational groups as diverse as secretaries, data entry clerks, lawyers, librarians, and scientists in his category of "information workers," Naisbitt observed that a majority of the work force in the United States was employed in the information sector. He argued that knowledge, unlike property, cannot be possessed by a small elite. Since a majority of the population is involved in creating, processing, and distributing information, society must be moving into a new, more democratic era. "The new source of power is not money in the hands of a few but information in the hands of many," he concluded (Naisbitt, 1982: 7).

While continuing to focus on knowledge workers in his book, *The Work of Nations*, Robert Reich disputes the arguments of Bell and Naisbitt about declining inequality. Reich distinguishes *symbolic analysts* (engineers, scientists, consultants, and so on) from the many individuals performing *routine production work* (most manufacturing employees, along with data entry clerks and many other lower-level white-collar workers) and from those providing *in-person services* (retail sales clerks, workers in the food services, and security guards, for example)

Source: Excerpted from *Work, Industry, and Canadian Society*, 3rd ed. (Toronto: ITP Nelson, 1998), pp. 24–36. Reprinted with permission.

Reich, 1991: 174–76). Reich recognizes that inequality has increased in American society in the past decades. He argues that the symbolic analysts whose skills are in great demand have become wealthier, while other American workers have become poorer (Reich, 1991: 174–76).

Why the optimism in the early theories of postindustrial society? These explanations of social and economic change were developed in the decades following the Second World War, a time of significant economic growth in North America.[2] White-collar occupational opportunities were increasing, educational institutions were expanding, and the overall standard of living was rising. This context influenced the optimistic tone of the social theories being developed. Yet other commentators paint a negative picture of the rise of service industries and an expanding white-collar work force. These critical perspectives point to job deskilling, reduced economic security, the dehumanizing impact of computers, and widening labour market polarization—trends that seem more pronounced since the early 1980s.

INDUSTRIAL RESTRUCTURING

Technological change is accelerating at a time when the international economy is in upheaval. The deep recessions of the early 1980s and early 1990s, fierce international competition, multinational free-trade arrangements, and the spectacular growth of Asian economies have had a major impact on Canada. In fact, it is becoming more difficult to think in terms of discrete national economies. In the words of Robert Reich (1991: 6), "money, technology, information, and goods are flowing across national borders with unprecedented rapidity and ease." This *globalization* of economic activity continues to bring about fundamental readjustments in the Canadian economy and labour market, including plant shutdowns; job loss through "downsizing," corporate reorganization, and mergers; and the relocation or expansion of company operations outside Canada.[3]

But are these new trends? Writing in the early twentieth century, economist Joseph Schumpeter considered *industrial restructuring* a basic feature of capitalism. According to Schumpeter, this process of "creative destruction" involved breaking down old ways of running industry and building up more competitive, efficient, and high-technology alternatives.[4] North American industry clearly is engaged in this process today. But while necessary for the economy as a whole, industrial restructuring can also have negative effects on the quality and quantity of work for individuals. Job losses may be part of the process for some, while others may find themselves with much less job security.

Industrial restructuring involves interrelated social, economic, and technological trends. Crucial is the shift from manufacturing to services. Canada's service industries have rapidly grown in recent decades, compared with declining employment in agriculture, resource, and manufacturing industries. Indeed, both Canada and the United States have experienced *deindustrialization*. This concept refers to declining employment due to factory closures or relocation, typically in once-prominent manufacturing industries: steel, automotives, textiles, clothing, chemicals, and plastics. Once mainstays of the Canadian and U.S. economies, these industries are now sometimes referred to as "sunset industries," because they have failed to adapt quickly to shifting consumer demands. Factories have been sold off, shut down, or relocated to areas such as Mexico, China, or other developing nations where labour is cheap and employment rights and environmental standards are lax. As Bluestone and Harrison (1982: 9) observe, "left behind are shuttered factories, displaced workers, and a newly emerging group of ghost towns."

Canada has been more vulnerable than the United States to deindustrialization. As Daniel Drache and Meric Gertler note, by 1990 dozens of large multinationals, encouraged by the Canada–U.S. free trade agreement, had announced or implemented plant closures in central Canada, seeking cheaper labour and fewer regulations.[5] More recently, after purchasing the Bauer hockey equipment company, Nike announced in 1997 that it was closing the Ontario factory. But Canadian-owned firms have also been making similar moves. As Canadian corporate giants like Bombardier and Nortel have become global competitors, they have shifted more of their operations (and many of the jobs they provide) out of the country. For example, at the beginning of the 1990s, Nortel reduced its Canadian work force by almost half while increasing recruitment in its U.S. operations.[6]

GLOBALIZATION

The term *globalization* has become part of everyday language, but what does it really mean, and can evidence document such a trend? As we noted regarding industrial restructuring, the basic idea is not new; in Canada's colonial past, the masters of the British Empire no doubt envisioned their reach as global. Yet searching for a definition of globalization, one is struck by the great many meanings it conveys. Advocates of globalization believe in the inevitable spread of capitalist markets, national convergence, and the postindustrial vision of economic progress through technology and information. As Gordon Laxer (1995: 287–88) explains, globalization typically refers to four interrelated changes:

> Economic changes include the internationalization of production, the harmonization of tastes and standards and the greatly increased mobility of capital and of transnational corporations. Ideological changes emphasize investment and trade liberalization, deregulation and private enterprise. New information and communications technologies that shrink the globe signal a shift from goods to services. Finally, cultural changes involve trends toward a universal world culture and the erosion of the nation-state.

Corporations, and often governments, promote globalization as a means by which expanding "free markets" will generate economic growth and elevate living standards. Signs of an increasingly global economy are visible in trade arrangements and financial markets. The following are good examples: regional trade liberalization agreements such as the North American Free Trade Agreement (NAFTA), the European Union, the Association of South East Asian Nations, and recent initiatives by the larger Asia-Pacific Economic Co-operation forum; international regulatory frameworks such as the World Trade Organization and the Multilateral Agreement on Investment (MAI); and the integration of financial markets through information technology. Critics—and there are many—detect more sinister aspects of globalization. For example, in Canada the proposed international investment treaty (MAI) has raised concerns reminiscent of the earlier debates over free trade. Such treaties are seen as threats to Canadian culture, workers' rights, environmental regulations, and, ultimately, national sovereignty (*The Globe and Mail*, April 3, 1997: A1).

In a truly global economy, corporations would operate in a completely transnational way, not rooted in a specific national economy. But research suggests that there are few such corporations (Hirst and Thompson, 1995). McDonald's, IBM, and General Motors may do business in many countries, but they are still U.S.-based. The United States, Japan, and several countries in Europe still account for most of the world's trade, largely through corporations located in these countries. While multinational corporations account for 25 percent of the world's production, they employ only 3 percent of the labour force (Giles, 1996: 6). Even so, global production is becoming more of a reality. Personal computers are a good example, with financing, design, manufacturing components, assembly, and marketing involving a network of suppliers from many countries. But as Anthony Giles (1996: 6) cautions, "Beyond the obvious technological, economic and logistical hurdles, there are a host of cultural, legal, political and linguistic factors which complicate the development of genuine globally integrated production systems."

It is much easier to imagine production systems spanning several continents than it is to envision a largely global labour force. Despite expanding international markets for some goods and services, labour is still a local resource. According to Hirst and Thompson (1995: 420), "Apart from a 'club-class' of internationally mobile, highly skilled professionals, and the desperate, poor migrants and refugees who will suffer almost any hardship to leave intolerable conditions, the bulk of the world's populations now cannot easily move." In fact, Canada plays an important role in this regard, being one of the few nations to accept relatively large numbers of immigrants annually.

Although labour might not be part of a global market, globalization may still have an impact on labour practices, notably through the public's growing concern about the labour practices of nationally based firms operating in developing countries (one could say the same about environmental practices). Global media coverage has helped to raise the awareness of North Americans. Recently, multinational corporations like Nike have been the targets of public campaigns because of their labour practices in Asian countries (Heinzl, 1997). Reflecting these concerns, a 1997 survey by the Montreal-based International Centre for Human Rights and Democratic Development of 98 of Canada's largest corporations found that while 42 percent of the responding firms agreed that international business has a role to play in promoting human rights and sustainable development, only 14 percent had a code of labour standards that protects basic human rights — freedom of association, nondiscrimination, and elimination of child labour and forced labour.[7]

CANADA AND FREE TRADE

The 1989 Free Trade Agreement (FTA) with the United States and the 1994 NAFTA, which included Mexico, committed Canada to a policy of more open, less regulated markets. As a NAFTA proponent commented: "Free trade is Darwinian. In the absence of tariff protection, the inefficient expect to be weeded out if incapable of competing" (Dana, 1992: 7). He was referring to inefficient industries and firms, but individuals, families, and communities end up being the real victims. It is not clear what the effects of the FTA have been, given that a severe recession began soon after the agreement was signed.[8] While claims of massive job losses directly from the FTA and NAFTA have not been borne out, the permanent factory closures and job losses that occurred in central Canada as the 1990s began have partly been linked to free trade. Significant industrial restructuring was already taking place, but the FTA probably accelerated the process, allowing the individuals and communities negatively affected less time to respond. Between the first quarter of 1990 and the second quarter of 1991, Canada lost 273 000 manufacturing jobs, a decline of 13 percent in the industry as a whole. As the Economic Council of Canada (1992a: 4) concluded, "Many of the jobs that were lost will not return." NAFTA does include an accord on labour as well as a commission for labour cooperation to track labour market trends in the three NAFTA countries and to address complaints about workers' rights, collective bargaining, and labour standards, so, presumably, these issues are being monitored.[9]

To put NAFTA in perspective, the three participating countries had a combined labour force of 183 million workers in 1995: 72 percent in the United States, 20 percent in Mexico, and 8 percent in Canada (Secretariat of the Commission for Labor Cooperation, 1996: 8). Mexico's labour force has been growing at a considerably faster rate than have the labour forces of its two northern neighbours, but since 1990 manufacturing employment in that country has actually declined (Arsen, 1996: 46). The migration of jobs from Canada or the United States to Mexico was a major concern of NAFTA opponents. There is little doubt that the *maquiladora* factories along Mexico's northern border have been booming. In January 1995, for example, there were 300 new maquilas started by Canadian and Japanese investors and 6000 new workers hired (Kopinak, 1996: 197). Were these "new" jobs, or relocated jobs from high-wage Canada or Japan? From available evidence, it seems that fewer jobs than expected have migrated south.[10] And much of the new foreign investment in Mexico is from firms based in Japan, East Asia, and Europe seeking a base from which to supply the North American consumer market.

Jobs may be migrating south, but only in some manufacturing industries, and if these employers are in search of low wages, they would likely relocate to China, not Mexico. Actually, there is as much concern that competitive pressures from NAFTA in some manufacturing industries, such as auto and auto parts manufacturing, have accelerated the trend toward *nonstandard or contingent* work (part-time, temporary, contract) in the United States and Canada (Roberts, Hyatt, and Dorman, 1996). Thus, perhaps the group most negatively affected by NAFTA is Mexican workers. Drawing our attention to Mexico's industrial and social development, one commentator notes: "Of the many arguments against NAFTA the most cogent was the case made by many Mexican opposition activists: that it would artificially prop up a decadent political monopoly, delaying democratic reform and ultimately making it harder for Mexico to modernize" (Orme, 1996: xxv).

It is not difficult to find supporting evidence for this view. Mexico's industrialization in the 1980s led to increased social and economic inequalities. The workers in the border maquiladora factories numbered about half a million prior to NAFTA. While their dollar-an-hour pay, lack of rights, and working conditions may be deplorable by Canadian standards, they were part of an emerging middle class in Mexico, able to "cross-border" shop in the United States. But few workers were spared the ravaging effects of the devaluation of the Mexican peso in late 1994, which saw per capita income instantly plummet from US $4000 to $2600 (Orme, 1996: xi). Maquiladora workers, already advantaged by Mexican standards, had the most militant response to this devaluation, and, through illegal strikes, did gain better pay and benefits (Kopinak, 1996: 199). Furthermore, NAFTA debates tended to overlook the circumstances of the majority of Mexicans — the rural poor. The Zapatista uprising in the rural state of Chiapas briefly drew the world's attention to those who would not benefit from NAFTA.

THE ROLE OF THE STATE IN TODAY'S ECONOMY

Clearly, the information technology revolution, industrial and labour market restructuring, and economic globalization are proceeding in a political context where laissez-faire beliefs that advocate free markets with little or no government interference are dominant.[11] In a sense, this political environment is also a key determinant of Canadians' future employment prospects. These three large trends have the potential to either improve employment opportunities for Canadians, or lead to further labour market disruptions. It is difficult to predict just what their ultimate impact might be, but it is important to consider how these forces could be shaped to our collective advantage. Public policy in other industrial countries in Europe and Asia has been more proactive in attempting to influence the course of technological, labour market, and economic change.

The FTA and NAFTA were negotiated by governments, and have been hotly contested political issues in all three countries affected. These trade agreements underscore the evolving role of the state (or government) in the economy and the labour market. The history of industrial capitalism is replete with instances of different forms of state intervention. For example, in the early Industrial Revolution, the French government forced unemployed workers into factories in an attempt to give manufacturing a boost. In the early nineteenth century the British government dealt harshly with the Luddite protests against new technologies. And the Canadian government adopted its National Policy in 1879 to promote a transcontinental railway and settlement of the West.

In fact, as Canada industrialized, the government heavily subsidized the construction of railways in order to promote economic development. It also actively encouraged immigration to increase skilled labour for factory-based production and unskilled labour for railway construction. At times, it provided military assistance to employers combatting trade unionists, and introduced laws discriminating against Chinese and other nonwhite workers. But the Canadian government also passed legislation that provided greater rights, unemployment insurance, pensions, and compensation for workplace injuries. While some might argue that these initiatives were designed mainly to ensure industrial harmony and to create an environment conducive to business, it is still true that these labour market interventions benefited workers.

A consensus, or compromise, was reached between employers and workers (mainly organized labour) in the prosperous post–Second World War period. Acting on *Keynesian economic principles*, which advocated an active economic role for the state, the Canadian government attempted to promote economic development, regulate the labour market, keep unemployment down, and assist disadvantaged groups — in short, develop a "welfare state." While the Canadian state was never as actively involved in the economy and the labour market as some European governments, it nevertheless saw itself playing an important role.[12]

But industrial restructuring in the 1980s was accompanied (some would say facilitated) by new conservative political doctrines based on free-market economics (Marchak, 1981; Saul, 1995; Kapstein, 1996). Ronald Reagan in the United States, Margaret Thatcher in Britain, and Brian Mulroney in Canada argued that economies would become more productive and competitive with less state regulation and intervention. Public policy was guided by the assumption that free markets can best determine who benefits and who loses from economic restructuring. The ideas of Adam Smith were used to justify the inevitable increases in inequality. High unemployment came to be viewed as normal. In some jurisdictions, labour rights were diluted, social programs of the welfare state came to be seen as a hindrance to balanced budgets and economic competitiveness, and government-run services were privatized.[13] As John Ralston Saul (1995) argues, these free-market ideologies erode democratic freedoms, threatening to result in what he calls "the great leap backward." Similarly, with the rapidly developing economies of East Asia, governments routinely use economic imperatives to restrict individual and collective rights.

Thus, in today's economic climate of globalization and restructuring, proponents of free-market economics seem to have more influence. But an unchecked marketplace generally leads to greater inequality. So, when answering the question, "what kind of society do we want?" it will be important to determine how the functions of the state will contribute toward this end. Given that Canadians are concerned about labour market inequalities, unemployment, workers' rights, and employers' responsibilities to communities, then clearly the state will continue to play an active role in economic life (Betcherman and Lowe, 1997; Tobin, 1996; Lonnroth, 1994).

NOTES

1. Bell (1973); current and more critical perspectives on postindustrial society are reviewed by Kumar (1995), Clement and Myles (1994), and Nelson (1995).
2. The managerial revolution perspective (Burnham, 1941; Berle and Means, 1968) was

developed earlier, during an era when corporate concentration in North America was proceeding rapidly and when concerns about the excessive power of the corporate elite were being publicly debated (Reich, 1991: 38).

3. See Betcherman and Lowe (1997) for analyses of industrial restructuring in the Canadian economy. Also see Drache and Gertler (1991), Boyer and Drache (1996), and Barnet and Cavanagh (1994: Part Three) for critical perspectives on restructuring, globalization, and work.

4. Schumpeter's views are discussed in Bluestone and Harrison (1982: 9).

5. Drache and Gertler (1991: 13); also see Lush (1987), Grayson (1985), and the Canadian Labour Congress (1991). See Heinzl (1997) on Nike's closure of the Bauer factory.

6. Drache and Gertler (1991: 12). Also see Mahon's (1984) analysis of restructuring in the Canadian textile industry.

7. International Centre for Human Rights and Democratic Development, 1997. A report on this survey is available at the organization's Web site: (http://www.ichrdd.ca).

8. The Canadian Labour Congress (1991) places the blame directly on the agreement. See the assessments of the FTA in Drache and Gertler (1991), as well as positions on both sides of the debate in Gold and Leyton-Brown (1988).

9. For current information, see the North American Institute's Web site (http://www.santafe.edu). The Institute monitors the North American Agreement on Labor Cooperation. Two recent complaints, one in Mexico and the other in the United States, concerned management opposition to union membership and collective bargaining.

10. Orme (1996: 13); Arsen, Wilson, and Zoninsein (1996); for different perspectives on NAFTA, see Bognanno and Ready (1993).

11. See Saul (1995) for a critique of this ideology.

12. Smucker and van den Berg (1991) provide a useful comparison of Swedish and Canadian labour market prices.

13. See Rubery et al. (1989) on British government labour market policies in the past decade; Kalleberg and Berg (1987: 208–12) and Rosenberg (1989) on the U.S. experience; Drache and Gertler (1991) on neoconservatism in Canada; and Haiven et al. (1991) for articles on Canada, Britain, and Sweden. Block (1990: 1–5) discusses how free market economics have come to dominate social and economic thought in North America.

REFERENCES

Arsen, David D. 1996. "The NAFTA Debate in Retrospect: U.S. Perspectives." *Policy Choices: Free Trade Among NAFTA Nations.* Karen Roberts and Mark I. Wilson, eds. East Lansing: Michigan State University Press.

Arsen, David D., Mark I. Wilson, and Jonas Zoninsein. 1996. "Trends in Manufacturing Employment in the NAFTA Region: Evidence of a Giant Sucking Sound?" *Policy Choices: Free Trade Among NAFTA Nations.* Karen Roberts and Mark I. Wilson, eds. East Lansing: Michigan State University Press.

Barnet, Richard J., and John Cavanagh. 1994. *Global Dreams: Imperial Corporations and the New World Order.* New York: Touchstone.

Bell, Daniel. 1973. *The Coming of Post-Industrial Society.* New York: Basic Books.

Berle, Adolf A., and Gardiner C. Means. 1968. *The Modern Corporation and Private Property*, rev. ed. New York: Harcourt Brace and World. [Originally published in 1932.]

Betcherman, Gordon, and Graham Lowe. 1997. *The Future of Work in Canada: A Synthesis Report.* Ottawa: Canadian Policy Research Networks.

Block, Fred. 1990. *Postindustrial Possibilities: A Critique of Economic Discourse.* Berkeley, CA: University of California Press.

Bluestone, Barry, and Bennett Harrison. 1982. *The Deindustrialization of America.* New York: Basic Books.

Bognanno, Mario F., and Kathryn J. Ready, eds. 1993. *The North American Free Trade Agreement: Labor, Industry, and Government Perspectives*. Westport, CT: Praeger.

Boyer, Robert, and Daniel Drache, eds. 1996. *States Against Markets: The Limits of Globalization*. London: Routledge.

Burnham, J. 1941. *The Managerial Revolution*. Harmondsworth, England: Penguin.

Canadian Labour Congress (CLC). 1991. *Two Years Under Free Trade: An Assessment*. Ottawa: CLC Free Trade Briefing Document no. 7.

Clement, Wallace, and John Myles. 1994. *Relations of Ruling: Class and Gender in Postindustrial Societies*. Montreal and Kingston: McGill–Queen's University Press.

Dana, Leo-Paul. 1992. "Why We Must Join NAFTA." *Policy Options* 13(27): 6–8.

Drache, Daniel, and Meric S. Gertler. 1991. "The World Economy and the Nation-State: The New International Order." In D. Drache and M.S. Gertler, eds., *The New Era of Global Competition: State Policy and Market Power*. Montreal and Kingston: McGill–Queen's University Press.

Economic Council of Canada. 1992a. *Pulling Together: Productivity, Innovation and Trade*. Ottawa: Supply and Services Canada.

Giles, Anthony. 1996. "Globalization and Industrial Relations." In Anthony Giles, Anthony E. Smith, and Gilles Trudeau, eds., *The Globalization of the Economy and the Worker*. Selected papers from the 32nd annual Canadian Industrial Relations Association Conference. Quebec, QC: CIRA.

The Globe and Mail. 1997. April 3: A1.

Gold, Mark, and David Leyton-Brown, eds. 1988. *Trade-Offs on Free Trade: The Canada–U.S. Free Trade Agreement*. Toronto: Carswell.

Grayson, Paul. 1985. *Corporate Strategies and Plant Closures: The SKF Experience*. Toronto: Our Times.

Haiven, Larry, Stephen McBride, and John Shields, eds. 1991. *Regulating Labour: The State, Neo-Conservativism and Industrial Relations*. Toronto: Garamond.

Heinzl, John. 1997. "Nike's Hockey Plans Put Bauer on Thin Ice." *The Globe and Mail* (July 2, 1997): B2.

Hirst, Paul, and Grahame Thompson. 1995. "Globalization and the Future of the Nation State." *Economy and Society* 24: 408–42.

Kalleberg, Arne, and Ivar Berg. 1987. *Work and Industry: Structures, Markets and Processes*. New York: Plenum.

Kapstein, Ethan B. 1996. "Workers and the World Economy." *Foreign Affairs* 75: 16–37.

Kopinak, Kathryn. 1996. *Desert Capitalism: Maquiladoras in North America's Western Industrial Corridor*. Tucson: University of Arizona Press.

Kumar, Krishnan. 1995. *From Post-Industrial to Post-Modern Society: New Theories of the Contemporary World*. Oxford: Blackwell.

Laxer, Gordon. 1995. "Social Solidarity, Democracy and Global Capitalism." *Canadian Review of Sociology and Anthropology* 32: 287–313.

Lonnroth, Juhani. 1994. "Global Employment: Issues in the Year 2000." *Monthly Labor Review* (September): 5–15.

Lush, Patricia. 1987. "Going, Going, Gone." *Report on Business* (January): 36–40.

Mahon, Rianne. 1984. *The Politics of Industrial Restructuring: Canadian Textiles*. Toronto: University of Toronto Press.

Marchak, M. Patricia. 1981. *Ideological Perspectives on Canada*. 2nd ed. Toronto: McGraw-Hill Ryerson.

Naisbitt, John. 1982. *Megatrends: Ten New Directions Transforming Our Lives*. New York: Warner.

Nelson, Joel J. 1995. *Post-Industrial Capitalism: Exploring Economic Inequality in America*. Thousand Oaks, CA: Sage.

Orme, Jr., W.A. 1996. *Understanding NAFTA: Mexico, Free Trade, and the New North America*. Austin: University of Texas Press.

Reich, Robert B. 1991. *The Work of Nations: Preparing Ourselves for 21st-Century Capitalism*. New York: Alfred A. Knopf.

Roberts, Karen, Doug Hyatt, and Peter Dorman. 1996. "The Effect of Free Trade on

Contingent Work in Michigan." *Policy Choices: Free Trade Among NAFTA Nations.* Karen Roberts and Mark I. Wilson, eds. East Lansing: Michigan State University Press.

Rosenberg, Samuel, ed. 1989. *The State and the Labor Market.* New York: Plenum.

Rubery, Jill, F. Wilkinson, and R. Tarling. 1989. "Government Policy and the Labour Market: The Case of the United Kingdom." In S. Rosenberg, ed., *The State and the Labor Market.* New York: Plenum.

Saul, John R. 1995. *The Unconscious Civilization.* Toronto: Anansi.

Secretariat of the Commission for Labor Cooperation. 1996. *North American Labor Markets: A Comparative Profile 1984–1995. Preliminary Findings.* Dallas: Commission for Labor Cooperation.

Smucker, Joseph, and Axel van den Berg. 1991. "Some Evidence of the Effects of Labour Market Policies on Workers' Attitudes Toward Change in Canada and Sweden." *Canadian Journal of Sociology* 16: 51–74.

Tobin, James. 1996. "Business Cycles and Economic Growth: Current Controversies about Theory and Policy." *Unnecessary Debts.* Lars Osberg and Pierre Fortin, eds. Toronto: Lorimer.

PART 5

CRIME AND DEVIANCE

Deviance is behaviour that departs from a norm. It ranges from harmless fads to the most violent crimes. In a sense, all deviance is anti-institutional because it seeks to achieve acceptable goals, such as getting rich or being happy, by means that are generally disapproved of, and often illegal. But deviance is also institutionalized behaviour because it is socially learned, organized, and persistent. Accordingly, an individual is more likely to become a deviant if he or she is exposed to more deviant than nondeviant role models. Moreover, the deviant role is learned by means of socialization; just as medical students are socialized into the role of doctor, so professional robbers must learn the moral code of thieves. And deviants, including criminals, establish counter-institutions — cliques, gangs, mafias, and so forth — with their own rules of behaviour and their own subcultural norms.

Criminal behaviour worries the Canadian public more today than it did even five years ago, and much more than it did ten or twenty years ago. There is much talk about crime waves and mounting random violence. Many people are afraid to walk alone outside at night. In big cities, many people have equipped their homes with burglar alarms and installed steel bars on their basement windows.

There is no doubt that crime rates have risen since the 1960s, but are current fears exaggerated? Most people rely on the mass media for information about crime trends. The police rely on information they collect in the course of doing their work. Reported criminal incidents, apprehensions, convictions, and incarcerations are all recorded in order to determine, among other things, whether crimes of various types are on the rise. Both public and police sources of information are, however, subject to bias. The mass media are often inclined to exaggerate the extent of criminal behaviour because doing so increases audience size and therefore the amount of money that businesses are willing to pay for advertising. The police may record more crime not just because there is more, but also because more officers are looking harder for criminals and because the public is more willing to report certain types of crimes.

Because of these biases, sociologists prefer to supplement official police statistics with **victimization surveys**, polls of representative samples of citizens that seek to determine whether and under what circumstances people are victims of crime. Victimization surveys often yield results that differ from official statistics. In Chapter 26, Rosemary Gartner and Anthony N. Doob of the University of Toronto compare the results of government-sponsored victimization surveys conducted in Canada in 1988 and 1993. Their findings lead to conclusions that differ from recent public and police perceptions of crime. They found that in both 1988 and 1993, just under a quarter of Canadians were victims of at least one crime in the preceding year. Overall, victimization rates remained steady or *decreased* during the five-year period, depending on the type of crime examined. They also discovered that while Canadians think crime rates are rising, they believe that the rise is occurring some place other than their own neighbourhood. Thus it is not personal experience that accounts for recent perceptions of rising crime rates. Rather, Gartner and Doob conclude that such perceptions result partly from mass media "hype" and partly from the fact that robberies and assaults occur more frequently in public settings than they used to. They conclude by arguing that discrepancies between police statistics and victimization surveys are partly due to the fact that the victims of some crimes, such as spousal assault and school violence, are more willing to report events to the authorities than they used to be. Increased reporting does not, however, necessarily mean increased crime.

When people claim that crime is on the rise, they tend to focus on "street crime" such as robbery, assault, homicide, and the like. But one large category of illegal behaviour scarcely enters the public consciousness, even though, according to some estimates, it costs the Canadian public more than street crime in terms of dollars and lives. I refer to corporate crime. A **corporate crime** is an act that breaks a law intended to regulate business activity. Such laws are designed to ensure worker safety and accurate advertising, and to prevent fraudulent financial manipulation, price fixing, market splitting, and environmental pollution. In Chapter 27, Carl Keane of Queen's University develops a theory of corporate crime. His review of the literature suggests that an adequate explanation of corporate crime needs to focus not just on the individual characteristics of corporate criminals, but also on characteristics of the corporation as a social organization and on the socioeconomic environment within which the corporation operates.

Some Canadians believe that crime is in part a racial phenomenon. Canadian Blacks in particular rank high in the public's perception of criminal villains. Some people—including a handful of academics, such as University of Western Ontario psychology professor Philippe Rushton—go so far as to claim that there is a *genetic* link between race and crime. Rushton contends that "Negroids" (Blacks) are genetically predisposed to commit more criminal acts than "Caucasoids" (whites), while whites are genetically predisposed to commit more criminal acts than "Mongoloids" (orientals). He cites crime statistics from the United States, the United Kingdom, and other countries showing that crime rates do indeed vary along racial lines, as he predicts.

In Chapter 28, Julian V. Roberts and Thomas Gabor of the University of Ottawa criticize Rushton's views. They show, among other things, that crime rates vary *within* racial groups, depending on historical period and society. Homicide rates are very low among Blacks in Africa and Chinese in Hong Kong, but very high among Blacks in the Bahamas and even higher among Filipinos in the Philippines. Yet if Rushton's genetic theory were correct, Blacks would have universally higher crimes rates than orientals. Roberts and Gabor also show that race-specific crime rates vary by type of crime. For instance, in the United States, whites have much higher rates of white-collar crime (fraud, embezzlement, etc.) than do Blacks. These and other facts analyzed by Roberts and Gabor demonstrate that genetic factors peculiar to each race do not cause crime. Roberts and Gabor instead attribute high rates of "street crime" among Blacks in the United States and the United Kingdom exclusively to social factors: where they face high levels of discrimination, widespread poverty, and differential treatment by the criminal justice system, Blacks are convicted of more street crime.

Crime statistics by race are not widely available in Canada, but those that are available often contradict Rushton's argument. For example, the homicide rate among aboriginal Canadians is more than ten times higher than that among whites, but Rushton's theory predicts the opposite since Aboriginal Canadians are of Mongoloid descent. Canadian Aboriginal people do, however, resemble American Blacks in terms of the social conditions in which they live, a fact that is consistent with Roberts and Gabor's theory.

In Chapter 29, Rhonda L. Lenton of McMaster University tackles yet another commonly held belief about crime in her comparative analysis of homicide rates in Canada and the United States. Crime rates in the United States—especially rates of violent crime—are higher than those in Canada. This difference is sometimes attributed to the greater anti-authoritarianism and lawlessness of American culture, which supposedly derives from the early frontier experience of the United States. In contrast, it is sometimes held that Canadians' greater respect for law and order keeps crime rates lower here. Our enduring ties to England, and the predominance of the relatively authoritarian Roman Catholic and Anglican churches in Canada, presumably reinforce that respect. Lenton, however, shows otherwise. Homicide rates in Canada are not highest in areas with relatively few people of British origin and few

Roman Catholics and Anglicans. Rather, they are highest in areas with the highest proportion of Aboriginal Canadians, the greatest percentage of families reporting no income, and the highest levels of infant mortality. This leads her to suggest that, in general, homicide rates vary with social-structural, not cultural, differences: high levels of racial discrimination and income inequality result in high homicide rates. In that light, it is not surprising that Canada has a lower homicide rate than the United States, since a smaller proportion of people suffer from racial discrimination in Canada and the level of income inequality is lower.

GLOSSARY

A **corporate crime** is an act that breaks a law intended to regulate business activity.

Deviance is behaviour that departs from a norm.

Victimization surveys are polls of representative samples of citizens that seek to determine whether and under what circumstances people are victims of crime.

CRITICAL THINKING QUESTIONS

1. Why are the results of victimization surveys different from recent public and police perceptions of crime?
2. What social factors contribute to crime?
3. What is corporate crime? What theories best explain corporate crime? Why are corporate crimes underrepresented in the news?
4. Does society make criminals, or is criminality based on biology?
5. Is the crime rate rising in Canada? What types of crimes are more likely to get reported to the police?
6. According to Rhonda Lenton, why are homicide rates higher in the United States than in Canada?

ANNOTATED BIBLIOGRAPHY

Erich Goode and Nachman Ben-Yehudah, *Moral Panics: The Social Construction of Deviance* (Cambridge, UK: Cambridge University Press, 1995). Drug panics and witch crazes illustrate the ways in which deviance and crime are not "given" but created by social reactions.

Jerome G. Miller, *Search and Destroy: African-American Males in the Criminal Justice System* (Cambridge, UK: Cambridge University Press, 1996). This infuriating book shows how the American justice system has been turned into a system of racial segregation and control. It can be read as a warning to Canadians about some of the potential effects of neoconservative, anti-welfare policies.

Robert A. Silverman, James J. Teevan, and Vincent F. Sacco, eds., *Crime in Canadian Society*, 5th ed. (Toronto: Harcourt Brace, 1996). The standard, comprehensive overview of Canadian criminology.

Chapter 26

Criminal Victimization in Canada, 1988–1993

ROSEMARY GARTNER

ANTHONY N. DOOB

In 1988, a survey on personal risk related to criminal victimization was initiated as part of the General Social Survey program. It examined the prevalence and the social and demographic distribution of eight specific types of criminal victimization experiences: sexual assault, robbery, assault, break and enter, motor vehicle theft, theft of personal property, theft of household property, and vandalism. Sexual assault, robbery, and assault were combined with theft of personal property to produce the cumulative category "personal victimization." The remaining specified types of victimization were collapsed in the aggregate category "household victimization." This survey also examined the victims' experience of crime, the reason victims decide to report offences to the police, and Canadians' perceptions of the level of crime around them. This survey was replicated in 1993.

The purpose of this report is to explore the changes that have occurred since 1988, as well as what has remained changed, rather than to look in detail at the nature and consequences of victimizations that were reported in the most recent survey.

METHODOLOGY

Early in 1988 and throughout 1993, the General Social Survey conducted telephone interviews with approximately 10 000 Canadian adults aged 15 years or older. Respondents were asked about their experiences with crime and the criminal justice system over a previous twelve-month period.[1] The sample in both cases covered the non-institutionalized population throughout the ten provinces. On the basis of these interviews, statistical estimates were made of the incidence of certain crimes in the general adult population and on Canadians' perceptions of risk and attitudes toward various components of the justice system.

Repeating a survey allows for the examination of changes over time. However, the types of questions and the context in which they are asked are important variables in interpreting results. In replicating surveys there is always a dilemma between whether to use the identical questions used in the previous cycle in order to compare survey results or to make improvements in the manner in which the questions are framed, based on knowledge gained from the previous survey.

Source: "Trends in Criminal Victimization: 1988–1993," Statistics Canada, *Juristat*, Catalogue no. 85-002, Vol. 14, No. 13 (Ottawa: Canadian Centre for Justice Statistics, June 1994), pp. 1–19. Reproduced by authority of the Minister of Industry, 2000. The data in all tables and figures are taken from surveys published by the *Service Bulletin of the Canadian Centre for Justice Statistics*, Statistics Canada, Catalogue no. 11-612. Reproduced by authority of the Minister of Industry, 2000.

For example, in the 1988 survey, respondents were asked about being "attacked." They were told that "an attack can be anything from being hit, slapped, pushed or grabbed, to being shot, raped or beaten." In 1993, a similar question was asked, but the word "raped" was omitted from the list of examples of an "attack." However, in addition, two further questions were asked: "has anyone forced you or attempted to force you into any sexual activity when you did not want to, by threatening you, holding you down or hurting you in some way" and "has anyone ever touched you against your will in any sexual way? By this I mean anything from unwanted touching or grabbing to kissing or fondling." Not surprisingly, the number of sexual assaults reported in 1993 was considerably higher than the number reported in 1988. Different questions were asked and, as one would expect, different results were obtained.

Clearly the 1993 questions on sexual assault are an improvement over the previous questions. Similarly, some of the other questions were changed so as to obtain a more thorough picture of respondents' views of crime and the criminal justice system.

It is felt, however, that the differences in the two survey instruments—other than for sexual assault—should have no significant impact on the levels of crime reported in the 1988 as compared with the 1993 survey. There is confidence, therefore, about the comparisons across time contained in this report.

RISK OF PERSONAL VICTIMIZATION

The data from the recent General Social Survey (GSS) describe the criminal victimization experiences of Canadians aged 15 and over. By comparing the victimization rates obtained from this survey with those from 1988, it can be determined whether Canadians experience more crime now than five years ago.

As shown in Table 26.1, the results of the 1993 survey indicate that overall victimization rates have not changed substantially since 1988 —that is, essentially the same proportion of the population (24 percent) experienced at least one instance of criminal victimization in 1993 as compared with 1988.[2]

The 1988 and 1993 data are reasonably consistent across crime categories (see Table 26.2 and Figure 26.1). GSS assault rates show little change over time; from 68 per 1000 population in 1988 to 67 per 1000 population in 1993. GSS robbery rates decreased by 31 percent, from 13 to 9 per 1000 population during this same time period. Personal theft rates also decreased by 14 percent from 59 per 1000 in 1988 to 51 per 1000 in 1993.

TABLE 26.1 PROPORTION OF POPULATION VICTIMIZED ONE OR MORE TIMES, BY VICTIM CHARACTERISTICS, AGE 15+, CANADA, 1988 AND 1993

| | VICTIMIZED BY FREQUENCY (%) | | | | | |
| | Once | | Twice or More | | Total | |
VICTIM CHARACTERISTICS	1988	1993	1988	1993	1988	1993
Canada	15	16	8	7	24	24
Males	16	17	9	7	25	24
Females	14	15	8	7	22	23
Urban	17	18	10	8	27	27
Rural	12	12	6	5	18	17

SOURCE: General Social Survey, 1988 and 1993.

TABLE 26.2   PERSONAL VICTIMIZATION RATES PER 1000 POPULATION, BY TYPE OF INCIDENT AND VICTIM CHARACTERISTICS, AGE 15+, CANADA, 1988 AND 1993

| | Theft Personal Property | | Sexual Assault | | Robbery | | Assault | |
VICTIM CHARACTERISTICS	1988	1993	1988*	1993	1988	1993	1988	1993
Canada	59	51	—	17	13	9	68	67
Urban	70	57	—	18	14	9	72	72
Rural	46	36	—	14	—	—	56	53
Age 15–24	123	93	—	48	39	23	145	155
25–44	65	61	—	17	10	9	80	69
45–64	22	29	—	—	—	—	19	38
65+	—	—	—	—	—	—	—	—
Male	58	51	—	—	17	12	74	68
Female	61	51	—	29	10	6	63	66

*There were too few cases reported in 1988 to make statistically reliable estimates. New questions concerning sexual assault were added to the 1993 survey.
— amount too small to be meaningful.

SOURCE: General Social Survey, 1988 and 1993.

CHARACTERISTICS OF PERSONAL VICTIMIZATIONS

In 1993, as seen in Table 26.3, violent victimizations were more likely to have been committed by strangers and were more likely to have been committed in public places than in 1988. The proportion of robberies committed by strangers increased from 45 percent to 67 percent. When interpreted in the context of the overall decrease in robbery victimizations, it would appear that the overall risk of being robbed by a stranger in Canada did not substantially change in the five-year period between the two surveys.[3] The proportion of assaults committed by strangers increased from 27 percent to 38 percent. Nevertheless, the majority of sexual assaults and assaults were committed by offenders known to the victim in 1993, as in 1988. Only in the case of robberies did strangers make up a majority of offenders.

The locations of victimizations reflect these patterns of victim–offender relationships and the shift toward more public victimizations. The majority of robberies and assaults occurred outside of a residence and this proportion increased over time.

Only sexual assaults were about as likely to take place in a residence as elsewhere.

In most victimizations recorded in 1988 and 1993, offenders acted alone and without weapons. However, according to the 1993 survey, the percentage of robberies committed by multiple offenders increased from 29 percent to 44 percent. Furthermore, weapon use decreased over time for violent victimizations in total and individually for assaults and remained too negligible to estimate for robberies and sexual assaults (see Table 26.3).

PERSONAL VICTIMIZATION RISK FACTORS — THE 1993 SURVEY

As with levels of crime, the social and demographic characteristics associated with overall personal victimization changed little between 1988 and 1993[4] (see Table 26.4). For example,

FIGURE 26.1 PERSONAL VICTIMIZATION RATES PER 1000 POPULATION, BY TYPE OF INCIDENT, AGE 15+, CANADA, 1988 AND 1993

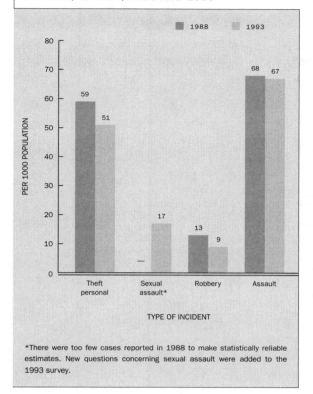

FIGURE 26.1 PERSONAL VICTIMIZATION RATES PER 1000 POPULATION, BY TYPE OF INCIDENT, AGE 15+, CANADA, 1988 AND 1993

*There were too few cases reported in 1988 to make statistically reliable estimates. New questions concerning sexual assault were added to the 1993 survey.

SOURCE: General Social Survey, 1988 and 1993.

robbery rate for men, however, was double that for women (12 per 1000 for men; 6 per 1000 for women).

Women's higher rates were especially apparent in urban areas, where their rates exceeded men's for each type of personal victimization, with the exception of robberies, and their total victimization rate was almost 20 percent higher than men's (168 versus 141 per 1000). Rural women reported a total victimization rate only marginally greater than rural men (110 versus 105 per 1000).

Gender differences in rates were also greater for certain marital statuses. While married women and men had the same total victimization rates (85 per 1000), the single women's rate was 27 percent higher than the single men's rate (311 versus 245 per 1000), and the rate for separated and divorced women was twice as high as the separated and divorced men's rate (374 versus 187 per 1000). In fact, separated or divorced women had the highest rate of personal victimization (see Figure 26.2).

urban dwellers and young Canadians continued to report higher rates of victimization than rural dwellers and older Canadians. Urban dwellers reported a total personal victimization rate almost 44 percent higher than rural dwellers (155 versus 108 per 1000). Those aged 15–24 reported a personal victimization rate three times that of those over the age of 24 (318 versus 106 per 1000).

In the 1993 survey, the total personal victimization rate for women was 11 percent higher than for men (151 versus 136 per 1000), largely because of the fact that sexual assaults are rarely perpetrated against males (Table 26.2). For the other personal crimes, women reported similar rates to men in the 1993 survey: personal theft rates were the same for women and men (51 per 1000) and assault rates were nearly the same (66 per 1000 for women; 68 per 1000 for men). The

FIGURE 26.2 PERSONAL VICTIMIZATION RATES PER 1000 POPULATION, BY SEX OF VICTIM, MARITAL STATUS, AGE 15+, CANADA, 1993

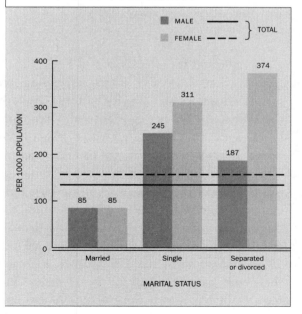

SOURCE: General Social Survey, 1993.

TABLE 26.3   VIOLENT VICTIMIZATIONS BY TYPE OF INCIDENT AND INCIDENT CHARACTERISTICS, AGE 15+, CANADA, 1988 AND 1993

| | INCIDENT TYPE | | | | | |
| | % of Sexual Assaults | | % of Robberies/Attempts | | % of Assaults | |
INCIDENT CHARACTERISTICS	1988	1993	1988	1993	1988	1993
Committed						
By stranger	—	22	45	67	27	38
By acquaintance	—	58	33	—	43	38
By relative	—	—	—	—	22	19
Unknown/not applicable	—	—	—	—	8	5
By single offender	—	81	68	54	73	81
By multiple offenders	—	—	29	44	20	15
Unknown	—	—	—	—	7	4
With weapon	—	—	28	—	19	14
Location						
Victim's home	—	30	32	—	41	31
Other residence	—	17	—	—	9	5
Restaurant/bar	—	17	—	—	9	10
Commercial	—	24	—	—	18	24
Public place/other	—	—	42	57	21	27
Not stated	—	—	—	—	—	—

SOURCE: General Social Survey, 1988 and 1993.

As indicated in Table 26.5 and Figure 26.3, victimization rates also differ depending on people's lifestyles and activity patterns. In both the 1988 and 1993 surveys, those who frequently engaged in evening activities away from home reported higher rates of personal victimization. Total personal victimization rates for those who were involved in 30 or more evening activities a month were over three times the rates of those who participated in fewer than 10 evening activities a month (243 versus 66 per 1000), according to the 1993 survey. Personal theft and assault rates for both males and females increase with the number of evening activities.

RISK OF HOUSEHOLD VICTIMIZATION

Respondents were asked about four crimes that might have occurred to their household: break and enters, theft of household property, motor vehicle theft or attempts, and vandalism. The 1993 GSS data on household victimization (Table 26.6 and Figure 26.4) show rates similar to or lower than those found in 1988. Reported rates of break and enters, motor vehicle theft or attempts, and vandalism were lower in 1993 than in 1988. The rate of break and enters decreased by 7 percent, from 54 to 50 per 1000 households; the rate of motor vehicle theft or

TABLE 26.5 VICTIMIZATION RATES PER 1000 POPULATION, BY TYPE OF INCIDENT, SEX, AND NUMBER OF EVENING ACTIVITIES, AGE 15+, CANADA, 1993

SEX OF VICTIM AND NUMBER OF EVENING ACTIVITIES (PER MONTH)	TYPE OF INCIDENT		
	Theft Personal Property	Assault	Total Personal
Both Sexes	51	67	143
<10 activities	20	34	66
10–19 activities	45	58	130
20–29 activities	48	59	129
30+ activities	89	113	243
Male	51	68	136
<10 activities	—	—	37
10–19 activities	42	55	116
20–29 activities	40	54	102
30+ activities	85	120	232
Female	51	66	151
<10 activities	19	46	84
10–19 activities	47	61	142
20–29 activities	56	64	156
30+ activities	94	104	258

SOURCE: General Social Survey, 1993.

TABLE 26.4 PERSONAL VICTIMIZATION RATES PER 1000 POPULATION, BY VICTIM CHARACTERISTICS, AGE 15+, CANADA, 1993

VICTIM CHARACTERISTICS	MALE	FEMALE	TOTAL
Total	136	151	143
Urban	141	168	155
Rural	105	110	108
Age 15–24	304	333	318
25–44	135	178	156
45–64	73	74	74
65+	—	—	—
Married/Common-law	85	85	85
Single	245	311	274
Separated or divorced	187	374	301

SOURCE: General Social Survey, 1993.

FIGURE 26.3 PERSONAL VICTIMIZATION RATES PER 1000 POPULATION, BY SEX OF VICTIM AND NUMBER OF EVENING ACTIVITIES, AGE 15+, CANADA, 1993

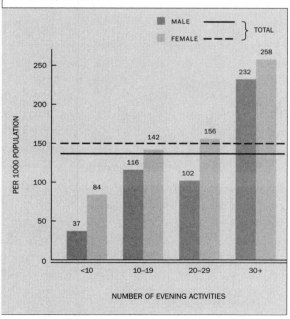

SOURCE: General Social Survey, 1993.

attempts decreased by 27 percent, from 51 to 37 per 1000 households; and the vandalism rate decreased by 13 percent, from 63 to 55 per 1000.

HOUSEHOLD VICTIMIZATION RISK FACTORS

Household victimization rates vary depending on location and economic status, according to both the 1988 and 1993 surveys (Table 26.6). For all types of household victimizations, rates for households in urban areas are higher than for households in rural areas. The total household victimization rate for urban households was 67 percent higher than the rate for rural households, according to the 1993 survey (222 versus 133 per 1000).

TABLE 26.6   HOUSEHOLD VICTIMIZATION RATES PER 1000 HOUSEHOLDS, BY TYPE OF INCIDENT, URBAN/RURAL RESIDENCE AND HOUSEHOLD INCOME, CANADA, 1988 AND 1993

	TYPE OF INCIDENT									
HOUSEHOLD CHARACTERISTICS	Break and Enter/Attempt		Motor Vehicle Theft/Attempt		Theft Household Property/Attempt		Vandalism		Total Household	
	1988	1993	1988	1993	1988	1993	1988	1993	1988	1993
Canada	54	50	51	37	48	48	63	55	216	190
Urban	64	56	59	45	54	56	76	64	252	222
Rural	32	40	36	—	35	38	42	38	146	133
Income Groups										
<$15 000	55	57	—	—	36	—	38	43	163	154
$15 000–$29 999	58	46	52	—	52	44	59	51	221	172
$30 000–$39 999	59	77	60	54	75	—	64	58	258	239
$40 000–$59 999	64	56	80	51	49	58	102	75	296	240
$60 000+	63	56	—	42	—	75	101	81	277	254

SOURCE: General Social Survey, 1988 and 1993.

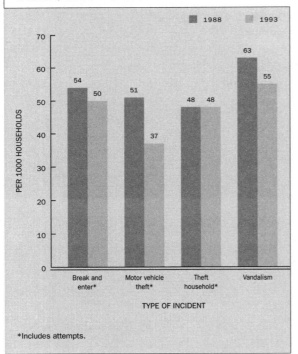

FIGURE 26.4   HOUSEHOLD VICTIMIZATION RATES PER 1000 HOUSEHOLDS, BY TYPE OF INCIDENT, CANADA, 1988 AND 1993

*Includes attempts.

SOURCE: General Social Survey, 1988 and 1993.

Household income is also linked to household victimization rates (Figure 26.5). While the pattern varies somewhat across different types of victimizations, the total household victimization rate rose steadily with household income in the 1993 survey. At the extremes, households with incomes of $60 000 or more had victimization rates 65 percent higher than households with incomes of less than $15 000 (254 versus 154 per 1000).

THE DECISION TO REPORT VICTIMIZATIONS TO THE POLICE

Police statistics and victimization surveys often give different pictures of crime. This is not surprising since the process by which an event gets recorded as a "crime" by police can be seen as a series of discretionary decisions, starting with the citizen identifying the event as a crime and ending with the police officer recording the event as a particular "founded" crime. At any stage in the process, a decision can be made that

FIGURE 26.5 HOUSEHOLD VICTIMIZATION RATES PER 1000 HOUSEHOLDS, BY HOUSEHOLD INCOME, CANADA, 1988 AND 1993

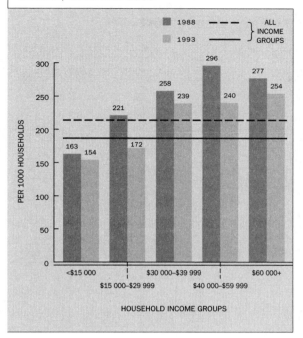

SOURCE: General Social Survey, 1988 and 1993.

has the effect of ensuring that the event never gets recorded as a crime.

Citizens do not automatically report all crimes to the police—the decision is a complex one based on a number of considerations. Reporting takes time, it may subject the victim to additional stress, and it may not be seen as sensible to report for a range of different reasons.

The likelihood of reporting a crime varies enormously from crime to crime. In 1993, of those crimes covered by the GSS, household break and enters were the most likely crimes to be reported to the police and sexual assaults were the most likely to remain unreported (Table 26.7). It is clear from these data that the police are informed about only a small fraction of these personal and household crimes.

Reporting rates for assaults, break and enters, motor vehicle thefts, household thefts, thefts of personal property, and vandalism did not differ much between the two surveys. Robbery was the only crime that showed evidence

of substantial change: a higher proportion of robberies were reported to the police in 1993 (47 percent) than were reported in 1988 (32 percent).

The reasons for not reporting criminal victimizations to the police are shown in Table 26.8 for the 1993 survey. Because fewer reasons for not reporting were offered to the respondent in 1988 than in 1993, comparisons were rendered impossible. The important finding in this table is that, for the most part, the reasons for non-reporting appear to relate to the perceived usefulness of reporting. Generally speaking, victims who did not report the incident to the police saw the event as one that was best dealt with another way, that was too minor to report, or that they thought the police could not do anything about. However, in about three of ten sexual assaults and in about a fifth of the assaults, one of the reasons that victims gave for not reporting was fear of revenge.

TABLE 26.7 VICTIMIZATIONS NOT REPORTED TO THE POLICE, BY TYPE OF INCIDENT, AGE 15+, CANADA, 1988 AND 1993

	% NOT REPORTED	
TYPE OF INCIDENT	1988	1993
Personal*		
Sexual assault	—	90
Robbery	68	53
Assault	65	68
Theft personal property/attempt	63	56
Household		
B&E/attempt	28	32
Motor vehicle theft/attempt	42	48
Theft household property/attempt	56	57
Vandalism	54	54
Total household	45	48

*Total "Personal" figures are not presented due to the non-comparability of sexual assault data.

SOURCE: General Social Survey, 1988 and 1993.

TABLE 26.8   VICTIMIZATIONS NOT REPORTED TO THE POLICE BY REASON FOR NOT REPORTING, BY TYPE OF INCIDENT, AGE 15+, CANADA, 1993

	REASON FOR NOT REPORTING TO POLICE (%)*								
INCIDENT TYPE	Dealt with Another Way	Too Minor	Fear of Revenge	Insurance Wouldn't Cover	Police Couldn't Do Anything	Police Wouldn't Help	Didn't Want to Get Involved with Police	Nothing Taken	Personal Matter
Theft personal property/attempt	43	54	—	26	47	21	34	—	32
Sexual assault	65	30	29	—	28	20	50	21	67
Robbery	70	—	—	—	—	—	—	—	—
Assault	64	48	19	7	27	13	47	22	49
Break & enter/attempt	46	48	—	—	42	—	—	36	—
Motor vehicle theft/attempt	33	65	—	—	52	—	—	—	—
Theft household property/attempt	36	58	—	—	38	—	27	—	29
Vandalism	45	60	—	—	47	—	37	20	33

*Proportions do not add to 100 as these are separate variables. Only proportion of affirmative responses shown.

SOURCE: General Social Survey, 1993.

PERCEPTIONS OF CRIME

Statistics about crime—almost always relating to crimes reported to the police—are quite often reported in the mass media. Increases in crime make news. Decreases or no changes in crime rates appear to get somewhat less press coverage. An ordinary Canadian consumer of the mass media, therefore, would likely have encountered a number of stories in the past five years suggesting that crime has increased. The source and meaning of these statistics may not always be considered carefully.

It is not surprising, therefore, that a large proportion of Canadians (46 percent) think that the level of crime in their neighbourhoods has increased (see Table 26.9). Those who live in rural areas are somewhat more likely to think that crime in their neighbourhoods has not changed and are somewhat less likely to think that it has increased than are people who live in urban areas.

Generally speaking, it appears that Canadians believe that their own neighbourhoods have about the same amount of crime or less crime than other areas of Canada (Table 26.10). Very few people—about 10 percent in 1993—indicate that they think their neighbourhoods have more crime than other places in Canada.

TABLE 26.9   PERCEIVED CHANGE IN THE LEVEL OF CRIME IN NEIGHBOURHOOD, DURING THE LAST 5 YEARS, BY URBAN/RURAL RESIDENCE, AGE 15+, CANADA, 1993

	PERCEIVED CHANGE IN THE LEVEL OF CRIME IN NEIGHBOURHOOD IN THE LAST 5 YEARS (%)				
AREA	Increased	Decreased	Same	Don't Know	Total
All	46	4	43	8	100
Urban	48	4	41	8	100
Rural	40	4	52	4	100

SOURCE: General Social Survey, 1993.

TABLE 26.10   PERCEIVED LEVEL OF CRIME IN NEIGHBOURHOOD COMPARED WITH OTHER AREAS, BY URBAN/RURAL RESIDENCE, AGE 15+, CANADA, 1988 AND 1993

PERCEIVED LEVEL OF CRIME IN NEIGHBOURHOOD COMPARED WITH OTHER AREAS (%)

	Higher		About Same		Lower		Don't Know/ Not Stated		Total	
AREA	1988	1993	1988	1993	1988	1993	1988	1993	1988	1993
All	8	10	29	29	57	57	6	4	100	100
Urban	10	11	32	31	53	54	5	4	100	100
Rural	4	5	22	19	71	74	4	2	100	100

SOURCE: General Social Survey, 1988 and 1993.

TABLE 26.11   FEELINGS OF SAFETY WALKING ALONE IN NEIGHBOURHOOD AFTER DARK, BY URBAN/RURAL RESIDENCE AND SEX, AGE 15+, CANADA, 1988 AND 1993

FEELINGS OF SAFETY WALKING ALONE IN NEIGHBOURHOOD AFTER DARK (%)

	Very Safe		Reasonably Safe		Total Unsafe		Somewhat Unsafe		Very Unsafe		Don't Know		Total	
VICTIM CHARACTERISTICS	1988	1993	1988	1993	1988	1993	1988	1993	1988	1993	1988	1993	1988	1993
Total	40	32	33	40	25	27	17	15	9	12	2	2	100	100
Male	58	48	29	41	11	10	9	6	3	4	1	1	100	100
Female	23	16	36	40	39	42	24	23	14	19	3	2	100	100
Urban Total	36	27	35	43	28	29	18	17	9	12	1	1	100	100
Male	55	43	32	45	12	11	9	7	3	3	1	1	100	100
Female	18	12	38	41	42	45	27	25	15	20	2	2	100	100
Rural Total	53	48	28	36	18	15	12	10	6	5	1	1	100	100
Male	70	63	22	30	8	6	6	3	2	2	—	—	100	100
Female	37	31	33	43	28	25	19	16	9	8	2	1	100	100

SOURCE: General Social Survey, 1988 and 1993.

Crime may be perceived to be a problem — but, for the most part, most of us see it as being located somewhere else. Canadians view their own neighbourhoods, in comparison to other parts of Canada, in much the same way as they did five years earlier.

Even though most Canadians view their own neighbourhoods as less dangerous than other parts of Canada, a substantial portion — 27 percent overall, in 1993 — indicated that they felt unsafe walking alone at night in their own neighbourhoods (Table 26.11). This is a slightly higher proportion of Canadians indicating that they feel "unsafe" than five years earlier. The important change occurring in the past five years was that fewer people indicated they felt "very safe" walking alone at night than was the case five years ago. In 1988, 40 percent indicated they felt very safe. In 1993, this proportion dropped to 32 percent.

As in the past, there is a dramatic difference between males and females with regard to perceptions of safety. Only 10 percent of males indicated that they felt unsafe walking alone at night in their own neighbourhoods whereas 42 percent of females felt unsafe. Those living in urban areas — both male and female — are more likely to feel unsafe than are those living in rural areas. As with other findings, the pattern is identical to that of five years ago.

As can be seen in Table 26.12, males and females over 65 years of age were more likely than those who were younger to indicate that they felt unsafe walking alone in their neighbourhoods. Between 1988 and 1993 the proportion of those over 65 who indicated that they felt "very unsafe" walking alone at night in their neighbourhoods increased substantially, particularly for

females. In 1993, 38 percent of females over 65 indicated that they felt very unsafe walking alone at night as compared with 24 percent in 1988.

The variation among different groups in the population is large. For example, in 1993, almost two-thirds of rural males (63 percent) indicated that they felt very safe walking alone in their neighbourhoods at night in comparison to 12 percent of urban females.

COMPARING THE GSS AND THE UNIFORM CRIME REPORTING (UCR) SURVEYS: DIFFERENT PERSPECTIVES RESULT IN DIFFERENT PICTURES

Victimization surveys were developed to provide an estimate of the likelihood of personal and household victimizations. They are designed to provide a way of looking at crime from the per-

TABLE 26.12   FEELINGS OF SAFETY WALKING ALONE IN NEIGHBOURHOOD AFTER DARK, BY SEX AND AGE GROUP, AGE 15+, CANADA, 1988 AND 1993

	FEELINGS OF SAFETY WALKING ALONE IN NEIGHBOURHOOD AFTER DARK (%)													
						Unsafe								
	Very Safe		Reasonably Safe		Total Unsafe		Somewhat Unsafe		Very Unsafe		Don't Know		Total Population 15+	
SEX AND AGE GROUP	1988	1993	1988	1993	1988	1993	1988	1993	1988	1993	1988	1993	1988	1993
Male														
15–24 years	61	50	29	43	9	7	6	5	3	1	—	—	100	100
25–44	61	51	29	40	9	9	7	6	2	3	—	—	100	100
45–64	57	47	28	42	13	11	10	7	3	4	1	—	100	100
65+	41	38	32	37	22	19	15	9	6	10	6	6	100	100
Female														
15–24 years	19	14	37	45	43	40	30	26	14	14	—	—	100	100
25–44	25	17	40	44	34	38	23	25	12	14	1	1	100	100
45–64	26	17	35	40	37	41	23	21	14	20	2	2	100	100
65+	15	13	25	22	49	57	25	19	24	38	11	7	100	100

SOURCE: General Social Survey, 1988 and 1993.

spective of individual victims. They describe what has happened to individual Canadians and they describe the way in which people have responded to their victimization experiences. As pointed out earlier, many crimes are not reported to the police. Hence police-reported crimes cannot capture the full experience that people have with crime.

There are, however, some limitations on the data that can be obtained from victimization surveys. They do not, for example, describe crimes (e.g., thefts or vandalism) in which organizations such as schools or corporations are the victims. In addition they do not describe crimes such as impaired driving or drug offences. The GSS has two other limitations: it samples only those people who were 15 years old and over and who are residents of Canada.

The most commonly cited crime statistics in Canada — those from the UCR survey — give a picture of crime through a different process. These are the reports of crimes that are recorded by the police. Typically, though not always, these crimes come to the attention of the police as a result of a call from a victim. Police departments respond to these calls and produce crime statistics. There is evidence to suggest that the type and frequency of calls for service to the police may change over time and vary according to location. For example, as society becomes more concerned about school violence, people may be more likely to report fights to the police rather than dealing with them informally. Similarly, as the police and other justice authorities are seen to be increasingly sympathetic to victims of family violence and sexual assault, those victims may be more willing to report these incidents, and authorities will be more likely to treat them as crimes.

The repetition in 1993 of the victimization component of the GSS survey, which was conducted by Statistics Canada in 1988, provides the opportunity to examine changes in victimization rates as reported by the victims themselves from one point in time to another. It also encourages one to compare these with the figures reported to the police over a similar time

period. Notwithstanding other limitations in comparability as described above, 1993 UCR data are not presently available. That is, it is not known at this time whether police-reported crime increased or decreased in 1993 as compared with 1988. However, UCR data from 1988 to 1992 suggest the existence of increases in violent crime (Table 26.13). These trends are not substantiated by the data from the GSS, but a direct comparison of these results is not possible.

Comparisons between UCR and GSS household victimization data are more problematic than personal victimizations due to the fact that UCR property offences generally include crimes against commercial establishments.[5] Once again, however, UCR-reported increases in the rate of many property crimes from 1988 to 1992 (break and enters, theft of motor vehicles, and mischief (vandalism)) are not reflected in GSS survey data.

These divergent trends support the contention that the extent and nature of criminal victimizations tapped by police-reported statistics differ from that tapped by victimization surveys. The results of these two surveys should be seen as complementary — they both measure crime but from different perspectives.

TABLE 26.13 POLICE REPORTED CRIME (UNIFORM CRIME REPORTING SURVEY), BY TYPE OF INCIDENT PER 1000 POPULATION, CANADA, 1988–1992

TYPE OF INCIDENT	1988	1989	1990	1991	1992
Sexual assault	1.0	1.0	1.0	1.1	1.2
Assault	6.4	6.7	7.2	7.8	7.9
Robbery	0.9	1.0	1.1	1.2	1.2
Break & enter residence	8.2	7.6	8.1	9.1	8.9
Theft motor vehicle	3.4	3.8	4.3	5.1	5.3
Mischief	13.9	14.2	15.7	17.0	16.4
Theft (other than shoplifting)	28.9	28.1	29.6	31.8	30.2

SOURCE: Uniform Crime Reporting Survey (UCR), 1988–1992.

CONCLUSION

The clear conclusion from the 1993 General Social Survey data is that individual and household victimization rates did not change appreciably in the five-year period between 1988 and 1993. A substantial portion of Canadians— about 24 percent—were touched by one or more of the crimes covered by the GSS in the 1993 survey. However, there is no indication that this proportion has changed since 1988.

In the areas where Canadians understandably show most concern—violent victimizations— the data are very clear. Canadians are not at a higher risk than they were five years earlier, overall. There is almost no evidence to support the view that Canadians 15 years and older were more at risk of being victims of any of the crimes examined in the survey in 1993 than they were in 1988. The likelihood of a person being the victim of an assault, robbery, or personal theft, and the likelihood of a household being victimized by way of a break and enter, motor vehicle theft, theft of household property, or vandalism have either decreased or not changed.

NOTES

1. For ease of presentation, the two surveys will be referred to as if they solely related to 1988 and 1993—the years in which they were carried out. Technically speaking, it is not quite that simple. The 1988 survey, carried out in the first few months of 1988, asked about victimizations that took place in the previous calendar year—1987. The 1993 survey, carried out over the twelve months of 1993, asked about victimizations that occurred in the previous twelve months —in this case, the one-year period often spanned two calendar years, 1992 and 1993. The "fear" questions related to their feelings at the time of the survey, 1988 and 1993.

2. It should be remembered that the 1993 survey included additional questions concerning sexual assault that were not included in the 1988 survey. Since the 1993 questions elicited victimizations that would not have been elicited from the questions used in 1988, the overall victimization rates are not strictly comparable.

3. In 1988, 45 percent of the 13 per 1000 robberies, or about 6 per 1000, were committed by strangers. In 1993, 67 percent of the 9 per 1000 robberies, or about 6 per 1000, were committed by strangers.

4. Overall personal victimization rates in 1988 and 1993 are not strictly comparable because of the change in the measurement of the incidence of sexual assaults.

5. The household victimization rates are expressed in terms of the rates per 1000 households (not total population as is normally the case with UCR). Hence the actual numbers are not comparable.

Chapter 27 | Corporate Crime
CARL KEANE

INTRODUCTION

Every day, middle-class individuals, holding positions of responsibility, and hiding behind veils of corporate bureaucracy, violate the laws of society. The few studies that have investigated corporate crime report that it is not uncommon. Yet few people are aware of the extent of such crime.

It was the groundbreaking work of Sutherland (1949) that first brought corporate crime into the spotlight. Sutherland analyzed the 70 largest U.S. manufacturing, mining, and mercantile corporations, examining the following legal violations: restraint of trade; misrepresentation in advertising; infringements of patents, trademarks, and copyrights; labour law violations; illegal rebates; financial fraud and violation of trust; violations of war regulations; and finally some miscellaneous offences. He found a total of 980 decisions had been made against the 70 corporations, an average of 14 decisions per corporation (1949: 29). More current research shows that his findings are not unusual. For example, focusing on illegal acts such as price fixing, overcharging, violation of environmental regulations and antitrust laws, bribes, fraud, patent infringements, and violations of other market regulations, a 1984 survey found that approximately two-thirds of the Fortune 500 largest industrial companies had been involved in illegal behaviour since the mid-1970s (Etzioni, 1985).

Perhaps the most extensive examination to date of corporate offending is the study conducted by Clinard and his colleagues (Clinard et al., 1979; Clinard and Yeager, 1980). This research involved the analysis of federal administrative, civil, and criminal actions either initiated or completed by 25 U.S. agencies during 1975–76 against the 477 largest publicly owned U.S. manufacturing companies and the 105 largest U.S. wholesale, retail, and service companies. Six main types of corporate illegal behaviour were discovered: administrative violations such as noncompliance with an order from a court or government agency; environmental violations such as pollution of the air or water; financial violations including bribery, tax violations, and accounting malpractices; labour violations involving employment discrimination, occupational safety and health hazards, and unfair labour practices; manufacturing violations such as violations of the Consumer Product Safety Act; and unfair trade practices, involving various abuses of competition such as price fixing as well as acts such as false advertising (Clinard and Yeager, 1980: 113–15). The researchers found that of the 582 corporations, approximately 60 percent had at least one federal action brought against them, and for those companies that had at least one action brought against them, the average was 4.4 cases (1980: 113).

Turning closer to home, and focusing on violations of the Combines Act in Canada, Goff and Reasons (1978) reported that between 1952 and 1972 a total of 157 decisions were made against the 50 largest Canadian corporations, an average of 3 decisions per corporation. Taken together, these studies demonstrate the wide extent of corporate offending, and reveal that individuals in the middle and upper socioeconomic classes, contrary to popular stereotypes, quite frequently engage in illegal behaviour.

Source: Adapted from "Corporate Crime," in *Crime in Canadian Society*, 5th ed., Robert A. Silverman, James J. Teevan, and Vincent F. Sacco, eds. (Toronto: Harcourt Brace, 1996), pp. 282–92. Reprinted by permission of the publisher.

What causes such crime? Reflecting on Sutherland's (1949) point that corporate offences cannot be explained by conditions of poverty, or by individual pathology, any search for the causes of corporate crime should begin with an examination of the context within which such crimes occur—the organization. This approach calls for an analysis of the corporation and its impact on the individuals who work there. As such, it is useful to first examine external and internal factors that affect the organization, followed by those factors that affect the employees of the organization.

EXTERNAL FACTORS OF INFLUENCE

Every organization both affects, and is affected by, its environment. Organizations are constrained by laws, and, at the same time, they may try to influence legislators. Some corporations conduct business in markets with numerous competitors, consumers, and suppliers—others with few. And organizations operate in economies ranging from capitalist to communist. To help us understand the influence of external factors, we can begin with an examination of the economic system.

CAPITALISM

Some criminologists argue that to understand corporate crime we should adopt a macro-perspective and focus on the features of our capitalist economy. They suggest that corporate capitalism, with its primary emphasis on the goals of maximizing profitability and minimizing costs, leads to unsafe products, environmental pollution, employee and consumer deception, and unsafe working conditions (see Henry, 1982: 85). At the same time, it is argued that the content and enforcement of laws against corporate crime reflect the interests of the economic elite, who through their economic dominance are able to influence the political elite, leading to weak legislation and lax enforcement of existing

laws (Snider and West, 1985; also see Snider, 1993, for a thorough examination of the problems of corporate regulation). However, organizational problems are not restricted to capitalist countries. For example, in an effort to meet productivity goals, former Soviet workers endured one of the worst records of industrial safety and occupational health in the world (Handelman, 1989). Others have reported a variety of economic crimes such as bribery, fraud, property theft, and "black-market" operations that have been widespread in communist countries (Los, 1982). Therefore, the economic system alone cannot provide a comprehensive explanation for organizational deviance.

COMPETITION

Some see competition, common to both the profit and not-for-profit sectors, as a precipitating factor in the genesis of corporate crime. The case of the Ford Pinto automobile can be cited as an example. Facing increasing competition from foreign small-car imports, the Ford Motor Company attempted to speed up the production process of the Pinto in order to meet the competition. When it was determined that a faulty fuel system could cause the car to explode on impact, Ford executives conducted a cost–benefit analysis, weighing the estimated number of injuries and deaths and resulting lawsuits that would occur, against the cost of recalling all the defective cars. In accordance with the results of the cost–benefit analysis, the company decided against recalling the Ford Pinto, a decision that ultimately resulted in numerous deaths and injuries (Cullen et al., 1987; Dowie, 1977). This example is but one manifestation of a "culture of competition" that exists in all industrialized countries. It is related to corporate crime in that it motivates individuals to succeed at virtually any cost (Coleman, 1987, 1989). In fact, at a session on business ethics at the World Economic Forum, it was reported that "corrupt practices such as bribery are considered inevitable—if not acceptable—in international business, and executives fear they will lose contracts to competitors unless they go along with the corrupt practices" (*The Globe and Mail*, 1994a: B7). Thus the quest for success is framed within a competitive milieu.

STRAIN THEORY

We have seen how companies pitted against each other in a "culture of competition" produce a situation of interfirm rivalry wherein some firms might violate the law to gain advantage over a competitor. What we have described is a setting where industrial culture promotes competition as a means of attaining corporate goals, but the market limits the opportunity for all companies to achieve success. This discrepancy between culture and structure produces a situation of strain that increases the possibility of corporate corruption (see Keane, 1993). A similar process can be seen as even internal to the organization. That is, in the planning and budgeting process, companies regularly set internal corporate goals. In this situation competition may exist between two divisions, between plants, and/or between time periods such as when a company budgets to decrease costs, or forecasts to increase sales, over the previous year. Again we have a situation where the corporate culture emphasizes competition, but the corporate structure may not provide the opportunity to achieve the corporate goal. According to Merton (1938) this type of situation may lead to illegal behaviour. Merton postulated that if individuals are thwarted in their quest to attain their desired goals, such as the culturally prescribed goal of success, they will become frustrated. This frustration, caused by a disjuncture between legal means and desired goals, will produce a situation of strain, and individuals will adapt to alleviate the strain. Some individuals, whom Merton called "innovators," while accepting the goal will reject conventional means and embrace illegal means of attaining the goal. With respect to strain, Clinard (1983) reported on the pressure exerted on middle managers from top management to increase profitability, decrease costs, and meet production and sales quotas, pressure that may result in illegal behaviour. Simply stated, some individuals faced with a discrepancy between goals and the legal means to achieve them will become corporate criminals.

Competition, however, is a necessary but not sufficient cause of corporate crime. For example, although competition exists in every industry, some industries are more crime prone than others. Also, even within the same industry, some firms violate the law more than others. As researchers of corporate crime, we must ask: What is there about particular industries, and particular firms, that produces a higher rate of corporate crime? This question calls for a closer examination of other aspects of the external environment of modern organizations.

ENVIRONMENTAL UNCERTAINTY

In examining the external structure of organizations, we can identify certain factors that vary among firms and industries. For example, while all organizations place an organizational priority on goal attainment (Finney and Lesieur, 1982), organizations may have a variety of goals, and goals will differ among organizations. Although profitability is often the primary goal, organizations may strive to maximize revenue, earnings per share, market share, growth, or production quotas; or the primary goal may be survival. Organizations, however, do not operate in a vacuum. The external environment of an organization comprises political, sociocultural, economic, physical, and technological factors, and perhaps most importantly, other organizations. The political environment may affect the organization through government legislation; the sociocultural environment through changing tastes and values; the economic environment through economic changes such as a recession or rapid growth of the economy; the physical environment through pollution levels; the technological environment through changes in technology used by the company or others; and other organizations may have an impact through their actions as competitors, suppliers, or consumers. These various elements of what has been referred to as an organization's "task environment" (Dill, 1958) produce a high degree of uncertainty. In order to meet corporate goals, an organization operating within an uncertain environment may attempt to reduce that uncertainty through illegal behaviour (see Aldrich, 1979). For example, to reduce uncertainty concerning pricing vis-à-vis competitors, as well as to reduce the uncertainty of profitability, an organization may collude with other firms in the same industry to set and maintain prices (see Simpson, 1986). This price-fixing conspiracy serves to reduce uncertainty by providing the company with some control over an important element of its external environment. Braithwaite (1984) provides an example of this when he describes a conversation he had with an executive of a pharmaceutical company who admitted:

> ... just recently we got together about 30 of us, all of the accountants and finance directors ... to sit around the table together and work out prices that we could all agree on in the submissions that we make to the Health Department. ... (Braithwaite, 1984: 172)

In general, as environmental uncertainty increases, thus threatening goal attainment, illegal behaviour may increase in attempts to control or minimize the uncertainty, and to increase the likelihood of goal achievement.

MARKET STRUCTURE

The admission reported above reveals that price fixing reduces uncertainty about profitability and competitive behaviour. The statement quoted also shows that for a price-fixing conspiracy to be successful, there must be agreement among the firms that prices will be maintained. Hence, the greater the number of firms in a particular industry, the harder it may be to coordinate a collusion, and thus the harder it will be for all to agree to maintain prices. Therefore, price

fixing may be more prevalent in concentrated industries dominated by a small number of firms. More specifically, Coleman (1989: 225) suggests, "it would seem that industries with many small, highly competitive firms would be characterized by a high rate of crimes that are intended to improve competitive performance, such as fraud, false advertising, and espionage, and that collusion and antitrust activities are most common in more concentrated industries." An example of the relationship between price fixing and a concentrated market structure can be seen in the case of the compressed gases industry in Canada. In this case, it was found that only five companies supplied 97 percent of the compressed gases sold in Canada. Representatives of these companies admitted in a statement of facts read in court that they met and agreed to adopt common prices for the sale of various compressed gases, thereby violating the Competition Act (*The Globe and Mail*, 1991a: B2; *The Globe and Mail*, 1991b: B3). So, the market structure of the industry is important with respect to the type of illegal activity most likely to occur. In addition, some situations may be particularly conducive to criminal behaviour in that there is an increased opportunity to violate the law. This leads us to a discussion of what can be termed opportunity theory.

OPPORTUNITY THEORY

The notion of "opportunity" differs slightly from the preceding discussion of industry concentration and corporate deviance by focusing on the increased likelihood of a firm to violate a specific type of law. For example, oil companies in the course of producing and/or shipping oil have a greater likelihood of polluting the environment (Clinard and Yeager, 1980: 250–51), while firms that are labour-intensive, placing a heavy reliance upon workers as opposed to equipment, are more likely to violate labour laws (Clinard and Yeager, 1980: 131–32). Thus some industries, and the firms and employees within them, may be more prone to committing certain offences than others.

At the same time, some industries more than others may find themselves the target of various regulatory agencies. For example, the pharmaceutical industry, the automobile industry, and the chemical and petroleum industries, because of the harm their products can cause, are more regulated than others (Coleman, 1989), and in turn, they have higher crime rates than others (Clinard and Yeager, 1980), if only because of the greater regulation imposed upon them. Also, because some industries may be more stringently regulated than others, it follows that organizations that are diversified into a number of stringently regulated industries are more likely to face "opportunities" to deviate and/or are more likely to attract regulatory attention (Clinard and Yeager, 1980: 131).

To summarize, companies are goal oriented, and with factors such as globalization of business and rapid social change, they may find themselves operating in uncertain environments. In the process of minimizing uncertainty and maximizing goal attainment, regulations peculiar to the industry may be violated. Nevertheless, differences in the rates of violation exist among companies in the same industry. That is, although some industries tend to violate the law more than others, there is still variation within industries with some firms more deviant than others (Clinard and Yeager, 1980: 58). This being the case, we must ask what characteristics distinguish criminal from non-criminal firms. Or, put another way, what are the characteristics of those firms that come to the attention of regulatory bodies? An examination of the internal environment of the corporation may provide an answer to these questions.

INTERNAL FACTORS OF INFLUENCE
INTERNAL CONTROL

The modern corporation is a large, diffuse, hierarchical system, oriented toward goal attainment through effective use of available resources in an uncertain environment. Employees of the corporation are one resource deployed to meet organizational goals. And, just as an organization will attempt to have some influence over its external environment, it must also manage its internal resources, including its employees. However, the internal structure of the corporation may make it difficult to control corporate illegality. For example, conditions associated with larger size may be conducive to corrupt behaviour (Clinard and Yeager, 1980). As companies increase their number of product lines, employees, and geographically dispersed locations, they become more difficult to manage, more difficult to control, and in short, more complex.

Deviant activities can remain hidden in this complex structure. In attempts to control the internal environment in the midst of complexity, lines of authority may become decentralized. Stated differently, complexity and diversification, resulting from corporate growth, may call for a decentralized corporate structure as a means of coping with the vast numbers of people and information. And it can be argued that a decentralized corporate structure in turn may be actually more conducive to corruption, rather than less, because visibility is decreased and responsibility is diffused (Finney and Lesieur, 1982; Keane, 1994). That is, when an individual is geographically distant, such as in a branch plant in another country, and/or shielded from senior management by several levels of staff, communication may suffer. In a decentralized system it is easier to withhold information. In turn, senior management can distance themselves from wrongdoing occurring at the divisional level and/or at a distant location and deny accountability—a tactic referred to by Sutherland (1949: 226) as "obfuscation as to responsibility." Pearce and Tombs (1993) provide an example of this process in their study of the Union Carbide disaster in Bhopal, India. They describe how the parent company attempted to shift responsibility for the disaster to the subsidiary, thereby minimizing the accountability of the parent company.

On the subject of accountability, Braithwaite (1984) has argued that corporations may intentionally create an impression of a diffusion of responsibility. He writes that "all corporate actors benefit from the protection afforded by presenting to outsiders an appearance of greatly diffused accountability. Yet when companies for their own purposes want accountability, they can generally get it" (Braithwaite, 1984: 138–39).

Earlier we argued that the organization's external environment is a contributing factor to corporate crime. Now we see that internal corporate factors are also important. But the picture is still incomplete. Although the form of the corporation may provide a setting where control is difficult and the potential for criminal activity is increased, certain individual-level variables are also necessary for crime to occur.

INDIVIDUAL-LEVEL FACTORS
CONTROL THEORY

Control theories of crime argue that individuals who have weak ties to the norms of conventional society are more likely to deviate than those who (1) are emotionally attached to conventional others and therefore reluctant to deviate for fear of displeasing these others; (2) are committed to conventional goals acquired through conventional means; (3) are involved in conventional/legal activities; and (4) believe in the validity of the laws of society and the need to obey those laws (Hirschi, 1969). In essence, control theorists argue that the more individuals are integrated into a legal, as opposed to an illegal, culture, the less likely they are to violate society's laws. Thus, at first glance, it appears that social control theory would be deficient in explaining crimes of the privileged, since unlike the stereotypical "street" criminal, the corporate executive appears to be strongly connected to conventional society. If we modify control theory, however, and examine the subculture of the organization, we can hypothesize that corporate offenders may be more tightly bonded to the culture of the organization than they are to larger society. This

suggests a socialization process whereby individuals come to identify closely with the organization and its goals. That is, through work-related activities and social interaction with other company employees, they intensify their bond of loyalty to the organization. This bond to the organization may then be strengthened through social mobility via promotions, and/or geographic mobility via transfers (Coleman, 1989: 220), both of which may make it difficult for individuals to develop long-term social ties outside the organization. Thus individuals may come to associate predominantly with other members of the organization for whom they come to care, and from whom they learn the behaviour required to attain corporate goals with which they come to strongly identify.

DIFFERENTIAL ASSOCIATION

Continuing with individual-level explanations of wrongdoing, Sutherland's (1949) interactionist theory of "differential association" also makes a contribution. A form of learning theory, differential association postulates that deviant behaviour is learned, just like any other type of behaviour. Differential association points to the importance of learning both the illegal methods as well as the beliefs supporting the use of the methods (Sutherland, 1949: 234). Clinard and Yeager (1980: 58) have confirmed the validity of differential association theory in explaining economic crimes, arguing that although the corporation is influenced by its external environment, the behaviour of a firm is also a product of cultural norms operating within a given corporation. With respect to corporate crimes, the theory suggests that executives become enmeshed in a corporate or professional subculture, and through association with deviant peers learn illegal behaviour. Two essential components of this theory are that (1) the individual must be exposed to an excess of definitions favourable to crime, and (2) the individual must be isolated from definitions unfavourable to crime. Given the loyalty and feelings of identification with the corporation that some organizations are able to instill in their employees, it is easy to see how an individual could be socialized to commit an unlawful act. For example, the former head of securities lending for Gordon Capital Corporation of Toronto, who was banned from trading for ten years for exposing the firm to improper risks by abusing the regulatory system, argued in his own defence that "the Gordon culture sacrificed compliance for profits." He also argued that "many others were involved in the transactions and ... no one indicated any concerns or problems to him" (*The Globe and Mail*, 1993b: B2).

Finney and Lesieur (1982: 277) wrote that internal organizational constraints against crime will vary along a continuum, "one end representing moral commitment against law violation, the middle representing a state of neutral receptivity, and the other end representing positive attitudes towards law violation." Accordingly, illegal behaviour is more likely if corporations selectively hire, selectively promote, and socialize a significant number of employees who adopt a stance on the continuum near the neutral or deviant end. Thus the presence of internal cultural constraints, or their absence, will have an influence on organizational members, and in turn the level of organizational deviance.

TECHNIQUES OF NEUTRALIZATION

Finally, how does the corporate criminal justify his or her deviant behaviour? Sykes and Matza (1957: 664–70) argued that individuals who periodically "drift" from conformity into illegal behaviour will rationalize their guilt by using various "techniques of neutralization." These techniques, which allow normally law-abiding people, such as corporate executives, to justify illegal behaviour are outlined below.

1. Denial of Responsibility

Vandivier (1987: 114–15) relates a conversation he had with a senior executive at the B.F. Goodrich Company, who when asked why he was not going to report to senior management that a faulty aircraft brake was being developed, replied: "Because it's none of my business, and it's none of yours. I learned a long time ago not to worry about things over which I had no control. I have no control over this." Not satisfied with this answer, Vandivier asked him if his conscience wouldn't bother him if, during test flights on the brake, something should happen resulting in death or injury to the test pilot. To this the executive replied: "I have no control over this thing. Why should my conscience bother me?"

2. Denial of Injury

In 1993, the U.S. government fined the Louisiana-Pacific Corporation $11.1 million (U.S.) for excessive emissions and giving false information to environmental officials. The violations occurred at fourteen facilities in eleven states. A spokesperson for the company later insisted that federal officials "aren't charging us with any significant emissions of anything hazardous into the air or any environmental harm. What they're saying is the proper procedures, as they see them, weren't followed" (*The Globe and Mail*, 1993a: B5).

3. Denial of Victimization

Continuing with the example given earlier of the Canadian compressed gas industry, in 1991 Union Carbide was fined $1.7 million while Canadian Oxygen Ltd. was fined $700 000 after pleading guilty to fixing prices. Officials at both companies claimed, however, that because of long-term contracts, no customers were penalized during the period from January to May 1990, when prices were fixed by the conspirators (*The Globe and Mail*, 1991a: B2).

4. Condemnation of the Condemners

An example of this technique is the case of Charles Keating, who was fined in excess of $260 million and sentenced to over twelve years in prison for his involvement in the Lincoln Savings and Loan Association fraud in the United States. Professing his innocence, he claimed that a vendetta by banking regulators caused Lincoln's collapse in 1989 and his ruination (*The Globe and Mail*, 1993c: B15).

5. Appeal to Higher Loyalties

When the chairman of France's largest private corporation was arrested and charged with fraud, embezzlement, and corruption, the country's minister of industry and trade argued that the country should have more important things to do in a recession than prosecute business leaders. He questioned whether the prosecution of this senior executive should be a priority in a country with 3.4 million people unemployed (*The Globe and Mail*, 1994c: B10).

To this point we have seen that at the macro-level, external factors have an impact on the organization and have some influence on the structure of the organization. Further, these macro-level factors, as well as micro-level influences, are felt at the individual level. Let us now synthesize these arguments.

THEORETICAL INTEGRATION

To gain a clearer picture of corporate crime, a theoretical integration of external, internal, and individual factors related to corporate offending may be useful. To begin, the economic condition of the industry and the extent of task-environment uncertainty are important, as is the degree of industry competition, which may lead to behaviour to reduce uncertainty. Also, the likelihood of a firm violating a particular law varies with the type of industry and the level of industry regulation. Further, large firms may be more likely to be deviant because of the diffusion of responsibility and diminished control. And, if the firm is not performing well, the potential for illegal behaviour increases.

Although this context may be conducive to illegal behaviour, individuals must also be exposed to a socialization process whereby they come to identify with the company and its goals, learn the illegal behaviour required to meet the objectives perceived to be unattainable through legal means, and rationalize their actions through various techniques. Hence, the external culture and the internal corporate culture interact to either promote or inhibit law violation.

An element of strain exists in both cultures of an offending corporation. At the external level the strain may be caused by competitors, suppliers, or government legislation, posing a threat to the corporation's objectives. At the internal level the strain may be caused by the potential failure to meet corporate objectives, but the pressure is imposed by internal rather than external actors. And, if cultural restraints such as values and regulations opposing and thus inhibiting corporate criminal behaviour are lacking or weak, both externally, in society in general, and internally, within the organization, corruption is more likely to occur. This being the case, can we control corporate crime?

CONTROLLING CORPORATE OFFENDING

Braithwaite (1989: 40) argued that "in modern capitalist societies there are many more statutes that criminalize the behaviour of corporations (anti-pollution laws, occupational health and safety laws, consumer protection laws, antitrust laws, laws to enforce compliance with standards) than there are laws that criminalize the behaviour of the poor." However, application of the law is another matter. That is, evidence suggests that crimes of the powerful are punished differently than crimes of the powerless. For example, focusing on Canadian securities violations, Hagan (1989; Hagan and Parker, 1985) examined all cases referred for prosecution under the Criminal Code or the Securities Act from 1966 to 1983. After categorizing offenders in terms of their class position, the researchers found that offenders in positions of power committed crimes larger in scope than those with less power, but they received proportionately less severe sanctions, because the powerful were less likely to be charged under the Criminal Code, and more likely to be charged under the Securities Act, which carries lesser sanctions.

Also considering the element of power is research by Goff and Reasons (1978). Their research involved an investigation of the major Canadian corporations that have violated the Combines Act and have been investigated by the Combines Branch from 1952 to 1973. Concentrating on the illegal acts of combinations, mergers, monopolies, resale price maintenance, misleading price advertising, predatory pricing, price discrimination, and violations of patents, they concluded that the "Combines Branch has centred its attentions upon the investigation, prosecution, and conviction of small- and medium-sized companies and corporations leaving the very largest corporations free to engage in their monopolistic practices" (Goff and Reasons, 1978: 86). Again, they suggested that this occurs because large corporations operating in oligopolistic industries have the ability to obscure their illegal practices.

Snider (1982) compared the punishments given to those offenders who commit traditional non-violent economic offences with those given to offenders who commit what she terms "upperworld" non-violent economic offences. Examples of upperworld non-violent economic offences are acts such as false advertising, misleading price representation, and violations of acts such as the Food and Drug Act, the Packaging and Labelling Act, the Weights and Measures Act, the Hazardous Products Act, and the Combines Investigation Act. Examples of traditional underworld non-violent economic offences are theft, possession of stolen goods, breaking and entering, and taking a motor vehicle without consent. In brief, she found that, over a considerable period of time, more traditional offenders were charged, and the sanctions for the traditional economic crimes were much heavier than for the upperworld economic crimes. Others have similarly argued that corporate criminals enjoy a legal advantage because of the types and combinations of legal sanctions that they experience (see Hagan and Nagel, 1982).

For example, although New York State had originally sued Occidental Chemical Corporation for almost $700 million in costs and damages toward the cleanup of Love Canal, the company recently agreed to pay only $98 million (U.S.) to settle a fourteen-year liability lawsuit over the toxic disaster that forced hundreds of families from their homes (*The Globe and Mail*, 1994b: B2).

CONCLUSIONS

In summary, corporate criminals have been spared the stigma of criminalization often imposed on those less privileged. Furthermore, given the evidence of recidivism reported by researchers such as Goff and Reasons (1978) and Clinard and Yeager (1980), the existing sanctions appear to have little deterrent effect. This being the case, to control corporate corruption perhaps we should recall that the roots of unethical behaviour are embedded in the organizational and cultural contexts.

Sanctions that have been suggested to inhibit organizational deviance include stiffer penalties for corporations and executives, negative publicity, nationalization of firms that are habitual offenders, and forced deconcentration and divestiture of offending firms, to name a few (Braithwaite, 1984; Clinard and Yeager, 1980; Coleman, 1989). These sanctions are similar in that they are imposed by others external to the organization, and they are imposed after the criminal act. It may also be possible to control corporate crime at the internal corporate level.

Internal corporate control can be increased by actions such as improving and strengthening the firm's self-regulatory systems (Braithwaite, 1984) and providing for public and/or union representation on corporate boards of directors (Clinard and Yeager, 1980). These internal corporate mechanisms would serve to control the actions of executives prior to any offence. Another method of controlling corporate crime that has received increased attention is the development of a stronger business ethic (Clinard and Yeager, 1980; Coleman, 1989). This proposal is directed at the culture of the organization and is preventive in its orientation. An increasing number of companies are finding that "good ethics is good business" (Etzioni, 1989). Unethical corporate behaviour may destroy a company's reputation, and given the increase in foreign competition experienced by many industries, a loss of customers may accompany the loss of reputation. In addition, failure to follow ethical business practices may result not only in consumer protest, but also in government intervention (Hilts, 1989). Many companies are taking steps to avoid this possibility. A survey conducted in 1984 of the Fortune 500 industrial and 500 service companies found that 80 percent of those responding were incorporating an ethics program into their organizations (Hoffman, 1986).

Whether the institutionalization of ethics is successful in decreasing corporate crime remains to be seen. However, it will be a step in creating a culture in which corporate crime is not tolerated, at least publicly. On a broader scale, Braithwaite (1989) has argued that what society needs "is punishment for organizational crime that maximizes the sense of shame and sends a message to executives that corporate crime is as despicable to society as street crime." He further asserts that "once members of the organization internalize this abhorrence of corporate wrongdoing, then the self-regulation of executive consciences and corporate ethics and compliance policies will do most of the work for the government" (1989: 143).

NOTE

The author would like to thank John Cairney and Shelley Garr for their research assistance.

REFERENCES

Aldrich, H.E. 1979. *Organizations and Environments*. Englewood Cliffs, NJ: Prentice-Hall.

Braithwaite, J. 1984. *Corporate Crime in the Pharmaceutical Industry*. London: Routledge & Kegan Paul.

———. 1989. *Crime, Shame and Reintegration*. Cambridge: Cambridge University Press.

Clinard, M.B. 1983. *Corporate Ethics and Crime: The Role of Middle Management*. Beverly Hills, CA: Sage.

Clinard, M.B. and P.C. Yeager. 1980. *Corporate Crime*. New York: Free Press.

Clinard, M.B., P.C. Yeager, J. Brissette, D. Petrashek, and E. Harries. 1979. *Illegal Corporate Behavior*. Washington, DC: U.S. Department of Justice.

Coleman, J.W. 1987. "Toward an Integrated Theory of White-Collar Crime." *American Journal of Sociology* 93(2): 406–39.

———. 1989. *The Criminal Elite: The Sociology of White-Collar Crime* (2nd ed). New York: St. Martin's Press.

Cullen, F.T., W.J. Maakestad, and G. Cavender. 1987. *Corporate Crime Under Attack: The Ford Pinto Case and Beyond*. Cincinnati: Anderson Publishing.

Dill, W.R. 1958. "Environment as an Influence on Managerial Autonomy." *Administrative Science Quarterly* 2 (March): 409–43.

Dowie, M. 1977. "Pinto Madness." *Mother Jones* Sept.–Oct.: 18–32.

Etzioni, A. 1985. "Will a Few Bad Apples Spoil the Core of Big Business?" *Business and Society Review* 55 (Fall): 4–5.

———. 1989. "Good Ethics Is Good Business—Really." *The New York Times*, February 12, p. F2.

Finney, H.C. and H.R. Lesieur. 1982. "A Contingency Theory of Organizational Crime." In S.B. Bacharach (ed.) *Research in the Sociology of Organizations*. Vol. 1. Greenwich, CT: JAI Press.

The Globe and Mail. 1991a. "Union Carbide Fined $1.7-Million for Price Fixing." September 7.

———. 1991b. "Pair Fined $75,000 Each for Price-Fixing Role." October 19.

———. 1993a. "Louisiana-Pacific Fined." May 25.

———. 1993b. "OSC Slaps Gordon Players." June 18.

———. 1993c. "Keating Fined $265-Million for Fraud." July 29.

———. 1994a. "To Bribe or Not To Bribe." February 14.

———. 1994b. "Love Canal Settlement." June 22.

———. 1994c. "Alcatel Boss Rejects Fraud Charges." July 6.

Goff, C.H. and C.E. Reasons. 1978. *Corporate Crime in Canada*. Scarborough, ON: Prentice-Hall.

Hagan, J. 1989. *Structural Criminology*. New Brunswick, NJ: Rutgers University Press.

Hagan, J. and I. Nagel. 1982. "White Collar Crime, White Collar Time: The Sentencing of White Collar Criminals in the Southern District of New York." *American Criminal Law Review* 20(2): 259–301.

Hagan, J. and P. Parker. 1985. "White-Collar Crime and Punishment: The Class Structure and Legal Sanctioning of Securities Violations." *American Sociological Review* 50: 302–16.

Handelman, S. 1989. "Fighting to Put People before Production." *The Toronto Star*, July 16, pp. H1–H2.

Henry, F. 1982. "Capitalism, Capital Accumulation, and Crime." *Crime and Social Justice* 18: 79–87.

Hilts, P.J. 1989. "Wave of Protests Developing on Profits from AIDS Drug." *The New York Times*, September 16, p. 1.

Hirschi, T. 1969. *Causes of Delinquency*. Berkeley: University of California Press.

Hoffman, W.M. 1986. "Developing the Moral Corporation." *Bell Atlantic Quarterly* 1 (Spring): 31–41.

Keane, C. 1993. "The Impact of Financial Performance on Frequency of Corporate Crime: A Latent Variable Test of Strain Theory." *Canadian Journal of Criminology* 35(3): 293–308.

———. 1994. "Loosely Coupled Systems and Unlawful Behaviour: Organization Theory and Corporate Crime." In F. Pearce and L. Snider (eds.) *Corporate Crime: Ethics, Law and the State*. Toronto: University of Toronto Press.

Los, M. 1982. "Crime and Economy in the Communist Countries." In P. Wickman and T. Dailey (eds.) *White-Collar and Economic Crime*. Toronto: D.C. Heath.

Merton, R.K. 1938. "Social Structure and Anomie." *American Sociological Review* 3: 672–82.

Pearce, F. and S. Tombs. 1993. "U.S. Capital versus the Third World: Union Carbide and Bhopal." In F. Pearce and M. Woodiwiss (eds.) *Global Crime Connections: Dynamics and Control*. Toronto: University of Toronto Press.

Simpson, S. 1986. "The Decomposition of Antitrust: Testing a Multi-Level, Longitudinal Model of Profit-Squeeze." *American Sociological Review* 51: 859–75.

Snider, D.L. 1982. "Traditional and Corporate Theft: A Comparison of Sanctions." In P. Wickman and T. Dailey (eds.) *White-Collar and Economic Crime*. Toronto: D.C. Heath.

———. 1993. *Bad Business: Corporate Crime in Canada*. Scarborough, ON: Nelson Canada.

Snider, D.L. and W.G. West. 1985. "A Critical Perspective on Law in the Canadian State: Delinquency and Corporate Crime." In T. Fleming (ed.) *The New Criminologies in Canada: Crime, State and Control*. Toronto: Oxford University Press.

Sutherland, E.H. 1949. *White Collar Crime*. New York: Holt, Rinehart and Winston.

Sykes, G.M. and D. Matza. 1957. "Techniques of Neutralization: A Theory of Delinquency." *American Sociological Review* 22: 664–70.

Vandivier, K. 1987. "Why Should My Conscience Bother Me?" In M.D. Ermann and R.J. Lundman (eds.) *Corporate and Governmental Deviance*. New York: Oxford University Press.

Chapter 28

Race and Crime:
A Critique

JULIAN V. ROBERTS

THOMAS GABOR

Canadian criminologists have been challenged recently by the work of a professor of psychology, Philippe Rushton, who claims to have uncovered evidence of significant interracial differences in many areas of human behaviour, including criminality (Rushton, 1987; 1988; 1989). In January 1987, Professor Rushton delivered a paper at the American Association for the Advancement of Science conference in San Francisco (Rushton, 1987). He proposed a genetically based hierarchy in which Blacks (who supposedly evolved earlier than whites or orientals) were, *inter alia*, less intelligent and law-abiding than whites and orientals. Rushton asserts that there are substantial interracial differences in crime rates, and that these are accounted for by genetic factors. We shall examine later the credibility of genetic explanations of variations in crime rates. First, it is important to address the context of these assertions, and their likely impact upon society.

Rushton's speculations about race and crime have achieved national coverage exceeding that accorded any research project undertaken by criminologists (*The Globe and Mail*, 1989). Part of the reason for this is the aggressive posture adopted by Rushton: he has been interviewed in several newspapers and has appeared on several television programs with national audiences. In contrast, the reaction from criminologists, but not other professional groups (*The Globe and Mail*, 1989), has

been muted. His monopolization of media coverage may, we believe, have had a detrimental impact upon public opinion. It is important, therefore, that criminologists in Canada respond to his statements. While Rushton's claims about racial influences upon intelligence have been challenged, his assertions about crime have not.

THE EFFECT OF RUSHTON'S VIEWS ON PUBLIC THEORIES OF CRIME CAUSATION

The race/crime controversy has important consequences for public opinion in the area of criminal justice. Many of the important questions in the field of criminology—such as the relative deterrent effect of capital punishment—cannot be addressed by experiments. Accordingly, criminologists have used sophisticated correlational procedures to untangle the relative effects on crime of correlated variables such as genetic and environmental factors. The existence of a simple statistic, then, such as the overrepresentation in some crime statistics of certain racial minorities, will by itself convince few scholars. Criminologists have become sensitized to the possibility of alternative explanations for apparently straightforward relationships. Members of the public, however, are not so sophisticated in drawing inferences from statistical information. In fact, a great deal of recent research in social psychology has documented numerous ways in which the layperson is led into making unjustified inferences from material such as that which appears in newspapers (Fiske and Taylor, 1984; Nisbett and Ross, 1980).

Rushton's theories may affect public opinion in this area for several reasons. First, as already noted, the average layperson may not readily seek alternative (i.e., nongenetic) explanations for the overrepresentation of Blacks in certain types of crime. Second, laypersons are less likely to realize that studies on race and crime are essentially correlational, rather than causal, in nature. Third, the race/crime hypothesis comes from a highly credible source, namely a well-published and tenured university professor. Fourth, it is vital to remember that, to the average member of the public, crime is a relatively unidimensional phenomenon: it usually involves violence, loss of property, and is a consequence of a "criminal disposition." Members of the public tend to regard offenders as a relatively homogeneous group (Roberts and White, 1986) varying somewhat in their actions but not their motivations. Criminologists have long been aware of the deficiencies of this perception of crime; the multidimensional nature of crime and the complexity of motivation render sweeping statements about the etiology of crime invalid. Finally, but not last in importance, some people may be particularly receptive to racial explanations of crime. Thus, views such as those expressed by Professor Rushton may have the unintended effect of inflaming racism in Canada.

Furthermore, Rushton's views received what many laypersons might interpret as substantial support within days of the news media's coverage of his San Francisco address. On February 16, a representative of the Toronto Police Force released statistics showing that Blacks were overrepresented in the crime statistics in the Jane–Finch area of Toronto (*The Toronto Star*, 1989). These data are likely to be misinterpreted by members of the public to constitute evidence supporting a genetic explanation of crime.

For the vast majority of the public, the mass media constitute their primary source of infor-

mation about crime and criminal justice. Public conceptions of deviance are a consequence of what people read, hear, and see in the media. An abundance of research has demonstrated a direct correspondence between public misperceptions of crime and distorted media coverage of criminal justice issues (Doob and Roberts, 1982). Since criminologists have failed to refute Rushton in the news media, we have also relinquished access to the one means of influencing public opinion on this issue. Criminologists may be highly skeptical of Rushton's opinions in the area of crime, but the only way that this skepticism can affect the public is through coverage in the news media. Once again, we note that while Rushton has been criticized by various behavioural geneticists (such as David Suzuki), his assertions regarding race and crime have remained uncontested.

We believe, therefore, that it is important to address the hypothesis that inherited racial traits affect crime rates. We shall examine some methodological issues relating criminality to race. A comprehensive survey of the literature on this topic would occupy a whole issue of a journal; we can only highlight the research findings and point out what we perceive to be the principal flaws in Rushton's argument. We shall draw upon data from Canada, the United States, and the United Kingdom. Finally, it should be made clear from the outset that we are addressing Rushton's theory as it pertains to the phenomenon of crime. We are not behavioural geneticists, to whom we cede the question of whether the general theory of racial differences withstands scientific scrutiny.

THE SCIENTIFIC ARGUMENT: EMPIRICAL RESEARCH ON RACE AND CRIME
PROBLEMS WITH THE DEFINITION OF RACE

Rushton relates an independent variable (race) to a dependent variable (crime). The interracial comparisons cited by Rushton are predicated on the assumption that people are racially pure. Each racial "category" is held to be homogeneous, but this is now accepted by contemporary anthropologists and biologists to be an antiquated and dangerous myth. Centuries of interbreeding reduce Rushton's rather crude tripartite classification (Black, white, oriental) to the level of caricature. For example, Radzinowicz and King (1977) note that in the United States, close to 50 percent of those classified as Black are over half white by lineage (see also Herskovits, 1930; and, for a study of offenders, Hooton, 1939). Many American whites, as well, have some Black ancestry; Haskell and Yablonsky (1983: 95) note that:

> Estimates of the number of blacks who have "passed" into the white society run as high as 7 million. In addition to those millions who have introduced an African mixture into the "white" population of the United States in the relatively recent past, there must have been millions of Africans who were assimilated into the population of Spain, Portugal, Italy, Greece, and other Mediterranean countries. Descendants of those people are now part of the "white" population of the United States.

Wolfgang and Cohen (1970) cite data showing that no more than 22 percent of all persons designated as Black, in the United States, were of unmixed ancestry. Fully 15 percent of persons classified as Black were more white than Black (Wolfgang and Cohen, 1970: 7). The pervasiveness of such racial overlap calls genetically based racial theories of crime into question. (For the rest of this article, for convenience only, we shall continue to refer to interracial differences. This does not mean we endorse the racial trichotomy of Blacks, orientals, and whites advanced by Professor Rushton.) Finally, it is important to bear in mind that crime statistics deal with race as a sociological and not a biological category. In short, the independent variable, as it were, is highly problematic. Now we turn to the dependent

measure, official and unofficial measures of crime.

THE ISSUE OF OVERREPRESENTATION IN OFFICIAL CRIME STATISTICS

Rushton's evidence for a genetic influence consists of the overrepresentation of Blacks in official statistics of crime in the United States, the United Kingdom, and elsewhere. Specifically he asserts that:

> African descended people, for example, while constituting less than one-eighth of the population of the United States or of London, England, currently account for over 50% of the crimes in both places. Since about the same proportion of victims say their assailant was black, the arrest statistics cannot really be blamed on police prejudice. (Rushton, 1987: 3)

There are at least two factually incorrect elements here, but first we offer a general comment regarding the issue of overrepresentation.

A simple correlation between two variables does not constitute evidence of a *causal* relationship. A multitude of other confounding factors must be ruled out before one can contemplate a causal relationship. Even if the relationship between race and crime holds up after careful secondary analyses, this is hardly convincing evidence of genetic influences. The fact that parental alcoholism is correlated with alcoholism in the offspring does not prove a genetic component to alcoholism. Alcohol abuse can be a learned behaviour as well. The same argument applies to the race/crime relationship.

Another point is relevant to the issue of a disproportionate involvement in crime. Virtually every society contains racial and ethnic groups, usually minorities, who are more criminally active in certain crimes than the rest of the population. According to Rushton's theory of criminal behaviour, Native Canadians should display lower, not higher, crime rates than the non-Native population. Unfortunately for the theory, this is not true. The overrepresentation of

Native offenders in the criminal justice statistics has been apparent for some time (Griffiths and Verdun-Jones, 1989; LaPrairie, 1989). Explanations in terms of the social strata in our society occupied by indigenous peoples can easily explain these findings; Rushton's racial theory cannot. According to Rushton's typology this group, being oriental or mongoloid, should display lower, not higher rates of criminality.

According to Rushton's genetic explanation of crime, the crime rates for Blacks should be higher than the white crime rates, *and* the rates for Native Canadians should be *lower* than the non-Native population. The two categories (Blacks and Native people) are genetically dissimilar; their rates of criminality should reflect this difference (relative to the white population). The fact is that both Black Americans and Native Canadians share an elevated risk of certain kinds of criminality (relative to the comparable white populations in their respective countries). Such an outcome is, of course, perfectly consistent with a sociological explanation: both minority groups share a protracted history of constrained social opportunity, as well as overt discrimination.

Also in Canada, French Canadians are the most active in the crime of robbery (Gabor et al., 1987). In England, Irish immigrants have been overrepresented in crimes of assault for years (Radzinowicz and King, 1977). In Israel, the Arab population and non-European Jews are more criminally active in conventional crimes than the European Jews (Fishman, Rattner, and Weimann, 1987). Such overrepresentation, then, is the rule rather than the exception across different societies.

To return to Rushton's suggestion, two errors can be identified. First, he cites data published in the *Daily Telegraph* (a British newspaper) showing that Blacks account for over 50 percent of the crimes in the United States and the United Kingdom (Rushton, 1988). By any measure, this is a considerable exaggeration. If he refers to all reported crimes and not merely index crimes, Blacks account for about 29 percent of all persons charged in the United States (United States Department of Justice, 1989). Index crimes are those included in official crime indices; they exclude many white-collar crimes, for example.

As well, aggregate statistics based on index crimes alone misrepresent the true picture. Crime is not, as suggested by Rushton's publications, a homogeneous category of behaviours. While Blacks in the United States account for over 60 percent of arrests for robbery and almost 50 percent of arrests for murder, they account for about 30 percent of arrests for burglary and theft, less than 24 percent of those arrested for arson and about 20 percent of those arrested for vandalism (United States Department of Justice, 1987). Using Rushton's own data, Blacks are underrepresented in crimes like tax fraud and securities violations. In fact, arrest statistics for white-collar crimes such as fraud and embezzlement are significantly higher for whites. Treating crime as a unitary phenomenon obscures this diversity. These variations reflect differential opportunities for offending, and not, we submit, offence-specific genetic programming.

Differential Treatment of Blacks by the Criminal Justice System

Finally, arrest statistics reflect, to a degree, the more rigorous surveillance by police to which minorities are subject. Data on this point are hard to obtain; the magnitude of the problem is hard to quantify. Nevertheless, the recent release of the "Guildford Four" in England, after fifteen years of imprisonment following a wrongful conviction based upon fabricated police evidence, reveals the dangers posed to minorities by an overzealous police force.

Research in the United States sustains the view that the police are more likely to arrest and charge Blacks (Black and Reiss, 1967; Lundman, Sykes, and Clark, 1978). Wolfgang and Cohen (1970: 71) summarize some of this research:

In comparing arrest statistics for blacks and whites, it is important to remember, then, that one reason for the high arrest rates among blacks is that they are more likely to be stopped, picked up on suspicion and subsequently arrested.

Furthermore, the bias does not remain at the police station: British data (Landau, 1981; Landau and Nathan, 1983) show that prosecution is more likely for persons of Afro-Caribbean origin. Bias persists at most critical stages of the criminal justice process. As Paul Gordon (1988: 309) noted, summarizing data on the issue:

> Black people's experience of the British criminal justice system shows clearly that the rhetoric of the law does not accord with the reality of its practice. The law is not colour-blind, but a means by which black people have been subject to a process of criminalization.

Most recently, Albonetti and her colleagues (1989) have demonstrated that while the influence of race upon pretrial decisions is complicated, white suspects have the edge over Black suspects.

To summarize the data on contact with the criminal justice process, American Blacks are clearly overrepresented in violent crime statistics, slightly overrepresented in property crimes, and underrepresented in white-collar crimes. In order to explain this diverse pattern, one has to strain the genetic explanation beyond the breaking point. Are Blacks genetically predisposed toward street crimes while whites are programmed to commit white-collar crimes? A far more plausible explanation exists: social groups commit crimes as a consequence of their social situations and in response to prevailing criminal opportunities. This environmental perspective explains more findings and requires fewer assumptions. The law of parsimony, then, clearly favours environmental over genetic theories of crime. In short, Rushton's explanation of crime by reference to genetic influences requires acceptance of the position that specific antisocial behaviours are directly related to genetic structure. Modern behavioural geneticists would undoubtedly reject this view.

OVERREPRESENTATION AND ALTERNATIVE SOURCE OF CRIME STATISTICS: VICTIMIZATION SURVEYS AND SELF-REPORTED CRIMINALITY

There is convincing evidence that arrest data exaggerate the true incidence of Black criminality. Two alternative sources of information on crime make this clear. Overall, FBI data indicate that 46.5 percent of all violent crimes reported to the police are committed by Blacks. However, the victimization survey conducted by the U.S. Department of Justice found that Blacks account for only about 24 percent of violent crimes (United States Department of Justice, 1986). Which source presents a more accurate picture of crimes actually committed? With regard to crimes of violence, data derived from victims would appear to be more accurate than arrest data. But it is not just victimization surveys that cast doubt upon the official statistics. A third source of information on crime patterns also shows discrepancies. Rojek (1983) compared police reports with self-reports of delinquency. In the police database, race was a significant factor in several offence categories, but this was not true for the self-reports. Other studies using the self-report approach (Williams and Gold, 1972) have found a similar pattern: no difference between Black and white respondents (Pope, 1979) or only slight differences (Hirschi, 1969).

Unreported versus Reported Crime

Another explanation for the elevated incidence of Black offenders in official crime statistics concerns the issue of unreported crimes. As we have noted, official crime data indicate that Blacks are more likely than whites to commit certain crimes (personal injury offences) and less likely than whites to commit other types of crimes. The problem with crime statistics is that the reporting rate is highly variable, depending upon the offence. The types of offences committed by Blacks are more likely to be reported than the offences committed by whites. Any examination of aggregate crime statistics is going to overestimate the true incidence of crime committed by Blacks relative to the amount of crime committed by whites.

To conclude, the extent of overrepresentation of Blacks, even in those offences where it occurs, has been exaggerated. In perhaps the most comprehensive study to date which relates crime to race, Michael Hindelang (1982) tested various theories that attempted to explain interracial differences. He concluded that the theories of delinquency that best explain the patterns of data were sociological rather than biological. These included Merton's reformulation of anomie theory (Merton, 1968), Cloward and Ohlin's opportunity theory (Cloward and Ohlin, 1960), and Wolfgang's subculture of violence theory (Wolfgang and Ferracuti, 1982).

A final word on the crime statistics utilized by Rushton consists of a caveat: recorded crime is exactly that: it is only a small fraction of all reported and unreported crime. A recent article by Tony Jefferson (1988: 535) makes the point succinctly:

> We do not *know* what the real rate of black crime is, nor whether it is on the increase. Take robbery for instance. The British Crime Survey reveals that only 8% of robberies were recorded. If those figures applied to London this would mean that there is a suspect for only 1 in 100 robberies. The comparable figure for burglaries would be 5 in 100. This means that *whatever* the arrest figures, and whatever the victim identifications, the "unknown" element is so great, especially for those crimes where black "over-representation" is seen as greatest, as to make all estimates of black offending strictly conjectural.

When there is sound reason to suppose that the police are more vigilant with regard to Black suspects and offenders, it is clear that if we were able to replace reported with unreported crime rates, the interracial differences would diminish still further.

Self-report studies provide insight in another area as well. While Professor Rushton associates "lawlessness" with being Black, there is overwhelming evidence indicating that most people, at one point or another, commit acts for which they could be prosecuted. As an example, in a now classic study, Wallerstein and Wyle (1947) surveyed 1700 New York City residents without a criminal record. Fully 99 percent admitted to involvement in at least one of 49 offences. This evidence suggests that rule breaking is normal activity on the part of most citizens in Western societies. The selection of norm violators to be prosecuted therefore is critical to an understanding of who becomes officially classified as a criminal. Many observers of the criminal justice system believe that race may be a key factor affecting that selection process. Another classic study, Hartshorne and May's (1928) investigation of children, also showed that dishonesty was both pervasive and situation-specific. There was little cross-situational consistency: children that were dishonest in one situation were honest in others. This emphasis on the social situation as the determinant of behaviour is consistent with an environmental view of crime, and inconsistent with Rushton's genetic theory. (A large body of evidence, drawn from longitudinal, self-report, experimental, and observational research, suggests that law breaking is widespread in North American society.)

WITHIN RACE COMPARISONS

Comparisons over Time

In the next two sections, we examine variation in crime rates within race, but across time and cultures. If genetic factors have an important impact upon crime, rates should be relatively stable within race, across both time and cultures. This, however, is not the case. Further undermining Rushton's thesis are the temporal and cross-cultural variations in crime patterns for the Black population. Street crime by Blacks in the United Kingdom has only recently increased significantly. Just over a decade ago, Radzinowicz and King (1977) were able to write that, with the exception of prostitution and other victimless crimes, the Black community was as law abiding as other Britons. Any increase in crime rates within a generation obviously cannot be attributed to genetic factors. This point was made recently by Anthony Mawson (1989) in the context of explanations of homicide in terms of Darwinian selection (Daly and Wilson, 1988). Mawson (1989: 239) notes the inability of biological explanations of homicide to account for fluctuations in homicide rates over a short period of time:

> Thus, it seems doubtful whether a selectionist explanation can be applied to changing homicide rates, even those occurring over a thousand years.

The same argument applies in the context of Rushton's work: increases in offending by Blacks over a period of ten to fifteen years cannot possibly be explained by reference to genetic influence.

In the United States as well, the proportional involvement of Blacks in crime has risen over the past few decades. One major factor in this rise has been the proliferation of illicit drug usage. Heroin use became pervasive in the 1950s, and "crack" cocaine is creating an explosion of violent crime in this decade. As well, the erosion of taboos relating to interracial crimes has been associated with increased victimization of whites by Blacks (Silberman, 1978). A third major development has been the greater accessibility of firearms. These are three potent environmental factors affecting Black criminality. One would be hard-pressed to find a genetic explanation for the changing criminal activity pattern of a race over such a short period of time.

Comparisons across Jurisdictions

The variations in Black, white, and oriental crime from one society to another also demonstrate the potency of environmental factors in the etiology of crime. Levels of violent crime in the American South are greater for both Blacks

and whites than they are in other parts of the country. As well, there is substantial variation in the homicide rates for Blacks in different American states. For example, in Delaware the homicide rate for Blacks is 16.7 per 100 000. This is considerably lower than the homicide rate for Black residents of other states; in Missouri, for example, the rate is 65 per 100 000 (Carroll and Mercy, 1989).

Cross-national, within-race comparisons make the same point. Black Americans have a higher homicide rate than their more racially pure counterparts in Africa: this fact directly contradicts Rushton's thesis. The author (Bohannan, 1960: 123) of a study of African homicide concludes:

> if it needed stressing, here is overwhelming evidence that it is a cultural and not biological factor which makes for a high homicide rate among American negroes.

More recent data (International Criminal Police Organization, 1988) demonstrate the same variations: the homicide rate per 100 000 inhabitants varies from .01 (Mali) to 29 (Bahamas) and 22.05 (Jamaica). It is noteworthy also that the Caribbean homicide rates are far in excess of even the African countries with the highest rates (e.g., Rwanda, 11 per 100 000; Tanzania, 8 per 100 000). This despite the fact that residents of the Caribbean are more racially mixed than Blacks from Africa. According to Rushton's theory, homicide rates should be higher not lower in the more racially pure African states.

Furthermore, orientals do not constitute a monolith of law-abiding citizens. The homicide rates in the Far East also vary considerably, from 39 per 100 000 residents in the Philippines to 1.3 per 100 000 in Hong Kong. In Thailand, the homicide rate exceeds the rate of homicide in Japan by a factor of twelve (International Criminal Police Organization, 1988). In all these comparisons, the genetic explanation falls short. The magnitude of these intraracial differences suggests that the potency of environmental factors to explain crime rates far exceeds that of genetic factors. In statistical terms, these data imply that the percentage of variation in crime rates explained by genetic factors is negligible, if it exists at all.

VICTIMIZATION PATTERNS

There is another form of overrepresentation of which Professor Rushton appears unaware: Blacks are at much higher risk of becoming the victims of violent crime. In the United States, Black males are 20 times more likely than whites to be shot, cut, or stabbed, and Black females are 18 times more likely to be raped than white women (Wolfgang and Cohen, 1981). Black Americans are also more likely than whites to be victims of burglary, motor vehicle theft, assault, robbery, and many other offences (United States Department of Justice, 1983). Although Blacks constitute only 12 percent of the general United States population, over 40 percent of homicide victims are Black. See Barnett and Schwartz (1989) for recent data showing Black victimization rates to be approximately four times higher than white rates. The same trends are apparent in other countries, such as England. The overrepresentation of Blacks as victims is substantial, yet no one has posited that such overrepresentation is due to a genetically based susceptibility to criminal victimization. While this finding is not inconsistent with an explanation based upon genetic factors, it does underscore the importance of environmental factors such as propinquity and accessibility. Violent crimes are a result of an interaction between offender and victim. To posit an overriding genetic basis of crime is to ignore the role of the victim and situational factors (Boyd, 1988; Wolfgang, 1958). When we examine the dynamics of the violent crime most commonly associated with Blacks—armed robbery—we readily see the importance of situational determinants. Actually, recourse to physical violence occurs only in a small minority of robberies. Usually the violence that does occur arises in response to victims who resist the

robbers' demands (Gabor et al., 1987). The violence, therefore, is often instrumental and situation-specific.

If Blacks are more likely to be both offenders and victims in relation to certain types of crime, then a plausible explanation for their overrepresentation on both counts is that they tend to live in areas in which violence is a normal consequence of stress, threat, and frustration. This essentially is Wolfgang and Ferracuti's (1982) subculture of violence thesis. Aside from living in environments where violence is normative behaviour, Blacks tend disproportionately to live in poverty. Furthermore, they are overrepresented among urban dwellers. Economic status and urban residence are linked to a number of crime indices. A fair examination of Black and white criminality would therefore necessitate comparison between persons situated similarly in society.

But even the presence of a correlation between race and certain indices of crime, after other plausible environmental factors have been pointed out, does not demonstrate a genetically based race/crime link. As Charles Silberman (1978) has pointed out, the experience of Black Americans has been very different from the experience of any other disadvantaged group. The generations of violence, deprivation, disenfranchisement, and exclusion from educational and vocational opportunities to which they have been subjected has not been shared by any other ethnic or racial group. Moreover, much of this racial discrimination persists, to this day, and in this country, as recent research has documented (Henry and Ginzberg, 1985). Discrimination of this kind can engender social patterns and attitudes toward authority that lead to law breaking.

Careful epidemiological research can result in samples of Black and white citizens that are "matched" on many important background variables such as social class, income, education, age, and family size and composition. Comparison between such groups is preferable to comparison based upon unmatched samples, but the effects of long-term discrimination, brutality, and oppression over generations cannot be captured by the most rigorous multiple regression analysis. As John Conklin (1989: 140) notes:

> to argue that blacks and whites of similar backgrounds will have the same crime rate is to argue that centuries of discrimination have had no long-term effects on blacks that are conducive to criminal behavior.

Our opposition to Rushton's views should not be interpreted to mean that we deny the existence of any genetic influences upon human behaviour. Rather, we take issue with the attribution of racial differences in criminality to genetic factors. In our view, there is little scientific basis for his rather sweeping assertions about the relative "law-abidingness" of different racial groups. The few statistics he provides are susceptible to a multitude of highly probable alternative explanations derived from an environmental perspective. Given the incendiary nature of the theory and its policy implications, we feel that the burden of proof is upon Professor Rushton to provide more convincing data than the few ambiguous statistics he has to date brought forth. We leave it to others (Lynn, 1989; Zuckerman and Brody, 1989) to evaluate the scientific credibility of Professor Rushton's genetic explanation of other phenomena such as: intelligence, sexual restraint, personality, political preferences, and the efficacy of the German army in the Second World War (*The Globe and Mail*, 1989). In the area of criminality, his evidence, in our view, falls short of discharging a scientific burden of proof.

NOTE

The authors would like to acknowledge that this manuscript has benefited from the comments of Michael Petrunik, from the University of Ottawa, the editorial committee of the *Canadian Journal of Criminology*, and two anonymous reviewers.

REFERENCES

Albonetti, Celesta, Robert Hauser, John Hagan, and Ilene Nagel. 1989. "Criminal justice decision making as a stratification process: The role of race and stratification resources in pre-trial release." *Journal of Quantitative Criminology* 5: 57–82.

Barnett, Arnold and Elliot Schwartz. 1989. "Urban homicide: Still the same." *Journal of Quantitative Criminology* 5: 83–100.

Black, D. and Albert Reiss. 1967. *Studies of Crime and Law Enforcement in Major Metropolitan Areas*. Washington, DC: Government Printing Office.

Bohannan, Paul. 1960. *African Homicide and Suicide*. Princeton, NJ: Princeton University Press.

Bonger, Willem. 1969. *Race and Crime*. New Jersey: Patterson Smith. (Originally published 1943).

Boyd, Neil. 1988. *The Last Dance: Murder in Canada*. Toronto: Prentice-Hall.

Carroll, Patrick and James Mercy. 1989. "Regional variation in homicide rates: Why is the west violent?" *Violence and Victims* 4: 17–25.

Cloward, Richard A. and Lloyd Ohlin. 1960. *Delinquency and Opportunity: A Theory of Delinquent Gangs*. New York: Free Press.

Conklin, John. 1989. *Criminology*. (Third edition) New York: Macmillan.

Curie, Elliot. 1985. *Confronting Crime*. New York: Pantheon.

Daly, Martin and Margo Wilson. 1988. *Homicide*. New York: Aldine.

Doob, Anthony N. and Julian V. Roberts. 1982. *Crime: Some Views of the Canadian Public*. Ottawa: Department of Justice.

Fishman, G., Arye Rattner, and Gabriel Weimann. 1987. "The effect of ethnicity on crime attribution." *Criminology* 25: 507–24.

Fiske, Susan T. and Shelley E. Taylor. 1984. *Social Cognition*. Reading, MA: Addison-Wesley.

Gabor, Thomas. 1991. "Crime by the public." In Curt Griffiths and Margaret Jackson, eds., *Canadian Criminology: Perspectives on*

Crime and Criminality. Toronto: Harcourt Brace Jovanovich.

Gabor, Thomas, Micheline Baril, M. Cusson, D. Elie, Marc LeBlanc, and André Normandeau. 1987. *Armed Robbery: Cops, Robbers, and Victims*. Springfield, Ill.: Charles C. Thomas.

The Globe and Mail. 1989. February 11: 14.

Gordon, Paul. 1988. "Black people and the criminal law: Rhetoric and reality." *International Journal of the Sociology of Law* 16: 295–313.

Gould, Stephen Jay. 1981. *The Mismeasure of Man*. New York: W.W. Norton.

Griffiths, Curt and Simon Verdun-Jones. 1989. *Canadian Criminal Justice*. Toronto: Butterworths.

Hartshorne, M. and M.A. May. 1928. *Studies in Deceit*. New York: Macmillan.

Haskell, M.R. and L. Yablonsky. 1983. *Criminology: Crime and Criminality*. Boston: Houghton Mifflin.

Henry, F. and E. Ginzberg. 1985. *Who Gets the Work: A Test of Racial Discrimination in Employment*. Toronto: Urban Alliance on Race Relations and the Social Planning Council.

Herskovits, Melville J. 1930. *The Anthropometry of the American Negro*. New York: Columbia University Press.

Hindelang, Michael. 1982. "Race and Crime." In Leonard D. Savitz and N. Johnston, eds., *Contemporary Criminology*. Toronto: John Wiley.

Hirschi, Travis. 1969. *Causes of Delinquency*. Berkeley: University of California Press.

Hooton, Ernest A. 1939. *Crime and the Man*. Cambridge: Harvard University Press.

International Criminal Police Organization. 1988. *International Crime Statistics* 1985–86.

Jefferson, Tony. 1988. "Race, crime and policing: Empirical, theoretical and methodological issues." *International Journal of the Sociology of Law* 16: 521–39.

Landau, Simha. 1981. "Juveniles and the police." *British Journal of Criminology* 21: 27–46.

Landau, Simha and G. Nathan. 1983. "Selecting delinquents for cautioning in the London metropolitan area." *British Journal of Criminology* 28: 128–49.

LaPrairie, Carol. 1989. *The Role of Sentencing in the Over-Representation of Aboriginal People in Correctional Institutions*. Ottawa: Department of Justice.

Lombroso, Cesare. 1968. *Crime: Its Causes and Remedies*. (English edition) Montclair, NJ: Patterson Smith. (Original publication: *Le Crime, causes et remèdes*, 1899).

Lombroso-Ferrero, Gina. 1972. *Criminal Man According to the Classification of Cesare Lombroso*. Montclair, NJ: Patterson Smith, 1972 (Originally published 1911).

Lundman, R., R. Sykes and J. Clark. 1978. "Police control of juveniles: A replication." *Journal of Research in Crime and Delinquency* 15: 74–91.

Lynn, Michael. 1989. "Race difference in sexual behaviour: A critique of Rushton and Bogaert's evolutionary hypothesis." *Journal of Research in Personality* 23: 1–6.

Mawson, Anthony. 1989. "Review of *Homicide*" (Daly and Wilson, 1988). *Contemporary Sociology* March: 238–40.

Merton, Robert K. 1968. *Social Theory and Social Structure*. Glencoe: Free Press.

Nisbett, Richard and Lee Ross. 1980. *Human Inference: Strategies and Shortcomings of Social Judgement*. Englewood Cliffs, NJ: Prentice-Hall.

Pope, Carl E. 1979. "Race and crime re-visited." *Crime and Delinquency* 25: 345–57.

Radzinowicz, Leon and Joan King. 1977. *The Growth of Crime: The International Experience*. London: Penguin.

Roberts, Julian V. and Nicholas R. White. 1986. "Public estimates of recidivism rates: Consequences of a criminal stereotype." *Canadian Journal of Criminology* 28: 229–41.

Rojek, Dean G. 1983. "Social status and delinquency: Do self-reports and official reports match?" In Gordon P. Waldo, ed., *Measurement Issues in Criminal Justice*. Beverly Hills: Sage.

Rushton, J. Philippe. 1987. "Population differences in rule-following behaviour: Race, evolution and crime." Paper presented to the

39th Annual Meeting of the American Society of Criminology, Montreal, November 11–14.

———. 1988. "Race differences in behaviour: A review and evolutionary analysis." *Personality and Individual Differences* 9: 1009–24.

———. 1989. "Race differences in sexuality and their correlates: Another look at physiological models." *Journal of Research in Personality* 23: 35–54.

Silberman, Charles. 1978. *Criminal Violence, Criminal Justice*. New York: Vintage.

The Toronto Star. 1989. February 17: 20.

United States Department of Justice. 1983. *Sourcebook of Criminal Justice Statistics*. Washington, DC: Bureau of Justice Statistics.

———. 1986. *Criminal Victimization in the United States*. Washington, DC: Bureau of Justice Statistics.

———. 1987. *Sourcebook of Criminal Justice Statistics*. Washington, DC: Bureau of Justice Statistics.

———. 1989. *Sourcebook of Criminal Justice Statistics*. Washington, DC: Bureau of Justice Statistics.

Wallerstein, James S. and Clement J. Wyle. 1947. "Our law-abiding lawbreakers." *Probation* 25: 107–12.

Williams, Jay and Martin Gold. 1972. "From delinquent behaviour to official delinquency." *Social Problems* 20: 209–29.

Wolfgang, Marvin. 1958. *Patterns in Criminal Homicide*. Philadelphia: University of Pennsylvania Press.

Wolfgang, Marvin and Bernard Cohen. 1970. *Crime and Race: Conceptions and Misconceptions*. New York: Institute of Human Relations Press.

———. 1981. "Crime and race: The victims of crime." In Burt Galaway and Joe Hudson, eds., *Perspectives on Crime Victims*. St. Louis: C.V. Mosby.

Wolfgang, Marvin and Franco Ferracuti. 1982. *The Subculture of Violence*. Beverly Hills: Sage.

Zuckerman, Marvin and Nathan Brody. 1989. "Oysters, rabbits and people: A critique of 'race differences in behaviour' by J.P. Rushton." *Personality and Individual Differences* 9: 1025–33.

Chapter 29

Culture and Homicide in Canada and the United States

RHONDA L. LENTON

One of the most striking and well-known differences between Canada and the United States concerns their crime rates. Americans are roughly four times more likely than Canadians to commit homicide and rape, two and one-half times more likely to commit robbery, and one and one-quarter times more likely to commit burglary. While some of these differences may result partly from cross-national variations in legal definitions of crime, methods of counting crime, and levels of police surveillance, it is generally agreed that for the most violent crimes — homicide in particular — official crime rates reflect real behavioural differences between the two countries (Hagan, 1984: 48–55).

John Hagan refers to the most serious forms of deviance as "consensus crimes." In his judgement members of society broadly agree that the most violent crimes are the most serious crimes, and that their perpetrators deserve the most severe forms of punishment. Violent crime involves avoiding, neutralizing, and rejecting deeply and widely held societal norms and values. The rate of violent crime therefore hinges on the ability of a culture to define achievable goals, impose constraints on behaviour, and prevent both the neutralization of community standards and the creation of subcultures that oppose the dominant value system (Hagan, 1984: 80–120).

In explaining Canadian–American differences in homicide rates, Hagan follows this cultural approach. Borrowing from the work of S.D. Clark (1976), Seymour Martin Lipset (1986), and others, Hagan argues that two sets of historical forces created Canadian and American value systems, which differ in important respects and account for the lower rate of homicide in Canada (Hagan, 1984: 117–18, 147–48, 230–35; Hagan and Leon, 1977). First, in the early years of North American economic development, Canada's frontier was "harder" than that of the United States. That is, Canada was a vast and inhospitable country compared with the United States, and its natural resources were less accessible. While the development of the American frontier could therefore be left to the initiative of the lone, relatively lawless entrepreneur, the exploitation of the Canadian frontier required the assistance of state-supported armies, police forces, and other social organizations such as the established Roman Catholic and Anglican Churches. The "wild West" shaped American attitudes toward authority, the state, and law and order quite differently from the way the harmonious development of the Canadian frontier influenced Canadians' attitudes: Canadians became more respectful of authority and less inclined to break the law.

Source: "Homicide in Canada and the U.S.A.: A Critique of the Hagan Thesis," *Canadian Journal of Sociology* 14, 2 (1989): 163–78. Reprinted by permission of the publisher.

According to Hagan, the second main historical force that produced lower Canadian rates of violent crime was the tenacity of Canada's ties to elitist and conservative Britain. Presumably, those ties were reinforced during the American Revolution, when loyalist tories migrated northward, and persisted well into the twentieth century. Canadians' characteristic deference to authority supposedly derived in part from the British connection. In contrast, the American Revolution severed the American bond to Britain and institutionalized a deep and abiding anti-authoritarianism in the American psyche. Presumably, that attitude is reflected in the greater propensity of Americans to commit violent crimes.

My purpose in this chapter is not to dispute the accuracy of the violent crime statistics, historical interpretations, or attitudinal differences discussed by Hagan. Other analysts have already raised serious questions about the precision of some of the "facts" he uncritically accepts. For example, there is a considerable body of historical scholarship contesting the old view, endorsed by Hagan, that the Loyalists were tories (Jones, 1985; Upton, 1967). Similarly, an analysis of recent sample survey data indicates that the purported Canadian–American value differences either do not exist or are in the opposite direction from that predicted by Hagan (and Clark and Lipset before him). According to Baer, Grabb, and Johnston (1990), Canadians are *less* respectful of government leaders and institutions than are Americans, and *less* traditional than Americans about the need for crime control.[1]

Whether or not the predicted Canadian–American value differences actually exist, my aim is to demonstrate that variation in homicide rates is better explained by structural factors. I argue that the relationship posited by Hagan between some measured value differences and homicide rates may be largely an artifact of his choice of data. Hagan bases his argument mainly on a comparison of only two cases over a relatively short period of time. By increasing the cross-sectional and longitudinal variation in his independent and dependent variables, however, I cast doubt on the accuracy of Hagan's generalizations.

I also suggest an alternative explanation of Canadian–American differences in homicide rates. I argue that certain features of American and Canadian social structure account for Canadian–American differences in homicide rates better than do alleged cultural differences. Specifically, variations in the racial composition of the two countries and in the level of income inequality stand out as the two most important determinants of cross-national differences in my analysis. In general, I agree with Ian Taylor's view that "[t]here is a clear need to examine the *structure* of ... society (its demography, political economy and social institutions) and to relate these to ... pathological social interactions like homicide" (Taylor, 1983: 97; emphasis in the original). Apart from criticizing Hagan's thesis, then, my paper adds modest empirical substance to Taylor's assertion.

The persuasiveness of my argument is compromised by the type of data I employ to make my case. It is by now widely recognized that, ideally, the study of homicide etiology should combine data on the characteristics of individual perpetrators and victims with structural data on community and regional characteristics. Such data would help researchers guard against making ecologically fallacious inferences and enable them to explain how individual-level behaviour accounts for aggregate statistical patterns. In practice, however, most analyses of homicide in North America are based on aggregated data for provinces and territories (in Canada), or states and Standard Metropolitan Statistical Areas (in the United States). Individual-level data are difficult to obtain from official sources, and when they are available they are usually presented in the form of nationwide, two- or three-variable contingency tables. Thus, my approach, if deficient, is at least standard. For the most part I use provinces and territories as units of analysis. I also inspect some Statistics Canada contingency tables containing individual-level data for Canada as a whole and report relevant results of the past fifteen years of (almost exclusively American) research on homicide etiology. The result is less a definitive refutation of Hagan's thesis than an attempt to underscore some of its weaknesses and propose an alternative approach. I do, however, claim that the alternative theoretical argument I offer is both plausible and apparently more consistent with available data than is Hagan's thesis.

VARIATION OVER TIME

A key argument in Hagan's thesis is that the ratio of American to Canadian homicide rates has remained about the same or increased over time. A relatively constant or increasing ratio suggests that values that first crystallized 100 to 200 years ago remain obdurate and that cultural differences between the two North American countries exert an enduring influence on criminal behaviour despite vast economic, political, and legal changes. A widely fluctuating or declining ratio of American to Canadian homicide rates, in contrast, would suggest that the values discussed by Hagan have no persistent effect on criminal behaviour.

When Hagan first made his case he compared American and Canadian homicide rates in 1957, 1960, 1967, 1968, and 1970. He concluded that the ratio of American to Canadian homicide rates is increasing over time (Hagan and Leon, 1977: 198–99). He later compared homicide rates for the years 1960–80 and concluded that the ratio has remained constant over time (Hagan, 1984: 50).

It is unclear why Hagan selected these particular years for comparison. It does, however, seem that he based his conclusions on a simple visual inspection of the data. Table 29.1 assembles American and Canadian homicide rates from 1954 (the first year for which Canadian data are readily accessible from secondary sources) to 1986 (the last year for which data are currently available). Although the ratio of

TABLE 29.1 HOMICIDE RATES (PER 100 000 POPULATION), CANADA AND U.S.A., 1954–1986

	CANADA	U.S.A.	U.S.A./CANADA RATIO
1954	1.2	4.8	4.0
1955	1.2	4.5	3.8
1956	1.3	4.6	3.5
1957	1.2	4.5	3.8
1958	1.4	4.5	3.1
1959	1.2	4.5	3.8
1960	.9	5.1	5.7
1961	1.2	4.8	4.0
1962	1.4	4.5	3.3
1963	1.3	4.6	3.5
1964	1.3	4.9	3.8
1965	1.4	5.1	3.6
1966	1.2	5.6	4.7
1967	1.7	6.2	3.7
1968	1.8	6.9	3.8
1969	1.8	7.3	4.1
1970	2.2	7.9	3.6
1971	2.2	8.6	3.9
1972	2.4	9.0	3.8
1973	2.5	9.4	3.8
1974	2.7	9.8	3.6
1975	3.1	9.6	3.1
1976	2.9	8.8	3.0
1977	3.0	8.8	2.9
1978	2.8	9.0	3.2
1979	2.7	9.7	3.6
1980	2.5	10.2	4.1
1981	2.7	9.8	3.7
1982	2.7	9.1	3.4
1983	2.7	8.3	3.0
1984	2.7	7.9	3.0
1985	2.8	7.9	2.8
1986	2.2	8.6	3.9

SOURCES: Canada, 1954–59: Statistics Canada (1973c: 8); Canada and U.S.A., 1960–80: Hagan (1984: 50); Canada, 1981–86: Statistics Canada (1987: 85); U.S.A., 1954–59: Bureau of the Census (1976: 414); U.S.A., 1981–86: Statistics Canada (1987: 83).

American to Canadian rates does not fluctuate widely from year to year, it appears to be very slowly *declining*. Rather than substantiating Hagan's thesis, these findings offer some support for Irving Louis Horowitz's contrary claim that homicide data reveal a tendency for the "cultural gap" between Canada and the United States to be closing over time. Horowitz asserts that this gap is narrowing due to the Americanization of Canada that is caused by such structural forces as increasing American economic and political influence (Horowitz, 1973: 341 and *passim*).

VARIATION BY REGION

A second problem with Hagan's analysis is that he considers only two cases—Canada and the United States—and is consequently unable to determine whether the relationship he observes between homicide rates and culture patterns is fortuitous or generalizable. One way of getting around this problem is by comparing units of analysis smaller than countries, such as provinces or states.[2] This seems sensible because there is more variation in homicide rates *within* both Canada and the United States than *between* the two countries. In 1986, the coefficient of variation (the standard deviation over the mean) of homicide rates within Canada was 1.534. Within the U.S. the coefficient of variation was .664, and between Canada and the U.S. it was only .593 (raw data sources: Department of Justice, 1987: 44–50; Statistics Canada, 1987: 61). The range of homicide rates across the Canadian provinces was almost the same in 1986 (27) as the range of homicide rates across the American states (30). The ranges and coefficients of variation show that national comparisons mask wide regional variations within the two countries. This raises the question of whether it makes much sense to assume national homogeneity in values and homicidal behaviour, as does a simple comparison of national mean rates.

In order to test the stability of correlations across time, I calculated zero-order correlations for 1986, 1981, 1976, and 1971.[3] In order to test the robustness of correlations across groups of cases, I used all twelve cases—that is, the ten provinces and two territories. Next, the Northwest Territories, which has the highest homicide rate and the second smallest population of the twelve jurisdictions, was removed and the correlations recalculated. Then the Yukon, which generally has the second highest homicide rate and the smallest population of the twelve jurisdictions, was removed and the correlations calculated for a third time. Finally, both the Northwest Territories and the Yukon were removed and the correlations calculated for a fourth time.[4]

In Hagan's view, one correlate of homicide rates is the strength of the "Imperial connection." Presumably, an indicator of British influence is the proportion of British-origin people in each province or territory: it follows from Hagan's argument that the greater the proportion British-origin, the lower the homicide rate. In fact, out of the sixteen correlations between proportion British and the homicide rate, only ten are in the predicted direction and statistically significant at the .05 level.[5] Proportion British is in the predicted direction and statistically significant across time only if the two northern territories are omitted; and proportion British is in the predicted direction and statistically significant across groups of cases only in 1971 and 1981.

Hagan also suggests that Canadian values have been profoundly influenced by the predominance of the Anglican and Roman Catholic Churches, which provided Canada with "a set of hierarchical and traditionally rooted control mechanisms" that reinforced the effects of the hard frontier and the British connection (Hagan and Leon, 1977: 184; cf. Lipset, 1986: 124–28). In contrast, Protestant sectarianism flourished in the United States, thus reinforcing individualism and lack of respect for authority in that country. Yet of the 32 correlations between provincial and territorial homicide rates, on the one hand, and proportion Catholic and proportion Anglican, on the other, none is in the predicted direction and statistically significant. Combining proportion Catholic and proportion Anglican into one index does not alter the conclusion that provincial and territorial homicide rates do not increase with the greater numerical prevalence of Catholics and Anglicans.

VARIATION BY RACE AND ECONOMIC CONDITION

The foregoing analysis generates only weak support for Hagan's thesis. The best that can be said for his argument is that proportion British predicts homicide rates well for the ten provinces. However, once the territories are included in the analysis, proportion British fails to perform very well. And proportion Catholic and proportion Anglican systematically fail to predict homicide rates.

An alternative explanation of the Canadian–American difference in homicide rates can be derived from research on homicide conducted mainly in the United States over the past fifteen years. Perhaps the best substantiated finding of both ecological and individual-level analyses of homicide etiology in the United States is that poor, young, urban Blacks and Hispanics are tremendously overrepresented among homicide offenders (e.g., Williams, 1984). In 1986, for example, Blacks accounted for 48.0 percent and Hispanics for 15.7 percent of American murderers, yet they composed, respectively, only 12 percent and 6 percent of the American population (Department of Justice, 1987: 182, 185). Significantly, Canadian homicide statistics for poor Native Canadians are equally startling. In 1986, for instance, Native Canadians accounted for 21 percent of Canadian murderers for whom race could be ascertained, yet Native people represented a mere 2 percent of the population (Statistics Canada, 1987: 95). There is a consistently strong and statistically significant association between homicide rates in the Canadian provinces and territories and the proportion of the population that is of Native origin: fifteen of the sixteen relevant correlations are in the predicted direction and statistically significant.

The racial skewedness of homicide in both Canada and the United States, and the dissimi-

lar racial compositions of the two countries have important implications for Hagan's thesis. Consider, for instance, that the 1986 non-Black, non-Hispanic American homicide rate was 3.1 (compared with 8.6 for the entire American population). The 1986 non-Native Canadian rate was 1.7 (compared with 2.2 for the entire Canadian population). If one compares American non-Blacks and non-Hispanics with Canadian non-Natives, then the 1986 American–Canadian homicide ratio of 3.9 falls to a much less dramatic 1.8.[6] Hagan virtually dismisses the significance of the racial composition of Canada and the United States in interpreting the two countries' different homicide rates (Hagan and Leon, 1977: 199; contrast Horowitz, 1973: 341). The fact is, however, that differences in racial composition account for over half the discrepancy that Hagan set out to explain.

Despite the fact that Hagan makes no mention of the higher level of poverty and inequality in the United States as compared with Canada, some portion of the remaining discrepancy is likely the result of the different distribution of economic advantages in the two countries (cf. Horowitz, 1973: 341). Consider the following:

1. We know from American research that measures of economic well-being, both at the aggregate and individual level, are associated with homicide rates (Blau and Blau, 1982; Loftin and Hill, 1974; Smith and Parker, 1980; Williams, 1984; Williams and Flewelling, 1988). To varying degrees in different studies, unemployment, poverty, levels of inequality, and so forth, have been reported to promote homicidal behaviour independent of the effects of race. While there has been some inconsistency in findings on the effects of economic variables, recent research suggests that that is because such effects are indirect and mediated by levels of family disruption (Sampson, 1987).

2. In Canada, too, economic condition appears to be associated with propensity to commit homicide. Thus, from 1961 to 1974, fully 56 percent of murder suspects had a primary education or less (compared with 35 percent

of the population in 1971); and only 3 percent of murder suspects had a university
education (compared with 10 percent of the
population in 1971) (Statistics Canada,
1976: 99). In that same period, 61 percent of
homicide suspects were blue-collar workers
or self-employed workers in the primary
sector (Statistics Canada, 1976: 102) compared with 36 percent of the population in
those occupational categories in 1971
(Kalbach and McVey, 1979: 290).

3. Cross-national studies including Canada and
   the United States as cases have also found
   that homicide rates are positively associated
   with levels of inequality (Krahn, Hartnagel,
   and Gartrell, 1986; Messner, 1982). In this
   connection it is of interest that the level of
   income inequality in Canada is considerably
   lower than that in the United States. In the
   mid-1970s the Gini index of income inequality was .33 in Canada and .41 in the United
   States (Krahn, Hartnagel, and Gartrell, 1986:
   295), and the gap between the two countries
   seems to have widened during the 1980s (cf.
   Banting, 1987, and Rothschild, 1988).

In my analysis, structural poverty (cf. Loftin
and Hill, 1974: 719) is operationalized as an
index constructed from two items: the infant
mortality rate and the proportion of households
reporting no income.[7] Scores on both these
items were standardized and added together to
create the index. Family disruption (cf. Sampson, 1987: 356) is operationalized as an index
constructed from three items: the proportion of
lone-parent families, the incidence of marital
separation, and the incidence of divorce. As with
the structural poverty index, scores on these
items were standardized and added together to
create the index.

As a predictor of homicide, structural poverty performs nearly as well as percent Native,
with thirteen of sixteen relevant correlations
attaining statistical significance. The correlations between family disruption and homicide
are much less robust and stable, with only four

of the sixteen relevant correlations attaining
statistical significance. I surmise that my family
disruption index performs poorly in the
Canadian context because it is derived from
research on Black Americans and therefore fails
to tap manifestations of family disruption
among Native Canadians. Divorce, separation,
and single-parent families are relatively common in American urban ghettos, but Native
Canadians do not appear to be more prone to
these forms of family breakdown than other
Canadians. For Native Canadians, family violence and incest seem to be more valid indicators of family breakdown (Shkilnyk, 1985).
Unfortunately, however, systematically collected national data on family violence and incest
by ethnic group are unavailable.

In the light of these findings it is tempting to
model my argument along the lines of Figure
29.1. I propose that structural poverty and racial
discrimination are the two principal causes of
homicide. Structural poverty exerts its impact
both directly and indirectly through its effects
on family disruption.

DISCUSSION

If murder is the prototypical crime of passion, it
seems evident that passion is much more likely
to take such a violent course in particular types
of communities. Cross-sectional data from both
Canada and the United States suggest that when
racial discrimination, endemic poverty, and family disruption cause hopelessness and rage, murder rates increase.

FIGURE 29.1 A CAUSAL MODEL OF HOMICIDE ETIOLOGY IN CANADA

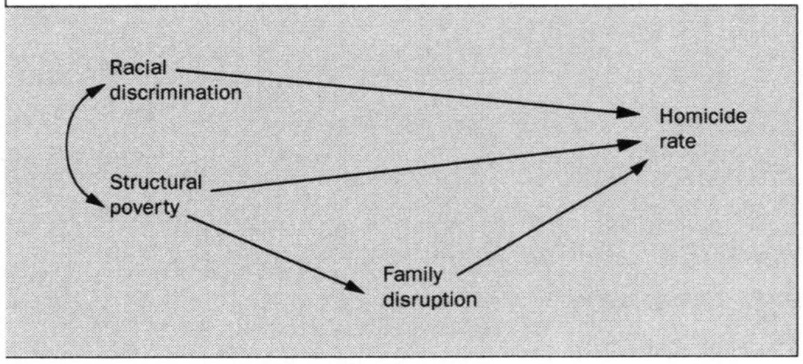

This social-structural interpretation is of course at variance with Hagan's argument, which borrows heavily from the "subculture of violence" thesis, until recently the dominant explanation of homicide in the United States (Wolfgang and Ferracuti, 1967). Darnell Hawkins, a student of homicide among American Blacks and a critic of the subculture of violence thesis, summarizes the thesis by noting that it

> tends to identify the value system of a given subculture as the locus of crime causation. Emphasis is also placed upon the role of social learning as the principal process by which aggressive behavior is acquired. While there is some attention paid to the social, economic and political deprivation within subcultures, such deprivation is itself seldom seen as a direct cause of crime. That is, the impact of deprivation on crime is mediated by social values—in particular the existence of a positive attitude toward the use of violence. (Hawkins, 1986: 112)

In like fashion, Hagan tries to account for American–Canadian differences in homicide rates by examining value differences between the two countries and, in the process, ignoring differences in racial composition and the distribution of economic advantages.

The data assembled here do not unequivocally undermine the cultural thesis and support a structural interpretation of variation in homicide rates across Canadian regions and between Canada and the United States. This is due partly to problems stemming from the highly aggregated nature of most of the data reviewed here and partly to measurement problems. Although my inspection of individual-level contingency tables from Canadian government sources does suggest that my argument is not ecologically fallacious, I cannot be absolutely certain that the relationships discovered here hold at lower levels of aggregation or at the individual level because most of my data are highly aggregated. Moreover, partly because I use ecological data, my independent variables are highly correlated, thus preventing the construction of a multivari-

ate model. On these grounds alone there is much room for additional research.

In addition, some of the measures used here —such as proportion British and proportion Native—are not unambiguously structural or cultural (cf. Loftin and Hill, 1974). Thus, it is unclear to what degree the prevalence of members of a given group indicates something about the value system of a particular region or about its social structure. Better measures are clearly needed. Until they are available, one is obliged to note that there is apparently considerable variation in homicide rates across Native Canadian groups (compare, for example, Fisher, 1987; French, 1988; and Shkilnyk, 1985). This casts doubt on the notion that there is some culturally uniform cause of homicide among Native Canadians.

All these qualifications notwithstanding, available evidence suggests that the conviction with which Hagan endorses the cultural theory of Canadian–American differences in homicide rates is unwarranted. The evidence supporting a structural theory is somewhat stronger, but considerably more research is needed before one can hope to call closure on the debate.

CONCLUSION

I noted at the beginning of this chapter that homicide is considered by Hagan to be one variant of a broad class of "consensus" crimes, including murder, rape, incest, and kidnapping. According to Hagan, these are the most violent crimes and, as a result, members of society generally agree that they are the most serious crimes; their perpetrators receive the most severe forms of punishment; attitudes toward these crimes are weakly, if at all, related to status group membership; social and economic forces play a relatively small role in designating such acts as deviant; and these crimes are best explained by consensus theories, which focus on how cultures succeed or fail in imposing constraints on deviant behaviour. Hagan argues that, in contrast, crimes that do not match the criteria listed above are better explained by labelling, conflict, and Marxist theories, which emphasize the historical variability of crime and the manner in which dominant groups define and punish criminal behaviour.

My critique has questioned the applicability of a consensus theory to one of the most violent types of crime in two countries. But, more broadly, the foregoing analysis calls into question the utility of viewing the most violent crimes as consensus crimes. For in two senses—one concerning social definition, the other etiology—even homicide is a conflict crime. Consider, first, that some types of widespread killing are not socially defined as serious crimes because to do so would harm corporate interests; in contrast, homicide is "allowed" to be socially defined as a serious crime because it does not harm corporate interests. Thus, deaths that result from industrial pollution and the failure to implement more stringent worker safety legislation account for many more deaths per year than homicide. Yet these acts are not consensually defined as serious crimes, they are not subject to strict surveillance, they are often not detected and counted by authorities, and their perpetrators are typically not punished severely when detected. Corporate influence is surely a major socioeconomic force that prevents such killing from being classified as a crime on a par with homicide. As these examples illustrate, to the degree that there is consensus about what kind of killing is a serious crime, that consensus is not "given" by culture but is manufactured by the distribution of power in society.[8] Crimes like homicide are *mala en sa* (wrong in themselves), but they are also *mala prohibita* (wrong by prohibition).

Homicide is also a conflict crime from an etiological point of view. The distribution of homicide by race, class, sex, age, and level of inequality indicates that most homicide is a manifestation of social conflict, a violent response to racial, class, and sexual antagonism.[9] As Ian Taylor (1983: 84) writes, "antagonistic or competitive social relationships in patriarchal, capitalist societies tend to produce violent solutions to individuals' social, sexual or financial problems." Cultural interpretations of violent crime like Hagan's deflect our attention from the ways in which homicide and other violent crimes are, like all forms of deviance, socially constructed and socially caused.[10] Such interpretations should therefore be treated with appropriate sociological skepticism.

NOTES

I would like to thank Robert Brym, John Fox, Graham Lowe, and three anonymous *CJS* reviewers for helpful comments on an earlier version of this paper.

1. More generally, Hagan fails to cite some published evidence that refutes the subculture of violence thesis (e.g., Erlanger, 1974).
2. One could also compare more countries. This strategy is adopted by Tom Truman (1971), for example, whose findings, like mine, are inconsistent with Hagan's argument.
3. I correlated 1986 and 1981 homicide data with 1981 data on the ethnic and religious composition and family disruption rates of the provinces and territories and 1980–81 data on structural poverty. Similarly, I correlated 1976 and 1971 homicide data with 1971 data on the ethnic and religious composition and family disruption rates of the provinces and territories and 1970–71 data on structural poverty. This was mainly because of limitations on the availability of published data (e.g., 1986 data on the ethnic and religious composition of the provinces and territories are not yet available from Statistics Canada). In addition, over the course of a decade the provinces and territories are unlikely to change their ranks on a variable like the rate of divorce or the infant mortality rate, so I collected data on these variables for only one year per decade for the sake of parsimony.
4. Although there are some outliers in the provincial–territorial scatterplots, there are none in the province-only scatterplots.

5. The use of tests of significance on population data is now fairly common and is justified by Blalock (1979: 241–43) on the grounds that such tests help eliminate "explanations" based on the existence of chance processes.

6. American Native people and Canadian Blacks also seem to have higher homicide rates than one would expect on the basis of their representation in the population, but they are relatively small groups and their overrepresentation is not as striking as that of the racial minorities mentioned above. Thus, in 1986 American Native people amounted to very roughly 0.5 percent of the American population and accounted for 0.9 percent of homicide arrests (Department of Justice, 1987: 183). In the period 1961–74, about 1.2 percent of murders in Canada were committed by Blacks, very roughly double the proportion of Blacks in the population (Statistics Canada, 1976: 86–87).

7. I also constructed a measure of income inequality, but it performed poorly as a predictor of homicide, reaching statistical significance in only five of the sixteen relevant cases. This is probably because large regional differences in the cost of living make income inequality a problematic measure of economic disadvantage in Canada.

8. In fact, where homicide is economically beneficial it may be positively sanctioned. See, for example, Eisenberg's (1981: 300) discussion of infanticide among the !Kung San of the Kalahari and the Netsilik Inuit of northwestern Hudson Bay — peoples who are warm and indulgent toward their children and yet defend the practice of infanticide because of an "unpredictable subsistence base."

9. This by no means implies that the violence is directed principally at superordinate groups. Quite the contrary: most suspect–victim relationships do not in fact cross racial, class, and family lines. For example, from 1961 to 1974, 39.3 percent of suspect–victim relationships in Canada were domestic relationships and another 30.2 percent were social or business relationships (Taylor, 1983: 101).

10. My argument holds even more emphatically for violent crimes other than homicide that Hagan classifies as consensus crimes, such as rape and incest. All aspects of rape and incest reflect power imbalances and social conflict (Toronto Rape Crisis Centre 1985; Lenton, 1989). For example, there is dissensus, especially between men and women, over how rape should be defined, over how serious a crime rape is, and over how severely rapists should be punished; and the likelihood of detection, apprehension, and punishment appears to vary inversely with the ratio of the victim's to the perpetrator's power.

REFERENCES

Baer, Doug, Edward Grabb, and William A. Johnston. 1990. "The values of Canadians and Americans: A critical analysis and reassessment." *Social Forces* 68: 693–713.

Banting, Keith. 1987. "The welfare state and inequality in the 1980s." *Canadian Review of Sociology and Anthropology* 24: 309–38.

Blalock, Hubert M., Jr. 1979. *Social Statistics*. Rev. 2nd ed. New York: McGraw-Hill.

Blau, Judith R. and Peter M. Blau. 1982. "The cost of inequality: Metropolitan structured and violent crime." *American Sociological Review* 47: 114–29.

Bureau of the Census. 1976. *The Statistical History of the United States*. Washington, DC: U.S. Bureau of the Census.

Clark, S.D. 1976. *Canadian Society in Historical Perspective*. Toronto: McGraw-Hill Ryerson.

Department of Justice. 1983. *Report to the Nation on Crime and Justice*. Washington DC: U.S. Department of Justice.

———. 1987. *Uniform Crime Reports, 1986*. Washington, DC: U.S. Department of Justice, Federal Bureau of Investigation.

Devine, Joel A., Joseph F. Sheley, and M. Dwayne Smith. 1988. "Macroeconomic and social-control policy influences on crime rate changes, 1945–1985." *American Sociological Review* 53: 407–20.

Eisenberg, Leon. 1981. "Cross-cultural and historical perspectives on child abuse and neglect." *Child Abuse and Neglect* 5: 299–308.

Erlanger, Howard S. 1974. "The empirical status of the subculture of violence thesis." *Social Problems* 22: 280–92.

Fisher, A.D. 1987. "Alcoholism and race: The misapplication of both concepts to North American Indians." *Canadian Review of Sociology and Anthropology* 24: 81–98.

French, Orland. 1988. "Where man belongs to the land." *The Globe and Mail* (24 September), D5.

Hagan, John. 1984. *The Disreputable Pleasures: Crime and Deviance in Canada*. 2nd ed. Toronto: McGraw-Hill Ryerson.

Hagan, John and Jeffrey Leon. 1977. "Philosophy and sociology of crime control." *Sociological Inquiry* 47: 181–208.

Hawkins, Darnell F. 1986. "Black and white homicide differentials: Alternatives to an inadequate theory." In Darnell F. Hawkins, ed., *Homicide among Black Americans*, 109–35. New York: University Press of America.

Horowitz, Irving Louis. 1973. "The hemispheric connection: A critique and corrective to the entrepreneurial thesis of development with special emphasis on the Canadian case." *Queen's Quarterly* 80: 327–59.

Jones, Elwood. 1985. "The Loyalists and Canadian history." *Journal of Canadian Studies* 20(3): 149–56.

Kalbach, Warren E. and Wayne W. McVey. 1979. *The Demographic Bases of Canadian Society*. 2nd ed. Toronto: McGraw-Hill Ryerson.

Krahn, Harvey, Timothy F. Hartnagel, and John W. Gartrell. 1986. "Income inequality and homicide rates: Cross-national data and criminological theories." *Criminology* 24: 269–95.

Lenton, Rhonda L. 1989. "Parental discipline and child abuse." Unpublished PhD dissertation. Toronto: Department of Sociology, University of Toronto.

Lipset, Seymour Martin. 1986. "Historical traditions and national characteristics: A comparative analysis of Canada and the United States." *Canadian Journal of Sociology* 11: 113–55.

Loftin, Colin and Robert H. Hill. 1974. "Regional subculture and homicide: An examination of the Gastil-Hackney thesis." *American Sociological Review* 39: 714–24.

Messner, Steven F. 1982. "Societal development, social equality, and homicide: A cross-national test of a Durkheimian model." *Social Forces* 61: 225–40.

Rothschild, Emma. 1988. "The real Reagan economy." *New York Review of Books* 35 (11) June 30: 46–53.

Sampson, Robert J. 1987. "Urban black violence: The effect of male joblessness and family disruption." *American Journal of Sociology* 3: 348–82.

Shkilnyk, Anastasia M. 1985. *A Poison Stronger than Love: The Destruction of an Ojibwa Community*. New Haven, CT: Yale University Press.

Smith, M. Dwayne and Robert Nash Parker. 1980. "Type of homicide and variation in regional rates." *Social Forces* 59: 136–47.

Statistics Canada. 1973a. *1971 Census of Canada. Families: Family by Size and Type*. Ottawa: Statistics Canada.

———. 1973b. *1971 Census of Canada. Population: Ethnic Groups*. Ottawa: Statistics Canada.

———. 1973c. *Murder Statistics, 1971*. Ottawa: Statistics Canada, Judicial Division.

———. 1973d. *Murder Statistics, 1961–1970*. Ottawa: Statistics Canada, Judicial Division.

———. 1974. *Vital Statistics*. Volume 3. *Deaths: 1971*. Ottawa: Statistics Canada.

———. 1975. *1971 Census of Canada. Families: One-Parent Families*. Ottawa: Statistics Canada.

———. 1976. *Homicide in Canada: A Statistical Synopsis*. Ottawa: Statistics Canada, Justice Statistics Division.

————. 1978. *Homicide Statistics, 1976*. Ottawa: Statistics Canada, Justice Statistics Division.

————. 1982a. *1981 Census of Canada. Census Families in Private Households: Persons, Children at Home, Structure and Type, Living Arrangements*. Ottawa: Statistics Canada.

————. 1982b. *1981 Census of Canada. Population: Age, Sex and Marital Status: Canada, Provinces, Urban Size Groups, Rural Non-Farm and Rural Farm*. Ottawa: Statistics Canada.

————. 1982c. *Crime and Traffic Enforcement Statistics, 1981*. Ottawa: Statistics Canada, Canadian Centre for Justice Statistics.

————. 1983a. *1981 Census of Canada. Population: Religion*. Ottawa: Statistics Canada.

————. 1983b. *Vital Statistics*. Volume 1. *Births and Deaths: 1981*. Ottawa: Statistics Canada.

————. 1984a. *1981 Census of Canada. Ethnic Origin: Canada, Provinces, Urban Size Groups, Rural Non-Farm and Rural Farm*. Ottawa: Statistics Canada.

————. 1984b. *1981 Census of Canada. Private Households: Income: Canada, Provinces, Urban Size Groups, Rural Non-Farm and Rural Farm*. Ottawa: Statistics Canada.

————. 1986. *Homicide in Canada, 1984: A Statistical Perspective*. Ottawa: Statistics Canada, Canadian Centre for Justice Statistics, Law Enforcement Programme.

————. 1987. *Homicide in Canada, 1986*. Ottawa: Statistics Canada, Canadian Centre for Justice Statistics, Law Enforcement Programme.

Taylor, Ian. 1983. "Some reflections on homicide and violence in Canada." In *Crime, Capitalism and Community: Three Essays in Socialist Criminology*, 83–115. Toronto: Butterworths.

Toronto Rape Crisis Centre. 1985. "Rape." In Connie Guberman and Margie Wolfe, eds., *No Safe Place: Violence against Women and Children*, 61–86. Toronto: Women's Press.

Truman, Tom. 1971. "A critique of Seymour Martin Lipset's article, 'Value differences, absolute or relative: The English-speaking democracies.' " *Canadian Journal of Political Science* 4: 473–96.

Upton, L.F.S., ed. 1967. *The United Empire Loyalists: Men and Myths*. Toronto: Copp Clark.

Williams, Kirk R. 1984. "Economic sources of homicide: Reestimating the effects of poverty and inequality." *African Sociological Review* 49: 283–89.

Williams, Kirk R. and Robert L. Flewelling. 1988. "The social production of criminal homicide: A comparative study of disaggregated rates in American cities." *American Sociological Review* 53: 421–31.

Wolfgang, Marvin E. and Franco Ferracuti. 1967. *The Subculture of Violence: Towards an Integrated Theory in Criminology*. London: Tavistock.

PART 6 | GLOBAL DEVELOPMENT AND THE ENVIRONMENT

The Industrial Revolution began in Britain in the 1780s. For over two centuries it spread and brought prosperity to Western Europe, North America, Japan, and some other parts of Asia. Today, China, India, Brazil, Mexico, Indonesia, and other countries constituting over half the world's population are in the throes of rapid industrialization. At the same time, parts of Latin America and Asia and most of Africa south of the Sahara Desert remain economically stagnant and poor. This pattern of economic development raises two main questions. First, what accounts for the relative economic success of some countries over the past few decades and the relative economic failure of others? Second, how will the world cope with the environmental strain that results from the industrialization of most of the world?

The Chinese, Indians, and others want electricity, cars, VCRs, Pepsi, and Guess jeans just as much as Canadians do. They cannot, however, afford expensive pollution control measures. Consider only the fact that motor vehicles accounts for roughly half the carbon dioxide pollution in the world, which in turn is largely responsible for global warming. Imagine the consequences when the proportion of car owners in the populous, industrializing areas of Asia and Latin America increases from 5 percent to even 25 percent of the adult population!

Economic development is very difficult to achieve, as Yale University's Paul Kennedy, one of the most popular historians in the English-speaking world, shows in Chapter 30. Kennedy demonstrates that the countries that have managed to undergo rapid economic growth in the past 25 years — South Korea, Taiwan, Singapore, and Hong Kong — all emphasize the need for education (in order to create a highly trained work force), personal saving (to make investment capital readily available), centralized economic coordination (to help plan and subsidize industrial development), and export-led growth (to stimulate economic expansion). He predicts that while a few more countries in Asia and Latin America may move from "have-not" to "have" status in the twenty-first century, most countries, especially those in Africa, will remain destitute because they lack one or more of the four main social and political conditions that encourage economic growth.

From a demographic point of view, the less-industrialized countries are now in the position that Europe and North America were in between 1700 and 1870. Their populations are growing very rapidly because people are living longer and birth rates are high and barely falling. Today's 6 billion inhabitants of the planet are expected to multiply to about 10 billion in a century, and during that period the less developed countries are expected to increase their share of world population from 75 percent to 86 percent of the total.

A frequently voiced and increasingly popular solution to the problem of overpopulation in the less-industrialized countries is compulsory sterilization and other forms of coercive birth control. Some advocates even claim that economic development aid should be redirected to coercive family planning. In Chapter 31, Harvard University's Amartya Sen, one of the world's leading economic demographers and students of famine, shows how misguided such recommendations are. By carefully analyzing the situation in China, India, and other countries, he demonstrates that forced birth control often results in higher infant mortality and discrimination against female children, while the surest way to bring down the birth rate in the less-industrialized countries is to encourage economic development and improve the economic status and education of women. Once women enter the nonagricultural paid labour force, they quickly recognize the advantages of having few children, and the birth rate plummets.

For the first two centuries after the Industrial Revolution began in Britain, nature seemed exploitable without limit, a thing to be subdued and dominated in the name of economic progress and human development. In the last few decades of this century, however, circumstances have forced a growing number of people to recognize that industrial-era attitudes toward nature are not just naive, but also arrogant and foolhardy. For example:

- Since the Industrial Revolution, humans have been using increasing quantities of fossil fuels (coal, oil, gasoline, and so on). When burned, they release carbon dioxide (CO_2) into the atmosphere. The accumulation of CO_2 allows more solar radiation to enter the atmosphere and less solar radiation to escape. The result of this "greenhouse effect" is global warming and, eventually, potentially catastrophic climactic change, including the partial melting of the polar ice caps and the flooding of heavily populated coastal regions.

- CFCs (chlorofluorocarbons) are widely used in industry and by consumers, and they are burning a hole in the atmosphere's ozone layer. Ozone is a form of oxygen that blocks ultraviolet radiation from the sun. Let more ultraviolet radiation reach ground level and, as we are now witnessing, rates of skin cancer and crop damage increase.

- A wide range of toxic gases and liquids enter the environment as a result of industrial production, often with devastating consequences. For example, sulphur dioxide and other gases emitted by coal-burning power plants, pulp and paper mills, and motor-vehicle exhaust help to form an acid in the atmosphere that rains down on the earth, destroying forests and lakes.

- The world's forests help to clean the air, since photosynthesis uses carbon dioxide and produces oxygen. The tropical rain forests contain a varied plant life that is an important source of new drugs. The rain forests also produce moisture that is carried by wind currents to other parts of the globe and falls as rain. Despite the enormously important role the forests play, however, they are being rapidly depleted as a result of strip mining, the construction of huge pulp and paper mills and hydroelectric projects, and the deforestation of land by farmers and cattle grazers.

- A huge fleet of trawlers belonging to the highly industrialized countries has been equipped with sonar to help locate large concentrations of fish. Some of these ships use fine mesh nets to increase their catch. They have been enormously "successful." Fish stocks in some areas of the world, such as off the coast of Newfoundland, have been greatly depleted, devastating fishing communities and endangering one of the world's most important sources of protein.

Two main lessons may be drawn from these examples. First, issues of economic development can no longer be separated from those of the environment. Second, development problems have become **globalized**: increasingly, local developments have worldwide repercussions, while worldwide developments shape local events.

In general, because less-industrialized countries are poor and relatively powerless, the people living there suffer disproportionately from the effects of environmental degradation. Only the rich countries can enjoy the luxury of locating some of their dirtiest industries far from their population centres (including abroad) and cleaning up some of the local mess. The difficulty that the less-industrialized countries have in paying for pollution prevention and control, clean water, vaccines, soil irrigation, and basic sanitation services is closely related to the problem of international debt. The prices paid on world markets for the raw materials exported by less-developed countries have dropped by more than

50 percent since 1974. As a result, the less-developed countries have been forced to borrow enormous sums from banks in the rich industrialized countries. Some people in the rich countries complain that they are giving too much aid to the poor countries of the world, but the plain fact is that the poor countries now receive about U.S. $100 billion less per year in the form of aid than they pay to the rich countries in the form of interest and repayments of debt principal.

In Chapter 32, Lester R. Brown of the Worldwatch Institute in Washington, DC, outlines the main environmental challenges that face humanity in the twenty-first century. Brown is a firm believer in **sustainable growth**. In his view, economic growth and environmental degradation do not have to go hand in hand. To ensure sustainable growth, he calls for a shift from economics to ecology, from irrational markets to the rational deployment of resources for the benefit of all humankind. He makes several practical recommendations for how this can be achieved. For example, one of his proposals involves levying substantial "green taxes" on products and processes that pollute, deplete, or degrade natural systems while simultaneously cutting income taxes.

Whether individuals and governments in the rich industrialized countries will be willing to act along the lines recommended by Brown is an open question. My guess is that it will probably take many serious environmental disasters to convince us to do so; public opinion polls show that while many people pay lip service to environmental concerns, most are unwilling to do much about them unless it is convenient and cheap. One thing is, however, crystal clear. If people continue to think of themselves only as members of a particular nation, class or race, then Brown's recommendations are likely to fall on deaf ears. In that event, many citizens of the privileged countries will believe that it is in their self-interest to cut aid to the less-industrialized countries, to use just as many scarce resources as they wish to and can afford, and to object to the imposition of high environmental taxes on fossil fuels. They will be blind to the fact that such a narrow definition of self-interest may devastate all of humanity.

Much now seems to depend on whether we will be able to think and act as members of a single human group whose members share a common interest in survival. If we fail to take such a global view, if we insist instead on fighting to protect our narrow group privileges rather than humanity's general interest, we may not go the way of the dinosaurs, but future generations will in all likelihood suffer an existence that is nastier, more brutish, and shorter than that which we now enjoy.

GLOSSARY

Globalization is the increasing tendency for local social processes to have implications for the entire planet, and the increasing tendency for worldwide social forces to shape local events.

Sustainable growth refers to environmentally sound economic development.

CRITICAL THINKING QUESTIONS

1. What does it take to turn a "have not" into a "have" nation? Give examples to support your answer.
2. "We are sitting on a population time bomb." Do you agree or disagree? Explain your position.
3. How can industrial countries go through rapid economic growth and bring down their birth rates? Give examples to support your answer.
4. Is forced birth control the best way to reduce the birth rate? What are other methods of lowering the birth rate in the less-industrialized countries? Use examples from your readings in this section to support your answer.

5. How have countries like Hong Kong, South Korea, and Singapore achieved rapid economic growth? Can these countries serve as models for less-industrialized countries in Asia and Africa?

6. What would a technological advanced but environmentally sustainable economy look like?

7. What are some of the social forces that are facilitating and blocking the emergence of a technologically advanced but environmentally sustainable economy?

ANNOTATED BIBLIOGRAPHY

Benjamin R. Barber, *Jihad vs. McWorld: How Globalism and Tribalism Are Reshaping the World* (New York: Ballantine, 1996). The central conflict of our times is incisively analyzed in this heralded work.

Lester R. Brown et al., *State of the World 2000* (New York: W.W. Norton, 2000). In this definitive and widely acclaimed annual, the authors give up-to-the-minute details on the world's environmental crisis and its political, economic, and social ramifications.

Eric Hobsbawm, *Age of Extremes: The Short Twentieth Century, 1914–1991* (London: Abacus, 1994). It's long, it's opinionated, and it's a masterpiece by one of the world's greatest historians. Magnificently expands one's understanding of global twentieth-century development.

Chapter 30

Winners and Losers in the 21st Century

PAUL KENNEDY

1.

Everyone with an interest in international affairs must be aware that broad, global forces for change are bearing down upon humankind in both rich and poor societies alike. New technologies are challenging traditional assumptions about the way we make, trade, and even grow things. Automated workplaces in Japan intimate the end of the "factory system" that first arose in Britain's Industrial Revolution and spread around the world. Genetically engineered crops, cultivated in biotech laboratories, threaten to replace naturally grown sugar, vanilla, coconut oil, and other staple farm produce, and perhaps undermine field-based agriculture as we know it. An electronically driven, twenty-four-hour-a-day financial trading system has created a global market in, say, yen futures, over which nobody really has control. The globalization of industry and services permits multinationals to switch production from one country to another (where it is usually cheaper), benefitting the latter and hurting the former.

In addition to facing these technology-driven forces for change, human society is grappling with the effects of fast-growing demographic imbalances throughout the world. Whereas birth rates in richer societies plunge well below the rates that would replace their populations, poorer countries are experiencing a population explosion that may double or even treble their numbers over the next few decades. As these fast-swelling populations press upon the sur-rounding forests, grazing lands, and water supplies, they inflict dreadful damage upon local environments and may also be contributing to that process of global warming first created by the industrialization of the North a century and a half ago. With overpopulation and resource depletion undermining the social order, and with a global telecommunications revolution bringing television programs like *Dallas* and *Brideshead Revisited* to viewers everywhere from Central America to the Balkans, a vast illegal migration is under way as millions of families from the developing world strive to enter Europe and North America.

Although very different in form, these various trends, from global warming to twenty-four-hour-a-day trading, are *transnational* in character, crossing borders all over our planet, affecting local communities and distant societies at the same time, and reminding us that the earth, for all its divisions, is a single unit. Every country is challenged by these global forces for change, to a greater or lesser extent, and most are beginning to sense the need to prepare themselves for the twenty-first century. Whether *any* society is at present "well prepared" for the future is an open question;[1] but what is clear is that the regions of the globe most affected by the twin impacts of technology and demography lie in the developing world. Whether they succeed in harnessing the new technologies in an environmentally prudent

Source: "Preparing for the 21st Century: Winners and Losers," *The New York Review of Books* 40, 4 (February 11, 1993): 32–44. Copyright © 1993 Nyrev, Inc. Reprinted with permission from *The New York Review of Books*.

fashion, and at the same time go through a demographic transition, will probably affect the prospects of global peace in the next century more than any other factor. What, then, are their chances?

Before that question can be answered, the sharp contrasts among the developing countries in the world's different regions need to be noted here.[2] Perhaps nothing better illustrates those differences than the fact that, in the 1960s, South Korea had a per capita GNP exactly the same as Ghana's (US $230), whereas today it is ten to twelve times more prosperous.[3] Both possessed a predominantly agrarian economy and had endured a half-century or more of colonial rule. Upon independence, each faced innumerable handicaps in its effort to "catch up" with the West, and although Korea possessed a greater historical and cultural coherence, its chances may have seemed less promising, since it had few natural resources (apart from tungsten) and suffered heavily during the Korean War in the early 1950s.

Decades later, however, West African states remain among the most poverty-stricken countries in the world—the per capita gross national products of Niger, Sierra Leone, and Chad today, for example, are less than $500[4]—while Korea is entering the ranks of the high-income economies. Already the world's thirteenth largest trading nation, Korea is planning to become one of the richest countries of all in the twenty-first century,[5] whereas the nations of West Africa face a future, at least in the near term, of chronic poverty, malnutrition, poor health, and underdevelopment. Finally, while Korea's rising prosperity is attended by a decrease in population growth, most African countries still face a demographic explosion that erodes any gains in national output.

This divergence is not new, for there have always been richer and poorer societies; the prosperity gap in the seventeenth century—between, say, Amsterdam and the west coast of Ireland, or between such bustling Indian ports as Surat and Calcutta[6] and the inhabitants of New Guinean hill villages—must have been marked, although it probably did not equal the gulf between rich and poor nations today. The difference is that the twentieth-century global communications revolution has made such disparities widely known. This can breed resentments by poorer peoples against prosperous societies, but it can also provide a desire to emulate (as Korea emulated Japan). The key issue here is: What does it take to turn a "have not" into a "have" nation? Does it simply require imitating economic techniques, or does it involve such intangibles as culture, social structure, and attitudes toward foreign practices?

This discrepancy in performance between East Asia and sub-Saharan Africa clearly makes the term "third world" misleading. However useful the expression might have been in the 1950s, when poor, nonaligned, and recently decolonized states were attempting to remain independent of the two superpower blocs,[7] the rise of super-rich oil-producing countries a decade later already made the term questionable. Now that prosperous East Asian societies —Korea, Taiwan, and Singapore—possess higher per capita GNPs than Russia, Eastern Europe, and even West European states like Portugal, the word seems less suitable than ever. With Taiwanese or Korean corporations establishing assembly plants in the Philippines, or creating distribution networks within the European Community, we need to recognize the differences that exist among non-Western economies. Some scholars now categorize *five* separate types of "developing" countries in assessing the varied potential of societies in Asia, Africa, and Latin America.[8]

Relative national growth in the 1980s confirms these differences. Whereas East Asian economies grew on average at an impressive annual rate of 7.4 percent, those in Africa and Latin America gained only 1.8 and 1.7 percent respectively[9]—and since their populations grew faster, the net result was that they slipped backward, absolutely and relatively. Differences of economic structure also grew in this decade:

African and other primary commodity-producing countries were eager for higher raw-material prices, whereas the export-oriented manufacturing nations of East Asia sought to keep commodity prices low. The most dramatic difference occurred in the shares of world trade in manufactures, a key indicator of economic competitiveness (see Figure 30.1). Thus, while some scholars still refer to a dual world economy[10] of rich and poor countries, what is emerging is increasing differentiation. Why is this so?

The developing countries most successfully catching up with the West are the trading states of the Pacific and East Asia. Except for Communist regimes there, the Pacific rim countries (including the western provinces of Canada and the United States, and in part Australia) have enjoyed a lengthy boom in manufacturing, trade, and investment; but the centre of that boom is on the *Asian* side of the Pacific, fuelled chiefly by Japan's own spectacular growth and the stimulus given to neighbouring economies and trans-Pacific trade. According to one source:

> In 1962 the Western Pacific (notably East Asia) accounted for around 9 percent of world GNP, North America for 30 percent, and Western Europe for 31 percent. Twenty years later, the Western Pacific share had climbed to more than 15 percent, while North America's had fallen to 28 percent and Europe's to 27 percent. By the year 2000 it is likely that the Western Pacific will account for around one-quarter of world GNP, with the whole Pacific region increasing its share from just over 43 percent to around half of world GNP.[11]

East Asia's present boom is not, of course, uniform, and scholars distinguish between the different stages of economic and technological development in this vast region. Roughly speaking, the divisions would be as follows:

1. Japan, now the world's largest or second largest financial centre and, increasingly, the most innovative high-tech nation in the nonmilitary field;

2. the four East Asian "tigers" or "dragons," the newly industrialized economies (NIEs) of Singapore, Hong Kong, Taiwan, and South Korea, of which the latter two possess bigger populations and territories than the two port-city states, but all of which have enjoyed export-led growth in recent decades;

3. the larger Southeast Asian states of Thailand, Malaysia, and Indonesia, which, stimulated by foreign (chiefly Japanese) investment, are becoming involved in manufacturing, assembly, and export—it is doubtful whether the Philippines should be included in this group;

4. finally, the stunted and impoverished Communist societies of Vietnam, Cambodia, and North Korea, as well as isolationist Myanmar pursuing its "Burmese Way to Socialism."

FIGURE 30.1 SHARES OF WORLD TRADE IN MANUFACTURES

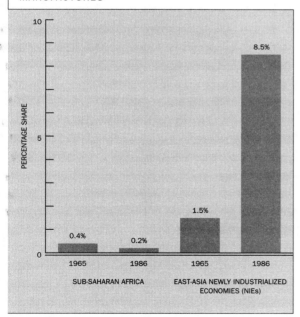

SOURCE: S. Fardoust and A. Dhareshwan, *Long-Term Outlook for the World Economy: Issues and Projections for the 1990s*, World Bank Policy and Research Report, No. 12 (February 1990), p. 9, Table 3.

Because of this staggered level of development, economists in East Asia invoke the image of the "flying geese," with Japan the lead bird, followed by the East Asian NIEs, the larger Southeast Asian states, and so on. What Japan produced in one decade—relatively low-priced toys, kitchenware, electrical goods—will be imitated by the next wave of "geese" in the decade following, and by the third wave in the decade after that. However accurate the metaphor individually, the overall picture is clear; these birds are flying, purposefully and onward, to an attractive destination.

Of those states, it is the East Asian NIEs that have provided the clearest example of successful transformation. Although distant observers may regard them as similar, there are notable differences in size, population,[12] history, and political system. Even the economic structures are distinct; for example, Korea, which began its expansion at least a decade later than Taiwan (and democratized itself even more slowly), is heavily dependent upon a few enormous industrial conglomerates, or *chaebol*, of whom the top four alone (Samsung, Hyundai, Lucky-Goldstar, and Daewoo) have sales equal to half Korea's GNP. By contrast, Taiwan possesses many small companies, specializing in one or two kinds of products. While Taiwanese are concerned that their firms may lose out to foreign giants, Koreans worry that the *chaebol* will find it increasingly difficult to compete in large-scale industries like petrochemicals and semiconductors and shipbuilding at the same time.[13]

Despite such structural differences, these societies each contain certain basic characteristics, which, *taken together*, help to explain their decade-upon-decade growth. The first, and perhaps the most important, is the emphasis upon education. This derives from Confucian traditions of competitive examinations and respect for learning, reinforced daily by the mother of the family who complements what is taught at school.

To Western eyes, this process—like Japan's—appears to concentrate on rote learning and the acquisition of technical skills, and emphasizes consensus instead of encouraging individual talent and the habit of questioning authority. Even if some East Asian educators would nowadays admit that criticism, most believe that their own educational mores create social harmony and a well-trained work force. Moreover, the uniformity of the system does not exclude intense individual competitiveness; in Taiwan (where, incidentally, twelve members of the fourteen-member cabinet of 1989 had acquired PhDs abroad), only the top one-third of each year's 110 000 students taking the national university entrance examinations are selected, to emphasize the importance of college education.[14]

Perhaps nothing better illustrates this stress upon learning than the fact that Korea (43 million population) has around 1.4 million students in higher education, compared with 145 000 in Iran (54 million), 15 000 in Ethiopia (46 million), and 159 000 in Vietnam (64 million); or the further fact that already by 1980 "as many engineering students were graduating from Korean institutions as in the United Kingdom, West Germany and Sweden combined."[15]

The second common characteristic of these countries is their high level of national savings. Through fiscal measures, taxes, and import controls to encourage personal savings, large amounts of low-interest capital were made available for investment in manufacture and commerce. During the first few decades of growth, personal consumption was constrained and living standards controlled—by restrictions upon moving capital abroad, or importing foreign luxury goods—in order to funnel resources into industrial growth. While average prosperity rose, most of the fruits of economic success were plowed back into further expansion. Only when economic "take-off" was well under way has the system begun to alter; increased consumption, foreign purchases, capital investment in new homes, all allow internal demand to play a larger role in the country's growth. In such circumstances, one would expect to see overall savings ratios decline. Even in the late 1980s, however, the East Asians NIEs still had high national savings rates (see Table 30.1).

The third feature has been a strong political system within which economic growth is fostered. While entrepreneurship and private property are encouraged, the "tigers" never followed a laissez-faire model. Industries targeted for growth were given a variety of supports—export subsidies, training grants, tariff protection from foreign competitors. As noted above, the fiscal system was arranged to produce high savings ratios. Taxes assisted the business sector, as did energy policy. Trade unions operated under restrictions. Democracy was constrained by the governor of Hong Kong, *dirigiste* administrations in Singapore, and the military regimes in Taiwan and Korea. Only lately have free elections and party politics been permitted. Defenders of this system argued that it was necessary to restrain libertarian impulses while concentrating on economic growth, and that democratic reforms are a "reward" for the people's patience. The point is that domestic politics were unlike those in the West yet did not hurt commercial expansion.

The fourth feature was the commitment to exports, in contrast to the policies of India, which emphasize locally produced substitutes for imports, and the consumer-driven policies of the United States. This was traditional for a small, bustling trading state like Hong Kong, but it involved substantial restructuring in Taiwan and Korea, where managers and workers had to be trained to produce what foreign customers wanted. In all cases, the value of the currency was kept low, to increase exports and decrease imports. Moreover, the newly industrialized economies of East Asia took advantage of favourable global circumstances: labour costs were much lower than in North America and Europe, and they benefitted from an open international trading order, created and protected by the United States, while shielding their own industries from foreign competition.

Eventually, this led to large trade surpluses and threats of retaliation from European and American governments, reminding us of the NIEs' heavy dependence upon the current international economic system. The important thing, however, is that they targeted export-led growth in manufactures, whereas other developing nations continued to rely upon commodity exports and made little effort to cater to foreign consumers' tastes.[16] Given this emphasis on trade, it is not surprising to learn that Asia now contains seven of the world's twelve largest ports.

Finally, the East Asian NIEs possess a local model, namely Japan, which Yemen, Guatemala, and Burkina Faso simply do not have. For four decades East Asian peoples have observed the dramatic success of a non-Western neighbour, based upon its educational and technical skills, high savings ratios, long-term, state-guided targeting of industries and markets, and determination to compete on world markets, though this admiration of Japan is nowadays mixed with a certain alarm at becoming members of a yen block dominated by Tokyo. While the Japanese domestic market is extremely important for the East Asian NIEs, and they benefit from Japanese investments, assembly plants, engineers, and expertise, they have little enthusiasm for a new Greater East Asia co-prosperity sphere.[17]

TABLE 30.1   COMPARATIVE SAVINGS RATIOS, 1987*

Taiwan	38.8%
Malaysia	37.8%
Korea	37.0%
Japan	32.3%
Indonesia	29.1%
United States	12.7%

*Lest this 1987 figure appear too distant, note that Korea's sixth Five-Year Plan calls for a national savings rate of 33.5 percent in the early 1990s: see *Trends in Developing Economies*, p. 300.

SOURCE: T. Fukuchi and M. Kagami, eds., *Perspectives on the Pacific Basin Economy: A Comparison of Asia and Latin America* (Tokyo: Asian Club Foundation, Institute of Developing Economics, 1990), p. 31, Table 10.

The benefits of economic success are seen not merely in East Asia's steadily rising standards of living. Its children are on average four or five inches taller than they were in the 1940s, and grow up in some of the world's healthiest countries:

A Taiwanese child born in 1988 could expect to live 74 years, only a year less than an American or a West German, and 15 years longer than a Taiwanese born in 1952; a South Korean born in 1988 could expect 70 years on earth, up from 58 in 1965. In 1988 the Taiwanese took in 50 percent more calories each day than they had done 35 years earlier. They had 200 times as many televisions, telephones and cars per household; in Korea the rise in the possession of these goods was even higher.[18]

In addition, the East Asian NIEs enjoy some of today's highest literacy rates, once again confirming that they are altogether closer to "first" world nations than poor, developing countries (see Table 30.2).

Will this progress last into the twenty-first century? Politically, Hong Kong's future is completely uncertain, and many companies are relocating their headquarters elsewhere; Taiwan remains a diplomatic pariah-state because of Beijing's traditional claims; and South Korea still worries about the unpredictable, militarized regime to the north. The future of China—and of Siberia—is uncertain, and causes concern. The 1980s rise in Asian stock-market prices (driven by vast increases in the money supply) was excessive and speculative, and destined to tumble. Protectionist tendencies in the developed world threaten the trading states even more than external pressures to abandon price supports for local farmers. A rise in the value of the Korean and Taiwanese currencies has cut export earnings and reduced their overall rate of growth. Some Japanese competitors have moved production to neighbouring low-cost countries such as Thailand or southern China. Sharp rises in oil prices increase the import bills. High wage awards (in Korea they increased by an average 14 percent in 1988, and by 17 percent in 1989) affect labour costs and competitiveness. The social peace, precarious in these recent democracies, is damaged by bouts of student and industrial unrest.[19]

On the other hand, these may simply be growing pains. Savings ratios are still extremely high. Large numbers of new engineers and technicians pour out of college each year. The workers' enhanced purchasing power has created a

TABLE 30.2   COMPARATIVE LIVING STANDARDS

	LIFE EXPECTANCY AT BIRTH (YEARS), 1987	ADULT LITERACY RATE (%), 1985	GNP PER CAPITA, 1988 U.S.$
Niger	45	14	300
Togo	54	41	310
India	59	43	340
Singapore	73	86	9 070
South Korea	70	95	5 000
Spain	77	95	7 740
New Zealand	75	99	10 000

SOURCES: For the first two columns, "Development Brief," *The Economist*, May 26, 1990, p. 81. Copyright © 1990 The Economist Newspaper Group, Inc. Reprinted with permission. Further reproduction prohibited. www.economist.com: the GNP per capita comes from *World Development Report* (New York: Oxford University Press, 1990), pp. 178–79.

booming domestic market, and governments are investing more in housing, infrastructure, and public facilities. The labour force will not grow as swiftly as before because of the demographic slowdown, but it will be better educated and spend more.[20] A surge in overseas investments is assisting the long-term balance of payments. As the populous markets of Indonesia, Thailand, and Malaysia grow at double-digit rates, there is plenty of work for the trading states. A hardening of the currency can be met by greater commitment to quality exports, high rates of industrial investment, and a move into newer, high-technology manufacture — in imitation of the 1980s retooling of Japanese industry when its currency hardened swiftly. Nowhere else in the world would growth rates of "only" 5 or 6 percent be considered worrying, or a harbinger of decline. Barring a war in East Asia, or a widespread global slump, the signs are that the four "tigers" are better structured than most to grow in wealth and health.

2.

For confirmation of that remark, one need only consider the present difficult condition of Latin America, which lost ground in the 1980s just as East Asia was gaining it. Here again, distinctions have to be made between various countries within the continent, with its more than 400 million people in an area about 18 million square kilometres stretching from the Rio Grande to Antarctica, and with a range of political cultures and socioeconomic structures. Argentina, which around 1900 had a standard of living suggesting that it was a "developed" economy, is very different from Honduras and Guyana. Similarly, population change in Latin America occurs in three distinct forms: such nations as Bolivia, the Dominican Republic, and Haiti have high fertility rates and lower life expectancies; a middle group — Brazil, Colombia, Mexico, Venezuela, Costa Rica, and Panama — is beginning to experience declines in fertility and longer life expectancy; and the temperate-zone countries of

Argentina, Chile, and Uruguay have the demographic characteristics of developed countries.[21]

Despite this diversity, there are reasons for considering Latin America's prospects as a whole: the economic challenges confronting the region are similar, as are its domestic politics — in particular, the fragility of its recently emerged democracies — and each is affected by its relationship with the developed world, especially the United States.

Several decades ago, Latin America's future appeared encouraging. Sharing in the post-1950 global boom, benefitting from demand for its coffee, timber, beef, oil, and minerals, and enjoying foreign investments in its agriculture, industry, and infrastructure, the region was moving upward. In the 30 years after 1945, its production of steel multiplied twenty times, and its output of electric energy, metals, and machinery grew more than tenfold.[22] Real gross domestic product (GDP) per person rose at an annual average of 2.8 percent during the 1960s and spurted to an annual average increase of 3.4 percent in the 1970s. Unfortunately, the growth then reversed itself, and between 1980 and 1988 Latin America's real GDP per person steadily fell by an annual average of 0.9 percent.[23] In some states, such as Peru and Argentina, real income dropped by as much as one-quarter during the 1980s. With very few exceptions (Chile, Colombia, the Dominican Republic, Barbados, the Bahamas), most Latin American countries now have per capita GDPs lower than they were a decade earlier, or even two decades earlier (see Table 30.3).

The reasons for this reversal offer a striking contrast to the East Asian NIEs. Instead of encouraging industrialists to target foreign markets and stimulate the economy through export-led growth, many Latin American governments pursued a policy of import substitution, creating their own steel, cement, paper, automobiles, and electronic-goods industries, which were given protective tariffs, government subsidies, and tax-breaks to insulate them from international competition. As a result, their products became less

TABLE 30.3   PER CAPITA GDP OF LATIN AMERICAN COUNTRIES (1988 U.S. DOLLARS)

COUNTRY	1960	1970	1980	1988
Chile	1 845	2 236	2 448	2 518
Argentina	2 384	3 075	3 359	2 862
Uruguay	2 352	2 478	3 221	2 989
Brazil	1 013	1 372	2 481	2 449
Paraguay	779	931	1 612	1 557
Bolivia	634	818	983	724
Peru	1 233	1 554	1 716	1 503
Ecuador	771	904	1 581	1 477
Colombia	927	1 157	1 595	1 739
Venezuela	3 879	4 941	5 225	4 544
Guyana	1 008	1 111	1 215	995
Suriname	887	2 337	3 722	3 420
Mexico	1 425	2 022	2 872	2 588
Guatemala	1 100	1 420	1 866	1 502
Honduras	619	782	954	851
El Salvador	832	1 032	1 125	995
Nicaragua	1 055	1 495	1 147	819
Costa Rica	1 435	1 825	2 394	2 235
Panama	1 264	2 017	2 622	2 229
Dominican Republic	823	987	1 497	1 509
Haiti	331	292	386	319
Jamaica	1 610	2 364	1 880	1 843
Trinidad & Tobago	3 848	4 927	8 116	5 510
Barbados	2 000	3 530	3 994	4 233
Bahamas	8 448	10 737	10 631	11 317

SOURCE: Taken from G.W. Landau et al., *Latin America at a Crossroads* (New York: The Trilateral Commission, 1990), p. 5, which reports the source as being *Economic and Social Progress in Latin America: 1989 Report* (Washington, DC: Inter-American Development Bank, 1989), Table B1, p. 463.

attractive abroad.[24] Moreover, while it was relatively easy to create a basic iron and steel industry, it proved harder to establish high-tech industries like computers, aerospace, machine-tools, and pharmaceuticals—most of these states therefore still depend on imported manufactured goods, whereas exports consist chiefly of raw materials like oil, coffee, and soybeans.[25]

Secondly, economic growth was accompanied by lax financial policies and an increasing reliance upon foreign borrowing. Governments poured money not only into infrastructure and schools but also into state-owned enterprises, large bureaucracies, and oversized armed forces, paying for them by printing money and raising loans from Western (chiefly U.S.) banks and international agencies. The result was that public spending's share of GDP soared, price inflation accelerated, and was further increased by index-linked rises in salaries and wages. Inflation became so large that it was difficult to comprehend, let alone to combat. According to the 1990 *World Resources* report, "in 1989, for example, annual inflation in Nicaragua was more than 3,400 percent; in Argentina inflation reached 3,700 percent, in Brazil almost 1,500 percent, and in Peru nearly 3,000 percent. Ecuador, with only 60 percent inflation, did comparatively well."[26] In such circumstances the currency becomes worthless, as does the idea of seeking to raise national savings rates for long-term capital investment.

Another result is that some Latin American countries find themselves among the most indebted in the world, as Table 30.4 shows. Total Latin American indebtedness now equals about $1000 for every man, woman, and child. But instead of being directed into productive investment, that money has been wasted domestically or disappeared as "capital flight" to private accounts in U.S. and European banks. This has left most countries incapable of repaying even the interest on their loans. Defaults on loans (or suspension of interest payments) then produced a drying up of capital from indignant Western banks and a net capital *outflow* from Latin America just when it needed capital to aid economic growth.[27] Starved of foreign funds and with currencies made worthless by hyperinflation, many countries are in a far worse position than could have been imagined twenty-five years ago.[28] For a while, it was even feared that the region's financial problems might undermine parts of the international banking system. It now appears that the chief damage will be in the continent itself, where 180 million people (40 percent) are living in poverty—a rise of 50 million alone in the 1980s.

Given such profligacy, and the conservative, "anti–big government" incumbents in the White House during the 1980s, it was predictable that Latin America would come under pressure—from the World Bank, the International Monetary Fund, private bankers, Washington itself—to slash public spending, control inflation, and repay debts. Such demands were easier said than done in the existing circumstances. Islands of democracy (e.g., Costa Rica) did exist, but many states were ruled by right-wing military dictatorships

TABLE 30.4   GROWTH OF LATIN AMERICAN INDEBTEDNESS (SELECTED COUNTRIES)

COUNTRY	TOTAL EXTERNAL DEBT (BILLION U.S.$)			LONG-TERM PUBLIC DEBT AS A PERCENTAGE OF GNP		
	1977	1982	1987	1977	1982	1987
Argentina	8.1	32.4	53.9	10	31	62
Brazil	28.3	68.7	109.4	13	20	29
Chile	4.9	8.5	18.7	28	23	89
Guyana	0.4	0.9	1.2	100	158	353
Honduras	0.6	1.6	3.1	29	53	71
Jamaica	1.1	2.7	4.3	31	69	139
Mexico	26.6	78.0	93.7	25	32	59
Venezuela	9.8	27.0	29.0	10	16	52

SOURCE: *World Resources 1990–91*, p. 246. Copyright © by the World Resources Institute. Reprinted by permission of World Resources Institute, Washington, DC.

or social revolutionaries; internal guerrilla wars, military coups d'état, labour unrest were common. Even as democracy began to reassert itself in the 1980s, the new leaders found themselves in a near-impossible situation: inheritors of the high external debts contracted by the outgoing regimes, legatees in many cases of inflationary index-linked wage systems, targets of landowner resentment and/or of guerrilla attacks, frustrated by elaborate and often corrupt bureaucracies, and deficient in trained personnel. While grappling with these weaknesses, they discovered that the Western world, which applauded the return to democracy, was unsympathetic to fresh lending, increasingly inclined to protectionism, and demanding unilateral measures (e.g., in the Amazon rain forests) to stop global warming.

Two other weaknesses have also slowed any hoped-for recovery. One is the unimpressive accomplishments of the educational systems. This is not due to an absence of schools and universities, as in parts of Africa. Many Latin American countries have extensive public education, dozens of universities, and high adult literacy rates; Brazil, for example, has 68 universities, Argentina 41.[29] The real problem is neglect and underinvestment. One citizen bemoaned the collapse in Argentina as follows:

> Education, which kept illiteracy at bay for more than a century, lies in ruins. The universities are unheated and many public schools lack panes for their window frames. Last summer [1990] an elementary school teacher with ten years' experience earned less than $110 a month. An associate professor at the Universidad de Buenos Aires, teaching ten hours a week, was paid $37 a month. A doctor's salary at a municipal hospital was $120 a month. ... At times, teachers took turns teaching, or cut their class hours, because they and their students could not afford transportation.[30]

Presumably, if resources were available, those decaying educational and health-care structures could be resuscitated, helping national recovery; but where the capital can be raised under the present circumstances is difficult to see. Moreover, in the strife-torn countries of Central America there is little education to begin with; in Guatemala, the latest census estimated that 63 percent of those 10 years of age and older were illiterate, while in Honduras the illiteracy rate was 40 percent.[31] Unfortunately, it is in the educationally most deprived Latin American countries that resources are being eroded by swift population increases.

Despite these disadvantages, recent reports on Latin America have suggested that the "lost decade" of the 1980s will be followed by a period of recovery. The coming of democratic regimes, the compromises emerging from protracted debt-recycling talks, the stiff economic reforms (cutting public spending, abandoning indexation) to reduce inflation rates, the replacement of "state protectionism with import liberalization and privatization,"[32] the conversion of budget deficits into surpluses—all this has caused the Inter-American Development Bank to argue that "a decisive and genuine takeoff" is at hand, provided the new policies are sustained.[33] Growth has resumed in Argentina, Mexico, and Venezuela. Even investment bankers are reported to be returning to the continent.

Whether these changes are going to be enough remains uncertain, especially since the newly elected governments face widespread resentment at the proposed reforms. As one commentator put it, "Much of Latin America is entering the 1990s in a race between economic deterioration and political progress."[34] Whereas Spain, Portugal, and Greece moved to democracy while enjoying reasonable prosperity, Latin America (like Eastern Europe) has to make that change as its economies flounder —which places immense responsibilities upon the political leadership.

Although it can be argued that the region's future is in its own hands, it will also be heavily influenced by the United States. In many ways, the U.S.–Latin American relationship is similar to that between Japan and the East Asian NIEs, which are heavily dependent upon Japan as their major market and source of capital.³⁵ Yet there is more to this relationship than Latin America's economic dependence upon the United States, whose banking system has also suffered because of Latin American indebtedness. U.S. exports, which are 50 times larger to this region than to Eastern Europe, were badly hurt by Latin America's economic difficulties, and they would benefit greatly from a resumption of growth. The United States' own environment may now be threatened by the diminution of the Amazon and Central American rain forests. Its awful drug problem, driven by domestic demand, is fuelled by Latin American supplies—more than 80 percent of the cocaine and 90 percent of the marijuana entering the United States are produced in or move through this region.

Finally, the population of the United States is being altered by migration from Mexico, the Caribbean, and Central America; if there should be a widespread socioeconomic collapse south of the Rio Grande, the "spillover" effects will be felt across the United States. Instead of being marginalized by the end of the cold war, Latin America may present Washington with formidable and growing challenges—social, environmental, financial, and ultimately political.³⁶ Thus, while the region's own politicians and citizens have to bear the major responsibility for recovery, richer nations—especially the United States—may find it in their own best interest to lend a hand.

3.

If these remarks disappoint readers in Brazil or Peru, they may care to glance, in grim consolation, at the world of Islam. It is one thing to face population pressures, shortage of resources, educational/technological deficiencies, and regional conflicts, which would challenge the wisest governments. But it is another when regimes themselves stand in angry resentment of global forces for change instead of (as in East

Asia) selectively responding to such trends. Far from preparing for the twenty-first century, much of the Arab and Muslim world appears to have difficulty in coming to terms with the nineteenth century, with its composite legacy of secularization, democracy, laissez-faire economics, industrial and commercial linkages among different nations, social change, and intellectual questioning. If one needed an example of the importance of cultural attitudes in explaining a society's response to change, contemporary Islam provides it.

Before analyzing the distinctive role of Islamic culture, one should first note the danger of generalizing about a region that contains such variety. After all, it is not even clear what *name* should be used to describe this part of the earth. To term it the "Middle East"³⁷ is, apart from its Atlantic-centred bias, to leave out such North African states as Libya, Tunisia, Algeria, and Morocco. To term it the "Arab World"³⁸ is to exclude Iran (and, of course, Israel), the Kurds, and the non-Muslim tribes of southern Sudan and Mauritania. Even the nomenclature Islam, or the Muslim world, disguises the fact that millions of Catholics, Copts, and Jews live in these lands, and that Islamic societies extend from West Africa to Indonesia.³⁹

In addition, the uneven location of oil in the Middle East has created a division between super-rich and dreadfully poor societies that has no equivalent in Central America or sub-Saharan Africa.⁴⁰ Countries like Kuwait (2 million), the United Arab Emirates (1.3 million), and Saudi Arabia (11.5 million) enjoy some of the world's highest incomes, but exist alongside populous neighbours one-third as rich (Jordan, Iran, Iraq) or even one-tenth as rich (Egypt, Yemen). The gap is accentuated by different political systems: conservative, antidemocratic, traditionalist in the Gulf sheikdoms; demagogic, populist, militarized in countries such as Libya, Syria, Iraq, and Iran.

The 1990 Iraqi attack upon Kuwait, and the different responses of the Saudi elites on the one hand and the street masses in Amman or

Rabat on the other, illustrated this divide between "haves" and "have-nots" in the Muslim world. The presence of millions of Egyptian, Yemeni, Jordanian, and Palestinian *Gastarbeiter* (literally "guest workers" — temporary foreign workers) in the oil-rich states simply increased the mutual resentments, while the Saudi and Emirate habit of giving extensive aid to Iraq during its war against Iran, or to Egypt to assist its economic needs, reinforces the impression of wealthy but precarious regimes seeking to achieve security by bribing their larger, jealous neighbours.[41] Is it any wonder that the unemployed, badly housed urban masses, despairing of their own secular advancement, are attracted to religious leaders or "strongmen" appealing to Islamic pride, a sense of identity, and resistance to foreign powers and their local lackeys?

More than in any other developing region, then, the future of the Middle East and North Africa is affected by issues of war and conflict. The region probably contains more soldiers, aircraft, missiles, and other weapons than anywhere else in the world, with billions of dollars of armaments having been supplied by Western, Soviet, and Chinese producers during the past few decades. In view of the range and destructiveness of these weapons, another Arab–Israeli war would be a nightmare, yet many Muslim states still regard Israel with acute hostility. Even if the Arab–Israeli antagonism did not exist, the region is full of other rivalries, between Syria and Iraq, Libya and Egypt, Iran and Iraq, and so on. Vicious one-man dictatorships glare threateningly at arch-conservative, antidemocratic, feudal sheikdoms. Fundamentalist regimes exist from Iran to the Sudan. Terrorist groups in exile threaten to eliminate their foes. Unrest among the masses puts a question mark over the future of Egypt, Algeria, Morocco, Jordan.[42] The recent fate of Lebanon, instead of serving as a warning against sectarian fanaticism, is more often viewed as a lesson in power politics, that the strong will devour the weak.

To the Western observer brought up in Enlightenment traditions — or, for that matter, to economic rationalists preaching the virtues of the borderless world — the answer to the Muslim nations' problems would appear to be a vast program of *education*, not simply in the technical, skills-acquiring sense but also to advance parliamentary discourse, pluralism, and a secular civic culture. Is that not the reason, after all, for the political stability and economic success of Scandinavia or Japan today?

If that argument is correct, then such an observer would find few of those features in contemporary Islam. In countries where fundamentalism is strong, there is (obviously) little prospect of education or advancement for the female half of the population.[43] Where engineers and technicians exist, their expertise has all too often been mobilized for war purposes, as in Iraq. Tragically, Egypt possesses a large and bustling university system but a totally inadequate number of jobs for graduates and skilled workers, so that millions of both are underemployed. In Yemen, to take an extreme example, the state of education is dismal. By contrast, the oil-rich states have poured huge resources into schools, technical institutes, and universities, but these alone are insufficient to create an "enterprise culture" that would produce export-led manufacturing along East Asian lines. Ironically, possession of vast oil reserves could be a disadvantage, since it reduces the incentive to rely upon the skills and quality of the people, as occurs in countries (Japan, Switzerland) with few natural resources. Such discouraging circumstances may also explain why many educated and entrepreneurial Arabs, who passionately wanted their societies to borrow from the West, have emigrated.

It is difficult to know whether the reason for the Muslim world's troubled condition is cultural or historical. Western critics pointing to the region's religious intolerance, technological backwardness, and feudal cast of mind often forget that, centuries before the Reformation, Islam led the world in mathematics, cartography, medicine, and many other aspects of science and industry; and contained libraries, universities, and observatories, when Japan and America possessed none and Europe only a few. These assets were later sacrificed to a revival of traditionalist thought and the sectarian split between Shi'ite and Sunni Muslims, but Islam's retreat into itself—its being "out of step with History," as one author termed it[44]—was probably also a response to the rise of a successful, expansionist Europe.

Sailing along the Arab littoral, assisting in the demise of the Mughal Empire, penetrating strategic points with railways, canals, and ports, steadily moving into North Africa, the Nile Valley, the Persian Gulf, the Levant, and then Arabia itself, dividing the Middle East along unnatural boundaries as part of a post–First World War diplomatic bargain, developing American power to buttress and then replace European influences, inserting an Israeli state in the midst of Arab peoples, instigating coups against local popular leaders, and usually indicating that this part of the globe was important only for its oil—the Western nations may have contributed more to turning the Muslim world into what it is today than outside commentators are willing to recognize.[45] Clearly, the nations of Islam suffer many self-inflicted problems. But if much of their angry, confrontational attitudes toward the international order today are due to a long-held fear of being swallowed up by the West, little in the way of change can be expected until that fear is dissipated.

4.

The condition of sub-Saharan Africa—"the third world's third world," as it has been described—is even more desperate.[46] When one considers recent developments such as perestroika in the former Soviet Union, the coming integration of Europe, and the economic miracle of Japan and the East Asian NIEs, remarked a former president of Nigeria, General Olusegun Obasanjo, and "contrasting all this with what is taking place in Africa, it is difficult to believe that we inhabit the same historical

time."[47] Recent reports on the continent's plight are extraordinarily gloomy, describing Africa as "a human and environmental disaster area," as "moribund," "marginalized," and "peripheral to the rest of the world," and having so many intractable problems that some foreign development experts are abandoning it to work elsewhere. In the view of the World Bank, virtually everywhere else in the world is likely to experience a decline in poverty by the year 2000 *except* Africa, where things will only get worse.[48] "Sub-Saharan Africa," concludes one economist, "suffers from a combination of economic, social, political, institutional and environmental handicaps which have so far largely defied development efforts by the African countries and their donors."[49] How, an empathetic study asks, can Africa survive?[50]

The unanimity of views is remarkable, given the enormous variety among the forty-five states that constitute sub-Saharan Africa.[51] Nine of them have fewer than one million people each, whereas Nigeria contains about 110 million. Some lie in the desert, some in tropical rain forests. Many are rich in mineral deposits, others have only scrubland. While a number (Botswana, Cameroon, Congo, Gabon, Kenya) have seen significant increases in living standards since independence, they are the exception—suggesting that the obstacles to growth on East Asian lines are so deep-rooted and resistant to the "development strategies" of foreign experts and/or their own leaders that it may require profound changes in attitude to achieve recovery.

This was not the mood 30 years ago, when the peoples of Africa were gaining their independence. True, there was economic backwardness, but this was assumed to have been caused by decades of foreign rule, leading to dependency upon a single metropolitan market, monoculture, lack of access to capital, and so on. Now that Africans had control of their destinies, they could build industries, develop cities, airports, and infrastructure, and attract foreign investment and aid from either Western powers or the

USSR and its partners. The boom in world trade during the 1950s and 1960s, and demand for commodities, strengthened this optimism. Although some regions were in need, Africa as a whole was self-sufficient in food and, in fact, a net food exporter. Externally, African states were of increasing importance at the United Nations and other world bodies.

What went wrong? The unhappy answer is "lots of things." The first, and perhaps most serious, was that over the following three decades the population mushroomed as imported medical techniques and a reduction in malaria-bearing mosquitoes drastically curtailed infant mortality. Africa's population was already increasing at an average annual rate of 2.6 percent in the 1960s, jumped to 2.9 percent during the 1970s, and increased to over 3 percent by the late 1980s, implying a doubling in size every twenty-two years; this was, therefore, the highest rate for any region in the world.[52]

In certain countries, the increases were staggering. Between 1960 and 1990, Kenya's population quadrupled, from 6.3 million to 25.1 million, and Côte d'Ivoire's jumped from 3.8 million to 12.6 million. Altogether Africa's population — including the North African states — leapt from 281 to 647 million in three decades.[53] Moreover, while the majority of Africans inhabit rural settlements, the continent has been becoming urban at a dizzying speed. Vast shanty-cities have already emerged on the edges of national capitals (such as Accra in Ghana, Monrovia in Liberia, and Lilongwe in Malawi). By 2025, urban dwellers are predicted to make up 55 percent of Africa's total population.

The worst news is that the increase is unlikely to diminish in the near future. Although most African countries spend less than 1 percent of GNP on health care and consequently have the highest infant mortality rates in the world — in Mali, for example, there are 169 infant deaths for every 1000 live births — those rates are substantially less than they were a quarter century ago and will tumble further in the future, which is why demographers forecast that Africa's population in 2025 will be nearly three times that of today.[54]

There remains one random and tragic factor that may significantly affect all these (late 1980s) population projections — the AIDS epidemic, which is especially prevalent in Africa. Each new general study has raised the global total of people who are already HIV positive. For example, in June 1991, the World Health Organization abandoned its earlier estimate that 25–30 million people throughout the world would be infected by the year 2000, and suggested instead that the total could be closer to 40 million, and even that may be a gross underestimate.[55] Without question, Africa is the continent most deeply affected by AIDS, with entire families suffering from the disease. Tests of pregnant women in certain African families reveal that 25–30 percent are now HIV positive.[56] Obviously, this epidemic would alter the earlier projections of a doubling or trebling of Africa's total population over the next few decades — and in the worst possible way: family sizes would still be much larger than in most other regions of the globe, but tens of millions of Africans would be dying of AIDS, further crushing the world's most disadvantaged continent.

The basic reason why the present demographic boom will not otherwise be halted swiftly is traditional African belief-systems concerning fecundity, children, ancestors, and the role of women. Acutely aware of the invisible but pervasive presence of their ancestors, determined to expand their lineage, regarding childlessness or small families as the work of evil spirits, most Africans seek to have as many children as possible; a woman's virtue and usefulness are measured by the number of offspring she can bear. "Desired family size," according to polls of African women, ranges from five to nine children. The social attitudes that lead women in North America, Europe, and Japan to delay childbearing — education, career ambitions, desire for independence — scarcely exist in African societies; where such emerge, they are swiftly suppressed by familial pressures.[57]

This population growth has not been accompanied by equal or larger increases in Africa's productivity, which would of course transform the picture. During the 1960s, farm output was rising by around 3 percent each year, keeping pace with the population, but since 1970 agricultural production has grown at only half that rate. Part of this decline was caused by drought, hitting countries south of the Sahara. Furthermore, existing agricultural resources have been badly eroded by overgrazing—caused by the sharp rise in the number of cattle and goats—as well as by deforestation in order to provide fuel and shelter for the growing population. When rain falls, the water runs off the denuded fields, taking the top-soil with it.

None of this was helped by changes in agricultural production, with farmers encouraged to grow tea, coffee, cocoa, palm oil, and rubber for export rather than food for domestic consumption. After benefitting from high commodity prices in the early stages, producers suffered a number of blows. Heavy taxation on cash crops, plus mandatory governmental marketing, reduced the incentives to increase output; competition grew from Asian and Latin American producers; many African currencies were overvalued, which hurt exports; and in the mid-1970s, world commodity prices tumbled. Yet the cost of imported manufactures and foodstuffs remained high, and sub-Saharan Africa was badly hurt by the quadrupling of oil prices.[58]

These blows increased Africa's indebtedness in ways that were qualitatively new. Early, postcolonial borrowings were driven by the desire for modernization, as money was poured into cement works, steel plants, airports, harbours, national airlines, electrification schemes, and telephone networks. Much of it, encouraged from afar by international bodies like the World Bank, suffered from bureaucratic interference, a lack of skilled personnel, unrealistic planning, and inadequate basic facilities, and now lies half-finished or (where completed) suffers from lack of upkeep. But borrowing to pay for imported oil, or to feed half the nation's population,

means that indebtedness rises without any possible return on the borrowed funds. In consequence, Africa's total debt expanded from $14 billion in 1973 to $125 billion in 1987, when its capacity to repay was dropping fast; by the mid-1980s, payments on loans consumed about half of Africa's export earnings, a proportion even greater than for Latin American debtor nations. Following repeated debt reschedulings, Western bankers—never enthusiastic to begin with—virtually abandoned private loans to Africa.[59]

As a result, Africa's economy is in a far worse condition now than at independence, apart from a few countries like Botswana and Mauritius. Perhaps the most startling illustration of its plight is the fact that "excluding South Africa, the nations of sub-Saharan Africa with their 450 million people have a total GDP less than that of Belgium's 11 million people"; in fact, the entire continent generates roughly 1 percent of the world GDP.[60] Africa's share of world markets has shrivelled just as East Asia's share has risen fast. Plans for modernization lie unrealized. Manufacturing still represents only 11 percent of Africa's economic activity—scarcely up from the 9 percent share in 1965; and only 12 percent of the continent's exports is composed of manufactures (compared with Korea's 90 percent). There is a marked increase in the signs of decay: crumbling infrastructure, power failures, broken-down communications, abandoned projects, and everywhere the pressure of providing for increasing populations. Already Africa needs to import 15 million tons of maize a year to achieve minimal levels of food consumption, but with population increasing faster than agricultural output, that total could multiply over the next decade—implying an even greater diversion of funds from investment and infrastructure.[61]

Two further characteristics worsen Africa's condition. The first is the prevalence of wars, coups d'état, and political instability. This is partly the legacy of the European "carve-up" of Africa, when colonial boundaries were drawn without regard for the differing tribes and ethnic groups,[62] or even of earlier conquests by successful tribes of neighbouring lands and peoples; Ethiopia, for example, is said to contain 76 ethnic groups and 286 languages.[63] While it is generally accepted that those boundaries cannot be unscrambled, most of them are clearly artificial. In extreme cases like Somalia, the "state" has ceased to exist. And in most other African countries, governments do not attract the loyalty of citizens (except perhaps kinsmen of the group in power), and ethnic tensions have produced innumerable civil wars—from Biafra's attempt to secede from Nigeria, to the conflict between Arab north and African south in the Sudan, to Eritrean struggles to escape from Ethiopia, to the Tutsi–Hutu struggle in Burundi, to clashes and suppressions and guerrilla campaigns from Uganda to the Western Sahara, from Angola to Mozambique.[64]

These antagonisms have often been worsened by struggles over ideology and government authority. The rulers of many new African states rapidly switched either to a personal dictatorship or single-party rule. They also embraced a Soviet or Maoist political economy, instituting price controls, production targets, forced industrialization, the takeover of private enterprises, and other features of "scientific socialism" that—unknown to them—were destroying the Soviet economy. Agriculture was neglected, while bureaucracy flourished. The result was the disappearance of agricultural surpluses, inattention to manufacturing for the world market, and the expansion of party and government bureaucracies, exacerbating the region's problems.

The second weakness was the wholly inadequate investment in human resources and in developing a culture of entrepreneurship, scientific inquiry, and technical prowess. According to one survey, Africa has been spending less than $1 each year on research and development per head of population, whereas the United States was spending $200 per head. Consequently, Africa's scientific population has always trailed the rest of the world (see Table 30.5).

In many African countries—Malawi, Zambia, Lesotho—government spending on education has fallen, so that, after some decades of advance, a smaller share of children are now in school. While there is a hunger for learning, it cannot be satisfied beyond the secondary level except for a small minority. Angola, for example, had 2.4 million pupils in primary schools in 1982–83, but only 153 000 in secondary schools, and a mere 4700 in higher education.[65] By contrast, Sweden, with a slightly smaller total population, had 570 000 in secondary education and 179 000 in higher education.[66]

Despite these relative weaknesses, some observers claim to have detected signs of a turnaround. With the exception of intransigent African socialists,[67] many leaders are now attempting to institute reforms. In return for "structural adjustments," that is, measures to encourage free enterprise, certain African societies have secured additional loans from Western nations and the World Bank. The latter organization has identified past errors (many of them urged on African governments and funded by itself), and encouraged economic reforms. Mozambique, Ghana, and Zambia have all claimed recent successes in reversing negative growth, albeit at considerable social cost.

TABLE 30.5 NUMBERS OF SCIENTISTS AND ENGINEERS PER MILLION OF POPULATION

Japan	3548
United States	2685
Europe	1632
Latin America	209
Arab States	202
Asia (minus Japan)	99
Africa	53

SOURCE: T.R. Odhiambo, "Human Resources Development: Problems and Prospects in Developing Countries," *Impact of Science on Society*, UNESCO, No. 155 (1989), p. 214. Reprinted by permission of UNESCO, Paris, France.

Democratic principles are also returning to the continent: the dismantling of apartheid in South Africa, the cease-fire in Angola, the independence of Namibia, the success of Botswana's record of democracy and prosperity, the cries for reforms in Gabon, Kenya, and Zaire, the rising awareness among African intellectuals of the transformations in East Asia, may all help — so the argument goes — to change attitudes, which is the prerequisite for recovery.[68] Moreover, there are local examples of economic self-improvement, cooperative ventures to halt erosion and improve yields, and village-based schemes of improvement.[69] This is, after all, a continent of enormous agricultural and mineral resources, provided they can be sensibly exploited.

Despite such signs of promise, conditions are likely to stay poor. Population increases countered only by the growing toll of AIDS victims, the diminution of grazing lands and food supplies, the burdens of indebtedness, the decay of infrastructures and reduced spending on health care and education, the residual strength of animist religions and traditional belief-systems, the powerful hold of corrupt bureaucracies and ethnic loyalties ... all those tilt against the relatively few African political leaders, educators, scientists, and economists who perceive the need for changes.

What does this mean for Africa's future? As the Somalian disaster unfolds, some observers suggest that parts of the continent may be taken over and administered from the outside, rather like the post-1919 League of Nations mandates. By contrast, other experts argue that disengagement by developed countries might have the positive effect of compelling Africans to begin a *self-driven* recovery, as well as ending the misuse of aid monies.[70] Still others feel that Africa cannot live without the West, although its leaders and people will have to abandon existing habits, and development aid must be more intelligently applied.[71] Whichever view is correct, the coming decade will be critical for Africa. Even a partial recovery would give grounds for hope; on the other hand, a second

decade of decline, together with a further surge in population, would result in catastrophe.

5.

From the above, it is clear that the developing countries' response to the broad forces for global change is going to be uneven. The signs are that the gap between success and failure will widen; one group enjoys interacting beneficial trends, while others suffer from linked weaknesses and deficiencies.[72]

This is most clearly the case with respect to demography. As noted earlier, the commitment of the East Asian trading states to education, manufacturing, and export-led growth produced a steady rise in living standards, and allowed those societies to make the demographic transition to smaller family sizes. This was in marked contrast to sub-Saharan Africa, where, because of different cultural attitudes and social structures, improved health care and rising incomes led, *not* to a drop in population growth, but to the opposite. Just before independence in 1960, for example, the average Kenyan woman had 6.2 children, whereas by 1980 she had 8.2[73] — and that in a period when Africa's economic prospects were fading.

In Africa's case the "global trend" that drives all others is, clearly, the demographic explosion. It spills into every domain — overgrazing, local conflicts over water and wood supplies, extensive unplanned urbanization, strains upon the educational and social structures, reliance upon imported food supplies (at the cost of increasing indebtedness), ethnic tensions, domestic unrest, border wars. Only belatedly are some African governments working to persuade families to limit their size, as people become aware that access to family planning plus improved educational opportunities for women produce significant declines in birth rates. Against such promising indications stand the many cultural, gender-related, and economic forces described above that encourage large families. This resistance to change is aided by Africa's general lack of resources. Raising Somalia's female literacy rate (6 percent) to South Korea's (88 percent) to produce a demographic transition sounds fine until one considers how so ambitious a reform could be implemented and paid for. Unfortunately, as noted above, the projections suggest that, as Africa's population almost trebles over the next few decades, the only development curtailing it could be the rapid growth of AIDS.[74]

In many parts of Latin America, the demographic explosion will also affect the capacity to handle globally driven forces for change. While wide differences in total fertility rates exist between the moderate-climate countries and those in the tropics, the overall picture is that Latin America's population, which was roughly equal to that of United States and Canada in 1960, is increasing so swiftly that it will be more than double that of those two countries in 2025.[75] Even if birth rates are now declining in the larger countries, there will still be enormous increases: Mexico's population will leap to 150 million by 2025 and Brazil's to 245 million.[76] This implies a very high incidence of child poverty and malnutrition; further strain upon already inadequate health care and educational services; the crowding of millions of human beings into a dozen or more "mega-cities"; pollution; and the degradation of grazing land, forests, and other natural resources. In Mexico, for example, 44 million people are without sewers and 21 million without potable water, which means that when disease (e.g., cholera) strikes, it spreads swiftly.[77] These are not strong foundations upon which to improve the region's relative standing in an increasingly competitive international economic order.

In this regard, many Muslim states are in a similar or worse position; in no Arab country is the population increasing by less than 2 percent a year,[78] and in most the rate is considerably higher. The region's total population of more than 200 million will double in less than 25 years, and city populations are growing twice as fast as national averages. This puts enormous pressures upon scarce food, water, and land resources, and produces unbalanced populations. Already, in most Arab countries at least four out of every ten people are under the age of 15 — the classic recipe for subsequent social unrest and political revolution. One in five Egyptian workers is jobless, as is one in four Algerian workers.[79] In what is widely regarded as the most turbulent part of the world, therefore, demography is contributing to the prospects of future unrest year by year. Even the Israeli–Palestine quarrel has become an issue of demography, with the influx of Soviet Jews seen as countering the greater fertility of the Palestinians.

There is, moreover, little likelihood that population growth will fall in the near future. Since infant mortality rates in many Muslim countries are still high, further improvements in prenatal care will produce rises in the numbers surviving, as is happening in the Gulf States and Saudi Arabia (see Table 30. 6).

As elsewhere, politics intrudes; many regimes are deliberately encouraging women to have large families, arguing that this adds to the coun-

TABLE 30.6 COMPARATIVE INFANT MORTALITY RATES (INFANT DEATHS PER 1000 LIVE BIRTHS)

	1965–70	1985–90
Algeria	150	74
Egypt	170	85
Sudan	156	108
Yemen Arab Republic	186	116
Saudi Arabia	140	71
Kuwait	55	19
Iraq	111	69
Japan	16	5
United States	22	10
Sweden	13	6

SOURCE: *World Resources 1990–91*, pp. 258–59. Copyright © by the World Resources Institute. Reprinted by permission of World Resources Institute, Washington, DC.

try's military strength. "Bear a child," posters in Iraq proclaim, "and you pierce an arrow in the enemy's eye."[80] Countries such as Iraq and Libya offer many incentives for larger families, as do the Gulf States and Saudi Arabia, anxious to fill their oil-rich lands with native-born rather than foreign workers. Only in Egypt are propaganda campaigns launched to curb family size, but even if that is successful—despite resistance from the Muslim Brotherhood—present numbers are disturbing. With a current population of over 55 million Egyptians, six out of ten of whom are under 20, and with an additional one million being born every eight months, the country is in danger of bursting at the seams during the next few decades.

6.

For much the same reasons, we ought to expect a differentiated success rate among developing countries in handling environmental challenges, with the newly industrializing East Asian economies way ahead of the others. This is not to ignore significant local schemes to improve the ecology that are springing up in Africa and the interesting proposals for "sustainable development" elsewhere in the developing world,[81] or to forget that industrialization has caused environmental damage in East Asia, from choked roads to diminished forests. Yet the fact is that nations with lots of resources (capital, scientists, engineers, technology, a per capita GNP of over U.S. $4000) are better able to deal with environmental threats than those without money, tools, or personnel. By contrast, it is the poorer societies (Egypt, Bangladesh, Ethiopia) that, lacking financial and personnel resources, find it difficult to respond to cyclones, floods, drought, and other natural disasters—with their devastated populations augmenting the millions of refugees and migrants. Should global warming produce sea-level rises and heightened storm surges, teeming island populations from the Caribbean to the Pacific are in danger of being washed away.[82]

Finally, it is the population explosion in Latin America and South Asia and Africa that is the major cause of overgrazing, soil erosion, and salinization, as well as the clearing of the tropical rain forests that, while contributing to global warming, also hurts the local populations and exacerbates regional struggles for power. Elsewhere, in the Middle East, for example, supplies of water are the greatest concern, especially in view of growing demographic pressures. The average Jordanian now uses only one-third the amount of domestic water consumed in Israel and has little hope of increasing the supply, yet Jordan's population, which is now roughly equal to Israel's, is expected to double during the next twenty years.[83]

With all governments in the region striving to boost agricultural output and highly sensitive to famine and unrest among their peasant farmers, the search for secure water influences domestic politics, international relations, and spending priorities. Egypt worries that either the Sudan or Ethiopia might dam the Nile in order to increase irrigation. Syria and Iraq are alarmed about Turkey's new Ataturk dam, which can interrupt the flow of the Euphrates. Jordan, Syria, and Israel quarrel over water rights in the Litani, Yarmuk, and Jordan river valleys, as do Arabs and Jews over well supplies in the occupied West Bank. Saudi Arabia's ambition to grow wheat is draining its aquifers, and the same will occur with Libya's gigantic scheme to tap water from under the Sahara.[84] As more and more people struggle for the same—or diminishing—amounts of water, grand ideas about preparing for the twenty-first century look increasingly irrelevant; surviving *this* century becomes the order of the day.

What are the implications for these societies of the new technologies being developed by Western scientists? The revolution in biotech farming, for example, is of great relevance to developing countries, even if the consequences will be mixed. Improved strains of plants and more sophisticated pesticides and fertilizers could, potentially, enhance yields in the developing world, reduce pressures upon marginal lands, restore agricultural self-sufficiency, improve the balance of payments, and raise standards of living. Since much biotech does not involve expensive enterprise, we could witness farmers' groups experimenting with new seeds, improved breeding techniques, cultivation of gene tissue, regional gene-banks, and other developments.

Yet it is also possible that giant pharmaceutical and agro-chemical firms in the "first" world may monopolize much of the knowledge — and the profits — that this transformation implies. Surpluses in global foodstuffs caused by the biotech revolution could be used to counter malnutrition. They could also undermine commodity prices and hurt societies in which most inhabitants were employed in agriculture. Removing food production from the farm to the laboratory — which is what is implied by recent breakthroughs in biotech agriculture — would undercut agrarian societies, which is why some biotech experts in the development field call for serious planning in "agricultural conversion," that is, conversion into other economic activities.[85]

While the uses of biotechnology are relatively diverse, that is not the case with robotics and automated manufacture. The requirements for an indigenous robotics industry — capital, an advanced electronics sector, design engineers, a dearth of skilled labour — suggest that countries like Taiwan and Korea may follow Japan's example out of concern that Japan's automation will make their own products uncompetitive. On the other hand, automated factories assembling goods more swiftly, regularly, and economically than human beings pose a challenge to *middle-income* economies (Malaysia, Mexico), whose comparative advantage would be undercut. As for countries without a manufacturing base, it is difficult to see how the robotics revolution would have any meaning — except to further devalue the resource they possess in abundance — masses of impoverished and undereducated human beings.

Finally, the global financial and communications revolution and the emergence of multinational corporations threaten to increase the gap between richer and poorer countries, even in the developing world. The industrial conglomerates of Korea are now positioning themselves to become multinational, and the East Asian NIEs in general are able to exploit the world economy (as can be seen in their trade balances, stock-markets, electronics industries, strategic marketing alliances, and so on). Furthermore, if the increasingly borderless world rewards entrepreneurs, designers, brokers, patent-owners, lawyers, and dealers in high value-added services, then East Asia's commitment to education, science, and technology can only increase its lead over other developing economies.

By contrast, the relative lack of capital, high-technology, scientists, skilled workers, and export industries in the poorer countries makes it difficult for them to take part in the communications and financial revolution, although several countries (Brazil, India) clearly hope to do so. Some grimmer forecasts suggest the poorer parts of the developing world may become more marginalized, partly because of the reduced economic importance of labour, raw materials, and foodstuffs, partly because the advanced economies may concentrate upon greater knowledge-based commerce among themselves.

7.

Is there any way of turning these trends around? Obviously, a society strongly influenced by fundamentalist mullahs with a dislike of "modernization" is unlikely to join the international economy; and it does not *have* to enter the borderless world if its people believe that it would be healthier, spiritually if not economically, to remain outside. Nor ought we to expect that countries dominated by selfish, authoritarian elites bent upon enhancing their military power — developing world countries spent almost $150 billion on weapons and armies in 1988 alone—will rush to imitate Japan and Singapore.

But what about those societies that wish to improve themselves yet find that they are hampered by circumstances? There are, after all, many developing countries, the vast majority of which depend upon exporting food and raw materials. With dozens of poor countries seeking desperately to sell their cane sugar or bananas or timber or coffee in the global market, prices fall and they are made more desperate.[86] Moreover, although much international aid goes to the developing world, in fact far more money flows out of impoverished countries of Africa, Asia, and Latin America and *into* the richer economies of Europe, North America, and Japan—to the tune of at least $43 billion each year.[87] This outward flow of interest repayments, repatriated profits, capital flight, royalties, fees for patents and information services makes it difficult for poorer countries to get to their feet; and even if they were able to increase their industrial output, the result might be a large rise in "the costs of technological dependence."[88] Like their increasing reliance upon Northern suppliers for food and medical aid, this has created another dependency relationship for poorer nations.

In sum, as we move into the next century the developed economies appear to have all the trump cards in their hands—capital, technology, control of communications, surplus foodstuffs, powerful multinational companies[89]—and, if anything, their advantages are growing because technology is eroding the value of labour and materials, the chief assets of developing countries. Although nominally independent since decolonization, these countries are probably more dependent upon Europe and the United States than they were a century ago.

Ironically, three or four decades of efforts by developing countries to gain control of their own destinies—nationalizing Western companies, setting up commodity-exporting cartels, subsidizing indigenous manufacturing to achieve import substitution, campaigning for a new world order based upon redistribution of the existing imbalances of wealth—have all failed. The "market," backed by governments of the developed economies, has proved too strong, and the struggle against it has weakened developing economies still further—except those (like Korea and Taiwan) that decided to join.

While the gap between rich and poor in today's world is disturbing, those who have argued that this gap is unjust have all too often supported heavy-handed state interventionism and a retreat from open competition, which preserved indigenous production in the short term but rendered it less efficient against those stimulated by market forces. "Scientific socialism for Africa" may still appeal to some intellectuals,[90] but by encouraging societies to look inward it made them less well equipped to move to newer technologies in order to make goods of greater sophistication and value. And a new "world communications order," as proposed a few years ago by UNESCO to balance the West's dominance, sounds superficially attractive but would in all likelihood become the pawn of bureaucratic and ideological interests rather than function as an objective source of news reporting.

On the other hand, the advocates of free market forces often ignore the vast political difficulties that governments in developing countries would encounter in abolishing price controls, selling off national industries, and reducing food subsidies. They also forget that the spectacular commercial expansion of Japan and the East Asian NIEs was carried out by strong states that eschewed laissez-faire. Instead of copying either socialist or free market systems, therefore, the developing countries might imitate East Asia's "mixed strategies," which combine official controls and private enterprise.[91]

Although the idea of a mixed strategy is intriguing, how can West or Central African countries imitate East Asia without a "strong state" apparatus, and while having a weak tradition of cooperation between government and firms, far lower educational achievements, and a

350 PART 6 · GLOBAL DEVELOPMENT AND THE ENVIRONMENT

different set of cultural attitudes toward family size or international economics? With the global scene less welcoming to industrializing newcomers, how likely are they to achieve the same degree of success as the East Asian NIEs did, when they "took off" a quarter-century ago?[92] Even if, by an economic miracle, the world's poorest 50 nations *did* adopt the Korean style of export-led growth in manufactures, would they not create the same crisis of overproduction as exists in the commodity markets today?

How many developing nations will be able to follow East Asia's growth is impossible to tell. The latest *World Development Report* optimistically forecast significant progress across the globe, provided that poorer nations adopted "market friendly" policies and richer nations eschewed protectionism.[93] Were Taiwan and Korea to be followed by the larger states of Southeast Asia such as Malaysia and Thailand, then by South Asia and a number of Latin American countries, that would blur the North–South divide and make international economic alignments altogether more variegated. Moreover, sustained manufacturing success among developing countries *outside* East Asia might stimulate imitation elsewhere.

At the moment, however, the usual cluster of factors influencing relative economic performance—cultural attitudes, education, political stability, capacity to carry out long-term plans—suggests that while a small but growing number of countries is moving from a "have-not" to a "have" status, many more remain behind. The story of winners and losers in history will continue, therefore, only this time modern communications will remind us all of the growing disparity among the world's nations and regions.

NOTES

1. Discussed further in Paul Kennedy, *Preparing for the Twenty-First Century* (New York: Random House, 1993).

2. For reasons of size and organization, China and India (containing around 37 percent of the world's population) are not treated here: for coverage, see chapter 9, "India and China," of *Preparing for the Twenty-First Century*.

3. *World Tables 1991* (Washington, DC: World Bank, 1991), pp. 268–69, 352–53.

4. *World Tables 1991*, pp. 268–69, 352–53.

5. See the World Bank publication *Trends in Developing Economies* (Washington, DC: 1990), pp. 299–303, for Korea.

6. For descriptions, see F. Braudel, *Civilization and Capitalism: Vol. 3, The Perspective of the World* (New York: Harper and Row, 1986), pp. 506–11.

7. See P. Lyon, "Emergence of the Third World," in H. Bull and A. Watson, eds., *The Expansion of International Society* (New York: Oxford University Press, 1983), p. 229 ff.; G. Barraclough, *An Introduction to Contemporary History* (Harmondsworth, UK: Penguin, 1967), chapter 6, "The Revolt against the West."

8. J. Ravenhill, "The North–South Balance of Power," *International Affairs*, Vol. 66, No. 4 (1990), pp. 745–46. See also J. Cruickshank, "The Rise and Fall of the Third World: A Concept Whose Time Has Passed," *World Review*, February 1991, pp. 28–29. Ravenhill's divisions are high-income oil-exporting countries; industrializing economies with strong states and relatively low levels of indebtedness (Taiwan, etc.); industrializing economies with the state apparatus under challenge and/or with debt problems (Argentina, Poland); potential newly industrializing countries (Malaysia, Thailand); primary commodity producers (in sub-Saharan Africa, Central America).

9. Ravenhill, "The North–South Balance of Power," p. 732.

10. W.L.M. Adriaansen and J.G. Waardenburg, eds., *A Dual World Economy* (Groningen: Wolters-Noordhoff, 1989).

11. P. Drysdale, "The Pacific Basin and Its Economic Vitality," in J.W. Morley, ed., *The*

Pacific Basin: New Challenges for the United States (New York: Academy of Political Science with the East Asian Institute and the Center on Japanese Economy and Business, 1986), p. 11.

12. While Korea has a population of around 43 million and Taiwan about 20 million, Hong Kong possesses 5.7 million and Singapore only 2.7 million.

13. See especially, "Taiwan and Korea: Two Paths to Prosperity," *The Economist*, July 14, 1990, pp. 19–21; also "South Korea" (survey), *The Economist*, August 18, 1990. There is a useful comparative survey in L.A. Veit, "Time of the New Asian Tigers," *Challenge*, July–August 1987, pp. 49–55.

14. N.D. Kristof, "In Taiwan, Only the Strong Get US Degrees," *The New York Times*, March 26, 1989, p. 11.

15. Figures taken, respectively, from J. Paxton, ed., *The Statesman's Yearbook 1990–1991* (New York: St. Martin's Press, 1990); and from R.N. Gwynne, *New Horizons? Third World Industrialization in an International Framework* (New York/London: Wiley, 1990), p. 199.

16. See also H. Hughes, "Catching Up: The Asian Newly Industrializing Economies in the 1990s," *Asian Development Review*, Vol. 7, No. 2 (1989), p. 132 (and Table 32.3).

17. "The Yen Block" (survey), *The Economist*, July 15, 1989; "Japan Builds a New Power Base," *Business Week*, March 20, 1989, pp. 18–25.

18. "Taiwan and Korea: Two Paths to Prosperity," *The Economist*, p. 19; "South Korea: A New Society," *The Economist*, April 15, 1989, pp. 23–25.

19. "When a Miracle Stalls," *The Economist*, October 6, 1990, pp. 33–34 (on Taiwan); *Trends in Developing Economies*, 1990, pp. 299–300 (Korea); R.A. Scalapino, "Asia and the United States: The Challenges Ahead," *Foreign Affairs*, Vol. 69, No. 1 (1989–1990), especially pp. 107–12; "Hong Kong, In China's Sweaty Palm," *The Economist*,

November 5, 1988, pp. 19–22.

20. See the detailed forecasts in "Asia 2010: The Power of People," *Far Eastern Economist Review*, May 17, 1990, pp. 27–58. On industrial retooling, see pp. 8–9 of "South Korea" (survey), *The Economist*, August 18, 1990, pp. 8–9.

21. N. Sadik, ed., *Population: The UNFPA Experience* (New York: New York University Press, 1984), chapter 4, "Latin America and the Caribbean," pp. 51–52.

22. A.F. Lowenthal, "Rediscovering Latin America," *Foreign Affairs*, Vol. 69, No. 4 (Fall 1990), p. 34.

23. Figure from "Latin America's Hope," *The Economist*, December 9 1989, p.14.

24. As mentioned earlier, Japan and its East Asian emulators also sought to protect fledgling domestic industries, but that was in order to create a strong base from which to mount an export offensive — *not* to establish an economic bastion within which their industries would be content to remain.

25. For details, see the various national entries in *The Statesman's Year-Book 1990–91* (London: Macmillan); and *The Economist World Atlas and Almanac* (Englewood Cliffs, NJ: Prentice-Hall, 1989), pp. 131–57. R.N. Gwynne's *New Horizons?* has useful comments on Latin America's "inward-oriented industrialization" (chapter 11), which he then contrasts with East Asia's "outward orientation" (chapter 12).

26. World Resources Institute, *World Resources 1990–91* (New York: Oxford University Press, 1990), p. 39.

27. In 1989, the net transfer of capital leaving Latin America was around $25 billion.

28. For the above, see *World Resources 1990–91*, pp. 33–48; "Latin America at a Crossroads," B.J. McCormick, *The World Economy: Patterns of Growth and Change* (New York: Oxford University Press, 1988), chapter 13; "Latin American Debt: The Banks' Great Escape," *The Economist*, February 11, 1989, pp. 73–74.

29. For educational details, see *The Statesman's Year-Book 1990–91*, pp. 95, 236; for literacy rates, see especially those of Uruguay, Costa Rica, Argentina, and Venezuela in the table "Development Brief," *The Economist*, May 26, 1990, p. 81.

30. T.E. Martinez, "Argentina: Living with Hyper-inflation," *The Atlantic Monthly*, December 1990, p. 36.

31. *The Statesman's Year-Book 1990–91*, pp. 584, 605.

32. T. Kamm, "Latin America Edges toward Free Trade," *The Wall Street Journal*, November 30, 1990, p. A10.

33. C. Farnsworth, "Latin American Economies Given Brighter Assessments," *The New York Times*, October 30, 1990; "Latin America's New Start," *The Economist*, June 9, 1990, p. 11; N.C. Nash, "A Breath of Fresh Economic Air Brings Change to Latin America," *The New York Times*, November 13, 1991, pp. A1, D5.

34. "Latin America's Hope," *The Economist*, December 9, 1989, p. 15; Nash, "A Breath of Fresh Economic Air Brings Change to Latin America."

35. J. Brooke, "Debt and Democracy," *The New York Times*, December 5, 1990, p. A16; P. Truell, "As the U.S. Slumps, Latin America Suffers," *The Wall Street Journal*, November 19, 1990, p. 1.

36. For these arguments, see especially Lowenthal's fine summary, "Rediscovering Latin America," in *Foreign Affairs*; also G.A. Fauriol, "The Shadow of Latin American Affairs," *Foreign Affairs*, Vol. 69, No. 1 (1989–90), pp. 116–34; and M.D. Hayes, "The U.S. and Latin America: A Lost Decade?" *Foreign Affairs*, Vol. 68, No. 1 (1988–89), pp. 180–98.

37. This is the subdivision preferred by *The Economist World Atlas and Almanac* (Englewood Cliffs, NJ: Prentice-Hall, 1989), pp. 256–71, which discusses the North African states (except Egypt) in a later section, under "Africa."

38. "The Arab World" (survey), *The Economist*, May 12, 1990.

39. See "Religions" in the *Hammond Comparative World Atlas* (New York: Hammond, 1993 edition), p. 21.

40. The few oil-producing countries in Africa, such as Gabon and Nigeria, still have relatively low per capita GNPs compared with the Arab Gulf states.

41. G. Brooks and T. Horwitz, "Shaken Sheiks," *The Wall Street Journal*, December 28, 1990, pp. A1, A4.

42. "The Arab World," *The Economist*, p. 12.

43. In 1985, adult female literacy in the Yemen Arab Republic was a mere 3 percent, in Saudi Arabia 12 percent, in Iran 39 percent. On the other hand, many women from the middle and upper-middle classes in Muslim countries are educated, which suggests that poverty, as much as culture, plays a role.

44. M.A. Heller, "The Middle East: Out of Step with History," *Foreign Affairs*, Vol. 69, No. 1 (1989–90), pp. 153–71.

45. See also the remarks by S.F. Wells and M.A. Bruzonsky, eds., *Security in the Middle East: Regional Change and Great Power Strategies* (Boulder, CO: Westview Press, 1986), pp. 1–3.

46. D.E. Duncan, "Africa: The Long Good-bye," *The Atlantic Monthly*, July 1990, p. 20.

47. J.A. Marcum, "Africa: A Continent Adrift," *Foreign Affairs*, Vol. 68, No. 1 (1988–89), p. 177. See also the penetrating article by K.R. Richburg, "Why Is Black Africa Overwhelmed While East Asia Overcomes?" *The International Herald Tribune*, July 14, 1992, pp. 1, 6.

48. C.H. Farnsworth, "Report by World Bank Sees Poverty Lessening by 2000 Except in Africa," *The New York Times*, July 16, 1990, p. A3; Marcum, "Africa: A Continent Adrift"; Duncan, "Africa: The Long Good-bye"; and "The Bleak Continent," *The Economist*, December 9, 1989, pp. 80–81.

49. B. Fischer, "Developing Countries in the Process of Economic Globalisation," *Intereconomics* (March/April 1990), p. 55.

50. J.S. Whitaker, *How Can Africa Survive?* (Washington, DC: Council on Foreign Relations Press, 1988).

51. As will be clear from the text, this discussion excludes the Republic of South Africa.

52. T.J. Goliber, "Africa's Expanding Population: Old Problems, New Policies," *Population Bulletin*, Vol. 44, No. 3 (November 1989), pp. 4–49, an outstandingly good article.

53. *World Resources 1990–91*, p. 254.

54. *World Resources 1990–91*, p. 254 (overall population growth to 2025), and p. 258 (infant mortality). L.K. Altman, "W.H.O. Says 40 Million Will Be Infected with AIDS Virus by 2000," *The New York Times*, June 18, 1991, p. C3 (for percentage of GNP devoted to health care).

55. L.K. Altman, "W.H.O. Says 40 Million Will Be Infected with AIDS Virus by 2000"; and for further figures, see Kennedy, *Preparing for the Twenty-First Century*, chapter 3.

56. K.H. Hunt, "Scenes from a Nightmare," *The New York Times Magazine*, August 12, 1990, pp. 26, 50–51.

57. See Whitaker, *How Can Africa Survive?* especially chapter 4, "The Blessings of Children," for a fuller analysis; and J.C. Caldwell and P. Caldwell, "High Fertility in Sub-Saharan Africa," *Scientific American*, May 1990, pp. 118–25.

58. "The Bleak Continent"; Whitaker, *How Can Africa Survive?* chapters 1 and 2; Goliber, "Africa's Expanding Population," pp. 12–13.

59. Whitaker, *How Can Africa Survive?*; Duncan, "Africa: The Long Good-bye."

60. "Fruits of Containment" (op-ed), *The Wall Street Journal*, December 18, 1990, p. A14, for the Africa–Belgium comparison; H. McRae, "Visions of Tomorrow's World," *The Independent* (London), November 26, 1991, for Africa's share of world GDP.

61. "Aid to Africa," *The Economist*, December 8, 1990, p. 48.

62. In this regard, East Asian nations like Taiwan and Korea, possessing coherent indigenous populations, are once again more favourably situated.

63. *The Economist World Atlas and Almanac*, p. 293.

64. Apart from the country-by-country comments in *The Economist World Atlas and Almanac*, see also K. Ingham, *Politics in Modern Africa: The Uneven Tribal Dimension* (London: Routledge, 1990); "Africa's Internal Wars of the 1980s — Contours and Prospects," United States Institute of Peace, *In Brief*, No. 18 (May 1990).

65. *The Statesman's Yearbook 1989*, p. 84; Goliber, "Africa's Expanding Population," p. 15.

66. *The Statesman's Yearbook 1989*, pp. 1, 159–60 (certain smaller groups of students are excluded from these totals).

67. P. Lewis, "Nyere and Tanzania: No Regrets at Socialism," *The New York Times*, October 24, 1990.

68. "Wind of Change, but a Different One," *The Economist*, July 14, 1990, p. 44. See also the encouraging noises made — on a country-by-country basis — in the World Bank's own *Trends in Developing Economies*, 1990, as well as in its 1989 publication *Sub-Saharan Africa: From Crisis to Sustainable Growth* (summarized in "The Bleak Continent," *The Economist*, pp. 80–81).

69. See especially P. Pradervand, *Listening to Africa: Developing Africa from the Grassroots* (Westport, CT: Greenwood Press, 1989); B. Schneider, *The Barefoot Revolution* (London: I.T. Publications, 1988); K. McAfee, "Why the Third World Goes Hungry," *Commonweal*, June 15, 1990, pp. 384–85.

70. See Edward Sheehan's article "In the Heart of Somalia," *The New York Review*, January 14, 1993. See also Duncan, "Africa: The Long Good-bye," p. 24; G. Hancock, *Lords of Poverty: The Power, Prestige, and Corruption of the International Aid Business* (New York: Atlantic Monthly Press, 1989); G.B.N. Ayittey, "No More Aid for Africa," *The Wall Street Journal*, October 18, 1991 (op-ed), p. A14.

71. Whitaker, *How Can Africa Survive?* p. 231.

72. See, for example, the conclusions in B. Fischer, "Developing Countries in the Process of Economic Globalisation," pp. 55–63.

73. Caldwell and Caldwell, "High Fertility in Sub-Saharan Africa," p. 88.

74. "AIDS in Africa," *The Economist*, November 24, 1989, p. 1B; E. Eckholm and J. Tierney, "AIDS in Africa: A Killer Rages On," *The New York Times*, September 16, 1990, pp. 1, 4; C.M. Becker, "The Demo-Economic Impact of the AIDS Pandemic in Sub-Saharan Africa," *World Development*, Vol. 18, No. 12 (1990), pp. 1, 599–619.

75. *World Resources 1990–91*, p. 254. The US–Canada total in 1960 was 217 million to Latin America's 210 million; by 2025 it is estimated to be 332 million to 762 million.

76. *World Resources 1990–91*, p. 254.

77. Apart from chapters 2 and 4 above, see again *World Resources 1990–91*, pp. 33–48; T. Wicker, "Bush Ventures South," *The New York Times*, December 9, 1990, p. E17; T. Golden, "Mexico Fights Cholera but Hates to Say Its Name," *The New York Times*, September 14, 1991, p. 2.

78. "The Arab World," *The Economist*, p. 4.

79. "The Arab World," p. 6; Y.F. Ibrahim, "In Algeria, Hope for Democracy but Not Economy," *The New York Times*, July 26, 1991, pp. A1, A6.

80. As quoted in "The Arab World," p. 5.

81. See again Pradervand, *Listening to Africa*. Also important is D. Pearce et al., *Sustainable Development: Economics and Environment in the Third World* (Brookfield, VT: Gower, 1990).

82. F. Gable, "Changing Climate and Caribbean Coastlines," *Oceanus*, Vol. 30, No. 4 (Winter 1987–88), pp. 53–56; G. Gable and D.G. Aubrey, "Changing Climate and the Pacific," *Oceanus*, Vol. 32, No. 4 (Winter 1989–90), pp. 71–73.

83. "The Arab World," p. 12.

84. *World Resources 1990–91*, pp. 176–77; *State of the World 1990*, pp. 48–49.

85. C. Juma, *The Gene Hunters: Biotechnology and the Scramble for Seeds* (Princeton, NJ: Princeton University Press, 1989).

86. D. Pirages, *Global Technopolitics: The International Politics of Technology and Resources* (Pacifiic Grove, CA: Brooks-Cole, 1989), p. 152.

87. McAfee, "Why the Third World Goes Hungry," p. 380.

88. See P.K. Ghosh, ed., *Technology Policy and Development: A Third World Perspective* (Westport, CT: Greenwood Press, 1984), p. 109.

89. C.J. Dixon et al., eds., *Multinational Corporations and the Third World* (London: Croom Helm, 1986).

90. For a good example, see B. Onimode, *A Political Economy of the African Crisis* (Atlantic Highlands, NJ: Humanities Press International, 1988), especially p. 310 ff.

91. M. Clash, "Development Policy, Technology Assessment and the New Technologies," *Futures*, November 1990, p. 916.

92. L. Cuyvers and D. Van den Bulcke, "Some Reflections on the 'Outward-Oriented' Development Strategy of the Far Eastern Newly Industrialising Countries," especially pp. 196–97, in Adriaansen and Waardenburg, *A Dual World Economy*.

93. *World Development Report 1991: The Challenge of Development*, a World Bank report (New York: Oxford University Press, 1991). See also the World Bank's *Global Economic Prospects and the Developing Countries* (Washington, DC: 1991).

Chapter 31

Population: Delusion and Reality

AMARTYA SEN

1.

Few issues today are as divisive as what is called the "world population problem." With the approach this autumn of the International Conference of Population and Development in Cairo, organized by the United Nations, these divisions among experts are receiving enormous attention and generating considerable heat. There is a danger that in the confrontation between apocalyptic pessimism, on the one hand, and a dismissive smugness, on the other, a genuine understanding of the nature of the population problem may be lost.[1]

Visions of impending doom have been increasingly aired in recent years, often presenting the population problem as a "bomb" that has been planted and is about to "go off." These catastrophic images have encouraged a tendency to search for emergency solutions, which treat the people involved not as reasonable beings, allies facing a common problem, but as impulsive and uncontrolled sources of great social harm, in need of strong discipline.

Such views have received serious attention in public discussions, not just in sensational headlines in the popular press, but also in seriously argued and widely read books. One of the most influential examples was Paul Ehrlich's *The Population Bomb*, the first three sections of which were headed "Too Many People," "Too Little Food," and "A Dying Planet."[2] A more recent example of a chilling diagnosis of imminent calamity is Garrett Hardin's *Living within Limits*.[3] The arguments on which these pessimistic visions are based deserve serious scrutiny.

If the propensity to foresee impending disaster from overpopulation is strong in some circles, so is the tendency, in others, to dismiss all worries about population size. Just as alarmism builds on the recognition of a real problem and then magnifies it, complacency may also start off from a reasonable belief about the history of population problems and fail to see how they may have changed by now. It is often pointed out, for example, that the world has coped well enough with fast increases in population in the past, even though alarmists had expected otherwise. Malthus anticipated terrible disasters resulting from population growth and a consequent imbalance in "the proportion between the natural increase of population and food."[4] At a time when there were fewer than a billion people, he was quite convinced that "the period when the number of men surpass their means of subsistence has long since arrived." However, since Malthus first published his famous *Essay on Population* in 1798, the world population has grown nearly six times larger, while food output and consumption per person are considerably higher now, and there has been an unprecedented increase both in life expectancies and in general living standards.[5]

The fact that Malthus was mistaken in his diagnosis as well as his prognosis 200 years ago

Source: "Population: Delusion and Reality," *The New York Review of Books* 41, 15 (September 22, 1994): 62–71. Copyright © 1994 Nyrev, Inc. Reprinted with permission from *The New York Review of Books*.

does not, however, indicate that contemporary fears about population growth must be similarly erroneous. The increase in the world population has vastly accelerated over the last century. It took the world population millions of years to reach the first billion, then 123 years to get to the second, 33 years to the third, 14 years to the fourth, 13 years to the fifth billion, with the sixth billion to come, according to one UN projection, in another 11 years.[6] During the last decade, between 1980 and 1990, the number of people on earth grew by about 923 million, an increase nearly the size of the total world population in Malthus's time. Whatever may be the proper response to alarmism about the future, complacency based on past success is no response at all.

IMMIGRATION AND POPULATION

One current worry concerns the regional distribution of the increase in world population, about 90 percent of which is taking place in the developing countries. The percentage rate of population growth is fastest in Africa—3.1 percent per year over the last decade. But most of the large increases in population occur in regions other than Africa. The largest absolute increases in numbers are taking place in Asia, which is where most of the world's poorer people live, even though the rate of increase in population has been slowing significantly there. Of the worldwide increase of 923 million people in the 1980s, well over half occurred in Asia— 517 million in fact (including 146 million in China and 166 million in India).

Beyond concerns about the well-being of these poor countries themselves, a more self-regarding worry causes panic in the richer countries of the world and has much to do with the current anxiety in the West about the "world population problem." This is founded on the belief that destitution caused by fast population growth in the Third World is responsible for the severe pressure to emigrate to the developed countries of Europe and North America. In this view, people impoverished by overpopulation in the "South" flee to the "North." Some have claimed to find empirical support for this thesis in the fact that pressure to emigrate from the South has accelerated in recent decades, along with a rapid increase in the population there.

There are two distinct questions here: first, how great a threat of intolerable immigration pressure does the North face from the South, and second, is that pressure closely related to population growth in the South, rather than to other social and economic factors? There are reasons to doubt that population growth is the major force behind migratory pressures, and I shall concentrate here on that question. But I should note in passing that immigration is now severely controlled in Europe and North America, and insofar as Europe is concerned, most of the current immigrants from the Third World are not "primary" immigrants but dependent relatives— mainly spouses and young children—of those who had come and settled earlier. The United States remains relatively more open to fresh immigration, but the requirements of "labour certification" as a necessary part of the immigration procedure tend to guarantee that the new entrants are relatively better educated and more skilled. There are, however, sizable flows of illegal immigrants, especially to the United States and, to a lesser extent, to southern Europe, though the numbers are hard to estimate.

What causes the current pressures to emigrate? The "job-worthy" people who get through the immigration process are hardly to be seen as impoverished and destitute migrants created by the sheer pressure of population. Even the illegal immigrants who manage to evade the rigours of border control are typically not starving wretches but those who can make use of work prospects in the North.

The explanation for the increased migratory pressure over the decades owes more to the dynamism of international capitalism than to just the growing size of the population of the Third World countries. The immigrants have allies in potential employers, and this applies as much to illegal farm labourers in California as to the legally authorized "guest workers" in automobile factories in Germany. The economic incentive to emigrate to the North from the poorer Southern economies may well depend on differences in real income. But this gap is very large anyway, and even if it is presumed that population growth in the South is increasing the disparity with the North—a thesis I shall presently consider—it seems unlikely that this incentive would significantly change if the Northern income level were, say, 20 times that of the Southern as opposed to 25 times.

The growing demand for immigration to the North from the South is related to the "shrinking" of the world (through revolutions in communication and transport), reduction in economic obstacles to labour movements (despite the increase in political barriers), and the growing reach and absorptive power of international capitalism (even as domestic politics in the North has turned more inward-looking and nationalistic). To try to explain the increase in immigration pressure by the growth rate of total population in the Third World is to close one's eyes to the deep changes that have occurred—and are occurring —in the world in which we live, and the rapid internationalization of its cultures and economies that accompanies these changes.

FEARS OF BEING ENGULFED

A closely related issue concerns what is perceived as a growing "imbalance" in the division of the world population, with a rapidly rising share belonging to the Third World. That fear translates into worries of various kinds in the North, especially the sense of being overrun by the South. Many Northerners fear being engulfed by people from Asia and Africa, whose share of the world population increased from 63.7 percent in 1950 to 71.2 percent by 1990, and is expected, according to the estimates of the United Nations, to rise to 78.5 percent by 2050.

It is easy to understand the fears of relatively well-off people at the thought of being surround-ed by a fast-growing and increasingly impoverished Southern population. As I shall argue, the thesis of growing impoverishment does not stand up to much scrutiny; but it is important to address first the psychologically tense issue of racial balance in the world (even though racial composition as a consideration has only as much importance as we choose to give it). Here it is worth recollecting that the Third World is right now going through the same kind of demographic shift—a rapid expansion of population for a temporary but long stretch—that Europe and North America experienced during their industrial revolution. In 1650 the share of Asia and Africa in the world population is estimated to have been 78.4 percent, and it stayed around there even in 1750.[7] With the industrial revolution, the share of Asia and Africa diminished because of the rapid rise of population in Europe and North America; for example, during the nineteenth century while the inhabitants of Asia and Africa grew by about 4 percent per decade or less, the population of "the area of European settlement" grew by around 10 percent every decade.

Even now the combined share of Asia and Africa (71.2 percent) is considerably *below* what its share was in 1650 or 1750. If the United Nations' prediction that this share will rise to 78.5 percent by 2050 comes true, then the Asians and the Africans would return to being proportionately almost exactly as numerous as they were before the European industrial revolution. There is, of course, nothing sacrosanct about the distributions of population in the past; but the sense of a growing "imbalance" in the world, based only on recent trends, ignores history and implicitly presumes that the expansion of Europeans earlier on was natural, whereas the same process happening now to other populations unnaturally disturbs the "balance."

COLLABORATION VERSUS OVERRIDE

Other worries involving the relation of population growth to food supplies, income levels, and the environment reflect more serious matters.[8]

Before I take up those questions, a brief comment on the distinction between two rival approaches to dealing with the population problem may be useful. One involves voluntary choice and a collaborative solution, and the other overrides voluntarism through legal or economic coercion.

Alarmist views of impending crises tend to produce a willingness to consider forceful measures for coercing people to have fewer children in the Third World. Imposing birth control on unwilling people is no longer rejected as readily as it was until quite recently, and some activists have pointed to the ambiguities that exist in determining what is or is not "coercion."[9] Those who are willing to consider — or at least not fully reject — programs that would use some measure of force to reduce population growth often point to the success of China's "one-child policy" in cutting down the national birth rate. Force can also take an indirect form, as when economic opportunities are changed so radically by government regulations that people are left with very little choice except to behave in ways the government would approve. In China's case, the government may refuse to offer housing to families with too many children — thus penalizing the children as well as the dissenting adults.

In India the policy of compulsory birth control that was initiated during the "emergency period" declared by Mrs Gandhi in the 1970s was decisively rejected by the voters in the general election in which it — along with civil rights — was a major issue. Even so, some public health clinics in the northern states (such as Uttar Pradesh) insist, in practice, on sterilization before providing normal medical attention to women and men beyond a certain age. The pressures to move in that direction seem to be strong, and they are reinforced by the rhetoric of "the population bomb."

I shall call this general approach the "override" view, since the family's personal decisions are overridden by some agency outside the family — typically by the government of the country in question (whether or not it has been pressed

to do so by "outside" agencies, such as international organizations and pressure groups). In fact, overriding is not limited to an explicit use of legal coercion or economic compulsion, since people's own choices can also be effectively overridden by simply not offering them the opportunities for jobs or welfare that they can expect to get from a responsible government. Override can take many different forms and can be of varying intensity (with the Chinese "one-child policy" being something of an extreme case of a more general approach).

A central issue here is the increasingly vocal demand by some activists concerned with population growth that the highest "priority" should be given in Third World countries to family planning over other public commitments. This demand goes much beyond supporting family planning as a part of development. In fact, proposals for shifting international aid away from development in general to family planning in particular have lately been increasingly frequent. Such policies fit into the general approach of "override" as well, since they try to rely on manipulating people's choices through offering them only some opportunities (the means of family planning) while denying others, no matter what they would have themselves preferred. Insofar as they would have the effect of reducing health care and educational services, such shifts in public commitments will not only add to the misery of human lives, they may also have, I shall argue, exactly the opposite effect on family planning than the one intended, since education and health care have a significant part in the *voluntary* reduction of the birth rate.

The "override" approach contrasts with another, the "collaborative" approach, that relies not on legal or economic restrictions but on rational decisions of women and men, based on expanded choices and enhanced security, and encouraged by open dialogue and extensive public discussions. The difference between the two approaches does not lie in government's activism in the first case as opposed to passivity in the second. Even if solutions are sought through the decisions and actions of people themselves, the chance to take reasoned decisions with more knowledge and a greater sense of personal security can be increased by public policies, for example, through expanding educational facilities, health care, and economic well-being, along with providing better access to family planning. The central political and ethical issue concerning the "override" approach does not lie in its insistence on the need for public policy but in the ways it significantly reduces the choices open to parents.

THE MALTHUS–CONDORCET DEBATE

Thomas Robert Malthus forcefully argued for a version of the "override" view. In fact, it was precisely this preference that distinguished Malthus from Condorcet, the eighteenth-century French mathematician and social scientist from whom Malthus had actually derived the analysis of how population could outgrow the means of living. The debate between Condorcet and Malthus in some ways marks the origin of the distinction between the "collaborative" and the "override" approaches, which still compete for attention.[10]

In his *Essay on Population*, published in 1798, Malthus quoted—extensively and with approval—Condorcet's discussion, in 1795, of the possibility of overpopulation. However, true to the Enlightenment tradition, Condorcet was confident that this problem would be solved by reasoned human action: through increases in productivity, through better conservation and prevention of waste, and through education (especially female education), which would contribute to reducing the birth rate.[11] Voluntary family planning would be encouraged, in Condorcet's analysis, by increased understanding that if people "have a duty toward those who are not yet born, that duty is not to give them existence but to give them happiness." They would see the value of limiting family size "rather than foolishly ... encumber the world with useless and wretched beings."[12]

Even though Malthus borrowed from Condorcet his diagnosis of the possibility of overpopulation, he refused to accept Condorcet's solution. Indeed, Malthus's essay on population was partly a criticism of Condorcet's Enlightenment reasoning, and even the full title of Malthus's famous essay specifically mentioned Condorcet. Malthus argued that

> there is no reason whatever to suppose that anything beside the difficulty of procuring in adequate plenty the necessaries of life should either indispose this greater number of persons to marry early, or disable them from rearing in health the largest families.[13]

Malthus thus opposed public relief of poverty: he saw the "poor laws" in particular as contributing greatly to population growth.[14]

Malthus was not sure that any public policy would work, and whether "overriding" would in fact be possible: "The perpetual tendency in the race of man to increase beyond the means of subsistence is one of the great general laws of animated nature which we can have no reason to expect will change."[15] But insofar as any solution would be possible, it could not come from voluntary decisions of the people involved, or acting from a position of strength and economic security. It must come from overriding their preferences through the compulsions of economic necessity, since their poverty was the only thing that could "indispose this greater number of persons to marry early, or disable them from rearing in health the largest families."

DEVELOPMENT AND INCREASED CHOICE

The distinction between the "collaborative" approach and the "override" approach thus tends to correspond closely to the contrast between, on the one hand, treating economic and social development as the way to solve the population problem and, on the other, expecting little from development and using, instead, legal and economic pressures to reduce birth rates.

Among recent writers, those such as Gerard Piel,[16] who have persuasively emphasized our ability to solve problems through reasoned decisions and actions, have tended—like Condorcet—to find the solution of the population problem in economic and social development. They advocate a broadly collaborative approach, in which governments and citizens would together produce economic and social conditions favouring slower population growth. In contrast, those who have been thoroughly skeptical of reasoned human action to limit population growth have tended to go in the direction of "override" in one form or another, rather than concentrate on development and voluntarism.

Has development, in fact, done much to reduce population growth? There can be little doubt that economic and social development, in general, has been associated with major reductions in birth rates and the emergence of smaller families as the norm. This is a pattern that was, of course, clearly observed in Europe and North America as they underwent industrialization, but that experience has been repeated in many other parts of the world.

In particular, conditions of economic security and affluence, wider availability of contraceptive methods, expansion of education (particularly female education), and lower mortality rates have had—and are currently having—quite substantial effects in reducing birth rates in different parts of the world.[17] The rate of world population growth is certainly declining, and even over the last two decades its percentage growth rate has fallen from 2.2 percent per year between 1970 and 1980 to 1.7 percent between 1980 and 1992. This rate is expected to go steadily down until the size of the world's population becomes nearly stationary.[18]

There are important regional differences in demographic behaviour; for example, the population growth rate in India peaked at 2.2 percent a year (in the 1970s) and has since started to diminish, whereas most Latin American countries peaked at much higher rates before coming down sharply, while many countries in Africa currently have growth rates between 3 and 4 percent, with an average for sub-Saharan Africa of 3.1 percent. Similarly, the different factors have varied in their respective influence from region to region. But there can be little dispute that economic and social development tends to reduce fertility rates. The regions of the Third World that lag most in achieving economic and social development, such as many countries in Africa, are, in general, also the ones that have failed to reduce birth rates significantly. Malthus's fear that economic and social development could only encourage people to have more children has certainly proved to be radically wrong, and so have all the painful policy implications drawn from it.

This raises the following question: in view of the clear connection between development and lower fertility, why isn't the dispute over how to deal with population growth fully resolved already? Why don't we reinterpret the population problem simply as a problem of underdevelopment and seek a solution by encouraging economic and social development (even if we reject the oversimple slogan "development is the most reliable contraceptive")?

In the long run, this may indeed be exactly the right approach. The problem is more complex, however, because a "contraceptive" that is "reliable" in the long run may not act fast enough to meet the present threat. Even though development may dependably work to stabilize population if it is given enough time, there may not be, it is argued, time enough to give. The death rate often falls very fast with more widely available health care, better sanitation, and improved nutrition, while the birth rate may fall rather slowly. Much growth of population may meanwhile occur.

This is exactly the point at which apocalyptic prophecies add force to the "override" view. One claim, then, that needs examination is that the world is facing an imminent crisis, one so urgent that development is just too slow a process to deal with it. We must try right now, the argument goes, to cut down population growth by drastic and forceful means if necessary. The second claim that also needs scrutiny is the actual feasibility of adequately reducing population growth through these drastic means, without fostering social and economic development.

2.

POPULATION AND INCOME

It is sometimes argued that signs of an imminent crisis can be found in the growing impoverishment of the South, with falling income per capita accompanying high population growth. In general, there is little evidence for this. As a matter of fact, the average population of "low-income" countries (as defined by the World Bank) has been not only enjoying a rising gross national product (GNP) per head, but a growth rate of GNP per capita (3.9 percent per year for 1980–92) that is much faster than those for the "high-income" countries (2.4 percent) and for the "middle-income" ones (0 percent).[19]

The growth of per capita GNP of the population of low-income countries would have been even higher had it not been for the negative growth rates of many countries in sub-Saharan Africa, one region in which a number of countries have been experiencing economic decline. But the main culprit causing this state of affairs is the terrible failure of economic production in sub-Saharan Africa (connected particularly with political disruption, including wars and military rule), rather than population growth, which is only a subsidiary factor. Sub-Saharan Africa does have high population growth, but its economic stagnation has contributed much more to the fall in its per capita income.

With its average population growth rate of 3.1 percent per year, had sub-Saharan Africa suddenly matched China's low population growth of 1.4 percent (the lowest among the low-income countries), it would have gained roughly 1.7 percent in per capita GNP growth. The real income per person would still have fallen, even with that minimal population growth,

for many countries in the region. The growth of GNP per capita is *minus* 1.9 percent for Ethiopia, *minus* 1.8 percent for Togo, *minus* 3.6 percent for Mozambique, *minus* 4.3 percent for Niger, *minus* 4.7 percent for Ivory Coast, not to mention Somalia, Sudan, and Angola, where the political disruption has been so serious that no reliable GNP estimates even exist. A lower population growth rate could have reduced the magnitude of the fall in per capita GNP, but the main roots of Africa's economic decline lie elsewhere. The complex political factors underlying the troubles of Africa include, among other things, the subversion of democracy and the rise of combative military rulers, often encouraged by the cold war (with Africa providing "client states"—from Somalia and Ethiopia to Angola and Zaire—for the superpowers, particularly from the 1960s onward). The explanation of sub-Saharan Africa's problems has to be sought in these political troubles, which affect economic stability, agricultural and industrial incentives, public health arrangements, and social services —even family planning and population policy.[20]

There is indeed a very powerful case for reducing the rate of growth of population in Africa, but this problem cannot be dissociated from the rest of the continent's woes. Sub-Saharan Africa lags behind other developing regions in economic security, in health care, in life expectancy, in basic education, and in political and economic stability. It should be no great surprise that it lags behind in family planning as well. To dissociate the task of population control from the politics and economics of Africa would be a great mistake and would seriously mislead public policy.

POPULATION AND FOOD

Malthus's exact thesis cannot, however, be disputed by quoting statistics of income per capita, for he was concerned specifically with food supply per capita, and he had concentrated on "the proportion between the natural increase of population and food." Many modern commentators, including Paul Ehrlich and Garrett Hardin, have said much about this, too. When Ehrlich says, in his *Population Bomb*, "too little food," he does not mean "too little income," but specifically a growth shortage of food.

Is population beginning to outrun food production? Even though such an impression is often given in public discussions, there is, in fact, no serious evidence that this is happening. While there are some year-to-year fluctuations in the growth of food output (typically inducing, whenever things slacken a bit, some excited remarks by those who anticipate impending doom), the worldwide trend of food output per person has been firmly upward. Not only over the two centuries since Malthus's time, but also during recent decades, the rise in food output has been significantly and consistently outpacing the expansion of world population.[21]

But the total food supply in the world as a whole is not the only issue. What about the regional distribution of food? If it were to turn out that the rising ratio of food to population is mainly caused by increased production in richer countries (for example, if it appeared that U.S. wheat output was feeding the Third World, in which much of the population expansion is taking place), then the neo-Malthusian fears about "too many people" and "too little food" may have some plausibility. Is that what is happening?

In fact, with one substantial exception, exactly the opposite is true. The largest increases in the production of food — not just in the aggregate but also per person — are actually taking place in the Third World, particularly in the region that is having the largest absolute increases in the world population, that is, in Asia. The many millions of people who are added to the populations of India and China may be constantly cited by the terrorized — and terrorizing — advocates of the apocalyptic view, but it is precisely in these countries that the most rapid rates of growth in food output per capita are to be observed. For example, between the three-year averages of 1979–81 and

1991–93, food production per head in the world moved up by 3 percent, while it went up by only 2 percent in Europe and went down by nearly 5 percent in North America. In contrast, per capita food production jumped up by 22 percent in Asia generally, including 23 percent in India and 39 percent in China[22] (see Table 31.1).

During the same period, however, food production per capita went down by 6 percent in Africa, and even the absolute size of food output fell in some countries (such as Malawi and Somalia). Of course, many countries in the world — from Syria, Italy, and Sweden to Botswana in Africa — have had declining food production per head without experiencing hunger or starvation, since their economies have prospered and grown; when the means are available, food can be easily bought in the international market if it is necessary to do so. For many countries in sub-Saharan Africa the problem arises from the fact that the decline in food production is an integral part of the story of overall economic decline, which I have discussed earlier.

Difficulties of food production in sub-Saharan Africa, like other problems of the national economy, are not only linked to wars,

TABLE 31.1 INDICES OF FOOD PRODUCTION PER CAPITA		
	1979–81 BASE PERIOD	1991–93
World	100	103
Europe	100	102
North America	100	95
Africa	100	94
Asia	100	122
including		
India	100	123
China	100	139

SOURCE: *FAO Quarterly Bulletin of Statistics*, Food and Agriculture Organization of the United Nations.

dictatorships, and political chaos. In addition, there is some evidence that climatic shifts have had unfavourable effects on parts of that continent. While some of the climatic problems may be caused partly by increases in human settlement and environmental neglect, that neglect is not unrelated to the political and economic chaos that has characterized sub-Saharan Africa during the last few decades. The food problem of Africa must be seen as one part of a wider political and economic problem of the region.[23]

THE PRICE OF FOOD

To return to "the balance between food and population," the rising food production per capita in the world as a whole, and in the Third World in general, contradicts some of the pessimism that characterized the gloomy predictions of the past. Prophecies of imminent disaster during the last few decades have not proved any more accurate than Malthus's prognostication nearly two hundred years ago. As for new prophecies of doom, they cannot, of course, be contradicted until the future arrives. There was no way of refuting the theses of W. Paddock and P. Paddock's popular book *Famine—1975!* published in 1968, which predicted terrible cataclysm for the world as a whole by 1975 (writing off India, in particular, as a basket case), until 1975 actually arrived. The new prophets have learned not to attach specific dates to the crises they foresee, and past failures do not seem to have reduced the popular appetite for this creative genre.

However, after noting the rather dismal forecasting record of doomsayers, we must also accept the general methodological point that present trends in output do not necessarily tell us much about the prospects of further expansion in the future. It could, for example, be argued that maintaining growth in food production may require proportionately increasing investments of capital, drawing them away from other kinds of production. This would tend to make food progressively more expensive if there

are "diminishing returns" in shifting resources from other fields into food production. And, ultimately, further expansion of food production may become so expensive that it would be hard to maintain the trend of increasing food production without reducing other outputs drastically.

But is food production really getting more and more expensive? There is, in fact, no evidence for that conclusion either. In fact, quite the contrary. Not only is food generally much cheaper to buy today, in constant dollars, than it was in Malthus's time, but it also has become cheaper during recent decades. As a matter of fact, there have been increasing complaints among food exporters, especially in the Third World, that food prices have fallen in relation to other commodities. For example, in 1992 a United Nations report recorded a 38 percent fall in the relative prices of "basic foods" over the last decade.[24] This is entirely in line with the trend, during the last three decades, toward declining relative prices of particular food items, in relation to the prices of manufactured goods. The World Bank's adjusted estimates of the prices of particular food crops, between 1953–55 and 1983–85, show similarly steep declines for such staples as rice (42 percent), wheat (57 percent), sorghum (39 percent), and maize (37 percent).[25]

Not only is food getting less expensive, but we also have to bear in mind that the current increase in food production (substantial and well ahead of population growth, as it is) is itself being kept in check by the difficulties in selling food profitably, as the relative prices of food have fallen. Those neo-Malthusians who concede that food production is now growing faster than population often point out that it is growing "only a little faster than population," and they are inclined to interpret this as evidence that we are reaching the limits of what we can produce to keep pace with population growth.

But that is surely the wrong conclusion to draw in view of the falling relative prices of food, and the current difficulties in selling food, since it ignores the effects of economic incentives that govern production. When we take into account the persistent cheapening of food prices, we have good grounds to suggest that food output is being held back by a lack of effective demand in the market. The imaginary crisis in food production, contradicted as it is by the upward trends of total and regional food output per head, is thus further debunked by an analysis of the economic incentives to produce more food.

DEPRIVED LIVES AND SLUMS

I have examined the alleged "food problem" associated with population growth in some detail because it has received so much attention both in the traditional Malthusian literature and in the recent writings of neo-Malthusians. In concentrating on his claim that growing populations would not have enough food, Malthus differed from Condorcet's broader presentation of the population question. Condorcet's own emphasis was on the possibility of "a continual diminution of happiness" as a result of population growth, a diminution that could occur in many different ways—not just through the deprivation of food, but through a decline in living conditions generally. That more extensive worry can remain even when Malthus's analysis of the food supply is rejected.

Indeed, average income and food production per head can go on increasing even as the wretchedly deprived living conditions of particular sections of the population get worse, as they have in many parts of the Third World. The living conditions of backward regions and deprived classes can decline even when a country's economic growth is very rapid on the average. Brazil during the 1960s and 1970s provided an extreme example of this. The sense that there are just "too many people" around often arises from seeing the desperate lives of people in the large and rapidly growing urban slums—*bidonvilles*—in poor countries, sobering reminders that we should not take too much comfort from aggregate statistics of economic progress.

But in an essay addressed mainly to the population problem, what we have to ask is not whether things are just fine in the Third World (they obviously are not), but whether population growth is the root cause of the deprivations that people suffer. The question is whether the particular instances of deep poverty we observe derive mainly from population growth rather than from other factors that lead to unshared prosperity and persistent and possibly growing inequality. The tendency to see in population growth an explanation for every calamity that afflicts poor people is now fairly well established in some circles, and the message that gets transmitted constantly is the opposite of the old picture postcard: "Wish you weren't here."

To see in population growth the main reason for the growth of overcrowded and very poor slums in large cities, for example, is not empirically convincing. It does not help to explain why the slums of Calcutta and Bombay have grown worse at a faster rate than those of Karachi and Islamabad (India's population growth rate is 2.1 percent per year, Pakistan's 3.1), or why Jakarta has deteriorated faster than Ankara or Istanbul (Indonesian population growth is 1.8 percent, Turkey's 2.3), or why the slums of Mexico City have become worse more rapidly than those of San José (Mexico's population growth rate is 2.0, Costa Rica's 2.8), or why Harlem can seem more and more deprived when compared with the poorer districts of Singapore (U.S. population growth rate is 1.0, Singapore's is 1.8). Many causal factors affect the degree of deprivation in particular parts of a country—rural as well as urban—and to try to see them all as resulting from overpopulation is the negation of social analysis.

This is not to deny that population growth may well have an effect on deprivation, but only to insist that any investigation of the effects of population growth must be part of the analysis of economic and political processes, including the effects of other variables. It is the isolationist view of population growth that should be rejected.

THREATS TO THE ENVIRONMENT

In his concern about "a continual diminution of happiness" from population growth, Condorcet was a pioneer in considering the possibility that natural raw materials might be used up, thereby making living conditions worse. In his characteristically rationalist solution, which relied partly on voluntary and reasoned measures to reduce the birth rate, Condorcet also envisaged the development of less improvident technology: "The manufacture of articles will be achieved with less wastage in raw materials and will make better use of them."[26]

The effects of a growing population on the environment could be a good deal more serious than the food problems that have received so much attention in the literature inspired by Malthus. If the environment is damaged by population pressures, this obviously affects the kind of life we lead, and the possibilities of a "diminution in happiness" can be quite considerable. In dealing with this problem, we have to distinguish once again between the long and the short run. The short-run picture tends to be dominated by the fact that the per capita consumption of food, fuel, and other goods by people in Third World countries is often relatively low; consequently the impact of population growth in these countries is not, in relative terms, so damaging to the global environment. But the problems of the local environment can, of course, be serious in many developing economies. They vary from the "neighbourhood pollution" created by unregulated industries to the pressure of denser populations on rural resources such as fields and woods.[27] (The Indian authorities had to close down several factories in and around Agra, since the façade of the Taj Mahal was turning pale as a result of chemical pollution from local factories.) But it remains true that one additional American typically has a larger negative impact on the ozone layer, global warmth, and other elements of the earth's environment than dozens of Indians and Zimbabweans put together. Those who argue for the immediate

need for forceful population control in the Third World to preserve the global environment must first recognize this elementary fact.

This does not imply, as is sometimes suggested, that as far as the global environment is concerned, population growth in the Third World is nothing to worry about. The long-run impact on the global environment of population growth in the developing countries can be expected to be large. As the Indians and Zimbabweans develop economically, they too will consume a great deal more, and they will pose, in the future, a threat to the earth's environment similar to that of people in the rich countries today. The long-run threat of population to the environment is a real one.

3.

WOMEN'S DEPRIVATION AND POWER

Since reducing the birth rate can be slow, this and other long-run problems should be addressed right now. Solutions will no doubt have to be found in the two directions to which, as it happens, Condorcet pointed: (1) developing new technology and new behaviour patterns that would waste little and pollute less, and (2) fostering social and economic changes that would gradually bring down the growth rate of population.

On reducing birth rates, Condorcet's own solution not only included enhancing economic opportunity and security, but also stressed the importance of education, particularly female education. A better-educated population could have a more informed discussion of the kind of life we have reason to value; in particular it would reject the drudgery of a life of continuous child bearing and rearing that is routinely forced on many Third World women. That drudgery, in some ways, is the most immediately adverse consequence of high fertility rates.

Central to reducing birth rates, then, is a close connection between women's well-being and their power to make their own decisions and bring about changes in the fertility pattern.

Women in many Third World countries are deprived by high birth frequency of the freedom to do other things in life, not to mention the medical dangers of repeated pregnancy and high maternal mortality, which are both characteristic of many developing countries. It is thus not surprising that reductions in birth rates have been typically associated with improvement of women's status and their ability to make their voices heard — often the result of expanded opportunities for schooling and political activity.[28]

There is nothing particularly exotic about declines in the birth rate occurring through a process of voluntary rational assessment, of which Condorcet spoke. It is what people do when they have some basic education, know about family planning methods and have access to them, do not readily accept a life of persistent drudgery, and are not deeply anxious about their economic security. It is also what they do when they are not forced by high infant and child mortality rates to be so worried that no child will survive to support them in their old age that they try to have many children. In country after country the birth rate has come down with more female education, the reduction of mortality rates, the expansion of economic means and security, and greater public discussion of ways of living.

DEVELOPMENT VERSUS COERCION

There is little doubt that this process of social and economic change will over time cut down the birth rate. Indeed the growth rate of world population is already firmly declining — it came down from 2.2 percent in the 1970s to 1.7 percent between 1980 and 1992. Had imminent cataclysm been threatening, we might have had good reason to reject such gradual progress and consider more drastic means of population control, as some have advocated. But that apocalyptic view is empirically baseless. There is no imminent emergency that calls for a breathless response. What is called

for is systematic support for people's own decisions to reduce family size through expanding education and health care, and through economic and social development.

It is often asked where the money needed for expanding education, health care, and so on would be found. Education, health services, and many other means of improving the quality of life are typically highly labour-intensive and are thus relatively inexpensive in poor countries (because of low wages).[29] While poor countries have less money to spend, they also need less money to provide these services. For this reason many poor countries have indeed been able to expand educational and health services widely without waiting to become prosperous through the process of economic growth. Sri Lanka, Costa Rica, Indonesia, and Thailand are good examples, and there are many others. While the impact of these social services on the quality and length of life has been much studied, they are also major means of reducing the birth rate.

By contrast with such open and voluntary developments, coercive methods, such as the "one-child policy" in some regions, have been tried in China, particularly since the reforms of 1979. Many commentators have pointed out that by 1992 the Chinese birth rate had fallen to 19 per 1000, compared with 29 per 1000 in India, and 37 per 1000 for the average of poor countries other than China and India. China's total fertility rate (reflecting the number of children born per woman) is now at "the replacement level" of 2.0, compared with India's 3.6 and the weighted average of 4.9 for low-income countries other than China and India.[30] Hasn't China shown the way to "solve" the population problem in other developing countries as well?

4.
CHINA'S POPULATION POLICIES

The difficulties with this "solution" are of several kinds. First, if freedom is valued at all, the lack of freedom associated with this approach must be seen to be a social loss in itself. The importance of reproductive freedom has been persuasively emphasized by women's groups throughout the world.[31]

The loss of freedom is often dismissed on the grounds that, because of cultural differences, authoritarian policies that would not be tolerated in the West are acceptable to Asians. While we often hear references to "despotic" Oriental traditions, such arguments are not more convincing than a claim that compulsion in the West is justified by the traditions of the Spanish Inquisition or of the Nazi concentration camps. Frequent references are also made to the emphasis on discipline in the "Confucian tradition"; but that is not the only tradition in the "East," nor is it easy to assess the implications of that tradition for modern Asia (even if we were able to show that discipline is more important for Confucius than it is for, say, Plato or Saint Augustine).

Only a democratic expression of opinion could reveal whether citizens would find a compulsory system acceptable. While such a test has not occurred in China, one did in fact take place in India during "the emergency period" in the 1970s, when Indira Gandhi's government imposed compulsory birth control and suspended various legal freedoms. In the general elections that followed, the politicians favouring the policy of coercion were overwhelmingly defeated. Furthermore, family planning experts in India have observed how the briefly applied programs of compulsory sterilization tended to discredit voluntary birth control programs generally, since people became deeply suspicious of the entire movement to control fertility.

Second, apart from the fundamental issue of whether people are willing to accept compulsory birth control, its specific consequences must also be considered. Insofar as coercion is effective, it works by making people do things they would not freely do. The social consequences of such compulsion, including the ways in which an unwilling population tends to react when it is coerced, can be appalling. For example, the demands of a "one-child family" can lead to the

neglect—or worse—of a second child, thereby increasing the infant mortality rate. Moreover, in a country with a strong preference for male children—a preference shared by China and many other countries in Asia and North Africa—a policy of allowing only one child per family can easily lead to the fatal neglect of a female child. There is much evidence that this is fairly widespread in China, with very adverse effects on infant mortality rates. There are reports that female children have been severely neglected as well as suggestions that female infanticide occurs with considerable frequency. Such consequences are hard to tolerate morally, and perhaps politically also, in the long run.

Third, what is also not clear is exactly how much additional reduction in the birth rate has been achieved through these coercive methods. Many of China's longstanding social and economic programs have been valuable in reducing fertility, including those that have expanded education for women as well as men, made health care more generally available, provided more job opportunities for women, and stimulated rapid economic growth. These factors would themselves have reduced the birth rates, and it is not clear how much "extra lowering" of fertility rates has been achieved in China through compulsion.

For example, we can determine whether many of the countries that match (or outmatch) China in life expectancy, female literacy rates, and female participation in the labour force actually have a higher fertility rate than China. Of all the countries in the world for which data are given in the *World Development Report 1994*, there are only three such countries: Jamaica (2.7), Thailand (2.2), and Sweden (2.1)—and the fertility rates of two of these are close to China's (2.0). Thus the additional contribution of coercion to reducing fertility in China is by no means clear, since compulsion was superimposed on a society that was already reducing its birth rate and in which education and jobs outside the home were available to large numbers of women. In some regions of China, the compulsory program needed little enforcement, whereas in other — more backward — regions, it had to be applied with much severity, with terrible consequences in infant mortality and discrimination against female children. While China may get too much credit for its authoritarian measures, it gets far too little credit for the other, more collaborative and participatory, policies it has followed, which have themselves helped to cut down the birth rate.

CHINA AND INDIA

A useful contrast can be drawn between China and India, the two most populous countries in the world. If we look only at the national averages, it is easy to see that China with its low fertility rate of 2.0 has achieved much more than India has with its average fertility rate of 3.6. To what extent this contrast can be attributed to the effectiveness of the coercive policies used in China is not clear, since we would expect the fertility rate to be much lower in China in view of its higher percentage of female literacy (almost twice as high), higher life expectancy (almost ten years more), larger female involvement (by three-quarters) in the labour force, and so on. But India is a country of great diversity, whose different states have very unequal achievements in literacy, health care, and economic and social development. Most states in India are far behind the Chinese provinces in educational achievement (with the exception of Tibet, which has the lowest literacy rate of any Chinese or Indian state), and the same applies to other factors that affect fertility. However, the state of Kerala in southern India provides an interesting comparison with China, since it too has high levels of basic education, health care, and so on. Kerala is a state within a country, but with its 29 million people, it is larger than most countries in the world (including Canada). Kerala's birth rate of 18 per 1000 is actually lower than China's 19 per 1000, and its fertility rate is 1.8 for 1991, compared with China's 2.0 for 1992. These low rates have been achieved without any state coercion.[32]

The roots of Kerala's success are to be found in the kinds of social progress Condorcet hoped for, including, among others, a high female literacy rate (86 percent, which is substantially higher than China's 68 percent). The rural literacy rate is in fact higher in Kerala — for women as well as men — than in every single province in China. Male and female life expectancies at birth in China are respectively 67 and 71 years; the provisional 1991 figures for men and women in Kerala are 71 and 74 years. Women have been active in Kerala's economic and political life for a long time. A high proportion do skilled and semi-skilled work, and a large number have taken part in educational movements.[33] It is perhaps of symbolic importance that the first public pronouncement of the need for widespread elementary education in any part of India was made in 1817 by Rani Gouri Parvathi Bai, the young queen of the princely state of Travancore, which makes up a substantial part of modern Kerala. For a long time, public discussions in Kerala have centred on women's rights and the undesirability of couples marrying when very young.

This political process has been voluntary and collaborative, rather than coercive, and the adverse reactions that have been observed in China, such as infant mortality, have not occurred in Kerala. Kerala's low fertility rate has been achieved along with an infant mortality rate of 16.5 per 1000 live births (17 for boys and 16 for girls), compared with China's 31 (28 for boys and 33 for girls). And as a result of greater gender equality in Kerala, women have not suffered from higher mortality rates than men in Kerala, as they have in China. Even the ratio of females to males in the total population in Kerala (above 1.03) is quite close to that of the current ratios in Europe and America (reflecting the usual pattern of lower female mortality whenever women and men receive similar care). By contrast, the average female-to-male ratio in China is 0.94 and in India as a whole 0.93.[34] Anyone drawn to the Chinese experience of compulsory birth control must take note of these facts.

The temptation to use the "override" approach arises at least partly from impatience with the allegedly slow process of fertility reduction through collaborative, rather than coercive, attempts. Yet Kerala's birth rate has fallen from 44 per 1000 in the 1950s to 18 by 1991—not a sluggish decline. Nor is Kerala unique in this respect. Other societies, such as those of Sri Lanka, South Korea, and Thailand, which have relied on expanding education and reducing mortality rates —instead of on coercion—have also achieved sharp declines in fertility and birth rates.

It is also interesting to compare the time required for reducing fertility in China with that in the two states in India, Kerala and Tamil Nadu, which have done most to encourage voluntary and collaborative reduction in birth rates (even though Tamil Nadu is well behind Kerala in each respect).[35] Table 31.2 shows the fertility rates both in 1979, when the one-child policy and related programs were introduced in China, and in 1991. Despite China's one-child policy and other coercive measures, its fertility rate seems to have fallen much less sharply than those of Kerala and Tamil Nadu. The "override" view is very hard to defend on the basis of the Chinese experience, the only systematic and sustained attempt to impose such a policy that has so far been made.

FAMILY PLANNING

Even those who do not advocate legal or economic coercion sometimes suggest a variant of the "override" approach—the view, which has been getting increasing support, that the highest priority should be given simply to family planning, even if this means diverting resources from education and health care as well as other activities associated with development. We often hear claims that enormous declines in birth rates have been accomplished through making family planning services available, without waiting for improvements in education and health care.

The experience of Bangladesh is sometimes cited as an example of such success. Indeed, even

TABLE 31.2 FERTILITY RATES IN CHINA, KERALA, AND TAMIL NADU

	1979	1991
China	2.8	2.0
Kerala	3.0	1.8
Tamil Nadu	3.5	2.2

SOURCES: For China, Xizhe Peng, *Demographic Transition in China* (New York: Oxford University Press, 1991), Li Chengrui, *A Study of China's Population* (Beijing: Foreign Language Press, 1992), and *World Development Report, 1994* (New York: Oxford University Press, 1996). For India, *Sample Registration System, 1979–80* (New Delhi: Ministry of Home Affairs, 1982) and *Sample Registration System: Fertility and Mortality Indicators, 1991* (New Delhi: Ministry of Home Affairs, 1993).

though the female literacy rate in Bangladesh is only around 22 percent and life expectancy at birth no higher than 55 years, fertility rates have been substantially reduced there through the greater availability of family planning services, including counselling.[36] We have to examine carefully what lessons can, in fact, be drawn from this evidence.

First, it is certainly significant that Bangladesh has been able to cut its fertility rate from 7.0 to 4.5 during the short period between 1975 and 1990, an achievement that discredits the view that people will not voluntarily embrace family planning in the poorest countries. But we have to ask further whether family-planning efforts may themselves be sufficient to make fertility come down to really low levels, without providing for female education and the other features of a fuller collaborative approach. The fertility rate of 4.5 in Bangladesh is still quite high—considerably higher than even India's average rate of 3.6. To begin stabilizing the population, the fertility rates would have to come down closer to the "replacement level" of 2.0, as has happened in Kerala and Tamil Nadu, and in many other places outside the Indian subcontinent. Female education and the other social developments connected with lowering the birth rate would still be much needed.

Contrasts between the records of Indian states offer some substantial lessons here. While Kerala and, to a smaller extent, Tamil Nadu have surged ahead in achieving radically reduced fertility rates, other states in India in the so-called "northern heartland" (such as Uttar Pradesh, Bihar, Madhya Pradesh, and Rajasthan), have very low levels of education, especially female education, and of general health care (often combined with pressure on the poor to accept birth control measures, including sterilization, as a qualifying condition for medical attention and other public services). These states all have high fertility rates—between 4.4 and 5.1. The regional contrasts within India strongly argue for the collaborative approach, including active and educated participation of women.

The threat of an impending population crisis tempts many international observers to suggest that priority be given to family planning arrangements in the Third World countries over other commitments such as education and health care, a redirection of public efforts that is often recommended by policy makers and at international conferences. Not only will this shift have negative effects on people's well-being and reduce their freedoms, it can also be self-defeating if the goal is to stabilize population.

The appeal of such slogans as "family planning first" rests partly on misconceptions about what is needed to reduce fertility rates, but also on mistaken beliefs about the excessive costs of social development, including education and health care. As has been discussed, both these activities are highly labour-intensive, and thus relatively inexpensive even in very poor economies. In fact, Kerala, India's star performer in expanding education and reducing both death rates and birth rates, is among the poorer Indian states. Its domestically produced income is quite low—lower indeed in per capita terms than even the Indian average—even if this is somewhat deceptive, for the greatest expansion of Kerala's earnings derives from citizens who work outside the state. Kerala's ability to finance adequately both educational expansion and health coverage depends on both activities being labour-intensive; they can be made available even in a low-income economy when there is the political will to use them. Despite its economic backwardness, an issue that Kerala will undoubtedly have to address before long (perhaps by reducing bureaucratic controls over agriculture and industry, which have stagnated), its level of social development has been remarkable, and that has turned out to be crucial in reducing fertility rates. Kerala's fertility rate of 1.8 not only compares well with China's 2.0, but also with the United States' and Sweden's 2.1, Canada's 1.9, and Britain's and France's 1.8.

The population problem is serious, certainly, but neither because of "the proportion between the natural increase in population and food" nor because of some impending apocalypse. There are reasons for worry about the long-term effects of population growth on the environment; and there are strong reasons for concern about the adverse effects of high birth rates on the quality of life, especially of women. With greater opportunities for education (especially female education), reduction of mortality rates (especially of children), improvement in economic security (especially in old age), and greater participation of women in employment and in political action, fast reductions in birth rates can be expected to result through the decisions and actions of those whose lives depend on them.

This is happening right now in many parts of the world, and the result has been a considerable slowing down of world population growth. The best way of dealing with the population problem is to help to spread these processes elsewhere. In contrast, the emergency mentality based on false beliefs in imminent cataclysms leads to breathless responses that are deeply counterproductive, preventing the development of rational and sustainable family planning. Coercive policies of forced birth control involve terrible social sacrifices, and there is little evidence that they are more effective in reducing birth rates than serious programs of collaborative action.

NOTES

1. This chapter draws on a lecture by Amartya Sen arranged by the "Eminent Citizens Committee for Cairo '94" at the United Nations in New York on April 18, 1994, and also on research supported by the National Science Foundation.

2. Paul Ehrlich, *The Population Bomb* (New York: Ballantine, 1968). More recently Paul Ehrlich and Anne H. Ehrlich have written *The Population Explosion* (New York: Simon and Schuster, 1990).

3. Garrett Hardin, *Living within Limits* (New York: Oxford University Press, 1993).

4. Thomas Robert Malthus, *Essay on the Principle of Population As It Affects the Future Improvement of Society with Remarks on the Speculation of Mr. Godwin, M. Condorcet, and Other Writers* (London: J. Johnson, 1798), chapter 8; in the Penguin classics edition, *An Essay on the Principle of Population* (Harmondsworth, UK: Penguin, 1982), p. 123.

5. See Simon Kuznets, *Modern Economic Growth* (New Haven, CT: Yale University Press, 1966).

6. Note by the Secretary-General of the United Nations to the Preparatory Committee for the International Conference on Population and Development, Third Session, A/Conf.171/PC/5, February 18, 1994, p. 30.

7. Philip Morris Hauser's estimates are presented in the National Academy of Sciences publication *Rapid Population Growth: Consequences and Policy Implications*, Vol. 1 (Baltimore, MD: Johns Hopkins University Press, 1971). See also Kuznets, *Modern Economic Growth*, chapter 2.

8. For an important collection of papers on these and related issues, see Sir Francis Graham-Smith, F.R.S., ed., *Population — The Complex Reality: A Report of the Population Summit of the World's Scientific Academies*, issued by the Royal Society and published in the United States by North American Press, Golden, Colorado. See also D. Gale Johnson and Ronald D. Lee, eds., *Population Growth and Economic Development, Issues and Evidence* (Madison: University of Wisconsin Press, 1987).

9. Hardin, *Living within Limits*, 274.

10. Paul Kennedy, who has discussed important problems in the distinctly "social" aspects of population growth, has pointed out that this debate "has, in one form or another, been with us since then," and "it is even more pertinent today than when Malthus composed his Essay," in *Preparing for the Twenty-First Century* (New York: Random House, 1993), pp. 5–6.

11. On the importance of "Enlightenment" traditions in Condorcet's thinking, see Emma Rothschild, "Condorcet and the Conflict of Values," forthcoming in *The Historical Journal*.

12. Marie Jean Antoine Nicholas de Caritat Marquis de Condorcet's *Esquisse d'un Tableau Historique des Progrès de l'Esprit Humain*, Xᵉ Epoque (1795). English translation by June Barraclough, *Sketch for a Historical Picture of the Progress of the Human Mind*, with an introduction by Stuart Hampshire (London: Weidenfeld and Nicolson, 1955), pp. 187–92.

13. T.R. Malthus, *A Summary View of the Principle of Population* (London: John Murray, 1830); in the Penguin classics edition (Harmondsworth, UK: Penguin, 1982), p. 243; emphasis added.

14. On practical policies, including criticism of poverty relief and charitable hospitals, advocated for Britain by Malthus and his followers, see William St. Clair, *The Godwins and the Shelleys: A Biography of a Family* (New York: Norton, 1989).

15. Malthus, *Essay on the Principle of Population*, chapter 17; in the Penguin classics edition, *An Essay of the Principle of Population*, pp. 198–99. Malthus showed some signs of weakening in this belief as he grew older.

16. Gerard Piel, *Only One World: Our Own to Make and to Keep* (New York: Freeman, 1992).

17. For discussions of these empirical connections, see R.A. Easterlin, ed., *Population and Economic Change in Developing Countries* (Chicago: University of Chicago Press, 1980); T.P. Schultz, *Economics of Population* (London: Addison-Wesley, 1981); J.C. Caldwell, *Theory of Fertility Decline* (New York: Academic Press, 1982); E. King and M.A. Hill, eds., *Women's Education in Developing Countries* (Baltimore, MD: Johns Hopkins University Press, 1992); Nancy Birdsall, "Economic Approaches to Population Growth," in *The Handbook of Development Economics*, H.B. Chenery and T.N. Srinivasan, eds. (Amsterdam: North Holland, 1988); Robert Cassen et al., *Population and Development: Old Debates, New Conclusions* (New Brunswick, NJ: Overseas Development Council/ Transaction Publisher, 1994).

18. World Bank, *World Development Report 1994* (New York: Oxford University Press, 1994), Table 25, pp. 210–11.

19. World Bank, *World Development Report 1994*, Table 2.

20. These issues are discussed in Jean Drèze and Amartya Sen, *Hunger and Public Action* (New York: Oxford University Press, 1989), and the three volumes edited by them, *The Political Economy of Hunger* (New York: Oxford University Press, 1990), and also in Amartya Sen, "Economic Regress: Concepts and Features," in *Proceedings of the World Bank Annual Conference on Development Economics 1993* (Washington, DC: World Bank, 1994).

21. This is confirmed by, among other statistics, the food production figures regularly presented by the United Nations Food and Agricultural Organization (see the *FAO Quarterly Bulletin of Statistics,* and also the *FAO Monthly Bulletins*).

22. For a more detailed picture and references to data sources, see Amartya Sen, "Population and Reasoned Agency: Food, Fertility and Economic Development," in *Population, Economic Development, and the Environment*, Kerstin Lindahl-Kiessling and Hans Landberg, eds. (New York: Oxford University Press, 1994); see also the other contributions in this volume. The data presented here have been slightly updated from later publications of the FAO.

23. On this see Amartya Sen, *Poverty and Famines* (New York: Oxford University Press, 1981).

24. See *UNCTAD VIII, Analytical Report by the UNCTAD Secretariat to the Conference* (New York: United Nations, 1992), Table V-S, p. 235. The period covered is between 1979–81 and 1988–90. These figures and related ones are discussed in greater detail in Amartya Sen, "Population and Reasoned Agency."

25. World Bank, *Price Prospects for Major Primary Commodities*, Vol. II (Washington, DC: World Bank, March 1993), Annex Tables 6, 12, and 18.

26. Condorcet, *Esquisse d'un Tableau Historique des Progrès de l'Esprit Humain*; in the 1968 reprint, p. 187.

27. The importance of "local" environmental issues is stressed and particularly explored by Partha Dasgupta in *An Inquiry into Well-Being and Destitution* (New York: Oxford University Press, 1993).

28. In a forthcoming monograph by Jean Drèze and Amartya Sen called *India: Economic Development and Opportunity* [New York: Oxford University Press, 1995], they discuss the importance of women's political agency in rectifying some of the more serious lapses in Indian economic and social performance —not just pertaining to the deprivation of women themselves.

29. See Drèze and Sen, *Hunger and Public Action,* which also investigates the remarkable success of some poor countries in providing widespread educational and health services.

30. World Bank, *World Development Report 1994,* p. 212; and *Sample Registration Sys-*

tem: *Fertility and Mortality Indicators 1991* (New Delhi: Ministry of Home Affairs, 1993).

31. See the discussions, and the literature cited, in Gita Sen, Adrienne German, and Lincoln Chen, eds., *Population Policies Reconsidered: Health, Empowerment, and Rights* (London: Harvard Center for Population and Development Studies/International Women's Health Coalition, 1994).

32. On the actual processes involved, see T.N. Krishnan, "Demographic Transition in Kerala: Facts and Factors," in *Economic and Political Weekly*, Vol. 11 (1976), and P.N. Mari Bhat and S.I. Rajan, "Demographic Transition in Kerala Revisited," in *Economic and Political Weekly*, Vol. 25 (1990).

33. See, for example, Robin Jeffrey, "Culture and Governments: How Women Made Kerala Literate," in *Pacific Affairs*, Vol. 60 (1987).

34. On this see Amartya Sen, "More Than 100 Million Women Are Missing," *New York Review of Books*, December 20, 1990; Ansley J. Coale, "Excess Female Mortality and the Balance of the Sexes: An Estimate of the Number of 'Missing Females,' " *Population and Development Review*, No. 17 (1991); Amartya Sen, "Missing Women," *British Medical Journal*, No. 304 (March 1992); Stephan Klasen, " 'Missing Women' Reconsidered," *World Development*, Vol. 22 (1994).

35. Tamil Nadu has benefited from an active and efficient voluntary program of family planning, but these efforts have been helped by favourable social conditions as well, such as a high literacy rate (the second highest among the sixteen major states), a high rate of female participation in work outside the home (the third highest), a relatively low infant mortality rate (the third lowest), and a traditionally higher age of marriage. See also T.V. Antony, "The Family Planning Programme — Lessons from Tamil Nadu's Experience," *Indian Journal of Social Science*, Vol. 5 (1992).

36. World Bank and Population Reference Bureau, *Success in a Challenging Environment: Fertility Decline in Bangladesh* (Washington, DC: World Bank, 1993).

Chapter 32

Challenges of the New Century

LESTER R. BROWN

As we look back at the many spectacular achievements of the century just ended, the landing on the Moon in July 1969 by American astronauts Neil Armstrong and Buzz Aldrin stands out. At the beginning of the century, few could imagine humans flying, much less breaking out of Earth's field of gravity to journey to the Moon. And few could imagine how quickly the world would go from air travel to space exploration.

Indeed, when the century began, the Wright brothers were still working in their bicycle shop in Dayton, Ohio, trying to design a craft that would fly. Just 66 years elapsed from their first precarious flight in 1903 on the beach at Kitty Hawk, North Carolina, to the landing on the Moon. Although their first flight was only 36 metres, it opened a new era, setting the stage for a century of breathtaking advances in technology.[1]

In 1945, engineers at the University of Pennsylvania's Moore School of Electrical Engineering successfully designed what many consider to be the first electronic computer, the ENIAC (Electronic Numerical Integrator and Computer). This advance was to have an even more pervasive effect than the Wright brothers' invention, as it set the stage for the evolution of the information economy. Computer technology progressed even more rapidly, going from the era of large mainframes to personal computers in just a few decades.[2]

A new industry evolved. New firms were created. IBM, Hewlett-Packard, Dell, Apple, Microsoft, Intel, and America On-Line became household names. Fortunes were made overnight. When the listed stock value of Microsoft overtook that of General Motors in 1998, it marked the beginning of a new era—a shift from a period dominated by heavy industry to one dominated by information.[3]

The stage was set for the evolution of the Internet, a novel concept that has tied the world together as never before. Although still in its early stages as the new century begins, the Internet is already affecting virtually every facet of our lives—changing communication, commerce, work, education, and entertainment. It is creating a new culture, one that is evolving in cyberspace.

In the United States, the information technology industry, including computer and communications hardware, software, and the provision of related services, was a major source of economic growth during the 1990s. Creating millions of new, higher-paying jobs, it has helped fuel the longest peacetime economic expansion in history. It has also induced a certain economic euphoria, one that helped drive the Dow Jones Industrial Average of stock prices to a long string of successive highs, raising it from less than 3000 in early 1990 to over 11 000 in 1999.[4]

Caught up in this economic excitement, we seem to have lost sight of the deterioration of environmental systems and resources. The contrast between our bright hopes for the future of the information economy and the deterioration of Earth's ecosystem leaves us with a schizophrenic outlook.

Source: Excerpted from "Challenges of the New Century," in Lester R. Brown et al., *State of the World 2000* (New York: W.W. Norton, 2000), pp. 3–21. Reprinted by permission of Worldwatch Institute.

Although the contrast between our civilization and that of our hunter-gatherer ancestors could scarcely be greater, we do have one thing in common—we, too, depend entirely on Earth's natural systems and resources to sustain us. Unfortunately, the expanding global economy that is driving the Dow Jones to new highs is, as currently structured, outgrowing those ecosystems. Evidence of this can be seen in shrinking forests, eroding soils, falling water tables, collapsing fisheries, rising temperatures, dying coral reefs, melting glaciers, and disappearing plant and animal species.

As pressures mount with each passing year, more local ecosystems collapse. Soil erosion has forced Kazakhstan, for instance, to abandon half its cropland since 1980. The Atlantic swordfish fishery is on the verge of collapsing. The Aral Sea, producing over 40 million kilograms of fish a year as recently as 1960, is now dead. The Philippines and Côte d'Ivoire have lost their thriving forest-product export industries because their once luxuriant stands of tropical hardwoods are largely gone. The rich oyster beds of the Chesapeake Bay that yielded more than 70 million kilograms a year in the early twentieth century produced less than 2 million kilograms in 1998. As the global economy expands, local ecosystems are collapsing at an accelerating pace.[5]

Even as the Dow Jones climbed to new highs during the 1990s, ecologists were noting that ever growing human demands would eventually lead to local breakdowns, a situation where deterioration would replace progress. No one knew what form this would take, whether it would be water shortages, food shortages, disease, internal ethnic conflict, or external political conflict.

The first region where decline is replacing progress is sub-Saharan Africa. In this region of 800 million people, life expectancy—a sentinel indicator of progress—is falling precipitously as governments overwhelmed by rapid population growth have failed to curb the spread of the virus that leads to AIDS. In several countries, more than 20 percent of adults are infected with HIV. Barring a medical miracle, these countries will lose one-fifth or more of their adult population in the first decade of the twenty-first century. In the absence of a low-cost cure, some 23 million Africans are beginning a new century with a death sentence imposed by the virus. With the failure of governments in the region to control the spread of HIV, it is becoming an epidemic of epic proportions. It is also a tragedy of epic proportions.[6]

Unfortunately, other trends also have the potential of reducing life expectancy in the years ahead, of turning back the clock of economic progress. In India, for instance, water pumped from underground far exceeds aquifer recharge. The resulting fall in water tables will eventually lead to a steep cutback in irrigation water supplies, threatening to reduce food production. Unless New Delhi can quickly devise an effective strategy to deal with spreading water scarcity, India—like Africa—may soon face a decline in life expectancy.[7]

ENVIRONMENTAL TRENDS SHAPING THE NEW CENTURY

As the twenty-first century begins, several well-established environmental trends are shaping the future of civilization. This section discusses seven of these: population growth, rising temperature, falling water tables, shrinking cropland per person, collapsing fisheries, shrinking forests, and the loss of plant and animal species.

The projected growth in population over the next half-century may more directly affect economic progress than any other single trend, exacerbating nearly all other environmental and social problems. Between 1950 and 2000, world population increased from 2.5 billion to 6.1 billion, a gain of 3.6 billion. And even though birth rates have fallen in most of the world, recent projections show that population is projected to grow to 8.9 billion by 2050, a gain of 2.8 billion. Whereas past growth occurred in both industrial and developing countries, virtually all future growth will occur in the developing world, where countries are already overpopulated,

truding from a melting glacier in the Yukon Territory of western Canada. Our ancestors are emerging from the ice with a message for us: Earth is getting warmer.[14]

(3)   One of the least visible trends that is shaping our future is falling water tables. Although irrigation problems, such as waterlogging, salting, and silting, go back several thousand years, aquifer depletion is a new one, confined largely to the last half-century, when powerful diesel and electric pumps made it possible to extract underground water at rates that exceed the natural recharge from rainfall and melting snow. According to Sandra Postel of the Global Water Policy Project, overpumping of aquifers in China, India, North Africa, Saudi Arabia, and the United States exceeds 160 billion tons of water per year. Since it takes roughly 1000 tons of water to produce 1 ton of grain, this is the equivalent of 160 million tons of grain, or half the U.S. grain harvest. In consumption terms, the food supply of 480 million of the world's 6 billion people is being produced with the unsustainable use of water.[15]

The largest single deficits are in India and China. As India's population has tripled since 1950, water demand has climbed to where it may now be double the sustainable yield of the country's aquifers. As a result, water tables are falling in much of the country and wells are running dry in thousands of villages. The International Water Management Institute, the world's premier water research body, estimates that aquifer depletion and the resulting cutbacks in irrigation water could drop India's grain harvest by up to one-fourth. In a country that is adding 18 million people a year and where more than half of all children are malnourished and underweight, a shrinking harvest could increase hunger-related deaths, adding to the 6 million worldwide who die each year from hunger and malnutrition.[16]

In China, the quadrupling of the economy since 1980 has raised water use far beyond the sustainable yield of aquifer recharge. The result is that water tables are falling virtually every-where the land is flat. Under the north China plain, which produces 40 percent of the country's grain harvest, the water table is falling by 1.6 m a year. As aquifer depletion and the diversion of water to cities shrink irrigation water supplies, China may be forced to import grain on a scale that could destabilize world grain markets.[17]

(4)   Also making it more difficult to feed the projected growth in population adequately over the next few decades is the worldwide shrinkage in cropland per person. Since the mid-twentieth century, grainland area per person has fallen in half, from 0.24 ha to 0.12 ha. If the world grain area remains more or less constant over the next half-century (assuming that cropland expansion in such areas as Brazil's cerrado will offset the worldwide losses of cropland to urbanization, industrialization, and land degradation), the area per person will shrink to 0.08 ha by 2050.[18]

Among the more populous countries where this trend threatens future food security are Ethiopia, Nigeria, and Pakistan—all countries with weak family planning programs. As a fixed area of arable land is divided among ever more people, it eventually shrinks to the point where people can no longer feed themselves. Unfortunately, in the poorer nations of sub-Saharan Africa and the Indian subcontinent, subsistence farmers may not have access to imports. For them, land scarcity translates into hunger.

Pakistan's population, for example, is projected to grow from 146 million today to 345 million in 2050, shrinking the grainland area per person in this crowded nation to a minuscule 0.04 ha by 2050—less than half of what it is today, and an area scarcely the size of a tennis court. A family of six will then have to produce all its food on roughly one-fifth of a hectare—the equivalent of a small suburban building lot in the United States. Similar prospects lie ahead for Nigeria, where numbers are projected to double to 244 million over the next half-century, and for Ethiopia, where more than half the children are undernourished and where population is projected to nearly triple. In these and dozens of other developing countries, grainland area per person will shrink dramatically.[19]

If world grainland productivity, which climbed by 170 percent over the last half-century, were to rise rapidly over the next half-century, the shrinkage in cropland area per person might not pose a serious threat. Unfortunately, the rise is slowing. From 1950 to 1990, world grain yield per hectare increased at more than 2 percent a year, well ahead of world population growth. But from 1990 to 1999 it grew at scarcely 1 percent a year. While biotechnology may reduce insecticide use through insect-resistant varieties, it offers little potential for raising yields.[20]

Humanity also depends heavily on the oceans for food, particularly animal protein, From 1950 until 1997, the oceanic fish catch expanded from 19 million tons to more than 90 million tons. This fivefold growth since mid-century has pushed the catch of most oceanic fisheries to their limits or beyond. If, as most marine biologists believe, the oceans cannot sustain an annual catch of more than 95 million tons, the catch per person will decline steadily in the decades ahead as world population continues to grow. This also means that all future growth in demand for food will have to be satisfied from land-based sources.[21]

These three parallel trends—falling water tables, shrinking cropland area per person, and the levelling off of the oceanic fish catch—all suggest that it will be far more difficult to keep up with the growth in world demand for food over the next half-century if the world remains on the United Nations medium population trajectory of adding nearly 3 billion people and if incomes continue to rise.[22]

Forests, too, are being overwhelmed by human demands. Over the past half-century, the world's forested area has shrunk substantially, with much of the loss occurring in developing countries. And the forested area per person worldwide is projected to shrink from 0.56 ha today to 0.38 ha in 2050. This figure reflects both population growth and the conversion of some forestland to cropland. In many situations, the rising worldwide demand for forest products—lumber, paper, and fuelwood—is already overwhelming the sustainable yield of forests.[23]

In some ways, the trend that will most affect the human prospect is an irreversible one—the accelerating extinction of plant and animal species. The share of birds, mammals, and fish vulnerable or in immediate danger of extinction is now measured in double digits: 11 percent of the world's 8615 bird species, 25 percent of the world's 4355 mammal species, and an estimated 34 percent of all fish species. The leading cause of species loss is habitat destruction, but habitat alterations from rising temperatures or pollution can also decimate both plant and animal species. As human population grows, the number of species with which we share the planet shrinks. As more and more species disappear, local ecosystems begin to collapse; at some point, we will face wholesale ecosystem collapse.[24]

REPLACING ECONOMICS WITH ECOLOGY

As noted earlier, global economic trends during the 1990s were remarkably bullish, but environmental trends were disastrous. The contrast could scarcely be greater. An economic system that worked well in times past when the demands of a small economy were well within the capacities of Earth's ecosystems is no longer working well. If the trends outlined in the last section cannot be reversed, we face a future where continuing environmental deterioration almost certainly will lead to economic decline. The challenge is to redesign the economic system so that it will not destroy its environmental support systems, so that economic progress can continue.

The time has come for what science historian Thomas Kuhn describes as a paradigm shift. In his classic work *The Structure of Scientific*

Revolutions, Kuhn observes that as the scientific understanding of reality in a field advances, reaching a point where existing theory no longer adequately explains reality, then theory has to change. It has to be updated, replacing the old paradigm with a new one. Perhaps history's best-known example of this is the shift from the Ptolemaic view of the world, in which the sun revolved around Earth, to the Copernican view, which argued that Earth revolved about the sun. Once the Copernican model was accepted, relationships not only within the solar system but between the solar system and the rest of the universe suddenly made sense to those who studied the heavens, leading to an era of steady advances in astronomy.[25]

We are now facing such a situation with the global economy. The market is a remarkably efficient device for allocating resources and for balancing supply and demand, but it does not respect the sustainable yield thresholds of natural systems. In a world where demands of the economy are pressing against the limits of natural systems, relying exclusively on economic indicators to guide investment decisions is a recipe for disaster. Historically, for example, if the supply of fish was inadequate, the price would rise, encouraging investment in additional fishing trawlers. This market system worked well. But today, with the fish catch already exceeding the sustainable yield of many fisheries, investing in more trawlers in response to higher seafood prices will simply accelerate the collapse of fisheries. A similar situation exists with forests, rangelands, and aquifers.

The gap between economists and ecologists in their perception of the world as the new century begins could not be wider. Economists look at grain markets and see the lowest grain prices in 20 years—a sure sign that production capacity is outrunning effective demand, that supply constraints are not likely to be a problem for the foreseeable future. But ecologists see water tables falling in key food-producing countries. Knowing that 480 million of the world's 6 billion people are being fed with grain produced by

overpumping aquifers, they are worried about the effect of eventual aquifer depletion on food production.[26]

Economists see a world economy that has grown by leaps and bounds over the last half-century, but ecologists see growth based on the burning of vast quantities of cheap fossil fuels, which is destabilizing the climate. They are keenly aware that someone buying a litre of gasoline pays the cost of pumping the oil, of refining it into gasoline, and of distributing the gasoline to the service station, but not the cost to society of future climate disruptions. Again, while economists see booming economic indicators, ecologists see an economy that is altering the climate with consequences that no one can foresee.

Today ecologists look at the deteriorating ecosystem and see a need to restructure the economy, the need for a paradigm shift. For example, stabilizing Earth's climate now depends on reducing carbon emissions by shifting from fossil fuels to a solar/hydrogen energy economy. Solar is here defined broadly, including not only direct sunlight but also indirect forms of solar energy—wind power, hydropower, and biological sources, such as wood. Fortunately, the technologies for tapping this enormous source of energy already exist. We can now see electricity generated from wind being used to electrolyze water and to produce hydrogen. Hydrogen then becomes the basic fuel for the new economy, relying initially on the distribution and storage facilities of the natural gas industry. Put simply, the principles of ecological sustainability now require a shift from a carbon-based to a hydrogen-based energy economy.

There is a similar need for restructuring the world food economy. Some 40 percent of the world's food is produced on irrigated land, with much of the water used for irrigation being heavily subsidized. Encouraging water use with subsidies at a time when water tables are falling sends the wrong signal, one that encourages the inefficient use of water. As world water use has tripled over the last half-century, often pressing against the limits of local supply, water has become scarcer than land. With water emerging as the principal constraint on efforts to expand food production, restructuring the world food economy to make it more water-efficient is a necessary, though not sufficient, precondition to feeding an expanding world population adequately. Among other things, this means shifting to more water-efficient crops and more grain-efficient sources of animal protein, such as poultry.[27]

As the global economy outgrows the various natural capacities of Earth, as just described, it imposes new demands on the political system that is responsible for managing the interaction between the two. Managing this increasingly stressed relationship between the global market economy, which is expanding by a trillion dollars per year, and Earth's ecosystems, whose capacities are essentially fixed, becomes ever more demanding. The demands on political institutions to reverse deterioration will intensify. At issue is whether our political institutions are capable of incorporating ecological principles into economic decision making.[28]

CROSSING THE SUSTAINABILITY THRESHOLD

Most environment ministers understand the need to restructure the global economy so that progress can continue, but unfortunately not enough of their constituents understand this. The ministers must also contend with interests that are vested in the existing economic system, interests that are more than willing to bribe political leaders either directly or in the form of campaign contributions and to mount disinformation campaigns to confuse the public about the need for change. Eventually, if enough people in a country are convinced of the need for change, they can override these vested interests, crossing a threshold of social change.

A threshold—a concept widely used in ecology in reference to the sustainable yield of natural systems—is a point that, when crossed, can bring rapid and sometimes unpredictable change. In the social world, the thresholds of sudden change are no less real, though they may be more difficult to identify and anticipate. Among the more dramatic recent threshold crossings are the ones that led to the political revolution in eastern Europe and to the dramatic decline in cigarette smoking in the United States.

Signs that the world is approaching a key environmental threshold are perhaps as strong within the corporate community as in any sector. The shifts have been particularly dramatic in the oil industry, led by Royal Dutch Shell and British Petroleum. And in February 1999, Mike Bowlin, the chief executive officer of ARCO, startled an energy conference in Houston by saying: "We've embarked on the beginning of the Last Days of the Age of Oil." He went on to discuss the need to convert our carbon-based energy economy into a hydrogen-based energy economy.[29]

Two months later, Shell Oil and Daimler-Chrysler announced they were leading a consortium of corporations whose goal is to make Iceland the world's first hydrogen-based economy. Iceland—with an abundance of geothermal energy, widely used for heating buildings, and cheap hydropower—is an ideal place to begin. Cheap electricity from hydropower makes it economically feasible to split the water molecule by electrolysis, producing hydrogen that can be used in new, highly efficient fuel-cell engines that are under development. DaimlerChrysler, a leader in the development of these engines, plans to market its new fuel-cell powered automobiles in Iceland within the next few years. Shell has also opened its first hydrogen station—the future equivalent of today's gasoline station—in Hamburg, Germany.[30]

In the United States, the threshold for responsible forest management appears to have been crossed. In effect, the principles of ecology are replacing basic economics in the management of national forests. After several decades of building roads with taxpayers' money to help logging companies clearcut publicly owned forests, the Forest Service announced in early 1998 that it was imposing a moratorium on road building. For decades the goal of the forest management system, which had built some 600 000 km of roads to facilitate clearcutting, had been to maximize the timber harvest in the short run.[31]

The new chief of the Forest Service, Michael Dombeck, responding to a major shift in public opinion, introduced a new management system — one designed to maintain the integrity of the ecosystem and to be governed by ecology, not by economics. Henceforth, the 78 million ha of national forests — more than the area planted to grain in the United States — will be managed with several goals in mind. The system will recognize the need, for example, to manage the forest so as to eliminate the excessive flooding, soil erosion, and silting of rivers, and the destruction of fisheries associated with the now banned practice of clearcutting. Under the new policy, the timber harvest from national forests, which reached an all-time high of 12 billion board feet per year during the 1980s, has been reduced to 3 billion board feet.[32]

The United States is not the only country to institute a radical change in forest management. In mid-August 1998, after several weeks of near-record flooding in the Yangtze river basin, Beijing acknowledged for the first time that the flooding was not merely an act of nature but was exacerbated by the deforestation of the upper reaches of the watershed. Premier Zhu Rongji personally ordered a halt not only to the tree-cutting in the upper reaches of the Yangtze basin, but also to the conversion of some state timbering firms into tree-planting firms. The official view in Beijing now is that trees standing are worth three times as much as those cut, simply because of the water storage and flood control capacity of forests.[33]

Oil companies investing in hydrogen and reformed forest management in the United States and China — these are just some of the signs that the world may be approaching the kind of paradigm shift that Thomas Kuhn wrote about. Across a spectrum of activities, places, and institutions, attitudes toward the environment have changed markedly in just the last few years. Among giant corporations that could once be counted on to mount a monolithic opposition to serious environmental reform, a growing number of high-profile CEOs have begun to sound more like environmentalists than representatives of the bastions of global capitalism.

If the evidence of a global environmental awakening were limited to only government initiatives or a few corporate initiatives, it might be dubious. But with the evidence of growing momentum now coming on both fronts, the prospect that we are approaching the threshold of a major transformation becomes more convincing. The question is, Will it happen soon enough? Will it happen before the deterioration of natural support systems reaches a point of no return?

TWO KEYS TO REGAINING CONTROL OF OUR DESTINY

The overriding challenges facing our global civilization as the new century begins are to stabilize climate and stabilize population. Success on these two fronts would make other challenges, such as reversing the deforestation of Earth, stabilizing water tables, and protecting plant and animal diversity, much more manageable. If we cannot stabilize climate and we cannot stabilize population, there is not an ecosystem on Earth that we can save. Everything will change. If developing countries cannot stabilize their population soon, many of them face the prospect of wholesale ecosystem collapse.

The exciting thing about the climate and population challenges is that we already have the technologies needed to succeed at both. Restructuring the energy economy to stabilize climate requires investment in climate-benign energy sources. It is the greatest investment opportunity in history. Stabilizing population, though it requires additional investment in reproductive health services and in the education of young women in developing countries, is more a matter of behavioural change — of couples having fewer children and investing more in the health and education of each.

Stabilizing climate means shifting from a fossil-fuel or carbon-based energy economy to alternative sources of energy. Nuclear power, once seen as an alternative to fossil fuels, has failed on several fronts. Within a few years, the closing of aging power plants is expected to eclipse the new plants still coming online, setting the stage for the phaseout of nuclear power. Electricity from the power source that was once described as "too cheap to meter" has now become too costly to use. The issue is no longer whether it is economical to build nuclear power plants but — given the high operating costs — whether it even makes economic sense in many situations to continue using those already built.

The only feasible alternative is a solar/hydrogen-based economy, one that taps the various sources of energy from the sun, such as hydropower, wind power, wood, or direct sunlight. The transition to a solar/hydrogen economy has already begun, as can be seen in energy use trends from 1990 to 1998 (see Table 32.1). Coal burning, for example, did not increase at all during this period. Meanwhile, wind power and photovoltaic cells — two climate-benign energy sources — were expanding at 22 percent and 16 percent a year, respectively. But the transition is not moving fast enough to avoid potentially disruptive climate change.

Although the use of all sources of energy that derive from the sun directly and indirectly will probably expand, wind and solar cells are likely to be the cornerstones of the new energy economy. Already Denmark gets 8 percent of its electricity from wind. For Schleswig-Holstein, the northernmost state in Germany, the figure is 11 percent. Navarra, a northern industrial state in Spain, gets 20 percent of its electricity from wind. In the United States, wind generating capacity is moving beyond its early stronghold

TABLE 32.1 TRENDS IN GLOBAL ENERGY USE, BY SOURCE, 1990–1998

ENERGY SOURCE	ANNUAL RATE OF GROWTH (PERCENT)
Wind power	22
Solar photovoltaics	16
Geothermal power	4
Hydroelectric power*	2
Oil	2
Natural gas	2
Nuclear power	1
Coal	0

*1990–97 only.

SOURCE: Worldwatch estimates based on UN, BP, DOE, EC, Eurogas, PlanEcon, IMF, LBL, IAEA, BTM Consult, and *PV News*.

in California as new wind farms come on-line in Minnesota, Iowa, Oregon, Wyoming, and Texas, dramatically broadening the industry's geographic base.[34]

Within the developing world, India, with 900 MW of generating capacity, is the unquestioned leader. With the help of the Dutch, China began operation in 1998 of its first commercial wind farm, a 24-MW project in Inner Mongolia, a region of vast wind wealth.[35]

The world wind energy potential can only be described as enormous. Today the world gets over one-fifth of all its electricity from hydropower, but this is dwarfed by the wind power potential. For example, China is richly endowed with wind energy and could double its national electricity generation from wind alone. An inventory of wind resources in the United States by the Department of Energy indicates that three states — North Dakota, South Dakota, and Texas — have enough harnessable wind energy to satisfy national electricity needs.[36]

With the costs of wind electric generation dropping from $2600 per kilowatt in 1981 to

$800 in 1998, wind power is fast becoming one of the world's cheapest sources of electricity, in some locations undercutting coal, traditionally the cheapest source. Once cheap electricity is available from solar sources, it can be used to electrolyze water, producing hydrogen—an ideal means of both storing and transporting solar energy.[37]

In 1998, sales of solar cells, the silicon-based semiconductors that convert sunlight into electricity, jumped 21 percent, reaching 152 MW. This growth reflected the sharp competition emerging among major industrial countries in the solar cell market as the world looks for clean energy sources that will not destabilize climate. The development of a solar cell roofing material in Japan has set the stage for even more rapid future growth in solar cell use. With this technology, the roof becomes the power plant for the building.[38]

In Japan, nearly 7000 rooftop solar systems were installed in 1998. The German government announced in late 1998 the goal of 100 000 solar roofs in that country. In response, Royal Dutch Shell and Pilkington Solar International jointly are building the world's largest solar cell manufacturing facility in Germany. Italy joined in with a goal of 10 000 solar rooftops.[39]

While wind and solar cell use are soaring, the worldwide growth of oil use has slowed to less than 2 percent a year and may peak and turn downward as early as 2005. The burning of natural gas, the cleanest of the three fossil fuels, is growing by 2 percent per year. It is increasingly seen as a transition fuel, part of the bridge from the fossil fuel–based energy economy to the solar/hydrogen energy economy.[40]

The goal is to convert small positive growth rates for fossil fuels into negative rates, as they are phased down, and to boost dramatically the growth in wind power and solar cells. Because wind energy is starting from such a small base, and because the urgency of stabilizing climate is mounting, it should perhaps be growing at triple-digit annual rates, not just in the double digits.

One way of dramatically boosting the growth in wind power would be to reduce income taxes and offset them with a carbon tax on fossil fuels, one that would more nearly reflect the full costs associated with air pollution, acid rain, and climate disruption. Such a move would raise investment not only in wind power, but also in solar cells and energy efficiency. It could push wind power growth far above the current rates, greatly accelerating the shift to a solar/hydrogen energy economy.

Sharply accelerating the wind power growth rate depends on restructuring tax systems to reduce taxes on income and wages while increasing those on environmentally destructive activities, such as carbon emissions from fossil fuel burning. Some countries have already begun to do this, including Denmark, Finland, the Netherlands, Spain, Sweden, and the United Kingdom. And in late 1998, the new coalition government in Germany announced the first step in a massive restructuring of the tax system, one that would simultaneously reduce taxes on wages and raise them on energy use. In April 1999, the first of four annual tax shifts was implemented. This ecological tax shift of some $14 billion—the largest yet contemplated by any government—was taken unilaterally, not bogged down in the politics of the global climate treaty or contingent on steps taken elsewhere. The framers of the new tax structure justified it primarily on economic grounds, mainly the creation of additional jobs. It would also help reduce carbon emissions.[41]

This bold German initiative is setting the stage for tax restructuring in other countries. If the world is going to make the economic changes needed in the time available, tax restructuring must be at the centre of the effort. No other set of policies can bring about the needed changes quickly enough. In an article in *Fortune* magazine, which argued for a 10 percent reduction in U.S. income taxes and a 50¢-per-gallon hike in the tax on gasoline, Professor N. Gregory Mankiw of Harvard noted: "Cutting income taxes while increasing gasoline taxes would lead to more rapid economic growth, less traffic congestion, safer roads, and reduced risk of global warming — all without jeopardizing long-term fiscal solvency. This may be the closest thing to a free lunch that economics has to offer.[42]

While stabilizing climate is largely a matter of investing in new energy sources, stabilizing population is more a matter of changing reproductive behaviour. The annual addition to world population increased steadily from 38 million in 1950 to the historical peak of 87 million in 1989. After that, it dropped to 78 million in 1998. While the annual additions in many developing countries have been increasing, they have been declining elsewhere. Some 32 countries — virtually all of industrialized Europe, from the United Kingdom to Russia, plus Japan and Canada — have succeeded in stabilizing their population size. Births and deaths are essentially in balance, as they must be in a sustainable society. This group of countries contains some 15 percent of the world population.[43]

Another, much larger group of countries has reached replacement level of fertility of 2.1 children per couple, but this does not immediately translate into population stability because of the disproportionately large number of young people moving into their reproductive years. This group, containing over 40 percent of the world's people, includes two of the most populous countries: China and the United States. In each of these, population is growing at just under 1 percent a year.[44]

One of the keys to the needed changes in reproductive behaviour is information that will help people understand the consequences of not shifting quickly to smaller families. Few people intentionally want their children or grandchildren to be deprived of adequate water supplies or of education because they themselves have too many children. Thus information is vital. Governments can provide this information through national carrying capacity assessments — studies to determine how many people the cropland, water, grassland, and forest resources of a country can sustain. This also involves a tradeoff between the size of population and the level of consumption. The carrying capacity calculations provide the information needed for that choice.

The key to stabilizing world population is for national governments to formulate strategies for stabilizing population humanely rather than waiting for nature to intervene with its inhumane methods, as it is in Africa. Once these strategies are developed, it is in the interest of the international community to support the stabilization effort.

At the UN Conference on Population and Development in Cairo in 1994, it was estimated that the annual cost of providing quality reproductive health services to all those in need in developing countries would be $17 billion in the year 2000. By 2015, this would climb to $22 billion. Industrial countries agreed to provide one-third of the funds, with developing countries providing the remainder. While developing countries have largely honoured their commitments, industrial countries — including the United States — have regrettably reneged on theirs. And, almost unbelievably, in late 1998 the U.S. Congress withdrew all funding for the UN Population Fund, the principal source of international family planning assistance.[45]

Fortuitously, the same family planning services that provide reproductive health counselling and that supply the condoms to help slow population growth also help to check the spread of HIV. Investment in efforts to slow population growth can thus also help to check the spread of the virus.

In stabilizing climate and stabilizing population, there is no substitute for leadership. Examples of this abound in both initiatives. Denmark, for instance, has simply banned the construction of coal-fired power plants. Meanwhile, it has adopted a series of economic incentives for investment in wind power that has fostered the development of the world's largest wind turbine manufacturing industry. As a result, in 1998 wind turbines of Danish design accounted for half of all turbines installed worldwide. Though scarcely a major industrial power, Denmark has a commanding position in this fast-expanding new industry.[46]

In every developing country where population growth has slowed dramatically, family planning programs have enjoyed strong government support. The same is true for containing the HIV epidemic. In the two countries that have successfully curbed the spread of HIV after it reached epidemic proportions—Uganda and Thailand—the heads of state led the containment campaign. In Uganda, President Museveni personally led the effort and continuously referred not only to the dangers of the virus but also to the behavioural changes needed to check its spread. In Thailand, Prime Minister Anand Punyarachun both provided the personal leadership to direct the campaign and was instrumental in raising the appropriations for containing the virus from $2.6 million in 1990 to $80 million in 1996.[47]

Leadership and time are the scarce resources. The world desperately needs more of both. Saving the planet, including the stabilization of climate and the stabilization of population, is a massive undertaking by any historical yardstick. This is not a spectator sport. It is something everyone can participate in. Few activities offer more satisfaction.

We can participate not only as individuals, but also in an institutional sense. All of society's institutions—from organized religion to corporations—have a role to play. Although many individuals and corporations want to do something about the environment, few recognize the need for systemic change. Corporations take pride in listing in their annual reports the steps they have taken to help protect the environment. They will cite gains in office paper recycling or reductions in energy use. These are obviously moves in the right direction. And they are to be applauded. But they do not deal with the central issue, which is the need to restructure the global economy quickly. This is not likely to happen unless corporations use some of their political leverage with governments to actively support tax restructuring.

There is no middle path. The challenge is either to build an economy that is sustainable or to stay with our unsustainable economy until it declines. It is not a goal that can be compromised. One way or another, the choice will be made by our generation, but it will affect life on Earth for all generations to come.

NOTES

1. Wright brothers flight from *Encyclopedia Britannica* on-line, www.britannica.com, viewed October 25, 1999.
2. Martin Campbell-Kelly and William Aspray, *Computer: A History of the Information Machine* (New York: Basic Books, 1996).
3. Nicholas Denton, "Microsoft Capitalisation Exceeds $200bn," *Financial Times*, February 26, 1998.
4. Dow Jones Industrial Average from Dow Jones & Company, averages.dowjones.com, viewed 25 October 1999.
5. Cropland in Kazakhstan from U.S. Department of Agriculture (USDA), *Production, Supply, and Distribution*, electronic database, Washington, DC, updated November 1999; Atlantic swordfish from Lisa Speer et al., *Hook, Line and Sinking: The Crisis in Marine Fisheries* (New York: Natural Resources Defense Council, February 1997); Aral Sea from Sandra Postel, *Pillar of Sand* (New York: W.W. Norton, 1999); forest products industries from Janet N. Abramovitz, *Taking a Stand: Cultivating a New Relationship with the World's Forests*, Worldwatch Paper 140 (Washington, DC: Worldwatch Institute, April 1998); Chesapeake Bay from John Jacobs, Maryland Department of Natural Resources, unpublished printout sent to author, August 3, 1994.
6. Population of sub-Saharan Africa from Population Reference Bureau (PRB), "1999 World Population Data Sheet," wall chart (Washing-

ton, DC, June 1999); prevalence and number infected in sub-Saharan Africa from Joint United Nations Programme on HIV/AIDS (UNAIDS), *AIDS Epidemic Update: December 1998* (Geneva: UNAIDS, December 1998).

7. Water pumping in India from David Seckler et al., "Water Scarcity in the Twenty-First Century" (Colombo, Sri Lanka: International Water Management Institute, July 27, 1998).

8. United Nations, *World Population Prospects: The 1998 Revision* (New York: United Nations, December 1998).

9. Carbon Dioxide Information Analysis Center, *Trends: A Compendium of Data on Global Change* (Oak Ridge, TN: Oak Ridge National Laboratory, 1998), cdiac.esd.ornl.gov, viewed October 25, 1999; C.D. Keeling and T.P. Whort, "Atmospheric CO_2 Concentrations (ppmv) Derived from In Situ Air Samples Collected at Mauna Loa Observatory, Hawaii," Scripps Institute of Oceanography, La Jolla, CA, July 1999.

10. Figure 1.1 from James Hansen et al., Goddard Institute for Space Studies, Surface Air Temperature Analyses, "Global Land-Ocean Temperature Index," www.giss.nasa.gov/update/gistemps, viewed November 4, 1999.

11. Tom M.L. Wigley, *The Science of Climate Change: Global and U.S. Perspective* (Arlington, VA: Pew Center on Global Climate Change, June 1999).

12. Paul Epstein et al., *Marine Ecosystems: Emerging Diseases as Indicators of Change*, Health, Ecological and Economic Dimensions of the Global Change Program (Boston: Center for Health and Global Environment, Harvard Medical School, December 1998).

13. Melting ice caps and glaciers from Greenpeace International, "Climate Change and the Earth's Mountain Glaciers: Observations and Implications," May 1998, www.greenpeace.org/~climate/arctic99/reports/glaciers2.htm, viewed October 25, 1999; "Melting Himalayan Glaciers Pose Flooding Dangers," *Reuters*, June 3, 1999;

Liu Jun, "Cold Comfort for Yangtze Glaciers," *China Daily*, January 20, 1999; Richard Monastersky, "Sea Change in the Arctic," *Science News,* February 13, 1999; Joby Warrick, "As Glaciers Melt, Talks on Warming Face Chill," *Washington Post*, November 2, 1998; William K. Stevens, "Dead Trees and Shriveling Glaciers as Alaska Melts," *New York Times*, August 18, 1998; U.S. and British report from "Melting of Antarctic Ice Shelves Accelerates," *Environment News Service*, April 9, 1999.

14. Alps discovery from John Noble Wilford, "Move Over, Iceman! New Star from the Andes," *New York Times*, October 25, 1995; Yukon discovery from James Brooke, "Remains of Ancient Man Discovered in Melting Canadian Glacier," *New York Times*, August 25, 1999.

15. Postel, *Pillar of Sand*; 480 million being fed with food produced with the unsustainable use of water based on an average annual diet of 300 kg, or 0.3 tons, of grain.

16. Seckler et al., "Water Scarcity"; annual addition to India's population from United Nations, *World Population Prospect*s; malnourished children in India from UN Food and Agriculture Organization (FAO), *The State of Food Insecurity in the World* (Rome: FAO, 1999); 6 million children from World Health Organization, *The World Health Report 1998* (Geneva: WHO, 1998).

17. Liu Yonggong and John B. Penson, "China's Sustainable Agriculture and Regional Implications," paper presented to the symposium on Agriculture, Trade and Sustainable Development in Pacific Asia: China and Its Trading Partners, Texas A&M University, College Station, TX, February 12–14, 1998; for a more detailed analysis, see Lester R. Brown and Brian Halweil, "China's Water Shortage Could Shake World Food Security," *World Watch*, July/August 1998.

18. World grainland from USDA, *Production, Supply, and Distribution*; population from United Nations, *World Population Prospects*.

19. Grainland from USDA, *Production, Supply, and Distribution*; population from United Nations, *World Population Prospects*.

20. USDA, *Production, Supply, and Distribution*.

21. FAO, *Yearbook of Fishery Statistics: Catches and Landings* (Rome: FAO, various years), with 1990–97 data from Maurizio Perotti, fishery statistician, Fishery Information, Data and Statistics Unit, Fisheries Department, FAO, Rome, letter to Anne Platt McGinn, Worldwatch Institute, November 10, 1998; marine biologists from FAO, *The State of World Fisheries and Aquaculture, 1996* (Rome: FAO, 1997).

22. United Nations, *World Population Prospects*.

23. Forested area from Dirk Bryant, Daniel Nielsen, and Laura Tangley, *The Last Frontier Forests: Ecosystems and Economies on the Edge* (Washington, DC: World Resources Institute, 1997); population from United Nations, *World Population Prospects*.

24. Jonathan Baillie and Brian Groombridge, eds., *1996 IUCN Red List of Threatened Animals* (Gland, Switzerland: World Conservation Union–IUCN, 1996).

25. Thomas Kuhn, *The Structure of Scientific Revolutions*, 3rd ed. (Chicago: University of Chicago Press, 1996).

26. Overpumping from Postel, *Pillar of Sand*; 480 million being fed with food produced with the unsustainable use of water based on an average annual diet of 300 kg, or 0.3 tons, of grain.

27. Share of world's food from irrigated land from Postel, ibid.

28. Annual growth in global economy from Worldwatch update of Angus Maddison, *Monitoring the World Economy 1820–1992* (Paris: Organisation for Economic Cooperation and Development, 1995), and from International Monetary Fund, *World Economic Outlook* (Washington, DC: December 1998).

29. Mike R. Bowlin, ARCO, "Clean Energy: Preparing Today for Tomorrow's Challenges," presented at Cambridge Energy Research Associates 18th Annual Executive Conference: Globality & Energy: Strategies for the New Millennium, Houston, TX, February 9, 1999.

30. Corporate plans and Shell hydro station from Fred Pearce, "Iceland's Power Game," *New Scientist*, May 1, 1999.

31. Road moratorium from USDA, Forest Service, "Forest Service Limits New Road Construction in Most National Forests," press release (Washington, DC: February 11, 1999).

32. Tom Kenworthy, "Major Change Sought in Forest Regulations," *Washington Post*, October 1, 1999.

33. Wang Chuandong, "Logging Ban to Transform Timber Industry," *China Daily*, September 7, 1998; "Forestry Cuts Down on Logging," *China Daily*, May 26, 1998.

34. Denmark from Birger Madsen, BTM Consult, Ringkobing, Denmark, letter to Christopher Flavin, Worldwatch Institute, February 29, 1999; Schleswig-Holstein from Andreas Wagner, Fordergesellschaft Windenergie, Hamburg, Germany, e-mail to Christopher Flavin, Worldwatch Institute, January 20, 1999; Navarra from Energia Hidroelectrica de Navarra, S.A., "Projects and Scope of Action of Energia Hidroelectrica de Navarra" (Pamplona, Spain: August 1998); U.S. wind farms from Kent Robertson, American Wind Energy Association, Washington, DC, e-mail to Christopher Flavin, Worldwatch Institute, February 26, 1999.

35. India generating capacity from Madsen, letter; Dutch project in China from Niall Martin, "First Commercial Wind Farm in China," *Windpower Monthly*, September 1998.

36. Share of world electricity from hydroelectric is a Worldwatch estimate based on United Nations, *Energy Statistics Yearbook 1995* (New York: UN, 1997), and on British Petroleum, *BP Statistics Review of World Energy 1997* (London: Group Media and Publications, 1997); wind potential in China is Worldwatch estimate based on World Bank, Asia Alternative Energy Unit, "China: Renew-

able Energy for Electric Power" (Washington, DC: September 11, 1996), and on U.S. Department of Energy, Energy Information Administration, *International Energy Outlook 1999* (Washington, DC: U.S. Department of Energy, March 1999); D.L. Elliott, L.L. Windell, and G.L. Gower, *An Assessment of the Available Windy Land Area and Wind Energy Potential in the Contiguous United States* (Richland, WA: Pacific Northwest Laboratory, 1991).

37. Electric Power Research Institute, *Renewable Energy Technology Characterizations* (Palo Alto, CA: Electric Power Research Institute, 1997).

38. Paul Maycock, "1998 World Cell/Module Shipments," *PV News*, February 1999.

39. Paul Maycock, "Japan Expands '70,000 Roofs' Program," *PV News*, July 1998; Paul Maycock, "German '100,000 Roofs' Program Details," *PV News*, March 1999; Shell/Pilkington facility from Paul Maycock, Photovoltaic Energy Systems, Inc., Warrenton, VA, e-mail to Brian Halweil, Worldwatch Institute, November 1, 1999; Paul Maycock, "Italian 10,000 Roofs Program Takes Shape," *PV News*, July 1998.

40. Growth in oil and natural gas use from BP Amoco, *BP Amoco Statistical Review of World Energy* (London: Group Media and Publications, 1999); oil peak from Colin J. Campbell and Jean H. Laherrere, "The End of Cheap Oil," *Scientific American*, March 1998.

41. Countries that are restructuring their tax system from David Malin Roodman, "Building a Sustainable Society," in Lester R. Brown et al., *State of the World 1999* (New York: W.W. Norton, 1999); German tax shift of 1998 from Peter Norman, "SPD and Greens Agree German Energy Tax Rises," *Financial Times*, October 19, 1998; Michael Kohlhaas, "Ecological Tax Reform in Germany: Impact and Implications," presentation at American Institute for Contemporary German Studies, Washington, DC, April 21, 1999.

42. N. Gregory Mankiw, "Gas Tax Now!" *Fortune*, May 24, 1999.

43. U.S. Bureau of the Census, *International Data Base*, electronic database, Suitland, MD, updated, November 30, 1998; PRB, "1999 World Population."

44. PRB, "1999 World Population."

45. U.N. Population Fund (UNFPA), *The State of World Population* (New York: UNFPA, 1999); UNFPA, "Executive Director's Statement on Withdrawal of U.S. Funding from UNFPA," New York, October 20, 1998.

46. Madsen, letter.

47. UNAIDS, *AIDS Epidemic Update*; Uganda from World Bank, *Confronting AIDS: Public Priorities in a Global Epidemic* (New York: Oxford University Press, 1997); funding for HIV/AIDS in Thailand from Phil Guest, Population Council, Horizons Program, Bangkok, Thailand, e-mail to Mary Caron, Worldwatch Institute, March 5, 1999.

INDEX